REACHING INTO THE SILENCE

REACHING INTO THE SILENCE

Literary Scholarship in the Tradition of Catholic Humanism

Words, after speech, reach
Into the silence.
T.S. ELIOT, *Burnt Norton*

Rodney Delasanta

René Fortin

Brian Barbour

CLUNY
Providence, Rhode Island

CLUNY MEDIA EDITION, 2023

For more information regarding this title
or any other Cluny Media publication,
please write to info@clunymedia.com, or to
Cluny Media, P.O. Box 1664, Providence, RI 02901

❦ VISIT US ONLINE AT WWW.CLUNYMEDIA.COM ❦

....

For this Cluny edition, errata and select citations from
the original works have been updated and developed,
as needed, for the purposes of clarity and consistency.

ISBN (paperback) | 978-1685952402

ISBN (hardcover) | 978-1685952419

Cover design by Clarke & Clarke
Cover image: J. M. W. Turner, *Ruins of Tintern Abbey*,
c. 1794, watercolour with pencil tracing on paper
Courtesy of Google Arts and Culture

CONTENTS

For

Frances Delasanta *and* June Barbour

and in memory of

Jeannine Fortin

And also for

Mario DiNunzio, Suzanne Fournier, *and* Richard Grace

and in memory of

Paul van K. Thomson

NOTES ON CONTRIBUTORS

Rodney Delasanta (1932–2007) was born in Winchendon, Massachusetts, and grew up in Woonsocket, Rhode Island, where he attended public schools. He graduated B.A. *summa cum laude* from Providence College in 1953 and Ph.D. from Brown University in 1962, *Phi Beta Kappa*. He taught at Brown from 1955 to 1957 as an Instructor and in 1983 as a Visiting Professor. He also taught as Visiting Professor at the Universities of Fribourg (Switzerland), 1968–1970, and Neuchatel, 1969–1970. But his main teaching career was from Assistant Professor to Professor at Providence College, 1961–2007, where he chaired the English Department from 1972–1974, and where he was Director of the Liberal Arts Honors Program from 1988–2005. Delasanta won a Sears Roebuck Award for excellence in teaching. He was a co-founder of the Rhode Island Humanities Forum and from 1998–2002 he chaired the Rhode Island Rhodes Scholarship Nominating Committee. He was also a professional musician who as a teenager toured with Horace Heidt's big band, performing on national radio, and later he taught music. He was the author of *The Epic Voice* and of some thirty scholarly articles.

René Fortin (1934–1991) was born and grew up in Woonsocket, Rhode Island, where he attended parochial schools. He graduated B.A. *summa cum laude* from Providence College in 1955 and Ph.D. from Brown University in 1964, *Phi Beta Kappa*. He taught at Providence College, advancing from Instructor to Professor from 1958 to 1991, winning an E. Harris Harbison Prize for Gifted Teaching in 1968. He was Director of the Liberal Arts Honors Program from 1967–1970, chaired the English Department from 1970–1972, and was Director of the Development of Western Civilization Program (DWC) from 1972–1987. He was the primary intellectual architect of the curricular reforms that produced DWC. Fortin published some twenty scholarly articles, many of which were collected in his posthumous collection, *Gaining upon Certainty*, which was edited by Brian Barbour and Delasanta.

Brian Barbour (1943–) was born in Lorain, Ohio, and grew up there and in Lakeland, Florida, and was educated in parochial schools. He graduated B.A. from the University of Notre Dame in 1965 (where he studied for six semesters under Frank O'Malley and was a member of the Blue Circle Honor Society) and Ph.D. from Kent State University in 1969. He taught at Providence College from 1969–2014, advancing from Assistant Professor to Professor. He was Director of the American Studies Program from 1981–1984; Chair of the English Department from 1986–1988; and Director of the Development of Western Civilization Program from 1994–2004. He is a Visiting Fellow at St. Edmund's College, Cambridge, as from 1992–1993, and was Editor of *Providence: Studies in Western Civilization* from 1995–2000. He has edited six books and authored some fifteen scholarly articles, several of which won guild awards.

INTRODUCTION

Brian Barbour

> *Words, after speech, reach*
> *Into the silence.*
>
> (T. S. ELIOT, *Burnt Norton*)

The papers gathered in this volume range across seventeen major authors and some twelve-hundred years of literary history. They are a selection from the work of three friends who taught together for decades in the English Department at Providence College and who shared a roughly similar background and had a fairly similar outlook. Nearly every paper had its origins in classroom teaching, and each one inevitably exemplifies an outlook that can only be called Catholic Humanism: grounded in the Creed and blending a love of letters and the arts with a conviction that reality is sacramental; that human beings live in a metaphysically grounded and morally ordered universe in which good and evil are real alternatives about which decisions have to be made; that the human person is a unity of body and spirit with an eternal destiny and not just a rationalizing bundle of self-interest, appetites and desires; and that, in Newman's words, "the human race is implicated in some terrible aboriginal calamity" from which we need redemption—a redemption won by Christ. We were Catholics who came to maturity in the pre-Vatican II Church and who embraced the Council's varying attempts at reform, never faltering in our commitment even if we occasionally winced at certain things done in the Council's name or "spirit." And we were also affected by some forms of renewal that moved through the Church in the 1960s and later. In philosophy we were instinctively, though not dogmatically, Thomists, consistent with the work of Gilson, Maritain, and Pieper, though René Fortin was also strongly drawn to Pascal and his sense of existential crisis.

Catholicism, then, was in our deep background together with our conviction that great literature, like philosophy, begins in wonder, in awed silence, and that without an ability to receive and respond criticism (or any reading) is fruitless, external, a waste of time. So it was literature itself, great literature, the excitement, the joy that comes in that moment of inwardness when one finally sees, finally "gets," finally takes possession of the ever-deepening meaning of a great work—even when what one sees there is in itself quite terrible, as, for example, *King Lear*—it was this that excited us, nourished our thinking, brought us together, kept us talking together all our lives. We were blessed and we knew it.

I once saw René Fortin spend what must have been five or six classroom minutes explicating the meaning and showing the importance of the letter "Q" in the Roman standard SPQR, *Senatus Populusque Romanus*, and how that differed from the equally correct *Senatus et Populus Romanus*, how the Q embodied grammatically the pretense and deceit of unity with the plebs claimed by the senatorial class and, here, by the conspirators in the play. The play was *Julius Caesar*, of course, in which Cicero's key lines about perception and self-deception—

> Indeed it is a strange-disposed time.
> But men may construe things after their fashion,
> Clean from the purpose of the things themselves

—govern so much of the action. It must have been my second year at the college. As a young instructor I was struggling to find my way in the classroom and since everyone recognized Fortin as a great teacher (he had already won a Harbison Prize), I asked him if I could sit in for a few classes. Later I asked Rodney Delasanta the same thing, and in that way I served my apprenticeship, eventually "taking" six full courses from the two men, assimilating as well as I could classroom instruction of the very highest order. What nature had scanted me, I reflected, Providence was providing.

Spending six or seven minutes on the letter Q was neither posturing nor pedantry (Fortin was incapable of either). Rather it illustrates a key point about the papers in this collection. They are not the product of any Theory or Method; rather they begin with a primary concern with "the words on the page," to use again the once honored phrase, and from there they work out the meaning and the significance of those words. If we had no fixed Method in the classroom, nor followed any Theory in these papers, T. S. Eliot's demanding and humbling admonition certainly rang in our ears: "the only method is to be as intelligent as possible."

But without having a method, how then did we get from reception of the words on the page to a full critical understanding? Although possessed of neither Theory nor Method we did share a few general principles, usually phrased as quite basic questions. The first was, *What is this that I am looking at?*—a question deceptively simple since to accurately describe a literary work is a highly demanding intellectual exercise. The second question followed: *How does this work of art generate its meaning*? Which are the artistic elements at play here—imagery, tone, structure, rhythm, ironies, conventions, contrasts and so forth—and how are they being used? And then came the third: *What is its meaning*? At every point the questions would act upon each other and modify one's growing perception. If the first question is broadly about *theme*, the second is about *art*, about how the theme is realized, made real in this specificity. And the third would often lead to a judgment: from meaning to larger significance. From *What?* to *How?* to *Significance?* was quite enough to be excited by, to take great pleasure in, to take great riches from, the literary work.

So if we were primarily concerned with the words on the page, with *explicatio de texte*, were we then not New Critics? Well, yes and no. We certainly knew our Brooks and Warren. But we knew our Northrop Frye as well. And setting aside the silly but common caricature of the New Critic as someone who approached a poem as though it existed in an historical void while paying obeisance to the Intentional Fallacy, what separated us from the autotelic temptation were the demands and possibilities of our second home—in Providence College's once-legendary (now, sad to say, eviscerated) Development of Western Civilization Program. In four semesters the course moved from the ancient Near East to almost the present day with four lectures a week and one discussion session. "Civ" was General Education at its best. It was taught by teams of four—an historian, a theologian, a philosopher, and a literary scholar—and we sat for one another's lectures, so that by the nature of the case we were obliged to read literary works within and against their full historical and cultural context, to approach them with a sense of the past. In Eliot's terms, we saw the individual talent take its place modifying the tradition.

Moreover, the presence of theology and philosophy meant that the literary scholar was not constrained by the secular horizon that closes off vast ranges of discussion in many universities. We were free to follow the words as they reached into the silence, into mystery. And we could not be satisfied with just *meaning*, however rich and resonate and subtle, but we had to go on to consider *significance*, the larger questions raised by the greatest works—about truth and goodness, for example and about what it means to be a person, about the nature of the good life and the nature of our relationships with each other and with the Divine. We were able to recognize more easily in literary works not just the Christian paradigm —which, after all, was part of the consciousness of nearly all Western authors until the early twentieth century—in its overt or allegorical form, but also its presence by archetype or non-reductive parody, or by implication, or by allusion, or by denial. It is here, wrestling with these matters, that we saw literature illuminate the depths of human nature and explore the exigencies of the human condition.

To approach literature under these conditions was a great joy both for instructors and students. And the cross-fertilization of background and ideas strengthened our grasp of the philosophical and theological issues in our work for the English Department. Delasanta taught Chaucer so he was keenly interested in the problem of the Universal, its rejection by Ockham, its effect on Chaucer's art, and its associated theological Fideism; Fortin taught Shakespeare and thus explored Renaissance epistemological skepticism and the Reformation creedal issues; while Barbour taught American Literature and was concerned with Descartes and with utilitarianism ("Franklinian" in its American form) and Romanticism/secularism as religion substitutes. But in raising such questions, and in exploring them analogically in art and music, we certainly moved away from the caricature of the New Critic and became just teachers trying to fully understand, properly value, and open up for others the beautiful work we had before us.

At any one moment there were thirty-two instructors engaged in teaching Civ, many of them Full Professors, in eight teams of four—four First Year teams and four Second. Each day at 12:30 a dozen or more, whoever was free, gathered together at the lunch table to trade ideas and insights culled from the morning's work, or the week's, or the semester's. My experience of lunching and dining at High Table in various Oxbridge colleges is that the talk there is wide-ranging, witty, allusive and charming, of course, but generally not as intellectually stimulating as was the Civ Lunch Table in its golden age. Rodney Delasanta, who was a professional musician as well as a Professor of English and who shared with us his extraordinary knowledge of art history, usually presided. Manifesting his characteristic exuberance and energy he would start things off, generally with some form of the phrase, "*Listening to Professor X this morning, it occurred to me that...*" and the insights and ideas *sic et non* would begin to fly about—literature alive in our joyful grasp and sharing, a living force, quickening our minds, and enriching our own work going forward; a community of scholars *in actu*.

All well and good, one might say, but also ancient history, so why be concerned *now* with literary scholarship that in some cases stretches back half a century and that would not be acceptable in most academic journals today? Two reasons immediately present themselves. First, during the last twenty-five years American colleges and universities have seen a precipitous decline in the number of English majors and in students taking English electives. This decline has gone hand-in-glove with the rise of, first, Theory, and then, slightly later, various types of politicized approaches that together define the way literature is studied in graduate school and taught to undergraduates. This "turn to Theory" has had ruinous consequences. Each of these approaches is anti-humanist (and proudly so) and none has any patience with the imaginative exploration of the individual moral life that great literature provides. This is not the place to rehearse the sad story of the displacement of a sense of wonder by a hermeneutics of suspicion, but at bottom all the regnant approaches graduate students are permitted are both ahistorical and broadly Cartesian (in that they *start with ideas*) and then either force the literature to fit the ideas or use the literature to exemplify some favored social pathology. Students have fled in droves; they need examples of a better way. Earlier criticism may not have been universally good in the classroom or on the page but at least the point was always to understand the moral and spiritual dimensions of life in the work. Thus the shift from *understanding* literature to *using* it has been a disaster. Why should an undergraduate waste his time "studying literature" if (a) all literature says pretty much the same thing—that life is more or less meaningless; or (b) she can hear the same social accusations being made in her sociology and political science and grievance studies classes? What she wants from literary study is to sense that the individual life really matters, that it has moral weight, that its joys and sorrows can be explored in their depth and subtlety, and that great literature can give insight into Truth (and Appearance), Goodness (and Evil), Beauty (and the Meretricious). Unless you love literature as literature and not as an instrument for social change there is no point to studying it.

Second, the damage done in English Departments is but one part of a wider problem for universities, their loss of vision, their attenuated and mis-directed sense of purpose. Colleges and universities today, when they turn to education at all, are mainly interested in business, the social sciences, and the STEM departments, all of which are rationalistic and mostly treat human beings not as individuals but as numbers, as units in a group. Surely Kierkegaard brought down this temple upon Hegel's head? Surely the aim of education has to be more than the easy anger of factitious righteousness and/or a good entry-level position with full benefits? What of Friendship? Charity? Sincerity? Self-knowledge? What of not going gentle into that good night? *If* English Departments are to again be a living force at the center of the Humanities, they will need to recover the ability to talk seriously about literature itself, not to use it instrumentally to bring about social change, and that means a return to "the words on the page" as start-point, to *What* works are saying and *How*. And English professors will need to regain the ability and see the need to discriminate between major and minor works and between minor works and the weightless and worthless. For major literature has an unmatched ability to nurture the moral imagination; it should not be abandoned. And *if* the Liberal Arts and the Humanities are ever going to regain their position at the center of the Academy as the definers of its mission, then they are going to need to draw on good examples of solid work in the older but still vital tradition of Humanist scholarship such as this volume provides. Newman, to cite him again, said that the aim of education was to develop a philosophic habit of mind and to understand the relative disposition of things. His contemporary, Matthew Arnold, argued that the question, *How to live?* was one none of us could avoid. But STEM courses and the social sciences are agnostic on such matters. Rationalism avoids mystery even though that is what lies all around us. *If* American colleges and universities are ever to regain their equilibrium and an adequate sense of purpose, one important contributing factor will be this: that young people will have re-discovered the love of literature *qua* literature, its joys and truths, and want to discuss it in ways such as these papers exemplify–within the vital tradition of the receptive imagination's joyful encounters with the beautiful and complex truths of great works—even as they attempt to make sense out of their own lives. As it happens the Catholic Humanist Tradition is particularly well-placed to provide, not easy answers, but recognition of the depth and complexity and importance of these questions. Besides that, all colleges, but Catholic colleges in particular, ought to be willing to resist the winds of fashionable doctrine and to be counter-cultural.

The reader will notice the broad range of literature covered in these papers—some seventeen different authors. And yet this is only a selection from a body of our work that goes back to Greek drama and Aeschylus and then forward to C. S. Lewis, Flannery O'Connor, and Aleksandr Solzhenitsyn. This breadth is because as critics our primary concern was with *literature* and its power, not the secondary scholarship; because we were not restricted in teaching to our specialist areas (although we knew the scholarship well); and because Delasanta and Fortin with their great pedagogical gifts at one time or another taught both years of Civ. These papers, then, illustrate our joy in all great literature, its truth, its goodness, and its beauty, and that enlargement of vision and being to be found even in the literature that demonstrates, or relieves, life's terrible moments. In all of the papers we can recognize how great literature, "living and active and sharper than a two-edged sword," can open and illuminate both our own lives and the world around us.

Ours is a restless, noisy, superficial world terrified by silence, enthralled with politics, disdainful of interiority. When the modern secular person looks out, perhaps even with pride, at its bleak utilitarian contours, blinking, yet slouching towards metaphysics, he beholds, with the eyes of Wallace Stevens' Snow Man,

Nothing that is not there and the nothing that is,

But the Catholic humanist, fortified perhaps by Emily Dickinson's declaration that

This world is not conclusion;

and remembering with a certain grateful awe Gerard Manley Hopkins' insight that

The world is charged with the grandeur of God;

ponders once again the mystery,

Words, after speech, reach
Into the silence,

and rejoices.

REACHING INTO THE SILENCE

Literary Scholarship in the Tradition of Catholic Humanism

BEOWULF AND THE HYPOSTATIC UNION

Rodney Delasanta and James Slevin

Recent critical theories of *Beowulf* have insisted that the poem, however pagan its origins, is in its final form Christian. How Christian may never be agreed upon, of course. Did the essentially heathen story accept baptism reluctantly, like the hundred thousand Saracens under Charlemagne's sword in *The Song of Roland*, or did it, like Bramimunde in the same poem, "hear so many sermons and parables that she...asked to be made a Christian"? This paper will cast its lot with the converted queen.

In our own day, the religious sophistication of the poem has commanded scholarly respect. Recent critics, unwilling to accept the poem's Christianity as mere "coloration," have argued for a much deeper Christian dye. Hamilton, Robertson and Bloomfield have emphasized its patristic lore, Cabaniss its liturgical subtleties, Goldsmith its catechetical qualities, and Father McNamee the poem's mission: a delicate Christian allegory fulfilling but never destroying its pagan base.[1] It is the intention of this paper to add to this evidence by suggesting that, in attempting to perfect the pagan heroic ideal by submerged references to Christ, the poet was successful in dramatizing not only his *person* but his *dual nature* as well: that by means of plot, character-contrast and imagery the poet drew his Christ-figure in *Beowulf* with hypostatic lines. Of course, this theory will take for granted most of the parallel relationships that Father McNamee has pointed out between the Beowulf story and the Christian story of salvation: Beowulf as savior, as harrower of hell, and as sacrificial victim.[2] It would qualify, however, Father McNamee's contention that the two parts of the poem are artistically intertwined merely because whereas "part one tells the story of salvation emphasizing the historical facts of the Savior, part two repeats the story but dramatizes the kind of Savior Who saved by yielding up His own life."[3] Instead, this paper will offer the suggestion that the structural dichotomy of the poem—the dual mission of Beowulf separated by fifty years—is brilliantly related to the dual mission of Christ, that is, to his Redemptive Act both as *God* and *Man*.

The chief theological concern of the early Ecumenical Councils of the Church was in defining the relationship of Christ to God. In 325, the Council of Nicaea defined the divinity and consubstantiality of Christ, and later councils continued to refine that dogma. The Council of Ephesus in 431 defined the personal union of the two natures in Christ and the divine maternity of Mary; and as late as 680 the Third Council of Constantinople was still at work defining the two wills in Christ. By the time the Beowulf poet was composing his poem, the early medieval Church had clarified the dogma of the hypostatic union; and the heresies against the dogma—Arianism in the West, Monophysitism and Nestorianism in the East—were quite dead. And yet it is interesting to recall that, with the exception of the Franks, all the Germanic tribes who overran the western Roman Empire in the fourth, fifth and sixth centuries had been converted by Arian missionaries. Even though Clovis's sword had by the eighth century succeeded in keeping an orthodox peace in the Western Church, it would seem that the tenacious, Germanic-disseminated heresy would have to be reckoned with, if only catechetically, in any apologetics of the Christian faith.

Certainly, the Anglo-Latin writers—particularly Bede and Alcuin—display an extraordinary precision in their theological works about the divinity and humanity of Christ. Their knowledge of St. Augustine, for example, whom they regarded "as second only to the Scriptures in authority,"[4] was intimate and far-reaching, even to those Augustinian treatises in some way concerned with the problems of hypostasis—*Enchiridion*, *Liber contra Sermonem Arianorum*, *Contra Maximinum Arianum*, *De Doctrina Christiana*, and *De Trinitate*.[5] Indeed, Alcuin's famous participation in the Council of Frankfurt in 794, at which the Adoptionist heresy was condemned, depended in great measure upon his knowledge of the hypostatic union as Augustine expressed it in the *Enchiridion*.[6]

None of this suggests, of course, that the Beowulf poet was engaged in any catechetical exercise about the natures of the God-man; but it does suggest that the theological air must have been charged with controversy, and that then as now no committed Christian could for very long ignore questioning and examining and meditating upon this central claim of the Christian revelation. Would it be improbable to assume that a cleric-poet whose function it was to baptize the pagan poem—however subtly—in the name of the Father, Son and Holy Ghost and who had probably cut his theological teeth on Augustine[7] would have thought once or twice of frustrating the Arian? If it is not mere fancy to suggest, as Father McNamee has suggested, that the Beowulf poet was reshaping and reorganizing his materials in order "to shadow forth the essential facts of the new story of salvation," then it is entirely probable that his dark conceit may have been intended to dramatize the union of the Son of God and the Son of Man as well.

Even a swift reading of the poem reveals a significant contrast between the Beowulf of part one and the Beowulf of part two, a contrast obviously related to the youth-age dichotomy but at the same time transcending it. One feels that the "two" Beowulfs—their "twoness" emphasized by the fifty-year hiatus—dramatize particularly well the distinction between what Northrop Frye has called the romance hero and the high mimetic hero.[8] The former—a god-like being—is superior not only to other men but also to his environment, whereas the latter, although superior to his fellow men, is subject to the limitations of his environment. When Beowulf comes to assist the Danes, he comes clearly as a romance, or even mythic, figure. We are told that he had the greatest strength among the men of his day ("se wæs moncynnes mægenes strengest/ on þæm dæge," 196–97); that he was the greatest man in the world ("monig oft gecwæð / þætte suð ne norð be sæm tweonum / ofer eormengrund oþer nænig/ under swegles begong selra nære / rondhæbbendra rices wyrðra," 857–61); that he had the strength of thirty men ("he þritiges / manna mægencræft on his mund-gripe/ heaþorof haebbe," 379–81); that he was born of superior people ("þæt ðes eorl wære / geboren betera!" 1702–3). His superiority to his environment as well as to his fellow men—obvious in many instances—is particularly well dramatized by his power over water. In his swimming match with Breca (530–90), he swims clad in armor for five days before defeating the whales at the bottom of the sea; and when he dives into the pool in order to reach Grendel's dam's lair, he sinks through the waves for hours before meeting his adversary (1495–96). Later, the poet reminds us that when the Hetwares killed Hygelac, Beowulf came away from West Frisia by swimming the expanse of the sea (2367–68). Moreover, his voyage from Geatland to Denmark, although not miraculous, is surrounded by an aura of wonder and majesty, particularly from the reactions of the coastwarden.

When he comes to fight the dragon, however, Beowulf is no longer a romance or mythic figure superior in a god-like way to his environment. He has become vulnerable, assailable, human: in Frye's language—high mimetic. He is still, of course, superior to other men, for he himself tells us that he alone is capable of slaying the dragon (2532–34). But Beowulf is not stronger than the dragon, and this human vulnerability is emphasized by more than his death. In part two, Beowulf not only fails to perform any supra-environmental feats, but there are definite suggestions that he *cannot*. Whereas in the first part his superiority to the environment was particularly dramatized by his power over water, in the second part he is especially vulnerable—metaphorically at least—to this very phenomenon. In his first encounter with the dragon, Beowulf sees a *stream* bursting forth from the barrow, the *flood* of the stream hot with deadly flames ("*stream* ut þonan / brecan of beorge wæs þære burnam *wælm* / heaðofyrun hat," 2545–47). Before the dragon emerges from the barrow, Beowulf sees a hostile *vapor* ("hildeswat," 2558) announcing his rage. At the second attack, after Wiglaf has remained faithful, a *wave* of flame burns Beowulf's shield clear to the edge ("Ligyðum forborn / bord wið rond," 2672–73); and when the dragon succeeds in enclosing Beowulf with his sharp teeth, the hero's blood (significantly, this is the first time Beowulf's blood is mentioned) *welled* out in *waves* ("he geblodegod wearð / sawuldriore swat *yðum weoll*," 2692–93). By relating this imagery to the Biblical account of Christ's power over water—his walking on the waves (Matthew 14:22ff.) and his controlling of the tempestuous sea (Mark 4:39), the reader recognizes that the poet's repeated references in the first part to Beowulf's power over water allusively underscore his divinity and that his vulnerability to water in the second part intimates his humanity.

The difference between the two natures is evident also in the two missions, in both their cause and their result. When Beowulf arrives to assist the

Danes, he is performing a merciful and supererogatory act. His father's debt, to be sure, disposed him to be concerned with the Danes' well-being, but the specific assistance he rendered them was *not* something he was *compelled* to do. Although related to the Danes, he was not of them. Whatever aid he brought them was entirely gratuitous, God-sent, and from afar. Hrothgar reminds his thanes of this on two occasions. Before the battle with Grendel, he rejoices that Holy God has sent Beowulf as a help to the Danes against the terror of Grendel ("Hine halig God / for arstafum us onsende / to West-Denum þæs ic wen haebbe / wið Grendles gryre," 381–83); and after the battle he exults that a warrior through God's might has accomplished the deeds which the Danes with their own skill were unable to bring to pass ("Nu scealc hafað / þurh Drihtnes miht dæd gegremede / ðe we ealle ær ne meahton / snyttrum besyrwan," 939–42).

In the battle with the dragon, however, Beowulf as the king of the Geats is *compelled* to destroy the monster who is terrorizing *his own* people; and he makes it clear to them that no one else can do what needs to be done:

> Nis þæt eower sið,
> ne gemet mannes, nefn(e) min anes,
> þæt he wið aglæcean cofoðo dæle,
> eorlscype efne. (2532–35)

The gratuitousness of the first act and the necessity of the second relate significantly to the Redemption; for it is a commonplace of Redemption theology that God's decision to send the Son to redeem mankind was an entirely gratuitous act, one which justice alone could not have demanded, whereas man's ability to satisfy the demands of divine justice depended totally on his offering himself through the merits of the God-man. Thus, Beowulf's gratuitous offer to slay Grendel and his glorious return to his "far-off" home after he has succeeded in doing so dramatize the Divine role in the story of the Redemption, whereas Beowulf's suffering and death in his slaying of the dragon dramatize that part of the Redemption that is particularly human.

This interpretation of the missions is reinforced, moreover, by the "nature" of the different creatures which Beowulf slays. Whereas the dragon is referred to only as a beast, a humanly imaginable entity exactly fifty feet long who fights in daylight for Beowulf and others to see, Grendel's appearance and his parentage are shrouded in almost diabolical mystery. His image is a *shadow* of death in the darkness ("deorc deaþ scua," 160); he rules the misty moors in perpetual night ("sinnihte heold / mistige moras," 161–62) always unseen; and his race is of Cain. This air of mystery which pervades both our image of Grendel and our understanding of what, exactly, he is gives the entire section dealing with Beowulf's slaying of him and his mother an un-natural, and indeed something of a supra-natural or diabolical, cast. One would expect a man to slay a dragon, but only a god can slay his own adversary, the "hellegast."

Texturally, too, both missions underscore the distinction between the two natures in Beowulf. The prominent imagery of the first mission is related in almost all cases to the supernatural aspects of Christ's life. Hrothgar's praise directed to the woman who bore him (942–46), as McNamee has pointed out, subtly echoes the woman's greeting of Christ in Luke 11:27.[9] But the praise, when related to its Biblical source, suggests an awe occasioned by a higher being; for all mortals have mothers, but only mythic men have mothers worthy of honor. Moreover, when we recall that Hrothgar's praise comes immediately *after* Beowulf has cleansed Heorot of Grendel's visitations, we recognize a further allusion to Christ's divinity; for in the gospel passage, the praise of Christ's mother is occasioned by Jesus's exorcism of the devil out of the dumb man and his subsequent insistence, when challenged by his detractors, of his divine power in such an act. "By the finger of God...I cast out devils" (Luke 11:20). The awe of the coastwarden at the appearance of Beowulf and his retinue—"Næfre ic maran geseah / eorla ofer eorþan, ðonne is eower sum" (246–47)—is a further example of the praise directed to the God nature of the God-man, for the remark has echoes of the precursing worshipful remarks of John the Baptist about Christ in John 4:27–36. And the coastwarden's desire to know about Beowulf's origins—"ofost is selest / to gecyðanne, hwanan eowre cyme syndon" (256–57)—echoes the Baptist's wishes that Christ reveal his mission in Luke 7:19. The purging effect of Beowulf's descent into the underworld which transforms the monsters' lake from blood-stained and swirling to calm and clean has already been read as an echo of Christ's harrowing of hell,[10] but not as a detail particularly revelatory of the Divine Nature. The glorious re-appearance of Beowulf after most of the onlookers had given him up for dead and his gift-laden return to his "far-off" home, amid the sorrow of those he has left behind, suggest respectively the Resurrection and the Ascension, two further aspects of Christ's redemptive mission which point to his Divinity. These details allude subtly not to the suffering and dying humanity of the God-man, but to his supernature and the triumph of his Divinity.

On the other hand, most of the significant Christ imagery in the second mission is concerned with the *human* aspects of Christ's Redemption, an imagery which underscores his suffering and death. McNamee has already commented upon the slave's betrayal as an obvious allusion to Judas's betrayal of Christ and Wiglaf's fidelity as a strong suggestion of St. John's fidelity to his lord.[11] The desertion of Beowulf's men, those whom he chose from all his great army, is a further detail alluding to Christ's humiliation. So indeed is the "male Cinderella" quality in Beowulf—"Hean wæs lange / swa hyne Geata bearn godne ne tealdon / ne hyne on medobence micles wyrðne/ drihten Wedera gedon wolde" (2183–86)—allusive of Christ's brethren failing to recognize him as a prophet: "A prophet is not without honor, but in his own country and in his own house and among his own kindred" (Mark 6:4). All these details allude to the Gospel story, and some critics have recognized some of the parallels, but it is important to note that they relate particularly to the betrayal or humiliation of the Son of Man, to those aspects of Christ's life in which he is revealed not in his transfigured or glorified state but in which he is revealed as a man suffering, humiliated, and betrayed by other men. Finally, the image of the funeral smoke rising so high that it seems to be swallowed by Heaven has already been read by Paul B. Taylor as a sign of Beowulf's state of grace[12]; but in contrast to the triumphal "ascension" to his far-off home in the first part, this scene seems particularly revelatory of the human death and seeming destruction that precedes the glory.

In *Beowulf*, then, we see a mythic and glorious hero contrasted with a high mimetic and painfully mortal one; a gratuitous and merciful act contrasted with a necessary and just one; a glorious plot contrasted with a tragic one; a supra-natural monster contrasted with a natural one; and a divine Christ imagery contrasted with a human one. It is true that most of these contrasts function to emphasize the ancient, and not exclusively Christian, *Lif is læne* motif which runs through so much of Anglo-Saxon poetry. But if *Beowulf* is a Christian poem, as so many of its recent commentators have insisted, then these contrasts function in still another, and quite precise, way by forcefully suggesting the Divine-human Redemptive act, the glorious-infamous, joyful-sad triumph-failure of Christ.

Notes to *Beowulf* and the Hypostatic Union

1. Lewis E. Nicholson has conveniently collected some of these critics in *An Anthology of Beowulf Criticism* (University of Notre Dame Press, 1963): Marie Padgett Hamilton, "The Religious Principle in *Beowulf*," D. W. Robertson, Jr., "The Doctrine of Charity in Medieval Literary Gardens: A Topical Approach Through Symbolism and Allegory," Morton W. Bloomfield, "Patristics and Old English Literature: Notes on Some Poems," Allen Cabaniss, "*Beowulf* and the Liturgy," M. B. McNamee, S. J., "*Beowulf*—An Allegory of Salvation?"
2. This theory would quibble at the same time with his use of the word "allegory" to describe the parallels, substituting perhaps "submerged allusion" or "archetypal relationship." It would agree with Marie Padgett Hamilton that "the blend is not allegory, that the Iron shield of Beowulf is not yet the breastplate of Righteousness" (Nicholson, p. 135). Whatever one calls the parallels, however, they remain strikingly present and answer to Father McNamee's contention that "the Beowulf-poet was proceeding in a manner exactly opposite to the procedure of the authors of poems like the *Andreas*. There an explicit Christian subject matter is told in the language and literary conventions of the old Nordic sagas; whereas in *Beowulf* the old pagan sagas are subtly reshaped and reorganized to shadow forth the essential facts of the new story of salvation" (Nicholson, p. 350).
3. Nicholson, pp. 351–52.
4. J. D. A. Ogilvy, *Books Known to Anglo-Latin Writers from Aldhelm to Alcuin, 670–804* (Cambridge, MA, 1936), p. 13.
5. Ogilvy, pp. 13–20.
6. Ogilvy has pointed out that what Alcuin wrote about the relationship between the Father and the Son in his epistle *Contra Felicem* (*Patrologiae Cursus Completus,* ed. J. Migne, vol. 101 [Paris, 1863], p. 134) had its source in Augustine's *Enchiridion*: but no exact parallel is pointed out. Quoted below are the central passages from Augustine and Alcuin that relate to the hypostatic union. Augustine says: "Christ Jesus the Son of God is both God and man: God before all ages, man in this age of ours; God because He was the Word of God...man because in the unity of His person there was joined to the Word a body and rational soul. Accordingly, insofar as He is God, Himself and the Father are one; insofar as He is man, the Father is greater than He.... He has Himself both natures, and from these two natures is one Christ. 'Though he was in the form of God, he thought it not robbery to be'—what He

was by nature—'equal with God, but emptied Himself, taking the form of servant,' Phil. 2. 6–7, neither losing nor diminishing the form of God. Accordingly, He both became less and remained equal, being both in one.... As the Word, He was one of these; as man, the other: as Word, He is equal with the Father; as man, He is less." (*The Fathers of the Church,* ed. R. J. Deferrari et al., vol. 4 [*Writings of Saint Augustine*], pp. 400–401.)

. Alcuin writes: "Catholica enim fides habet...in Christo duas naturas esse proprias et perfectas, divinam scilicet, qua ex Deo Patre ante omnia tempora consubstantialiter natus est: humanum vero qua in plenitudine temporarum ex Virgine idem ipse Filius Dei carnem assumpsit, et factus est verus homo, qui est verus Filius Dei totus in suo...et totus in nostro, idem in utroque, non alter in suo, et alter in nostro." (*Patrologiae*, p. 134)

7. Ogilvy has concluded about Augustine's influence on the English clergy: "it would be much safer to assume that the English knew any given work of Augustine than they did not" (p. 14).
8. Northrop Frye, *Anatomy of Criticism* (Princeton, 1957), p. 33.
9. Nicholson, p. 347, n. 23.
10. In Nicholson, see Allen Cabaniss, "Beowulf and the Liturgy," pp. 223–32; and McNamee, pp. 338–46.
11. In Nicholson, p. 349.
12. Paul Beekman Taylor, "Heofon Riece Swealg: A Sign of Beowulf's State of Grace," *PQ* (April 1963), pp. 257–259..

NOMINALISM AND TYPOLOGY IN CHAUCER

Rodney Delasanta

I.

When Sir Lewis Clifford returned from a diplomatic trip to France in 1386, he presented Geoffrey Chaucer with a ballade from Eustace Deschamps in which the French poet apostrophized his English counterpart as a "Socrates plain de philosophie" and a "Seneque en meurs." At about the same time, while Thomas Usk was awaiting execution in Newgate and lucklessly importuning friends in high places with his *Testament of Love*, he saw fit to address Chaucer therein as "the noble philosophical poete in Englissh."

These well known anecdotal glimpses into Chaucer's life attest to a perception in the late 1380s about some qualities of his genius more honored in his own time than in ours. When Deschamps and Usk praised Chaucer for being "philosophical," they did not use the word as Wordsworth did four hundred years later in the "Intimations Ode"—while romanticizing those advancing years "that bring the philosophic mind"—to mean serene resignation. Nor would they have quite understood Yeats's disavowals when he exclaimed that "the abstract is not life and everywhere draws out its contradictions." On the contrary, for them philosophy meant the sum of speculative human knowledge and wisdom, distinct from theology while remaining its handmaiden, and accessible by the systematic study of its components: logic, physics (philosophy of nature), rational psychology, ethics, politics and, in its upper reaches, metaphysics.

Notwithstanding their high praise of philosophy, medieval thinkers would have been shocked to see the rationalist direction that it was to take later in the history of thought, particularly in the seventeenth century with Descartes and again in the nineteenth with Hegel. What both of these philosophers did, of course, was to disengage philosophy from the service of theology and thereby—if I may tinker with the language of the well-known medieval metaphor—transmute the handmaiden into the queen herself. Whereas some medieval thinkers like Anselm and Aquinas claimed much for human reason—that it could, for example, prove the existence of God Himself—they also acknowledged the paradox that whatever Reason could know on its own was dim indeed compared to the mysterious incandescence of Revelation. They were unembarrassed by the role of philosophy as handmaiden, dutiful and self-abnegating in the service of her queen. It is an attitude appropriate to the direction of this paper, which intends to approach the issue of typological themes in Chaucer via the prolegomena of philosophy as handmaiden to both theology and esthetics.

Up to Chaucer's time, the greatest achievement of medieval art was superintended by an Augustinianism that presupposed a universe in which truth, goodness, and beauty existed transcendentally as *ante rem* universal ideas in the mind of God. From this divine source, these noumena overflowed into the phenomena of created being that were in turn understood by medieval artists—whether they "imitated" them in stone, paint, or words—to be *vestigia* of a higher reality traceable back to the mind of God Himself. As Erwin Panofsky has reminded us:

> The relationship of the artistic mind to its inner notions and its external works...could well be paralleled with the relationship of the Divine Intellect to its inner Ideas and to the world it created; so that the artist, even if he does not have an Idea as such, can nevertheless be thought of as having a "quasi-idea" ... This is in fact how medieval philosophy represented the creative artistic process—comparing the artist with the *deus artifex* or *deus pictor*, not in order to honor art but in order to make it easier to understand the nature and working of the divine mind.[1]

On the theological side, such a metaphysics of *ante rem* universals was perfectly reconcilable to the ancient system of typology whose first principles antedated even Augustine's thought. If *ante rem* universals were metaphysically understood to function as God's exemplary ideas, as his "preconceptions" so to speak, from which created phenomena emanated and in which they participated, they could comfortably coexist in the divine mind with those *typoi* or *figurae* that constituted the providential ordering of human history in patterns which theologians had come to call typological. Erich Auerbach has said it better:

> the [figural] event is enacted according to an ideal model which is a prototype situated in the future and thus far only promised. This model situated in the future and imitated in the figures (one is reminded of the term *imitatio veritatis*) recalls Platonistic notions. It carries us still further. For every future model, though incomplete as history, is already fulfilled in God and Has existed from all eternity in His providence. The figures in which He cloaked it, and the incarnation in which He revealed its meaning, are therefore prophecies of something that has always been, but which will remain veiled for men until the day when they behold the Saviour *revelata facie*, with the sense as well as in spirit. Thus the figures are not only tentative; they are also the tentative form of something eternal and timeless; they point not only to the concrete future, but also to something that always has been and always will be.[2]

Indeed, both the *ante rem* universal and the *typos* or *figura*, addressed respectively in the philosophical and theological enterprises of the time, presupposed residence in a divine mind which begot them, a divine mind in which universals were analogous, as it were, to transcendental "nouns" and *typoi* or *figurae* to transcendental "verbs."

Such was the frame of mind, whether conscious or unconscious, that informed the works of hundreds, perhaps thousands, of mute, inglorious artisans in the millennium of Christian art that preceded Chaucer's time, either nameless or with names on the edge of anonymity like Gislebertus and the Vezelay Master. Despite formidable competition in the later Middle Ages, this Augustinianism continued to wield some influence deep into the fifteenth century in overt allegorical works like *Everyman*; and with the reemphasis on Neo-Platonism and Augustine during the Renaissance and Reformation, it reemerged triumphantly in the sixteenth century with works like *The Faerie Queene*. For those who look at reality and art thus, as Sheila Delany has reminded us, "the world itself is an allegory, and we the exegetes."[3] To the artist functioning under the suzerainty of this metaphysic/esthetic, allegory ministers ideally to narrative, for its preconceptions generate symbols that "provide in advance the correct interpretation of those symbols."[4]

With the coming of the post-Augustinian school of philosophers, whose hallmark was experimentation with Aristotelian epistemology, the allegorical/typological mode found competition, whether consciously or unconsciously, in a revised esthetic. Thomas Aquinas did not argue with Augustine about the *ante rem* nature of divine ideas, but he certainly denied that human knowledge started there. In concert with Aristotle, he insisted that human knowledge was generated from particulars apprehended by the senses, particulars from which universals *in re* could only be abstracted *post rem* by the active intellect. Although *ante rem* universals remained exemplars in the mind of God, man knew reality, in the Thomistic synthesis, not by any illumination emanating therefrom but by a process of abstraction that proceeded from sense experience to image to idea: *nihil in intellectu quod prius in sensu*. Thus, to repeat the well-known Thomistic formula: essence precedes existence ontologically, but existence precedes essence psychologically.

The implications of such a synthesis for art were significantly different from its Augustinian predecessor. Although the medieval masterpieces that gestated under the midwifery of this new philosophy did not totally disengage from the older typological regimen, they nevertheless appeared more naturalistic and less overtly allegorical than their predecessors by virtue of a *tabula rasa* epistemology which denied any nexus to *ante rem* universals. *Chefs d'oevure* such as the sculpture in the west façade of the Strasbourg Cathedral, or the works of Giovanni Pisano, or even the paintings of Giotto may be categorized under the imperatives of this genre. But the *Divine Comedy* is perhaps the best example because, although its *ante rem* allegorical intention [revealed clearly in the letter to Can Grande and in Dante's admonitions to his readers (*Inferno* 9, 61)] controls the literal steps of the journey, the reader never loses the impression of experiencing *existential* reality while following Virgil and Dante down the treacherous footing of the nine circles and up the tortuous purgatorial mount. In other words, although from the perspective of the poet/creator, the allegorical essence of the work precedes its existential incarnations in the specific fictions (just as *ante rem* universals in the divine mind precede their *in re* incarnations in created phenomena), still from the perspective of the reader the essence of the poem cannot be grasped until it is first experienced step by step, *terza rima* by *terza rima*, canto by canto, in its existential totality. As such, the work is a narrative manifestation of the Thomistic doctrine that, although essence precedes existence in the ontological order, existence precedes essence in the psychological.

By the late fourteenth century, the nominalism of William of Ockham had overwhelmed both Augustinian exemplarism and Thomistic moderate realism (which had been badly wounded by the Condemnations of 1277).[5] Nominalism's refusal to accommodate phenomena to noesis in traditional ways would not only dethrone the reigning philosophies and theologies, but it would also filter many of its speculations down to the studios of artist and poet. Whereas both Augustine and Thomas had sought to explain the Many in terms of the One (in epistemologies that ultimately derived from Plato and Aristotle respectively), Ockham insisted on the exclusivity of the Many while denying altogether the ontological existence of the One. If universals existed at all, they were to be found neither *ante rem* in the mind of God, nor *in re* in particulars. They were in fact only mental constructs with no *real* connection to the objective world. Ockham taught that, because the order of the world was ruled by the inscrutable and inaccessible divine *will* and not by the intermediary of more scrutable and accessible ideas in the divine intellect, there was no reason to multiply the existence of universal ideas anywhere else except in the *human* mind. The famous formula from Ockham reads: "*Numquam ponenda est pluralitas sine necessitate.*" By denying the ontological *pluralitas* of universals, either *ante rem* in the mind of God or *in re* in the created order outside of the human intellect, Ockham held for the utter individuality, singularity, and particularity of all being. The only place he allowed universals was in the human mind and only as arbitrary generic signs for all the individuals that alone had real existence.

The implications of this kind of nominalism for late medieval art were profound and much more revolutionary than the earlier shift from Augustinianism to Thomism. I have said elsewhere that the gradual ascendancy of the singular over the universal (the Many chasing out the One) contributed to the slow diminution of allegory as the dominant artistic mode and to the substitution of a competing naturalism.[6] One need only compare the "Augustinian-inspired" sculpture of Gislebertus and the Vezelay Master at Autun and Vezelay, respectively, with the radically naturalistic sculpture of the ambulatory screen at Notre Dame de Paris or the rout of singular figures at St. Maclou in Rouen to realize that a major shift in style occurred from thirteenth- to early fifteenth-century modes—a shift inadequately expressed by words like *romanesque*, *gothic*, or *late gothic*. Against the Gislerbertian emphasis on the bare essentials of the biblical figure is the Parisian and Rouenian celebration of singulars. Erwin Panofsky was more than a generation ahead of literary scholars when he perceptively saw this kind of late medieval art as "comparable indeed to the *philosophia moderna* of those nominalists who found the quality of real existence only in things 'individual by virtue of themselves and by nothing else.'"[7]

But typology too suffered an inevitable impairment at the hands of the new philosophy. As a way of interpreting salvific history, typology depends upon an understanding of God that necessarily assumes the existence of Divine Ideas. Whether these Ideas are understood, in the philosophical sense, as *ante rem* universals or, in the theological sense, as *typoi* that manifest themselves providentially over the march of history is less important than the assurance that they belong to a Divine Mind that is accessible to human knowledge—whether by the analogical vehicle of metaphysical thought or by the benign strategies of Revelation. It is this sense of proportional accessibility, however infinitely distant, of the human to the Divine mind that for centuries sustained a belief in Predestination and in Revelation as an infallible sign of God's foreknowledge. In Thomas Aquinas's famous definition, predestination is "a certain Divine pre-ordination *from eternity* of those things which are to be done *in time* by the grace of God" (*ST* III, q. 24, a. 1): Accordingly, predestination implies a certain antecedence in regard to that which is predestined, an antecedence that traditionally had its *locus* in the Divine Intellect. But when, by Chaucer's time, nominalist thinkers had emptied the Divine Mind of Ideas in favor of an utterly radical Will, both the certitude of Predestination and the reliability of Revelation as a sign of God's immutable plan suffered a rude shock. By rendering supernatural habits and forms dispensable in a salvific order now less fixed than ever before, Ockham in effect rejected the view that predestination is a *real* relation between God, the predestinate person, and blessedness[8]—i.e., he denied that predestination or reprobation signify anything *really* existing as agenda in the Divine Mind, so that man is free even to "act contrary to the antecedent divine will."[9] Indeed, a nominalist like the Carmelite John Kenningham, for example, could make the startling claim that "every future act...is necessarily contingent; even a prophecy, which is the affirmation of the certainty of a future event, cannot necessitate that event. So if Christ himself should make a revealed prophecy, it would remain a contingent statement until the moment of its actual occurrence."[10] The consequence of all this "pelagianism," as Thomas Bradwardine called it, was that the process of salvation was no longer approachable by human intelligence. And the further impact of these ideas on art could not but have variously "deconstructed" the elaborate system of typology upon which so much of medieval art was built. It is not to be wondered that in scanning the poetry of Chaucer we should discover the bare ruined choirs of that typology.

2.

Despite the staying power of the Augustinian critics, the poetry of Chaucer has begun to be examined against this shift of emphasis away from the controlling universal—away from the assumptions of an *ante rem* intention that seeks to incarnate its existential fictions in allegorical modes.[11] The *Canterbury Tales*, for example, carries few suggestions of overt allegory, and that apparent disengagement is what has endeared Chaucer to the modern sensibility, which is militantly anti-allegorical. Never would Chaucer have been able to exclaim in concert with Dante: "O voi, che avete gl'intelleti sani, / Mirate la dottrina che s'asconde / Sotto il velame degli versi strani" (*Inferno* 9, 61). [O you who have sound minds, look closely at the teaching hidden under the covering of my strange verses.] Rather, the quotidian life Chaucer describes for us, especially in his later works, is much more recalcitrant with genera and much more indulgent with separables: in C. S. Lewis's phrase, "incorrigibly plural." The cause, as some commentators have claimed, was at least in part a nominalist skepticism uncomfortable with cheap universals inherited from an intellectual tradition that for too long had gone unexamined.

The befuddled testimony of Chaucer's surrogate narrator, Geoffrey the Pilgrim (and in his earlier incarnations Geoffrey the Dreamer, Geoffrey the Unrequited Lover, Geoffrey the Historian, Geoffrey the Maligned Chauvinist), dramatizes a limited intelligence, overtaxed by the burden of discrete singulars, from which it is incapable of abstracting valid universal truths. This radical dependence on particulars splinters whatever omniscience had been traditionally accorded the poet into plural narrations at deliberate cross-purposes: from the uncertain voices of Geoffrey the Pilgrim to Harry Bailly to twenty-one more of the pilgrims. This comic *que sais-je?* seems to assure only the unascertainability of truth by distancing it at farther and farther removes from the controlling intelligence of Chaucer the Poet, who by willfully distancing himself from omniscience into a kind of *auctor absconditus* forces questions upon his readers usually left to philosophers: What kind of knowledge is possible when universals have been banished from their former *ante rem, in re*, and *post rem* loci? How is analogical language, including the language of typological indirection, affected by such a debilitated epistemology?

If Chaucer was introduced to these questions from the philosophical debates of his century, he would have known the differences between the traditional position (of a Thomist like his friend and neighbor Ralph Strode, for example) and that of the nominalists. Whereas traditional theology had sought to confer upon philosophy the dignity of a handmaiden—*fides quaerens intellectum*—the Ockhamists hoped to humble it in order to exalt faith. More particularly, by demoting the function of the universal, they expected to inaugurate a series of ultimately benign reductions or deflations within the epistemological process: from demonstration to possibility; from necessity to conditionality; and—of special interest to us as it relates to esthetic practice—from an epistemology comfortable with *analogical* predication to one that admitted only *univocal* or *equivocal* predication. As staples of medieval epistemology, the terms repay investigation in this context.

Whereas *univocity* and *equivocity* are no more difficult to understand in the medieval sense than in the modern, *analogy* presents greater problems. (1) *Analogy* is the applicability of a concept to a corresponding object in a manner that acknowledges *both* the similarity and the difference of the analogate to the analogue. What analogy recognizes is that, in spite of the great differences between the term and the object (in the case of man and God a difference in the actual mode of being—i.e., man *has* being in the participative sense, whereas God *is* being), some conformity obtains notwithstanding the differences, and *that conformity can be validly articulated.* (2) *Univocity* is the applicability of a concept to an object in only one, unambiguous, specific sense, so that exactly the same thing answers to it. (3) *Equivocity* is the applicability of a concept to an object in more than one sense so that multiple ambiguous meanings answer to it.

To a traditional Thomist for whom concepts, and by extension words too, represent *real* things, the *object* is the criterion of the truth of the sign, whether that sign is involved in judgments about natural objects or about God Himself. Because man bears a likeness to God and because that likeness is a *real* relation of common attributes which the universal idea adequates (however distinct the mode of being is between man and God), knowledge about mankind from an experiential starting point allows the knower to have a proportional knowledge about God. Accordingly, even the partial, proportional representation of truth present in analogical predication, which reasons "from the existence of things seen to the existence of things unseen"[12]—or, as Thoreau wrote in his journal, "from our hands to our head"—is capable of providing valid similitudes. Indeed, even the similitude of paralleling the artist's mind (with its inner notions) to God's (with its *ante rem* Ideas), as Erwin Panofsky has already reminded us, constitutes valid analogical knowledge. While such an epistemology is aware of the tension "between man's God-given ability to speak about God and the impossibility of his ever saying anything truly commensurate with Him"[13] (the tension, in other words, between God's accessibility and ineffability), it nevertheless functions as a guarantor of symbolic statement because, simply said, it trusts the sign. To quote Thoreau again: "All perception of truth is the detection of an analogy."

To a nominalist, by contrast, for whom propositions are made up of terms that by their very nature *cannot* adequate the object (because *in re* or *ante rem* universals do not exist ontologically), knowledge by analogical predication, especially about God, is at best inadequate and at worst impossible; and thus one must be content with a *reductio* toward univocal or equivocal predication.[14] Such an epistemology, which rises inevitably from the nominalist insistence on the inviolate individuality of all being, functions as a guarantor only of mimetic or ambiguous statement because it does not trust the sign to perform feats of proportionality.[15]

That, on one level, Chaucer's art acknowledges univocal predication requires little commentary here. It has been amply attested to in the twentieth century by critics, from Kittredge to Lumiansky and, more recently, Derek Pearsall, who have based their criticism on the assumption that, as a reporter mimetically recording the glories and foibles of his time, Chaucer meant pretty much what he said. Obvious ironies are admitted, of course, *pace* Sister Madeleva's famous defense of the Prioress, but symbols are suspect. Therefore, although the univocal school has said something unimpeachable, if only partial, about the Chaucerian intention, it was inevitable that someone sooner or later would "discover" a level of analogical predication that an Augustinian esthetic, however debilitated by fourteenth-century challenges, virtually guaranteed. Led by scholars like Robertson and Huppé since the late 1950s, the patristic school has insisted, sometimes with doctrinaire stridency, that Chaucer meant considerably *more* than what he said, and that by way of an iconography long since lost to the twentieth century. By impressive scholarly efforts of iconographic reclamation, patristic scholars have succeeded in forcing readers into a sometimes reluctant acknowledgement of analogical predication in Chaucer's work. By now even the most unreconstructed univocal critic would find it hard to deny that Chaucer's emphasis on certain images does in fact connect to universal meanings beyond the particular: that the pilgrimage, for example, means considerably more than "the only way" varied estates could confront each other in order to enhance realistic clashes of personality; that the Wife's deafness is not merely a "realistic incident" but an analogical nexus leading beyond aural disability to the iconographic tradition of those who have ears and hear not; that January's blindness leads beyond merely ocular infirmity to an iconographic tradition of those who have eyes and see not. Notwithstanding the overstatement of the allegorical school that unconvincingly theorizes in defense of its own exclusivity that late medieval style does not display "imitations of actions actually carried out by individuals," it is evident that something inestimably valuable has been said here, at least about one level of Chaucerian discourse.

But if both the univocal and analogical schools have variously addressed epistemological strategies in Chaucerian narrative, it remained for those who detected a nominalist/equivocal dimension in Chaucer to stake their claims as well. Sheila Delany has argued, for example, that because the century in which Chaucer lived was uniquely complex and ambiguous in its assumptions and challenges, it was "precisely this sense of the ambiguity or complexity of life that allegory [was] not suited to convey."[16] "The limitation of allegory," she continues, "[became] apparent...when the experiences and attitudes to be portrayed pass[ed] a certain degree of complexity...[when] the complexity or simultaneity of motive and implication which exists at any given point"[17] made it ill-suited for the systematizations of allegory. Accordingly, as Stewart Justman has argued, Chaucer's artistic strategies "represent a major break with the [traditional] view that the world of the senses—the literal world—is necessarily a sacred cipher or 'analogy,' and that 'signs' are necessarily spiritually inscribed." For him, indeed, "The *Canterbury Tales* abound with mock signs, false expectations, [and] allegory that fails"[18]—a strategy, I submit, of equivocal discourse born of nominalist epistemology.

3.

Much of what has already been said about the epistemology of Chaucerian narrative assumes a distinction so simple between Chaucer the Poet and Chaucer the Pilgrim that when it first appeared in a *PMLA* article by E. Talbot Donaldson in 1954[19] it sent Chaucerians of all stripes back to the text for another look. What he said about the *Canterbury Tales*, of course, is a *sine qua non* of narrative criticism everywhere: i.e., the reader must not assume that the writer and the narrator he has invented are the same person and duplicate the same consciousness; Chaucer the Pilgrim is no more to be identified with Chaucer the Poet, Donaldson reminded us, than Lemuel Gulliver is to be identified with Jonathan Swift. To do so would remove from the Chaucerian intention a broad range of ironic discourse that is one of the glories of the *Canterbury Tales* because, in terms Donaldson did not himself use, it filters much of the observation of the human condition through the nominalist consciousness of an unreliable witness.

Much refinement of position followed that piece: *contra* Donaldson, it was correctly asserted, for example, that Chaucer the Poet sometimes unaccountably abandons his *auctor absconditus* detachment and enters the poem with his own voice. Donald Howard even invented a felicitous phrase that designated those moments of authorial intrusion: *unimpersonated artistry*.[20] Barbara Nolan has gone on to refine the refinement by positing three voices in the General Prologue: the "clerkly" voice of authority; the pilgrim's voice of the fallen world in which "chance, change, unpredictability hold sway"; and the "boold" voice of Harry Bailly which, "empowered by the pilgrim voice, assumes control over the design of the tales."[21] Notwithstanding the refinements, the basic distinction holds true for most Chaucerians; Chaucer the Poet has seen fit to separate himself, more often than not, from Chaucer the Pilgrim.

If I may be allowed a refinement of my own, I should like to suggest that the pilgrim narrator, despite his differentiation from Chaucer the Poet and despite his frequent victimization at the ironic hands of his creator, is almost always allowed by the end of the work to arrive at some kind of epiphany, however less than luminous it may be. This is not to claim that Chaucer the narrator ends his spiritual odyssey contemplating the Ineffable, as Dante does in the *Paradiso*, but neither does universal darkness bury all, as it does for Lemuel Gulliver. Barbara Nolan has maintained that Chaucer the pilgrim "eschew[s]...the comforts of enlightenment,"[22] but even a cursory survey of Chaucer's peripities suggests the opposite to be true. The languorous narrator of *The Book of the Duchess*, for example, who reveals himself in the first twenty-nine lines as oppressed by "sorwful ymagynacioun," profits as much from his dream as does his chief character, the Black Knight, for by the end of the elegy the narrator quickens from his despondency and vows to "put this sweven in ryme / as I kan best, and that anoon." The self-righteous interpreter of dreams at the opening of *The House of Fame* comes to a paradoxical awareness, after a comically Dantesque journey to the higher spheres, that even without the testimony of the "man of gret auctoritee" "fals and soth" cannot be cleanly demarcated one from the other but necessarily exist "compouned." For the first fifty-six lines of *Troilus and Criseyde*, the narrator introduces himself as a victimized poet of courtly love, a stranger to experience who has come to know love only through the vicarious world of books; but by the end of the poem we observe him experiencing a conversion away from the "love twaddle" (to quote James Smith) that had debilitated him for so long to an awareness of its "brotelnesse" and "vanyte." And, finally, the pilgrim/narrator of the *Canterbury Tales*, who refuses to make earnest out of game early in the journey, is convinced by the time of the Parson's Prologue that the pilgrimage is "greet mateere" indeed and that, in unison with his fellow pilgrims, it should end in "vertuous sentence."

What is important is that in each case mentioned above, Chaucer the Poet, by leading his Narrators from benign befuddlement to feeble epiphany, has resisted *permanent* entrapment in the univocal or equivocal snares of nominalist epistemology. It may be true, as Stewart Justman has maintained, that Chaucer "is interested more in the violabilty than the inviolability of the word...more in the loophole, quibble, or trick case than in the categorical standard,"[23] but that is because to have proclaimed inviolabilities and categorical standards in the late fourteenth century would have constituted a cavalier dismissal of everything that a century of philosophical "disputisoun" had fought over. Such a dismissal would have necessitated the espousal of overt allegorical narrative, which Chaucer obviously found to be inadequate in his vision of a world made irrevocably more complex by that very "disputisoun." Yet to say that Chaucer seemed to prefer quibbles to categories is *not* to proclaim the *final* victory of the quibble. He may, for reasons of artistic feint, have hidden his light under a bushel, but only for a time and without any final intention of seeing it extinguished there. Indeed, it is this tension between the bushel and the light, between the voluble asseverations of Chaucer the Pilgrim and the tacit assumptions of Chaucer the Poet, that vivifies much of the art of the *Canterbury Tales.*

At its philosophical/esthetic base, I contend that while Chaucer the *Pilgrim* serves as the spokesman for a *nominalist* epistemology that, by limiting its vision to the palpably empirical, unwittingly dramatizes the inadequacies of reason, Chaucer the *Poet* continues to uphold a more traditional epistemology that has abandoned neither those *ante rem* ideas located "perdurabely in the devyne thought" (*Boece*, V, Prosa 4, 170) nor the *in re* and *post rem* universals whose *locus* is "yplounged" and "yhyd" deep in the "rote of sothfastnesse" (*Boece*, III, Metrum 11).[24] Such a tension between what the Pilgrim says and what the Poet means is the very *urstoff* of Chaucerian parody, which so many commentators have seen as a major fictive strategy in his art. The word itself—para/oide—which etymologically means one song sung alongside another, implies a double consciousness, a comic imitation of a serious manner which paradoxically cannot be articulated without an almost loving appreciation of the original. Yet although that original, like Keats's spirit ditty of no tone, remains unplayed, it remains in its very tacitness infinitely sweeter than the heard melody. What is actually heard in the *Canterbury Tales*, of course, is the raucous music of the Miller's bagpipes and the perverted duet of the Summoner and Pardoner, which "burdoun[s]" the great trumpet voice of the one against the small, thin, goat-bleat of the other. But the unheard music of the spheres, which these pilgrims distort, has a title nonetheless—one that, in fact, Chaucer the Poet has allowed his unwitting narrator to supply as the *leitmotif* of pilgrimage: "Com hider, love, to me!"

In this respect, Stewart Justman is only half right when he argues that, because the *Tales* "abound with mock signs, false expectations, [and] allegory that fails," they "represent a major break with the view that the...literal world is necessarily a sacred cipher or analogy."[25] If I may attempt to flesh out his argument with terms I have used earlier, it would proceed thus: Because an esthetic of efficacious signs is dependent upon a realist (or, like Aquinas's, a moderate realist) epistemology, any disfunction of the *ante rem* universal will effect a correspondent disruption in the efficacy of analogical predication. If the particular is discouraged, as it is in nominalism, from pointing proportionally (or analogically) to a reality beyond itself, the whole ancient apparatus of efficacious signs collapses. Whereas, philosophically speaking, a predictable though contingent world ordered by *ante rem* ideas in the mind of God connects, theologically speaking, to a typological/figural interpretation of history in which Revelation is understood to be a sign of God's foreknowledge and predestination its guarantor, a nominalist world stripped of *ante rem* universals and subject to the asymmetries of God's *potentia absoluta* (with its attendant dismissal of the certitudes of foreknowledge, Revelation, and predestination) connects only fitfully to any typological system of salvific history and may in fact produce the mock signs, false expectations, and failed allegory of which Justman speaks.

But, as I have insisted above, the mock signs do not answer to Chaucer's *final* intention. We must not confuse their ubiquity in the *Canterbury Tales* with their entelechy. When the pilgrim/narrator describes the Summoner and the Pardoner singing a debased duet while the Miller's bagpipes equivocally lead the pilgrims "oute of towne," the discord is simply *not* Chaucer's final word. We may be witnessing a typology of signs gone awry, and those ruptured signs may dominate our attention for a time, but by the end of the pilgrimage we will have observed that Chaucer the Poet has—in Raymond P. Tripp's words—put "new fruit into the old chaff."[26] We will have witnessed that Chaucer has in fact deliberately fractured received ideas in order to recover the spiritual meanings within them[27]; and what will have been recovered by the time the Parson urges his charges to *confiteor* is that "Com hider, love, to me," in spite of the papuliferous and androgynous mockery issuing from the mouths of its unholy cantors, has been exactly the right song after all.

4.

As the central *topos* of the *Canterbury Tales,* the pilgrimage is broad enough to bear these tensions not only *univocally*, but also *equivocally* and *analogically*, for its range of meanings extends from percept through parody to paradigm. Univocal, equivocal, analogical—these are the three ways of experiencing pilgrimage that Chaucer "assays" from Southwark to Bobbe-up-and-Doun: *by assigning univocal perception, born of nominalist epistemology, to his dull, sublunary narrator while transmuting that literalness into analogical or typological paradigm by means of parody.* Indeed, the ongoing dispute between the traditional critics of Chaucer, for whom the pilgrimage is only dramatic or satiric occasion, and the patristics, who interpret it uncompromisingly as salvific way, has oversimplified this larger, more complex intention. To graph the tensions pertaining to that complexity, we must remind ourselves of the obvious: that pilgrimage was both quotidian journey and a metonymy of the questing life in the Middle Ages and thus reflected the purity or the perversion of that experience as it waxed and waned across the centuries.

If Chaucer were to have written a history of his own time, he could not but have anticipated Christopher Dawson's judgment that the later Middle Ages—of which the waning pilgrimage was symptomatic—failed to fulfill the spiritual promise of its beginnings: "From the tenth to the thirteenth century, European culture under the urge of a powerful religious impulse had been centripetal, towards unity and towards the ideal of Catholic universalism. From the beginning of the fourteenth century, this tendency [was] reversed and centrifugal movement set in which ultimately culminated...in the complete destruction of the religious unity of Christendom."[28] To an age buffeted by the storms of dynastic contention, peasant revolts, black deaths, interminable wars, unprecedented schisms, radical heresies, and—especially germane to our study—philosophical revolutions, the "spiritual promise" of its antecedents must have seemed an idle hope. Nor under the circumstances could the centripetally produced unity of thirteenth-century religious art have maintained its "deep and perfect harmony" (the phrase is Emile Mâles') throughout the centrifugal dislocations of the fourteenth. The earlier harmonies so confidently preached, taught, and sung by its philosophers, theologians, and artists must have rung somewhat hollow to those who saw clearly that the age of Aquinas, Dante, and the great cathedrals was nearly over. (The repeated collapses of the choir of Beauvais Cathedral from 1284 might well have seemed a metonymic prophecy of the collapse of an age.)

Certainly, pilgrimage was one victim of that centrifugal dislocation. As an exercise in religious devotion, it had by Chaucer's time lost much of its pristine purity so that a century later it would come to earn the scorn of Erasmus and

More. This is not to say that, for some, it did not remain a significant penitential act; but for many, baubled like Langland's pilgrim with tokens from faraway shrines, Saint Truth was conspicuously missing from among the relics. Indeed, for most of its fifty-four miles from tavern to thrope's end, the Canterbury pilgrimage reads more like a mock sign than a true token of spiritual odyssey—just as the Pardoner's sales pitch for indulgences is a mock sign of penitential earnestness and the Monk's corpulence a mock sign of holy asceticism. In terms which by now have become familiar, we are tempted to say that the pilgrimage serves as a mock universal, under which perverted genus Chaucer has gathered a host of mock particulars, an antipilgrimage, as Donald Howard describes it, "in which things traditionally peripheral are brought to the fore and things traditionally central allowed to lapse into the background."[29]

Had his spiritual sense been less acute, Chaucer could well have dismissed the entire peregrination as unregenerate muddle and added his voice to the Lollard William Thorpe's in choleric denunciation of pilgrimage and pilgrims: "everie towne that they come through, what with the noise of their singing, and with the sound of their piping, and with the jangling of their Canterburie bels, and with the barking out of dogges after them...they make more noise, then if the king came there away, with all his clarions, and many other minstrels. And if these men and women be a moneth out in their pilgrimage, many of them shall be an halfe yeare after, great janglers, tale-tellers and liers."[30] But Chaucer's temper, happily, was not so proto-Puritan. If there is one Catholic teaching to which Chaucer testifies by his art, above all others, it is that man both *bears* and *distorts* the divine image. What the virtuous Thorpe saw and chastised with his weak univocal vision was what Malvolio would later see: the distortion alone. What Chaucer the pilgrim saw through his rose-colored spectacles was the *curiositas* of Cockaigne. But what Chaucer the Poet detected behind the distortion was the true substance of pilgrimage "yhyd" beneath the debased accidents, a reality whose appearance had been besmirched by time and custom but whose *ding an sich* remained inviolate. Despite his disdain in the *House of Fame* for "pilgrimes / With scrippes bret-ful of lesynges," Chaucer could still in a later lyric appeal to the ideal of pilgrimage as undebased analogy for the Way:

> Her is non hoom, her nis but wildernesse:
> Forth pilgrim, forth! Forth, beste, out of thy stal!
> Know thy contree, look up, thank God of al;
> Hold the heye wey, and lat thy gost thee lede... ("Truth," 17–20)

He was well aware that the remnant of sanctity in late fourteenth-century pilgrimage, what Coulton has called its "far-off halo," possessed in earlier times more integrity. Then, pilgrimage had been a more solemn matter, encouraged and often imposed by the Church as penitential practice (without carping from the heterodox like Thorpe or even the orthodox like Archbishop Sudbury), and canonized by her in the liturgy. Indeed its ideal meaning had been typologically fixed in pilgrimage votive masses centuries before by scriptural readings that, well into Chaucer's day and beyond, would have reminded the *nouveaux voyageurs* of holier pilgrims in holier times, such as the pilgrim-patriarch Abraham sent out of Ur by Yahweh to find a new land and the pilgrim-apostles sent by Jesus to convert the world before the final day. The *Sarum Missal* juxtaposed these scriptural voyages from Genesis and the gospel of Matthew as typological commemorations intended to direct quotidian pilgrims, in the Parson's words, to "the righte wey of Jerusalem celestial" (X, 79). In the *lectio* of the *Missa pro iter agentibus*,[31] for example, we read these words of Abraham, noteworthy for the divine promise of a future land:

> The Lord God of heaven, who took me out of my father's house, and out of my native country...spoke to me, and swore to me, saying: To thy seed will I give this land; he will send his angel before thee. (Genesis 24:7)

And immediately thereafter, as typological complement in the gospel selection, we read this imperative of Jesus to his apostles, noteworthy for enjoining upon them a poverty that extends to scrip and staff, but also for its reminder of the connection between pilgrimage and eschaton:

> And going, preach, saying: The kingdom of heaven is at hand. Heal the sick, raise the dead, cleanse the lepers, cast out devils. Freely have

> you received: freely give. Do not possess gold, nor silver, nor money in your purses. Nor scrip for your journey, nor two coats, nor shoes, nor a staff... And whatsoever city or town you shall enter, inquire who in it is worthy: and there abide till you go thence.... And whosoever shall not receive you, nor hear your words: going forth out of that house or city shake off the dust from your feet. Amen, I say to you, it shall be more tolerable for the land of Sodom and Gomorrah in the day of judgment than for that city. (Matthew 10:7–15)

What these votive readings urged, then, was a typological ideal that connected pilgrimage backward to promise and forward to eschaton: by counting themselves among Abraham's seed for whom a new land had been prepared after a long journey, and by enrolling themselves in the ranks of the poor pilgrim-apostles of the Lord sent as witnesses to the imminence of the Kingdom of Heaven, the pilgrims were expected to equip themselves spiritually for the final day of judgment when the unreceptive *civitas terrena* would be punished even more severely than Sodom or Gomorrah and when the *civitas dei* would open its holy gates. Unfortunately by Chaucer's day eschatological expectation had been crowded out by tourist *curiositas*[32] so that pilgrimage had been diverted from its apocalyptic direction. The extraordinary popular response in the late fourteenth and fifteenth centuries to Mandeville's *Travels* (three hundred surviving manuscripts!) exposes the often debased motive for pilgrimage in this burgeoning secular age in which the *straunge strondes* of this world were of greater attraction than the *ferne halwes* heralding the next.

Yet notwithstanding the distractions of latter-day pilgrims away from the eschatological compulsions of pilgrimage, distractions that seem to have occupied most of Chaucer the Pilgrim-Narrator's nominalist attention, at the end of this worldly pageant Chaucer the Poet offers penance—however mixed or even talismanic its motives—as the most efficacious antidote to the religious, moral, and philosophical confusion that was the inheritance of the age. Accordingly, it is not unpurposeful that Chaucer the Poet should "direct" the Host to turn the control of the pilgrimage over to the Parson as the pilgrims approach the Holy City. Having been dismissed as Jankin and Lollard, having been put off as a spoilsport of their *divertissements* until this penultimate moment, the good priest is finally acknowledged as appropriate instrument of sentence:

> For, as it seemed, it was for to doone,
> To enden in som vertuous *sentence*,
> And for to yeve hym space and audience. (X, 62–64)

But, as I have argued elsewhere,[33] the "sentence" to which the pilgrims unanimously agree is a "word with two visages"—and even three. Although the obvious denotation of "sentence" here is meant as a term of rhetoric (as distinct from "solaas"), it also implies, in addition to the sentence of eschatological judgment, epistemological confidence in the ascertainability of truth (because "sentence" proceeds from "sense," as concept proceeds from percept, or as idea proceeds from image). Moreover, as Paul B. Taylor has convincingly argued, the Parson's "sentence" on penitence—by insisting on both the moral and epistemological corrective of contrition, confession and satisfaction—reestablishes the harmony between thought, word, and deed that had been disrupted in the nominalistic disordering of tales and tellers.[34] Pilgrimage, therefore, despite its apparent reduction into *curiositas*, is reconstituted by parody into what it had been in the beginning, a nimble metonymy for the Christian Way.

And so it goes with each of the great typological themes that Chaucer will trot out for inspection during the journey to Canterbury. Although we may be tempted to read them nominalistically, with Chaucer the Pilgrim, as mock signs, we must delay judgment about their efficacy until Chaucer the Poet plumbs the "rote of sothfastnesse" to find first parody and then paradigm there.

Notes to Nominalism and Typology in Chaucer

1. Erwin Panofsky, *Idea: A Concept in Art Theory*, trans. Joseph J. S. Peake (Columbia: University of South Carolina Press, 1968), p. 40.

2. Erich Auerbach, "Figura," in *Scenes from the Drama of European Literature* (Gloucester, MA: Peter Smith, 1973), p. 59.
3. Sheila Delany, "The Late Medieval Attack on Analogical Thought: Undoing Substantial Connection," in Kenneth McRovine, ed., *Chaos and Form: History and Literature/Ideals and Relationships* (Winnipeg: University of Manitoba Press, 1972), p. 42.
4. Delany, p. 41.
5. The most comprehensive exposition of Ockham's thought is Gordon Left, *William of Ockham: The Metamorphosis of Scholastic Discourse* (Manchester: Manchester University Press, 1975). But note that Notre Dame Press has just published a two-volume work on Ockham by Marilyn McCord Adams, *William Ockham*, 2 vols. (Notre Dame: University of Notre Dame Press, 1987). Also useful is Leff's *The Dissolution of the Medieval Outlook* (New York: Harper & Row, 1976). Of the standard histories of philosophy, I have made most use of Etienne Gilson, *History of Christian Philosophy in the Middle Ages* (New York: Random House, 1955), but Armand A. Maurer, "Some Aspects of Fourteenth-Century Philosophy," *Mediaevalia et Humanistica*, 7 (1976), pp. 175–88 is the best short treatment. Some of Ockham translated into English may be read in *Ockham: Philosophical Writings*, trans. Philotheus Boehner (Indianapolis: Bobbs-Merrill, 1964) and Marilyn McCord Adams and Norman Kretzmann, eds., *William of Ockham: Predestination, God's Foreknowledge, and Future Contingents* (New York: Appleton-Century-Crofts, 1969).
6. "Chaucer and the Problem of the Universal," *Mediaevalia*, 9 (1986), p. 148.
7. *Early Netherlandish Painting* (Cambridge, MA: Harvard University Press, 1953), I, p. 35.
8. Adams and Kretzmann, p. 16.
9. Adams and Kretzmann, p. 19.
10. J. A. Robson, *Wyclif and the Oxford Schools* (Cambridge: Cambridge University Press, 1961), p. 167.
11. *The House of Fame* seems to be especially fertile ground for nominalist theories of poetry as they apply to Chaucer. See, for example, Laurence Eldredge, "Chaucer's *House of Fame* and the *Via Moderna*," *Neuphilologische Mitteilungen*, 71 (1970), pp. 105–119; Sheila Delany, *Chaucer's House of Fame: The Poetics of Skeptical Fideism* (Chicago: University of Chicago Press, 1972); and Piero Boitani, "Chaucer's Labyrinth: Fourteenth-Century Literature and Language," *Chaucer Review*, 17 (1983), pp. 197–220.
12. Laurence Eldredge, "Boethian Epistemology and Chaucer's *Troilus* in the Light of Fourteenth-Century Thought," *Mediaevalia*, 2 (1976), p. 53.
13. Marcia Colish, *The Mirror of Language: A Study in the Medieval Theory of Knowledge* (New Haven: Yale University Press, 1968), p. 208.
14. Leff, *William of Ockham*, p. 163.
15. Delany, "Late Medieval Attack," p. 52.
16. Delany, p. 55.
17. Delany, p. 56.
18. Stewart Justman, "Literal and Symbolic in the *Canterbury Tales*," *Chaucer Review*, 14 (1980), p. 199.
19. "Chaucer the Pilgrim," *PMLA*, 69 (1954), pp. 928–36.
20. *The Idea of the Canterbury Tales* (Berkeley: University of California Press, 1976), p. 243
21. Barbara Nolan, "'A Poet Their Was': Chaucer's Voices in the General Prologue to the *Canterbury Tales*," *PMLA*, 101 (1986), pp. 158–64.

22. Nolan, p. 160.
23. Stewart M. Justman, "Abuse of Authority in Chaucer," *DAI*, 37 (1976), 3607A.
24. For a more fully argued Chaucerian nexus to Boethius in this regard, see my "Chaucer and the Problem of the Universal," pp. 154–61. For an opposite view, see Russell A. Peck, "Chaucer and the Nominalist Question," *Speculum*, 57 (1978), pp. 745–60.
25. "Literal and Symbolic," p. 199.
26. Raymond P. Tripp, Jr., *Beyond Canterbury* (Denver: Society for New Language Study, 1977), p. 121.
27. Russell A. Peck, "Public Dreams and Private Myths," *PMLA*, 90 (1975), p. 158.
28. *Medieval Essays* (New York: Image Books, 1959), p. 101.
29. Howard, p. 162.
30. Quoted in G. G. Coulton, *Chaucer and his England* (London: University Paperback 1963), p. 125.
31. J. Wickham Legg, ed. *The Sarum Missal* (Oxford: Clarendon Press, 1969), p. 405.
32. Christian Zacher, *Curiosity and Pilgrimage* (Baltimore: Johns Hopkins University Press, 1976).
33. "The Theme of Judgment in the *Canterbury Tales*," *MLQ*, 31 (1970), pp. 298–307.
34. "Chaucer's *Cosyn to the Dede*," *Speculum*, 57 (1982), pp. 315–27.

CHAUCER AND THE PROBLEM OF THE UNIVERSAL

Rodney Delasanta

From the beginning, Christianity has paid court to Lady Philosophy: at first briefly and with dubious success, as we read in Paul's wooing of the Athenian Epicureans and Stoics in Acts 17; then more forcefully among the early Fathers, as we may infer from Tertullian's reactionary lament —"What has Athens to do with Jerusalem?"; and later with paternal blessing from the premier Father of the Western Church, the Neoplatonist St. Augustine.[1] By the High Middle Ages, as we are all aware, a marriage between the two was finally consummated. The double impediments of extreme realism raised by William of Champeaux and extreme nominalism raised by Roscelin in the eleventh century had been largely resolved, or so it seemed, first by the moderate realism of Abelard and later by the champion matchmaker, Thomas Aquinas, who clasped Reason's hand in Revelation's and asserted their distinct but complementary roles in the pursuit of truth.

Among the major issues that prevented the marriage for so long (and one that shortly thereafter was to force a divorce) was the problem of the *universal*, that Proteus of Form which took sundry shapes among sundry philosophers in order to elude truth-telling. For the Christian thinker, of course, the universal's precise placement in the accommodation of *noesis* to phenomenon had serious implications for the Faith. Platonize the universal to the extent that phenomena are reduced to mere shadows of transcendent truth, and one necessarily does violence to the existential value of God's creation and, moreover, to human history, which according to Christian thought God had redeemed by the Incarnation of Christ. Impugn the reality of the flesh, in other words, and suffer the dangers of an inevitable Gnosticism. On the other hand, Aristotelianize the universal to the extent that the only objective reality is reduced to the phenomenon, and one traps the noumenon in his own mind, does violence to the essentiality of the real, and makes inaccessible to rational man a metaphysical and moral order. Impugn the reality of the *Idea*, in other words, and suffer the dangers of skepticism or, worse, fideism.

The solution was found, it has been averred, by the compromising genius of Thomas Aquinas, who sought to settle the question by locating the universal *ante rem* in the mind of God (so preserving the ordination of divine reason in the created universe), the universal *in re* in phenomena (so preserving the existential integrity of individual creation), and the universal *post rem* in the mind of man (so preserving the demonstrability of objective truth by a spiritual faculty capable of knowing it). Thus, to repeat the philosophical formula, in the Thomistic synthesis essence precedes existence in the ontological order, but existence precedes essence in the logical order.

The implications of such a synthesis for aesthetics should have been significant. By reasserting the universal *ante rem* in the mind of God, art can never move very far from interpreting reality according to the rational ordinations of an exemplary cause; and thus a symbolic or allegorical vehicle urging doctrinal and didactic truth can never be very far from its intention. At the same time, by submerging the universal *in re* in phenomena, art is bound to the concrete, never loath to number the streaks of a tulip, for it is only by the accidents of streaks that the substance of the tulip can be known. Concomitantly, the abstracting of the universal *post rem* frees art from the incommunicability of individual cognition trapped in experience and assures the transmissibility of truth.

With the exception of the *Divine Comedy*, however, most medieval works came to light under a different illumination. Thomas' influence upon medieval culture was sporadic and late, soon to be dissipated by the subtle detractors encouraged by the Condemnations of 1277. Up to Thomas' time and even beyond it, the greatest efflorescence of medieval art was effected by an Augustinian *Weltanschauung*—accommodated as it was whether consciously or unconsciously to Neoplatonism—that stressed exemplary and final cause over efficient and formal cause. As a Christian, of course, Augustine had to insist on the existentiality of literal and historical phenomena (which served in their rhetorical emanations as a restraint upon allegorical flight). But even so, the virtuosity of his exegesis of Scripture was obviously directed in large part toward the explication of allegorical meanings therein. And so Augustine's famous imperative against mistaking the figurative for the literal presupposed a universe in which universal truth, goodness, and beauty transcendentally and exemplarily existed in the mind of God, from which they overflowed—as signs of those Ideas—into all created phenomena. These phenomena were to be treated by artists not as self-sufficient objects of contemplation, like William Carlos Williams' red wheelbarrow, but as signs of higher reality ultimately traceable to Ideas in the mind of God. Such notions were ideally suited (pun fully intended) to ministrations of allegory, and Christian art is rife with examples of such an aesthetic.

By the middle of the fourteenth century, with Augustinian exemplarism showing signs of age and Thomistic moderate realism forced into desuetude by Scotist detractors, a new—and largely original philosophy initiated by William of Ockham had invaded the lecture halls of the great European universities. Its refusal to accommodate phenomenon to *noesis*—an accommodation that had taken place in traditional Christian philosophy—would have a profound effect upon reigning philosophies and theologies and would filter many of its *quodlibet* down to the studios of the artist and the poet.

What Ockham did, as anyone who has studied fourteenth-century thought is quite aware, was to reverse the direction of Christian philosophy as it had developed from the days of Augustine.[2] Rather than try to explain the individual as a derivative from the universal, Ockham strove to understand how the universal could be derived from a world made up of intuitively known singulars. In a way, this had been Aristotle's problem, too, and the problem as well of his thirteenth-century godfather, Thomas Aquinas. But whereas Aquinas taught that whatever the mind abstracted from the singular thing was its essence or form adhering in similar individuals as the source of their likeness, Ockham insisted that the mind's recognition of likenesses among similar individuals (and its reduction of these likenesses into species and genera) did *not* represent any essence or form distinct from the individuals themselves, not even archetypally distinct in the mind of God where they had enjoyed transcendental status from the time of Plotinus. On the contrary, Ockham's first axiom asserted that, because the order of the world is utterly contingent on the divine will and is not controlled by the mutability of divine Ideas or necessitated by secondary causes, only individual things exist ontologically and all human knowledge derives from intuitive cognition of them. Like Scotus, Ockham denied the ancient notion—as old indeed as Plato's *Dialogues*—that the proper object of the intellect could only be the Idea freed from its unknowability in the senses; and he insisted upon the intellect's intuitive ability to know the individual. The traditional concept that the superiority of the intellect over the senses resulted from its transforming of the expendably concrete phantasm into the lofty universal, the image into the Idea, was thus stood on its head. To Ockham, the universal was utterly more imperfect a mental construct than the singular because as a mere abstraction it could be known only conceptually in the intellect and not outside of it. Possessing no extra-mental reality, the universal could only make claim to logical, and not ontological, reality.

The implications of this philosophy for late medieval art were profound. Inevitably, the gradual ascendancy of the singular over the universal (the Many chasing out the One) contributed to the slow diminution of allegory as the dominant artistic mode and to the intro-mission of naturalism as a competing style. (With apologies to Zola, I shall henceforth use the word *naturalism* instead of *realism* to designate artistic technique so as to distinguish narrative realism from the philosophical system of the same name.) Even without artistic expertise, one need only compare the Platonistically inspired sculpture of the north porch of Chartres Cathedral, for example, with the naturalistic sculpture of the ambulatory screen at Notre Dame de Paris to realize that a major shift in style occurred from thirteenth- to early-fifteenth-century modes. Against the Chartrean emphasis on the essentiality of the Biblical figures—with their studied neglect of detail—is the Parisian celebration of existential singulars—with every gesture, facial feature, or garment fold chiseled into a festive naturalism. Or perhaps a comparison of the universalized geometricities of Duccio with the particularized grotesques of Pieter Brueghel will suffice to remind us that, late in the medieval period, the age of the singular had dawned and that of the universal had receded.

The poetry of Chaucer deserves to be re-examined against this shift of emphasis away from the controlling universal, away from the assumption of an *ante rem* intention that purports to incarnate its existential fictions in allegorical modes. If the *Canterbury Tales* is *not* anything overtly, it is *not* overtly allegorical. Whatever the merits of the claims of patristic critics, those claims have been made against a common-sense view of Chaucer that recognizes his greatest talent to be the purveying of plenty in which universal types are not easily espied. Indeed, one comes away from Chaucer's work, when critical theories have been put out of mind, charmed with a sense—to use Auden's phrase—of "the happy eachness of things." The "collision" of singulars in Chaucer, to modify the phrase from Professor Shelley, requires few explicators; it is the alleged "collusion" of these singulars into a pattern of universality that has been the *causa belli literari*. Certainly, from Chaucer the Pilgrim's point of view, the *Canterbury Tales* seem recollected in confusion as a plethora of people and events, a flux of experience over which the narrator has only tenuous control, despite his protestations of competence, "accordaunt to resoun."[3] The effect is of life recalcitrant to genera. (Indeed, on the few occasions when Chaucer's chief marshal, Harry Bailly, forces his charges into hierarchy, he is spectacularly unsuccessful: e.g., the drunken Miller insisting on requiting the Knight instead of bowing to the social prerogatives of the Monk in Fragment I; or the Cook so sodden with wine that his only response to Harry's command to tell his tale in Fragment IX is to fall off his horse into the mire. Can one conceive of Virgil the guide suffering such indignities in the *Inferno*?)

Some recent commentators, usually in opposition to the Robertsonian refusal to acknowledge the hegemony of singulars in Chaucer's work, have begun to find in Ockhamist epistemology an antidote to the doctrinaire *allegoresis* that they find objectionable in their Augustinian colleagues.[4] Some of their prelusive observations tempt us into *amplificatio*. For example, the plenitude of Chaucer's observations in the *Canterbury Tales*, made with his Brueghel-like attention to discrete singulars from which, with few exceptions, universal types do not readily emerge, depends for its effect upon the testimony of the restricted narrator, Geoffrey the Pilgrim. Chaucer's radical dependence on singulars experientially and intuitively apprehended necessarily transforms the omniscience of the traditional narrator into unreliability and produces a fiction that tilts narrator against narrator and tale against tale in a dialectical joust that seems to unhorse almost all the players and force the audience into a confrontation with the contingencies and relativities of truth-telling. "So as it semed me" is the unwitting epistemological disclaimer by which he sets the tone of the *General Prologue*, and most of the tales that he "delegates" to the other pilgrims contribute to this compendium of uncertainty by asking questions usually left to philosophers: Can man verify truth by his own experience? Can he know with any certitude? Is certitude still possible in a world despoiled of ontological universals? How is language affected by a delimited epistemology?

The Ockhamists had hoped, of course, that by reducing universals from an ontological to a merely logical status they would cripple philosophical certitude in a contingent world where certitudes had no business competing with fideistic truth. Their intention was to aggrandize the Faith by diminishing Philosophy. For the older scholastic axiom that true knowledge equates the intellect with the thing, the Ockhamists substituted the notion of asymmetry, or discrepancy, between the intellect and the thing (the phrase is Gordon Leff's). The result, they expected, would be a series of ultimately benign reductions or deflations within the philosophical enterprise: from demonstration to mere possibility; from necessity to conditionality; and—of considerable importance to aesthetic practice—from an epistemology quite comfortable with analogical predication (and thus a guarantor of symbolic statement) to an epistemology more comfortable with equivocal predication (and thus a guarantor of ambiguity).

How far modern critics have come in recognizing ambiguity in Chaucer's work since the days of Thomas Lounsbury, who in 1892 found only two puns in the whole of the canon! In our day, learned articles and even book-length studies testify to Chaucer's alertness to the function of ambiguity in his language. Even though it would require a tome to investigate the relationship between an epistemology of equivocity and a poetic language attracted to ambiguity (a project I would urge on other Chaucerians), still it is not mere ingenuity to suggest that Chaucer's experimentation with ambiguity may indeed reflect a fourteenth-century detraction of universals that had earlier been understood to be expressible either univocally or analogically but never equivocally.

That Chaucer was aware of the issue of equivocity in language is evident by his own poetic practice which often hangs a tale's meaning on a pun. Certain famous puns leap to mind: "Goddes pryvetee" and "Nowelis flood" in the *Miller's Tale*, "the flour of il endyng" in the *Reeve's Tale*; "cheste" in the *Wife of Bath's Prologue*, "grope" and "ars-metrike" in the *Summoner's Tale*; "taillynge ynough" in the *Shipman's Tale*, etc. But in at least two places Chaucer addresses the issue directly. How much of a Chaucerian aesthetic of ambiguity may we read into Diomede's warning to Criseyde against expecting Troilus to survive the war? Calchas will lead the Greeks to victory, he gloats, "with ambages [ambiguities], That is to seyn, with *double wordes slye*, / Swiche as men clepen *a word with two visages* (*Troilus and Criseyde*, V. 897–99). And what are the full implications of the famous line repeated at both ends of the *Canterbury Tales* that overtly addresses the epistemology of truth-telling in fiction: "The wordes moote be cosyn to the dede"?

Spoken first by Geoffrey the Pilgrim in the *General Prologue* as embarrassed justification of those brilliantly scurrilous tales that are to follow (I. 742) and then by the Manciple, a pilgrimage later, in similar justification for the impending cuckolding of Phoebus (IX. 210), this phrase seems to represent the aesthetic equivalent of the aforementioned epistemological axiom that knowledge is the adequation of the intellect with the thing. Its source in Plato's *Timaeus* and its reappearance in Book III of Boethius's *Consolation of Philosophy* confirm the impression that Chaucer's obvious attraction to this formula is related to the issue of whether or not words do transmit truth. Obviously, Chaucer the Pilgrim has been made to think so, or he would not have tagged his tales with this epistemological apologia. Whether Chaucer the Poet agrees that words can indeed "teilen as it was" is of course another matter.

The flurry of parodic readings of the *Canterbury Tales* in the last twenty years supports the suspicion that although Chaucer the Poet pretends to use a mimetic language that functions as "cousin" to the narrative deed, he in fact delights in a poetic diction that ambiguously "cozens" those deeds instead. Despite the lack of lexicographical evidence that a deliberate ambiguity is being brilliantly exploited by the paronomasial possibilities of *cousin*, Chaucer seems to have manipulated his sources in order to advance the equivocal implications of the word. Although Boethius had not actually made use of the "cousin" metaphor in the *Consolation* (Book III, Prosa 12) but had only used the more generic word *cognatos* (relatives),[5] Chaucer translated this passage for his own *Boece* by drawing "cousin" from a version of the Boethian passage already translated in the *Romance of the Rose*.

> Li dis doit le fait resembler;
> Car les vois as choses voisines
> Doivent estre a lor faiz *cousines*.[6]

Which passage he Englished thus: "Thow hast lernyd by the sentence of Plato, that nedes the wordis moot be *cosynes* to the thinges of which they speken."[7]

By the time we see the word again in the *Canterbury Tales*, however, we may be justified in wondering whether *cousin* has retained its metaphorical innocence or whether, given the paronomasial transformation the word undergoes before our very eyes in the *Shipman's Tale*,[8] it can ever mean "cousin" univocally again. For, interestingly enough, although all poets would agree with the desideratum of the *Consolation* that "language we use ought to be related [cognatos] to the subject of our discourse," yet in Chaucer one cannot help but detect a *sotto voce* by which his words ironically "cozen" as well as mimetically "cousin" his narrative material. Chaucer the Pilgrim's protestations of the need for mimetic adequation between the word and the deed almost beg to be balanced by the suspicion that Chaucer the Poet is experimenting with an equivocal rather than a univocal epistemology. If, in the long history of Chaucerian criticism, such cozening has been dismissed as mere punning japes by the Brahmins of high seriousness, it has also been hailed within the last generation as meaningful paronomasia by those for whom "earnest" need not exclude "game." To alter slightly the question from Donne, "are not our wits pleased with those jests that cozen our expectations?" Quite so, our poet might have answered, as he wondered perhaps whether truth was as accessible a commodity and reason as efficacious a faculty as traditional epistemology had been wont to assert.

In "Lack of Steadfastnesse," for example, a lyric contemporaneous with the *Canterbury Tales* and spoken in a voice manifestly free of ironies, Chaucer betrays a moral weariness with his times—"The world hath made a permutacioun / Fro right to wrong, fro trouble to fikelnesse"—in language that questions Truth's vaunted dominion or Reason's vaunted efficacy: in terms that lament, in fact, the separation of word from deed:

> Somtyme the world was so steadfast and stable
> That mannes word was obligacioun;
> And now it is so fals and deceivable
> That *word and deed*, as in conclusion
> *Ben nothing lyk*, for turned up-so-doun
> Is al this world for mede and wilfulnesse,
> That al is lost for lak of steadfastnesse....
> Trouthe is put doun, resoun is holden fable.
> Vertu hath now no dominacioun.

Upon examining Chaucer's corpus for further epistemologically addressed evidence of moral discontent, one is struck by the number of times his *Weltschmerz* finds expression in some variant of the word-deed dichotomy. "Unlyk is my word to my dede," Fals-Semblant boasts in his catalog of hypocritical actions in the *Romance of the Rose* (6360). And in the *House of Fame* Dido accuses Aeneas and his gender of treachery with similar sentiments: "O have ye men such goodly hede / In speche and never a dele of trouthe?" (I. 330). The antithesis is exploited for ironic effect frequently in *Troilus and Criseyde* (III. 1053; IV. 979; IV. 1471; IV. 1534) and in some of the *Canterbury Tales* (III. 1937; IV. 1916ff.; VI. 918; VII. 1507; VIII. 638). The *Parson's Tale*, as one would expect in such a homiletic context, is fond of expressing its do's and don't's in a catechetical language relating to words and deeds (see ll. 299, 517, 524, 534, 795, 946, 968). Occasionally, virtue is praised rather than vice excoriated by the unusual accord of word and deed (or word and sign), as in *The Legend of Good Women* (1736–39), the *Physician's Tale* (VI. 108), and the *Clerk's Tale* (IV. 708). But more typical is Chaucer's obvious attraction to the process of ambiguity with its "double wordes slye," such as we saw in Diomede's warning to Criseyde.

To be good Chaucerians, then, should we not prefer "cozen" to "cousin" and glory in the "double wordes slye" that manifestly characterize his mature style? Whatever the *final* commitment of Chaucer the Poet to epistemological and aesthetic equivocity (of that more anon), it is evident that Chaucer the Pilgrim at least cannot tell the whole truth because his is a language of inadvertent equivocal terms dependent upon the limitations of his own experience and upon an inadequate intuition of reality. In this respect he is most like the Wife of Bath, who, in her attempt to intuit the truth of the real meaning of marriage, for example, brazenly invokes the muse of experience, that same experience than which—for the nominalists—no greater knowledge could be conceived:

> Experience, though noon auctoritee
> Were in this world, is right ynogh for me
> To speke of wo that is in mariage (III. 1–3)

What the Wife is responding to, a response which the Ellesmere order places immediately after the *Man of Law's Tale*, is the pomposity of universalized "truth" spoken with the discredited rhetoric of self-satisfied Philistines like the Man of Law. Most readers find themselves responding in a fashion sympathetic to Alice's when they are confronted with other truth-poseurs who, like the Merchant, "spak hir resons ful solempnely." Yet, confusingly, even the Wife, with her nominalistic dependence on experience, is no more to be believed, if her muddled *Prologue* and self-serving *Tale* are any indication, than the safer epistemologies of her rivals. Indeed, the reader is tempted to see in the Clerk's Ockhamist language and themes[9] a response not only to the marriage heterodoxies of the Wife but also an ironic commentary on the inadequacy of her unwitting nominalism.

To what extent, then, is Chaucer the Poet inviting us to welcome the question mark and to delight in the confusion? Has John Gardner summed up the problem correctly by saying that Chaucer expresses in his poetry "a tension between an orthodox theory of reality and an unorthodox intuition of reality"?[10]

One is forced into a *sic et non* response here when putting aside an admittedly indecisive discussion of Chaucer's unorthodox intuitions about reality in order to examine his orthodox theories, for there is considerable contradictory evidence suggesting that his sympathies lay with earlier, more traditional doctrine. Despite all the studies of the influence of Boethius on Chaucer—particularly in areas relating to divine foreknowledge, predestination, and free will—no one to my knowledge has investigated the significance to Chaucer of those passages in the *Consolation of Philosophy* that address themselves to the universal.[11] Admittedly, one cannot assume that a translator need be sympathetic to the philosophical stand of his subject (although it is a truism that a good translation is often the end result of the translator's strong attraction to the original). But does not Chaucer's strong attraction to his original on major Boethian themes in tales like the Knight's and the Nun's Priest's suggest more than mere academic interest in his philosophical mentor? Why else in the ninth decade of the fourteenth century, in an age of *nouveauté* dominated by the nominalist thought of *au courant* Oxonian skeptics or crypto-skeptics like William of Ockham, Adam of Woodham, Thomas Buckingham, and their Parisian counterparts like John of Mirecourt and Nicholas of Autrecourt, would the mature Chaucer have interrupted the most creative decade of his life to translate a philosophical chestnut like the *Consolation*?

One simply cannot dismiss the obvious reply that, unlike his countrymen who, Delilah-like, razored the potency of reason into debility, Chaucer sought to retrieve from philosophy precisely what Boethius had claimed to offer in its name—consolation: consolation in a metaphysic that placed cosmic love at the center of being; consolation in a theodicy that reconciled divine foreknowledge and omnipotence to the efficacy of man's free will; and consolation, above all, in an epistemology that assumed the accessibility and transmissibility of truth by a process of intellection that adequated generic universals to discrete singulars. It is in this last consolation that Chaucer's involvement with Boethius has been most ignored.

One must remember that the central epistemological axiom dominating nominalistic thought in Chaucer's day categorically denied the traditional explanation of the universal as having any kind of ontological existence, either *in re* (as the Aristotelians would have it) or *ante rem* (as the Neoplatonists taught). The implications of such a revolutionary idea for art we have already examined, even to the point of suggesting that the *urstoff* of Chaucer's poetic in the *Canterbury Tales* involved a necessarily unreliable narrator lolling in an Ockhamist universe of splendidly unnegotiable singulars. Yet here is our Chaucer, not five years before the creation of Geoffrey the Pilgrim, spiritedly translating passages from Boethius which not only reasserted the traditional hierarchy of man's cognitive faculties leading from the senses to the intellect but which also reasserted the superiority of the universal over the singular, a superiority that is even given a divine *locus*:

> For the wit [senses] comprehendith withoute-forthe [outwardly] the figure of the body of the man that is establisschid in the matere subgett; but the ymaginacioun comprehendith oonly the figure withoute the matere; resoun surmountith ymaginacioun and comprehendith by an universal lokynge the comune spece that is in the singular speces; but the eighe of the intelligence is hyere, for it surmountith the envyrounyne of the universite, and loketh over that bi pure subtilte of thought thilke same symple forme of man that is *perdurablely in the devyne thought.*[12]

The distinction between the reason and the intelligence is original with Boethius and need not detain us here. But I italicize the last clause because it is probably original with Chaucer, appearing nowhere in the Boethian text. "Perdurablely in the devyne thought" is a phrase redolent of an *ante rem*, Platonic interpretation of the universal (or beyond the universal to the "symple forme," as Chaucer calls it) that caps what is otherwise an Aristotelian *post rem* explanation of universals abstracted from singulars.

Admittedly, the point of Boethius' discourse in Book V is not to make any special claims for the ontological integrity of the universal, for that integrity is a datum in a dialectic which proceeds to higher argument. Just as man's senses and imagination are incapable of knowing in the spiritual manner by which his reason and intelligence know (spiritual by virtue of his ability to abstract the universal from the singular: "oute of matere," Chaucer translates it), so by analogy is man incapable of knowing in the eternal manner (what the Nun's

Priest will call His "heigh ymaginacioun") by which God *fore*knows. But this Boethian point is not as important to our purposes here as are the happy circumstances of our being able to observe Chaucer painstakingly translating some complex passages from the *Consolation* that reveal him in lengthy and ostensibly sympathetic involvement with traditional epistemology. Here are some telling excerpts dealing with the respective objects of man's hierarchically ordered cognitive faculties. As one would expect, the universal and "symple forme" receives the honorifics:

> For wit [senses] ne mai no thing comprehende out of matere ne the ymaginacioun loketh nat the universels speces, ne resoun ne taketh nat the symple forme so as intelligence takith it; but intelligence, that lookith al aboven, whanne it hath comprehended the forme, it knoweth and demyth alle the thinges that ben undir that foorme. But sche knoweth hem in thilke manere in the whiche it comprehended thilke same symple forme that ne nevere ben knowen to noon of that othere *(that is to sayn, to non of the thre forseyde strengthis of the soule)*. For it knoweth the universite of [by] resoun, and the figure of [by] ymaginacioun, and the sensible material conceyved by wit.... Certes, resoun, whan it lokith any thing universel, it ne useth nat of ymaginacioun, nor of wit [senses]; and algates yit it comprehendith the thingis ymaginable and sensible. For resoun is she that diffynyscheth the universel of here conceyte [fancy].[13]

Shortly thereafter, we find Chaucer translating a long passage in which Boethius says, in sum, that just as man must prefer the testimony of his highest cognitive faculty—the reason—to that of his lower faculties—the senses and the imagination—so by analogy should he trust the testimony of the divine mind as regards foreknowledge and predestination over the inadequate surmises of human understanding in these mysterious matters. Again, my intention in quoting here is not to pursue the Boethian argument but rather to observe Chaucer hard at work Englishing the traditional epistemology:

> But resoun is al oonly to the lynage of mankynde, ryght as intelligence

> is oonly the devyne nature. Of which it folweth that thilke knowynge is more worth than thise oothre, syn it knoweth the subject...of alle othre knowynges. But how schal it thanne be, yif that wit and ymaginacioun stryven ayein resonynge, and seyn that, of thilke universel thingis that resoun weneth to seen, that it nis ryght naught? For wit and ymaginacioun seyn that that that [sic] is sensible or ymaginable, it ne mai nat ben universel. Thanne is either the jugement of resoun soth, ne that ther nis no thing sensible; or elles, for that resoun woot wel that many things ben subject to wit and to ymaginacioun, thanne is the concepcioun of resoun veyn and fais, which that lokith and comprehendith that that is sensible and singular as universel.[14]

As one would expect, the either/or argument translated here goes on to decide *against* the "veyn and fals" opinion that "lokith" at the singular as if it were the universal: not exactly a put-down of the nominalist position (for the nominalists did accept the *logical* integrity of the universal) but an argument that comes remarkably close to countering Ockham's central doctrine.

More evidence from Chaucer's *Boece* that seems to recommend his sympathy for traditional epistemology comes from two glosses—one of which is the longest in the entire *Consolation*—that he adapted from the Latin commentaries of Nicholas Trivet and the Pseudo-Aquinas.[15] In Metrum 11 of Book III, Boethius' encouragement to whoever "would seek the truth with thoughts profound" ("quisquis profunda mente vestigat verum") and his caveat to whoever "would not stray into false bypaths" ("cupitque nullis ille deviis falli") combine to lead to an apology for the Platonic doctrine of the soul's recollection of Ideas. The glosses, however, seem to stress more the ability of the human soul to connect the truth of what is naturally within itself to what is without, the adequation of the intellect to the thing, than to urge any doctrine of remembered ideas in the strict Platonic sense:

> Whoso wol soke the depe ground of soth in his thought, and wil nat ben disseyvid by false proposiciouns that goon amys fro the trouthe, lat hym wel examine and rolle withynne hymself the nature and the propretes of

> the thing; and let hym yet eftsoones examinen and rollen his thoghtes by good deliberacioun or [ere] that he deme, and lat hym techyn his soule that it hath, by natural principles kyndeliche yhyd withynne itself, al the trouthe the which he ymagineth to be in thinges withoute.... This is to seyn, how schulde men deme the sothe of any thing that were axid, yif ther nere a rote of sothfastnesse that were yplounged and hyd in the naturel principles, the which sothfastnesse lyvede within the depnesse of the thought?[16]

If I may be allowed to gloss a gloss, it would seem that Chaucer is urging certain points uncompromisingly in this passage while leaving some lesser points up to the reader: (1) Truth *is* accessible to the mind, but its accessibility may be "disseyvid" by false propositions. What the false propositions are he does not say, but they obviously would have to be at variance with numbers two and three following. (2) The seeker after truth must look within his mind and find there the properties and nature of the thing without. (3) Since "nature" obviously refers to the essence, or substance, or universal of the correspondent singular thing without, it is clear that the mind is capable of knowing truth only if it adequates itself to reality by a process of intellection that connects whatever is "yhyd" within itself to whatever is "in thinges withoute." The Platonist, of course, would interpret the inner principle to be an innate idea which the mind "recollects," rather than an acquired idea which the mind abstracts from phenomena, but either way the truth-giving value of the universal Idea, whatever its origin, is being celebrated.

Powerful phrases about the mind's operations like "natural principles kyndliche yhyd withinne itself' and "rote of sothfastnesse...yplounged and hyd in the naturel principles" underscore Chaucer's attraction, at least in this period, to the epistemology of *ante rem* Ideas from which man's ideas temporally derive. Such a theory, which Aquinas, despite his Aristotelian bent, incorporated into his philosophy, had been scorned by the avant-garde philosophers of the fourteenth century—except for two remarkable reactionaries whose influence on Chaucer has been well documented. One of them, Thomas Bradwardine, Chaucer immortalized by a single allusion in the *Nun's Priest's Tale*.[17] The other,

John Wycliffe, though never directly mentioned in Chaucer's pages, was the founder of the religious reform movement for which our poet betrayed considerable sympathy, and was patronized by the same great nobleman who, by a quirk of fate, was to become Chaucer's brother-in-law, John of Gaunt. Both men reacted with militant horror to the rampant nominalism of their time, conceiving of it as a danger rather than an aid to faith, and labored mightily to re-establish the priority of the idea in the ongoing confrontation between *noesis* and phenomenon. Their schoolmen's contribution to the "greet altercacioun" and the "greet disputicoun" to which Chaucer's Nun's Priest comically alludes has been admirably reviewed by scholars and needs no further commentary here.[18] But one must wonder whether Chaucer's motives for translating Boethius could have been related in some way to the antinominalist efforts of these latter-day realists. Is it possible, for example, that Bradwardine would have been enrolled unpurposefully on the side of the angels, Augustine and Boethius, in the divine foreknowledge-free will controversy that Chaucer comically celebrates in the *Nun's Priest's Tale*? (As realists, of course, all three philosophers variously agreed on the *ante rem* status of divine Ideas and, as a consequence, leaned hard on the what-that-God-forwoot-moot-needs-be" side of the argument that finally proves true against the skepticism of Pertelote.) And, as the most extreme realist of his time, could Wycliffe—whose militant enthusiasms extended philosophically to universals as well as to evangelical reform—have gone unnoticed by a contemporary like Chaucer, whose close friends, the knights Clifford and Stury, were prominent Lollards?

Thus does the preceding *sic et non* seem to vindicate John Gardner's aforementioned observation that Chaucer's art dramatizes "a tension between an orthodox theory of reality and an unorthodox intuition of reality." The "orthodox theory" appears conspicuously visible in the *Boece*, which must have given some comfort to the reaction against nominalism triggered earlier in the century by Bradwardine and culminating in Wycliffe. At the same time, the "unorthodox intuition" seems to inform a good deal of Chaucer's narrative method. If it is out of the fissures of such tension that great art bursts—like Shakespeare's tragedies exploding out of the igneous Mannerist challenge to the security of the Elizabethan Renaissance—it may be argued that the *Canterbury Tales* also erupted from two conflicting world views. For while one may readily detect in Chaucer's virtuoso use of ironic "ambages" a certain narrative acknowledgement of nominalist equivocity, one may also detect therein an ineradicable respect, even a preference, for that older system of adequating *noesis* to phenomenon which—though in his day obsolescent and unconsoling—awaited rediscovery and reconception.

Perhaps the manner of that reconception required an artistic feint—a nominalist surface cozening a realist depth; but the implications of this paradox must be pursued elsewhere. Suffice it to say here that just as Geoffrey the Pilgrim has been understood to serve the *de profundis* intentions of Chaucer the Poet, so too have the ambiguities of the surface voice resonated unwitting truth "deep down things." "Trouthe thee shal delivere," Chaucer assures us in his late lyric, but not via the cheap universals agile upon the lips of the rectitudinous—like the Man of Law, the Physician, and even perhaps Geoffrey himself in the *Melibee*. Against such, the irony resident in nominalist skepticism "cozens" correctively. Against such, even the heresiarch opinions of doubters like Dame Alice serve truth, if only to sear off its impurities. Like the burning coal that touched the mouth of Isaiah the prophet, irony has ever served to cauterize venerable truths debased into conventional wisdom by unworthy *nuntii*. But beneath the healed surface, if the *Boece* is to be believed, "yplounged" and "yhyd" deep in things, lies a "rote of sothfastnesse" deliverable, it would seem, only after the agony of pilgrimage.

Notes to Chaucer and the Problem of the Universal

1. "If those who are called philosophers, especially the Platonists, have said things which are indeed true and well accommodated to our faith, they should not be feared; rather what they have said should be taken from them as from unjust possessors and converted to our use." St. Augustine, *On Christian Doctrine*, trans. D. W. Robertson, Jr. (New York, 1958), p. 75.
2. The exposition of medieval nominalist thought in this paper is dependent upon a variety of sources, the most influential to my understanding being Gordon Leff's brilliant study, *Wil-*

liam of Ockham: The Metamorphosis of Scholastic Discourse (Manchester, 1975). Also useful are his *Medieval Thought, St. Augustine to Ockham* (Baltimore, 1958) and *The Dissolution of the Medieval Outlook* (New York, 1976). In addition, I have made considerable use of Frederick Copelston, *A History of Philosophy: Late Medieval and Renaissance Philosophy*, Vol. III (New York, 1963); Etienne Gilson, *History of Christian Philosophy in the Middle Ages* (New York, 1955); *Ockham: Philosophical Writings*, trans. Philotheus Boehner (Indianapolis, 1964); and Marilyn McCord Adams and Norman Kretzmann, eds., *William of Ockham: Predestination, God's Foreknowledge, and Future Contingents* (New York, 1969). Of ancillary value to this study are two books by Heiko Augustinus Oberman, *The Harvest of Medieval Theology* (Cambridge, MA, 1963) and *Forerunners of the Reformation* (New York, 1966).

3. Geoffrey Chaucer, *The Canterbury Tales: General Prologue*, l. 37. All citations of Chaucer's work are from *The Works of Geoffrey Chaucer*, ed., F. N. Robinson, 2nd ed. (Boston, 1957).
4. The fullest treatment of the question appears in the unpublished dissertation of Rosemary T. A. Wass, O.P., "Chaucer and Late Medieval Scholasticism: A Preliminary Study of Individuality and Experience," *DAI*, 34 (1974). The issue is also briefly addressed in two volumes by John Gardner, *The Life and Times of Chaucer* (New York, 1977) and *The Poetry of Chaucer* (Carbondale and Edwardsville, IL, 1977). The fideistic implications are the center of Sheila Delany's study, *Chaucer's House of Fame: The Poetics of Skeptical Fideism* (Chicago, 1972). Other treatments include Geoffrey Shepherd, "Religion and Philosophy in Chaucer," in *Geoffrey Chaucer: Writers and Their Background*, ed. Derek Brewer (Athens, OH, 1975), pp. 262–89, and Winthrop Wetherbee, "Some Intellectual Themes in Chaucer's Poetry," in *Geoffrey Chaucer: Contemporary Studies in Literature*, ed. George D. Economou (New York, 1975), pp. 75–91. The important study by Russell A. Peck ("Chaucer and the Nominalist Questions," *Speculum*, 53 [1978], pp. 745–60) involves issues largely unrelated to my observations, although his identification of voluntarist epistemology with "Chaucer's strongly Boethian orientation" (p. 746) is at odds with my own interpretation, which sees Ockham and Boethius on opposite sides of the philosophical fence. Two articles that appeared after I completed this essay are of major importance: P. B. Taylor, "Chaucer's *Cosyn to the Dede*," *Speculum*, 57 (1982), pp. 315–327 and Piero Boitani, "Chaucer's Labyrinth: Fourteenth-Century Literature and Language," *The Chaucer Review*, 17 (1983), pp. 197–220.
5. "Cum Platone sanciente didiceris *cognatos* de quibus loquuntur rebus oportere esse sermones." Boethius, *The Consolation of Philosophy*, Loeb Classical Library (Cambridge, MA, 1918), p. 292.
6. Quoted by Skeat in his edition of the *Complete Works of Geoffrey Chaucer, Notes to the Canterbury Tales*, 2nd ed. (Oxford, 1900), p. 57.
7. Chaucer, *Boece*, Book III, Metrum 11, ll. 205–07 (ed., Robinson, p. 357).
8. Ruth M. Fisher, "*Cosyn* and *Cosynage*: Complicated Punning in Chaucer's 'Shipman's Tale'?" *Notes & Queries*, 12 (1965), pp. 168–70. See also David H. Abraham, "*Cosyn* and *Cosynage*: Pun and Structure in the *Shipman's Tale*," *Chaucer Review*, 11 (1977), pp. 319–27. Admittedly, there is no evidence in the *Oxford English Dictionary* that *cozen* as a noun was understood in Chaucer's day to mean deceit or trick, even though anyone who reads the *Shipman's Tale* cannot but make the connection between "cosynage" and deception. Interestingly, however, the *Oxford English Dictionary* does list two items (see "cozen," No. 8) from the late sixteenth century in which *cousin*, meaning "cozen", is used as a noun in the phrase "to make a cousin of," and the *Medieval English Dictionary* offers similar meanings as early as 1453.

9. See Robert Stepsis, "*Potentia Absoluta* and the *Clerk's Tale*," *Chaucer Review*, 10 (1975), pp. 129–46; David C. Steinmetz, "Late Medieval Nominalism and the *Clerk's Tale*," *Chaucer Review*, 12 (1977), pp. 38–55.
10. *The Poetry of Chaucer*, p. xxvi.
11. Laurence Eldredge has written perceptively on the problem of Boethian epistemology with respect to *Troilus and Criseyde*: "Boethian Epistemology and Chaucer's *Troilus* in the Light of Fourteenth-Century Thought," *Mediaevalia*, 2, (1976), pp. 49–75.
12. Chaucer, *Boece*, Book V, Prosa 4, ll. 156–68 (ed., Robinson, p. 379).
13. Chaucer, *Boece*, Book V, Prosa 4, ll. 174–98 (ed., Robinson, p. 379).
14. Chaucer, *Boece*, Book V, Prosa 5, ll. 34–56 (ed., Robinson, p. 380).
15. Chaucer, *Boece*, Book III, Metrum 11, ll. 13–43 (ed., Robinson, p. 355).
16. Chaucer, *Nun's Priest's Tale*, l. 3242 (ed., Robinson, p. 203).
17. Bernard L. Jefferson, *Chaucer and the Consolation of Philosophy* (rpt. New York, 1968), pp. 11–13.
18. Gordon Leff, *Bradwardine and the Pelagians* (Cambridge, 1957) and "John Wycliff: The Path to Dissent," *Proceedings of the British Academy*, 52 (1966), pp. 143–80. See also Morton W. Bloomfield, "Fourteenth-Century England: Realism and Rationalism in Wycliff and Chaucer," *English Studies in Africa*, 16 (1973), pp. 59–70.

THE HORSEMEN OF *THE CANTERBURY TALES*

Rodney Delasanta

The well of English undefiled has in recent years been pumped hard by those critics who see Chaucer's art as inextricably bound to the orthodox tenets of medieval Christianity and patristic esthetics. Their testimony has been of inestimable value in asserting the "public" meaning of Chaucer's art, in tying his ostensibly private images and symbols to an iconographic tradition rooted deeply in the Bible and nourished by patristic exegesis. But as impressive as their theoretical testimony has been, the practical evidence they have offered from Chaucer's art has not always convinced.[1] I suspect that this fault can be laid more to the learned zeal of the defense than to the essential merits of their case, that in drawing up their briefs they have at times relied too heavily on the esoterica of patristic exegesis and too little on the Biblical texts which spawned the glossolia. It would seem more likely that with a life so short and a craft so long to learn Chaucer would have assayed harder with the Evangelists than with the Fathers, although certainly it would be folly to discount the influence of the latter.

Two ingenious (and convincing) readings by patristic critics of Chaucer's pilgrims' equestrian habits come to mind here. Both D. W. Robertson, Jr.,[2] and Beryl Rowland,[3] in pointing to the conventional medieval symbol of the horse and rider as representative of the restraining soul and the libidinous body, offer successful insights into the sexual irregularities of the Monk and the Wife of Bath by reference to their equestrian habits. In developing the sexual ambiguities of the phrase "an outridere, that lovede venerie," Robertson quotes one of the Fathers of the Church, St. Gregory the Great: "Indeed the horse is the body of any holy soul, which it knows how to restrain from illicit action with the bridle of continence and to release in the exercise of good works with the spur of charity."[4] In conjunction with this exegetical tradition which interconnects "woman/horse/flesh," Robertson glosses the sexually compromising meanings of "prikasour," "hunting for the hare," obesity, and "shameless staring eyes," in order to demonstrate Chaucer's castigation of his Monk's fleshly aberrations.[5] Rowland, in a more far-ranging survey of the symbol which leads her from the *Phaedrus* of Plato through the Fathers to a treatise on husbandry by Anthony Fitzherbert in 1523, investigates the equine-sexual implications in such works as the *Book of the Duchess* and *Troilus and Criseyde*, but even more specifically in the character of the Wife of Bath. I say these opinions are good, but that—ironically for patristic critics—their study is too little on the Bible. It seems curious, for example, that Robertson felt constrained to *go first* to St. Gregory for his interpretation rather than to the Scriptures (or indeed to Chaucer himself in his *Parson's Tale*) for a "public" airing of the symbol of the horse, the meaning of which in the *Canterbury Tales* extends, it seems to me, a considerable distance beyond the woman or the flesh. Rowland's interminable survey of extra-Scriptural sources is even more spectacular and more supererogatory than Robertson's.

It is obvious that by "inventing" a pilgrimage as central to the dramatic situation of the *Canterbury Tales* Chaucer has of necessity placed all his characters on horseback. Indeed, seventeen of the pilgrims are at one time or another described in relation to their horses; some in a line or two, others like the Monk and the Canon in considerable detail. Almost without exception Chaucer introduces or confirms an oblique moral judgment of these characters by reference to their riding habits. How appropriate, for example, that the Merchant, who speaks "his resons...ful solempnely," should ride "hye on horse" or that the reticent Clerk should ride as "coy and stille as dooth a mayde...newe spoused."

I will risk schematizing the essential dramatic truth of the *Canterbury Tales* by dividing Chaucer's equestrians into two groups, the characteristics of which would seem to confirm them in the judgments obliquely made elsewhere. The most obvious group includes those pilgrims who are either proud riders or who own horses of "greet estaat." The Monk is the chief representative. As an outrider for his community, he keeps for himself the best monastery horses ("Ful many a deyntee hors hadde he in stable"), rides ostentatiously on a palfrey with his bridle jingling as loud as the chapel bell. (That the horses in his stable are "deyntee," an adjective which in Middle English meant luxurious and rare as well as valuable, and that this particular horse is a palfrey, a small saddle-horse especially for lady riders, are significant details in reinforcing Robertson's reading of "venerie" as having sexual as well as the more obvious hunting connotations.) But certainly other pilgrims share his prideful horsemanship. Like the Merchant, who sits high on his horse, the Summoner also stands high "in his styropes" (D 1665); the Pardoner rides "al of the newe jet" (A 682); the Reeve sits "upon a ful good stot" (A 615); and the Wife of Bath sits "esily" upon her "amblere" (A 469), to which she applies "a paire of spores sharpe" (A 473). The word "amblere," of course, refers to a horse moving at a smooth or easy pace, distinct from trotting, but the *NED* lists connotations from the Middle Ages which suggest an affected walk, or an artificial or acquired pace, and even indeed a kind of dancing. Apparently Alisoun advertised her sexual wares on horseback too and "koude of that art the olde daunce" in every conceivable situation. The spurs, as Rowland has convincingly indicated suggest that the long-since-unvirginal Wife rides astride and that, contrary to the ideal, the wife rides the husband.[6]

Against these proud riders, Chaucer contrasts those who ride either poor or at least un-caparisoned horses. The most obvious example is the Clerk, whose horse, like him, is "as leene...as is a rake." And, as mentioned earlier, his riding habits are as humble as his horse, as the boisterous Host remarks. In his humble company we should include the Plowman, whose horse is a mare, the unmistakable badge of the very poor,[7] and the Nun's Priest, who is oppressed not only by the conventual humiliation of his position, but also by being forced to ride a jade patronizingly described by the Host as "foul and lene" (B 4003). The term *jade* is still in our time a contemptuous one for a horse, but in the Middle Ages it signified in addition a cart or draught horse, as opposed to a riding horse. Arthur Broes's description is apt: an English Rosinante. The Knight's horses, though obviously of quality, are described inside the general impression of their master's battered apparel: "His hors were goode, but he was nat gay. / Of fustian he wered a gypoun / Al bismotered with his habergeoun" (A 74–76). And finally the Parson, although his horse is not mentioned, is described in his parish visits at least as horseless like his master Christ, "upon his feet, and in his hand a staf" (A 495). Thus in one group we find the Monk, the Merchant, the Summoner, the Pardoner, the Reeve, and the Wife of Bath; in the other, the Clerk, the Nun's Priest, the Plowman, the Knight, and (by extension) the Parson. Chaucer was here at least too good a poet to divide his characters into mere goats and sheep, the damned and the saved, but the pattern produced by these distinct horsemen is unmistakable.

In still a third group, I would place those riders whose characters seem compromised by their *inefficiency* as horsemen. Chaucer places no opprobrium on excellent horsemanship as such. Witness his praise of the Squire, who "wel koude...sitte on hors and faire ryde," who had been "somtyme in chyvachie" in "Flaundres, in Artoys and Pycardie," and who had "born hym weel." But miserable horsemanship rates his censure. The prime example is the drunken Cook, who is incapable of remaining awake in the saddle and falls off into the "slough." "This was a fair chyvachee of a cook!" exclaims his antagonist, the Manciple (H 50). The drunken Miller—leading the Pilgrims from the Tabard while blowing his bagpipes (a grotesque image of his fleshliness)—like the Cook, also sits upon his horse "unnethe" (A 3121). And the Shipman, accustomed to more nautical modes of transportation, rides haltingly upon "a rouncy, as he kouthe" (A 390). Later in the pilgrimage, the Canon and his Yeoman join the company, and Chaucer makes mention of the abuse shown the horses in their attempt to intercept the pilgrims:

> His hakeney, that was al pomely grys,
> So swatte that it wonder was to see;
> It semed as he had priked miles three.
> The hors eek that his yeman rood upon
> So swatte that unnethe myghte it gon.
> Aboute the peytrel stood the foom ful hye:
> He was of foom al flekked as a pye. (G 559–65)

Again, the group representing poor horsemanship, like the group representing proud riders, includes an unexemplary variety: the Cook, the Miller, the Shipman, and the Canon.

If Chaucer was willing to expend such artistic energy on a complex pattern of horses and horsemanship, it is safe to assume that he expected that pattern to carry a meaning that extends beyond mere verisimilitude on the one hand or patristically precious exegesis on the other. I submit that in his description of these rider-pilgrims approaching Canterbury Chaucer is alluding to a Biblical event symbolically, liturgically, and homiletically close to Christians of all *saecula, Jesus Christ entering Jerusalem on Palm Sunday riding on a donkey.* No horse of great estate here, but an animal like his Master whose moment of glory was tied to his utter humility as a beast of burden—in Chesterton's words, a tattered outlaw of the earth, starved, scourged, derided, with shouts about his ears and palms before his feet. And each of the pilgrims in some measure will achieve his own entrance into Jerusalem, the "parfit glorious pilgrymage / That highte Jerusalem celestial" of which the Parson speaks, on a beast whose humility will exalt, or whose exaltedness will humble, its rider. Some, like their Master, will enter the New Jerusalem on humble beasts—the mare, the jade. Others, unaware of the glory that could be theirs if they die to themselves, sit high in the saddle on the palfrey and ambler.

The above reading draws strength, I believe, from Chaucer's own words. Recent critics have found in the language of the Parson's Sermon overt yet subtle judgments which apply retroactively to the characters and their tales that preceded and provoked the Parson's remarks. Bernard Huppe has brilliantly pointed to the Parson's undercutting of January's spiritual blindness in the *Merchant's Tale*, for example, by reminding us that in the Parson's view a man may indeed sin with his own wife as he could kill himself with his own knife.[8] January had used this very simile to exculpate himself from fleshly guilt. No less direct is the Parson's allusion to the equestrian habits of his colleagues on the pilgrimage: "Also the synne of aornement or of apparaille is in thynges that apertenen to ridynge, as in to manye delicat horses that been hoolden for delit, that been so faire, fatte, and costlewe; / and also in many a vicious knave that is sustened by cause of hem; and in to curious harneys, as in sadeles, in crouperes, peytrels, and bridles covered with precious clothyng, and riche barres and plates of gold and of silver. / For which God seith by Zakarie the prophete, *I wol confounde the rideres of siviche horses*" (I 430ff.).[9] Of course, the prophecy to which the Parson refers had looked forward to the events of Palm Sunday with an appropriateness startlingly effective here: "Rejoice greatly, O daughter of Sion, shout for joy, O daughter of Jerusalem: Behold thy King will come to thee, the just and saviour. He is poor and riding upon an ass and upon a colt, the foal of an ass. And I will destroy the chariot out of Ephraim and the horse out of Jerusalem" (Zacharias 9:9–10). And lest there be any doubt that the pilgrim riders and their horses are finally to be judged by another Chevalier, the Parson continues: "This folk taken litel reward of the ridynge of Goddes sone of hevene, and of his harneys whan he rood upon the asse, and ne hadde noon oother harneys but the povre clothes of his disciples; ne we ne rede nat that evere he rood on oother beest."

Perhaps a postscript would be useful here, appropriate both to my contention that patristic critics would do well to place practical priorities on Scripture over the Fathers and that Chaucer himself in the Parson's Sermon is probably the best clue to some Christian meanings in the *Canterbury Tales*.[10] For the Parson's commentary on proud riders is actually part of a longer disquisition on the prideful array of *clothing*, the wearers of which he excoriates as sinners: "For certes, if ther ne hadde be no synne in clothyng, Crist wolde nat so soone have noted and spoken of the clothyng of thilke riche man in the gospel" (I 412). Such an indictment reminds us of the lavish attention Chaucer devotes to the description of his pilgrims' clothing. Like his oblique judgments made in terms of horses and riders, indeed at times in conjunction with them, Chaucer's descriptions of the pilgrims' clothes undercut those "in outrageous array" and by contrast exalt those who sartorially humble themselves.

Whereas only two of the pilgrims, the Clerk and the Knight, are amply described in terms of unconcern for their appearance, and two more are briefly sketched so—the Plowman and Parson—at least eleven characters are described as being arrayed resplendently from sole to crown. I have already referred to the Knight's well-known "bismottered" look because of his recent return from the wars. The Clerk, like many of his inelegant academic colleagues from time immemorial, would prefer other than mere sartorial goods:

> Ful thredbare was his overeste courtepy;
> For he hadde geten hym yet no benefice......

> For hym was levere have at his beddes heed
> Twenty books...
> Than robes riche, or fithele, or gay sautrie. (A 290–91, 293–94,296)

The Plowman, as would be expected, is dressed in a "tabard," a smock-like, loose upper garment of coarse material worn out of doors by the members of the lower classes; and the Parson finds "suffisaunce" in "lytel thing," a general enough description but one which is clearly appropriate to his dress.

On the side of the exalted, we find the Monk, the Man of Law, and the Wife of Bath most inordinate in their pre-occupation with raiment. Indeed, some of the Parson's language alludes clearly to the garb of these fellow travelers. Certainly in his first example of "superfluity" in clothing the Parson's language must have stung at least the Monk and the Man of Law. Compare his first sentence with the language of the *General Prologue*: "As to the firste synne, that is in superfluitee of clothynge, which that maketh it so deere, to harm of the peple; / nat oonly the cost of embrowdynge, the degise endentynge or *barrynge*, owndynge, palynge, wyndynge or bendynge, and semblable wast of clooth in vanitee; / but ther is also costlewe *furrynge* in hir gownes, so muche pownsonynge of chisels to maken holes, so much daggynge of sheres..." (I 415 ff.). The Man of Law, remember, had been described as well stocked in "fees and robes," gifts presumably of clients.[11] He rides "in a medlee cote, / Girt with a ceint of silk, with *barres* smal" (A 328–29). (The "medlee cote," parti-colored of brown and green or of mixed weave, is ironically allusive, it would seem, to the simple seamless robe of Jesus.) The Monk's array, of course, is less justifiable than the Man of Law's. This ascetic makes his vows tolerable by wearing "sleves ypurfiled at the hond / With grys [an expensive gray fur],[12] and that the fyneste of a lond"; he also fastens his hood under his chin with a gold pin, and wears—no discalced monk he—"souple" boots. The Wife of Bath's pre-occupation with clothing, so well known in the famous description of her scarlet outfit, extends even to a talent for weaving.

Other pilgrims that may be rated as "superfluous" in their clothing include the Merchant, who, dressed like the Man of Law in "mottelee," wears a furred beaver hat on his head and "bootes clasped faire and fetisly" on his feet; the

Friar, another vowed ascetic like the Monk, who resembles a pope in his unwrinkled, rounded semycope of double worsted[13]; the Doctor, elegantly clad in "sangwyn and in pers... / Lyned with taffata and with sendal"; and perhaps the five gildsmen, who, prompted by their aspiring wives, are "clothed alle in o lyveree / Of a solempne and a greet fraternitee."

"The clothyng of thilke riche man in the gospel," of which the Parson speaks denigratively in his sermon, would thus seem to convict some of Chaucer's pilgrims of sin, of an inordinate concern for "what they shall put on." The allusion, of course, is to Luke 16:19ff., where a certain rich man, "clothed in purple and fine linen," ignores the beggar Lazarus only to end up in Hell himself begging for a drop of water to cool his tongue. More famous than this parable and equally appropriate to the motif of apparel in the *Canterbury Tales* is Jesus's admonition to his disciples in Luke 12:22ff: "Be not solicitous for your life, what you shall eat; nor for your body, what you shall put on. The life is more than the meat; and the body is more than the raiment.... Consider the lilies, how they grow: they labour not, neither do they spin. But I say to you, not even Solomon in all his glory was clothed like one of these. Now if God clothe in this manner the grass that is today in the field and tomorrow is cast into the oven: how much more you, O ye of little faith?"

The issue here, of course, is that for Chaucer the *pelerinage de la vie humaine* is peopled with many pilgrims of little faith whose primary concern is with what they shall eat and drink, what they shall put on, and indeed how they shall ride to their destiny. Chaucer's method was to remind them that their Master's own glorious destiny was achieved on a donkey and with a splendid unconcern for raiment. Each of the three synoptic gospels describes that specific event identically, but Luke's version will serve here. When the disciples bring the ass to the Lord, "*casting their garments on the colt,* they set Jesus thereon. And as he went, *they spread their clothes underneath in the way*" (Luke 19:35–36). Chaucer must have known the three passages intimately, particularly since two of them appear in the dominical gospel readings (the lilies of the field on the fourteenth Sunday after Pentecost and the donkey and garments on Palm Sunday) and one appears as the gospel reading for Thursday of the Second Week in Lent (Lazarus and the rich man). His parodic transformation of these Biblical images into powerful, but unobtrusive, commentary on the human condition continues to yield rich meanings to his readers, who six hundred years later seek the new Jerusalem for their own time.

Notes to The Horsemen of the Canterbury Tales

1. See the "opposition" essays in *Critical Approaches to Medieval Literature*, ed. Dorothy Bethurum (New York, 1960).
2. *A Preface to Chaucer* (Princeton, 1963), p. 254.
3. "The Horse and Rider Figure in Chaucer's Works," *UTQ*, 35 (1966), pp. 246–59. For a reading of the symbolic meaning of Bayard, the horse of the two clerks in the *Reeve's Tale*, see John Block Friedman, "A Reading of Chaucer's *Reeve's Tale*," *Chaucer Review*, 2 (1967), pp. 8–19.
4. Robertson, p. 254.
5. Ibid.
6. Rowland, p. 254.
7. See Albert C. Baugh, ed., *Chaucer's Major Poetry* (New York, 1963), p. 250, n. 541. All subsequent quotations of Chaucer's poetry will be from this volume.
8. *A Reading of the Canterbury Tales* (Baltimore, 1964), p. 152.
9. Quotations from the *Parson's Tale* are from *The Works of Geoffrey Chaucer*, ed. F. N. Robinson, 2nd ed. (Boston, 1957).
10. See, for example, the Parson's comments on pride as especially applicable to the Wife of Bath: "And yet is ther a privee spece of Pride, that waiteth first to be salewed er he wole salewe, al be he lasse worth than that oother is, peraventure; and eek he waiteth or desireth to sitte, or elles to goon above hym in the wey, or kisse pax, or been encensed, *or goon to offryng biforn his neighebor*, / and swiche semblable thynges" (I 406).
11. Robinson, p. 760, n. 317.
12. Baugh, p. 242, n. 194.
13. For a full treatment of the Friar's un-Franciscan attachment to expensive clothing, see Muriel Bowden, A *Commentary on the General Prologue* (New York, 1962), p. 137.

ALISOUN AND THE SAVED HARLOTS: A COZENING OF OUR EXPECTATIONS

Rodney Delasanta

Within the past few years, literary criticism has begun to claim that the muse of typology, hitherto considered one of the shyer sisters, had all along exerted considerable influence on the creative achievements of our more traditional literature. Works as diverse in time and genre as the Old English *Advent* and *Samson Agonistes*, we have been shown,[1] reveal an attitude toward poetic analogy (as well as toward the more obvious level of theme) that is less dependent upon the Hellenistically allegorical than upon the story of salvation as begun in the Old Testament and fulfilled in the New. To simplify a complex esthetic, one might say that it was the Hebraic characters, events, and images moving eschatologically across the two testaments that supplied the Christian poet with analogical vehicles more fitting than those to be found among the philosophical allegorizers; for the poet whose poetic vision was horizontal in history and time rather than vertical in philosophy and eternity remained close to his world and dramatized by his creations the prolongation of a real story that, in the words of the *Secunda Pastorum*, "semys to be told / Full oft."

Like most of the great Christian poets of Medieval and Renaissance Europe, Chaucer too must certainly have been aware of the typological motifs pressing him from every side of his experience: the invariable typological arrangement of cathedral statuary, painting, and stained glass, themselves a dramatization of the liturgical typology standardized in the Mass and Divine Office; the typological *pagina* of medieval drama wheeling its way from station to station; the rhetoric of the preacher urging his audience to a devotion often based upon typological correspondences; the exegesis of the scholar seeing in Christ and his saints the fulfillment of everything promised *in figura* from the Old Testament.

But whereas the minor artist settled for obvious typological parallels that had become familiar after more than a thousand years of use, Chaucer, like all great artists who keep their traditions alive by grafting upon them an individual talent, courted the covert and reserved his deeper meaning for those who have ears to hear.

One such typological motif that deserves attention in Chaucer studies is that of the saved harlot. The famous passage from Matthew's Gospel in which Jesus accuses the Jews of unbelief and then shocks them by asserting that "the publicans and harlots shall go into the kingdom of heaven before you" (21:31) is not fortuitous hyperbole. Nor is Luke's story of the woman in the city, a sinner, who anoints the Master's feet with precious balm as an act of loving penance (7:37) a mere episode hanging loose in the life of Jesus. These, conjoined with John's story of the much-married Samaritan Woman at the Well (4:4) and his story of the woman taken in adultery whom Jesus forgives after embarrassing her would-be stoners (8:3), contribute a recognizable design to the larger pattern introduced above. And later when patristic writers conflated Luke's "sinner" with Mary Magdalene, the woman from whom Jesus removed seven devils (Mark 16:9 and Luke 8:2), the typological tapestry received its major scene.

That Chaucer could not but have been aware of this theme of the saved harlot can be reasonably conjectured by the liturgical emphasis we can observe in any study of the missals, breviaries, and lectionaries used in his day. But the actual presence of some of these biblical characters in his own art offers impressive evidence that the analogical process described above must have been at least osmotically present in his work. What D. W. Robertson, Jr., has already noticed about the iconographic relationship between the Samaritan Woman at the Well and the Wife of Bath[2] should not close off discussion but rather, as his own title urges, preface it, for—as I hope to demonstrate—the implications of the thematic connection between the two loose women extend beyond Robertson's exordial insight.

To begin with, the tradition of the saved harlot would probably not have been limited in Chaucer's catholic imagination to the Samaritan Woman at the Well or even, I suspect, to the New Testament. Typological analogy, to accommodate a figure from Keats, sets a pretty peal of chimes at work by merely pulling an apron string. Few knowledgeable Christians could hear the story of Abel's worthy sacrifice of his first fruits, for example, without hearing echoes reverberating forward in time to Melchizidek's offering of bread and wine, Abraham's offering of Isaac, and God's sacrifice of Jesus on the Cross, the latter an obvious fulfillment of the previous types. But typological fulfillment did not necessarily end in the person of Christ. The apostles, for example, were anti-types of the prophets, Mary an anti-type of Eve, Elizabeth an anti-type of the late-bearing wives like Sarah and Rebecca. The Samaritan Woman at the Well and Mary Magdalene (both of whom serve Chaucer well analogically) also had their types in the Old Testament, believing harlots all, who, like those whom Jesus praised for their faith (Matthew 21:32), were themselves saved.

Among them is Rahab in the book of Joshua, who, with all her family, was preserved from the destruction of Jericho by the Jews because as a gentile she believed in the God of Israel and concealed in her dwelling some of Joshua's soldiers (chapter 2). The scarlet cord by which she let the spies down from the window of her house later functioned as the saving sign by which her house and all its inhabitants were recognized by the Jews and spared the destruction of the city. This episode does not go unnoticed in the New Testament. Matthew enters Rahab, the whore, into the genealogy of Jesus himself (1:5) in order presumably to underscore her paradoxical role in the salvific history of the Jews and also to underscore God's providence as extending to the Gentile nations.[3] She is mentioned again in the Epistle to the Hebrews (11:31), where the author demonstrates the efficacy of faith among the precursors of Jesus ("By faith Rahab the harlot perished not with the unbelievers, receiving the spies with peace"), and again in the Epistle of St. James (2:25), where the apostle demonstrates the efficacy of works ("And in like manner also Rahab the harlot, was not she justified by works, receiving the messengers and sending them out another way?"). For the Fathers of the Church, Rahab the harlot signified by typological analogy the saving blood of the Passover Lamb and thus of the Agnus Dei; for the image of the scarlet cord, because both it and lamb's blood are designated by the same Hebrew word, became the sign of the salvation from destruction by the agents of the Lord's vengeance.[4] Interestingly too, her house became a type of the Church itself: as Origen said, "if anyone wishes to be saved, let him come into the house of her that was a harlot..., into this house in which the blood of Christ is the sign of redemption. Let there be no mistake..., outside this house, there is no salvation."[5] And true to the typological function of relating things past to things to come, Rahab anticipates other saved harlots in other times: "There is prophetic reason in this reception of the spies of Joshua by a harlot," says St. Gregory. "We meet this harlot in many places of Scripture, not merely as a hostess, but as the bride of holy men."[6]

Hosea's harlot-wife, Gomer, whom God had commanded that he wed in order to symbolize Israel's temporary infidelity but ultimate reconciliation, is another famous example. After giving birth to three children, who are temporarily alienated from God's grace, Gomer is punished but then "allured" back to fidelity by her husband (2:14), who promises to espouse himself forever to her in faith (2:20). Like Rahab, she responds to God's call to put aside harlotry and reunite with him in holiness. The harlot of Ezekiel 16 has a similar salvific role. She too is chastised and punished for her prostitution but then promised restoration: "And I will remember my covenant with thee in the days of thy youth; and I will establish with thee an everlasting covenant" (16:60).[7]

The appearance of the saved harlot in the Gospel stories then is no accidental theme in the hands of the Evangelists but a conscious attempt to find in Jesus's mission a concretization of the types introduced in the Old Testament. The Samaritan Woman at the Well, who has had five husbands and whose extra-marital affair Jesus exposes, is the most obvious example and certainly of most immediate significance for Chaucer studies because the Wife of Bath makes overt reference to her prototype in the prologue of her tale (D 14ff.).[8] As Robertson has argued, "the 'five husbands' mentioned in the General Prologue and again at the beginning of the prologue to the tale, together with the hint of an analogy between a lady with five husbands from 'Biside Bath' and another five husbands 'biside a welle,' suggest that the Wife's marital condition may be an iconographic device based on the story of the Samaritan. The Samaritan learns to listen to the message of Christ, but the Wife is 'somdel deef,' an attribute which indicates that although she has ears, she hears not..."[9]

But it would seem that Chaucer intended his parodic allusions to extend to the wider tradition of saved harlot, as well as to the Samaritan. In fact, long before the Samaritan is mentioned—in the *General Prologue* itself—we detect a parodic iconographic strategy at work that seems to mask with deceptive realistic details the larger tradition outlined above. One of the central characteristics of the saved harlot, as we have already seen, is that she will precede the proud unbelievers into the kingdom of Heaven: "Amen, I say to you that the publicans and harlots shall go into the kingdom of God before you" (Matt. 21:31). The Fathers repeatedly stressed this paradox. "Let the gate of salvation be shut to the proud," said St. Augustine. "The meek, to whom God teaches His ways, will find all these things in the Scriptures, and those things which he does not see he will believe from what he sees.... He will see in Jericho, as in this perishing world, an harlot, *one of those of whom the Lord says that they go before the proud into the kingdom of heaven* putting out of her window a scarlet line symbolical of blood, as confession is made with the mouth for the remission of sins."[10] And in the *Paradiso* Dante himself emphasized this paradoxical primacy of the harlot by describing Rahab, whom he had assigned to the sphere of Venus (IX, 115–120), as having been brought to this Heaven by Christ *before* any other soul:

Or sappi che là entro si tranquilla
Raab; e a nostr'ordine congiunta,
di lei nel sommo grado si sigilla.

Da questo cielo, in cui l'ombra s'appunta
che'l vostro mondo face, *pria ch'altr' alma*
del triunfo di Cristo fu assunta.

Parodic of this iconography, the *General Prologue* contains the memorable description of the strumpet Wife crowding out all competition in leading the procession to the altar during the Offertory of the Mass while dressed in a finery that urges scarlet implications:

In al the parisshe wif ne was ther noon
That to the offrynge bifore hire sholde goon;

And if ther dide, certeyn so wrooth was she,
That she was out of alle charitee.
....
Her hosen weren of fyn scarlet reed,
Ful streite yteyd, and shoes ful moyste and newe. (A 449–52, 456–57.)

The fact that Chaucer dramatizes the Wife as proudly *preceding* other worshippers to the altar (which has traditionally been understood as a place sanctified by the divine presence)[11] would seem to indicate that he is deliberately playing ironic games with the typological motif. Like the aforementioned harlots, she too will be at the head of the heavenly queue, but in an "upsid-doun" version of the sense of Matthew 21:31. No chastened and forgiven harlot here with scarlet sins become as white as snow humbling by divine command the exalted behind her, but a scarlet-laced nymphomaniac insisting on first place upon pain of tantrum. Her motive for pilgrimage is hardly penitential but rather a boisterous abandonment to a way of life that contradicts the iconographic expectations summoned up from biblical types like Rahab, Gomer, and the Samaritan. She has played the harlot in pursuing her five husbands, not to mention "oother compaignye in youthe," and she has no intention of changing roles now: "Welcome the sixte, whan that evere he shal. / For sothe, I wol *nat* kepe me chaast in al" (D 45–46).

If the iconographic characteristics in the Wife of Bath can echo parodic allusions to these saved harlots, and particularly to the great theme of Matthew 21:31, another pull on the apron string should theoretically ring the pretty peal of typological chimes all the way to the most famous of the saved New Testament "sinners," Mary Magdalene. Western exegesis since the time of Gregory the Great, and until relatively recent times, had conflated three separately designated characters in the Gospels into the single formidable personage of Mary Magdalene. The "sinner in the city" of Luke 7 who comes to the house of the Pharisee where Jesus is dining in order to anoint his feet in repentance for her sins became identified with both Mary of Bethany, the sister of Martha and Lazarus, and then with Mary of Magdala, who after Jesus had removed seven devils from her ministered to his needs as far as the cross and sepulchre.

Her character contained many strains that medieval devotion came to venerate. First, she was the sinner who was greatly forgiven because she loved much: *Dismissa sunt ei peccata multa* are the liturgical words repeated like a refrain during the Canonical Hours on her feast day. By anointing the feet of her Master and drying the ointment and her tears of repentance with her hair (in Luke's version), Mary Magdalene continued the tradition of reformed harlot prefigured in Rahab, Gomer, the harlot of Ezekiel 16, and the Samaritan Woman at the Well. In this "peccatrix" God indeed concludes the covenant He solemnly promised to the harlots of old by granting to her the singular honor of being first witness to the Risen Christ (John 20:11–18). Moreover, it is she whom, after standing alone outside the sepulchre and weeping over the loss of her Lord, Jesus commissions as ambassador to his apostles in order to inform them of his Resurrection, a sacred embassy that moved medieval devotion to call her Apostle to the Apostles. In her eagerness to hear Christ's words, she is often described as sitting at his feet and listening to his teachings, much to the discomfiture of her sister Martha, who in Luke 10:38 grumbles in the kitchen while preparing Jesus's meal. His gentle rebuke to Martha—that Mary has chosen the better part—was traditionally interpreted in medieval theology as Divine ratification of the contemplative life: so that in addition to being known as the reformed harlot, the myrophore, and the weeping mourner, Mary Magdalene was also the contemplative *par excellence*.

Needless to say, her presence in the artistic, liturgical, and hagiographic life of the Middle Ages was ubiquitous. Victor Saxer's study of the Magdalenian liturgy shows that by Chaucer's day dioceses like Canterbury, Chester, and Salisbury celebrated her feast day, July 22, as a *duplex*, or a double rite, which indicates a certain pre-eminence in the sanctoral cycle.[12] Beverly Boyd's reproductions of the Calendar of St. Paul's Cathedral in London show the Magdalen's feast day honored with an inscription of colored ink in contrast to the ordinary ink used for simple feasts.[13] In the *Sarum Breviary*, hers is one of only fifty-five days of the sanctoral year in which there are three Nocturns, each of which consisted of three psalms, three lessons, and three responses—indicative of an important place in the celebration of the Divine Office.[14] (In the Middle Ages the Divine Office was sung and recited in secular as well as monastic churches, and hence diurnally available to the laity.) In medieval drama, there are several cycles in which Mary Magdalene is prominently included: those of Cornwall, Towneley, Chester, York, and Digby.[15] And very significant, it seems to me, was the popular medieval habit of compressing different characters into the single personage of Mary Magdalene. Helen Garth tells us that, in addition to the obvious conflations previously mentioned, Mary Magdalene was also associated with the woman taken in adultery of John 8 and, though far-fetched, with the woman of Samaria herself, the latter identification dramatized in the English ballad of the Maid and the Palmer.[16] Particularly interesting for Chaucer studies, too, was the curious identification of Mary Magdalene with St. Mary of Egypt, whose name turns up in one of the Man of Law's pious ejaculations (B[1] 500).

Now there can be no question that Chaucer was intimately knowledgeable about Mary Magdalene. In addition to the obvious reasons why any medieval Christian would be aware of her imposing presence, we find four separate references in the *Parson's Tale,* casually made, to some of the well-known attributes mentioned above. In his remarks against the sins of grumbling or murmuring, for example, the Parson alludes to Judas, who "grucched agayns the Magdaleyne, whan she enoynted the heved of oure Lord Jhesu Crist with hir precious oynement" (I 501). Another species of grumbler for the Parson was Simon the Pharisee, who "gruchched agayn the Magdaleyne, whan she approched to Jhesu Crist, and weep at his feet for hire synnes" (I 504).[17] As an example of the reformed "wommen that han doon leccherie and been releeved by penitence," the Parson refers to the odor of sanctity from the alabaster jar of Mary Magdalene: "They been the vessel or the boyste of the blissed Magdalene, that fulfilleth hooly chirche of good odour" (I 946). And finally as the model for forthright confession of sins, the Parson again alludes to her holy example: "The fourthe signe [of a good confession] is that he ne lette nat for shame to shewen his confessioun. Swich was the confessioun of the Magdalene, that ne spared, for no shame of hem that weren atte feeste, for to go to oure Lord Jhesu Crist and biknowe to hym hire synne" (I 995).

More intriguing evidence related to Chaucer's knowledge of Mary Magdalene, however, resides in his reference to a translation he once made, "goon ys a gret while," of "Origenes upon the Maudeleyne." The reference occurs in the

Prologue to the *Legend of Good Women* (F 427–28) in Queen Alceste's rebuttal of the charge against Chaucer that he had libeled the good name of women. Her list of his exculpating translations includes those "pro-feminist" tracts, the life of St. Cecelia (later transformed into the *Second Nun's Tale*) and the above mentioned work of Origen on Mary Magdalene, now lost. Whatever the quality of Chaucer's translation and wherever its whereabouts (perhaps some literary Schliemann will find it someday), at least there is no problem in examining the original, particularly since the recent exploratory work of John McCall. Entitled *De Maria Magdalena*, it was a Latin homily falsely attributed to Origen and probably written by a Benedictine monk in the thirteenth century in order to supply the required *lectio* during the Divine Office for the feast day of Mary Magdalene (July 22) and/or to supply the required homily for the Mass of the fifth feria after the Pasch.[18] It runs to about four thousand words and became enormously popular in the Middle Ages and beyond, surviving in at least one hundred and thirty manuscripts and editions and translated into a variety of languages, including an extant English version in 1585. Its interest for us lies in suggesting not only a possible source for Chaucer's rhetorical development (an approach which Professor McCall emphasizes in his article) but also as a dramatic and even iconographic reservoir from which Chaucer's later poetry—consciously or not—drew some draughts of inspiration.

Professor McCall seems certainly correct in suggesting that the character of Mary Magdalene, as the narrator develops it in the homily, has some kinship with the abandoned ladies in Chaucer's works. Just as the homilist dramatically exploits Mary's sense of loss as she stands outside the empty sepulchre, so the various narrators of Chaucer's early works exploit the sorrow of the desperate ladies in their respective dramatic situations: Alcyone in *The Book of the Duchess*, Dido in *The House of Fame*, the "wives" of *The Legend of Good Women*.[19] And this dramatic kinship would certainly seem to continue into the later works with characters like Constance, Griselda, Cecelia, Criseyde, and Dorigen.

But it is also true that dramatic kinships can be ironic as well as parallel and that, when they are connected by typological linkage, they may perform in the hands of a master ironist like Chaucer feats of prodigious dexterity. All of the dramatic and iconographic connections I will urge in the next few pages between the Wife of Bath and Mary Magdalene depend for their force upon the saved harlot motif already traced from the Old Testament to the famous passage of Matthew 21:31. Chaucer is saying, in effect, that contrary to the expectations of typological pattern, his world is "upsid-doun." Like the Summoner, who should have known justice, and the Pardoner, who should have known mercy, the Harlot should have exemplified repentance. But everywhere in Chaucer the ceremony of innocence is drowned.

Among the striking realistic details from the Gospel stories of Mary Magdalene that were later frozen into virtual iconographic stylization by medieval theologians and artists is the scene of the "peccatrix" anointing the feet of Jesus while weeping for her sins. In the *Parson's Tale*, as I have already observed, there are two allusions to this scene. And from the Latin original of the Pseudo-Origen's *De Maria Magdalena*, Chaucer would have translated references to this famous scene innumerable times. Among them for example, on the very first page of the homily, we read:

> As she had earlier wept tears on the feet of the Lord, so now she came in order to weep tears on his sepulchre. At one time she had wept and bathed his feet with her tears out of sorrow for the death of her soul [i.e., her sins], now she came to bathe the sepulchre with her tears because of the death of her Master.[20]

Again later in the sermon, we read:

> He praised you once when you anointed his feet, bathed them with tears, and dried them with your hair.... How quickly Mary arose when she heard [Jesus's call]; how quickly she came and in the same way as before fell at your feet, O good Jesus.[21]

It cannot be accidental that in the *Wife of Bath's Prologue* one of the most memorable descriptions of her habitual carnality comes at the moment of her fourth husband's funeral when she is stirred to lust by the *feet* of Jankyn as he helps bear the casket to the grave. The dramatic irony, and the euphemism, have always been noted, but the iconographic parody of a "grieving" *peccatrix* being stirred to concupiscence instead of repentance by the feet of a divinity student has never been related to its likely iconographic source.

> To chirche was myn housbonde born a-morwe
> With neighebores, that for hym maden sorwe;
> And Jankyn, oure clerk, was oon of tho.
> As help me God! whan that I saugh hym go
> After the beere, me thoughte he hadde a paire
> Of legges and of feet so clene and faire
> That al myn herte I yaf unto his hoold. (D 593–99)

As with the iconographic image of feet, so it is with the image of Magdalenian weeping. Our own word *maudlin*, of course, derives from the sentimental expansion of the Gospel stories which described Mary both weeping for her sins while anointing Jesus's feet and weeping at the sepulchre on the morning of the Resurrection over the presumed abduction of his body. As usual, the Gospel version shows dramatic restraint in describing Mary's tears, but later commentators and homilists refused to understate. The first maudlin passage translated above from the *De Maria Magdalena* is only one of the many passages in the homily that stresses the inconsolable flow of Mary's tears while she stands outside Jesus's sepulchre. Here is another:

> The more she cried, the greater the sense of his loss; and so Mary wept abundantly, with one sorrow being added to the other and she feeling in her heart two great sorrows which she wished to lessen with her tears, but without success. And thus totally oppressed with sorrow of mind and body, she became exhausted and knew not where to turn. For what could this woman do except cry, she who felt an insupportable sorrow and could find no consoler?[22]

Later in the homily, after the description of the angels at the tomb, the speaker even chides Mary for her tears:

> But O Mary, why do you remain behind, why do you torment yourself, why do you weep? You have the angels. The vision of the angels should suffice for you because he whom you seek, he for whom you weep, perhaps discerns something in you which keeps him from wishing to be seen by you. Give up your sorrow now. Let there be an end to your tears. Remember what he said to you and to the other women: do not cry over me. What is this then that you do since he has himself forbidden tears and you persist in weeping? I fear that by crying you may be offending him, considering how inordinately you weep.[23]

This iconographic cry is too rich an image for Chaucer, the translator and the parodist, not to have noticed. At the obsequies of her fourth husband, Alisoun too weeps, but in a manner travestying the famous inconsolable cry of the Gospels: no weeping Madeline here!

> Whan that my fourthe housbonde was on beere,
> I weep algate, and made sory cheere,
> As wyves mooten, for it is usage,
> And with my coverchief covered my visage,
> But for that I was purveyed of a make,
> I wepte but smal, and that I undertake. (D 587–92)

Moreover, the dramatic situation, as well as the crocodile tears, is the inverse of that described in the homily. When Mary reaches the tomb and discovers the body of Jesus gone, she is denied the administering of the obsequies she had expected to deliver, and thus her sorrow is aggrandized:

> But as she did not find the body in the sepulchre, the labor of anointing was obviated but the pain of weeping intensified. The obsequies were denied her but not the sorrow.[24]

In the case of the Wife, parodically, the obsequies were observed but none of the sorrow.

The fake tears, of course, are part of a larger casualness, indeed a niggardliness, about the expenditures related to her husband's burial. "It nys but *wast* to burye hym preciously," the Wife insists. "Lat hym fare wel, God yeve his soul reste! / He is now in his grave and in his cheste" (D 500–02). One cannot help but contrast this extreme parsimony against Mary's prodigal efforts at embalming Jesus's body:

> She had come to the sepulchre bringing with her perfumes and oils which she at an earlier time had prepared in order to anoint with precious balm the feet of the living, but now in order to anoint with oils and preserve with balm the entire body of the dead.[25]

And coming upon the empty tomb, she commits her very life to its honor and glory, with suggestions almost of sexual abandonment:

> I will stay and die here because at least I will be buried near the sepulchre of my Lord. O how blessed my body would be if it were entombed near my Lord, near my Master! How happy would my soul be which, leaving the fragile vessel of my body, would soon be able to enter my Lord's sepulchre.[26]

How parodically different is the Wife's mercantilistic attitude to her husband's sepulchre, his money box, and her own chastity! One might indeed conjecture about the extent to which Chaucer's elaborate punning on *chest* in the Wife's Prologue could have been provoked at least in part by this famous sepulchre scene that is the central dramatic situation of the *De Maria Magdalena*. For it is by a skillful manipulation of her *chastity* (sic!) that the Wife wins the keys of the *chest* (money box) away from her old husbands and awaits the moment when they can be safely laid away in their *chests* (coffins) in order to begin the game again. Can the interpolation at D 44a in the *Wife's Prologue* mean anything else? In most manuscripts the text merely reads:

> Yblessed be God that I have wedded fyve!
> Welcome the sixte, whan that evere he shal.
> For sothe, I wol nat kepe me *chaast* in al.
> Whan myn housbonde is fro the world ygon,
> Som Cristen man shal wedde me anon.... (D 44–48)

But despite the animadversions of some scholars about the quality of the six-line interpolation at D 44, it is my contention that it sets up a series of brilliant chaste-chest-chest puns that are extremely functional:

> Yblessed be God that I have wedded fyve!
> Of whiche I have pyked out the beste,
> Bothe of here nether purs and of here *cheste.* (D 44, 44a–b)

Later in her sample harangue of her fourth husband, the puns continue:

> But tel me this: why hydestow, with sorwe,
> The keyes of thy *cheste* awey fro me?
> It is my good as wel as thyn, pardee!
> ....
> What helpith it of me to enquere or spyen?
> I trowe thou woldest loke me in thy *chiste*! (D 308–10, 316–17)

And they culminate in the previously quoted apology for cheap burial·.

> It nys but wast to burye hym preciously,
> Lat hym fare wel, God yeve his soul reste!
> He is now in his grave and in his *cheste*. (D 500–02)

Further ironic correspondences suggest themselves at this point. Early in the homily, one side of the psychological conflict that the speaker exploits in his subject is the Magdalene's feeling that, unable to find Jesus, she could not go on living. His empty tomb had become her final end:

> She had lost her master whom she loved so familialy that because of him she could love or hope for nothing more. She had lost the life of her life, and she thought it would have been better for her to die than live; for certainly by dying she would find him whom, while she remained alive, she could not find and without whom it was not worth living.[27]

Quite evidently, no such monogamy of devotion inhibits the Wife. Her discourse is punctuated with expressions of habitual and exuberant widowhood whose major intention is to preserve that habituality. She had polished off her fourth with a certain dispatch—

> He is now in his grave and in his cheste.
> Now of my fifthe housbonde wol I telle. (D 502–03)

and, although her favorite, even the fifth —

> Yblessed be God that I have wedded fyve!
> Welcome the sixte, whan that evere he shal. (D 44–45)

As the homilist proceeds to explore the Magdalene's morbid psyche, as described and parodied above, he dramatizes her confrontation with the angels at the tomb as provoking her to a certain agitation of spirit that propels her into resolutions of seeking and questing, in language indeed that echoes the imagery of seeking from the Song of Songs:

> I looked for him in the sepulchre and did not find him: I called him and he did not answer me. Alas, where may I search for him, where may I find him? I will arise certainly and go to all the places that I can. I will not allow my eyes any sleep, I will not allow my feet any rest until I find him whom my soul loves.... Walk, O my feet, run and do not expect to rest.[28]

Such an attitude contrasts sharply with the Wife's own *habitus* of pilgrim. She too peregrinates—

> ...thries hadde she been at Jerusalem;
> She hadde passed many a straunge strem;
> At Rome she hadde been, and at Boloigne,
> In Galice at Seint-Jame, and at Coloigne—(A 463–66)

but the object of her quest is less *the* Lord than (to accommodate the language of the Miller) "*any* lord to leggen in his bedde." No single-minded devotion here to an all-consuming *caritas,* but rather a carnal celebration of flux and Fortune, and all in the accoutrements of religion:

> What wiste I wher my grace
> Was shapen for to be, or in what place?
> Therfore I made my visitaciouns
> To vigilies and to processiouns,
> To prechyng eek, and to thise pilgrimages.... (D 553–57)

But the final disposition of Mary Magdalene's psyche in the homily is quite opposite to the inveterate peregrinations of the Wife, who "koude muchel of wandrynge by the weye," for the Magdalene's ultimate intention is to remain fixed by the sepulchre of the Lord:

> My Lord's sepulchre will be rest and honor for me. Thus, during my life this sepulchre will be my consolation, and in my death it will be my repose. Living, I will remain close to it; dying I will be closer to him, but neither alive nor dead will I separate myself from him.[29]

It should be remembered, of course, that these iconographic images and dramatic situations relate directly in the legend of Mary Magdalene to her exemplary repentance. "Many sins are forgiven her because she hath loved much" is the biblical refrain of medieval devotion surrounding her, and it is a repentance of such efficacy that in some versions of the medieval pantheon she is placed—as Apostle to the Apostles—in a preeminent niche. By contrast, the most overt characteristic of the Wife of Bath is her intrepid unrepentance. Jesus "spak to hem that wolde lyve parfitly; / And lordynges, by youre leve, that am nat I," boasts the Wife early in her *Prologue* (D 111–12); and later she laments: "Allas! allas! that evere love was synne" (D 614) without the slightest purpose of amendment. On the contrary, in one of her most famous nostalgic moments, she weeps not for her sins but for the diminution of her power to sin:

> But, Lord Crist! whan that it remembreth me
> Upon my yowthe, and on my jolitee,
> It tikleth me aboute myn herte roote.
> Unto this day it dooth inyn herte boote.
> That I have had my world as in my tyme. (D 469–73)

And in a gesture of utter abandonment to unrepentance, she finds solace in a certain perverse fixity of purpose:

> Lat go, farewell the devel go therwith!
> The flour is goon, ther is namoore to telle;
> The bren, as I best kan, now moste I selle.... (D 476–78)

These efforts on the Wife's part to justify rather than mortify her celebrated carnality lead her into a posture that contrasts her in iconographic irony to one of Mary Magdalene's most significant attributes. That Mary had "chosen the better part" had always been medieval man's biblical justification for his preference of the contemplative over the active life.[30] Chaucer could not but have been impressed by this theme in his translation of the *De Maria Magdalena*. "Once he [Jesus] defended you against the pharisees and gently justified you to your sister," the homilist says to Mary. And later in the sermon, addressing Jesus directly in bewilderment over his seemingly careless treatment of her, the speaker says:

> Remember, O truthful Master and faithful witness, the testimony that you had once delivered to her sister Martha. You said that Mary had chosen the better part, which should not be taken from her....[31]

Again, the ironical relationship to the Wife seems evident. For Alisoun is a pseudo-contemplative of the first order. As a lay "exegete," she has gleaned theological leavings from a variety of sources, especially from her fifth husband Jankin, but always with an eye to self-justification, always with the intention—if one will excuse the pun—of exalting her own very active life. Her curious explanation of the "children of Mercurie and Venus" relate to this contrariety, Mercury representing in her own words "wysdam and science" and Venus "ryot and dispence" (D 699–700). As exegete, of course, the Wife should have been a child of Mercury, but by her own admission she is "al Venerien in feelynge."

Admittedly, the net effect of all this cannot be traced with genealogical precision back to an exclusive parentage.[32] The extent to which typological parody can be seen as a totally artful device on Chaucer's part will of necessity remain conjectural; for unlike allegory, which depends for its force upon the extended metaphor bureaucratically controlling all its minor offices, typology—within the dimensions of its given mythos—functions comfortably with free-wheeling, suggestive similitude and draws as much from associative and serendipitous connections as from any pre-ordained systematization. It is for this reason, as I have argued elsewhere, that medieval typology in its iconographic, dramatic, liturgical, and even rhetorical emanations served as the fair seed time of Chaucer's artistic soul. And it is for this reason too that one can see the Wife of Bath as another of his manipulations of a typological tradition—the saved harlot—that allows for dramatic development of a real character while urging concomitant meanings behind the literal. She is Chaucer's parody of the paradigm: an "upsid-doun," inside-out product of his strumpet age who, in Donne's apt words, has pleased our wits by cozening our expectations.

Notes to Alisoun and the Saved Harlots: A Cozening of Our Expectations

1. Robert B. Burlin, *The Old English Advent: A Typological Commentary* (New Haven: Yale Univ. Press, 1968) and Barbara Lewalski, "*Samson Agonistes* and the 'Tragedy' of the Apocalypse," *PMLA*, 85 (1970), pp. 1050–62.

2. D. W. Robertson, Jr., A *Preface to Chaucer* (Princeton: Princeton Univ. Press, 1963), pp. 318ff.
3. Jean Daniélou, *From Shadows to Reality*, trans. Dom Wulstan Hibberd (Westminster, MD: Newman Press, 1960), p. 245.
4. Ibid., p. 248.
5. Ibid., p. 251.
6. Quoted by Daniélou, ibid., p. 257.
7. Cf. also the story of Tamar in Genesis 36.
8. All subsequent references to Chaucer are to *The Works of Geoffrey Chaucer*, ed. F. N. Robinson, 2nd ed. (Boston: Houghton Mifflin, 1957).
9. Robertson, p. 320.
10. *Reply to Faustus the Manichean*, in *Nicene and Post-Nicene Fathers of the Christian Church*, vol. 4, ed. Philip Schaff (New York: Christian Literature Co., 1901), p. 193.
11. Jean Daniélou, *The Bible and the Liturgy* (Notre Dame, IN: Univ. of Notre Dame Press, 1956), pp. 129ff.
12. Victor Saxer, *Le Culte de Marie Madeleine en Occident des Origines à la Fin du Moyen Age* (Paris: Clavreuil, 1959), pp. 287ff.
13. Beverly Boyd, *Chaucer and the Liturgy* (Philadelphia: Dorrance, 1967), p. 8 (plate 7). In a letter to me, Professor Boyd has identified the color of the ink, not discernible in the black-and-white reproduction, as red.
14. *Breviarium ad Usum Insignis Ecclesie Sarum*, eds. Francis Procter and Christopher Wordsworth (Cambridge, England: Cambridge Univ. Press, 1886), pp. 511ff.
15. Helen Garth, "Saint Mary Magdalene in Medieval Literature," *The Johns Hopkins University Studies in Historical and Political Science*, 67 (1949), pp. 13–14.
16. Ibid., p. 21.
17. If I may anticipate some of the connections to be made later between the Wife and Mary Magdalene, it is interesting to note that in her *Prologue* she uses the same word, *grucchyng*, in boasting of her connubial victory over her old husbands:

    And thus of o thyng I avaunte me,
    Atte ende I hadde the bettre in ech degree,
    By sleighte, or force, or by som maner thyng,
    As by continueel murmur or grucchyng. (D 403–406)
18. John McCall, "Chaucer and the Pseudo Origen *De Maria Magdalena*: A Preliminary Study," *Speculum*, 46 (1971), pp. 491–509.
19. Ibid., p. 501.
20. The text I have translated is the London edition, printed separately c. 1504, available in microfilm (University Microfilms STC 18846) from the copy in the British Museum. "Et sicut prius ad pedes domini lacrimas fuderat: ita nunc ad monumentum lacrimas funderet. Fleverat prius et lacrimis suis pedes eius rigaverat pro morte animae suae. Veniebat nunc cum lacrimis monumentum rigare pro morte magistri sui."
21. "Olim laudabat te cum unguento pedes eius ungebas lacrimis rigabas, et capillis tergebas.... Quam cito surrexit Maria ut audivit, quam cito venit et solito modo ad pedes tuos cecidit, O bone ihesu."
22. "Eoque magis plorabat quo magis ille deerat. Plorabat itaque vehementer maria: quoniam additus erat dolor super dolorem duosque dolores eximios immo gestabat in corde quos

mitigare lacrimis volebat sed non valebat. Et ideo tota posita in dolore mente et corpore deficiebat et quid ageret nesciebat. Quid enim mulier ista poterat agere nisi plorae que intollerabilem habebat dolorem et nullum inveniebat consolatorem?"

23. "Sed O Maria, quid iam amplius moraris, quid turbaris, quid ploras? Habes angelos. Sufficit tibi angelorum visio quia ille forsitan quem queris, quem ploras, sentit aliquid in te propter quod non vult videri a te. Pone iam finem dolori tuo. Sit modus lacrimis tuis. Recordare quod dixit tibi et aliis mulieribus: nolite flere super me. Ergo quid est hoc quod facis ipse flere prohibuit et tu flere non desinis? Timeo ne ipsum plorando offendas pro quo sic instanter ploras."
24. "Cum autem non inveniret corpus in monumento labor ungendi periit, sed dolor lugendi crevit. Defuit obsequio qui dolori non defuit; defuit quem condiret sed non defuit quem ploraret."
25. "Venerat autem Maria ad monumentum deferens secum aromata et unguenta quae praeparaverat ut sicut antea pedes viventis unguento precioso unxerat, sic etiam nunc corpus defuncti totum et unguento ungeret et aromatibus condiret."
26. "Stabo igitur et hic moriar ut saltem iuxta sepulcrum domini mei sepeliar. O quam beatum erit corpus meum si fuerit sepultum iuxta dominum meum, prope magistrum meum. O quam felix erit anima mea que egrediens de fragili vase corporis mei mox poterit ingredi in sepulcrum domini mei."
27. "Perdiderat enim magistrum suum quem ita famigliariter diligebat ut propter illum nichil possit diligere et nichil possit sperare. Perdiderat vitam animae suae et melius arbitrabat fore sibi mori quam vivere quia forsitan inveniret moriens quem vivens invenire non poterat sine quo tamen vivere non valebat."
28. "Quesivi illum in monumento et non inveni; vocavi illum et non respondit michi. Heu me ubi illum queram, ubi illum inveniam? Surgam certe et circuibo omnia loca que potero. Non dabo sompnum oculis meis, non dabo requies pedibus meis donec inveniam illum quem diligit anima mea...ambulate pedes mei, discurrite et nolite quiescere."
29. "Sepulcrum domini mei erit illi requies et honor. Hoc ergo sepulcrum in vita mea erit consolacio mea, et in morte mea erit requies mea. Vivens iuxta illud manebo; moriens illi adherebo, nec viva mortua ab illo separabor."
30. Helen Garth conveniently lists a number of corroborating sources on pp. 85ff.: St. Augustine, *De Trinitate* 1, 20, trans. Dom Cuthbert Butler, *Western Mysticism: The Teaching of SS. Augustine, Gregory, and Bernard on Contemplation and the Contemplative Life* (London: Constable & Co., 1922), p. 202; St. Odo Abbas Cluniacensis II, *Sermo II*, in *Patrologia Latina* [*PL*] 133:716–17; Hugo de S. Victore, Opp. Pars I, *Exegetica Dubia, Cap. XIII: De Martha et Maria Sororibus Lazari*, in *PL* 175:816; S. Gregorius Magnus, *Moralium, Liber VII*, in *PL* 55:764; and others.
31. "O verax magister et fidelis testis, recordare testimonii quod olim reddidisti Martae sorori eius. Dixisti enim: Maria optimam partem elegit quae non auferetur ab ea. Vere Maria optimam partem elegit quia elegit te..."
32. I do not mean to imply, of course, that much of the Wife's *Prologue* has not already been amply charted from sources like Jerome's *Epistola Adversus J ovinianum*, the *Romance of the Rose*, or Deschamps' *Miroir de Mariage*. But what these sources supplied Chaucer, it would seem, is more the *inventio* of the literal meaning than its symbolic extension. And yet even in these more obvious sources we hear none of the major Magdalenian echoes I have described

above. In the *Miroir de Mariage*, for example, a wife's callousness about her husband's obsequies and her searching for another spouse in the funeral crowd are mentioned, but conspicuously missing are the important iconographic details of the concupiscent feet and the sepulchral weeping. Nor is there any mention of the parsimonious funeral except for a phrase about the sufficiency of a short mass. See *Sources and Analogues of Chaucers Canterbury Tales*, ed. W. F. Bryan and Germaine Dempster (Chicago: Univ. of Chicago Press, 1941), p. 220, ll. 1966ff. It is evident that these details represent Chaucer's reworking of his source from a totally different tradition.

QUONIAM AND THE WIFE OF BATH

Rodney Delasanta

None of the working editions of Chaucer define the Wife of Bath's curious use of the word *quoniam* (D 608) as anything more than a euphemism designating her pudendum.[1] Not that the context fails to make her meaning clear, certainly no less clear than her other euphemisms like "bele chose" (D 447, 510) and "queynte" (D 332, 444). But in the latter two instances the euphemisms are transparent. *Quoniam* is another matter.

In order to understand the word, we must take a second look at the Wife of Bath as amateur exegete. Perhaps as a result of her marriage to Jankin the clerk, the Wife has gleaned the leavings of much medieval theology so that part of the humor in her "Prologue" follows from her shameless attempt at justifying her heterodoxical positions by quoting Scripture to suit her purpose. The Samaritan Woman at the Well, Solomon, Lameth, Abraham, Jacob, St. Paul, St. Mark—these are only some of the unwitting catechumens of her new "secte." Yet although Chaucer amuses us with her exegetical legerdemain, his intention finally is to expose the upside-down character of her argument. And to keep that expose confidential, to keep himself unspotted from the world of strident moralizing, Chaucer the poet quietly points us, by means of unobtrusive reminders in the language of the Wife herself, to the Christian norm from which she has deviated.

A good example of this strategy is one that John Speirs briefly recognized, but neglected to exploit, twenty years ago.[2] Boasting of her use-it-or-lose-it life-style, the Wife brags thus about her "gaye scarlet gytes."

> Thise wormes, ne thise mothes, ne thise mytes,
> Upon my peril, frete hem never a deel;
> And wostow why? for they were used weel. (D 560–62)

It is curious that except for Speirs no one else had heard the echoes from Matthew 6:19–20 in those lines: "Lay not up to yourselves treasures on earth where the rust and moth consume and where thieves break through and steal. But lay up to yourselves treasures in heaven where neither the rust nor moth doth consume, and where thieves do not break through nor steal." Quite obviously, the Wife's boast about her unconsumed clothing is undercut by the ironically normative imagery from Scripture with which she has composed the boast. The irony cuts more sharply if one recalls the Wife's lament (only eighty lines earlier) in a moment of naked truth that time, the subtle thief of youth, had indeed consumed.

> But age, allas! that al wole envenyme,
> Hath me biraft my beautee and my pith. (D 474–75)

Thus has Chaucer implicitly asserted in the Wife's own imagery a biblical paradigm from which she has strayed.

Something similar to this technique is at work with the use of the word *quoniam*. It is evident from his introductory description in the "General Prologue" that Chaucer has characterized the Wife of Bath as an ecclesiastical camp follower. By her own admission she frequents—for perverse reasons—vigils, processions, predications, miracle plays, and marriages (D 555–58). She has visited shrines in Jerusalem, Rome, Boulogne, Galicia, and Cologne (A 463–66). She had plucked her fifth husband from his theological studies and, presumably, from clerical orders.[3] She always insists on primacy at the offertory procession during Mass (A 449–50). Thus her life has become a ragbag of ecclesiastical experiences from which she draws an indiscriminate and self-incriminating imagery. Indeed, her casual use of the word *quoniam* as a euphemism for her pudendum functions as a blasphemous translation of adoration away from God to the all-consuming pleasure of her sexual object. This translation, or transference, medieval theologians would have called idolatry, a detour away from adoration of the Creator to adoration of his creation. It involves not the use but the abuse of the world's pleasures; and as Robertson has convincingly pointed out, a typical figure for the idol in both testaments is the image of the fornicating woman[4]: "The beginning of fornication is the devising of idols" (Wisdom 14:12); "Whosoever shall look on a woman to lust after her, hath committed adultery with her in his heart" (Matthew 5: 28).[5]

The Wife's use of the word *quoniam* brings together her ecclesiastical preoccupations on the one hand and her sexual preoccupations on the other. For *quoniam* is the opening word of the final doxology of the Gloria, itself the preeminent hymn of praise in the opening moments of the Mass. It belongs to the Ordinary of the Mass, which is to say that, except for certain celebrations of a penitential or funereal character, the Gloria is sung or recited at every Mass. As such, its words, as well as the more popular Gregorian melodies to which the words arc committed, are obviously memorizable. Most schoolchildren, even in the new liturgy of our own day, can recite the Gloria without reference to the text. Its universality of appeal in the medieval liturgy is attested to by the total of fifty-six different melodies for the Gloria that have been catalogued, as well as the twenty-three that include interpolated tropes.[6] In Legg's edition of *The Sarum Missal*, which was, of course, the rite most commonly used in Chaucer's day in England, a total of sixteen Glorias are listed, some with various musical settings, three of which are fully reproduced.[7] The first is the standard Gloria, which has survived unrevised down to our own day. The other two are Glorias with tropes interpolated significantly at the *quoniam* passage. An examination of how the word *quoniam* works in the Gloria will reveal Chaucer's ironic intention in placing it on the "likerous mouth" of the Wife of Bath.

In both the troped and standard Glorias, the word *quoniam* (meaning simply "for" or "because") introduces a doxological finale in the Hymn of Praise to the Father and the Son. It is a triumphal tag, related to the rest of the Gloria as the final rhymed couplet is related to a Shakespearean sonnet. As finale, it sings of the *unique* holiness, lordship, and majesty of God, especially as related to Jesus Christ and the Holy Spirit: *Quoniam tu solus sanctus, tu solus dominus, tu solus altissimus, Ihesu Christe cum Sancto Spiritu in gloria Dei Patris. Amen.*

The listener is struck, whether during the recitation or during the chant by the repeated insistence on the word *solus*: "For you *alone* are holy, you *alone* are lord, you *alone* are most high, Jesus Christ, with the Holy Spirit in the glory of God the Father. Amen". By the Wife's use of *quoniam*, she is in effect glorifying her pudendum by attributing to it, and not to God, a unique holiness (as the First Cause in her sex "secte"), a unique dominion (repeatedly flaunted in her claims of "quaint governance"), and a unique majesty. It is a blasphemous challenge to the medieval vision that theocentrically saw the Wholly Other as the *sanctus, dominus, and altissimus*. It is not unlike the challenge of those French revolutionaries who placed a whore on the high altar of Notre Dame de Paris in order to worship her. It is the Wife's paean to pudendum, which in her own metaphor of the multiplied barley loaves of Jesus's miracle "refresshed many a man" (D 146).

An examination of the Marian Gloria in *The Sarum Missal* confirms this blasphemous attribution. For those masses which commemorate different aspects of Mary's life (such as the Annunciation, the Presentation, the Purification), one important trope is interpolated precisely in the *quoniam* section of the Gloria and in a manner provocatively related to the Wife's worldview. It reads: *Quoniam tu solus sanctus Mariam sanctificans, tu solus dominus Mariam gubernans, tu solus altissimus Mariam coronans*. Quite obviously, Mary functions here as the shared object of God's unique attributes of holiness, lordship, and majesty. This is not the occasion to explore the distinctions between *latria*, the worship due to God alone, and *hyperdulia*, the preeminent veneration due to Mary as the highest of the saints, nor is it the occasion to judge the characters of Chaucerian women against a Marian paradigm; but as this set of distinctions can be applied to the Prioress and the Second Nun, it does not seem contrived to expect that "Seinte Venus" the whore may be implicitly measured against Saint Mary the Virgin.

For to risk a blasphemy of my own, Mary's *quoniam* was an object of considerable interest in the Middle Ages.[8] Chaucer himself on at least two occasions showed himself astonishingly direct, though iconographically stylized, about the matter of Mary's maidenhead. In *An ABC* we read:

Moises, that saugh the bush with flawmes rede
Brenninge, of which ther never a stikke brende,
Was signe of thin unwemmed maidenhede. (ll. 89–91)

And in the "Prologue" to the *Prioress's Tale,* the Prioress invokes Mary thus:

O bussh unbrent, brennynge in Moyses sighte,
That ravyshedest doun fro the Deitee,
Thurgh thyn humblesse, the Goost that in th'alighte,
Of whos vertu, whan he thyn herte lighte,
Conceyved was the Fadres sapience. (B^2 468–72)

Contrariwise, note that in the Wife of Bath's "Prologue" one of the "parables" she lists for woman's destructive love is wild fire, the very opposite of the "bussh unbrent," that which in *An ABC* burned without consuming even a "stikke."

Thou liknest it also to wilde fyr;
The moore it brenneth, the moore it hath desir
To consume every thy ng that brent wole be. (D 373–75)

Unlike Mary, who is made holy by the sanctifying God (*Mariam sanctificans*), the Wife admits that she cannot live up to Christ's injunction to perfection: "He spak to hem that wolde lyve parfitly; / And lordynges, by youre leve, that am nat I" (D 111–12). Unlike Mary, whose will is governed by God (*Mariam governans*), the Wife insists on her own brand of heterodox governance: "I governed hem so wel, after *my* lawe" (D 219). Unlike Mary, who is crowned queen by God (*Mariam coronans*), the Wife ascribes sovereignty to herself by usurping it from the hands of her husbands: "whan that I hadde geten unto me, / By maistrie, al the soverayntee ... / After that day we hadden never debaat" (D 817ff.).

As a medieval Christian, Chaucer would have heard the Gloria and the Marian Gloria with their respective *quoniams* recited and chanted hundreds, perhaps thousands, of times during the course of a life inescapably tied to the liturgy. The phrase—*quoniam tu solus sanctus, tu solus dominus, tu solus altissimus* (along with its Marian trope) —must have been grooved deeply in his memory. And although the gap between memory and imagination in most mortals is seldom bridged, like the gap between two conductors in a dead electrical current, Chaucer was able to arc a tiny flame across that gap and charge a liturgical formula into new life.

Notes to Quoniam and the Wife of Bath

1. All references to Chaucer are from the *Works of Geoffrey Chaucer*, ed. F. N. Robinson, 2nd ed. (Boston, 1957).
2. John Speirs, *Chaucer the Maker* (London, 1951), p. 143.
3. See Eugene E. Slaughter, "Clerk Jankyn's Motive," *MLN*, 65 (1950): pp. 530–34.
4. D. W. Robertson, Jr., *A Preface to Chaucer* (Princeton, 1963), p. 112.
5. The theme is especially recognizable among the prophets. See Jer. 3:9, Isa. 23:17, Ezek. 16:17, and Hos. 2:2.
6. *The New Catholic Encyclopedia* (New York, 1967), 6:511.
7. *The Sarum Missal*, ed. J. Wickham Legg (Oxford, 1969), pp. 6–7.
8. See, for example, the variety of questions dealing with the fact and the manner of Mary's virginity before, during, and after the birth of Jesus in the *Summa Theologica* of St. Thomas Aquinas, III, q. 28.

AND OF GREAT REVERENCE: CHAUCER'S MAN OF LAW

Rodney Delasanta

I

Praise be to Alfred David for finally coming up with a credible motive for the *Man of Law's Tale.*[1] Critics had generally divided, at least when Bernard Duffey last kept score, between the older—those who "praised the tale for its sincerity of expression and genuine emotional appeal"—and the later: those who now "emphasize its conventionality and, by implication, its artificiality as well."[2] By a remarkable insight into the functional ambivalence of Chaucer's intention, David has theorized that Chaucer has constructed a faultless moral tale in order to fault its narrator: in his own words, to show a pilgrim who is "something of a fool and perhaps also something of a knave turn out to have extremely strait-laced notions about literature and tell an impeccably moral tale."[3] Chaucer always wrote for those who have eyes to see and ears to hear, and the *Man of Law's Tale is* no exception. The righteous audience of the fourteenth and later *saecula* are thus treated to a righteous tale about virtue for the most part triumphant while Chaucer—less certain than most about the certitudes—has amused himself with a wry undercutting of such medieval triumphalism.

We have seen this kind of thing before in Chaucer with different Tales serving their own didactic ends while compromising by means of distinct modes the characters of their narrators. Certainly, the Pardoner's perfect sermon and exemplum have always been read as serving this double intention. The *Wife of Bath's Tale* fits this pattern more loosely. Recent criticism has demonstrated similar, but less obvious, intentions operating in the *Prioress's Tale,*[4] and the *Monk's Tale,*[5] perhaps the *Franklin's Tale.*[6] In each instance, Chaucer's choice of genre has served to edify the larger audience while he has demolished for his private amusement a different species of *peccator narrator*: the religious charlatan, the self-justifying nymphomaniac, the gentle bigot, the philosophical lummox, the *bourgeois gentilhomme*. David's reading of the Man of Law as a "type of wealthy bourgeois who condescends to dictate his taste to the artist" adds to the group. As a highly successful professional man, "he insists that art be serious, dignified, and moral. But what he really appreciates in art is not morality, but respectability, which is the appearance that morality confers."[7] Thus, his subject matter is virtually hagiographic, his tone pious and sentimental, his style grave and solemn, but his character privately pilloried.

As satisfying as David's insights are, he falls short when he suggests that although the Tale is well "suited to the Man of Law's genteel, sentimental, and moralistic tastes...it could be difficult to maintain that it...dramatically develops the character of its narrator."[8] Some critics have pointed to scattered examples of the peccadillos that by punctuating the Tale characterize the narrator. David himself has revealed the lawyer's sententiousness as hiding a shallowness, pedantry, prudishness, and blunt materialism.[9] But these discrete observations need to be assembled from afar into a larger dramatic pattern.

First, it would be rewarding to examine Chaucer's dramatization of the Man of Law as cultural cognoscente, a pose that aggrandizes his public image of an aware, wise, discreet, reverent, knowledgeable, famous, and very busy lawyer. In an article that has too often been ignored by other critics, William L. Sullivan has suggested that it is a mistake to accept the Man of Law's cultural pronunciamentos as being coterminous with Chaucer's.[10] The assumption he attacks, of course, ignores all that Chaucerian criticism has taught us in recent years (indeed, since Sullivan's article appeared) about point of view and the unreliable narrator, and blurs the ironic distinctions that operate at the very heart of the *Canterbury Tales* between Chaucer the poet, Chaucer the pilgrim, and the individual narrator of each Tale.[11] Chaucer is *not* the Man of Law; he is quite obviously not fond of the Man of Law; and it is inconceivable that he would have allowed the Man of Law to shine in a story chosen for him without the attendant Chaucerian undercuttings. Curiously, although few critics would deny that Chaucer is quietly demolishing the lawyer in the *General Prologue*, most have hesitated to see the same pattern of demolition operating in the Tale itself, possibly because the pattern there is more subtle. Take the celebrated discrepancy between the memorized catalog of women recited to the pilgrims *alia bravura* by the Man of Law and the actual characters written about by Chaucer in the *Legend of Good Women*. Scholars have unconvincingly described the deuterocanonical list as a Chaucerian prospectus of additions.[12] This theory would account for the eight women *not* mentioned in the *Legend of Good Women* but would not explain the lawyer's *omission* of the two women whom Chaucer had included in his earlier work. Except for Sullivan, not enough attention has been paid to the possibility that the confusion results not from the unlikelihood of a revised plan, but from accepting the Man of Law's pronouncements as being omnisciently true. Consonant with the tone of the *General Prologue*, it is more likely that Chaucer is allowing this pretentious man to make a quasi-fool of himself, not by characterizing him as an obvious Mr. Malaprop (for that would be unrealistic considering the lawyer's professional accomplishments), but by allowing him just enough errata to bring an amused smile to the educated auditor's face. For the fact is that the Man of Law's introduction, prologue, and Tale are quietly networked with an interstitial pattern of errors about things literary—like this erroneous catalog of good women—that cannot be attributed to ignorance or planned revisions on Chaucer's part.

We are told in the catalog, for example, of "the crueltee of the, queen Medea, / Thy litel children hangynge by the hals" (B 72–73), despite the fact that the traditional story has Medea slaying her children by the sword. Richard Hoffman's new book on Chaucer and Ovid documents fully the extensive influences, direct and echoic, of the Roman upon our poet. Among his conclusions are that "Chaucer was both widely and deeply read in Ovid" and "most intimately acquainted with the *Metamorphoses*, the *Ars Amatoria*, the *Heroides*, and the *Fasti* in that order. The *Metamorphoses* served Chaucer regularly as a handbook of mythology, from which he gleaned not only entire stories but even minute details of mythological or iconographic significance."[13] In the *Metamorphoses* Medea's murder of her children is described in terms of "her blood-red steel piercing the bodies of her two sons" (VII, 397–98). Is it possible that Chaucer could have been so careless about such an important detail in the well-known Medea story, particularly when we find no reference in the rest of his own work to Medea hanging her children? (In the *Book of the Duchess*, Chaucer uses the verb *slough* to describe Medea's act in l. 727; one cannot slay by hanging one's victims.) Earlier in the same passage also appear the lawyer's reference to Ceys and Alcione (B 57—which accommodating editors have glossed obviously as *The Book of the Duchess*—and his reference to the "Seintes Legende of Cupide" (B 61), which with equal obviousness they identify as *The Legend of Good Women*. It is instructive to note, however, that Chaucer never identifies his own work metonymically in other places by reference to minor characters, but either by their full titles or by a reference to the chief characters or central subject matter. In the "Prologue" to the *Legend of Good Women*, the god of love explicitly mentions Chaucer's translations of the *Romance of the Rose* (F 329) and of Boethius (F 425), the full titles of the *Hous of Fame* and the *Parlement of Foules* (F 417, 419), the chief characters in their respective poems: Criseyde (F 332), Palamon and Arcite (F 420), and Seynt Cecile (F 426), and—most germane to our purposes here—the "Deeth of Blaunche the Duchesse" (F 418). Nowhere else in Chaucer do we find a reference to Ceys and Alcione as synonymous with the entire elegy, and the reason is that the content of the *Book of the Duchess* involves much more than the story of this Ovidian couple. Indeed, their function in the elegy, though important as a foreshadowing of the sorrow of the knight, is largely introductory. In a work of 1,334 lines, their function ceases at line 220, roughly where one would expect a pretentious literary dabbler like the Man of Law to have stopped in his reading. And the reference to the "Seintes Legende of Cupide" although Baugh sees it as a "playful" alternate title for the *Legend of Good Women*,[14] also suggests the lawyer's truncated knowledge of the "Prologue" alone.

The abounding errors continue in the famous denigration of Gower (and the attendant reluctant praise of Chaucer) that comes immediately after the catalog. Sullivan's description of this passage as a "grudging, one-thing-I'll-say-for-him [Chaucer] remark"[15] seems to identify the tone of prudish petulance. Yet nowhere in the *Confessio Amantis* had Gower described the incest scene offensively. Indeed there is no mention at all of Antiochus's throwing his daughter to the pavement (as the Man of Law describes it in line 85) in order to violate her. On the contrary, Gower's description of the incestuous deed is a model of understatement:

Bot whanne a man hath welthe at wille
The fleissh is frele and falleth ofte,
And that this made tendre and softe
Which in hir fadres chambres duelte,
Withinne a time wist and felte:
For likinge and concupiscence
Withoute insihte of conscience
The fader so with lustes blente,
That he caste al his hole entente
His oghne doghter forto spille.
This king hath leisir at his wille
With strengthe, and whanne he time sih,
This yonge maiden he forlih.[16]

Moral Gower can hardly be accused here—as the Man of Law has accused him—of sensationalism, of "cursed stories" or "horrible...tale[s]."[17] The suggestion that "Chaucer may possibly have been misremembering the suicide of Canace in the *Confessio*, or more likely, as suggested by the use of the word 'pavement' [misremembering] the assault of Antiochus in the Latin version"[18] is not convincing. If anyone is misremembering, it is most likely the pilgrim of vaunted memory, the Man of Law himself.

Ten lines later appears the much discussed Prologue to the Tale. The learned commentary about the relationship of the Prologue to Pope Innocent III's *De Miseria Humane Conditionis* has, until Robert Enzer Lewis's recent essay, been tangential to the central artistic issue of why Chaucer inserted the problem Prologue between the Introduction and the Tale proper.[19] Was he merely showing off a vestigial translation of Innocent mentioned elsewhere perhaps as *The Wreched Engendrynge of Mankynde*?[20] Lewis's answer contributes markedly to our understanding of Chaucer's characterization of the Man of Law as *cognoscente manqué*. Certainly, it is in character for a man preoccupied with the acquiring of wealth "to describe extensively...the evils of poverty and the hardships of poor men."[21] But the excising of that passage in Innocent where the pope scorns both poor *and* rich[22] suggests either that the lawyer is something of a knave for having suppressed evidence about the human condition which he himself has offered for the edification of the pilgrims or something of a fool for not having drunk deeply enough to have tasted of the pontifical spring. Either possibility would work dramatically, but I lean to the second because it brilliantly gives the lie to the lawyer's vaunted memory ("And every statu koude he pleyn by rote") and to his presumed knowledge and wisdom ("war and wys," he was greatly rewarded "for his science and for his heigh renoun").[23] Men might indeed "pynche" at his achievements.

The errors continue with unobtrusive tenacity into the Tale itself. Again, I must state that although Chaucer could on other occasions regale us with errors of the malaprop variety ("*In principio, mulier est hominis confusio*" crows Chauntecleer to his inamorata), such an excess in this case would falsify the legitimate accomplishments of this not-quite scholar. He is obviously learned in the law. He has also read in Scripture, history, and literature, but it has by now become more evident that he has pursued his extra-legal reading with an eye to intellectual posturing and didactic gesture, certainly not with the depth and understanding characteristic of pilgrims like the Clerk and the Nun's Priest. Among his scriptural allusions, for example, are three seeming matter-of-fact references to Old Testament heroes, but in each instance the narrator reveals a second-hand knowledge about the characters which does not square with the manner of their appearance in the Bible. Interestingly too, they appear in those passages which Chaucer did *not* derive from either Trivet or Gower but which are completely original with him: the apostrophe at B 470 where the narrator interrupts the action to declaim on God's Providence in saving Constance from being slain at her wedding feast or from being drowned in her Atlantic voyage; and the apostrophe at B 932 where he explains Constance's escape from the miscreant steward. Why was she not slain at the Syrian feast with the others, asks Man of Law? He answers with another question:

> Who saved Danyel in the horrible cave
> Ther every wight save he, maister and knave,
> Was with the leon fret er he asterte?
> No wight but God, that he bar in his herte. (B 473–76)

The pious answer is to be expected, but the lawyer's capsulized scripture lesson approaches the apocryphal. Nowhere in Daniel (cf. 6:17) do we read that the hero was accompanied by anyone else. Rather, he is thrust *alone* into the lion's den and released from it because of his refusal to apostasize *before* his accusers are cast in and devoured for their sins. The picture of a leonine feast where Daniel alone proves inedible reads like the embellishments of a fourteenth-century Fulton Oursler. And ten lines later, after asking how Constance escaped drowning in her perilous voyage from Syria to Britain, he again answers his own question with another:

> Now sith she was nat at the feeste yslawe,
> Who kepte hire fro the drenchyng in the see?
> Who kepte Jonas in the fisshes mawe
> Til he was spouted up at Nynyvee? (B 484–87)

The Book of Jonah is only four chapters long. As an Old Testament foreshadowing of Christ's harrowing of hell and his resurrection from the dead, it was extremely well-known in the Christian liturgy and readings of the Middle Ages. Thus, for the Man of Law to have conceived of Nineveh as a seaport where the whale disgorged Jonah is a misconception of large proportions. Nineveh, situated deep in Assyria on the Tigris River, was according to Jonah 3:3 a city of three days' journey inland. Jonah had attempted to escape the Lord's command to preach at Nineveh by embarking at Joppa where he found a ship going north to Tharsis (Jonah 1:3). When the great whale vomits Jonah out on dry land between Joppa and Tharsis, it is a considerable distance from Nineveh, whose only contiguity with water is the east bank of the Tigris River. Nor should this geographical knowledge be considered esoteric for Chaucer, like Shakespeare's seaport in Bohemia. For not only was Chaucer well-traveled himself (consider his various embassages to the continent), but he was also acutely interested in matters geographical (witness the famous itinerary of the Knight in the *General Prologue*). Moreover, and more important, Nineveh was no obscure city to the iconography of the Middle Ages. Rather it is frequently mentioned in the Bible as a city hated by the Jews because it was the capital of the Assyrian Empire. Its destruction is prophesied in Tobias 14, Nahum 1–3, and Sophonias 2:13 (Douay-Rheims translation) and averted, much to Jonah's discomfiture, in the fourth chapter of his own book. To conceive of it as a seaport, as the Man of Law has done, is to fail to recognize it as the capital of a hated enemy kingdom, a blunder that represents more than mere geographical miscalculation. That Chaucer could have been capable of such a mistake is unlikely, considering the evidence from patristic critics of his knowledge of scripture. That the Man of Law could be capable of such a misconception, however, seems more and more likely as we continue to examine the case against him.[24]

Less damaging an error than the two just mentioned, but indicative nonetheless of the scriptural popularizer, is another apostrophic reference, this time to Goliath at B 932. Constance had earlier been assaulted by a miscreant steward but had been preserved in her chastity by Jesus and Mary's intercession. Again, the Man of Law waxes eloquent over the miracle:

> How may this wayke womman han this strengthe
> Hire to defende agayn this renegat?
> O Golias, *unmesurable of lengthe,*
> Hou myghte David make thee so maat,
> So yong and *of armure so desolaat*? (B 932–36)

And again he reveals a flawed knowledge of the source, for the real sense of 1 Samuel 17:4 is the extent to which the writer indeed "measures" both Goliath and David so as to underscore the absurd discrepancy in their sizes. Rather than being "unmeasurable," Goliath is measured at "sly cubits and one span tall." And although David is "desolaat" of armor when actually confronting Goliath, he is earlier described as being fully armed by Saul before he decides that he would be more effective with a slingshot.

The spate of mini-errors in the *Man of Law's Tale* is not limited to Scripture. Elsewhere the lawyer unwittingly reveals a vincible ignorance about a miscellany of topics. Moreover, it is significant that the errors occur when the lawyer is clearly speaking in his own voice (as in an apostrophe, rather than within the dialogue of characters) and in those passages that Chaucer had added to Trivet. *None* of the errata which I find in the Tale are found in Trivet. All of them are Chaucerian interpolations. The allusion to Julius Caesar's "triumphe" at the death of Pompey, a detail attributed to Lucan by the Man of Law (B 401) although the *Pharsalia* explicitly describes Caesar's *sorrow* over Pompey's death,[25] is a case in point. So too is the lawyer's reference to Hannibal, which contains a curious detail of his having vanquished the Romans "tymes thre" (B 291). The number is improbable since a reading of the Second Punic War (even in Plutarch) reveals more than three Carthaganian victories before Hannibal is finally beaten by the Romans. The lawyer's "documentation" of the life of Maurice (the son of Constance and Alla) is also interpolated and inaccurate. "In the olde Romayn geestes may men fynde / Mauries lyf" says the Man of Law to his pilgrim audience. But, according to Robinson, "the life of Mauricius is not in the *Gesta Romanorum*, or, to judge from Loesche's analysis in the vast unpublished French compilation, in *Li Faits des Romains*."[26]

Of course, it is possible to read this deluge of misinformation and misinterpretation as unstrategic, as coming innocently from Chaucer the poet with no eye to quietly demolishing the Man of Law. If the errors I have pointed to had constituted a thin thread in the complex tapestry of Introduction, Prologue, and Tale, I would be inclined to agree. But the pattern has been stitched large, and I am old-fashioned enough to believe in the argument from design.

II

What has been said characterizes the Man of Law from only one perspective: that of being less than he pretends to be intellectually and culturally. It would seem, however, that Chaucer had other plans for his lawyer. In the *General Prologue*, Chaucer the pilgrim, who in so many other portraits is incapable of qualifying his praise and is thus himself ironically victimized in his judgments by Chaucer the poet, immediately hedges with the Man of Law. After describing him as "war and wys," "ful riche of excellence," "discreet" and—most revealing—"of greet reverence," our usually gullible reporter qualifies his praise with the famous line: "He semed swich, his wordes weren so wise." What "seems" in the Man of Law, as with so many other Pilgrims, is not what "is," and it is the "seems" of "greet reverence" that I will pursue in the rest of this essay.

I have indicated elsewhere that in an age that was not embarrassed about shouting its faith from the housetops, Chaucer showed remarkable restraint about bandying the central truths of Christianity.[27] He almost never indulged in facile affirmation (at least, to appropriate Northrop Frye's terms, in his *fictional*, as opposed to his *thematic*, modes), seldom cast his pearls before the feet of swine. Whenever one finds a voluble Christianity rhetorically flourishing in his work, therefore, it is safe to assume that Chaucer had other than the obvious catechetic intentions. It is no accident that one of the most overt expressions of Christian faith in Chaucer should have come in a Tale in which the triumphalism of its narrator is undercut by a brilliant characterization of her unfeeling bigotry: *The Prioress's Tale*.[28] Or conversely that the characters who seem most committed to the vocation of Christian men—the Clerk, the Plowman, the Knight, and the Parson—are the most involved in *deeds* and the most restrained in *words*. Although the Knight "full worthy was...in his lordes werre, / And thereto hadde he riden, no man ferre" (A 47–48), his speech is restrained ("He never yet no vileyne ne sayde"). The Clerk, hard at work at his studies and prayers—"And bisily gan for the soûles preye / Of hem that yaf hym wherwith to scoleye" (A 201–202)—is no stranger to silence ("Noght o word spak he moore than was neede"). Indeed, the Clerk eschews didactic utterance even in his Tale. The Parson, "ne of his speche daungerous ne digne" (A 517), practices before he preaches ("This noble ensample to his sheep he yaf / That first he wroghte, and afterward he taughte"). And the Plowman's perfect charity apparently needs no vocalization:

> Lyvynge in pees and parfit charitee,
> God loved he best with al his hoole herte,
> At alle tymes, though him gamed or smerte,
> And thanne his neighebore right as hymselve. (A 532–35)

The rhetorically hyperactive—whether learned or vulgar—on the other hand, are not among Chaucer's favorite people, especially those who are religious. The Pardoner's pulpit language, for example, is inflated ("I peyne me to han a hauteyn speche"). The Friar knows much of "daliaunce and fair langage." The Monk lards his tragedies with unremitting apostrophes. The Prioress in her Prologue cries out apostrophic ejaculations to Jesus and Mary. And among the laymen, the Merchant "spak his resons...ful solempnely"; the Physician is without equal "to speke of phisik and of surgerye"; the Summoner when drunk "wolde...speke and crie as he were wood"; the Host is "boold of his speche." Rhetorical declamation is simply not normal Chaucerian strategy unless it is mischievously directed *against* its practitioners, especially when we find it floating free of its dramatic anchor. One has the distinct impression that Chaucer removes rhetorical display from those narrators who are *simpatici* while reserving it for those narrators who are not. In the *Knight's Tale*, proportionate in length to the Man of Law's but of unquestioned seriousness, it is instructive to note that Chaucer uses rhetorical artifice with dramatic appropriateness by consigning it to an aristocratic speaker who uses it as textural support for a story rich in structural balance and symmetry. Verbal pyrotechnics for their own sake are simply absent. Indeed, we find here an almost complete exclusion of the interpolated apostrophe and even an inclusion of colloquial diction (what Robert W. Jordan describes as "humorous *lapses* into low style")[29] but what seems to me to be a deliberate humanization of an otherwise socially unapproachable narrator. In the *Clerk's Tale* too, although Chaucer allows the narrator occasional bursts of rhetorical anger at Walter's cruelty (E 460, 561, 621), elegant statement or apostrophe are forsaken, except for the "Lenvoy" in which the Clerk pays ironic homage to the "noble wyves" (E 1183) and the one incident in the Tale proper where a seldom apostrophe attacking the fickle multitudes is spoken not *obiter dictum* by the Clerk but dramatically by the "sadde folk" (E 995ff.).[30] In the *Franklin's Tale*, rhetorical elegance is quite plainly mocked. In his Prologue, the Franklin ironically apologizes for his "rude speche," his lack of rhetoric, his "bare and pleyn" utterance (F 718ff.), by indulging in the very language he claims no talent for:

> I sleep never on the Mount of Pernaso,
> Ne lerned Marcus Tullius Scithero.

> Colours ne knowe I none, withouten drede,
> But swiche colours as growen in the mode,
> Or elles swiche as men dye or peynte.
> Colours of rethoryk been to me queynte... (F 721–26)

Later in the Tale itself, describing the revels of Aurelius's friends, revels which the love-struck young man cannot participate in because of his sorrow over Dorigen's refusal of his suit, the Franklin tries his hand at elegant variation only to mock his own efforts:

> But sodeynly bigonne revel newe
> Til that the brighte sonne loste his hewe;
> For th'orisonte hath reft the sonne his lyght,
> This is as muche to seye as it was nyght! (F 1015–18)

And, of course, the brilliant repetition of apostrophes in the *Nun's Priest's Tale* is intimately related to the amount of requiting sweet Sir John is directing at Daun Pier's apostrophe for apostrophe. Indeed of all the Tales, I find more rhetorical kinship, more similarity of accent between the *Nun's Priest's Tale* and the Man of Law's than between any others. And since no critic would deny the mock epic strategies of the Priest's rhetorical flourishes, it would be useful to compare both narrations to determine how serious is Chaucer's intention in allowing the Man of Law his intrusive declamation.[31]

What is the relationship in Chaucer between rhetorical excess and religious exhibitionism? First it should be made quite clear that Chaucer is not mocking rhetoric *per se*. John Mathew Manly's observations about Chaucer's rhetorical methods have clearly shown his debt to the medieval rhetoricians, particularly Gaufred de Vinsauf and his *Nova Poetria*.[32] Manly has also observed, however, that Chaucer's poetic development "reveals itself...not as progress from crude, untrained native power to a style and method polished by fuller acquaintance with rhetorical precepts...but rather as a process of gradual *release* from the astonishingly artificial...art with which he began and the gradual replacement of formal rhetorical devices by methods of composition based upon close observation."[33] Equally important is Manly's contention that the difference between the successful and less successful tale is the extent to which rhetorical devices are made integral to the dramatic intention of the work. Unlike the tales of the Wife of Bath and the Nun's Priest, for example, in which rhetorical artificialities are made dramatic integers (usually humorous) of the tales' intentions, "in the tales of the Man of Law and the Doctor, the rhetoric is prevailingly, indeed almost exclusively, used by the narrator: that is, it is not incorporated and used dramatically but stands apart from the tale."[34]

It is this deliberate "apartness" of the rhetorical elements in the *Man of Law's Tale* (an apartness that Manly misreads as unfunctional) that reveals the lawyer's triumphalism. As I indicated earlier in this essay, it is curious to note that the flourishes (all of which unsubtly celebrate a religious mystery or moral triumph, or self-righteously castigate sin and sinners) represent Chaucer's additions to Trivet[35] and, as Manly has pointed out, represent not the language of dialogue but that of intrusion by the narrator. The amount of this un-dramatic interpolation, moreover, is prodigious: pompous allusions to classical or biblical or even contemporary figures serving as exempla; apostrophes directed didactically to objects both sacred and profane; rhetorical questions that curiously provoke their own answers; unremitting hyperbole; even imprecation. What all this implies is that the Man of Law, in Fr. Beichner's words, is "busy with his telling of the story."[36] He is self-consciously aware of his professional demeanor and anxious to reveal himself to the pilgrims by means of his narrative. What Chaucer the poet allows him to reveal, however, is at a considerable ironic distance from what ostensibly constitutes his self-aggrandizing intention. We have already observed Chaucer's subtle deflation of the Man of Law's cultural pretensions; however, the unveiling of the pharisee is yet to come.

With the telling of the Tale proper, we see the Man of Law introducing the matchless maiden, Constance, and the negotiations involved in her marriage to the Sultan of Syria. (It is significant, I believe, that the enemies endemic to the medieval Church Militant—the Mohammedans and the Jews—should appear in Chaucer only in those tales narrated by the pilgrims, the Man of Law and the Prioress, whose Christianity is comprised by its stridency. It is here that one recognizes the most obvious appropriateness of teller to tale, for the Man of Law lavishes much legalistic attention on the diversities of law, the canonical impediments to marriage, the mediation of the papacy, the Sultan's agreement to convert to Christianity, and the royal dowery attached to the conversion. These details, though also mentioned in Trivet (as they are in Gower), are strategically emphasized in Chaucer until one feels, as Fr. Beichner has suggested, "that the Man of Law was trying rather patronizingly to impress his fellow pilgrims with the amount of argumentation and subtle reasoning that the councilors employed."[37] Moreover, one hears in the expertise of such language as "privée conseil," "tretys," "embassadrie," "popes mediacioun," "Cristes lawe," "sufficient surtee," "purveiance," "ordinance," "clause," and all the rest (from B 204ff.) a canonist legality which identifies the Man of Law as pharisee, that peculiar combination of law and self-righteous religion so despised in the New Testament and in those later centuries (including our own) when the dead weight of the letter seems particularly oppressive to the spirit. It cannot be accidental that Chaucer took pains to include in his pilgrimage a man both learned in the law and rectitudinous in his religion. Commentators have repeatedly bemoaned Chaucer's revision of intention from the time he wrote the *General Prologue* to the time he allowed his lawyer to tell a story, but that attitude ignores even in the *General Prologue* Chaucer's preliminary designation of the man as both legalistic and "of *greet* reverence." What the lawyer's story succeeds in doing, it would seem, is to dramatize by its mode of narration the pharisaical spirit only hinted at in the Prologue which admits of no ambiguous mingling of good and evil but which rather pens the sheep away from the goat in every moment of human experience.

The characters of the *Man of Law's Tale* are thus defectively drawn because their narrator's legalistic attitude toward humankind is defective, alternately on the side of sentimentality or on that of anathema. For example, even though Edward A. Block, the great source critic of this Tale, finds nothing opprobrious redounding upon the narrator as a result of the pietistic additions to Trivet, he does admit that among other intentions Chaucer's "unmistakable purpose was to make the most of the 'good' characters, particularly Constance."[38] He points out too that Chaucer makes his good characters talk more and *pray* more than Trivet (eight hundred and fifty words of dialogue and three hundred and fifty words of prayer in Chaucer versus two hundred and fifty words of dialogue and *no prayer* in Trivet) and draws attention to certain additions "which emphasize the fact that her [Constance's] life was saved on various occasions only by God's miraculous intervention."[39] (It should be observed here that the interpolated passages referred to above in which the Man of Law facilely "miraculizes" are the same in which his Biblical allusions fail in accuracy.) Curiously, John Yunck has pointed to these pietistic interpolations as evidence of Chaucer's *intensifying* of religious attitudes for homiletic reasons and has found the results thus interpreted as artistically satisfying.[40] Such an attitude ignores the obvious fact that Chaucer disdains the didactic in his pilgrims unless they have "first wroghte," as the Parson has done and as the Man of Law has not, but more seriously such an attitude ignores the cursing and anathemas that punctuate the lawyer's narration, a stridency that Chaucer quite obviously never mistook for religious "intensification." (One has only to recall the Parson's reluctance to curse in the *General Prologue*: "Ful loth were hym to cursen for his tithes" (A 486).

The Man of Law's unremittingly black characterization and thumping condemnation of the Sultan's mother, for example, bespeak the other side of his pharisaical schizophrenia. In a veritable litany of malediction, anticipatory of *Tristram Shandy*, the Man of Law calls her a "welle of vices," "roote of iniquitee," "Semyrame the secounde," "serpent under femynyntee," "serpent depe in helle ybounde," "feyned womman," "nest of every vice," and "cursed krone."[41] Nor is this the only example of his unsubtle outrage against sinners. Later in the story he similarly condemns Donegild for her malicious reaction to the marriage of Alla and Constance. Characteristically, this mother-in-law too is outside the pale of the Faith, whereas her son "the kyng, and many another in that place, / Converted was, thanked be Cristes grace" (B 685–86). Like the Sultaness, Donegild is "full of tirannye"; she possesses a "cursed herte"; she is a feendlych spirit"; her "spirit is in helle." Nor do these execrations suffice. The speaker feels that he has no language capable of describing her evil and therefore resigns her to the fiend: "lat hym enditen of thy traitorie."[42] The only time in the entire Chaucer canon that one comes across venom of this kind, even for malicious characters, is when the speaker is among Chaucer's group of *peccator narrator*, or when, as in the *Nun's Priest's Tale*, the condemnation is tongue in cheek.[43] Nowhere, for example, in the characterizations of Pandarus, Walter, Aurelius, even the Wife of Bath, all of whom deserve some measure of censure, do we find condemnation. The reason, of course, is that the *speakers* of the respective Tales are sympathetically conceived by Chaucer and thus share his broadly tolerant view of human evil. In each of the Tales of Chaucer's militant or self-righteous pilgrims, however, the Prioress, the Man of Law, the Physician, and (by fakery) the Pardoner—the antagonists are all handled with choleric condemnation: the cursed Jews, the Sultaness and Donegild, Appius, and the three rioters. Moreover, the evil they are capable of is all-consuming and unmitigated by even the most elementary humanity. It is significant, for example, that in the *Man of Law's Tale* Chaucer does not follow Trivet in allowing three of the Christians at the feast to escape the Sultaness's wrath and return to Rome. Rather, he permits the Man of Law to narrate with martyrological glee the arranged slaughter of the converted Sultan "and the Cristen *everichone*" (B 429). "Ne ther was Surryen *noon that was converted*... That he nas al tohewe er he asterted" (B 435–37). It is as if Chaucer wished to emphasize the black and white rectitudinousness of his lawyer for whom Christians are all-good and all-suffering while the enemy is implacably hostile. It is probably this same kind of attitude that prompted Chaucer to revise another similar scene from Trivet later in the story. Block had pointed out in his catalog of differences between the two versions "that the Northumbrian knight who attempted to ravish Constance...was not only a Saxon but a *Christian*."[44] Chaucer's omission of this detail is consonant with his oblique characterization of the lawyer's clubby righteousness. For him Christians just don't behave that way. If one has left the club, however, then he is capable of all manner of mischief. Thus, it is not accidental that Chaucer allowed his source to go unrevised in describing another sexual assault upon Constance as having been perpetrated by a "theef that hadde reneyed oure creance" (B 915).

In such a universe in which "soth" and "fals" are never compounded (the kind of inevitable commingling Chaucer describes near the end of the *House of Fame*), vengeance serves as a natural correlative to condemnation. Again, it is instructive to note that in those Tales narrated by Chaucer's militants the evil antagonists suffer excruciating punishment for their sins, a punishment gleefully inflicted upon them by their fictional executioners. "Yvele shal have that evele wol deserve" is the Prioress's motto, and in her Tale the "cursed" Jews are first drawn by wild horses and then hanged "by the lawe" (B^2 1822–24). "Heere may men seen how synne hath his merite" (C 277) is the Physician's righteous response to Appius's suicide and the fate of his companions on the gallows. The two surviving rioters in the *Pardoner's Tale* suffer of poisoning beyond the experience even of the great physician Avicenna who "wroote never in no canon, ne in no fen, / Mo wonder signes of empoisonyng" (C 890–91). The vengeance of the *Man of Law's Tale* shares in this kind of eager sadistic justice. It is true that in Trivet the retaliatory slaughter of the Saracens is described in greater detail than in Chaucer, but it is also significant that in the original the slaughter is reported in the words of the emperor's envoy, the senator, whereas in the *Man of Law's Tale* Chaucer shifts the description to the mouth of the narrator himself:

> For which this Emperour hath sent anon
> His senatour, with roial ordinance,
> And other lordes, God woot, many oon,
> On Surryens to taken heigh vengeance.
> They brennen, sleen, and brynge hem to meschance
> Ful many a day... (B 960–65)

No less gleeful had been the lawyer's description of Donegild's miserable end, slain at the hands of her own son: "Thus endeth olde Donegild, with meschance!" (B 896).

III

It is always foolhardy to attempt to pinpoint the source of Chaucer's creative vision. The deep springs which fed the well of English undefiled are fortunately unplumbable even to those among us who pretend to be the most artesian of diggers. Although we are beguiled by those biographical theories that attempt to explain artistic activity as a realistic or allegorical response to people and events chronicled from an author's life, we recognize also that a poet of the first order is moved to creative activity only when the contemporary person or event assume a significance in his imagination which transcend their mere contemporaneity. Manly's famous designation of Thomas Pynchbek as the biographical source of Chaucer's satirical inspiration for the Man of Law is convincing. But other, more fetching, reasons must have provoked Chaucer to enroll a contemporary like Pynchbek into his Canterbury pilgrimage and transform him into the universal Man of Law. If Coleridge was right in defining the poetic imagination as that esemplastic power which reshapes our primary awareness of the world into symbolic avenues to the theological, then the medieval poet was especially fortunate in already having found those avenues to the theological amply charted for him in Scripture. That Chaucer knew the Biblical routes extraordinarily well has been convincingly demonstrated to us by the patristic critics. Whatever his "primary awareness" of the original Dame Alice may have been, for example, his subsequent reshaping of her into the Wife of Bath would not likely have been accomplished without the Scriptural presence in his imagination of the Samaritan woman at the well. It can be argued that similar Scriptural presences stand behind other pilgrims. One senses the Unjust Steward behind the Reeve, the ubiquitous Sadducee, Scribe and Pharisee behind the unholy ecclesiasts, perhaps the Faithful Centurion behind the Knight. What one finds standing behind the Man of Law is not so much a single figure as a medley of unnamed legalists who recur both in the Gospels as exemplary of Jesus's admonitions against self-satisfaction, self-righteousness, and self-exaltation and also in the Lollard literature of reform with which Chaucer must have been intimate. One senses, among other things, the presence of the lawyer anxious to justify himself before Jesus in our Man of Law: "And behold a certain lawyer stood up, tempting him and saying, Master, what must I do to possess eternal life? But he said to him: What is written in the law? How readest thou? He answering, said: Thou shalt love the Lord thy God with thy whole heart and with thy whole soul and with all thy strength and with all thy mind: and thy neighbor as thyself. And he said to him: Thou has answered right. This do: and thou shalt live. But he willing to justify himself, said to Jesus: And who is my neighbour?" (Luke 10: 25–29). Most ironically appropriate to the *Man of Law's Tale* is Jesus's challenging response to the lawyer's question: "And who is my neighbour?" For Jesus answers with the story of the Good Samaritan who represents the inclusive brotherhood of *all* humanity—inclusive even of the outcast, heretical, and hated Samaritan. The Man of Law's implicit definition of neighbor in his Tale is very similar to that of the pious Jews of the New Testament who refused to believe that "Samaritan" could possibly have meant "neighbor." As a self-righteous, militant, rectitudinous, and unmerciful Christian, the Man of Law represents the very opposite of all Jesus sought to portray in his story.

Other Biblical echoes must have reverberated in Chaucer's imagination. Certainly one can cautiously conjecture that Jesus's bitter rebuke of lawyers in Luke 11:45 would have had something further to do with Chaucer's unflattering portrait of his Man of Law: "And one of the lawyers answering, saith to him: Master, in saying these things [his condemnation of the pharisaical spirit] thou reproachest us also. But he said: Woe to you lawyers also, because you load men with burdens which they cannot bear and you yourselves touch not the packs with one of your fingers.... Woe to you lawyers, for you have taken away the key of knowledge. You yourselves have not entered in, you have hindered" (Luke 11:45–52). The echoes continue: in Jesus's seven-fold indictment of the scribes and pharisees in Matthew 23:13–36; in his condemnation of the yeast of the Pharisees and Sadducees in Matthew 16:5–12; in his famous parable of the Pharisee and the publican in Luke 18:9–14; in his reproach of the scribes "who like to walk about in long robes and love to be greeted obsequiously... while making a show of lengthy prayers" in Luke 20:45–47; in 1 John 3:18–20 where the apostle reminds his flock that "our love is not to be just words or mere talk, but something real and active"; and especially in Matthew 7:21 where Jesus reminds his followers that "not everyone that saith to me, Lord, Lord, shall enter into the kingdom of Heaven but he that doth the will of my Father who is in Heaven."

Similar echoes in the Lollard literature of reform tantalize us into admittedly undocumentable conjecture. It would be futile to reopen here the case of Chaucer and the Lollards, whether he was of their party or perhaps of their party without knowing it. But however orthodox (and therefore officially anti-Lollard) Chaucer's Catholicism might have been, it is inconceivable to me that their cause would not have stirred his sympathies and their literature his interest.[45] Indeed, one must concur with Dr. Shirley in his claim that if Wycliffe had died *before* his denial of transubstantiation "his name might have come down to us in another form, and miracles [would have been] wrought at the tomb of their founder by the brothers preachers of St. John Wycliffe."[46] Loomis has argued convincingly that in his presentation of the Knight, the Clerk, the Plowman, and the Parson Chaucer has sympathized with those social types most closely identified with the Lollard movement. His long friendship, moreover, with Sir Richard Stury and Sir Lewis Clifford, both well known in their support of the poor priests of Lollardry, strongly suggests an intimacy with Wycliffite affairs that shows up in his poetry.[47] I contend that Chaucer's discomfiture with the Man of Law as pharisaical legalist draws its inspiration at least in part from Wycliffite polemics. Repeatedly we see in those tracts condemnation of legal chicanery combined with outrage at the attendant religiosity. Muriel Bowden has already pointed to one passage:

> In men of lawe regneth moche gile, for thei meyntenen falsnes for wynnynge & maken lordis to meyntene wrongis, & don wrongis whanne lordis hopen to do right & plese god, & bi here coveitise & falsenesse thei purchasen londis & rentis ynowe and don many extorsions & beren don the right bothe of pore & riche, & *yet thei maken it so holy in signes outward as if thei weren angelis of hevene, to colour here falsenesse* & *blynde the peple thereby*.[48]

I italicize the telling passage because it is precisely this point that previous criticism (including Miss Bowden's) has overlooked. The "greet reverence" of which Chaucer the pilgrim speaks in the *General Prologue* did not go undisdained by his contemporaries. In another tract which F. D. Matthew cannot indisputably identify as Wycliffe's own, but which obviously belongs to the Lollard canon, we read the quintessential condemnation of pharisaism. After castigating lawyers for encouraging quarrels, suborning perjury, packing and intimidating juries, and an assortment of other evils, the polemicist is particularly outraged by their pretenses to religion;

> But most thei schullen be depe dampnyd for here grete ypocrisie, for thei maken it so holy bothe in word and signes, as knockynge here brest, knelynge & seiynge of matynes & evensong, & herynge of massis, & many others devocions to coloure here falsnesse, that symple men supposen no more rightwisnesse in ony man that leveth in herthe.[49]

What we finally come to see in the complex of Introduction, Prologue, and Tale, as well as in the brief introductory sketch of the *General Prologue*, is Chaucer's dramatization of still another kind of ersatz Christian man: the housetop shouter, the sober brow who blesses and approves with a text, the Pharisee who thanks God that he is not as other men, the whited sepulchre. Every Christian age has given birth to such a man who, confident of having grown in grace and wisdom before God, vouchsafes to impart these gifts to his fellow man.

Notes to And of Great Reverence: Chaucer's Man of Law

1. Alfred David, 'The Man of Law vs. Chaucer: A Case in Poetics," *PMLA*, 82 (1967), pp. 217–25.
2. Bernard Duffey, "The Intention and Art of the *Man of Law's Tale*," *ELH*, 14 (1947), p. 182.
3. David, p. 219. Chauncey Wood has agreed unawares in large outline with David (in "Chaucer's Man of Law as Interpreter," *Traditio*, 23 (1967), pp. 149–90) but has emphasized the lawyer's philosophical and theological, rather than esthetic, misinterpretations.
4. Richard J. Schoeck, "Chaucer's Prioress: Mercy and Tender Heart," *The Bridge: Yearbook of Judaeo-Christian Studies*, 2 (1956), pp. 239–55; reprinted in *Chaucer Criticism: The Canterbury Tales*, vol. 1, ed. Richard J. Schoeck and Jerome Taylor (Notre Dame, IN, 1961), pp. 245–48.
5. See my article, "'Namoore of This': Chaucer's Monk and Priest," *TSL*, 13 (1968), pp. 117–32.
6. Alan Gaylord, "The Promises in the *Franklin's Tale*," *ELH*, 30 (1964), pp. 331–65.
7. David, p. 221.
8. Ibid., p. 222.
9. Ibid., p. 220–21. Relative to this, Wood seems right in reading the Man of Law's religion as being ultimately materialistic. "God is to be thanked and praised not for strengthening us by trial, but for accomplishing our deliverance; not for the promise of heavenly joy, but for the arrangement of our temporal satisfaction" (p. 152).
10. William L. Sullivan, "Chaucer's Man of Law as a Literary Critic," *MLN*, 68 (1953), pp. 1–8.
11. E. Talbot Donaldson, "Chaucer the Pilgrim," *PMLA*, 69 (1954), pp. 928–36.

12. See Sullivan, pp. 4–5. Donaldson's brief suggestion is worth repeating here: "Perhaps Chaucer was laughingly trying to get credit for having completed more of that poem than his evident impatience with its subject permitted him to do. On the other hand, most of these stories had already been told by Gower in his *Confessio Amantis*, and it is possible that through the Man of Law Chaucer was reflecting a confusion in a nonliterary mind between poems on the same topics by Gower and Chaucer. This would lend at once more humor and less sharpness to his seeming preference for Chaucer." *Chaucer's Poetry: An Anthology for the Modern Reader* (New York, 1958), p. 912.
13. Richard Hoffman, *Ovid and the Canterbury Tales* (Philadelphia, 1967).
14. *Chaucer's Major Poetry*, ed. Albert C. Baugh (New York, 1963), p. 212.
15. Sullivan, "Literary Critic," p. 7.
16. *Confessio Amantis*, ll. 288–300, from *The Complete Works of John Gower*, ed. G. C. Macaulay (Oxford, 1901), vol. 3, p. 394.
17. David's commentary convinces: "The joke is really on the Man of Law, who only makes himself seem ridiculously prudish in professing to be more moral than the moral Gower" (p. 220).
18. John H. Fisher, *John Gower, Moral Philosopher and Friend of Chaucer* (New York, 1964), p. 289.
19. Robert Enzer Lewis, "Chaucer's Artistic Use of Pope Innocent III's *De Miseria Humane Conditionis* in the Man of Law's Prologue and Tale," *PMLA*, 81 (1966), pp. 485–92.
20. Robert Enzer Lewis, "What Did Chaucer Mean by *Of the Wreched Engendrynge of Mankynde*?", *Chaucer Review*, 2 (1968), pp. 139–58.
21. Lewis, "Chaucer's Artistic Use," p. 486.
22. Ibid., p. 487.
23. *General Prologue*, 327, 309, 316.
24. Perhaps I should abjure the trivial here, but I find still another example in the same apostrophe of scriptural error. At l. 491 the Man of Law identifies God himself as the power who called out to the Four Angels to hold back the winds from "annoying" neither "see, ne land, ne tree." This is a reference to Revelations 7:2 where it is another angel, rather than God, who does the commanding.
25. Baugh, *Major Poetry*, p. 320, n. 401; see also *Sources and Analogues of Chaucer's Canterbury Tales*, ed. W.F. Bryan and Germaine Dempster (Chicago, 1958), pp. 642–44.
26. *The Works of Geoffrey Chaucer*, ed. F. N. Robinson, 2nd ed. (Boston, 1957), p. 696, n. 1126.
27. "Christian Affirmation in the *Book of the Duchess*," *PMLA*, 84 (1969), pp. 245–51.
28. Richard J. Schoeck, "Chaucer's Prioress: Mercy and Tender Heart," in *Chaucer Criticism: The Canterbury Tales*, vol. 1, ed. Richard J. Schoeck and Jerome Taylor (Notre Dame, IN, 1961), pp. 245–48.
29. Robert W. Jordan, *Chaucer and the Shape of Creation: The Aesthetic Possibilities of Inorganic Structure* (Cambridge, MA, 1967), p. 180.
30. Paul G. Ruggiers' commentary on the contrasting modes of narration in the *Clerk's Tale* and the *Man of Law's Tale* confirms and expands my point. "The tale of Constance makes much—perhaps overmuch—of a didactic burden interpretable on an easily available *quid credas* level of statement. The tale of Griselda is virtually bare of flat didactic utterance, indeed *makes an effort to withhold statement* in favor of a more restrained, more rarefied, and ultimately a more spiritual vision...the level designated as *quo tendas*." *The Art of the Canterbury*

Tales (Madison, WI, 1965), p. 170. His distinction seems more descriptive than functional, however. What is Chaucer's intention in delegating a *quo tendas* narrative to a holy Clerk and a *quid credas* narrative to a holier-than-thou lawyer?

31. Examine, for example, the long intrusion of the lawyer into his narrative immediately after the Emperor of Rome negotiates to many his daughter, Constance, to the Sultan—

I trowe at Troye, whan Pirrus brak the wal,
Or Ilion brende, at Thebes the citee,
N'at Rome, for the harm thurgh Hanybal
That Romayns hath venquysshed tymes thre,
Nas herd swich tendre wepyng for pitee
As in the chambre was for hire departynge;
But forth she moot, wher so she wepe or synge. (B 288–94)

Compare this passage to the hilarious intrusion of the Nun's Priest into his own mock epic at the fox's abduction of Chauntecleer:

Certes, swich cry ne lamentacioun,
Was nevere of ladyes maad whan Ylioun
Was woone, and Pirrus with his streite swerd,
Whan he hadde hent kyng Priam by the herd,
And slayn hym, as seith us *Eneydos*,
As made alle the hennes in the clos,
Whan they had seyn of Chauntecleer the sighte.
But soverynly dame Pertelote shrighte
Ful louder than dide Hasdrubal es wyf,
Whan that hir housbonde hadde lost his lyf,
And that the Romayns hadde brend Cartage. (B 2, 4545–54)

The similarities of tone and even of allusion are striking, but not unique to these passages. After the epic allusion, the Man of Law apostrophizes astrological destiny as responsible for Constance's impending misfortune:

O firste moevyng, crueel firmament,
With thy diurnal sweigh that crowdest ay
And hurlest al from est til occident
That naturelly wolde holde another way... (B 295–98)

Again, the similarity to the Nun's Priest's apostrophe in the same passage is remarkable:

O destinee that mayst not been eschewed!
Allas, that Chauntecleer fleight fro the bernes!
Allas, his wyf ne roghte nat of dremes!
And on a Friday fil al this neschaunce. (B2 4528–31)

One could go on comparing, for example, the apostrophic reference to Mars made by the lawyer at B 305 and the Priest's apostrophe to Venus at B^2 4532, if more evidence is needed. The point, however, has already been made that Chaucer is not generally at home with declamation unless his purpose is slyly denigrative. In this respect, I would disagree with the second half of Robert Enzer Lewis's essay (see n. 19 above), in which he agrees with Block that the apostrophes, "along with other rhetorical traits of style, 'heighten the formal poetic effect' that Chaucer found lacking in Trivet's prose" and that they are "'intended to impart high moral seriousness'" (p. 489).

32. John M. Manly, "Chaucer and the Rhetoricians," *The Proceedings of the British Academy* (1926), pp. 95–113; reprinted in *Chaucer Criticism*, vol. 1, pp. 268–90.
33. Manly, p. 271 in *Chaucer Criticism.*
34. Ibid., p. 287.
35. Nor did Chaucer derive these additions from Gower. See Edward A. Block, "Originality, Controlling Purpose, and Craftsmanship in Chaucer's *Man of Law's Tale*," *PMLA*, 68 (1953), p. 601.
36. Paul E. Beichner, "Chaucer's Man of Law and *Disparitas Cultus*," *Speculum*, 23 (1948), p. 71.
37. Ibid.
38. Block, "Originality and Craftsmanship," lists the following examples of sanctifying additions to her character: 156–58, 276–77, 284, 451–62, 523, 624, 639–44, 689, 692, 719–21, 826–33, 841–54, 1023–29. See p. 587.
39. Ibid., 596, n. 66.
40. John Yunck, "Religious Elements in Chaucer's *Man of Law's Tale*," *ELH*, 27 (1960), 260.
41. B 323ff.
42. B 696ff.
43. B[2] 4416ff.
44. Block, "Originality and Craftsmanship," p. 579.
45. See Roger S. Loomis, "Was Chaucer a Laodicean?", from *Essays and Studies in Honor of Carleton Brown* (New York, 1940), pp. 129–48; reprinted in *Chaucer Criticism*, vol. 1, pp. 291–310.
46. *The English Works of Wyclif*, ed. F. D. Matthew (London, 1880), p. xvi.
47. Loomis, p. 304, in *Chaucer Criticism.*
48. Muriel Bowden, *A Commentary on the General Prologue to the Canterbury Tales* (New York, 1962), p. 169.
49. Matthew, *Wyclif*, p. 183.

"NAMOORE OF THIS": CHAUCER'S PRIEST AND MONK

Rodney Delasanta

In recent years, both Arthur T. Broes and Charles S. Watson have argued that *The Nun's Priest's Tale* offers more than mere autonomous narrative,[1] and that it answers to Kittredge's now generally accepted thesis that the pilgrims' stories are primarily significant "because they show the relations of the travelers to one another in the progressive action of the Pilgrimage."[2] Broes' argument that *The Nun's Priest's Tale* is satirically aimed at the Prioress is both convincing and incomplete; Watson's suggestion that *The Nun's Priest's Tale* "quyts" *The Monk's Tale* complements Broes's thesis but does so, it would seem, with a fusillade instead of a cannonade. So much more could have been argued.

It is my contention that the Priest's aim is directed not only at "discrediting the Prioress and establishing his own intellectual and moral superiority to her,"[3] but also at demolishing the one other ecclesiastic who deserves his erudite mockery—the Monk. The verb *deserves* is used here precisely, for a personal antagonism—although one-sided from the perspective of the Priest—is the only reasonable occasion for *The Nun's Priest's Tale.* To see the personal differences between the two as "distinctly secondary" in importance, as Watson has done,[4] is to misunderstand the raison d'etre of the tale. It is true, of course, that no sharp personal clash ever takes place between the Monk and the Priest, the kind that characterizes the relationship of the Miller and the Reeve, the Friar and the Summoner, the Manciple and the Cook, the Host and the Pardoner, and even the Host and the Parson. Rather, the antagonism is under the surface—much like that between the Clerk and the Wife of Bath. But under the surface or not, to the Priest the Monk represents the very antithesis of his own mien, personality, and sacerdotal destiny. In ecclesiastic discipline, in character, in physiology, in social station, and above all in intelligence, the two men are total opposites; and it is an opposition in which the "disgruntled cleric" has every right to be disgruntled.

As a member of the monastic community,[5] the Monk has taken vows to which the Nun's Priest—as a member of the diocesan clergy—need not answer. By virtue of his ordination to the Benedictine Order, the Monk is a cenobite; he has taken the vow of stability.[6] The Priest, obviously, is not a cenobite. By the ironies of ecclesiastical appointment, however, these functions have become reversed: it is the cloistered Monk who is the "outridere" and "prikasour," and the uncloistered Priest who is humiliatingly conventualized. In addition to the vow of stability, the Monk has taken the vow of poverty; the Priest has not. Yet it is the vowed ascetic who is "ful fat," who loves roast swan, who wears sleeves trimmed with fur and boots made of the finest leather, and who rides a valuable palfrey with a jingling bridle.[7] The Priest, no vowed ascetic, must make his way on a jade "foul and lene," "an English Rosinante, while meekly suffering the rude familiarity of the Host,"[8] and the genteel indifference of his Prioress. Even relative to the vows they *share*—obedience and chastity—there is an ironic inversion in their application. The Monk, "recchelees," pays little attention to the "reule of Seint Maure or of Seint Beneit" and refuses to study "as Austin bit." But the Priest, whose obedience is theoretically less stringent, must obey superiors of feminine rather than patristic eminence. In reference to chastity, the Monk's attitude can at least be inferred: his hood is fastened with a "ful curious pyn" in the shape of a love knot; he is a hunter who gives not a plucked hen for that text which says that hunters are not holy men and therefore loves *venery*, a functional ambiguity that Chaucer the Pilgrim treats with extreme reticence in *The General Prologue*, but which the Host amplifies in the introduction to *The Monk's Tale*. The Priest's chastity, whatever its actual state, must somehow be achieved in a house of women in which he is the only man.

The most significant opposition between the two men is also ironically related to their respective monastic and diocesan stations. As a member of the monastic clergy, one whose claustration is particularly conducive to prayer, work and study, the Monk would traditionally have been considered the intellectual superior to the Priest, who as a member of the diocesan clergy would not have been expected to achieve scholarly competence in philosophy and theology. The Benedictine Rule allowed more hours in the day for study (four) than it did for celebration of the Divine Office, and among its required readings Saint Augustine was of major importance, a point whose significance will be examined later.[9] The diocesan clergy, on the other hand, could have shown no such pretensions to learning. Their function, by its very nature, was more pastoral than contemplative or intellectual, and the plague of 1348–1349 had wiped out whatever gestures towards the intellectual life that they might ever have had. What the Nun's Priest hears, therefore, after the Monk proceeds to recite a few of his tragedies, is the opposite of what he would have expected to hear. The Monk is no true disciple of Augustine and Benedict, but a philosophical and theological simpleton, a grotesquely retarded Martha dressed in Mary's clothes.

When these outward signs of sacerdotal demeanor show such obvious opposition, it is not unreasonable to assume that the Nun's Priest should resent the very presence of the un-monastic Monk as much as he does the indifferent Prioress, and that his tale should in some measure serve as a subtle retaliation for the vagaries of ecclesiastical fortune. Watson is absolutely correct in arguing that the second tale is a requital of the first, "that the two together form one of the best pairs of tales in the series and an outstanding example of the linking of short fictional works."[10] His briefs, however, in addition to misreading the personal antagonism of the Priest to the Monk, fail to exploit further extraordinary evidence.[11]

The narrative opposition of the two tales is achieved both in theme and technique. Chaucer's strategy in having chosen the Monk to recite a series of "tragedies" exemplifying the arbitrary fall of men (and one woman) from positions of earned or unearned eminence has always puzzled critics, first, for his having composed the dreary accounts at all and, second, for having assigned them to the Monk. Charles W. Dunn's remarks are typical: "All readers regret that the graceful *Squire's Tale* and even the improper *Cook's Tale* were left unfinished, because both show real literary promise.... Some avid readers would prefer that Chaucer had concluded his *Tale of Sir Thopas*, self-sufficient though the fragment is; but no critic has wished that the Monk had been allowed to recite all of the hundred or more tragedies known to him."[12] And then he adds what seems to be at the same time a correct and incorrect assessment of the interruption: "Chaucer himself obviously approved of the Knight's interruption of the tale, for the Monk's pessimistic fatalism is incompatible with the warm sympathy for mankind and underlying faith in divine providence which Chaucer displays elsewhere."[13]

Chaucer's interruption implies that he had no intention of allowing the Monk to tell all the hundred tales he had in his cell. Indeed, we must assume that Chaucer's deliberate interruptions (as in the *Tale of Sir Thopas* and as opposed to mere fragmented narratives like *The Cook's Tale* and *The Squire's Tale*) are not mere excuses on his part for not finishing the narrative but rather that the narrative has served its purpose in characterizing its speaker. In short, the stories are unfinished by design. Dunn, therefore, is correct in assuming that Chaucer "approved" of the Knight's interruption, but he is correct for the wrong reasons.

To call the Monk a "pessimistic fatalist" is to misunderstand precisely what in *The Monk's Tale* the Priest is requiting in his own tale. Curiously (for a cleric) the Monk ascribes the fall of all his characters to Fortune without emphasizing their fall as a consequence of divine retribution[14] or divine testing, or even as the operation, of an inscrutable fate. Moreover, for the Monk, Fortune's decree is irrevocable: "Ther nas no remedie [apparently not even the Redemption] to brynge hem out of hire adversitee." Although at first glance this fortunal conception of tragedy seems pessimistically fatalistic (as well as clearly un-Christian), it must be remembered that for the Christian philosopher fortune and fate were not considered interchangeable terms; and Chaucer, whose translation of Boethius brought him close to this very problem, was well aware of the distinction. Although both concepts (when detached from Providence) deny man's freedom, fate at least allows for cosmic plan and order, however impersonal, cruel, and arbitrary that design may be. Fortune when it is understood philosophically as pure chance, denies the existence even of this.[15] "A world in which chance really exists...is remarkably different from a world in which necessity prevails, in which everything is determined by causes and there are no uncaused coincidences."[16] The doctrine of absolute fortuitousness is indeterminism in its most extreme form. Whereas Augustine and Aquinas, for example, were perfectly willing to reconcile fate to the Christian concept of Providence ("Fate is a disposition inherent to changeable things, by which Providence connects each one with its proper order"[17]), both had unambiguously anathematized Fortune. Moreover, the old Roman personification of Fortune as a goddess to be worshipped, one indeed who by the time of the disintegration of the Roman religion had achieved a pantheonic eminence by absorbing the functions of many of the other gods, was particularly reprehensible to the Christian theologians as a *personal* rival of the true God; and their polemical writings bristle with attempts to annihilate her influence.[18]

Now it is perfectly true that most Christian poets tried hard to allow Fortune a place inside the benevolent predestination of God. Unlike the theologians, they recognized that common sense dictated the presence of *apparent* chance in human experience, and so they tried to account for it. Chaucer himself subscribed to Dante's belief that Fortune is "a creature subordinate to the Christian God, a ministering angel who carries out the divine bidding,"[19] and he sprinkled his writings with numerous references to the fickle goddess. Influenced by Boethius, he accommodated Fortune into a hierarchical scheme in which Providence delegates executive power to Destiny which in turn "sends its influences outward and still further away from the stable center until they move upon still another blind and capricious force called Fortune, whose function it is. .. to rule over the checkered careers of human beings in this world."[20] But it is idle to suppose that Chaucer would *philosophically* have accepted the place of Fortune in the cosmic scheme of things. "One did not 'believe in' Fortune," says Professor Robertson, "any more than one believed in the goddess Venus, but Fortune, like Venus, was used to express a kind of behavior to which almost everyone is subject."[21] Or, as Professor Curry has pointed out, Chaucer agreed with Boethius that if Fortune is to be understood as chance or "hap," then "what through ignorance is called chance is nothing more than an occurrence whose causes are not understood.... The causes...for everything, though perhaps not perceived by finite men," stretch back in an unbroken order through Destiny to the divine plan in God's mind.[22]

In his own poetry Chaucer seldom fails to accommodate Fortune to the orthodox idea of God's ultimate "governaunce," an accommodation which, as we shall see, Chaucer denies to the Monk as speaker of his own tale. In the *Balade de Visage sanz Peinture*, for example, the poet defies Fortune by refusing to accept her "governaunce"—

> ...no force of thy reddour
> To him that over himself hath the maystrye!
> My suffisaunce shal be my socour;
> For fynally, Fortune, I thee defye! —(ll. 13–16)

but even the goddess's defense against the plaintiff's attack turns into a denial of her autonomous existence and an admission of her total dependence on Providence:

> Lo, th'execucion of the majestee
> That al purveyeth of his [God's] rightwysnesse,
> That same thing "Fortune" clepen ye... (ll. 65–68)

In *Troilus and Criseyde* Chaucer seems to admit Fortune's existence but makes her subordinate to fate, which in his system would be subordinate in turn to Providence. When Criseyde, after having visited her uncle's house, is prevented from leaving by a rainstorm, the poet exclaims:

> ... O Fortune, *executrice of wyrdes* [italics mine]
> O influence of thise hevenes hye!
> Soth is that under God ye ben oure hierdes,
> Though to us bestes ben the causes wrie. (III, 617–620)

In the next crisis too—at the moment when Criseyde proves unfaithful to Troilus—Fortune plays the role of "executrice"; for, as Patch explains, although "Fortune is again held responsible...again she is described as only the agent of God's will." Because both lovers freely decide to separate, "the business of Fortune...is therefore to prepare the way for the deliberate act of Criseyde."[23] In *The Man of Law's Tale* the poet prays that Constance's rudderless ship be steered by Him "that is lord of Fortune," (l. 448) another obvious allusion to the Christian God's control and "governaunce." In *The Merchant's Tale*, the poet's incertitude about which destinal force leads May to love Damian is resolved by an orthodox assertion about God's ultimate power of causality:

> Were it by destynee or aventure,
> Were it by influence or by nature,
> Or constellacioun, that in swich estaat
> The hevene stood...
> I kan nat seye; but grete God above,
> *That knoweth that noon act causelees,* [italics mine]
> He deme of al, for I wole holde my pees. (l. 1967ff.)

At other times, of course, Chaucer's references to Fortune are as conversationally un-philosophical as modern man's invocations to good luck or his deprecations of bad luck. And in still other instances, such as the familiar reference to the scorpion in *The Merchant's Tale* (l. 2057ff.), Chaucer hyperbolically alludes to Fortune's power for an ironical and humorous effect, and certainly not for philosophical commentary.

By almost incantatory repetition, however, the interminable references to Fortune in *The Monk's Tale* play a more significant role in dramatizing the speaker than in any of the works just cited. It cannot be unpurposeful that of the seventeen stories the Monk relates he should attribute the tragedy of twelve of them explicitly to Fortune or that he should allude to Fortune in the course of his narrative twenty-three times—while making only two perfunctory references in the middle of all this lamentation to God's punishment and "governaunce." All men from time immemorial have praised good luck and cursed bad luck; but if medieval man railed at Fortune as that blind force whose "activities *seem* in their infinite capriciousness and diversity to be entirely illogical and chaotic,"[24] he was at the same time philosophically convinced of its subordination to Divine Providence. The Monk, by vocation the most philosophically oriented of medieval men, should have been the first to promulgate this doctrine by (in a tale stuffed with tragedy) preaching its comforting paradox to the pilgrims. Instead, he fails to reconcile Fortune to Providence,[25] fails indeed even to make his tales function as doomsday evangelism.

Chaucer's strategy in choosing the Monk—and not another ecclesiastic—to carry the simplistic Fortune motif is an oblique stroke of comic genius. The ironic situation of a Benedictine monk committed *by vow* to the daily study of St. Augustine[26] yet demonstrating total ignorance of Augustine's teachings on such central matters as fortune, fate, predestination, providence and free will is rich Chaucerian humor at its best. A brief survey of some of the Augustinian attitudes toward Fortune will underscore the Monk's vincible ignorance and corroborate the petulantly ironic observation in the *General Prologue* that a monk should not have to "studie and make hymselven wood,/ Upon a book in cloystre alwey to poure."

In The *City of God*, explaining the fortuitous events that brought some Roman gods to popular favor while at the same time leading others to obscurity, Augustine with tongue in cheek insists that Fortune should have been enthroned higher in the pantheon:

> If, therefore, Felicity ought not perhaps to have been put among the select gods, because they did not attain to that noble position by merit, but by chance, Fortune at least should have been placed among them or rather before them; for they say that that goddess distributes to every one the gifts she receives, not according to any rational arrangement, but according as chance may determine. She ought to have held the uppermost place among the select gods, for among them chiefly it is she that shows what power she has. For we see that they have been selected not on account of some eminent virtue or rational happiness, but by that random power of Fortune which the worshippers of these gods think that she exerts.[27]

A few lines later, he repeats his argument, this time pressing that Fortune be allowed the *pre-eminent* place:

> Fortune herself ought to occupy the place of pre-eminence among the select gods, since over them also she has such pre-eminent power. Or

> must we suppose that the reason why she is not among the select is simply this, that even Fortune herself has had an adverse fortune? She was adverse, then, to herself, since, whilst ennobling others, she herself has remained obscure.[28]

In other places, however, Augustine demonstrates no such humor. His condemnation of those who worship her is more direct:

> How, therefore, is she good, who without any discernment comes both to the good and to the bad? Why is she worshipped, who is thus blind, running at random on any one whatever, so that for the most part she passes by her worshippers and cleaves to those who despise her? Or if her worshippers profit somewhat, so that they are seen by her and loved, then she follows merit and does not come fortuitously. What, then, becomes of that definition of fortune? What becomes of the opinion that she has received her very name from fortuitous events? For it profits one nothing to worship her if she is truly *fortune*. But if she distinguishes her worshippers, so that she may benefit them, she is not fortune.[29]

And, as would be expected, he clearly refuses to allow Fortune a place in God's "governaunce," attributing the decline and fall of kingdoms, for example, specifically to God's will:

> Therefore...God, the author and giver of felicity, because He is alone the true God. Himself gives earthly kingdoms both to good and bad. Neither does he do this rashly, and, as it were, fortuitously—because He is God not fortune—but according to the order of things and times, which is hidden from us, but thoroughly known to Himself; which same order of times, however, He does not serve as subject to it, but Himself rules as lord and appoints as governor.... The cause then of the greatness of the Roman empire is neither fortuitous nor fatal.... In a word, human kingdoms are established by divine providence.[30]

At times, indeed, his attitude toward Fortune approaches—if only ironically—the suggestion that she is diabolical: "Is it perhaps the ease that when she is bad she is not a goddess, but is suddenly changed into a malignant demon?"[31]

The Monk's ignorance of these famous pronunciamentos would have been obvious to anyone who had studied the patristic authors even cursorily; but the Monk has not studied (not even Austin) "as Austin bit," and the Nun's Priest wastes no opportunity to remind his eminent monastic colleague, and perhaps some of the more discerning pilgrims (the Clerk, for example), that he is a theological lummox.

The Nun's Priest's Tale answers in general the Monk's simplistic and heretical contention that when "Fortune list to flee" no "remedie" can bring man out of his "adversitee." Such a contention implicitly denies the operation of Divine Providence (along with its corollary "function"—Divine foreknowledge) and explicitly denies the operation of free will. More esoterically, it denies the seventy-second (and final) precept of the Benedictine Rule which Jean Canu reads as central to the Benedictine spirit: "And never to despair of the mercy of God."[32] For all its mock-heroic and bestiary qualities, therefore, *The Nun's Priest's Tale* in its major intention dramatizes the operation of Divine Providence-Divine foreknowledge in the world and the possibility of free will operating within that mystery.

Chaunticleer is forewarned of the impending disaster by a dream which, because it is true, is presumably of divine origin: "By God, me mette I was in swich meschief / Right now that yet myn herte is soore afright" (2894–95). (This opening epithet can as easily be read an ablative of agent as an expletive.) Pertelote's skepticism and elaborate physiological explanations—in the best modern way—fail to convince Chaunticleer that his dream does not foretell doom, and he counters with a series of stories in which the dream functions as an accurate foretelling of the future and even as a divine means by which the sinful are brought to justice: "O blisful God, that art so just and *trewe*, / Lo how that thow *biwreyest* mordre alway" (4240–41) [italics mine]. To prove his point, the cock alludes to the Biblical dreams of Daniel and Joseph (as well as to the classical examples of Croesus and Andromecha). The appeal to authority here, of course, reminds the audience that Christian doctrine has always recognized dreams to be potentially of divine origin, of a kind of human participation in Divine foreknowledge.[33] Other critics have demonstrated that in this episode about prescient dreams the Priest has merely picked up where the Monk has left off: Croesus's dream—interpreted by his daughter—of his own forthcoming tragedy.[34] What critics have overlooked, however, is that the Monk by including a prescient dream in the account of a tragedy brought about by Fortune, has fallen unwittingly into a serious philosophical and theological contradiction, one that the Priest subtly exposes and quietly resolves. Prescience—whether in dreams and visions (as experienced by men) or in revelations (as foreknown and revealed by the Divine mind)—depends entirely upon a causal order of things, one in which Fortune, understood as chance or contingency, by its very nature can have no part. To allow the victim of his own ultimate tragedy to foresee that tragedy in a dream is to admit that the tragedy is somehow inevitable, an inevitability related either to fate or Providence. But to attribute this *inevitable* tragedy (as the Monk has done) to Fortune—which by its very nature represents indeterminism—represents an act of theological illiteracy. *The Nun's Priest's Tale* offers at the same time a retroactive exposition of that illiteracy and an "orthodox" solution of the problem.

The dream episode dramatizes only half of the Priest's requital of the Monk's heresy. By attributing the fall of his illustrious men solely to Fortune, the Monk has denied not only Providence and Divine foreknowledge but also the possibility of man's freedom functioning with the Divine plan. And that is a heresy particularly opprobrious for the Monk because it represents the denial of a central Augustinian teaching: the concomitant operation of Divine and human will, with human will unrestrained by Divine foreknowledge.[35] The Priest's hyperbolic dialectic at the moment of Chaunticleer's capture by the fox, therefore, is more than rhetorical horse play. He is deliberately flaunting before the Monk's "ful fat" face his knowledge of the theological mystery that "Augustyn" and "Boece" and "Bradwardyn" have explored while at the same time disclaiming any such intention ("I wol nat han to do of swich matere"). And his words about the great scholastic controversies relative to these doctrines must also be interpreted as particularly galling to the Monk who, despite the fact that his habit would reveal him to be one of the "certyn clerkis" of whom the Priest speaks, is totally ignorant even of the existence of such doctrines. Can the Priest have been addressing anyone else but the Monk who, although he has been to "scole," has obviously experienced no "altercacioun"?

> Witnesse on hym that any parfit clerk is,
> That in scole is greet altercacioun
> In this matere and greet disputisoun,
> And hath been of an hundred thousand men. (ll. 3236–39)

But the "altercacioun" *is* solved in the tale by the cock's ultimate ability to *will* his own resolution of the forewarned and foreknown events. For although Chaunticleer's dream accurately foretells the circumstances that bring him to grief ("where-as I say a beest, / Was lyk an hound and wolde han made areest / Upon my body and han had me deed") (ll. 4089–91), the foreknowledge does not obviate the possibility of free choice within the foreknown events, particularly when the free choice operates with the help of grace. Chaunticleer's success in tricking the fox to release him is both "humanly" and divinely willed:

> "Sire, if that I were as ye,
> Yet sholde I seyn, *as wys God helpe me,* [italics mine]
> Turneth agayn, ye proud cherles alle!
> A verray pestilence upon yow falle!" (ll. 4597–4600)

As clear as the Priest's requital of the Monk seems to be (in our unhurried analysis of the structure), it would be incorrect to think of the tale itself (in its line-by-line dramatic unfolding) as a mere schematic indulgence in philosophical comeuppances. In much the same way that the Priest's bitterness for the Prioress remains submerged and is revealed only for those who have ears to hear, so does his outrage at the Monk surface in equally decoying strategies. The Monk had opened his tragedies with an immediate act of obeisance to Fortune's power. The Priest opens his tale, on the other hand, with an immediate recognition of God's "governaunce." While twitting the Prioress about her daintiness by constructing a foil in the person of the good widow,[36] the Priest immediately attributes the goodness and simplicity of her life to her own "pacience" and to the husbandry "of swich as God hire sente." The theme of the tale—the efficacy of man's will within God's supernal Providence—is thus quickly launched, but without dialectical fanfare. A few lines later in the honorific passage about Chaunticleer, the Priest compares his voice favorably to a church organ and then indicates that it is more accurate than "any *abbey* or logge." Professor Donovan has shown that the Fathers of the Church interpreted the cock as a symbol of clerical alertness—one who "knows the hours of the night and crows accordingly" in order to arouse slumberers, particularly other ministers of religion.[37] In this instance, it would seem, the cock crows more accurately—that is, shows more doctrinal alertness—than the *abbey* itself. Although an oblique thrust, the Monk must have suffered it.

More subtle perhaps than the above is the Priest's textual sprinkling of his tale—sometimes in his own voice, sometimes in the voice of his characters—with a diction that must remind the Monk (or at least his more clever colleagues on the pilgrimage) of the philosophical imbroglio into which he has fallen. The diction is arranged in no particular pattern; more often than not it deliberately re-creates—with almost absurdist non-sequiturs—the very confusion that the Monk excelled in creating. The best example occurs in Chaunticleer's insistence that dreams "ben significaciouns/ As wel of joye as of tribulaciouns / That folk enduren in this lyf present." Within seventeen lines the narrator humorously, ironically and unobtrusively juxtaposes the contradictory concepts of free will, fate and fortune—all inside an episode whose ostensible intention is to defend foreknowledge:

> Oon of the gretteste auctor that men rede
> Seith thus, that whilom two felawes wente
> On pilgrymage *in a ful good entente,*
> *And happed* so they coomen in a toun
> Where-as ther was swich congregacioun
> Of peple and eek so streit of herbergage
> That they ne founde as muche as a cotage
> In which they bothe myghte y-logged be.

> Wherefore *they mosten of necessitee,*
> As for that nyght, departen compaignye,
> And ech of hem gooth to his hostelrye
> And took his loggyng *as it wolde falle.*
> That oon of hem was logged in a stalle
> Fer in a yeerd with oxen of the plow.
> That oother man was logged wel know
> *As was his aventure or his fortune,*
> *That us governeth alle as in commune.* [italics mine] (ll. 4174–4190)

The same kind of absurd potpourri of contradictory concepts follows in the introduction to Chaunticleer's near tragedy. The narrator's mock-heroic opening—"Whan that the monthe in which the world bigan"—actually includes unresolved allusions to fate, fortune, and predestination. The astrological lines obviously carry the fatalistic idea of impending doom for the cock. But no sooner does the narrator finish his apostrophe than he attributes the cock's forthcoming fall to Fortune in a direct burlesque of a line that the Monk had used repeatedly: "For evere the latter ende of joye is wo" (l. 4395). Upon entering into the details of the colfox's "sly iniquitee," however, he interprets the fox's treachery as caused "by heigh imaginacioun forncast," followed seventeen lines later by the elaborate disputation on "what that God forwoot must nedes be." The bumping together of fate, fortune, and predestination cannot be accidental.

The contradictory apostrophes continue without letup—a textual reminder to the Monk of the absurdity of his own philosophical position. Immediately before Chaunticleer's capture, the narrator blames fate—"O destynee, that mayst nat been eschewed" (l. 4528)—then blames Pertelote's "modernist" disbelief in prescient dreams—"Allas, his wyf roghte nat of dremes!" (l. 4530)—then ties the tragedy to the superstitions of religious fatalism—"And on a Friday fil al this meschance" I. 4531)—and finally blames the gods—"O Venus...why woldestow sufre hym on thy day to dye?" (I. 4536). As if this confusion is not enough, the narrator muddles the philosophical puddle even more—just before the cock's clever strategy in tricking the fox to let him go—by praising

Fortune—"Lo, how Fortune turneth sodeynly" (l. 4593), an obvious reversal of the Monk's earlier blaming of the goddess for all Misfortune.

In a tale whose *structure* so carefully distinguishes between these warring philosophical and theological ideas in order to answer to the Monk's obfuscation of their meaning, it cannot be accidental that the *texture* of the same tale should "quyt" his foolishness in a different, but more dramatically effective, way. Even up to the final lines, the Priest's subtle mockery continues unrelenting. In summing up the obvious morality of the tale, his eye must have been fixed squarely on his sacerdotal adversary, for in both faith and morals the Monk has demonstrated himself to be one who "wynketh whan he sholde see," "jangleth when he sholde holde his pees," and in reference to his own Rule comported himself in a "recchelees" and "necligent" manner. Nor does the Monk escape the Nun's Priest's quiet wrath even in his final prayer. Although ostensibly confining his didactic remarks to the moral of his tale, the Priest urges his listeners to "take the fruyt and lat the chaf be stille," for, as St. Paul has said, "al that writen is, / To oure doctrine it is ywrite." One gleaner of the chaff, for whose fortunal interpretation of tragedy "there has no remedie," especially needed to be reminded of the "doctrine" of St. Paul, particularly as the clause complementing the quoted line from Romans 15:4 applied fruitfully to him: "that, through patience and the comfort of the scriptures, we might have hope."

Notes to "Namoore of This": Chaucer's Priest and Monk

1. Arthur T. Broes, "Chaucer's Disgruntled Cleric: *The Nun's Priest's Tale*," *PMLA*, 78 (1963), pp. 156–162; Charles S. Watson, "The Relationship of the 'Monk's Tale' and the 'Nun's Priest's Tale,'" *Studies in Short Fiction*, 1 (1964), pp. 277–288. Since this paper was written, William C. Strange has also argued for a coupling of the two tales in a dramatic dialectic, but his major concerns are with the suitability of the *Monk's Tale* to its teller ("*The Monk's Tale*: A Generous View," *Chaucer Review*, 1 [1967], pp. 167–180). Contrary to most conclusions about the Monk's dullness as a story teller, he reads the tale as the Monk's fully realized questioning of "that order and justice in the world's events which the Knight had asserted in his tale." Strange's admittedly generous view credits the deprecated ("What should he Studie and make hymselven wood"—A, 184) and self-deprecating Monk ("Have me excused of

myn ignoraunce"—B, 3180) with a philosophical sophistication—albeit one leading to dilemma—that he does not deserve. To praise the Monk as story teller, one must needs knock the Knight as critic; and this Strange does by describing the Knight's interruption as the advocating of "a narcotic art limited to pleasantness," a strange interpretation indeed.

2. George L. Kittredge, *Chaucer and His Poetry* (Cambridge, 1915), p. 155.
3. Broes, p. 157.
4. Watson, p. 278.
5. Scholars have disagreed about the actual identity of the Monk's order. Ramona Bressie (*Modern Language Notes*, 54, p. 483) sees the Monk as an Augustinian Canon, but Tatlock disagrees (*Modern Language Notes*, 55, pp. 350–354), insisting that he is a Benedictine. Chaucer himself, however, all learned evidence to the contrary notwithstanding, must have conceived Dan Piers as a Benedictine if the text can be believed. If the Monk were an Augustinian Canon, the line about his "passing by" the "reule of Seint Maure or of Seint Beneit" would have been meaningless because Augustinian Canons observe the general rule of St. Augustine, not the more detailed and "streit" rule of St. Benedict. Moreover, as Tatlock has pointed out, Chaucer himself distinguishes between "canon" and "monk" in the *Tales*. Under these circumstances, it seems unlikely that he would have called a canon regular a monk.
6. The vow of stability is defined by *A Catholic Dictionary*, ed. Donald Attwater (New York, 1958) p. 474, as "the characteristic and peculiar vow of Benedictine monks and nuns, contained in the traditional formula of profession, I promise, before God and his saints, stability, conversion of manners and obedience according to the rule of our holy Father Benedict." By it the monk registers his intention of persevering in community life, and that in the monastery of his profession, unless his superior shall send him elsewhere. The permission of the Holy See has to be obtained for a monk permanently to be transferred from one to another monastery."
7. For the full implications of these signs of looseness, see Muriel Bowden, *A Commentary on the General Prologue to the Canterbury Tales* (New York, 1962), pp. 107–118, and D. W. Robertson, Jr., *A Preface to Chaucer* (Princeton, 1962), pp. 253–256.
8. Broes, n. 6.
9. Jean Canu, *Religious Orders of Men*, Twentieth Century Encyclopedia of Catholicism, No. 85 (New York, 1960), p. 24.
10. Watson, p. 287.
11. This is not to denigrate what Watson actually has accomplished. The subjects he discusses—"ideas in the 'Monk's Tale' that reappear in the 'Nun's Priest's Tale,' contrasts, parody, concepts of Fortune, the cock and the fox as allegorical figures, the tales as sermons, and the second tale as a comedy" (pp. 278–79)—considerably amplify Samuel B. Hemingway's pioneering contention (Chaucer's Monk and the Nun's Priest," *Modern Language Notes*, 31 [1916], pp. 479–483) that the *Nun's Priest's Tale* burlesques *The Monk's Tale*. But much of what he says is fairly obvious: e.g., *The Monk's Tale* is a tragedy; whereas *The Nun's Priest's Tale* is a comedy (p. 285); "a principal theme of both is that pride goeth before a fall" (p. 281); "the Priest is good-natured and blithe, the Monk is the opposite" (p. 280). Even where he seems to aim at the heart of the matter—"the different views of Fortune" (p. 281)—he seems only to review Donovan's assertions about moral alertness. See n. 37 of this paper.
12. *A Chaucer Reader* (New York, 1952), p. 61.

13. Ibid.
14. Only in his tale of King Antiochus does the Monk refer to divine retribution: l. 3789ff. in *Chaucer's Major Poetry*, ed. Albert C. Baugh (New York, 1963), p. 366. All subsequent references to Chaucer's works will be to this volume.
15. I do not wish to suggest that the problem is peculiarly Christian, medieval, or scholastic. The either-or qualities of fate and fortune—with fortune understood as a more terrifying alternative even than dark fate—is central to Robert Frost's poem "Design." Better "design of darkness to appall," says Frost, than no design at all.
16. *The Great Ideas: A Syntopicon of Great Books of the Western World*, ed. Robert M. Hutchins, Great Books of the Western World, No. 2 (Chicago, 1952), p. 181.
17. p. 517.
18. Howard Rollins Patch, "The Tradition of the Goddess Fortuna in Roman Literature," *Smith College Studies in Modern Languages*, 3, p. 180.
19. Howard Rollins Patch, "Chaucer and Lady Fortune," *Modern Language Review*, 22, p. 378.
20. Walter C. Curry, *Chaucer and the Mediaeval Sciences* (New York: Barnes and Noble, 1960), rev. ed., p. 243.
21. D. W. Robertson, Jr., "Chaucerian Tragedy," *ELH*, 19 (1952), p. 2.
22. Curry, p. 245.
23. Patch, "Chaucer and Lady Fortune," pp. 384–385.
24. Curry, p. 244.
25. The Monk's most dramatic failure to effect this reconciliation comes in his tale of Balthasar. Daniel's interpretation of the writing on the wall includes the familiar warnings about God's punishment of Balthasar's father. Nabugodonosor, and the imminent destruction of the kingdom by the Persians and Medes. But the Monk himself fails to pick up Daniel's "moral," and his own dreary refrain about Fortune is—for a cleric—astoundingly free of even a single religious sentiment.
26. In one respect, much of the learned lumber cut to Boethian specifications for *The Monk's Tale* is irrelevant to its dramatic occasion. The speaker of the tale, after all, is not Boethian Chaucer but Benedictine (and thus Augustinian) Dan Piers. Thus, wherever we find a meaningful adherence to, or departure from, an intellectual tradition in the tale, the artistic significance of that adherence or departure should be related as much to the intellectual traditions of the narrator as to the poet.
27. St. Augustine, *The Confessions, The City of God, On Christian Doctrine*, trans. Marcus Dods, Great Books of the Western World, No. 18 (Chicago, 1952), p. 246.
28. Ibid.
29. p. 198.
30. pp. 206–207.
31. p. 197.
32. Canu, p. 23.
33. Scripture asserts that God may enter into communication with man through dreams (Numbers 12:6, Job 33:14ff.) and frequently describes God's use of dreams to reveal future events. The dreams of Jacob in Genesis 28 and of Joseph in Matthew 1:20 and 2:13 are representatively famous in the respective testaments. The Fathers of the Church have always agreed that certain dreams may be of divine origin, and St. Thomas Aquinas has summarized the positive teaching of the Scholastics toward dreams in II-II, q. 95, a. 6 of the *Summa Theologica*. Chau-

cer himself accepts the possibility of dreams foretelling future events. See his distinction between "avisioun" (mere fantasy) and "revelaciouns" (portent of things to come) in *The House of Fame*; in Baugh l. 7ff. and n. 7 on p. 28.

34. Watson, p. 279.
35. The following passage from *The City of God* (V, 10) is representative of Augustine's position: "Now, against the sacrilegious and impious darings of reason, we assert both that God knows all things before they come to pass and that we do by our free will whatsoever we know and feel to be done by us only because we will it.... It is not the case, therefore, that because God foreknew what would be in the power of our wills, there is for that reason nothing in the power of our wills. For H Who foreknew this did not foreknow nothing. Moreover, if He Who foreknew what would be in the power of our wills did not foreknow nothing, but something, assuredly, even though he did foreknow, there is something in the power of our wills. Therefore we are by no means compelled, either, retaining the prescience of God, to take away the freedom of the will, or, retaining the freedom of the will, to deny that He is prescient of future things, which is impious. But we embrace both. We faithfully and sincerely confess both. The former, that we may believe well: the latter, that we may live well" (p. 216).
36. Broes, p. 162.
37. Mortimer J. Donovan, "The Morality of the Nun's Priest's Sermon," *Journal of English and Germanic Philology*, 52 (1953), pp. 501–502.

SACRAMENT AND SACRIFICE IN THE *PARDONER'S TALE*

Rodney Delasanta

We may be grateful to Robert E. Nichols, Jr. for having nudged scholarly debate about the Pardoner's "ale and cake," which had long been stalled in disagreement over the actual *locus* of the tale, toward the symbolic direction of the altar table.[1] By urging us to recognize the ale and cake (C 321–22) as a Eucharist which brings death instead of life to its partakers, Nichols was really the first to see Chaucer making brilliant parodic play with the sacramental meaning of the Mass. But as with most pioneering articles in which the full implications of a valuable insight are seldom exploited, Nichols overlooked the *dual* mode—sacrificial as well as sacramental—by which medieval man would theologically have understood the Mass and by means of which Chaucer achieved a parodic intensity even more powerful than originally claimed. A year later, William B. Toole in an article concerned with different ironies hinted at some of the implications of Eucharistic sacrifice in the *Pardoner's Tale*[2]; and most recently Clarence H. Miller and Roberta Bux Bosse, heavily armed with Robertsonian documentation, have pressed the claim that the *Pardoner's Tale* allegorically parodies the Mass which was itself conceived of in the Middle Ages as allegorical of Christ's life, death, and resurrection.[3] Beholden to these colleagues but convinced that all has not been said on the subject, I should like to take a closer look at those implications of sacrifice in the *Pardoner's Tale* which Nichols overlooked, which Toole only touched upon, and which Miller and Bosse seem to have taken for granted. And instead of rummaging through commentary of the Fathers and the medieval exegetes, commentary that may or may not have been known to Chaucer, it would be *dignum et justum* to go directly to the language of the medieval Mass itself, where formulaic references to the sacrificial nature of the cultic meal could not but have impressed themselves on the medieval artistic consciousness.

As one would expect, the number of references in the text of the Sarum Missal[4] to *sacrificium* or *oblatio* is considerable, particularly in the Offertory and Canon where the ritual would obviously identify itself overtly. During the Offertory, for example, while the priest prepared the bread and wine for consecration, he said: "In spiritu humilitatis et in animo contrito suscipiamur domine a te et sic fiat *sacrificium* nostrum ut a te suscipiatur hodie et placeat tibi domine deus."[5] After invoking the Holy Spirit in the "Veni sancte spiritus benedic et santifica hoc *sacrificium*," he turned to the people and invited them to join him in prayer: "Orate fratres ut meum pariterque vestrum acceptum sit domino deo nostro *sacrificium*."[6] And the response of the faithful immediately followed: "Sancti spiritus gracia illuminet cor tuum et labia tua et accipiat dominus digne hoc *sacrificium* laudis de manibus tuis pro peccatis et offensionibus nostris."[7] Shortly thereafter the Preface introduced the most solemn part of the Eucharistic celebration, the Canon, which began with the words "Te igitur clementissime pater" and led directly to the supplication that God accept the Sacrifice about to take place: "Hec dona. Hec munera. Hec Santa *Sacrificia* illibata."[8] After the prayer for the whole Church, the priest prayed for specific individuals and those in attendance "vel qui tibi hoc *sacrificium* laudis."[9] The consecration of the bread and wine followed, after which the priest recalled the sacrifices of the Old Testament, all types of the Crucifixion: "et accepta habere, sicuti accepta dignatus es munera pueri tui iusti abel et *sacrificium* patriarche nostri abrahe et quod tibi optulet summus sacerdos tuus melchisedech sanctum *sacrificium* immaculatam hostiam."[10]

The teachings about the nature of Eucharistic Sacrifice implicit in these passages are commonplaces, perhaps, but they merit some review before any claims can be made in reference to the *Pardoner's Tale*. From time immemorial the Eucharist has been interpreted as a cultic meal which ritualistically represents the Sacrifice of the Cross. By the separate consecrations of the bread and wine and their consumption by the faithful, Christ is considered ritually slain on the altar in typological fulfillment of the Passover feast which was itself a recalling and reliving of the Sinai covenant by a blood sacrifice. Thus, the dual notions of Sacrament and Sacrifice are inseparable: by its very nature the Sacrament produces the mystical Sacrifice so that the Mass becomes a telescoping of the events of Maundy Thursday—the Last Supper when Jesus instructed his apostles to "do these things in remembrance of Me"—and of Good Friday when he died on the cross.

The biblical sanction for this teaching—aside from the obvious moment at the Last Supper during which Jesus identified the offered bread and wine of the Passover Feast as his body and blood "which shall be given up for you"—is in the famous phrase of St. Paul where the Apostle announces that "as often as you shall eat this bread and drink the chalice, you shall shew the death of the Lord, until he come."[11] It would belabor the obvious to marshal patristic arguments for the Sacrament-Sacrifice conjunction in the Eucharist, for it is common in the Fathers, but perhaps a passage from St. Augustine will convince the agnostic: "The congregation or community of the saints is offered to God as our sacrifice through the great High Priest, who offered Himself to God in His passion for us.... And this also is the sacrifice which the Church continually celebrates in the sacrament of the altar..." (*City of God* X.6).[12]

The manner in which Chaucer parodies this teaching in the *Pardoners Tale*, for the sake of reinforcing our sense of the Christian norm from which the Pardoner has strayed, is one of the brilliant ironic achievements of the *Canterbury Tales*. Certainly Nichols' suggestion—that the imagery of food and drink has parodic *sacramental* overtones—is valuable:

> Given the symbolic duality of food and the latticed allusions to Deity, Chaucer's introduction of the "substance into accident" passage is, itself, substance whose presence in the Pardoner's Tale cannot be considered simply accident. By his application of the phrase the poet astutely juxtaposes physical with spiritual. In the physical aspect earthy cooks prepare marrow, leaf, bark, and root to make delicacies for the lechers of a flesh-bound world. In the spiritual aspect the Eucharist implication lifts those earthly elements to parallel one of the supreme mysteries of the Church, the miracle wrought each day, the highlight of ritual and service. And it is in the tavern that this microcosm-macrocosm

correspondence coalesces about the company's wine and wafers, the Pardoner's ale and cake.[13]

But as it was earlier animadverted, in his recognition of the *prandial* implications of the Eucharist imagery, Nichols almost totally ignores its *sacrificial* character. Chaucer drops some large clues in the very beginning of the tale when he describes the rioters as eating and drinking inordinately "thurgh which they doon the devel *sacrifise*" (C 469).[14] The Host, of course, had launched the motif in the very first lines of the link from the *Physician's Tale* (C 288) when he swears by the crucifixion: "Harrow!" quod he, "by nayles and by blood!" And subsequent references to Christ's sacrificial death lace the tale:

Oure blissed Lordes body they totere,—
Hem thoughte that Jewes rente hym noght enough. (C 474–75)

I seye it now wepying, with pitous voys—
That they been enemys of Cristes croys. (C 531–32)

"By Goddes precious herte," and "By his nayles,"
And "By the blood of Crist that is in Hayles." (C 651–52)

Allas! mankynde, how may it bitide
That to thy creatour, which that the wroghte,
And with his precious herte-blood thee boghte,
Thou art so fals and so unkynde, allas? (C 900–904)

... by the croys which that Seint Eleyne fond... (C 951)

But it is the conjunction of this death *and* the meal (perhaps one should say *inside* the meal) that is our special concern. Notice that even the Pardoner's allusion early in the tale to the death of John the Baptist is made in terms of Herod's feast:

> Herodes, whoso wel the stories soghte,
> Whan he of wyn was repleet at his feeste
> Right at his owene table he yaf his heeste
> To sleen the Baptist John, ful giltlelees. (C 488–91)

Such a prandial sacrifice foreshadows a parodic eucharist in the main action of the tale, for death later surprises the three rioters in the context of their own meal, the first scheming crony riven through by the sword and the remaining two poisoned by the very wine they had schemingly instructed him to procure.

We remember, moreover, that it is the two *older* members of the trio who, after the drawing of the straws, send the *youngest* member to town for provisions while they remain with the treasure and then conspire to kill him under the tree when he returns. Chaucer must obviously have had something in mind when he described them as a trio who swear fellowship in the name of unity:

> Herkneth, felawes, *we thre been al ones:*
> Lat ech of us holde up his hand til oother,
> And ech of us bicomes otheres brother... (C 696–98)

These details, though seemingly casual, alert the reader into an awareness of a trinitarian paradigm that invests the entire action, including the prandial, with a continued parody of Sacrifice. In Christian teaching, the Son (metaphorically "younger" than the Father or the Paraclete) is sent to perform his ministrations on earth through the Incarnation—the enfleshing of the Son by the nativity of the Christ child. Although the Creeds taught that the Son is co-eternal and co-equal with the Father and the Holy Spirit, in his human manifestation he was born into the world to which he was sent in order to be sacrificed: "For God so loved the world, as to give his only begotten Son.... God sent not his Son into the world to judge the world but that the world may be saved by him" (John 3:16–17). It was not the popular Christian imagination alone which saw the Son as carrying the burden of the salvific scheme for mankind. Medieval theologians often wrote about the mission of the Son in relation to the other Persons of the Trinity, a mission which Jesus himself alluded to in the Gospels:

"From God I proceeded and came. For I came not of myself, but he sent me" (John 8:42). In his Tract on the Trinity in the *Summa Theologica*, St. Thomas Aquinas devotes the entirety of Question XLIII in Part III to the "mission" of the Divine Persons and argues for the fittingness of the Son's being sent. Chaucer may therefore be appealing to a well-known attribute of the Trinity—the Divine Mission—when he allows the youngest member to be sent from the triune guardianship of the treasure in order to secure provisions of bread and wine and then be slain upon completion of his fellows' business. And it is parodically appropriate that the nature of that sacrifice should relate, as we shall see in greater detail, to a meal.

It is the "worste" of the rioters who commissions the youngest to "renne to the towne" and "brynge us breed and wyn ful prively" (C 796–97).[15] Not only does the reference to bread and wine identify the Eucharistic parody, but also the "ful prively" adverb seems to echo the descriptions in the Synoptic Gospels of the upper-room secretiveness which Jesus employed in celebrating the Passover feast with his apostles so as not to be accosted by his enemies (Matthew 26:17: Mark 14:12; Luke 22:7). Moreover, the language of the apothecary describing the full potency of the deadly poison about to be slipped into the wine bottles perverts Jesus's words about the vivifying quality of the Eucharist. Jesus had claimed much for his spiritual food: "If any man eat of this bread, he shall live for ever: and the bread that I will give is my flesh, for the life of the world" (John 6:52). The apothecary, however, promises instant death:

In al this world ther is no creature,
That eten or dronketh hath of this confiture
Noght but the montance of a corn of whete
That he ne shal his lif anon forlete,
Ye sterve he shal, and that in lasse while
Than thou wold goon a paas nat but a mile
This poysoun is so strong and violent. (C 859–67)

That the poison is parodically eucharistic (in its sacrificial sense) is evident not only from these Johannine echoes but also from the specific reference to the amount of a "corn of whete" being sufficient to destroy life immediately. As with the phrase "turnen substaunce into accident" at line 539, Chaucer is deliberately loading his description with specific eucharistic connotations when he mentions the commingling of the poisonous "corn" [grain] in the wine. The allusion is probably to the part of the Mass called the Fraction of the Host when the priest, having broken the host, drops a particle into the wine before he drinks from the chalice at his Communion, an act signaling the reunion of Christ's body and blood after the separate consecrations of the bread and wine, and hence a vivifying repast for the communicant. The *Sarum Missal* describes the Fraction thus: "Hic mittat sacerdos particulam corporis quam tenet in dextera in calicem"; and then it prescribes the recitation of the following words: "Hec sacrosancta commixtio corporis et sanguinis domini nostri ihesu christi fiat mihi omnibusque sumentibus salus mentis et corporis et ad vitam eternam promerendam preparacio salutaris."[16] The rioters, however, will drink from another tun and the "corn of whete" dropped into their wine will bring not life everlasting but immediate (and presumably eternal) death.

The fact that they are victims of each other's treachery calls to mind still another aspect of the Eucharistic sacrifice that Chaucer seems to be parodying in the *Pardoner's Tale*. As he who offers the immolation of the Cross, Christ has been considered, from the time of the Epistle to the Hebrews (chapters 5, 6, and 7) as High Priest—in fulfillment of the Levitical priesthood who offered sacrifices in the name of the Hebrew people. But by substituting himself for the sacrificial Paschal Lamb, Christ has been concomitantly considered as Victim—the Agnus Dei. Sacramentally too, Christ at the Last Supper took the bread and wine and, in the person of Priest presenting the ritualistic immolation, offered these gifts to the Father. But because he identified the gifts as his own body and blood (under the species of bread and wine) what he was finally offering was himself. The Mass dramatized the Priest-Victim duality very well. Immediately after the priest spoke Jesus's words at the Last Supper, the priestly words of offering—"This is my body.... This is the chalice of my blood"—, the language turned to the immolated victim: "...nos servi tui...offerimus praeclarae maiestati tue de tuis donis ac datis. *Hostiam* puram. *Hostiam* sanctam.

Hostiam immaculatam."[17] In the *City of God*, St. Augustine makes reference to the Priest-Victim duality thus:

> ...the great High Priest...offered Himself to God in His passion for us, that we might be members of this glorious head, according to the form of a servant. For it was this form He offered, in this He was offered, because it is according to it He is Mediator, in this He is our Priest, in this the Sacrifice.[18]

In the *Summa Theologica*, St. Thomas devotes an entire article to the question *Whether Christ Was at the Same Time Priest and Victim?* (III, q. 22, a. 2). After the customary theological sparring, his conclusion is that "Christ Himself, as man, was not only priest, but also a perfect victim, being at the same time victim for sin, victim for a peace-offering, and a holocaust."

The action of the *Pardoner's Tale* would seem to revolve parodically around this very duality. The three rioters, who have proclaimed themselves a unity, function both as priests and victims in the sense that, by the end of the tale, each has offered the other in sacrifice and has been *slain by his fellow*. Such a diabolical offertory had been unwittingly spoken almost ritualistically earlier during the tavern scene:

> Lat ech of us holde up his hand til oother,
> And ech of us becomen otheres brother,
> And *we wol sleen* this false traytour Deeth.
> He *shal be slayn,* he that so many sleeth,
> By Goddes dignitee, er it be nyght. (C 697–701)

And the vow had been extended to the possibility of being slain as well:

> Togidres han thise thre hir trouthes plight
> To lyve and *dyen ech of hem for oother,*
> As though he were his owene ybore brother. (C 702–704)

After they discover the treasure under the oak tree, the unwitting prophecy begins to fulfill itself in the roles of priests and victims. The two older rioters conspire to slay the younger under the tree by riving him through the side. The youngest is to be, therefore, the victim of this "devil's sacrifice" concelebrated by the priesthood of the damned. But the youngest member of the trinity is plotting his own plans and seeks to function as priest over the victims in his own right by bringing them a meal of death over which he plans to officiate. Before his plan can materialize, he is slain by his brethren, and they celebrate his death (and participate in their own) by partaking of the wine which he has offered. The images obviously collide here with collusive effect: a victim lies dead under a tree, riven through the side by slayers who proclaim their sacrifice by a meal of bread and wine. Earlier they had promised to "pleye at dees" (C 834) when they had "acorded to sleen the thridde." The allusion to the Crucifixion is unmistakable, of course, particularly as it is strengthened by reference to the tree, which in medieval iconography represented both the tree of Eden, which brought death to the world, and the tree of the Cross, which restored life. By Chaucer's day, the Sacrifice of the Mass would have been celebrated on an altar dominated by an altar cross so that the sacramental meal would always be iconographically related to Calvary.[19] And whenever the feasts related to the Holy Cross and to Christ's Passion, the priest recited these words during the Preface to the Canon: "Qui salutem humani generis in ligno crucis constituisti ut unde mores orietabur inde vita resurgeret. Et qui in ligno vicerat in ligno quoque vinceretur per Christum dominum nostrum."[20]

We must not lose sight of the fact that these words were spoken at the Canon of the Mass as the priest prepared the bread and wine for consecration. Thus, Sacrament proclaimed Sacrifice, and Sacrifice was prolonged throughout time by Sacrament, a ritualistic conjunction that Chaucer must have experienced countless times, especially in the households of the great where, in a lifetime of public service that ranged from page to ambassador, he would have assisted frequently, perhaps daily, at the Sacrifice of the Mass. His transubstantiating of these forms into the eucharist of his own art, thus proclaiming in a way uniquely poetic the death of the Lord until he come, accounts for some of the miracle of the *Pardoner's Tale*.

NOTES TO Sacrament and Sacrifice in the *Pardoner's Tale*

1. Robert E. Nichols. Jr., "The Pardoner's Ale and Cake," *PMLA*, 82 (1967), pp. 498–504.
2. William B. Toole III, "Chaucer's Christian Irony: The Relationship of Character and Action in the *Pardoner's Tale*," *Chaucer Review*, 3 (1968), pp. 37–43.
3. Clarence H. Miller and Roberta Bux Bosse, "Chaucer's Pardoner and the Mass," *Chaucer Review*, 6 (1972), pp. 171–184.
4. According to Beverly Boyd, "books of worship according to the Use of Sarum are the best available evidence of the Roman Rite as it was in Medieval England to serve as a basis for investigating Chaucer's reference to the liturgy." *Chaucer and the Liturgy* (Philadelphia, 1967), p. 6.
5. *The Sarum Missal*, ed. J. Wickham Legg (Oxford, 1969), p. 219. All citations from the Mass are from this volume. Translations from the Latin where they are available are from *Saint Andrew Daily Missal* by Dom Gaspar Lefebvre, O.S.B. (St. Paul, MN, 1949): "In the spirit of humility and with a contrite heart receive us, O Lord, and grant that the sacrifice which we offer this day in Thy sight, may be pleasing unto Thee, O Lord God" (p. 546).
6. *Sarum*, p. 219. "Come O Sanctifier, almighty and eternal God, and bless this sacrifice prepared for Thy holy name" (p. 546). "Brethren, pray that my sacrifice and yours may be acceptable to the Lord our God" (a slight variation of the Orate Fratres of the St. Andrew text, p. 547).
7. *Sarum*, p. 219. This is a passage proper to *Sarum*, not in the St. Andrew text, which represents the Roman Rite only after the reforms of the Council of Trent. I translate the passage myself thus: May the grace of the Holy Spirit illuminate your heart and your lips and may the Lord accept this sacrifice of praise from your hands for our sins and offenses.
8. *Sarum*, p. 221. "These gifts, these offerings, these holy and unblemished sacrifices" (p. 549).
9. *Sarum*, p. 221. "...who offer up to Thee this sacrifice of praise" (p. 550).
10. *Sarum*, p. 223. "...and accept them as Thou wert pleased to accept the gifts of Thy just servant Abel, and the sacrifices of our Patriarch Abraham, and that which Thy high priest Melchisedech offered to Thee, a holy sacrifice, a spotless Victim" (p. 551).
11. 1 Cor. 11:26. All biblical citations are to the Douay-Rheims translation.
12. St. Augustine, *The Confessions, The City of God, On Christian Doctrine*, trans. Marcus Dods, Great Books of the Western World. No. 18 (Chicago, 1952), p. 302.
13. Nichols, p. 503.
14. *Chaucer's Major Poetry*, ed. Albert C. Baugh. (New York, 1963). All citations to the *Pardoner's Tale* are to this volume.
15. Ian Bishop has commented on Chaucer's narrative strategy in leaving the trio unnamed, but it seems to me that the "worste" and the "youngest" relate parodically to attributes of the Father and the Son: the Father is the author of all good, creator of heaven and earth, etc.; and the Son, in the language of the Creeds, is the "only begotten," metaphorically al least the youngest. Cf. Bishop. "The Narrative Art of the *Pardoner's Tale*," *Medium Aevum*, 36 (1967), pp. 15–24.
16. I translate the *Sarum* directive al the Fraction of the Host (p. 225) thus: Here the priest puts the particle of the body which he holds in his right hand into the chalice. And the words accompanying the gesture are translated: May this sacred commingling of the body and blood

of our Lord Jesus Christ mean for me and for all those who consume it health of mind and body and an effective preparation for achieving eternal life.

17. *Sarum*, p. 223. "...we Thy servants ...offer unto Thy most excellent Majesty, of Thy gifts and presents, a pure Victim, a holy Victim, a spotless Victim" (p. 551).
18. *City of God*, X. 6. In Dods, p. 302.
19. Robert Lesage, *Vestments and Church Furniture*, Twentieth Century Encyclopedia of Catholicism, No. 114 (New York, 1960), pp. 23–24.
20. *Sarum*, p. 214. "Who didst set the salvation of mankind upon the tree of the Cross, so that whence came death, thence also life might rise again, and that He Who overcame by the tree might also be overcome on the tree" (p. 565).

THE THEME OF JUDGMENT IN *THE CANTERBURY TALES*

Rodney Delasanta

Despite some recent animadversions on the architectonic function of the *Parson's Tale*,[1] most critics since Ralph Baldwin[2] have agreed that the Parson's answer to the Host's call to "knytte up wel a greet mateere" (X. 28)[3] makes a suitable finish for the *Canterbury Tales*. Penance, however besmirched its motives, is the final reason for pilgrimage; and the interposing of a visible sign of grace in the person of a holy confessor between the penitents and their destiny, if not obviously appropriate to us moderns, was strikingly significant to the pilgrims:

> For, as it seemed, it was for to doone,
> To enden in som vertuous sentence,
> And for to yeve hym space and audience. (X. 62–64)

Time—finally—for them to make earnest out of game; time for the "seke" to "seeke."

But the "sentence" to which they agree is teasingly ambiguous: although its primary meaning here is obviously rhetorical, it also carries suggestions of the judicatory. That the pilgrims had been preparing themselves for judgment—albeit of a variety ironically Chaucerian—was evident from the moment they assented to the Host's offer in the General Prologue to "stonden at my juggement" (I. 778). They agree "that he wolde been oure governour, / And of oure tales juge and reportour" (I. 813–14),[4] that "we wol reuled been at his devys / In heigh and lough; and thus by oon assent / We been acorded to his juggement" (I. 816–18). Moreover, whoever would be "rebel" to his "juggement /

Shal paye for al that by the wey is spent" (I. 833–34). Accordingly, the Host gathers together the pilgrims "alle in a flok" (I. 824) and promises them that whoever tells the best tale of sentence and solace "Shal have a soper at oure aller cost" (I. 799) when they return from Canterbury. In the course of the journey, the pilgrims forget neither his judicial authority nor his promise of prandial reward. The Clerk, for example, responds to the Host's uncouth command to tell a tale with the acknowledgment that "I am under youre yerde; / Ye han of us as now the governance, / And therfore wol I do yow obeisance" (IV. 22–24). The Squire too agrees to the Host's command to "sey somwhat of love" so as not to "rebelle / Agayn youre lust" (V. 2, 5–6); the Franklin "wole obeye / Unto your wyl" (V. 703–704); and the Knight urges his fellow pilgrims to prepare their stories after his in order to "se now who shal the soper wynne" (I. 891).

Thus the Host is early characterized as judge whose decrees must be obeyed upon pain of punishment, but who will reward the most meritorious with a supper upon completion of the journey. A recognizable Chaucerian strategy begins to emerge, one that I shall attempt to define in the rest of this paper as still another parody of Christian teaching—in this case, the Last Judgment—and once again by means of a decoying strategy of realism intended to shake off all but those hounds willing to follow Chaucer down the labyrinthine way of his art. Kemp Malone recognized the Host as a figure of a servant who is also master—"telling the pilgrims what to do and the pilgrims obeying his orders in comic reversal of the customary relationship between an innkeeper and his guests"—without, however, recognizing the typological figure of another Servant-Master in the background.[5] Moreover, that this servant-master should also establish himself as judge who will call the rebels among them to reckoning and, most important, will reward the best of them with a supper brings to mind the famous eschatological passage from the Gospel of Luke (22:27–30) which would seem to lend special parodic relevance to these deceptively innocent details:

> For which is greater, he that sitteth at table or he that serveth? Is not he that sitteth at table? But I am in the midst of you, as he that serveth.... And I dispose to you, as my Father hath disposed to me, a kingdom; that

> you may eat and drink at my table, in my kingdom, and may sit upon thrones, judging the twelve tribes of Israel.[6]

One need not conjecture that Chaucer knew the tradition of the eschatological supper well. The Parson overtly enjoins his fellow pilgrims to penance thus:

> "I was atte dore of thyn herte," seith Jhesus, "and cleped for to entre. He that openeth to me shal have foryifnesse of synne. I wol entre into hym by my grace, *and soupe with hym*," by the goode werkes that he shal doon, whiche werkes been the foode of God; "*and he shal soupe with me*," by the grete joye that I shal yeven hym. (p. 235; my italics)

This eschatological supper is, of course, a staple of biblical imagery, typologically foreshadowed in the paschal feast of the Old Testament, symbolically fulfilled in the eucharistic meal of the New, and utilized time and again by Jesus in revealing to his disciples the mysterious manner of salvation, the invitation, the preparation, and the comportment of the invited determining their destiny inside the Judgment of God.

It should be remembered that the Christians of the Middle Ages were unceasingly being called to judgment, often with a suddenness that modern man—for all his *Angst* over the Bomb—can scarcely appreciate. One needs only a cursory knowledge of the apocalypses visited cyclically upon medieval man to imagine his intimate acquaintance with doom: the rapine of foreign invasions and internal anarchy; the unvaccinatable horror of plagues (the most terrible of them having descended in 1348, at the very moment of the invention of gunpowder); the "justice" of an implacable capital punishment meted out for the most venial of offenses; and the superstitions of his pagan heritage often reinforced rather than assuaged by contact with a mysterious Christian rubric. And, at the end of his suffering, the Final Judgment—with Jesus, the merciful Savior, giving way to the parousial Judge, separating on that *dies irae* the sheep from the goats, the wheat from the cockle, and banishing those on his left into the hell-fire prepared for them from all eternity by the Father. The scene was sculpted deep into Christian man's imagination, not only by the word, usually most voluble and terrifying during Advent and Lent, but also by the omnipresent art surrounding him during divine worship. Indeed, he often could not enter his church without passing through the great central doors beneath the mighty tympanum which drummed home the terrible lesson of man's final end.

The design of that tympanum—its subject invariably the Last Judgment—was remarkably stylized from the thirteenth century on, as Emile Mâle has demonstrated,[7] and it had a profound influence upon the popular and artistic imagination of the later Middle Ages. In the center we find the risen Christ, usually enthroned, lifting his wounded hands as if to pronounce his implacable judgment; surrounding him, angels blowing their apocalyptic trumpets or holding the instruments of his Crucifixion, and the Twelve Apostles ready to share in his judgment of the twelve tribes of Israel; near him, the figures of the Virgin and St. John kneeling in supplication for the fate of mankind; beneath him and to his right, the saved—following St. Peter with his key to the door of glory; to his left, the damned—herded by demons anxious to usher their prey into the mouth of Hell. Often in their midst—and of special importance to our purposes in this paper—we see the figure of an angel with scales in hand weighing the virtues and vices of a trembling soul in the balance. Although the details are generally standardized, the scene remains essentially dramatic, for Jesus seems not to have completed his judgment; the tombs of the risen dead are half open; St. Peter has not yet unlocked the door; the Virgin and St. John continue their supplication; the devil attempts to upset the justice of the scales by weighing it in his favor. The moment, in short, is suspensefully penultimate (Baldwin, p. 90).

Such too is the moment of the Canterbury pilgrimage as Chaucer conceives it at the "thropes ende" (X. 12). Stylizations of thirteenth-century apocalyptic art have given way to a characteristic fourteenth-century realism which masks its larger intentions in deceptive details, but the moment—to use Baldwin's word again—remains penultimate. "Almoost fulfild is al myn ordinaunce" announces the Host (X. 19). "For every man, save thou," he tells the Parson, "hath toold his tale. / Unbokele, and shewe us what is in thy male" (X. 25–26). In one sense the tales have served as a necessary prelude to the judgment of the Host, but in another sense the tales, by being inadvertently confessional, will serve as prelude to the absolution of the Parson and to the greater Judgment beyond for which the pilgrimage is itself preparation. In the case of the Reeve, the Wife of Bath, and the Pardoner, for example, their Prologues are unequivocal confessions, public and strident, although their intentions are obviously self-aggrandizing and self-justifying rather than penitential. And the Host too by the end of journey comes to intuit that earnest has indeed emerged from these games and that his function as ironic judge over humanity in microcosm enjoins him to fulfill his sentence somewhat more seriously. The japes of his earlier demeanor give way to the recognition of the need for knitting up well "a greet matere," and the Parson, whom he had earlier dismissed as a "Jankin" and Lollard and whose preaching he succeeded in aborting, now becomes the delegate of his "sentence." Nor does the real significance of the Host's offer of a "soper" in the General Prologue escape the attention of the holy priest, for he agrees to "knytte up al this feeste" (X. 47) by insisting on "the sentence" of his "meditacioun" and preaching to the pilgrims of sin, confession, and judgment.

If the dramatic occasion clearly prepares the pilgrims for judgment, the imagery of the Parson's Prologue supports the same intention. We learn immediately, for example, that day is falling and that the sun was no more than "Degrees nyne and twenty as in highte" (X. 4). E. T. Donaldson reads the figure as appropriately recapitulatory of the original twenty-nine pilgrims,[8] but, in conjunction with some of the other extraordinary numerals of this prologue, it obviously means more. Chaucer's puzzling reference to Libra in line 11 would seem to suggest that—whether or not in error about the moon's exaltation—he attaches a symbolic significance to this zodiacal sign which, here in the coda of the pilgrimage, must at least equal the importance he had attached to the Ram in the General Prologue. The fact that the sun should be descending into the last thirty-degree segment of its daily revolution through the heavens while Libra is in the ascendancy suggests the penultimate moments of temporal decline on the one hand and the coming of eternal Judgment on the other. Because there are twelve zodiacal signs, each governs thirty degrees of the celestial circumference—an obvious fact with which Chaucer shows familiarity in his *Treatise on the Astrolabe* when he teaches his son Lewis that "every signe is departid in thre evene parties by 10 degrees" (p. 551) and, a little later, "evermo generaly the houre inequal of the day with the houre inequal of the night contenen 30 degrees of the bordure" (p. 552).[9]

Thus, in the Parson's Prologue twenty-nine serves conveniently as a number expressing the experience of the twenty-nine pilgrims with their final allotment of light before the always (and almost) coming on of the night. That their time left for "earnest" is agonizingly short before night and Judgment descend is strengthened by some curious details. As the sun descends,

> For ellevene foot, or litel moore or lesse,
> My shadwe was at thilke tyme, as there,
> Of swiche feet as my lengthe parted were
> In sixe feet equal of proporcioun. (X. 6–9)

These curiously constructed lines mean simply that if Chaucer's height were divided into six parts, his shadow would extend a distance of eleven such parts. Again, the numerals carry the theme of the penultimate. In medieval art, the mystical numbers seven and twelve signify, respectively, temporality and eternity. Seven, the sum of four (the number of the body with its four elements) and three (the number of the soul), expresses the number of ages allotted to man. With this allotment is associated the practice of the seven virtues and of the seven sacraments (even the seven supplications of the Pater Noster), as well as seven corporal and the seven spiritual works of mercy—all of which militate against the seven deadly sins.[10] Twelve, on the other hand, a multiple of the above four and three, heralds the Universal and Eternal Church transcending time—the triumph of the Mystical Body through its Head who is eternal life itself. Thus, the twelve tribes of Israel foreshadow the Twelve Apostles who will sit in judgment upon them and who, in their multiples of 144 and 144,000, represent the apocalyptic number of the saved before the throne of the Lamb. As a pilgrim to the City of God who has heard all *but one* story, Chaucer sees himself and his generation in the penultimate stage of human life: *almost* fulfilled is the "ordinaunce" of his judge. If his temporal body of six parts casts a shadow of eleven feet, there remains only the final step to the temporal finality of seven and to the eschatological finality of twelve.

That latter finality is zodiacally complemented by the reference to Libra at line 11. The sign of Libra is the scales; and we have already seen that a traditional detail of thirteenth-century tympanums was the figure of the angel weighing the virtues and vices of the defendant in his apocalyptic scales. The ascending Libra of the Parson's Prologue thus betokens for the Canterbury pilgrims approaching Judgment, parodically foreshadowed in the function of the Host, temporally fulfilled in the role of the Parson, who unequivocally calls the pilgrims to penance *and* judgment, and still awaiting the parousial Judge himself who, as the Parson warns, "may nat been deceyved ne corrupt." What we find at the "thropes ende" is Chaucer gathering his pilgrims under the tympanum of his own art.

To objections that the above reading may credit Chaucer with a subtlety that belongs more properly to the critic than to the poet, I should like to conclude with evidence from traditions that surrounded him, and even with evidence from his less imaginative work, that would point to these themes as pertinent to his artistic concerns. It is obvious that Chaucer would have known the symbol of the scales not only from the omnipresent figure of the weighing angel on the tympanums, but also from zodiacal lore as well—a lore that would have been known to him both "scientifically" and iconographically. It is significant, I believe, that even in a work of no artistic pretension, his *Treatise on the Astrolabe*, the contrast of Aries (the Ram) and Libra (the Scales) could be useful to him. In explaining the readings of the heavenly bodies in terms of the sun rising and setting, he writes that "every degre of Aries by ordir is nadir to every degre of Libra by ordre" (p. 552). He uses the same contrast in his example of the "special declaracioun of the homes of planetes": "The xiij day of March fyl upon a Saturday, peraventure, and atte risyng of the sonne I fond the secunde degre of Aries sittyng upon my west orisonte.... Than fond I the 2 degre of Libra, nadir of my sonne, discending on my west orisonte..." (p. 553).

Iconographically, the Middle Ages associated the signs of the zodiac with considerably more than celestial "science," and it is hardly presumptuous to assume that a major poet would have been privy to that iconography. Indeed, in many medieval cathedrals the signs are to be found on the tympanums themselves, often conspicuous in their association with the judging Christ and

Apostles. Long ago James Fowler noted the preservation of these figures on the chief doorways of the abbey church at Vézelay, the cathedrals of Amiens, Sens, and Rheims, and on the English churches of Iffley in Oxfordshire and St. Margaret's in York.[11] Curiously overlooked in his catalogue is the startling evidence at Canterbury Cathedral itself of the sign of Libra personified as a judge in his robes. And although this judicatory emblem does not appear on any Last Judgment portal, it is to be found—even more significantly—inlaid as a pavement medallion among the other zodiacal signs on the very spot of St. Thomas à Becket's shrine (emptied of its glory, of course, by Henry VIII's rapaciousness) behind and to the left of the high altar, not many feet in front of St. Augustine's chair. The date of the medallions, or roundels as they are also called, is almost certainly the first quarter of the thirteenth century, and the origin of these splendid pieces is probably Italian, thus further underscoring the universality of the symbol of the judging Libra. It is noteworthy that such a representation also exists conspicuously at Merton College, Oxford, again as a Judge in his robes holding the scales, and although that sculpture is post-Chaucerian by almost a hundred years, it attests to the traditional association between scales and judgment which, I contend, is the intention of line 11 of the Parson's Prologue.

As Mâle has pointed out (p. 376), that traditional association is as old as humanity itself, finding expression in ancient Egyptian and Indian art. Among the ancient texts that Chaucer could conceivably have known to exploit the association are those of the Old Testament and of the Fathers of the Church. In that most typologically apocalyptic book of the Old Testament, the Book of Daniel (whose name means the judgment of God), Daniel interprets for King Belshazzar the meaning of the handwriting on the wall in the second of the three phrases thus: "Thou art weighed in the balance and art found wanting" (5:27). (It is evident that Chaucer knew the Book of Daniel, certainly well enough to allude to it in his own work. In the *Man of Law's Tale*, a passage presumably original with him—because it is not found in Nicholas Trivet, his source—is an apostrophe to Daniel's adventure in the lion's den: II. 470–76.) Among the Fathers of the Church, we find allusions to the figure both in the East and West. St. John Chrysostom warns that "in that day our actions, our words, our thoughts will be placed in the scales, and the dip of the balance on either side will carry with it the irrevocable sentence." St. Augustine too used the metaphor: "Good and evil actions shall be as if hanging in the scales, and if the evil preponderate the guilty shall be dragged away to hell."[12]

If those critics are right who would interpret Chaucer's use of the Ram in the General Prologue as naturally provocative to pilgrimage,[13] then it is equally appropriate to interpret his use of Libra in the Parson's Prologue as supernaturally judicatory of pilgrimage. For it is the ascendancy of the scales of Libra which will bring justice and judgment to the City of Man and certify him for residence in the New Jerusalem. And if, up to this point, Chaucer has written straight with crooked lines, the *Parson's Tale* that follows will decode his calligraphy by unambiguously unfolding the significance of the eschatological motif. The Parson reminds the pilgrims in great detail that among other "causes" that ought to move a man to contrition is the approach of Judgment:

> For, as Seint Jerome seith, "At every tyme that me remembreth of the day of doom I quake; *for whan I ete or drynke* [the eschatological supper again], or what so that I do, evere semeth me that the trompe sowneth in myn ere: 'Riseth up, ye that been dede, and cometh to the juggement.' " O goode God, muchel oghte a man to drede swich a juggement, "ther as we shullen been alle," as Seint Poul seith, "biforn the seete of oure Lord Jhesu Crist"; whereas he shal make a general congregacioun, whereas no man may been absent.[14] For certes there availleth noon essoyne ne excusacioun. And nat oonly that oure defautes shullen be jugged, but eek that alle oure werkes shullen openly be knowe. And, as seith Seint Bernard, "Ther ne shal no pledynge availle, ne no sleigh te; we shullen yeven rekenynge of everich ydel word." There shul we han a juge that may nat been deceyved ne corrupt. (p. 231; my italics)

It is to be noted that as a result of this holy exhortation Chaucer himself comes forth repenting his sins—both personal and literary. The Retraction is as much a confession in dramatic response to the Parson's call—*inside* the confines of the Canterbury pilgrimage—as it is a Pisgah view of Chaucer's whole life. And it is in perfect keeping with the motif of Judgment enunciated above that we should hear his last words—his very last words in the *Canterbury Tales*—as a prayer for benign sentence: "that I may been oon of hem at the day of doom that shulle be saved."

Note for The Theme of Judgment in the *Canterbury Tales*

1. E. Talbot Donaldson, "Poetry and Sin in Medieval English Literature," a paper read to the Medieval Section of the MLA convention in December 1968.
2. *The Unity of the Canterbury Tales* (Copenhagen, 1955), pp. 83–105.
3. Quotations from Chaucer are from the *Works of Geoffrey Chaucer*, ed. E. N. Robinson, 2nd ed. (Boston, 1957).
4. "Reportour" here presumably means "that he was to report on their merits"; see Albert C. Baugh, ed., *Chaucer's Major Poetry* (New York, 1963), p. 255, n. 814.
5. *Chapters on Chaucer* (Baltimore, 1951), p. 193.
6. From the Douay-Rheims translation. It is noteworthy that Chaucer should refer to Harry Bailly's demeanor in the Reeve's Prologue as "lordly as a kyng" (I. 3900) and that Harry should earlier have sworn "by my fader soûle" (I. 781).
7. *The Gothic Image,* trans. Dora Nussey, from the 3rd French ed. (London, 1961), pp. 365ff.
8. *Chaucer's Poetry* (New York, 1958), p. 948. Russell A. Peck, "Number Symbolism in the Prologue to Chaucer's *Parson's Tale*," *ES*, 48 (1967), pp. 205–15, interprets the numbers "as metaphors of the spiritual welfare of the pilgrims in the company" (p. 207). He points out that, according to numerological exegesis, twenty-nine, as well as eleven, connotes "imperfection, concupiscence, and spiritual decrepitude...in short, a sign of sin" (p. 207), whereas thirty is a "Christian marriage number and a sign of fruitfulness and the active life" (p. 208), and twelve "a number of spiritual regeneration and fulfillment" (p. 212). Six, like thirty, he also reads as a marriage number and as a number of the soul. This pioneering article, more directed to numerological lore than mine, conveniently confirms the Judgment motif I have been suggesting by reference to the rich implications of the numerological symbols that I have pursued in a different (and less exhaustive) but complementary way. See especially Peck's eminently satisfying reading of the time of day in the Parson's Prologue ("foure of the clokke" in some manuscripts, "ten of the clokke" in the others) as relevant to the above. Four, for example, stands as a warning to the pilgrims because it is "a number of Fortune, a number...intimately associated with the world" (p. 210).
9. See Robinson's note to paragraph 4, lines 16ff. (p. 870).
10. See Mâle, pp. 11–12, but also Peck, p. 213, n. 28.
11. "On Mediaeval Representations of the Months and Seasons," *Archaeologia*, 44 (1873), pp. 137–89. For a study of the primitive Judaeo-Christian origins of the symbolic association between the Twelve Apostles and the signs of the zodiac, see Jean Daniélou, S.J., *Les Symboles chrétiens primitifs* (Paris, 1961), chap. 8.
12. Quoted in Mâle, p. 376.

13. Chauncey Wood, "Chaucer and Astrology," in *Companion to Chaucer Studies*, ed. Beryl Rowland (New York, 1968), pp. 180–81.
14. One is tempted to think that the Canon's embarrassed flight from the pilgrimage is relevant here.

PENANCE AND POETRY IN THE *CANTERBURY TALES*

Rodney Delasanta

No part of the *Canterbury Tales* has been more unloved than its ending. Fragment X has always been an irritant to its readers: to nonspecialists, who, having been promised a "feeste" by the Parson, often gag on its religiosity, and to specialists as well, who, having dutifully feasted, seldom agree on the value of the repast. Some early scholars, embarrassed by its overtly religious subject, denied parts of it a place in the canon altogether. Others, inhibited by manuscript evidence from banishing it to the apocrypha, simply resorted to lamenting its existence ("grucchyng," the Parson would say) and tried to explain it away biographically: Chaucer, in extremis, had deviated into piety after having fallen into monkish clutches at Westminster Abbey.[1] With the slow emergence of scholarly opinion that granted Chaucer s art an increasing religious respectability, however, the penitential ending began to be interpreted as a *confiteor* theme appropriate to pilgrimage in general and to the Parson's Tale and Retraction in particular. And there most critics have left it within the last generation—in varying degrees of approbation[2]—until some recent scholars, by urging an ironic reading of Fragment X, have called into question the penitential earnestness of Chaucer's ending. Thou shall not make earnest out of earnest seems to be their imperative.

It is not my intention to engage in a long polemic here against the ironist scholars of Fragment X. Rather, like Dr. Johnson, I prefer to kick the stone against their kind of revisionist eccentricity by insisting that, both dramatically and symbolically, the penitential earnestness of the ending is *dignum et justum*. In less complicated times it may even have been obvious, at least in its dramatic compulsions. But to find irony where it deliberately has been excluded, as

Judson Bovce Allen has done with the Parson's Tale and Olive Sayce with the Retraction,[3] requires one to abjure the obvious and embrace the arcane: to reduce one's argument to special pleading from outside texts that Chaucer may not even have known rather than to identify alleged ironies inside the Fragment or retroactive to previous tales. Predictably, footnotes multiply and citations to desperate sources expand into the same bloat of bibliography that characterizes the industry of some of the unrestrained allegorical critics of Chaucer. Inversely, exegesis of the text itself diminishes and sometimes disappears altogether.[4] Ignored are those lines in the Parson's Prologue that disarm irony by showing the pilgrims *unanimously* assenting to the propriety, and even the urgency, of the Parson's "vertuous sentence":

> Upon this word we han assented soone,
> For, as it seemed, it was for to doone,
> To enden in som vertuous sentence,
> And for to yeve hym space and audience
> And bade oure Hoost he sholde to hym seye
> That *alle* we to telle his tale hym preye.
> Oure Hoost hadde the wordes for us *alle*. (X. 61–67)[5]

In their stead we are introduced to exegetes like Hugh of St. Victor and rhetoricians like Herman the German (sic) whose dubiously interpreted testimony is intended to lead us to the conclusion that the Parson's Tale is not what it seems. To Hugh's positive penitential system of "faith, love. Christ," for example, Allen ironically contrasts the Parson's alleged *contemptus mundi* negativism (curiously described as a "*worldly* system of penance"), which Chaucer is supposed to be satirizing. But no hard evidence is offered from *inside* the text that would make the Parson's perfectly orthodox call to sacramental penance alien in any wav to "faith, love. Christ "[6] Then, even more unconvincingly, Herman the German's gobbled version of Aristotle's *Poetics* is cited to show us that our modem presuppositions about climactic endings in literature have no significance in medieval esthetics and that the Parson's Tale "is not by medieval doctrine likely to be Chaucer's governing statement because of pride of place." One can only wonder how Herman the German would have explained the *Paradiso* by this extraordinary poetic that the last shall not be last or, more germane to our purpose, how he would have explained Chaucer's own words about climactic endings put in the mouth of that consummate artist Pandarus, in *Troilus and Criseyde*:

> How so it be that som men hem delite
> With subtyl art hire tales for to endite.
> Yet for al that, in hire entencioun,
> *Hire tale is al for som conclusioun.*
> And...*th'ende is every tales strengthe* (II. 256–60—my italics)

But we should leave further shadowboxing with absent colleagues to the notes[7] and pursue the main business of the paper. Let us begin by keeping our eyes squarely upon the obvious dramatic occasion of Fragment X. All the pilgrims have told their tales, according to Chaucer's stated though unfinished plan, except one; and the entire company agrees that, having put off the Parson up to this penultimate point, it would be proper to end in some virtuous sentence. They are, after all, on a pilgrimage, and the ostensible reason for pilgrimage is penance, however besmirched either its motive or its execution. Even the most worldly of the pilgrims would have been expected to go through the motions. And what, exactly, were the motions upon approaching this holy place? The *New Catholic Encyclopedia* tells us that "pilgrims often assumed a penitential posture from the moment they arrived at the *mons gaudii*, the place from which they had their first glimpse of the object of their pilgrimage" and that "they retained this posture until they reached their destination."[8] It would seem that the "mountjoy" of Chaucer's pilgrims had been reached two miles from Canterbury as they emerged from the Blean forest at Bobbe-up-and-doun or—as it has been identified—Harbledown, the location overlooking Canterbury where even as recalcitrant a pilgrim as Henry II assumed his penitential posture two centuries earlier by stripping himself naked for the monks' lashes. It was here that the "Caunterbury Weye," of which Chaucer speaks in the Prologue to the Manciple's Tale, became the "righte wey of Jerusalem celestial," to which the Parson alludes in the opening lines of his tale. And "this wey is cleped Penitence."

Since 1215, as legislated by the Fourth Lateran Council, Catholics were required to confess themselves at least once a year[9]; and, because the other half of the decree required them to receive the Eucharist during the Easter season, most would perform their Easter "duty" by confessing themselves and taking communion immediately thereafter. (It remains a confessional habit to our own day for many.) Now we know that the journey takes place around 18 April (II. 5), if not in the Lenten season certainly within the Paschal season, which in Chaucer's day extended to Pentecost. We know that the Parson, rich of holy thought and works, has one last sacerdotal shot at his fellow travelers before their arrival. He has witnessed the tainted nature of the human condition on this *pèlerinage de la vie humaine*; and he has witnessed it existentially. He has, moreover, heard its cri de coeur: the Wife's lament over encroaching old age, the Merchant's disenchantment with his recent marriage, the Franklin's disappointment with his son, the Reeve's frightened boast that he still sports a green tail, the Canon's embarrassed flight from the exposing of his secret sin, the eunuch Pardoner's pitiful bravado, the Cook's militant drunkenness, the Prioress' dainty enmities. We know too that the Parson is "to synful men nat despitous....but Cristes loore and his apostles twelve he taughte" (Prologue, ll. 516, 527–28). And what, at this penultimate moment, is Christ's lore? Despite Allen's dismissal of the Parson's penitential way as "adinventiones vanas" (new, vain inventions in penance) (p. 157), the good priest's understanding of Christ's lore is as old as the gospels from which he "trewely wolde preche" (Prologue, l. 481). From Luke: "I have not come to call the just, but sinners, to repentance." From Matthew: "Repent, for the kingdom of heaven is at hand." From Acts: "God now calls upon all men everywhere to repent: inasmuch as he has fixed a day on which he will judge the world with justice by a Man whom he has appointed." And the form of that repentance, as dictated by the medieval church, involved this holy Parson as indispensable instrument: "Amen I say to you, whatever you bind on earth shall be bound also in heaven; and whatever you loose on earth shall be loosed also in heaven."

By Chaucer's time, of course, confession was auricular: sins were heard in order to be forgiven or retained, as the case may have been. But, before confession, came its sine qua non: the indispensable preparation that made possible "shrift of mouth." And that was *examination of conscience*. Because it was understood that confession should be complete, that it should possess sacramental integrity, the penitent was urged to compare his current moral condition against some positive or negative standard, like the Ten Commandments or the Seven Deadly Sins. It is here that the Parson's Tale, at this moment of priestly goad before impending confession, functions with dramatic appropriateness in the Canterbury pilgrimage. For, contrary to its popular designation, the Parson's Tale is not a sermon in the normal homiletic sense of the word. As H. G. Pfander pointed out forty years ago in an article that defined the genre, but not the intention, of the Parson's Tale, it is a confessional manual designed for the priest to use with the layman in performing the rubric of the sacrament.[10] Its structure, like many French confessionals with similar "orders," is as follows: (1) a discourse on penitence and confession, (2) a treatment of the deadly sins, (3) a treatment of the Commandments (bypassed deliberately in this work),[11] and (4) a treatment of satisfaction, or expiation. It is curious, even ludicrous, to read how often critics use the word "digression" to describe the section on the Seven Deadly Sins in the Parson's Tale or how often they describe it as a sermon on penance into which a disquisition on the deadly sins has been awkwardly intruded.[12] That a disquisition on the nature and species of mortal sins can be considered digressive in a tract intended to ascertain their existence in order to shrive them bespeaks an ignorance of the process of sacramental confession. On the contrary, the so-called digression is perfectly related to the tract on confession, the instrumental cause of which is mortal sin—and all its works. The old scholastic distinction between material and formal sin applies here. To quicken the pilgrims' consciences into *formal* awareness of their own specific sinfulness, the Parson must first remind them what it is that *materially* constitutes serious sin. With this reminder dramatically before them, the pilgrims will begin their descent from Harbledown, their consciences newly informed (in some cases specifically challenged) and as prepared as ever they will be for the "shrift of mouth" that awaits them below.

Admittedly, a certain novelistic realism is sacrificed by submitting the pilgrims to so formidable a prick of conscience, especially at four in the afternoon and in a form so bookish and treatise-like. But, as some scholars have observed, dramatic appropriateness need not be equated with novelistic realism (see, e.g., Howard's discussion of verisimilitude, p. 196): Chaucer cannot be faulted for not sounding like Balzac. At the same time, one should not be too casuistical in justifying mimetic theories beyond the bounds of common sense. In this regard, it seems fitting to close off my remarks about the dramatic appropriateness of Fragment X by appending here two observations from nonliterary scholars that may make both the length and the bookishness of the Parson's Tale a little more understandable to the modem reader. The first, by Jonathan Sumption, concerns pilgrimage sermons:

> The company who travelled with Canon Casola in 1494 were fortunate enough to have amongst them one Francesco Tivulzio, "a holy friar with a wonderful library in his head." Whenever the ship was becalmed, he would rise and deliver an elaborate and learned sermon which lasted from 5 p.m. to sunset, and promised to deliver the rest of it on the following day.[13]

The second, by John T. McNeill, is about penitential manuals:

> While the penitentials were primarily intended for the use of priests, it was sometimes found convenient to provide them in the vernacular in order, we may suppose, to make their contents comprehensible to the people.... In some instances confessors were enjoined to read the penitential aloud to the sinner.[14]

As for the Retraction, given the dramatic compulsion of the Parson's plea for penance and given the fact of the pilgrims' approach to the holy city from the *mons gaudii*—Upper Harbledown—I find it wholly appropriate that Chaucer the pilgrim—perhaps, too, Chaucer the poet—should himself be moved to formal penitential posture: to examination of conscience, to a *confiteor* that admits to sins of *cogitatione, verbo, et opere* and to expiative retraction of whatever may have offended—even unwittingly—over the course of a long and mixed career. By this act of penance, Donald Howard tells us, "he is practicing 'the art of dying,'" which meant "rejecting all the wrong choices of one's life as best one knew what they were. It was not a time for cavils and distinctions. Hence the ring of extravagance, even of falsity, which some hear in this passage" (pp. 172–73). What Olive Sayce heard, as I have already said, is irony, but her suggestion that the formulaic nature of the Retraction detracts from its sincerity misunderstands the formulaic structure of sacramental penance. Does formula necessarily neutralize sincerity and force a speaker's tongue into his cheek? If so, the history of Catholic spiritual writing is sham. Chaucer would have understood very well that, in moments of spiritual crisis, one reaches for the "second plank" that has usually been thrown by others. He would have understood very well the Offertory *exhortatio*: "Recordare mei, Domine, omni potentatui dominans; et da sermonem rectum in os ut placeant verba mea in conspectu principis."

Having examined the dramatic occasion for Fragment X, I should like to turn my attention to symbolic strategies. I have written elsewhere that the Host's role in the pilgrimage extends beyond the literal: that his function of *judge* over the tales and his promise of prandial reward for the most meritorious of them, along with a warning of punishment for those pilgrims who would be rebels to his will, urge a parodic interpretation relating to the Last Judgment. Thus, the images of "supper on the house" for the best of the pilgrims contrasting with images of "footing the bill" for the worst of them, to be determined inside the salvific journey of the pilgrimage by the judgment and *sentence* of the Host, collude to characterize him as parodic Servant-Master and parousial Judge, whose "game" begins to turn "earnest" as the pilgrims arrive at the "thropes ende." Indeed, the "earnest" emerges unmistakably in the Parson's Prologue when the Host turns his parodically judicatory role over to the Parson, who, true to the promise of the supper, agrees to "'knytte up al this greet feeste" by urging a *sentence* of confession and judgment in his tale. Supporting this motif are a cluster of "sentence" and "juggement" images surrounding the Host in the

General Prologue and another cluster of "sentence" and "juggement" images in the Parson's Prologue, among which are those of penultimate numerology and the scales of Libra.[15]

Now I should like to strengthen my evidence for some of the eschatological symbols that I found to have been used parodically in the General Prologue--Parson's Prologue complex. First the supper. It was originally intended, of course, as a prize to be awarded upon the pilgrims' return to the Tabard. Was it abandoned when Chaucer revised his original plan for a one-way journey? I think not, for the Parson's intention to tell a final tale in order to "knytte up this greet feeste" seems to transfigure the visible supper into an image of the messianic banquet: *visibilium omnium* et *invisibilium.* It is a potent image that has arrested the attention of both medieval and modem man. Even though the present-day Mass has been despoiled of much of its medieval iconography by Vatican II, we continue to hear the formulaic phrase that reminds the faithful of the eschatological meaning of the sacramental meal: "Happy are those who are called to his supper." "Happy," of course, is a liturgical neologism for "blessed," and the whole line is a compression of similar formulas repeated in both the Old and the New Testaments to express the summum bonum, the *totaliter aliter*, the beatific vision. In Isaiah, in Esdras, even in the intertestamental Henoch, we hear the same motif: "The Lord of Spirits will dwell with them and they will eat with the Son of Man; they will take their places at his table for ever and ever" (Henoch 52:14). In the New Testament, it becomes almost a refrain. In Luke's gospel, the parable of the messianic banquet is prefaced with the line, "Blessed is he who shall feast in the kingdom of God" (15:25). In Revelations we hear, "Blessed are they who are called to the marriage supper of the Lamb" (19:9); and a few chapters earlier St. John had used a startlingly appropriate conjunction of the need for repentance and the salvific meal: "Be earnest therefore and repent. Behold I stand at the door and knock. If any man listens to my voice and opens the door to me, I will come in to him and will sup with him and he with me" (3:19).

There can be no question of Chaucer's intimate knowledge either of the salvific supper motif in general or of this apocalyptic passage in particular. In the Second Nun's Tale, Cecelia's angel, responding to Valerian's request that his brother too be converted to the faith, says:

> ... God liketh thy requeste,
> And bothe, with the palm of martirdom.
> Ye shullen come unto his blisful feste. (VIII.239–41)

And in the Parson's Tale the holy priest enjoins his fellow pilgrims to repentance with an exhortation directly alluding to the passage just quoted from Revelations: "I was atte dore of thym herte, seith Jhesus, and cleped for to entre. He that openeth to me shal have foryifnesse of synne. I wol entre into hym by my grace, and soupe with hym...and he shal soupe with me..." (X.288–89).

If the supper symbolizes eschatological reward, the haste of Harry Bailly, who is preoccupied during the pilgrimage with a fear of lapsed time, parodically signifies eschatological foreboding before the *dies illa*. "Say forth thy tale, and tarie nat the tyme" (I.3905), he warns the Reeve. "Lordynges, I warne yow... / The fourthe party of this day is gon. / Now for the love of God and of Seint John, / Leseth no tyme" (II.16–19), he admonishes the Man of Law, and so on with a command of haste to Chaucer the pilgrim before each of his two tales (VII.706 and VII. 2121); to the Monk before his (VII.3116): and finally to the Parson himself: "But hasteth yow, the sonne wol adoune: / Beth fructuous, and that in litel space" (X. 70–71). "HURRY UP PLEASE ITS TIME," another bartender will say about a different kind of wasteland centuries later. Can all this be thematically unpurposeful, serving only the demands of realistic dialogue?

Certainly, the Clerk had not reacted so on the previous day. Ever alert for a moralizing opportunity, he had used Harry's admonitions to haste as an occasion for his own memento mori. Harry had taunted the Clerk for studying some sophism or rhetorical figure instead of preparing his tale ("it is no tyme for to Studien heere"—IV.8) and had then appealed to the authority of Solomon, who was made to say, in the Host's inelegant translation, that "every thyng hath tyme" (IV.6). Knowing belter than Harry Bailly what the proto-eschatological passage from Ecclesiastes means, the Clerk had answered with an account of the glorious career and the recent death of his "auctour," Francis Petrarch. Death "wol nat suffre us dwellen heer. / But as it were a twynklyng of an ye...and alle shul we dye" (IV.35–37).

If both the dramatic and symbolic occasions compel us to see the pilgrimage as *via* and the pilgrims as *viatores*, then these exhortations to haste and these concomitant intimations of mortality resonate with overtones of impending doom. E. Talbot Donaldson has suggested that by the time of the Parson's Prologue "there comes something of the chill and urgency of late afternoon.... The shadows are lengthening and the sun has but twenty-nine degrees to sink before darkness falls on the nine-and-twenty pilgrims."[16] But St. John the Evangelist, the object of the Host's earlier hurry-up expletive to the Man of Law, had composed a better paradigm for eschatological haste: "Yet a little while the light is among you. He who walks in the darkness does not know where he goes. While you have the light, believe in the light, that you may become sons of light" (12:35–36). For Chaucer's pilgrims, too, "the sonne wole adoune."

It would require another paper to show how, as the pilgrims approach Canterbury, Chaucer has prepared them, in Fragments VII and IX, for the final eschatological pronunciamento of the Parson in Fragment X: the imagery of heaven informing the Second Nun's Tale, for example, and the imagery of hell and parodic confession informing the Canon's Yeoman's Tale.[17] But perhaps a brief explication of a deceptively casual exchange among the Host, the Cook, and the Manciple will strengthen my reading of eschatological haste. In the Manciple's Prologue, the pilgrims have arrived at Bobbe-up-and-doun during the morning of the last day of their journey. The Host, still frisky, notices the Cook hopelessly drunk and unable to respond to his call for a tale: "Is ther no man...that wole awake oure felawe al bihynde?" he asks (IX.6–7). But the Host's imperative to awake, to use the morning hours for the telling of the promised tale rather than for drunken sleep, fails to rouse the vinolent Cook to much of a response:

> Awake, thou Cook, quod he, God yeve thee sorwe!
> What eyleth thee to slepe by the morwe?
> Hastow had fleen alnyght, or artow dronke?
> Or hastow with some quene al nyght yswonke.
> So that thow mayst nat holden up thyn heed? (IX.15–19)

A few lines earlier the Host, with characteristic hyperbole, had claimed that the Cook was so drunk a thief could quite easily rob him:

> A theef myghte hym ful lightly robbe and bynde.
> See how he nappeth! see how, for cokkes bones.
> That he wol falle fro his hors atones. (IX.8–10)

It is my contention that Chaucer is here masking his larger eschatological intentions with a parodic realism that is preparatory of the Parson's final call to repentance; for what he has done is first to purloin and then artfully to disguise details of the doomsday admonition from St. Paul. In a famous passage from 1 Thessalonians, the Apostle refers especially to the dangers of *sleep* and *morning drunkenness* as metaphors of unpreparedness before the Day of Judgment, while connecting, in a striking simile, the unexpected coming of the Lord with a *thief* in the night:

> You yourselves know well that the day of the Lord is to come as a thief in the night.... But you, brethren, are not in darkness, that that day should overtake you as a thief: for you are all children of the light and children of the day. We are not of night nor of darkness. Therefore, let us not sleep as do the rest, but let us be wakeful and sober. For they who sleep, sleep at night, and they who are drunk, are drunk at night. But let us, who are of the day, be sober. (V.2–8)

The simile of the thief in the night is almost formulaically eschatological in the New Testament; for we find it—in addition to this passage in 1 Thessalonians—in Matthew 24:43, Luke 12:39–40, 2 Peter 3:10, and Revelations 3:3. Chaucer's use of it in the Manciple's Prologue, therefore, conjoined as it is with the other Pauline images of darkness-sleep-drunkenness in opposition to morning-wakefulness-sobriety, is well designed and as purposeful as Alison's casual response to the second coming of Absolon in the Miller's Tale in a scene also parodic of the eschaton: "Who is ther / That knokketh so? I warrante it a theef" (I.3790–91).

Thus has Chaucer laid his scenario of the Penultimate very well. The judgment scales of Libra ascend in the late afternoon sky while the Host urges his charges to eschatological haste before the sun sets. The promise of the supper does not go forgotten, but the pilgrims must merit it by their personal response to the call of repentance. Below them, from the Pisgah of their *mons gaudii*, lies Canterbury, which in the alchemy of the divine will and through the alembic of the Parson will become the golden Jerusalem celestial described in Revelations. A few miles back, at Boughton-under-the-Blean forest, an anti-Christ[18] had appeared briefly among them whose yeoman had boasted that his lord with his worldly alchemy could transform the road "til that we come to Caunterbury toun" into a pavement of silver and gold, a parody of the resplendent Jerusalem that St. John saw in his apocalyptic vision. But the way of the Canon is the wav of the world, not the *verace via*, and, as the Parson will shortly remind them, it is the "olde pathes" that are safest, upon which way they who walk will find refreshment for their souls.

Perhaps now the Parson's reason for abjuring fables takes on a special meaning. It is true, of course, that his dramatic justification is taken from Paul's Epistles to Timothy, but as the *alter Christus* seals the foreheads of the penitents on their way to the New Jerusalem, another more compelling reason offers itself. In Jesus' last discourse to his disciples before entering the Old Jerusalem in preparation for his passion and death, he had spoken to them cryptically of sin, justice, and judgment (John 16:8–24). And then, in response to the bewilderment of his disciples, he says: "These things I have spoken to you in parables. The hour cometh when I will no more speak to you in parables, but will show you plainly of the Father" (John 16:25). Like his Master, whose doctrine he teaches without gloss, the Parson knows that the pilgrims have arrived at their moment of truth. The time for parables has ceased. The time for plain speaking is ahead. Sin, justice, and judgment: these are the themes that must be clearly understood so that the scales of divine judgment may be weighed with terrifying exactitude. The "game" of poetry, parable, and play is over. And although a "man may seye ful soth in game and pley," the time for earnest has finally arrived.

Notes to Penance and Poetry in the *Canterbury Tales*

1. For a review of early scholarship relating to both the Parson's Tale and the Retraction, see F. N. Robinson, ed., *The Works of Geoffrey Chaucer,* 2nd ed. (Cambridge, MA: Houghton, 1957), pp. 765–66, and James D. Gordon, "Chaucer's *Retraction*: A Review of Opinion," in *Studies in Medieval Literature in Honor of Professor Albert Croll Baugh*, ed. MacEdward Leach (Philadelphia: University of Pennsylvania Press, 1961), pp. 81–96. See also Robert K. Root's complaint "that in the sadness of his latter days the poet's conscience was seized upon by the tenets of a, narrow creed, "which in the days of his strength he had known how to transmute into something better and truer," in *The Poetry of Chaucer* (Boston: Houghton, 1906), p. 238: and J. M. Manly's wish, as late as 1940, that he be "allowed to doubt whether Chaucer himself was responsible for the choice of the two prose treatises which are put together to form PsT and for the melancholy Retraction...," in *The Text of the Canterbury Tales*, ed. J. M. Manly and Edith Rickert. 8 vols. (Chicago: University of Chicago Press, 1940), IV, p. 527.
2. The most influential example of the scholarship of approbation is Ralph Baldwin's monograph. *The Unity of the* Canterbury Tales, *Anglistica*, 5 (Copenhagen: Rosenkilde and Bagger, 1955), pp. 83–110. Equally approving is Paul G. Ruggiers, *The Art of the Canterbury Tales* (Madison: University of Wisconsin Press. 1967), pp. 23–30. See also D. W. Robertson. Jr., *A Preface to Chaucer* (Princeton: Princeton University Press, 1962), pp. 335–36; and Bernard F. Huppé, *A Reading of the Canterbury Tales* (Albany: State University of New York Press, 1964), pp. 19–20. While distancing himself from the methodology of the aforementioned critics, Donald Howard clearly accepts the penitential theme as appropriate to the ending: *The Idea of the Canterbury Tales* (Berkeley: University of California Press, 1976). esp. pp. 68–74.
3. Judson Boyce Allen, "The Old Way and the Parson's Way: An Ironic Reading of the Parson's Tale," *Journal of Medieval and Renaissance Studies*, 3 (1973), pp. 255–71. Olive Sayce, "Chaucer's 'Retractions': The Conclusion of the *Canterbury Tales* and Its Place in Literary Tradition," *Medium Aevum*, 40 (1971), pp. 230–48.
4. Of all the ironist critics, John Finlayson is the most believable because his arguments stay closest to the text ("The Satiric Mode and the *Parson's Tale*," *Chaucer Review*, 6 [1971], pp. 94–116). But. curiously for an ironist, his denial "that the spiritual significance of the pilgrimage is the dominating preoccupation of the work" (p 104) is predicated on the unironic fact that Chaucer, unlike Dante and others, does not overtly announce his symbolic intention. Allegorists of the time, he observes, "manifest this concern most directly, as if they had little faith in their audience's ability to discern the sentence beneath the matter" (p. 104). But Chaucer is not Dante. His symbolic mode, parodically tilted as it often is, uses a decoying realism to put the "sentence seekers" off the scent. The work of scholars like Kaske, Reiss. Levy. Levitan. Wimsatt, and others has certainly documented this tactic. My own work has attempted to demonstrate that "game" in Chaucer is often "earnest," and by a parodic method that makes the word both "cousin" and "cozen" to the deed.
5. *The Works of Geoffrey Chaucer*, ed. F. N. Robinson, 2nd ed. (Cambridge, MA: Houghton, 1957), p. 228. All subsequent references to Chaucer's poetry are to this volume.
6. On the contrary, the text of the Parson's Tale reveals that the Parson's penitential counsels do not exclude "faith, love, Christ," particularly when he urges their reception as *remedia contra peccatum*. There would be little point in responding to Allen's misreading of the Parson's Tale by countering with some of the numerous passages about "faith, love, Christ" that belie his

claim. One could point out, for example, that Jesus is not exactly absent from the Parson's ruminations; rather, he is addressed with reverence at least eighty-six times. But perhaps quoting just one passage will suffice to correct Allen's allegation that the negative penitential tone of the Parson s Tale is "a likely target of Chaucerian irony" (p. 260). "But war thee wel that swiche manere penaunces on thy flessh ne make nat thyn bene bitter or angry or anoyed of thyself for bettre is to caste a we y thyn heyre (hairshirt), than for to caste awey the swetenesse of Jhesu Crist" (X.1052).

7. Olive Sayce's reading of the Retraction suffers, it seems to me, by failing to connect alleged ironies in the Retraction to the Parson's Tale itself, which she largely ignores. To convince us that Chaucer is indulging in ironies in the Retraction, it would be necessary to identify a consonant tone in the Parson's Tale. But, despite the extraordinary documentation of placing the Retraction within a literary tradition, her thesis—that the very conventionality of the language can reveal only an ironic intention—simply does not convince. Conventional language need not militate against sincerity. The "spring-song" opening of the General Prologue is also conventional in its rhetorical and imagistic patterns. No one to my knowledge has ever seen irony lurking there.
8. (New York: McGraw-Hill, 1967), XI, p. 370.
9. Chaucer alludes to the practice in the Parson's Tale: "And certes, oones a yeere atte leeste wey it is laweful for to been housled; for certes, oones a yeere alte thynges renovellen" (X.1027).
10. "Some Medieval Manuals of Religous Instruction in England and Observations on Chaucer's *Parson's Tale*," *Journal of English and Germanic Philology*, 35 (1936), pp. 243–58.
11. "Now after that I have declared yow, as I kan, the sevene deedly synnes, and somme of hire braunches and hire remedies, soothly, if I koude, I wolde telle yow the ten commandemantz. But so high a doctrine I lete to divines. Nathelees, I hope to God, they been touched in this tretice, everich of hem alle" (X.955–56).
12. Root's stricture is typical: "the digression hopelessly destroys the unity and proportion of the whole.... So inartistic is this combination, that many critics...have been unwilling to believe that the tale as preserved to us is Chaucer's authentic work" (pp. 286–87). And as recent a commentator as John Norton-Smith continues to use the word: "The "tract' falls into three main divisions, with the *summa peccatorum* as a central digression in the midst of the two continuous sections dealing with penance." *Geoffrey Chaucer* (London: Routledge and Kegan Paul, 1974), p. 154, n. 107.
13. *Pilgrimage: An Image of Mediaeval Religion* (London: Faber and Faber, 1975), p. 187.
14. With Helena M. Gamer, *Medieval Handbooks of Penance* (New York: Octagon, 1965). p. 3. For the practice of reading treatises aloud to the laity, see also Pfander, p. 247, and W. A. Pantin, *The English Church in the Fourteenth Century* (Cambridge: Cambridge University Press, 1955), pp. 193–94.
15. Rodney Delasanta, 'The Theme of Judgment in the *Canterbury Tales*," *Modern Language Quarterly*, 31 (1970), pp. 298–307.
16. *Chaucer's Poetry* (New York: Ronald, 1958), p. 948.
17. Lawrence V. Ryan, "The Canon's Yeoman's Desperate Confession," *Chaucer Review*, 8 (1974), pp. 297–310. Also, with reference to Fragment IX, see Roy J. Pearcy. "Does the *Manciple's Prologue* Contain a Reference to Hell's Mouth?" *English Language Notes*, 11 (1974), pp. 167–75.
18. The insight is Bruce A. Rosenberg's in "Swindling Alchemist, Antichrist," *Centennial Review*, 6 (1962), pp. 566–80.

HOPE, DESPAIR, AND FAUSTUS' "MANGLED LIMBS"

René Fortin

The evidence of the final scenes of *Dr. Faustus* in both A and B Texts strongly suggests that Faustus dies in despair and is thus denied the grace that would save him. Though he does see "Christ's blood streaming in the firmament," he is physically unable to reach for it, and his final vision seems to be that of a God of inexorable wrath who, like the Christ of Michelangelo's *Last Judgment*, "stretcheth out his arm and bends his ireful breast."

> My God, my God, look not so fierce on me;
> Adders and serpents, let me breathe a while:
> Ugly hell gape not; come not Lucifer,
> I'll burn my books; ah, Mephostophilis! (V. ii. 191–94)

The last word from Faustus, "Mephistophilis," suggests his inability to invoke the name of Christ who could, despite all, ransom him, and Faustus remains in the clutches of him to whom he had earlier sold himself. The following morning, the horrified scholar reports his dire fate:

> O help us heaven, see, here are Faustus' limbs,
> All torn asunder by the hand of death. (V. iii. 5–6)

The argument that we are to view Faustus as irretrievably damned is indeed strong, particularly since it is corroborated elsewhere in the play. The Old Man, sympathetic to the plight of Faustus, is able, even in Act V, Scene i, to assure Faustus that salvation lies still within his grasp:

> Ah stay good Faustus, stay thy desperate steps.
> I see an Angel hover o'er thy head,
> And with a vial full of precious grace,
> Offers to pour the same into thy soul,
> Then call for mercy, and avoid despair. (V. i. 68–72)

Faustus is clearly moved by the Old Man's plea—"Hell strives with grace for conquest in my breast: / What shall I do to shun the snares of death?"—but he is then deterred by the wrath of Mephistophilis and the Old Man abandons all hope:

> Accursed Faustus, miserable man,
> That from thy soul excluds't the grace of heaven,
> And fliest the throne of his tribunal seat. (V. i. 127–29)

The choral voices of the Scholars and of the Chorus itself (omitted in the A Text) add their judgments: the end of Faustus is such a death, says the Second Scholar, "as every Christian heart laments to think on," while the Chorus uses the "hellish fall" of Faustus to warn the wise against practicing "more than heavenly power permits." The most telling evidence of Faustus' damnation is the response of the Good Angel, who had earlier in the play insisted upon the inexhaustible mercies of God: "Never too late, if Faustus will repent." But even the Good Angel feels compelled to abandon Faustus to Lucifer: "O, thou hast lost celestial happiness, / Pleasures unspeakable, bliss without end."

In the face of this evidence, it would seem that we must inevitably conclude that Faustus is damned; the controversies about the play—and they are there in abundance—have to do rather with the significance of his damnation. But is our absolute certitude about the damnation warranted? I suggest that it may not be, particularly if we take the B Text seriously, for the "mangled limbs" of Faustus described by the Second Scholar in the final scene represent the fulfillment of an image system carefully elaborated throughout the play and offer the possibility that Faustus has indeed escaped from the coils of damnation.

First of all, the precise terms of Faustus' compact with Lucifer must be noted: Faustus cautions Lucifer that he is selling not only his soul but his body as well; he describes the document as a "deed of body and soul" and is careful to specify this condition in the actual pact:

> I John Faustus of Wittenberg, Doctor, by these presents, do give both body and soul to Lucifer, Prince of the East, and his minister Mephistophilis, and furthermore grant unto them...full power to fetch or carry the said John Faustus, body and soul, flesh and blood, into their habitation wheresoever. (II. 1. 105–111)

The terms of the contract are repeated once more several lines later, when Mephistophilis reminds Faustus that "thou hast given thy soul to Lucifer," and Faustus answers, "Ay, and body too. But what of that?" Faustus, who believes that there is no such thing as a physical hell, deprecates the importance of the sale of his body but it should be noted that the play attaches more importance by far to the fate of Faustus' body. Both Lucifer and Mephistophilis are more impressed by their possession of Faustus' body than he is, threatening on various occasions to tear his limbs if he should call upon God:

> If thou repent, devils will tear thee in pieces.
> Revolt, or I'll in piecemeal tear thy limbs. (II. ii. 82–83)

And Faustus himself testifies to the physical agonies awaiting him when he calls upon God.

> ... The devil threatened to tear me in pieces if I named God, to fetch me, body and soul, if I once gave ear to divinity. (V. ii. 72–73)

> Rend not my heart for naming of my Christ!
> Yet will I call upon him. O, spare me, Lucifer! (V. ii. 152–53)

What, then, are we to make of the "mangled limbs" which are left behind after the putative abduction of Faustus? It appears evident that Lucifer does not have, as the original pact proposed, Faustus' body and soul, and it may in fact be that he does not even have his soul, for we recall that the tearing of limbs had been cited as a penalty for calling upon God: "If thou repent, devils will tear thee in pieces."

A closer look at the final scene of the play would appear to be in order; especially significant, I think, is the Third Scholar's description of Faustus' final hour:

> The devils whom Faustus served have torn him thus;
> For 'twixt the hours of twelve and one, methought
> I heard him shriek and call aloud for help,
> At which self time, the house seemed all on fire
> With dreadful horror of these damned fiends. (V. iii. 8–12)

Though the Third Scholar dwells upon the horror of Faustus' infernal visitation and proffers little hope of salvation, his description of Faustus' final moments includes two facts worthy of further consideration: first, the abduction of Faustus occurred, not at twelve—as the original pact proposed—but "'twixt the hours of twelve and one"; secondly, the Scholar reports that he heard Faustus "call aloud for help." It should be noted that, despite the explicit stage direction at the end of Act V, Scene i ("Exeunt with him" in the A Text), Faustus' abduction does not take place on schedule nor without some resistance from Faustus. Because we are not audience to this final moment, the Third Scholar's description of what he has observed (and even he is not present at the scene itself) allows us to speculate that something may have gone awry. The delay in the fulfillment of the bargain intimates that Lucifer may have encountered some unexpected resistance, presumably in the form of Faustus' call for help. The torn limbs observed by the Scholars may then be the result of the fulfillment of Lucifer's threat—"to tear [Faustus] in pieces" if he repents.

A third fact reported by the Scholar, the apparent engulfment of the house of Faustus by the diabolical flames, seems at first sight an indication that Faustus is already suffering his fiery torment. But another possibility emerges when one recalls the invulnerability of the Old Man to similar flames; asked by Faustus to torment the Old Man, Mephistophilis despairs of success:

> His faith is great; I cannot touch his soul.
> But what I may afflict his body with,
> I will attempt, which is but little worth. (V. i. 95–96)

The Old Man is then exposed to hellish fire but remains undaunted:

> Satan begins to sift me with his pride.
> As in this furnace God shall try my faith.
> My faith, vile hell, shall triumph over thee. (V. i. 130–31)

The physical jeopardy of the Old Man, the afflictions of his body, do not endanger his soul. And perhaps neither the mangled limbs of Faustus nor his immersion in the "furnace" of Lucifer have endangered his soul, being only of "little worth." The mercy of God may indeed be as inexhaustible as the Second Scholar suggests: "Yet Faustus, look up to heaven, and remember mercy is infinite."

The apparently irrelevant and misdirected comedy of the play's subplot seems to provide some justification for this re-consideration of Faustus' fate. As several scholars have noted, Marlowe's comic "middle" is not so aimless as it was formerly thought to be: several episodes serve as comic parallels or ironic commentaries on the central plot. Among these, I suggest, is the Horse-Courser episode, which centers upon the violation of a bargain and the victim's desire for retaliation. Faustus sells his horse to the horse-courser, but the horse turns to hay when it is exposed to water. The irate victim of Faustus, seeking retaliation, "pulls off his leg" (s.d. IV. iv. 46) in retaliation. Faustus' delight in yet another prank is obvious:

> Stop him! Stop him! Ha. Ha. Ha. Faustus hath his leg again, and the courser a bundle of hay for his forty dollars.

The episode is not, I think, an instance of "undirected frivolity," but rather a reflection on the larger pact within the play: Faustus' hoodwinking of the horse-courser suggests that he will get the better of the larger pact as well and will be able to frustrate Lucifer in his revenge, the tearing of his limbs.

Faustus' mangled limbs need not, then, be seen as a sign of his damnation: rather they may be seen as an answer to a prayer that, though misdirected, eventually reaches God:

> Now draw up Faustus like a foggy mist
> Into the entrails of yon laboring clouds
> That when they vomit forth into the air,
> *My limbs you issue from your smoky mouths.*
> *So that my soul may but ascend to heaven.* (My emphasis) (V. ii. 162–66)

The prayer seems answered, not by "the stars that reigned at [Faust's] nativity," but by a God whose mercy "droppeth as the gentle rain from heaven."

What is being urged is not that Faustus should be viewed as triumphant—with flights of angels singing him to his rest—but rather that there is enough evidence in the play to warrant our suspending judgment. An argument for suspending judgment on the fate of Faustus must, of course, surmount major obstacles, not the least of which is the textual problem. Even if the argument for Faustus' possible salvation were absolutely persuasive, the fact remains that the surviving "mangled limbs" as well as the last-minute call for help reported by the Third Scholar are present only in the B Text and may thus be regarded as spurious interpolations. And yet, the A Text also highlights, if less insistently, the imagery of torn limbs and Faustus' selling of both soul and body to Lucifer; one may then argue that the B Text completes what exists in the A Text as an inchoate pattern.

A more troubling obstacle is the general view that Marlowe's art is one of bold strokes rather than subtle limning, a view still commonly held though challenged in recent scholarship. The choric scholars, the concluding Chorus, and the Old Man (who is perceptive enough to see the invisible "vial of grace" poised over the head of Faustus) all agree upon the imminent damnation of Faustus. And even more convincingly, the Good Angel, whose angelic identity would seem to make his testimony unimpeachable, accepts Faustus' damnation as a *fait accompli*. Is it at all plausible that Marlowe intends these as unreliable mediators, as characters limited in their knowledge and therefore unaware of the real fate of the hero?

A backward glance at a major play in the morality tradition, *The Castell of Perseverance*, reveals that such a dramatic strategy is not entirely without precedent, for the hero of the play, Mankind, faces his death impenitently and, *after* his death, is deserted by his Good Angel:

> Yea, alas, and welawoe!
> Against covetousness can I not tell.
> Reason while I from thee go,
> For, wretched soul, thou must to hell!

The Good Angel then departs, and Mankind is dragged off to Hell by the Bad Angel—but only to be saved by the intercession of Mercy, a mercy beyond even the capacity of the Good Angel to predict. The mercy of God extends even beyond death.

What I am proposing is that Marlowe has not entirely discounted the possibility of some ultimate saving stroke of God and that he has surrounded the death of Faustus with ambiguity in order to give dramatic form to the theological anxieties of the time. Schooled in the Calvinistic ambiance of Cambridge University, Marlowe was familiar with the God of the Reformers, the voluntaristic "Hidden God" whose plans and purposes are utterly beyond the ken of men and of angels. As Paul Sellin has argued, the dramatization of this concept of God required that the audience itself be submitted to this awesome mystery:

> ... In shaping his drama, what Marlowe seems to have assumed was an audience prepared to yield to the notion of an indecipherable Providence whose processes are hidden both to the onlooker and to the protagonists on whom they work.

What adds plausibility to this conjecture is that the play itself focusses—as in Faustus' attempts to delve into the divine mysteries contained in Scripture—on the hubris of presuming to know the hidden secrets of God; the intimations—and they, once again, are no more than that—of salvation in Faustus' final and private moments are an attempt to re-assert the mystery of God's judgments, a warning to the "forward wits" in the audience that they should not ""practice more than heavenly power permits." We are asked rather to submit to the eschatological mystery. As Judith Weil has observed.

> ... How can the audience feel confident of its capacity for understanding, when the play itself dramatizes the vanity of all reason not informed by wisdom and grace? ... [Marlowe] has checked our forward wits, reminding us of our blindness and leaving us in a fallen world of shadows.

LAUNCELOT AND THE USES OF ALLEGORY IN *THE MERCHANT OF VENICE*

René Fortin

Few critics now harbor any doubts about the structural sophistication of *The Merchant of Venice*. Despite its relative earliness in the canon, this drama nevertheless gives every indication of Shakespeare's incomparable ability to fuse disparate elements into an aesthetic whole and to wring ethical significance from the common properties of Elizabethan drama. The one apparently wasted motion is Launcelot Gobbo, who is most often overlooked as an awkward irrelevance or written off as a low-grade apprentice clown who has not yet realized the dramatic potential of his role.

I think, however, that Launcelot deserves a better press, for a closer look at his foolery suggests that he is very much involved in the play's central issues and that in fact, he adds much to its meaning. Specifically, he seems intended to provide an allegorical counter-statement to the major allegorical statement of the play, thereby offering a corrective to the one-sidedness and reductiveness of interpretation that the naive allegory invites.

However diverse the interpretation of *The Merchant of Venice* may be, there seems to be general agreement that the play communicates its meaning through allegory and that this meaning is centrally concerned with the tensions, theological and sociological, between Judaism and Christianity.[1] On the most naive level, the allegory contrasts the vindictiveness of Shylock, representing the Old Testament Law of Justice, with the tender mercy of the Christians, representing the New Testament Law of Love. Accordingly, in the defeat of Shylock in the trial scene, we are invited to relish the absolute vindication of the Christian way:

> The trial scene climaxes the action at all the levels of meaning that have been established. As has been suggested, it portrays at the moral level Shylock's degradation to a cur and a monster through his commitment to revenge, and by contrast, Antonio's attainment of the fullness of Christian love through his abjuration of revenge. Allegorically, the scene develops the sharpest opposition of Old Law and New in terms of their respective theological principles, Justice and Mercy, Righteousness and Faith; it culminates in the final defeat of the Old Law and the symbolic conversion of the Jew.[2]

Such a reading is firmly grounded in the facts of the play and is therefore quite compelling. But there nevertheless remain ironic overtones throughout the play, especially detectible in the persistent intolerance—despite their ethical principles—of the Christians toward Shylock. One cannot but be disturbed by the callous exultation of the minor characters over the misfortunes of Shylock or by the overt contempt of Antonio, who would indeed spit upon Shylock's "Jewish gaberdine" (I. iii. 108).[3] And even the most chauvinistic Christian sensibility cannot shrug off the truth of Shylock's assertion that he has learned his lesson of revenge from Christians. Thus the allegorical interpreter is compelled to acknowledge the existence of "thematic counterpoints" that cut across the grain of the naive allegory and to view the play as one that "does not present arbitrary, black-and-white moral estimates of human groups, but takes into account the shadings and complexities of the real world."[4]

So insistent, in fact, are the ironies of the play that the very integrity of the allegory is jeopardized. Burckhardt, for example, by rigorously studying only those patterns of plot and imagery intrinsic to the play, virtually inverts the thesis that the play celebrates the triumph of Love over Law; for him the true meaning of the play resides in the image of circularity which vindicates the concept of the bond: "Portia, won through the bond, wins Antonio's release from it; what is more, she wins it, not by breaking the bond, but by submitting to its rigor more rigorously than even the Jew had thought to do.... [The play] asks how the vicious circle of the bond's law can be transformed into the ring of love. And it answers: through a literal and unreserved submission to the bond as absolutely binding."[5]

Thus Burckhardt, ignoring the biblical allusions that constitute meaning for Lewalski, emerges from his involvement with the play's intrinsic structures with a quite different meaning, a meaning which qualifies severely the Christian reading of the play.[6]

Both readings of the play have much to recommend them, but I suggest that the meaning of *The Merchant of Venice* is product of a subtle synthesis of the two interpretations, a synthesis which does full justice to the biblical analogues discerned by Lewalski and the irony-laden patterns explored by Burckhardt. The key to this synthesis is, remarkably, Launcelot the Clown.

Launcelot first appears, in what seems to be a comic version of the central bond motif, in a moment of "spiritual crisis," being tormented by the decision whether to dissolve the master-servant "bond" with Shylock or risk damnation by continuing to serve the "devil" (II. ii). It is obvious that in his reasoning he adopts the attitudes of the medieval morality play (he is fittingly given a name with glittering medieval connotations) which identify the Jew with the devil, thus clearly betraying his unabashed and simple-minded contempt for Judaism.[7] In a similar vein, he later taunts Jessica about her probable damnation for being the daughter of a Jew (III. v. 1–16) and also expresses fear that the conversion of the Jews would raise the price of pork (III. v. 19–23). His moral crudity, in effect, caricatures the more genteel and discreet insensitivity of other Christians, who voice somewhat similar opinions throughout; as Barber has stated, "The solidarity of the Venetians includes the clown, in whose part Shakespeare can use conventional blacks and whites about Jews and misers without asking us to take them too seriously."[8] Lorenzo seems, however unwittingly, to have hit upon the truth that Launcelot is only slightly more a fool than the other supposedly sophisticated Christians:

> The fool hath planted in his memory
> An army of good words; and I do know
> A many fools that stand in better place,
> Garnished like him, that for a tricksy word
> Defy the matter. (III. v. 59–63)

In this role, Launcelot is delightful, useful, but not really necessary, since he is essentially restating what a reasonably perceptive and unbiased reader could conclude for himself, the discrepancy between Christian theory and practice. In Portia's words, "If to do were as easy as to know what were good to do, chapels had been churches, and poor men's cottages princes' palaces. It is a good divine that follows his own instructions...." (I. ii. 12–15). His crucial scene in the play is, rather, his encounter with his father, a scene which offers an oblique commentary on the tensions between the Judaic and Christian traditions.

This father-son encounter must be seen in the larger context of other father-child relationships, involving Portia, Bassanio, and Jessica as well as Launcelot. Each of these relationships offers a different version of the father-child relationship and serves to highlight the theme of filial piety which emerges as a central concern.

Portia's father, though physically absent, plays a thematically vital role in exemplifying the father who rules through Law. For the casket lottery which he has devised as a condition for the marriage of Portia demands her unquestioning obedience. It is clear that Portia would prefer things otherwise, that she would prefer to be given the freedom of choosing her mate on the basis of love; her references to the lottery, which she enjoys certainly far less than the audience, are tinged with, at best, an impatience at the arbitrariness of the test:

> O me, the word "choose"! I may neither choose who I would nor refuse who I dislike, so is the will of a living daughter curbed by the will of a dead father. Is it not hard, Nerissa. that I cannot choose one, nor refuse none? (I. ii. 21–25)

> Besides, the lott'ry of my destiny
> Bars me the right of voluntary choosing.
> But if my father had not scanted me,
> And hedged me by his wit to yield myself
> His wife, who wins me.... (II. i. 15–19)

One effect of the casket lottery is to blur the differences between Venice and Belmont. Though we are increasingly tempted as the play progresses to associate love and spiritual freedom with Belmont, we are here reminded that Belmont, like Venice, has its own stringent laws; as Burckhardt has correctly stated, "the rule which governs Belmont—the covenant of the caskets—seems even more rigidly positive than that of Venice. More rigidly even than the law of the bond, it puts obedience above meaning, the letter above the spirit."[9]

Nerissa, of course, reassures Portia of her father's good intentions, pointing out that her father was reputed to be a holy man and that the test could very well be the product of "good inspirations" granted to her father at the moment of death (I. ii. 26–27). But Portia needs no reassurance; despite her impatience, she is utterly obedient: "If I live to be as old as Sibylla, I will die as chaste as Diana unless I be obtained by the manner of my father's will" (I. ii. 98–100).

There is no question that the casket scene depicts an exemplary father-child relationship, but one that dwells primarily upon the legal aspect of the ideal relationship; the other aspect of the filial piety is revealed in the Antonio-Bassanio relationship. Though the relationship between the two is literally one of friendship, the discrepancy in age between the two invites us to fit this relationship into the pattern of father-child relationships and to view Antonio as Bassanio's protector and father-surrogate; it is a relationship reminiscent of that in *Twelfth Night* between Sebastian and Antonio's namesake.[10] Therefore, despite his love for Bassanio, Antonio seeks nothing but Bassanio's happiness and is eager to help him in his courting of Portia. Bassanio himself offers the best clue to this relationship in identifying himself as a "prodigal" son (I. i. 129); in contrast to the "legal" relationship existing between Portia and her father, this is one of love, with Antonio as the quintessential generous and forgiving father ready to sacrifice himself for the welfare of his son. Bassanio, by the same token, expresses his own filial piety by rushing to the support of Antonio in his peril, even when he is absolved by Antonio of any obligation, any bond:

> But life itself, my wife and all the world
> Are not with me esteemed above thy life.

> I would lose all, ay sacrifice them all
> Here to this devil, to deliver you. (IV. i. 282–285)

It is in the context of these exemplary father-child relationships, one based primarily on Law and the other based primarily on Love, that the Jessica-Shylock relationship is located. This relationship can be described only as a monstrous inversion of filial piety, a relationship lacking utterly in both Law and Love. Jessica, admitting to the "legal" bond, the bond of blood, states that she is ashamed of her father:

> Alack, what heinous sin is it in me
> To be ashamed to be my father's child.
> But though I am a daughter to his blood,
> I am not to his manners. (II. iii. 16–19)

She then severs all bonds with Shylock, sharing, in fact, in the Gentiles' identification of her father as a devil (II. iii. 2) and feeling no compunction whatever in her thievery of his fortune. Nor does she, while rejoicing in her own conversion, express any hope that her father will be similarly converted. She seems to have taken his damnation for granted. There is probably no more telling sign of her disregard for filial piety than her exchange of Shylock's ring, given to him by his wife Leah, for a monkey: "It was my turquoise; I had it of Leah when I was a bachelor. I would not have given it for a wilderness of monkeys" (III. i. 106–108).

Shylock, superficially at least, seems similarly lacking in paternal love; no thought of his daughter's elopement is ever unaccompanied by somber thoughts about the fortune she has taken with her, both ducats and daughter apparently occupying the same level in his hierarchy of values:

> *Solanio.* I never heard a passion so confused,
> So strange, outrageous, and so variable
> As the dog Jew did utter in the streets:
> "My daughter! O my ducats! O my daughter!
> Fled with a Christian! O my Christian ducats!" (II. viii. 12–16)

However, it is possible, as others have done, to attach some importance to the "confused passion" of Shylock and to detect beneath his bitter denunciations of Jessica genuine suffering over her betrayal of him.[11] I find personally moving, in fact, his concern over the loss of Leah's ring, which he seems to treasure for sentimental reasons, as a memento of happier days of love and domestic warmth.[12] But this suggestion of personal depth in Shylock is elsewhere overwhelmed by his vehemence, and the complex human being recedes again into the stereotype: "I would my daughter were dead at my foot, and the jewels in her ear! Would she were hearsed at my foot, and the ducats in her coffin!" (III. i. 77–79). The Jessica-Shylock relationship seems predominantly a complete inversion of filial piety, a relationship neither based on law nor leavened by love.

What then, in view of Jessica's ironic relationship to one of the major themes of the play, are we to make of the "allegorical" Jessica? It is my belief that Jessica transcends her realistic limitations and does serve to shadow forth the relationship between Jewish and Christian traditions; it is not inconsistent to see her invitation to Belmont as an invitation to participate in a "higher truth"; I would, in short, agree that "As Shylock's daughter and as a voluntary convert to Christianity, Jessica may figure forth the filial piety relationship of the New Dispensation to the Old."[13] Admittedly, to see her in this way poses a grave problem because of the apparent discontinuity between the "real" Jessica and the allegorical Jessica, but the problem is not unresolvable if we understand that we have here, not an irreparable split between literal and allegorical levels, but rather an elaborate structure in which a naive allegory is subtly complemented and corrected by a sophisticated allegory.

This correction is provided by Launcelot in his encounter with Old Gobbo. The encounter takes place immediately after Launcelot's decision to leave the service of his Jewish master and seek service with the Christian Bassanio. Launcelot is interrupted by the arrival of his father carrying a "dish of doves" (II. ii. 124) and looking for his son. In what seems initially to be a mere comic interlude, Launcelot decides to taunt his father: "O heavens, this is my true-begotten father who, being more than sand-blind, high-gravel blind, knows me not. I will try confusions with him" (II. ii. 31–33). After some not quite harmless mischief—Launcelot leads Gobbo to believe that his son is dead—Launcelot finally identifies himself:

> *Laun.* Do you not know me, father?
> *Gobbo.* Alack, sir, I am sand-blind! I know you not.
> *Laun.* Nay, indeed if you had your eyes you might fail of the knowing me; it is a wise father that knows his own child. Well, old man, I will tell you news of your son. [Kneels] Give me your blessing....
> Pray you let's have no more fooling about it, but give me your blessing. I am Launcelot—your boy that was, your son that is, your child that shall be.
> *Gobbo.* I'll be sworn, if thou be Launcelot thou art mine own flesh and blood. Lord worshipped might he be, what a beard hast thou got!
> (II. ii. 67–87)

This seems to be little more than pointless folly, but the scene would have important reverberations for a viewer conversant with the Bible; the Launcelot-Gobbo encounter closely parallels the Isaac-Jacob incident in Genesis 27.[14] In this famous biblical narrative, Jacob dupes the blind Isaac into blessing him, rather than the first-born Esau, by simulating with the skins of kids the hairy body of Esau. Isaac, touching the hairy hands of Jacob, extends the blessing that grants him and his race primacy over Esau and his progeny; Isaac then eats a ritual meal offered to him by Jacob in order to solemnize the blessing.

The recognition scene contains many of the elements of the narrative, including the blessing requested by Launcelot of Old Gobbo, the dish of doves carried by Gobbo, which recalls the ritual meal of Isaac[15]; Gobbo's fascination with the beard of Launcelot, which recalls the device of the hair; and, most conspicuously, the blindness of the father which prevents him from knowing his own child. The scene, moreover, is prepared for by Shylock's several references to Jacob (see esp. I. iii. 67–84), and by Shylock's reference to Rebecca, who devised Jacob's deception, in the "wise mother who wrought in his [Jacob's] behalf" (I. ii. 69).

That this richly allusive scene occurs in a play focusing upon Jewish-Christian relations and occurs, moreover, at the precise moment when Launcelot has decided to change from a Jewish to a Christian master underscores the need to explore carefully its implications. The scripturally-sophisticated viewer would be aware, for example, of St. Paul's commentaries on the narrative, which he considered prefigurative; Paul sees the twin "elections" in successive generations—of Isaac over Ishmael and of Jacob over Esau—as allegories of God's secret election of the Gentiles as his new "children of the promise." In his Epistle to the Romans, in which he grieves over the rejection of the Jews, Paul writes that

> All they are not Israel, which are of Israel:
>
> Neither are thei all children, because thei are the sede of Abraham: but, In Isaac [Geneva gloss: "That is, of Jacob whose name was also Israel"] shal thy sede be called:
>
> That is, they which are the children of the flesh, are not the children of God: but the children of the promes are counted for the sede.
>
> For this is a word of promes, In this same time wil I come, and Sara shal have a sonne.
>
> Nether he onlie felt this, but also Rebecca when she had conceived by one, even by our father Isaac.
>
> For yet the children were borne, & when they had neither done good, nor evil (that the purpose of God might remaine according to election not by workes, but by him that calleth)
>
> It was said unto her, The elder shal serve the younger.
>
> As it is written, I have loved Jacob, & have hated Esau. (9: 6–13)[16]

Thus what is symbolically re-enacted here is an allegory of the transferral of divine favor from the Jewish to the Christian Dispensation; but it is an allegory that unsparingly exposes the ironies of the situation. Just as the biblical narrative is itself steeped in irony (since Jacob's blessing is obtained by guile),[17] its counterpart in *The Merchant of Venice* releases ironic suggestions calculated to daunt the most zealous allegorist.

There is a strong emphasis to begin with on the bond of filial piety, for Old Gobbo's suit to Bassanio on behalf of Launcelot adumbrates the fact that the preferment of the Christian Dispensation was made possible by the centuries of integrity of the older faith. More obviously, the scene insists upon the mutual blindness of father and son, the *involuntary* blindness of Gobbo—and by extension, of the Jewish tradition—and the *willed* blindness of Launcelot—and by extension of the Christian tradition, which chooses to ignore its indebtedness to the older tradition from which it derives its richness. The shallow Lorenzo again utters a thought, profoundly true beyond his knowing, when he flippantly states: "Here dwells my father Jew" (II. iv. 25). Despite their father-son relationship, both traditions, in their mutual blindness, overlook the bond between them. Launcelot has stated it tersely: "It is a wise father that knows his own child"; and one might add, "It is a wise child who acknowledges his own father," who accepts the fact that, again in Launcelot's words, he is "your boy that was, your son that is, your child that shall be" (II. ii. 78–79). The point finally made by this allegorical expression of father-son relationships is that we are not to choose between Jewish Law and Christian Love, as most critics of the play suggest, but to recognize that an indissoluble bond of filial piety exists between the two traditions, a bond that should engender a mutual respect.

The traditional case for this shared heritage is put most strongly by St. Paul, a convert from Judaism: the same Epistle to the Romans which speaks of the passing of Divine favor from Jew to Christian nevertheless warns the Christians that the Jews remain mysteriously the Chosen People of God and that they will eventually be returned to a place of favor. Paul likens the Christian faith to a branch grafted to an olive tree and reminds Christians to be mindful of their origins:

> And though some of the branches be broken of, and thou being a wild olive tre, wast grafte in for them, and made partaker of the roote and the fatness of the olive tre. / Boast not thyself against the branches; and if thy boast thyself, thou bearest not the roote, but the roote thee. (Romans 11:17, 18)

> For I wold not, brethren, that ye sholde be ignorant of the secret (lest ye should be arrogant in yourselves) that partely obstinacie is come to

> Israel; until the fulness of the Gentiles be come in. / And so all Israel shal be saved, as it is written, the Deliverer shall come out of Sion, and shal turne away the ungodliness from Jacob. And this is my covenant to them, when I shal take away their sinnes. / As concerning the Gospel, they are enemies for your sakes; but as touching the election, they are beloved for the fathers sake. (Romans 11:25–28)

Launcelot's primary function in the play, then, is to focus our attention upon the theme of filial piety; in so doing he exposes the limitations of a naive allegory that would force upon the viewer an "either-or" choice when a "both-and" is in order. It is important to note that he, in a sense, duplicates the allegorical function of Jessica who, as we have seen, figures forth the relationship of the New Dispensation to the Old. But Launcelot's scene, though concerned with the same event, is actually in counterpoint to Jessica's naive allegory, for his allegory stresses the complexity of the relationships; it exposes, through the blindness motif especially, the *failure* of filial piety between Christian and Jew and compels us to recognize the distance between the idea shadowed forth in the naive allegory—the Higher Truth of Christianity—and the imperfect realization of that Idea in the commerce of everyday life, where, as Matthew points out, "one iote, or one title of the Law shal not scape, til all things be fulfilled" (Matt. 5:17, 18). We are reminded that Christianity, though a fulfillment of the Old Law, remains itself to be perfectly fulfilled. And until "all things be fulfilled," it must continue to respectfully observe the Law and not flout it as Jessica does.

The enigmatic fifth act confirms this view. Its central theme, which sheds a retrospective light on the entire play, seems to consist of a distinction between the absoluteness of the Heavenly Idea and the relativity of earthly experience.[18] The scene begins with Lorenzo and Jessica cataloguing the imperfection of earthly realities: the references to Cressida, Thisbe, Dido, and Medea are various reminders of the vicissitudes of human love; and the theme of imperfection persists in Lorenzo's taunting of Jessica about her theft from her father and Jessica's imputation of insincerity in Lorenzo's love. The dialogue is interrupted by the arrival of Portia, at which point Lorenzo, in more overt terms, refers to the disparity between the Heavenly Idea and earthly reality:

Sit Jessica. Look how the floor of heaven
Is thick inlaid with patens of bright gold.
There's not the smallest orb which thou behold'st
But in his motion like an angel sings,
Still quiring to the young-eyed cherubins;
Such harmony is in immortal souls,
But whilst this muddy vesture of decay
Doth grossly close it in, we cannot hear it. (V. i. 58–65)

But, though none can hear it, the existence of the music of the spheres, this absolute harmony, is attested to by the power of earthly music over men and even animals, whose "savage eyes [are] turned to a modest gaze, / By the sweet power of music" (V. i. 78–79). The Platonic imagery is sustained by Portia, who alludes to the other dominant image in Plato, light:

That light we see is burning in my hall;
How far that little candle throws his beams!
So shines a good deed in a naughty world. (V. i. 89–91)

Portia, in my opinion, refers to no specific good deed, but rather to the nature of human experience in general, which participates on a lower level of being in perfections fully existent only in a higher order of being. The implication seems to be that perfection is not to be hoped for in this world, and that only relative goodness can be expected:

So doth the greater glory dim the less.
A substitute shines brightly as a king
Until a king be by.... (V. i. 93–95)[19]

But the lone earthly candle which lights up this naughty world is nonetheless a true image of heavenly light, though it is not to be confused with that greater glory.

The relevance of this apparent lyric interlude to the major themes of the play becomes evident: Belmont is indeed, as the allegorists would have it, an image of the "higher truth" of Christianity and not, as Burckhardt argues, a locale where "scapegrace lovers have an unearned, nocturnal grace which transcends all that is earned and useful."[20] The imagery of Act V, in fact, seems to be derived from the Gospel of Matthew, which likens the New Law to a city on a hill and to a candle shining its light before men: "Ye are the light of the worlde. A citie that is set on a hill, can not be hid. / Neither do men light a candel, and put it under a bushel, but on a candlesticke, and it giveth light unto all that are in the house. / Let your light so shine before men, that they may se your good workes, and glorifie your Father which is in Heaven" (5:14–16).

The affirmation survives the ironies of the play, just as the above passage from Matthew, which focuses on the glory of Christianity, retains its force despite the passage which immediately follows it: "Thinke not that I am come to destroye the Law, or the Prophetes. I am not come to destroye them, but to fulfill them. For truely I say unto you, Til heaven, and earth perish, one iote, or one title of the Law shal not scape, til all things be fulfilled" (Matt. 5:17, 18).

Despite the new order introduced by Christianity, the Law survives. This co-existence of Love and Law seems to be the burden of the ring motif as well, for the ring is given as a bond of love entailing "legal" obligations; the ring is a reconciling symbol suggesting that Love, i.e., spiritual freedom, and Law, i.e., moral responsibility, must co-exist in human relationships.[21]

Thus the conclusions to which we are guided by Lancelot in his symbolic role are reiterated and developed in the fifth act; through the complex allegory which insists upon the co-existence of values, *The Merchant of Venice* suggests that, despite the truth contained in its naive allegory of love, man can expect only relative perfection in a world far too complex for naive allegory to be given full credit.

NOTES TO Launcelot and the Uses of Allegory in *The Merchant of Venice*

1. See J. R. Brown's brief survey of several allegorical approaches in J. R. Brown ed., The Arden Edition of *The Merchant of Venice* (New York, 1964), pp. 1-liii; see also the important study by Barbara K. Lewalski, "Biblical Allusion and Allegory in *The Merchant of Venice*," *Shakespeare Quarterly*, 13 (1962), pp. 327–343. The continuing popularity of the allegorical approach is attested to by Alan Holaday's recent study, "Antonio and the Allegory of Salvation," *Shakespeare Studies*, 4 (1968), pp. 109–118.
2. Lewalski, p. 338.
3. All references to the play will be to Brents Stirling, ed., *The Merchant of Venice*, in *The Complete Pelican Shakespeare*, gen. ed. Alfred Harbage (Baltimore, 1969).
4. Lewalski, p. 334.
5. Sigurd Burckhardt, "The Merchant of Venice: The Gentle Bond," *Shakespearean Meanings* (Princeton, 1968), p. 210; the article first appeared in *ELH*, 29 (1962).
6. I shall use the term "allegory" throughout this paper to mean generally an image or series of images referring figuratively to a doctrine or thesis. It is beyond the scope of this paper to elaborate a concept of Shakespearean symbolism that would, for example, effectively distinguish "allegory" from "symbol," but a further refinement in our critical language is much needed.
7. Lewalski, p. 335. I do not recall any attempt to account for the name "Gobbo"; the New Variorum editors, p. 62, find "Gobbo" spelled "Iobbe" and even "Job" in several early texts but dismiss the variant as "apparently one of those wild and inexplicable freaks...."—*New Variorum Merchant of Venice*, ed. H. H. Furness (Philadelphia, 1916), p. 62. But Launeclot's Jewish surname would probably be suggestive in this context, hinting at the unrecognized wedding of the two traditions. I am not insisting on this point, however.
8. C. L. Barber, *Shakespeare's Festive Comedy* (Cleveland and New York, 1963), p. 173.
9. Burckhardt, p. 215.
10. See Graham Midgley, "*The Merchant of Venice*: A Reconsideration," *Essays in Criticism*, 10 (1960), pp. 119–133; Midgley finds a discreet homosexual attraction between Antonio and Bassanio. E. M. W. Tillyard considers and rejects this theory in *Shakespeare's Early Comedies* (New York, 1965), pp. 197–200. Critics have also been uncomfortable with the Antonio-Sebastian relationship in *Twelfth Night*, but it seems even clearer to me here that Antonio should be understood as something of a "spiritual father" to Sebastian.
11. A tradition of sympathy for Shylock existed, of course, throughout the nineteenth century; see the *New Variorum*, pp. 427–435. For a more recent study in the spirit of this tradition, see Harold Goddard, *The Meaning of Shakespeare* (Chicago, 1962), I, pp. 92–101.
12. Tillyard comments sensitively on this scene, p. 192: "Shylock's house was a hell of gloom, puritanical and museless; and his Jessica is justified in leaving it in favour of light and the prospects of a Christian heaven. But in the background there is the synagogue and the antique world of the Old Testament; and I think we are justified in thinking that Shylock's reference to his wife and her ring is meant to denote a kind of ordered domestic life in past days. And as to his daughter, at least he was vulnerably dependent on her and perhaps loved her in his harsh way."
13. Lewalski, p. 334.

14. Cf. Dorothy C. Hockey, "The Patch Is Kind Enough," *Shakespeare Quarterly*, 10 (1959), pp. 448–450; after perceptively pointing out the parallels, the author then denies them any real thematic relevance beyond suggesting Shakespeare's comic view of Shylock.
15. The doves also recall the doves or pigeons offered as sacrifice in the Presentation of Jesus (Luke 2:22–24); the passage lays stress upon this ritual as being according to the Law of Moses and highlights the fact that Jesus was himself observant of the Law.
16. All biblical references are to The Geneva Bible (1560), facsimile edition (Madison, 1969). See also Galatians 4:24, where Paul sees Sara (mother of Isaac) and Hagar (Mother of Ishmael) as allegorical foreshadowings respectively of the New and Old Testaments: "By the which things another thing is ment: for the mothers are the two Testaments...."
17. Both Hosea (12:4) and Jeremiah (9:3, 4) express disapproval of Jacob's actions, however much they serve God's plan.
18. For similar views, see Burckhardt, pp. 226–227; Tillyard, p. 202; and Holaday, pp. 115–117.
19. It is tempting to read Act V as containing a Shakespearean theory of symbolism; not only is the system of correspondences affirmed, but also we are reminded of the latent irony in symbolism because the symbol is an imperfect image, a "substitute" for the higher reality.
20. Burckhardt, p. 227.
21. See Burckhardt's view that "the ring is the bond transformed, the gentle bond" (p. 234), a view that parallels mine.

JULIUS CAESAR: AN EXPERIMENT IN POINT OF VIEW

René Fortin

Recent studies of *Julius Caesar* reveal a significant trend in Shakespearean criticism; for better or for worse, critics have become increasingly tentative in their interpretations. Where in the past they plunged confidently into a play to pluck out the heart of its mystery, they are now inclined to submit reverently to the complexity of Shakespeare's vision and accept as an integral part of the meaning a dilemma which must not be violated. Perhaps some of the color of Shakespearean criticism has been lost; it was comforting for the neophyte to discover one critic arguing vehemently that *Julius Caesar* was intended as a bitter denunciation of the tyrant Caesar, while another critic would insist with equal vigor and certitude that the play was intended as an exposé of Brutus and a resounding affirmation, therefore, of the monarchical principle.[1] But if recent interpretations lack the flair and gusto of earlier criticism, they have gained, in my opinion, in accuracy.

The focal point of recent studies of *Julius Caesar* has been the very ambivalence of a play which has allowed for such contradictory responses. Bonjour, noting the confusion of good and evil which marks every character in the play, has concluded, for example, that the play is intended to reveal "the value of suspended judgment."[2] Traversi has also recognized the fundamental equivocality of the play; he finds that Caesar is cast as an ambivalent figure, but this

> is balanced by a similar ambivalence in the conspirators who oppose him. Their fear of Caesar is shown to be in part, though only in part, justified. But equally, once the object of their hostility has been removed by their own action, they collapse disastrously into rivalry and

> self-annihilation. The play, in fact, concentrates rather on the deed and the behavior of those concerned in it than upon the abstract political principles involved?[3]

It is indeed this complexity of human experience, the confusion of good and evil that one encounters in every sphere of human endeavor, that the play seeks to dramatize. To understand this much places one closer to the meaning of the play. And yet there lingers the suspicion that Shakespeare's intention is more than the dramatization of what is virtually a commonplace: if this is Shakespeare's point, why is it so subtly presented as to allow for such a diversity of interpretation? Thus, another critic has probed the enigmatic characterization of Caesar as the key to the play. Noting that Caesar as a character refuses to take on a definite outline, assuming a different identity according to who is evaluating him, he concludes:

> It is a dramatic treatment of Caesar in the manner of Pirandello. "Which of all these is the real Caesar?" Shakespeare seems to ask. And he takes care not to provide an answer. But does not Shakespeare further anticipate Pirandello by making us feel that perhaps there is no real Caesar, that he merely exists as a set of images in other men's minds and his own?[4]

Schanzer goes on to interpret the kaleidoscopic characterization as a dramatic strategy intrinsic to the problem play: Caesar is kept ambiguous to preserve the moral dilemma with which the play is concerned. The insight is quite perceptive; but it is my suspicion that if *Julius Caesar* assumes the form of a problem play, it does so for a specific purpose.

This specific purpose reveals itself if one considers *Julius Caesar* as a deliberate experiment in point of view, intended to reveal the limitations of human knowledge. Specifically, the play is a dramatization of the impact of point of view upon one's perception of truth: truth, the play suggests, is at least partially subjective, modified by the perspective from which one looks at it. Accordingly, Shakespeare directs us to look upon the spectacle before us as a colossal monument of human fallibility; the two "mighty opposites," Caesar and Brutus, play their part in history enveloped by the mists of error, victims of deception and self-deception. Not only are they incapable of interpreting accurately their outer experience; they are incapable of fathoming their inner experience, of knowing themselves.

In accordance with this epistemological focus, the structure of the play may best be understood as consisting of a series of subject-object relationships, with Caesar at the center of the play as the primary object of knowledge. And, as Schanzer has so provocatively suggested, this Caesar evokes a number of different reactions: to Cassius he is the tyrant who is even now suppressing the liberty of the people; to Brutus he is the friend and ruler who may eventually become a tyrant; to Casca he is the master-politician, the play-actor manipulating the emotions of the people; to Antony he is the noble, compassionate, generous ruler with the best interests of the people at heart; to Caesar himself he is of such Spartan virtues that he rises above ordinary human frailties; and finally, to the audience as he reveals himself immediately before the assassination, he seems to be a proud, intransigent ruler, susceptible to flattery and eminently capable of becoming the tyrant described by Cassius.[5]

This, then, is the object in a series of epistemological relationships. The principal subject, evidently, is Brutus; it is above all the personality of Brutus that Shakespeare explores. Recent commentaries almost universally agree upon his ambivalence; despite his apparently noble image—an image which he himself has done much to project—he seems to be impeached by irony because of his role in the assassination. In his own estimation he has committed an honorable act in the killing of Caesar who, because of his ambitions for the crown, posed a threat to the liberty of the Roman people; Brutus insists that what he is doing is "for the general" (II. i. 12) and harbors no doubt about "the even virtue of our enterprise" (II. i. 133).[6]

We as spectators, however, cannot forget that we have been given another version of him which is inconsistent with Brutus' own version; Cassius has intimated after their first encounter that Brutus is not entirely beyond reproach:

> Well, Brutus, thou art noble; yet I see
> Thy honourable mettle may be wrought

> From that it is dispos'd: therefore 'tis meet
> That noble minds keep ever with their likes;
> For who so firm that cannot be seduc'd?
> Caesar doth bear me hard; but he loves Brutus.
> If I were Brutus now, and he were Cassius,
> He should not humour me. (I. ii. 305–12)

Cassius, it is evident, believes that Brutus is essentially an honorable man but that there is a flaw in him that disposes him to be seduced. Brutus himself has admitted that he has been bothered "of late with passions of some difference / Conceptions only proper to myself" (I. ii. 39–40), and it is these conceptions that Cassius exploits to win Brutus over to his cause. We are not told precisely what it is that Cassius has found within Brutus, but he obviously appeals to Brutus' patrician pride: "There was a Brutus once," taunts Cassius, "that would have brook'd / Th' eternal devil to keep his state in Rome / As easily as a king" (I. ii. 157–59). And significantly, Brutus' reaction to the mysterious note urging him to "Awake, and see thyself" (II. i. 46) is to recall his ancestors who "did from the streets of Rome / The Tarquin drive, when he was call'd a king" (II. i. 53–54). An objective viewer of the play cannot fail to perceive, despite the play's reticence, that Brutus is motivated to a considerable extent by pride, a pride which he himself fails to recognize.

And these ironies cling to Brutus throughout the play. Even at the very end of the play, an ironic conception of the hero vies for acceptance with the more popular conception of Brutus as the heroic assassin. Both Octavius and Antony, it is true, look upon the dying Brutus with an emotion approaching solemn awe (V. v. 68–81),[7] but we cannot allay our suspicions even now that Brutus' "apt thoughts" (V. iii. 68) have blinded his reason and led him to misconstrue his own motives and actions. His self-deception persists throughout the play, for despite all of the indications to the contrary (his troubled sleeplessness, the surrender of his cause to expediency and the "itching palm" of Cassius, the succession of Caesar by unworthy triumvirs) he still feels himself vindicated: "Judge me, you gods; wrong I mine enemies? / And if not so, how should I wrong a brother?" (IV. ii. 38–39). Similarly, he continues to esteem Cassius, who has revealed to the audience his private grievances against Caesar, as "the last of the Romans" (V. iii. 99). Finally, when he is dying, Brutus is still able to boast: "My heart doth joy that yet in all my life / I found no man but he was true to me" (V. v. 34–35). If we have been attentive to the irony of his situation, we must conclude that Brutus dies with all of his illusions intact, unable or unwilling to recognize the horror of the action in which he has taken part. As Dorsch has suggested, "A man who committed Brutus's crime could not be portrayed as a wholly sympathetic character; but Shakespeare shows him as blind, not evil. And finally he buries Brutus's crime in his virtues, and ends the play with Antony's tribute...."[8]

This equivocal portrayal of Brutus has been sufficiently developed in several recent studies, and it is not my intention to rehearse the commonplaces of criticism. But it would be useful to examine in greater depth Brutus' epistemological situation, the roots of the deception and self-deception in which he is involved. For it is through Brutus especially that Shakespeare dramatizes the complexity of the act of knowing. The play suggests that because the act of knowing requires a subject-object relationship, man, unable to be present to himself wholly as object, cannot truly know himself. It is Brutus himself who is the source of this epistemological principle: "the eye sees not itself / But by reflection, by some other things" (I. ii. 51–52). The problem of Brutus, that is, is precisely that which Coleridge singled out as a principle of Shakespearean characterization: "the character himself sees himself through the medium of his character, not exactly as he is."[9] The intrusion of subjectivity frustrates true self-knowledge. Furthermore, the play suggests that because man cannot know himself, he cannot know external reality; thus Brutus, lacking in this vital self-knowledge, fails to detect the self-interest which colors his views of Caesar and the other conspirators.

These epistemological principles rather than any abstract political principles form the thematic center of the play. Commentators on *Julius Caesar* have failed, in my opinion, to appreciate the significance of Cicero's comment, which offers the governing principle of the action:

> Indeed, it is a strange-disposed time:
> But men may construe things, after their fashion,
> Clean from the purpose of the things themselves. (I. iii. 33–35)

The motif of misconstruction introduced by Cicero is remarkably pervasive in the play. As if to guide us to this motif, Shakespeare provides a "mirror-scene"[10] which suggests metaphorically the central action of the play. While Brutus and Cassius confer in private, Decius and Cinna herald the break of day, each pointing to it, however, in different quarters of the sky; but then Casca points in yet another direction: "You shall confess that you are both deceiv'd. / Here, as I point my sword, the sun arises..." (II. i. 105–106).

This motif of misconstruing, of misinterpreting the significance of events, is the point of several other scenes: the cosmic storms are variously interpreted by Casca, Cassius, Caesar, and Calpurnia; an anonymous poet barges into the tent of Cassius and Brutus under the impression that they are quarreling violently, only to find them reconciled; the poet Cinna, mistaken for Cinna the conspirator, is murdered by an angry mob; and even the first scene of the play, which is marked by seemingly pointless quibbles, focuses upon the motif of misconstruing:

> *Mar.* You, sir, what trade are you?
> *Cobbler.* Truly, sir, in respect of a fine workman, I am but, as you would say, a cobbler.
> *Mar.* But what trade art thou? Answer me directly.
> *Cob.* A trade, sir, that I hope I may use with a safe conscience; which is, indeed, sir, a mender of bad soles.
> *Mar.* What trade, thou knave? thou naughty knave, what trade?
> (I. i. 9–15)

Marullus constantly misconstrues the meaning intended by the cobbler. But, having finally determined the trade of the cobbler, Marullus berates the commoners for misconstruing the nature of Caesar, for celebrating as a hero one "Who...would soar above the view of man / And keep us all in servile fearfulness" (I. i. 74–75). There is no guarantee, however, that the Tribunes are not themselves construing things in their own fashion, for it is possible to suspect them, like Cassius, of having a private grievance against Caesar. Thus the central theme of the subjectivity of truth is introduced in the very first scene.

The motif is particularly prominent in the suicide of Cassius. Cassius commits suicide as a result of the limitations of physical sight; from the vantage point which he occupies, his armies seem to be losing the battle, and Cassius commits suicide in despair of the outcome. The lament of Messala offers a penetrating commentary on the action of the play:

> O hateful Error, Melancholy's child,
> Why dost thou show to the apt thoughts of men
> The things that are not? O Error, soon conceiv'd,
> Thou never com'st unto a happy birth,
> But kill'st the mother that engender'd thee. (V. iii. 67–71)

And Titinius looks upon the dying Cassius with the same observation: "Alas, thou hast misconstrued everything" (V. iii. 84). The "everything," the attentive reader perceives, includes much more than the immediate situation surrounding the suicide. For to some degree the central action of misconstruing touches all the characters of the play.

But there is yet another dimension to this theme of misconstruction; it is crucial to note that the audience has also become involved in the same epistemological situation as the characters. The wide range of opinion about the meaning of this play seems to arise from Shakespeare's intention to plunge the audience itself into the ambiguities of Brutus' world; as Schanzer has expressed it:

> ... Shakespeare seems to be playing on his audience's varied and decided views of Caesar, encouraging and discouraging in turn each man's preconceptions. And since on our view of Caesar depends, very largely, our judgment of the justifiability of the entire conspiracy, the whole drama is thus kept in the area of the problem play. For though, as it seems to me, Shakespeare makes abundantly clear the folly and the disastrous consequences of the murder, he does not, I think, make clear its moral indefensibility. His enigmatic presentation of Caesar's character and motives allows responses like that of Dover Wilson to be formed. (p. 33)

What has transpired in the play can best be described in terms of point-of-view strategy: the particular strategy of Shakespeare seems to be to involve the audience in the fallible judgments of the characters. It is made to shift its valuation of the action from time to time, accepting alternately the incompatible appraisals of Brutus, Antony, and Cassius; and the technique which makes these contradictory estimates possible is the dramatic equivalent of the unreliable narrator. The characters of the play represent limited, and hence fallible, points of view; their judgments, therefore, cannot be taken at face value but must be continually assessed by a wary audience with no guarantee of infallibility in its own judgment. Ultimately, Cicero's comment would extend to the audience's reception of the play; as the history of criticism has so well borne out, interpreters of this play may indeed "construe things after their fashion / Clean from the purpose of the things themselves" (I. iii. 33–35). It is the audience's reaction that bears the most eloquent testimony to the epistemological principles that underlie the play.

Julius Caesar becomes a richer play, more complex and more universal in its significance, if it is interpreted as an exploration of man's epistemological situation. Shakespeare develops in several dimensions his belief in the fallibility of human judgment, stressing especially the intrusion of "apt thoughts" into the act of knowing. Man, in his limited human situation, cannot aspire to intuitive, angelic knowledge; he must, on the contrary, painstakingly glean truth from the chaff of experience. The theme is at once traditional and modern. The play echoes on the one hand the Stoic doctrine that man's passions are inimical to his understanding, implying as an ideal the man whose Stoic "apathy" will allow him to judge dispassionately and objectively. The classical precept, "Know thyself," is then intimately involved in the play's meaning.

But there is, on the other hand, an urgent modern concern in this probing of the problem of knowledge, for Shakespeare, attuned to his times, seems to be dramatizing the "new" scepticism about human reason that is set forth, for example, in Montaigne:

> I must adapt my history to the moment. I may presently change, not only by chance but also by intention. It is a record of diverse and changeable

> events, of undecided and, when the occasion arises, contradictory ideas; whether it be that I am another self, or that I grasp a subject in different circumstances and see it from a different point of view.[11]

Man's natural condition, according to Montaigne, is incertitude; he is continually deluded by his sense experience and led unto error by the intrusion of subjectivity into the act of knowing. Retreating then into reason, with every judgment founded upon a previous and dubious judgment, he finds his fallibility confirmed. Man's only recourse is to probe his own mind, constantly redefining himself in relation to his present situation. Knowledge is difficult of access, tentative, and limited to particulars.[12]

This epistemological concern, which Shakespeare shares to some degree with Montaigne, is also recognizably modern, for in considering the impact of point of view on truth, Shakespeare is anticipating the concern of such modern thinkers as Ortega y Gasset; in a trans-subjective universe of reality, says Ortega y Gasset,

> truths are eternal, unique and invariable. How, then, can there be, in the knower, any process by which they can be identified? The reply of rationalism is narrow and arbitrary: knowledge is only possible if reality can penetrate it without the least disturbance of its own fabric. The knower, therefore, must be of a transparent medium, lacking any sort of special quality or characteristic colour: he must be the same yesterday as to-day or tomorrow: he must be ultra-vital and extra-historical....
>
> The reply of relativity is equally narrow and arbitrary. Knowledge is impossible; there is no such thing as transcendent reality, for the reason that every real knower resembles an arena that has its own special formation. Reality would have to alter its own fabric in order to enter such an arena, and the particular alteration made would in each case be falsely construed as reality.[13]

Admittedly, all of this would not be immediately evident to the viewer or even the reader of *Julius Caesar*, but the implications of the point-of-view strategy eventually reveal themselves to the reader who seriously considers the problem. As his abiding interest in the reality-appearances motif suggests, Shakespeare was vitally concerned with the problem of knowledge, and such a correlation with a modern philosopher like Ortega y Gasset is not, in my opinion, forcing the point, for Shakespeare seems to have conceived of the problem in remarkably modern terms. The problem of relativism is not at all foreign to the world of *Julius Caesar*.

Furthermore, the increasing tendency to see Shakespeare as a direct prototype of Pirandello has some warrant. For Shakespeare, in submitting the audience through a sophisticated point of view to the ambiguity of experience, anticipates not only the themes but the refined dramatic artifices of the modern playwright.[14]

But Shakespeare is not, in my opinion, propounding a Pirandellian relativism. He is, without denying the reality of objective truth, undercutting the godlike claims of man to absolute knowledge and stressing instead the complexity of human experience.[15] He would agree, I think, with Ortega y Gasset that the knower cannot be ultra-vital and extra-historical; man's perception of truth is modified by his existential situation.

Notes to *Julius Caesar*: An Experiment in Point of View

1. See J. Dover Wilson, ed., *Julius Caesar*, New Shakespeare Edition (Cambridge, 1949), p. xxx; J. E. Phillips, *The State in Shakespeare's Greek and Roman Plays* (New York, 1940), pp. 172–204.
2. Adrien Bonjour, *The Structure of Julius Caesar* (Liverpool, 1958), p. 3.
3. Derek Traversi, *Shakespeare: The Roman Plays* (London, 1963), p. 12.
4. Ernest Schanzer, *The Problem Plays of Shakespeare* (New York, 1963), p. 32.
5. Schanzer, pp. 24–36.
6. All references to *Julius Caesar* will be to The Arden Edition, ed. T. S. Dorsch (Cambridge, MA, 1958).
7. It is important to note the exact meaning of Antony's speech: Brutus is the "noblest Roman of them all"—i.e., of all the *conspirators*, not, as at first sight, of all the Romans. The next line begins, "All the conspirators..." (V. v. 69), an important qualification.
8. Arden Edition, p. xliv.

9. *Shakespearean Criticism*, ed. Thomas M. Raysor (London, 1960), I, 301.
10. See Hereward T. Price. "Mirror-Scenes in Shakespeare", in *Joseph Quincy Adams Memorial Studies* (Washington, 1948), pp. 101–113, eds. James McManaway and others.
11. Cited in Erich Auerbach, *Mimesis: The Representation of Reality in Western Literature* (Garden City, NY, 1957), p. 251.
12. See Auerbach's "L'Humaine Condition" in *Mimesis*, pp. 249–273, for a useful discussion of Montaigne's attitudes.
13. Jose Ortega y Gasset, "The Doctrine of Point of View," in *The Modern Theme*, trans. James Cleugh (New York, 1961), p. 87.
14. See, for example, Schanzer, p. 32; the view is implicit in Lionel Abel's *Metatheater* (New York, 1963); pp. 57–58 are especially relevant.
15. It is significant that there is in the play an "omniscient" point of view which subtly guides us out of the labyrinth of relativism; e.g., in the symbolic sleep of innocence enjoyed by Lucius, which highlights the suppressed guilt of the insomniac Brutus, thus transcending the limited point of view. Another example is the symbolic "mirror-scene," which unequivocally indicates that the conspirators are mistaken.

THE THEME OF REDEMPTION IN *I HENRY IV*

Rodney Delasanta

What I propose to say about the meaning of *I Henry IV*[1] in general and about the characters of Prince Hal and Falstaff in particular, if reduced to an abstract, would sound anti-revisionist, even establishmentarian. Witness: Prince Hal, despite the efforts of literary revisionists who have struggled mightily to convict him of sham, remains—for all his moral ambiguities—Shakespeare's representative of redemption; Falstaff, despite the unction of sentimentalists who have larded him with moral praise, remains—for all his endearing old charms—Shakespeare's representative of unregeneracy. Instinctively, one struggles to escape the righteous tone of such attributions by resorting to the kind of palliative subterfuge engaged in by Dr. Johnson when he described Falstaff as a study in "sense and vice: of sense which may be admired but not esteemed and of vice which may be despised but hardly detested." But it will take the rest of the essay to qualify the praise and blame humanely, even though my peroration will claim that what we finally witness in the play is, on the one hand, the emergence of the New Adam and, on the other, the fixture of the Old.

The establishment view of Hal sees him, of course, as prodigal become prince, madcap become monarch; and the word most used to describe this transformation has obviously been *redemption*. Taken in any of its multiple senses, *redemption* has come to mean in Hal's case a sloughing off of private vices and a putting on of public virtues which, if not entirely invisible up to the moment of his reformation, had lain in him dormant and unexpected. Yet by the end of the play Hal has become more than serendipitous majesty. Rather, Shakespeare has prepared his metamorphosis, if not completely in the fully visible area of drama, certainly in those imagistic crevices between action and thought that demand closer scrutiny if the play's fuller intention is to be realized.

Much has been said recently about the Pauline allusion to the redemption of time in Hal's famous "I-know-you-all" soliloquy. J. A. Bryant, Jr., and D. J. Palmer, especially, have pointed out for us that the theological implications of Hal's redemption have never been sufficiently explored: "Redeeming and casting off the 'old man' are, in this play as in Ephesians and in Romans, part of the same process, which involves recognizing clearly and casting off the old penchant for sin."[2] What they and others have said is accurate and valuable, but it is curious that in these studies relating to Hal's redemption the classical meaning of the word as it is repeated time and time again in the New Testament is only hinted at. To any Christian of the sixteenth century (whether his confession was Roman, Anglican, or Dissenting), its precise theological meaning would have meant more than moral refurbishment. Simply stated, the doctrine of Redemption taught "by sin man incurs, as a debt to divine justice, the punishment of death demanded by the Old Law. To ransom mankind from this slavery of sin and death, Christ is to pay the ransom and discharge the debt with the price of his blood."[3]

The key image in this powerful concept is that of discharging the debt, paying the ransom, often by means of an adjunctive image of blood-letting. We need not read very far in the New Testament of the Geneva Bible to be struck by the motif, one which Shakespeare would have known very well in those bible-reading and predicant days and one which, I submit, Shakespeare uses in this play as an imagistic paradigm against which to measure his characters. Here are some typical passages.

> Matthew 20:28 (and repeated almost word for word in Mark 10:45): "The sonne of man came not to be served, but to serve, and to give his life *for the ransome* of many."

> 1 Corinthians 6:20: "For ye are *boght* for a price: therefore glorifie God in your bodie, and in your spirit..."

> 1 Corinthians 7:23: "Ye are *boght* with a price: be not the servants of men."

> 1 Timothy 2:5–6: "For there is one God and one mediator between God and man...who *gave himself a ransome* for all men..."

> 1 Peter 1:18: "...ye were not *redemed* with corruptible things, as silver and golde..."

> 2 Peter 2:1: "...there shall be false teachers among you...even denying the Lord, *that hathe boght them...*"

Just as plentiful are passages which add to the image of paying the debt in blood.

> Acts 20:28: "...the Holie Gost made you Overseers to fede the Church of God, which he hathe *purchased with his owne blood.*"

> Hebrews, 9:12: "Nether by the blood of goates and calves: but *by his owne blood* entred he in once unto the holie place, and *obteined* eternal redemption for us.

> Hebrews 9:22: "And almost all things are by the Law purged with blood, and *without sheading of blood is no remission.*"

> Ephesians 1:7: "By whome we have *redemption through his blood,* even the forgivenes of sinnes, according to his riche grace."

> Colossians 1:14: "In whome we have redemption through his blood, that is, the forgivenes of sinnes."

> Revelation 5:9–10: "...thou wast killed, and hast *redemed us to God by thy blood* out of everie kinred, and tongue, and people, and nation, and hast made us unto our God Kings and Priests, and we shall reigne on the earth."

It cannot be accidental that in large structural terms—one might with Northrop Frye even say archetypal or typological terms—*I Henry IV* begins with a king's refusal to ransom and ends with his son's decision to free an enemy who has been rebel against that king. (I speak, of course, in the first instance of King Henry's refusal to ransom the pretender Mortimer in return for Hotspur's prisoners and, in the second, of Hal's gratuitous freeing of Douglas after the battle of Shrewsbury.) Nor can it be accidental that the preponderant imagery—and in some cases the dramatic action itself—involved in Hal's reformation should characterize him as paying off debts, either literal or metaphorical. And while at least two critics have recognized that "the language of settling debts is heard throughout Part One,"[4] none to my knowledge has pointed out that it is Hal's *willingness to pay others' debts* (in contrast to his foils like Falstaff, the King, and Hotspur who are reluctant or refuse to pay) that symbolically ties him in the Renaissance imagination to another Son of another King, who like Hal at the battle of Shrewsbury also paid a bloody price for victory.

To the reader's weary rejoinder that he is not willing to read about another contrived Christ figure, one should answer that in an age when Christ was the Alpha and Omega, when he served as the final exemplum for all human emulation, it should hardly be surprising that a prince of the blood royal be examined through the insistent refraction of the *lumen Christi*. Certainly Richard II was so examined by Shakespeare, although this is not to mean that the examinee cannot, under this refractory gaze, be found wanting—even ironically or parodically so. By measuring Hal's reformation (and Falstaff's unregeneracy) against the submerged, or implied, or paradigmatic metaphor of Redemption, Shakespeare has urged a thematic intention in *I Henry* IV which reveals itself as anagogically normative. It is devoutly to be wished that this claim will not dampen the comedy that is the major glory of *I Henry IV*. On the contrary, in an age of Faith (especially in its declination) comedy most successfully fulfills itself as it stretches its meanings to touch the hem of the sacred, and as it offers—in a history play like *I Henry IV*—a tone alternate to the high seriousness of the Chronicle. That Shakespeare could stitch his Redemption design both on and behind the nap of his remarkable garment the rest of this paper will try to prove.

Almost immediately upon being introduced to Falstaff and Hal in Act I, Scene ii, we hear the motif—comic, to be sure—of Hal's paying for Falstaff's debts:

> *Prince.* Why what a pox have I to do with my hostess of the tavern?
> *Falstaff.* Well, thou hast called her to a reckoning many a time and oft.
> *Prince.* Did I ever call for thee to pay thy part?
> *Falstaff.* No, I'll give thee thy due, thou hast paid all there.
> *Prince.* Yea, and elsewhere, so far as my coin would stretch, and where it would not I have used my credit.[5]

Hal's comic willingness to pay is strengthened at the end of the same scene when he seriously announces that he will "this loose behaviour...throw off, / And pay the debt I never promised" (I. ii. 203–204). Even the simile of "bright metal on a sullen ground" (l. 207) calls up connotations of a bright coin eventually to be put to use. And too the allusion to Ephesians 5 in the phrase "redeeming time," as a number of critics have pointed out, can certainly be interpreted to mean paying for a past evil with future virtuous actions.

What is dramatically ironic about this last passage in Scene ii—and what critics like Bryant and Palmer have overlooked—is that it is followed in Scene iii by Hal's father's irascible *refusal* to pay off Glendower in order to free his imprisoned cousin, Mortimer: "...shall our coffers then / Be empty'd to *redeem* a traitor home? / Shall we buy treason...I shall never hold that man my friend / Whose tongue shall ask me for one penny cost/ To *ransom* home revolted Mortimer." Hotspur's hyperbolic rejoinder introduces the adjunctive image of blood into the Redemption pattern, one that punctuates the rest of the play and comes to exclamatory fullness in the battle of Shrewsbury. But here we must suffer Hotspur's fulmination:

> Three times they breath'd and three times did they drink
> Upon agreement of swift Severn's flood,
> Who then affrighted with their bloody looks
> Ran fearfully among the trembling reeds,

And hid his crisp head in the hollow bank,
Bloodstained with these valiant combatants. (I. iii. 101–106)

Perhaps it would not be presumptuous to add another associative coupling of images to Professor Armstrong's well-known list,[6] for it shall become evident here that Shakespeare repeatedly associates images of purchase and ransom with blood, an association which—conscious or not—must have come from the Redemption-in-blood passages punctuating the New Testament and the liturgy of those more eucharistic, pre-Cromwellian times. Note the peculiar confluence of the two images thirty lines later as Hotspur explains the King's irascibility to Worcester, though here the connection is more associative than thematic:

Hotspur. And when I urg'd the ransom once again
Of my wife's brother, then his cheek look'd pale,
And on my face he turn'd an eye of death,
Trembling even at the name of Mortimer.
Worcester. I cannot blame him: was not he proclaim'd
By Richard that dead is, the next of *blood*? (I. iii. 139–144)

Note too the inversion of the motif when Hotspur uses it to urge his uncle and father to rebellion:

Hotspur. Revenge the jeering and disdain'd contempt
Of this proud King, who studies day and night
To answer all the debt he owes to you,
Even with the bloody payment of your deaths. (I. iii. 181–184)

And picking up the figure later in the scene, though with the allusion to blood only implicit, Worcester warns:

Worcester. The King will always think him [Hotspur] in our *debt*,
And think we think ourselves unsatisfy'd,
Till he hath found a time to *pay* us home. (I. iii. 280–282)

Like Hotspur, we too "apprehend a world of figures" and suspect a strategy at work.

The strategy becomes more palpable in Act II with the Gadshill robbery. Critics have pointed out that the activities of the comic thieves in Act II mirror the larger political thefts throughout the tetralogy.[7] Just as thieves (Poins and Hal) prey upon thieves (Falstaff and his men) in the Gadshill comedy, so it is thieves (Hotspur and the rebels) who prey upon thieves (the usurper Henry IV and his supporters) in the political action of the play. For the purposes of this paper, however, it is important to be reminded that Hal's role in both thefts, Gadshill and the kingdom, is innocent and finally redemptory. Certainly he was not responsible for his father's usurpation of Richard's throne, and his involvement with Falstaff's "squires of the night's body" is more a jest than a serious act. (We remember that it was Poins who convinced Hal to join in the theft in order to comically reprove Falstaff's lies. Obviously Hal showed no desire to steal for its own sake.) Yet by the end of Act II both "thefts" involve Hal in a course of action which depends solely upon him for resolution. First, the King's messenger comes to the Boar's Head with news of rebellion, and then the Sheriff comes to the tavern asking restitution for the Gadshill victims. To both "calls" Hal offers payment, literally in the comic theft ("The money shall be paid back again with advantage" [interest] and ironically in the political theft ("Give him as much as will make him a royal man [a royal being worth ten shillings] and send him back again to my mother").[8] But in the latter case, the irony is only temporary as Hal promises to commit himself martially to his father's case: "I'll to the court in the morning. We must all to the wars..."

Two scenes later comes the famous interview between Hal and his father, during which the King accuses his son of "vile participation" and degeneracy: only to be answered with protestations of filial piety and reform. Again Hal's language sings a Redemption motif, but this time in full-throated aria. It is convenient to quote the most telling lines:

> ... God forgive them that so much have sway'd
> Your Majesty's good thoughts away from me!
> I will redeem all this on Percy's head,

> And in the closing of some glorious day
> Be bold to tell you that I am your son.
> When I will wear a garment *all of blood*,
> And stain my favours *in a bloody mask*,
> Which, wash'd away, shall scour my shame with it. (III. ii. 130–137)

It is possible, at the risk of agnostic censure, to detect Christological echoes in this passage: overtones of the Bloody Scourge and apocalyptic images of being washed in the blood of the Lamb seem present, not to mention famous scriptural passages like "forgive them for they know not what they do" and "this is my beloved Son in whom I am well pleased." But most evident is the conjunction of redemption and blood. In one sense, it is a direct response to the King's lamentation that Hal's misdeeds represent God's revenge upon Henry's blood:

> I know not whether God will have it so
> For some displeasing service I have done,
> That in his secret doom out of my blood
> He'll breed revengement and a scourge for me. (III. ii. 4–7)

However, it is not "revengement" but redemption that God will breed out of blood. Hal promises his father that at the "closing of some glorious day," after having stained his features in the bloody mask of battle and wearing a garment soaked in blood, he shall wash and scour both blood and shame away. And he will perform this ritual cleansing by redeeming it all on Percy's head. Lest the classical religious connotations of Redemption be missed, Shakespeare loads Hal's following lines with images from the tally sheet:

> For the time will come
> That I shall make this northern youth *exchange*
> His glorious deeds for my indignities.
> Percy is but my factor, good my lord,
> To engross up glorious deeds on my behalf,
> And I will call him to so *strict account*

That he shall render every glory up,
Yea, even the slightest worship of his time,
Or I will tear the reckoning from his heart.
This in the name of God I *promise* here,
The which if He be pleas'd I shall perform,
I do beseech your Majesty may salve
The long-grown wounds of my intemperance;
If not, the end of life *cancels all* bands
And I will die a hundred thousand deaths
Ere break the *smallest parcel of* this vow. (III. ii. 144–159)

At Shrewsbury, Hal's prophecy comes true. Bloodied by the battle and urged by the King and Westmoreland to retire to his tent, Hal plunges back into the breach and shortly thereafter rescues his father from Douglas, who is at the point of killing the King. Hal's heroic interjection ("It is the Prince of Wales that threatens thee, / Who never *promiseth* but he means *to pay*") continues the redemption motif but, as we shall shortly see, in a singular way. In the meantime, the exhausted Henry praises his son's valor ("Thou hast *redeem'd* thy lost opinion, / And show'd thou mak'st some tender of my life" [V. iv. 47–48]) in language which continues the connotative exploitations already mentioned. (Although the notes tell us that "mak'st some tender" means "hast some regard for" [Arden, p. 157, n. 48], it also quite clearly carries the fiduciary meaning of an offer of money made to satisfy an obligation in order to avoid prosecution.)

I skip over the climactic battle with Hotspur because it is allied in Shakespeare's intention with Falstaff's "death," the redemptive implications of which I shall defer till later, and proceed to the final scene. It is here that the theme of Redemption comes full circle from the play's beginning. It is inconceivable that King Henry, who had refused to ransom his kinsman and ally, Mortimer, in the first act would now show mercy instead of justice to the rebels, Worcester and Vernon, as they are led before him, And, of course, our expectations are not deceived when the King, after justifiably rebuking Worcester's treachery, sends him and, in an apparent afterthought the noble Vernon, too, to their deaths.

The parousial justice had known no mercy, knows no mercy, although admittedly he decides to "pause upon" other offenders. At this penultimate point, Hal reports the capture of Douglas and beseeches his father to allow him to be the instrument of judgment. Upon the King's agreement, Hal instructs his brother to "go to the Douglas" and "deliver him up to his pleasure, *ransomless and free*" (V. v. 27–28). In his struggle with Douglas, the Prince had promised to pay, and here in a moment of merciful luminosity pays off the noble Scot's debt with his freedom. The distinction between the father's strict justice and the son's redemptive mercy could not have been more singularly drawn.

If Hal is thus finally portrayed as the prolific, it is Falstaff who is the devourer. Despite his reiterated promises to reform, Falstaff, unlike Hal, remains fixed in his vice; and although it is that very complexity of vice that makes him the unparalleled comic figure that he is, Shakespeare's final judgment comes down hard on the huge hill of flesh. We have heard much of Falstaff's biblical language, and certainly it is the incongruity of the biblical tone and the epicurean volume that provokes so much of our laughter. But he who would in the *final* analysis sentimentalize the old sinner as a triumph of morality would do well to measure the manner of Hal's redemption of his debts against Falstaff's.

We have already seen in Act I, Scene ii, Falstaff's admission that it is Hal who pays and Sir John who does not. The fact that his inability or refusal to pay in that early scene is intermixed with promises of reform contrasts him with Hal who, as we have already seen, "never promiseth but he means to pay." Falstaff's only efficacious transaction, as Poins jocularly avers, has been with the devil, to whom on Good Friday last in return for a cup of Madeira and a cold capon's leg Sir John sold his soul. His earthly creditors, however, are never so fortunate, and it is always Hal who picks up the tab. We remember those two gentlemen who "lost three hundred marks" in the Falstaffian robbery and whom Hal "pays back again with advantage.") Indeed, it is not reductive to affirm that the cosmic implications of the comic scenes in *I Henry IV* can often be summed up by the symbolic tallying of debts and payments. The broad comedy of Act III, Scene iii, is a good example. As in Act, I, Scene ii, Falstaff's reluctance to pay his debts is intermixed with protestations of remorse:

> Well, I'll repent, and that suddenly, while I am in some liking; I shall be out of heart shortly, and then I shall have no strength to repent. And I have not forgotten what the inside of a church is made of, I am a peppercorn, a brewer's horse: that inside of a church! Company, villainous company, hath been the spoil of me. (III. iii. 4–10)

But his remorse is never accompanied by redemption, and to Mistress Quickly's demand of payment for twenty-four pounds, Falstaff can only answer that his pocket has been picked in her tavern and that he will not pay. Let Bardolph pay, he insists, who has "had his part of it." At this point Hal enters, recruiting men for the march to Shrewsbury. Both Falstaff and the Hostess press him to arbitrate their differences, in the course of which the Hostess charges that Falstaff has slandered the Prince by having claimed that Hal owes him a thousand pounds. The verbal exchange, humorous as it is, does not allow the larger redemption motif to slacken:

> *Prince.* ... he slanders thee most grossly.
> *Hostess.* So he doth you, my lord, and said this other day you ought him a thousand pounds.
> *Prince.* Sirrah, do I owe you a thousand pounds?
> *Falstaff.* A thousand pound, Hal? A million, thy love is worth a million, thou owest me thy love. (III. iii. 130–136)

Finally, Hal admits that he has indeed picked Falstaff's pocket—while Sir John was asleep and drunk in order to pay off the Sheriff after the Gadshill robbery—but found there only "tavern reckonings, to make thee long-winded." Falstaff's famous rejoinder—"thou knowest in the state of innocency Adam fell, and what should poor Jack Falstaff do in the days of villainy"—overpowers Hal, who, exasperated with the old man's titanic unregeneracy and having admitted to picking Falstaff's pocket, is now presumably liable for his tavern debt. Then, in answer to Falstaff's question about the outcome of the Gadshill robbery, Hal explains that he must continue to "be good angel to thee--the money is *paid back again*." Apparently the eschatological overtones of the phrase annoy Falstaff, however, eschatological implications he has been repressing in his futile gestures of repentance, for he exclaims: "O I do not like that paying back, 'tis a double labour."

The very next comic scene, Act IV, Scene ii, opens with still another example of Falstaff's indifference to debt. Instructing Bardolph to "fill me a bottle of sack" before his soldiers reach Coventry, his subordinate is not above making demands for payment: "Will you give me money, captain? ... This bottle makes an angel [6s. 8d.]." Falstaff's assurance that he will "answer the coinage," however, sounds familiarly dead-beat (Shakespeare would have loved the colloquialism). After Bardolph leaves, Falstaff soliloquizes his shame in having "misused the King's press damnably." But we have by now familiarized ourselves to this pattern of remorse followed by an utter failure to redeem. And once again Falstaff does not disappoint. After a brilliant description, laden with biblical imagery, of his tactics of bribery by which he impresses only those who are too willing to buy out of their conscription and then filling his roll with slaves, Falstaff tries to justify his army of beggars to Hal by calling them "food for powder, food for powder, they'll fill a pit as well as better." His monetary tactics here, of course, are the exact opposite of Hal's, who has freed his charges by redemptivelv paying off their debts. Falstaff, on the contrary, frees his charges by collecting from them rather than paying for them and then proceeds to impress "slaves" in their place—"villains who "march wide betwixt the legs as if they had gyves [chains] on—for indeed I had the most of them out of prison" (IV. ii. 40–41). The echoes of Redemption from the New Testament carry brutally ironic overtones here: "Ye are bought with a price, be not the servants [in Douay-Rheims, *bondslaves*] of men."

These are the men who will fill the pit as they march to Shrewsbury under the command of Sir John, and by now the rollicking good fun of the tavern scenes gives way to the reckonings of death. As bloody pawns in their commander's death-dealing transactions, not three of Falstaff's hundred and fifty draftees survive the battle, we learn in Act V, and Falstaff himself, as Hal reminds him, owes God a death. " 'Tis not due yet," answers the frightened Sir John, "I would be loath to pay him before his day." Falstaff's language now begins to teem with images of accounts and reckonings as death duns him from every side. "A trim reckoning," he calls honorable death in his famous catechism on honor at the end of Act V, Scene i. And after Douglas kills Blunt two scenes later, Falstaff longs for the safety of the Boar's Head in London where he could "scape shot-free," a brilliant pun combining the idea of an escape from wounds or death and an escape as well from paying the "shot," or reckoning, a pun exploiting wounds and reckoning.

Falstaff's participation in the redemptive scheme of the play, therefore, is the reverse of Hal's. Rather than characterizing him imagistically as paying others' debts, often with an extra installment of blood, Shakespeare paints Falstaff's hands as being full of bribes and his conscience spotted with the blood of his elected conscripts. But it is at Hal's climactic battle against Hotspur that Falstaff's brilliantly perverse involvement with the Redemption comes to full parodic flower. Hal, we remember, had promised his father that at the end of that day Henry would be proud to call him son because he would redeem himself on Hotspur's head and scour away his shame with blood. The power of that speech must not obscure its allusion to the biblical Redemption of mankind through the payment of Christ's blood, a cardinal article of which is that the Redemption begun on Calvary will be complete when deliverance from death is secured by the resurrection of the body. Any number of passages from St. Paul's Epistles would remind us of this central teaching of Christianity, but these excerpts from Romans will suffice:

> But if the Spirit that raised up Jesus from the dead, dwell in you, he that raised up Christ from the dead, shal also quicken your mortal bodies... Therefore, brethren, we are detters not to the flesh, to live after the flesh: For if ye live after the flesh, ye shal dye: but if ye mortifie the dedes of the bodie by the Spirit, ye shal live... Because the creature also shal be delivered from the bondage of corruption into the glorious libertie of the sonnes of God... And not only the creature, but we also which have the first frutes of the Spirit, even we do sigh in our selves, waiting for the adopcion, even the redemption of our bodie. (Romans 8:11–23)

During Hal's battle with Hotspur, Douglas interrupts Falstaff's sideline cheering to engage him in combat. The cowardly Falstaff counterfeits a wound and falls down as if dead, immediately after which Hal mortally wounds Hotspur. Hal's tribute to Hotspur's valor and then his farewell to Falstaff are some of the most moving lines in the entire play, charged with dramatic irony in Falstaff's case, of course, because we in the audience know he is counterfeiting. But it is dramatic irony for us only because we know Shakespeare's play better even than the biblical event it is parodying here. Shakespeare's first-night audience certainly would not have known that Falstaff was faking it, and the sight of this considerable flesh rising from the dead after Hal's prophetic redemption had been fulfilled by his defeat of Hotspur must have struck them with a full thunderclap of dramatic power. For Falstaff does indeed rise from the dead, in a manner powerfully parodic of the General Resurrection promised in Scripture and brilliantly timed here against Hal's offered sacrifice, coming as it does immediately after the payment of Hal's ultimate debt. The comic effect is unparalleled in Shakespeare, for it balances precariously on the very brink of cosmic blasphemy.

Nor does Shakespeare cease with his parodic exploitations here. Falstaff, so that Percy too may seem to rise again, stabs the already slain rebel once more and carries the body to the Prince to whom he relates his titanically mendacious story of having fought with Hotspur "a long hour by Shrewsbury clock" before finally slaying him. At the Prince's astounded answer that "if a lie may do thee grace, I'll gild it with the happiest terms I have," a trumpet sounds and calls Hal to a reckoning of "what friends are living, who are dead." Falstaff follows the promise of judgment, his last words a parodic hope for reward and sorrow for sin:

I'll follow, as they say, for reward. He that rewards me, God reward him! If I do grow great, I'll grow less, for I'll purge and leave sack, and live cleanly as a nobleman should do. (V. iv. 161–164)

What remains after parodic redemption, resurrection, apocalyptic trumpet, and hope for reward is final judgment; and in the last scene of the play, as we have seen, Shakespeare gives us precisely that. Justice and mercy reveal themselves in the persons of the father and son respectively, the King condemning Worcester and Vernon to their deaths and the Prince by a redemptive and intercessionary mercy freeing Douglas "ransomless."

THE artistic device I have urged recognition of in *I Henry IV* has no satisfactory name, despite the fact that Shakespeare was not alone in employing its strategies. *Parody* is a term which suggests itself to us in the critical terminology of our day (and I have used it in this paper), but the word is not exact, for parody normally denigrates that which is being parodied, whereas what I have described here is hardly denigrative in intention. For the same reason that Milton was not abusing the Trinity in his parody of Satan, Sin, and Death in *Paradise Lost* or that Chaucer was not abusing Pentecost or the Flood in the Summoner's and Miller's Tales respectively, so Shakespeare cannot have intended to parody denigratively the Redemption in *I Henry IV*. This play is no kin to—say—*Northanger Abbey* or *Peter Bell III.*

Perhaps we come closer to the mark if we designate the phenomenon as archetype, for the submerged quality of the recurrent imagery seems to answer to Northrop Frye's description of archetype in The *Anatomy of Criticism*:

> In looking at a picture, we may stand close to it and analyze the details of brush work and palette knife... At a little distance back, the design comes into clearer view, and we study rather the content represented... The further back we go, the more conscious we are of the organizing design. At a great distance from, say, a Madonna, we can see nothing but the archetype of the Madonna, a large centripetal blue mass with a contrasting point of interest at its center. In the criticism of literature, too, we often have to "stand back" from the poem to see its archetypal organization... If we "stand back" from the beginning of the fifth act of *Hamlet*, we see a grave opening on the stage, the hero, his enemy, and the heroine descending into it, followed by a fatal struggle in the upper world.[9]

Certainly we discern the mythopoeic design of Redemption in *I Henry IV* more readily if we too "stand back" and espy its structure and texture from a distance. From this vantage point we make our prophetic promises of redemption;

watch a hero paying debts which he did not incur and ransom family, friends and enemies alike; observe a "slain" disciple resurrected: hear a trumpet calling men to judgment. And yet *archetype*, because it implies a certain *unconscious* recurrence of universal image or symbol, will not really do either. However unconscious certain details of the Redemption motif might be in *I Henry IV* (e.g., I. iii. 137ff.), it seems to me that Shakespeare has introduced it into the play with great deliberation in order to urge certain palpably thematic ends: to set up a series of correspondences which should alert the reader to the implicit presence of a controlling set of values.

I hesitate, however, lest these phrases suggest that I am beckoning the reader to allegory. There are few figures who can be laced into allegorical corsets with more difficulty than Falstaff, to name only one—though perhaps the most formidable—of the clearly un-allegorical characters in the play. Indeed, his girth represents the very fullness of that existential reality which defies the ordinary moralistic circumscriptions found in allegory. Yet Shakespeare was no dramatist of the absurd either. Although he refused to reduce the complexities of his art to the pet categories of philosophers, one is not justified in assuming that in his plays the centers do not hold. Like most of the great Christian artists of Medieval and Renaissance Europe, Shakespeare measured existential reality not by some rarefied and noumenal ideal but rather by another existential reality, which for him, I suspect, deepened rather than resolved mystery: the story of salvation as it unfolds from Genesis to Revelation.[10] Belatedly, literary criticism has come to press the claim that at the imaginative center of many of the classical works of our literature (before the Romantic Age, of course) lies *typological* analogy. Works as diverse in time and intention as *Beowulf* and *Samson Agonistes*, we have been shown, share a common imaginative involvement with the salvific story begun in the Old Testament and fulfilled in the New. What this means for a more mature understanding of Western Literature is beyond the scope of this paper, but nevertheless I find the term extremely germane to our purposes in understanding *I Henry IV*. To capsulize an opinion, I suspect that any writer of the first order like Shakespeare, if his creative imagination was impelled into motion by the example of typological analogy instead of by allegorical equation, would preserve in his creative moments deep memory of those powerful forces and proceed to measure human behavior against their submerged presences. By measuring Hal's reformation and Falstaff's unregeneracy against the submerged metaphor of Redemption, Shakespeare has urged a thematic intention in *I Henry IV* which reveals itself as anagogically normative. For it must be stressed that the typological presences in Christian art, despite their differences in kind from the allegorical certitudes, relate nonetheless to the teleological and look forward—inside history—to ultimate meanings. Thus, although the typological sense must not be confounded with the allegorical, it is only existentially reasonable to expect it to take moral measurements as it proceeds towards its teleological ends: especially if those measurements do not abandon the Christian injunction (as allegory invariably does) to love the sinner while hating the sin.

Thus we find ourselves loving Falstaff and Hotspur as we could never love Cymochles and Pyrochles, because the former are sinful (and delightful) men while the latter are only vices. We love Hal as we could never love Guyon because the Prince is also a man, while Gloriana's knight is only a mean. Yet to expect us to love Falstaff and Hal indiscriminately or indeed, as some would have it, to discriminate so as to aggrandize Falstaff and diminish Hal, is to expect us to applaud the tempter and scorn the deliverer. Like Falstaff, Hal too is a sinner, but his are sins from which he has delivered himself by having willingly paid off his debts, for others as well as for himself. Falstaff, on the other hand, remains in this great schema of Redemption as a debtor, who owes his creditors unpayable sums: to Mistress Quickly, the tavern tab; to Hal, the Gadshill interest; to King Henry, the conscription bribes; to Bardolph, the angel; to his impressed soldiers, their lives; to God, an honorable death. Even in Part Two our final glimpse of Falstaff catches him in his fixed role as debtor: this time to Justice Shallow for a thousand pounds. Is it possible that Shakespeare would have supplied us with the yardstick of anagogical measurement in the typological metaphor of Redemption without urging us to discriminate between the ultimate worth of Falstaff and Hal? No. To confound them in the final tally is to come away from the play confusing debits for credits, promissory notes for cancelled receipts. I am confident that Shakespeare expects us to keep better books.

Notes to The Theme of Redemption in *I Henry IV*

1. I do not extend my analysis to Part Two because I conceive of Part One as the only Henry IV play that Shakespeare originally intended to write. Although it is impossible to disprove the theory that the two parts constitute a "ten-act" intention, I find the arguments (both historical and critical) of scholars who see Part Two as an addendum to, rather than an integer with, Part One considerably more convincing. Almost irrefutable, it seems to me, is their contention that if Shakespeare had intended a Part Two from the beginning he would not have effected Hal's redemption with such finality in Part One. Hal. we must remember, solemnly promises, and succeeds in achieving, his redemption in the first five acts. That redemption is dramatically and thematically convincing, not only to the reader or audience but also, inside the play, to the other characters: Hal's father, his friends, even his foes. Could Shakespeare have intended from the beginning that in Part Two Hal should "pay as if not paid before"? It seems unlikely, despite the desperate arguments of some scholars, that Shakespeare expected Hal to step through his paces twice. More likely is the theory that the commercial success of Falstaff moved Shakespeare to revise his planned trilogy into a somewhat padded tetralogy in order to accommodate his great comic creation. I would think that *Henry V* coming immediately after a *Henry IV* without an intervening Part Two could easily have included the leftover material (like the defeat of the remaining rebels. Hal's accession to the throne, and the banishment of Falstaff) before continuing with the French wars as finale. (The fact that the early quarto editions of *Henry IV never* called themselves Part One is of some small comfort to the argument.)
2. J. A. Bryant, Jr., "Prince Hal and the Ephesians," *Sewanee Review*, 67 (1959), p. 217; D. J. Palmer, "Casting off the Old Man: History and St. Paul in *Henry IV*," *Critical Quarterly*, 12 (1970), pp. 267–283. See also Paul A. Jorgensen, *Redeeming Shakespeare's Words* (Berkeley and Los Angeles, 1962), pp. 52–69.
3. *The Jerusalem Bible* (New York. 1966), "The New Testament," Matthew 20: 28, pp. 47–49, note g.
4. Palmer, p. 270. In a recent article ("*I Henry IV*: The Metaphor of Liability," *Studies in English Literature* [1970], pp. 287–195). E. Rubinstein makes much of the debt imagery in the play but ignores completely the connection between redemption and Redemption. Rubinstein is certainly correct, it seems to me, in arguing that the ethical obligation of the characters is expressed in terms of their financial indebtedness, but like many New Critics he allows his discerned pattern of imagery to float free of historical and cultural anchor so that it functions only as metaphor. I hope to show that the imagery of indebtedness surpasses the metaphorical and touches the symbolic, perhaps the archetypal and typological.
5. All citations are from the Arden Shakespeare Edition of *King Henry IV, Part I*, ed. A. R. Humphreys (London, 1960).
6. Edward A. Armstrong, *Shakespeare's Imagination* (Lincoln, NE, 1963).
7. See, for example, Robert Hapgood, "Falstaff's Vocation," *Shakespeare Quarterly*, 16 (1965), pp. 91–98.
8. We remember too Hal's willingness to pay in the seemingly digressive game with Francis, the drawer, that opened this same scene. S. P. Zitner has argued ("Anon, Anon: or a Mirror for a Magistrate," *Shakespeare Quarterly*, 19 [1968], pp. 63–70) that Francis represents the Prince

torn between the attractions of the tavern and the responsibilities of kingship. It is noteworthy that even in his tipsy attempt to draw Francis away from his indenture to the innkeeper (a metaphor for his own prodigal temptations to flight) Hal proposes to pay Francis's way by offering him a thousand pounds for a pennyworth of sugar (II. iv. 60).

9. Shakespeare must have known very well the iconographic representations of the Final Judgment that, I submit, he is parodying here. English cathedrals, like their continental counterparts, often decorated the typanums of their portals with stylized scenes depicting the Judging Son flanked, among others, by angelic trumpeters. St. Michael holding the scales, and the dead rising from their tombs. But one need not search farther than the Guild Chapel across the street from New Place itself in Stratford-upon-Avon to find a large fresco, now badly faded, above the chancel arch depicting the Last Judgment. A copy of the fresco drawn by Thomas Fisher in 1804 suggests many of the traditional details of Judgment Day iconography dating back to the Middle Ages. Conjectured figures above Jesus are four angelic figures (crowned and winged), at least two of whom-if the stylized imagery of other similar scenes is any criterion-must have been blowing the apocalyptic trumpets.

10. Northrop Frye, *The Anatomy of Criticism* (Princeton, 1957). p. 140.

HAMLET AND THE MYTHIC HYPOTHESIS

René Fortin

The various archetypal approaches to *Hamlet*, which see Hamlet's mission as essentially a ritual purgation of his society, are generally satisfying in that they at least suggest reasons for the play's incomparable power. But they are nonetheless disappointing in that they fail to account adequately for the surface features of the play. The problem lies, I think, in our premature identification of Hamlet as a full-fledged mythic hero while ignoring the ironies that surround the several mythic actions he attempts.[1]

The key to Shakespeare's ironic strategy in this play is suggested by Robertson's familiar description of Hamlet as a "super-subtle Elizabethan" stranded in a primitive, barbaric setting.[2] Although Robertson attributed the dual time-frame of *Hamlet* to Shakespeare's difficulties with his intractable source materials, more recent studies consider the anachronisms as deliberate strategies rather than an accident of composition. Peter Alexander, for example, sees as a central feature of the play the confrontation of two ages, each with its distinct claim upon the hero: "Wittenberg, the University, is face to face with the heroic past."[3] Similarly, Willard Farnham has argued that *Hamlet* stands "between whole worlds of truths in our culture: between the world of an uncivilized heroic past going back even behind Christianity and that of a civilized present; between the world of medieval faith and otherworldliness and that of modem doubt and this-worldliness."[4]

It might be said, therefore, that Hamlet's mighty opposites are time and history, that Hamlet's problem is that he is asked to take on a mythic task—to renew the kingdom—in an anti-heroic age that is unresponsive to myth. His frustrated quest for heroic identity, I shall try to demonstrate, is reflected in the structure of the play, which consists of several mythic patterns which are projected and then ironically distorted as Hamlet fails to give life to his mythic roles.

Modem mythic studies of *Hamlet* begin with Gilbert Murray's analysis of the affinities between Orestes and Hamlet. Above and beyond their general situations, the revenge mission imposed upon them, Murray points out such other parallels as the hostile or latently hostile mother-relationships, the madness which afflicts both heroes, the misogyny which obsesses them, and finally their tendency to assume the role of fool.[5] The parallels were, for Murray, too striking to be dismissed as sheer coincidence; he concluded rather that they pointed to some universal psychic intuition:

> we finally run the Hamlet-saga to earth in the same ground as the Orestes-saga: in that prehistoric and world-wide ritual battle of Summer and Winter, of Life and Death, which has played so vast a part in the mental development of the human race.... Hamlet, also, like Orestes, has the notes of the Winter about him. Though he is on the side of right against wrong he is no joyous and triumphant slayer. He is clad in black, he rages alone, he is the bitter Fool who must slay the King.[6]

The shared venture of Hamlet and Orestes is therefore the re-enactment of a vegetation ritual, depicting the killing of the Summer King by the Winter King in order to bring about the restoration of Nature's vitality or, alternately, the killing of the Year King by a wintry slayer who "weds the queen, grows proud and royal, and then is slain by the Avenger of his predecessor."[7]

The Hamlet-Orestes parallels are susceptible to other interpretations, such as the existential one proposed by Jan Kott. Kott sees the tragic myths as dramatizations of the human condition, enforcing a decision between the two orders,

> the order of action, whose measure is efficacy, and the order of value, in which all gestures count and in which a gesture dearly bought by death gives meaning to fleeting human existence. The dramatic world of Hamlet-Orestes contains all human situations in which choice is

> enforced by the past, but has to be made on one's own responsibility and on one's own account.[8]

Hamlet and Orestes, then, share in the existential agony of moral decision in the face of necessity (or, in Kott's term, "prediction"), but Hamlet responds to this situation in a way that is in keeping with his Elizabethan situation. The quality of his response, as we shall see, is markedly different from that of Orestes.

Hamlet's affinities with Oedipus, his other heroic prototype, have been more extensively studied. Freud and Jones are, of course, foremost among the critics who have traced Hamlet back to Oedipus, both finding the Hamlet story to be a version of a fundamental sexual myth.[9] According to this view Hamlet is a victim of sexual repression, paralyzed by his suppressed guilt over an infantile incest-wish. His inability to kill Claudius results specifically from his feelings of complicity, from his unconscious identification with the person who has consummated his most secret wishes, to kill his father and wed his mother. Among more recent critics, Fergusson grants at least a partial validity to the Freudian reading but concludes that the sexual myth is too restrictive. Instead he locates the center of the Oedipus-Hamlet stories in the scapegoat roles to which both heroes are driven:

> The themes of Oedipus are, from many points of view, strikingly similar to those of Hamlet.... it is clear that in both plays a royal sufferer is associated with pollution, in its very sources, of an entire social order. Both plays open with an invocation of the well-being of an endangered body politic. In both, the destiny of the individual and of society are closely intertwined; and in both the suffering of the royal victim seems to be necessary before purgation and renewal can be achieved.[10]

Thus Oedipus begins as hero, as priest-king of his society, but because of his uncovered guilt and consequent suffering, he becomes a "scapegoat, a witness and a sufferer for the hidden truth of the human condition."[11] And Hamlet, in Fergusson's reading, follows the same general pattern, though admittedly more obscurely, and achieves some sort of purgation for himself and Denmark by his tragic ordeal.[12] Certainly the parallels are suggestive; moreover, their shared obsession for the knowledge that plunges them into tragic experience warrants our giving serious thought to the ties between Oedipus and Hamlet.

But Hamlet's mythic credentials do not establish him exclusively as a hero. Lord Raglan has pointed out as a recurrent pattern in literature and myth the strange symbiosis between hero and fool, an observation that seems especially pertinent to *Hamlet*.[13] Murray, without pursuing the point, noted vestiges in Hamlet of the Amloth figure of the sources and expressed wonder that Shakespeare had created "his greatest hero out of a Fool transfigured."[14] Later critics have developed this hint; Fergusson finds the Fool figure prominent in the improvisational activities of Hamlet, who is at times clown-and-ritual-head of state, gag-man and royal victim, and finally a Fool figure with unmistakable religious overtones.[15] Levin, while also sensitive to the archetypal implications of the Fool, sees Hamlet especially as a distant echo of the classical *eiron*, "the Socratic ironist whose ignorance concealed a deeper wisdom"; more immediately, he conjectures that Shakespeare was dramatizing in the Hamlet-Fool the humanistic critique of the intellect "in the grand Erasmian manner."[16] Both agree, in any case, that there is within Hamlet a peculiar coalescence of two antithetical mythic figures, the Hero and the Fool.

The archetypal accretions of the Fool figure considerably enrich the significance of Hamlet's tragedy, for the fool in antiquity was widely recognized as a central figure in ritual; the fool, after reigning for a time as mock-king, served as the scapegoat to be killed as a surrogate of the king.[17] Chambers emphasizes the importance of the fool's madness in the scapegoat ritual; though originally the fool's primary qualification for the role seems to have been his dispensability, "the common belief in madness or imbecility as a sign of divine possession may perhaps have contributed to make the village fool or natural seem a particularly suitable victim."[18] The fool, therefore, precisely because of his madness, is surrounded by a religious aura; in this identity the fool comes to be associated with the Saint, the Poet, and the Seer.[19]

This murky but rich mythic background accounts in part for our difficulty in denoting Hamlet truly; if we are attentive to the archetypal suggestions of the play, Hamlet emerges as a character of many masks, encompassing in his mythic dimensions the Winter King, the incest-driven Oedipal son, the royal victim, the Fool, and the existential striver for Truth who defies fate in the name of humanity. The guises are many, but they all seem to be directed toward a single mythic function, the restoration of a social order, either by ritual sacrifice or by revelation of a healing truth.

A general review of the plot of *Hamlet* suggests at first that the hero successfully lives up to his mythic responsibilities. Returning from a prolonged stay at Wittenberg, Hamlet finds a kingdom suffering a spiritual disease, the cause of which, he is told by the Ghost, is a murder "most foul, strange, and unnatural" (I. v. 28).[20] The murder is, in fact, a regicide, which makes Hamlet's mission a public as well as private responsibility. He must, that is, do nothing less than cleanse the state of pollution: "Let not the royal bed of Denmark be / A couch for luxury and damned incest" (I. v. 82–83). Claudius is more than a murderer; he is the usurper of the kingship, an institution that in Elizabethan times was regarded with religious awe, having absorbed some of the "holy and religious fear" (III. iii. 8) formerly accorded the Pope and the Church. The rightful monarch—in this case, presumably Hamlet—was to be the ruler, high-priest, and father of the community; he was to be the person on whom, as Laertes states, the "sanity and health of the whole state" would depend (I. iii. 21), or, in the figure used by Rosencrantz, the "massy wheel... To whose huge spokes ten thousand lesser things / Are mortised and adjoined" (III. iii. 17–20).[21]

Hamlet's activities in the play must therefore be seen in the context of his royal status, and, more specifically, of the preemption of his royal office by Claudius. He accepts the "sacred" mandate to set right the time, but finds, that, unlike his heroic prototypes, he cannot act decisively. An early indication of Hamlet's discomfort with his heroic role is expressed in his first soliloquy, when he describes Claudius as "my father's brother, but no more like my father / Than I to Hercules" (I. ii. 152–53). The reference to Hercules has far-reaching implications, indicating the persistence in the Renaissance of primitive concepts of heroism. Hercules, according to one side of the tradition, is the simple man of deeds, representing "a core of primitive strength never completely transmuted by the refining power of more civilized ideals"[22]; thus Hamlet's reference to Hercules hints at a nostalgia for the primitive heroic situation that would make the deed of blood accessible to him. Later, finding his revenge machinery stalled, Hamlet recalls Pyrrhus, son of Achilles, again a simple-minded warrior "roasted in wrath and fire" (II. ii. 449) and unwaveringly committed to violence.

It is significant in this context that Hamlet voices admiration for Fortinbras, the man of "unimproved mettle hot and full" (I. i. 99), for his audacity in war. Fortinbras, Hamlet perceives, is capable of venturing "all that fortune, death and danger dare, / Even for an eggshell" (IV. iv. 52–53) and will "find quarrel in a straw / When honour's at the stake" (IV. iv. 55–56). But Hamlet's admiration is tempered by his awareness of the horrible pointlessness of Fortinbras' Polish campaign, waged "to gain a little patch of ground / That hath in it no profit but the name" (IV. iv. 18–19). Fortinbras, in short, is the simple man of action that Hamlet, given a less critical temperament, might have been. But Hamlet cannot accept the simple soldierly code of Fortinbras, for it belongs to another, simpler age. As soldier-hero in the mold of Fortinbras, Hamlet would be able to fulfill without hesitation the command of the Ghost; but Hamlet cannot evade the subtleties of his predicament: the command, as many have observed, results in an extraordinary confusion of two moralities, the pagan Teutonic and the Christian, and there is no reconciling middle ground. Where the revenge code would enjoin Hamlet, in the name of honor and filial piety, to avenge his father's death, the Christian code expressly prohibits revenge. Thus Hamlet is inhibited by "craven scruples" (IV. iv. 40) and finds that "conscience does make cowards of us all" (III. i. 83).

Unable to bring himself to commit the cleansing act of killing Claudius, Hamlet is forced progressively to isolate himself from the polluted society whose center he, as rightful ruler, should normally have been. As Holloway describes it, Hamlet has assumed a role which "takes him from being the cynosure of his society to being estranged from it, and takes him through a process of increasing alienation to a point at which what happens to him suggests the expulsion of a scapegoat or the sacrifice of a victim, or something of both."[23]

It is in this isolation that Hamlet resorts to the role of fool, where he serves as counter-image or "shadow" to the King. His riddles and quibbles link him with the abusive fool of mythology, who characteristically confounds the wisdom of the king by his cunning simplicity.[24] Moreover, riddles in antiquity were often thought of as reflecting preternatural knowledge, and the Hamlet sources reveal that this mythic residue is present in the Hamlet story. Saxo credits his hero with "a wisdom too high for human wit under a marvelous disguise of silliness," while Belleforest, granting Hamlet powers of divination, agonizes at some length over their origin—even considering it probable that "the minister of Satan therein played his part."[25]

In any case, the fool role is immensely suggestive; Hamlet, finding himself incapable of the heroic deed, resorts to the instrument of the fool, the ironic (or prophetic) word. It could be said, in fact, that the tension between word and deed, which many have noted in Hamlet, is at least partially understandable as the result of a tension between two conflicting mythic roles: the royal prince and the fool. Because he is dispossessed by Claudius, Hamlet must express his somber truths by indirection, and the abusive clown seems increasingly to assume the religious identity of an inspired madman or prophet. As Fergusson has stated:

> if Hamlet is the joking clown, he is also like those improvising Old Testament prophets who, gathering a handful of dust or a few little bones, or a damaged pot from the potter's wheel, present to a blind generation a sudden image of their state.[26]

Through the first part of the play, therefore, the language of Hamlet is remarkably dominant as the play's center of interest. Having assumed his antic disposition, Hamlet is in a position to use language as an instrument of exploration, of concealment, or of correction. His language is used to taunt Polonius, to thwart the spying of Rosencrantz and Guildenstern, to instruct the players (largely about the proper use of language!), to castigate Ophelia, to chastise Gertrude with "words [that] like daggers enter in mine ears" (III. iv. 96), and to "unkennel" the "occulted guilt" of Claudius (III. ii. 77–78). But the word finally yields to the deed, in Hamlet's sudden killing of Polonius.

The first phase of Hamlet's ordeal ends with his "casual slaughter" of Polonius, an act which results in his being sent to England. This sea-voyage is for many critics fraught with archetypal implications; it is seen as a symbolic death-rebirth pattern, and the Hamlet who is "set naked on your kingdom" (IV.

vii. 43) has evidently undergone a sea-change, being finally reconciled to his task.[27] Significantly, both Saxo and Belleforest seem to attach great symbolic significance to the voyage, for in both narratives the hero before his departure instructs his mother to arrange "pretended obsequies" for him on the anniversary of his departure, and it is at this mock-funeral that Hamlet—in a symbolic rebirth of sorts—makes his appearance.[28]

The apparent transformation of Hamlet is manifested by the serenity of his disposition and the religious tone of his language, which communicate that Hamlet is now sure of his way, acquiescent in all things to the will of God. He is by his own testimony the man of "perfect conscience" (V. ii. 67), reliant upon the "divinity that shapes our ends" (V. ii. 10). Moreover, because of his newly acquired faith in a "special providence," he is ready to "defy augury" (V. ii. 208–209), explicitly linking his powers of divination, which he hinted at earlier,[29] to heavenly guidance.

Thus, according to the mythic script, Hamlet is then guided darkly to his martyrdom, the death that he must suffer in order to cleanse Denmark. There is, asserts Maud Bodkin, a powerful "spiritual power" in Horatio's invocation of "flights of angels" (V. ii. 349) over the body of Hamlet,[30] and many respond with a similar exultation to the promise of the "soldiers' music and the rites of war" (V. ii. 388) which will attend Hamlet's passage. Miss Bodkin has observed that our exultation in the death of Hamlet is related in direct line of descent to the religious exultation felt by the primitive group that made sacrifice of the divine king or sacred animal, the representative of the tribal life, and by the communion of its shed blood, felt that life strengthened and renewed.[31]

Such readings are admittedly quite moving, but how consistent are they with the facts of the play? Recent criticism has demonstrated the need for delicacy and tact in approaching myth in Shakespeare[32]; caution, I suggest, is particularly essential in *Hamlet* since the principle of this play seems to be to outline bold patterns only to expose them as ultimately abortive. Specifically, *Hamlet* apparently evokes images of mythic heroism only to point out the inability of its hero to perform as mythic hero, to provide, that is, either the sacrificial cleansing or the healing revelation. Fergusson himself, despite his final acceptance of the mythical Hamlet, calls attention to the ironic distortions of Hamlet's role:

> In *Hamlet* it is as though everyone of these [mythic] elements had been elaborated by a process of critical analysis. Hamlet himself, though a prince, is without a throne: though a sufferer for the truth, he can appear in public as a mere infatuated or whimsical youth.... Shakespeare provides many ironic parallels to his story—and to this I may add that it takes both Hamlet and Claudius to represent the royal victim of the tradition.[33]

The essential feature of a mythic action is its social impact, but the redemptive act of Hamlet has been widely questioned precisely because of its inefficacy. Even Fergusson, while affirming the final integrity of the mythic pattern, seems nevertheless sensitive to the dubious success of the hero: "He feels his way toward [his martyr-like death], not with public sanction, but with the faithless worldliness of the Danes."[34] Other critics are less able to overcome their doubts: Tillyard finds in Hamlet "no great revelation or reversal of direction, or regeneration"; Knights finds that Hamlet, unlike Lear, "cannot break out of the closed circle of self-contempt and loathing...the awareness that he embodies is at best an intermediate stage, at worst a blind alley"; Vyvyan similarly denies that there is any renewal, insisting that *Hamlet* is a "study of degeneration from first to last."[35] Finally, Kott points out that Hamlet differs crucially from Orestes in resisting the choice that he must make: "Unlike all the Orestes of antiquity, Hamlet will not accept this choice (to kill or not to kill). He will be forced to make it, forced by others."[36] The existential affirmation that we expect is never made, and the final scene is for Kott extremely bleak:

> The return of legality is without any motivation, deprived even of any semblance of necessity. It does not mean anything. It follows from the very logic of a structure, without any justification, without reference to any hierarchy of values.[37]

It is hardly astonishing that many critics fail to see any religious or quasi-religious affirmation in Hamlet's final moments, however devoutly such a consummation might be wished.[38] For above and beyond Hamlet's general fumbling, we must face the strongest evidence of all, the fact that Hamlet, despite his alleged reconciliation with Heaven, is utterly unrepentant—in fact, quite cavalier—about sending Rosencrantz and Guildenstern to their deaths "not shriving time allowed" (V. ii. 47). It is perhaps the one major action in the play that cannot be explained away, even by appealing, as Cruttwell does, to the fact that Hamlet is literally at war with Claudius.[39] The return of the ambassadors from England with news of the killing of Rosencrantz and Guildenstern is *dramatically* unnecessary and therefore seems to be a pointed reminder that Hamlet's order for their execution is to have an important bearing on our final estimate of him. We must come to the inescapable conclusion that Hamlet's insistence on killing their souls as well as their bodies is an appalling act in any moral context.[40]

Despite Horatio's invocation of the flights of angels, what we witness, if we look with our judgment rather than with our eyes, is a scene of stark desolation, of almost random slaughter. It takes something like an act of faith to feel exultation in Hamlet's death and in the deaths for which he is directly or indirectly responsible. And if we are unable to bring ourselves to perform this act of faith, we are merely following the precedent of Horatio, who himself finally abandons his religious language to interpret the action in wholly secular terms:

> ...let me speak to th'yet unknowing world
> How these things came about; so shall you hear
> Of carnal, bloody, and unnatural acts.
> Of accidental judgments, casual slaughters.
> Of deaths put on by cunning and forced cause.... (V. ii. 368–72)

It is a dreary catalogue of human fallibility that Horatio recites, and there is precious little indication that any good will come from the disaster which burdens the stage. If new life is to germinate from death, this new life is most inauspiciously embodied in Fortinbras, who, by whatever standard one measures him, seems unequal to his destiny. This, the cession of the kingdom to Fortinbras, the man of "unimproved mettle hot and full" (I. i. 96), is the upshot of Hamlet's mythic activity: as Winter King, as scapegoat or royal victim, Hamlet accomplishes little.

The other side of Hamlet's mythic function, serving as prophet of a healing truth, is fulfilled no more adequately. It is obvious that the sexual myth, first of all, is not brought to its completion, for what seems to be crucial in this myth is a process of recognition of guilt, leading to remorse, and eventually to a growth of insight into the human condition. On this plane, the hero must come to terms with the radical ambivalence of the parent-son relationship. Thus Miss Bodkin traces in the sufferings of Oedipus a progression from unconscious guilt to a "final expression of respect and loyalty" to the parent-figures; in Hamlet, however, she can appeal only to a vague "intuitive apprehension" in the hero (and, by extension, in the onlooker).[41] And Freud's own uneasiness about the reticence of Hamlet can be inferred from his treatment of the two heroes:

> As the poet brings the guilt of Oedipus to light by his investigation, he forces us to become aware of our inner-selves, in which the same truths are still extant, even though they are suppressed.... In *Oedipus Rex* the wish-fantasy of the child is brought to light and realized as it is in dreams; in *Hamlet* it remains repressed, and we learn of its existence—as we discover the relevant facts in a neurosis—only through the inhibitory effects which proceed from it. In the more modern drama, the curious fact that it is possible to remain in complete uncertainty as to the character of the hero has proved to be quite consistent with the overpowering effect of the tragedy.[42]

The *Oedipus* plot, in short, is therapeutic, liberating us from the dark demons of the unconscious by exposing repressed impulses to the light of consciousness, but *Hamlet* has that within that passeth show; it fails to dramatize the repressed life of its hero, lacking—in Eliot's famous dictum—the objective correlative of Hamlet's emotion. Hamlet, it can be convincingly argued, achieves neither self-knowledge nor revelation.

A brief review of the main outlines of the Oedipus story underscores the great distance between the two heroes as vessels of truth. The fate of Oedipus is inextricably bound with the experience of knowing: it is through his sagacity in answering the riddle of the Sphinx that Oedipus is called to be sacred king of

Thebes and is revered almost as a god. But because of his unrelenting pursuit of truth, Oedipus then discovers the guilt of his marriage, and with this advance in knowledge obtained at great personal cost, takes upon himself the guilt of his society, effecting its purgation by suffering in exile. In *Colonus*, finally, his guilty knowledge is transformed into prophetic wisdom, and Oedipus emerges from his tragic ordeal as seer and saint, favored of the gods.[43]

In Hamlet too there is promise of the truth that saves, but where Oedipus gains renown as the solver of riddles, Hamlet is best known as the *creator* of riddles. And, although these riddles suggest, as Dover Wilson has observed, "unfathomed and unfathomable depths,"[44] what they most clearly disclose is the fatal ignorance of a hero whose ultimate revelation is the vision of death in the graveyard scene, a confrontation with the ultimate riddle:

> Where be your gibes now? Your gambols, your songs, your flashes of merriment, that were wont to set the table on a roar? Not one now to mock your own grinning? Quite chop-fallen? Now get you to my lady's chamber, and tell her, let her paint an inch thick, to this favour she must come. (V. i. 177–82)

In this part of the play what we are invited to witness is the failure of language. Having just experienced the degradation of the word in his dialogue with the gravedigger ("We must speak by the card, or equivocation will undo us"—V. i. 128–29) and about to meet Osric, whose foppish language he will contemptuously burlesque, Hamlet here meditates upon the death of the fool, "a fellow of infinite jest" (V. i. 173), and ultimately upon the death of language. "The rest is silence" could, in fact, be borrowed from its more familiar context to serve as a commentary on this scene.

Hamlet has much to say about language in the course of the play, instructing the players, for example, to "suit the action to the word, the word to the action" (III. ii. 16–18) and to "let those that play your clowns speak no more than is set down for them..." (III. ii. 37–38). But the decorum and moderation in language that he pleads for is precisely what Hamlet is himself unable to achieve. Despite Horatio's rebuke about his "wild and whirling words" (I. v.

133), Hamlet indulges continually in linguistic extravagance, in a verbal hypertrophy that constantly damages his cause.[45] He eventually reproaches himself about his lack of discipline:

> This is most brave,
> That I, the son of a dear father murdered,
> Prompted to my revenge by heaven and hell,
> Must like a whore unpack my heart with words,
> And fall a-cursing like a very drab,
> A scullion! (II. ii. 568–73)

Something of this verbal extravagance is seen in the nunnery scene, when he castigates Ophelia; in the closet scene, when he "roars so loud and thunders in the index" (III. iv. 53); and in the burial scene, when he tries to out-rant Laertes. In each of these scenes we note that Hamlet, far from using language to convey the privileged wisdom of the fool-prophet, succeeds only in venting his ineffectual passion or his cynicism. The language of Hamlet, we must conclude, is a flawed instrument which simply thickens the darkness of his world and leaves us at last as the "yet unknowing world." And the fool-prophet lapses finally into silence.

It is evident, I think, that the mythic patterns elaborated by several critics are integral parts of the play's structure and must find a place in any critical consideration of the play. It seems, however, equally evident that the critic must be extremely discriminating in his handling of the patterns, for Shakespeare's handling of myth in this tragedy is profoundly ironic. Hamlet does indeed try to perform mythic actions, but a careful analysis of the consequences of his actions indicates that he fails dismally in his mythic roles. In an age which had already been considerably demythologized, Shakespeare's hero searches racial memory for a mythic conception of heroism that would give significance to his life. His tragedy, precisely, is that his life, and death, are meaningless: the society that he entrusts to Fortinbras is neither renewed by his death nor in possession of any saving truth.

NOTES TO *Hamlet* and the Mythic Hypothesis

1. For a sensitive study of the ironies surrounding Hamlet's quest for heroism, see G. K. Hunter, "The Heroism of Hamlet," in *Stratford-Upon-Avon Studies, 5: Hamlet,* gen. eds. John Russell Brown and Bernard Harris (London: Edward Arnold, 1963), pp. 90–109.
2. J. M. Robertson, *The Problem of Hamlet* (New York: Harcourt, Brace and Howe, 1920), p. 74.
3. Peter Alexander, *Hamlet, Father and Son* (Oxford: Clarendon Press, 1967), p. 35.
4. Willard Farnham, "Introduction," Pelican *Hamlet,* in *The Complete Pelican Shakespeare,* gen. ed. Alfred Harbage (Baltimore: Penguin Books, 1969), p. 932.
5. Gilbert Murray, *Hamlet and Orestes: A Study in Traditional Types* (New York: Oxford University Press, 1914). Israel Gollancz refers to an earlier interpretation of the Hamlet story as a nature myth by A. Zinzow (Halle, 1877) in *The Sources of Hamlet* (1924; rpt. New York: Octagon Books, 1967), p. 35.
6. Murray, pp. 20–21.
7. Murray, p. 17; he points out that two distinct patterns are often confused.
8. Jan Kott, "Hamlet and Orestes," *PMLA,* 82 (1967), p. 313.
9. Sigmund Freud, *The Interpretation of Dreams,* trans. A. A. Brill (New York: Macmillan, 1913), p. 225; Ernest Jones, *Hamlet and Oedipus* (Garden City, NY: Doubleday, 1954). See especially pp. 77–79.
10. Francis Fergusson, "Hamlet, Prince of Denmark: The Analogy of Action," in *The Proper Study: Essays on Western Classics,* eds. Quentin Anderson and Joseph A. Mazzco (New York: St. Martin's Press, 1962), p. 348. The essay first appeared in *The Idea of a Theater* (Princeton: Princeton University Press, 1949) and has been reprinted in several collections.
11. Fergusson, p. 354.
12. Fergusson, pp. 361–62.
13. Lord Raglan, *The Hero: A Study in Tradition, Myth, and Drama* (London: Methuen, 1936), p. 213.
14. Murray, p. 7.
15. Fergusson, pp. 351, 357.
16. Harry Levin, *The Question of Hamlet* (New York: Oxford University Press, 1959), pp. 124–25.
17. E. K. Chambers, *The Medieval Stage* (Oxford: Clarendon Press, 1925), I, p. 136; Enid Welsford, *The Fool: His Literary and Social History* (1935; rpt. Gloucester, MA: P. Smith, 1966), esp. pp. 68–73.
18. Chambers, I, p. 137.
19. Welsford, pp. 76ff.; inevitably a Christian culture would also recall St. Paul's description of the Christian as a "fool for Christ" in 1 Corinthians 4:10.
20. All references are to *The Complete Pelican Shakespeare,* gen. ed. Alfred Harbage (Baltimore: Penguin Books, 1969).
21. See Fergusson, p. 353; for the symbolic importance of kingship, see Harold Toliver, "Shakespeare's Kingship: Institution and Dramatic Form," in *Essays in Shakespearean Criticism,* eds. James Calderwood and Harold Toliver (Englewood Cliffs, NJ: Prentice-Hall, 1970), pp. 58–82.
22. Eugene M. Waith, *The Herculean Hero in Marlowe, Chapman, Shakespeare, and Dryden* (New York: Columbia University Press, 1962), p. 17. Cf. also Hamlet's reference to "the

Nemean lion's nerve" (I. iv. 83). Although the Hercules references seem to focus on Hercules as the man of action, the Hercules myth is much richer. See Marcel Simon, *Hercule et le christianisme* (Paris: Société d'Editions, 1955). Simon shows how Hercules was transformed into a symbol of virtue, and even into a pagan "type" of Christ. But Hamlet's allusions do not seem to evoke this part of the tradition.

23. John Holloway, *The Story of the Night* (London: University of Nebraska Press, 1961), p. 135.
24. Welsford, pp. 88–89.
25. Gollancz, pp. 131; 237–45.
26. Fergusson, p. 357.
27. This interpretation is by now almost critical dogma. For typical readings, see Maynard Mack, "The World of Hamlet," *The Yale Review*, 41 (1952), pp. 521–22, an essay also available in several collections; and Paul N. Siegel, *Shakespearean Tragedy and the Elizabethan Compromise* (New York: New York University Press, 1957), pp. 112–13.
28. Gollancz, pp. 117–27; 231–51.
29. These hints of preternatural insight include Hamlet's reference to his "prophetic soul" (I. v. 41) and his statement to Claudius: "I see a cherub that sees them [the plans of Claudius]" (IV. iii. 47).
30. Maud Bodkin, *Archetypal Patterns in Poetry* (1934; rpt. London: Oxford Univ. Press, 1968), pp. 20–21.
31. Bodkin, p. 31.
32. See Robert G. Hapgood, "Shakespeare and the Ritualists," *Shakespeare Survey* 15 (1962), pp. 111–23, for a judicious appraisal of myth criticism.
33. Fergusson, p. 354.
34. Fergusson, p. 362.
35. E. M. W. Tillyard, *Shakespeare's Problem Plays* (London: Chatto and Windus, 1957), p. 26; L. C. Knights, *An Approach to Hamlet* (Stanford, Stanford University Press, 1961), p. 90; John Vyvyan, *The Shakespearean Ethic* (London: Chatto and Windus, 1959), p. 55.
36. Kott, p. 312.
37. Kott, p. 312.
38. I am not intimating that the play lacks affirmation; Hamlet's point of view is not necessarily Shakespeare's.
39. Patrick Cruttwell, "The Morality of Hamlet—'Sweet Prince' or 'Arrant Knave,'" in *Stratford-Upon-Avon Studies, 5: Hamlet*, p. 128.
40. The point has been made elsewhere; seem for example, Harold Skulsky, "Revenge, Honor, and Conscience in *Hamlet*," *PMLA*, 85 (1970), p. 86.
41. Bodkin, p. 14.
42. Freud, pp. 224–25; Freud implies that *Oedipus Rex* is more explicit in its handling of the theme because it is the product of an earlier and less self-conscious age.
43. Louis Martz, in "The Saint as Tragic Hero," *Tragic Themes in Western Literature*, ed. Cleanth Brooks (New Haven: Yale University Press, 1955), pp. 166–67.
44. John Dover Wilson, ed. *New Cambridge Hamlet* (Cambridge, England: Cambridge University Press, 1936), p. xxxix.
45. Brents Stirling has a perceptive discussion of Hamlet's language and its relation to his "madness" in *Unity in Shakespearean Tragedy* (New York: Columbia University Press, 1966), pp. 91–94.

KING LEAR: TRAGEDY AND THE ANATOMY OF EVIL

René Fortin

The disappearance of the Fool in *King Lear* is one of the play's many oddities: a character who has grown larger and larger in stature as the play has developed is unobtrusively dispatched with a final riddling message: hearing Lear's announcement that "We'll go to supper i' the morning," the Fool replies, "And I'll go to bed at noon." The reply is unwittingly prophetic, for we later learn that the Fool is indeed "put to bed at noon," at a point when much remains unresolved, when the major business of Lear's education, hitherto entrusted to the Fool, remains woefully incomplete.

The disappearance of the Fool is almost universally noticed by critics, but is only vaguely accounted for; perhaps the most cogent explanations have associated the Fool's disappearance with the imminent return of Cordelia, who is in some ways his alter ego, and who therefore makes his character redundant. I suggest, however, that the Fool's departure can be accounted for in more precise terms: the Fool is dispatched because of his inadequacy in the major business of the play, the anatomy of evil. He is replaced by Edgar who, as Poor Tom, will be the chief anatomist of the play to its bitter end.

I

The crucial importance of the Fool in the early scenes of the play is that he posits a world that rewards reasonable and prudent behavior. For the Fool reason is an adequate guide to human behavior, and the miseries that are visited on humans are in his view the logical and predictable consequences of human folly. The opening scenes of the play indeed seem to bear out this wisdom: as Lear's predicament intensifies, it is all-too-evident that what he suffers at the hands of his daughters is of his own doing, the result of his ill-advised love-contest. Though there have been but the slightest intimations of Lear's vulnerability, the "most faint neglect of late" that Lear himself has barely noticed, the Fool is evidently aware of the dangers the future holds for his master. In his first words to Lear, he taunts him for being a Fool, in fact a fool twice over, for trusting both of his daughters:

> *Fool.* How now, nuncle? Would I had two coxcombs and two daughters!
> *Lear.* Why, my boy?
> *Fool.* If I gave them all my living, I'd keep my coxcombs myself. There's mine, beg another of thy daughters. (I. iv. 103–07)[1]

Lear's division of the kingdom, the Fool suggests, was unconscionable folly; his decision to vest his daughters jointly with all his "power / Pre-eminence, and all the large effects / That troop with majesty" was so egregiously foolish that it has turned his world up-side down:

> When thou clov'st thy crown in the middle, and gav'st away both parts, thou bor'st thine ass on thy back o'er the dirt. (I. iv. 157–59)

> ...thou mad'st thy daughters thy mothers...when thou gav'st them the rod and put'st down thine own breeches. (I. iv. 169–70)

The Fool's jibes repeatedly taunt Lear with the absurdity of his act and the consequent absurdity of the world he has created for himself: "Thou wast a pretty fellow when thou hadst no need to care for her frowning, now thou art an O without a figure. I am better than thou art now, I am a Fool, thou art nothing" (I. iv. 188–190). The Fool's reiterated lesson is clear: Lear is in trouble because of a failure in wisdom, a flouting of the rules of common sense that are accessible to all. Prudence is the key to a prosperous and untroubled life, as the Fool's ditty suggests:

Have no more than thou showest,
Speak less than thou knowest,
Lend less than thou owest,
Ride more than thou goest,
Learn more than thou throwest,
Set less than thou throwest,
Leave thy drink and thy whore,
And keep in a' door
And thou shalt have more
Than two tens to a score. (I. iv. 116–25)

This has been described, by William Elton, as a "bourgeois ethic" reminiscent of the banalities uttered by Polonius, but I suspect that the Renaissance audience would have thought otherwise, tracking the counsels instead to a more familiar source, the Wisdom books of the Old Testament, and especially the Book of Proverbs, which offers much the same counsels of prudence as the Fool does:

> He who guards his mouth protects his life; to open one's lips brings downfall. (13:13)

> One man pretends to be rich, yet has nothing; another pretends to be poor, yet has great wealth. (13:7)

> He who spares his words is truly wise, and he who is chary of speech is a man of intelligence. (17:27)

> Listen to counsel and receive instruction, that you may become wise. (19:20)

> Wine is arrogant, strong drink is riotous; none who goes astray for it is wise. (20:1)

> The harlot is a deep ditch, and the adulteress is a narrow pit; yes, she lies in wait like a robber, and increases the faithlessness among men. (23:27–28)

> The rich rules over the poor, and the borrower is the slave of the lender. (22:7)

> Let your foot be seldom in your neighbor's house, lest he have more than enough of you, and hate you. (25:17)

The proverbs, in a book considered to be inspired, are notable for two reasons, both of them highly relevant to *King Lear.* First, they are guides to good living based, not upon religious revelation, but upon the accumulated wisdom of the race. They do, to be sure, advocate ethical behavior, mandating, for example, that the rich give of their affluence to the poor, but by far the majority of the counsels concern themselves with cautions against self-destructive behavior, against the follies that jeopardize health and wealth.

Secondly, the proverbs are notable in their assurance that this world is one in which God transparently cherishes rational and virtuous behavior and decisively rebukes iniquity. The person who listens to wisdom and fears the Lord will thus prosper: "Be not wise in your own eyes, fear the Lord and turn away from evil; this will mean health for your flesh and vigor for your body" (3:7).

That confidence in the rule of reason provides the pith of the Fool's instructions to Lear. But the bitter torments undergone by the King and the Fool—Lear's betrayal by his daughters, his banishment from the castle, the physical ravages of the storm, and, above all, the psychic anguish of having to envisage a world now grown hostile—betray the shallowness of the proverbial wisdom. It is Lear's folly, of course, that has provided the daughters with their opportunity to torment him, but as we come to know the daughters more thoroughly, we cannot but conclude that their malice is so ingrained that even the most prudent behavior could not have deterred indefinitely the eruption of malice. If not this opportunity, then another would present itself—or be created by them: in the words of Hamlet, "The cat will mew, the dog will have its day"

(*Ham.* V. i. 22). Both Lear and the Fool at last realize that prudence offers no guarantee in a society where power and privilege hold sway:

> Tremble, thou wretch,
> That has within thee undivulged crimes
> Unwhipt of justice! Hide thee, thou bloody hand.
> Thou perjur'd, and thou simular of virtue,
> That art incestuous! Caitiff, to pieces shake,
> That under covert and convenient seeming
> Has practic'd on man's life! (III. ii. 51–57)

The Fool, though, is not entirely surprised by his discovery that the world has depths he has not yet fathomed, for from the beginning his comfortable rationalism has been belied by his actions, specifically by his loyalty to King Lear against his better wisdom. It is the rationalist Fool who, in his very first speech, chides Kent for following Lear, "for taking one's part that's out of favor." But the complexity of the Fool, that which gives him both appeal and strength as a dramatic character, is in evidence in a later speech, where we find both wisdoms, the wisdom of this world and the deeper wisdom of moral concern:

> Let go thy hold when a great wheel runs down a hill lest it break thy neck with following; but the great one that goes upward, let him draw thee after. (II. iv. 71–74)

But this cynical recognition that self-interest is, or should, dominate one's life is rejected by what immediately follows, the Fool's resolve to follow Lear despite everything:

> That sir that serves and seeks for gain,
> And follows but for form,
> Will pack when it begins to rain,
> And leave thee in the storm.
> But I will tarry, the Fool will stay,

And let the wise man fly.
The knave turns fool that runs away.
The Fool no knave, perdie. (II. iv. 78–85)

Reason for the Fool can explain neither the sudden hostility of the world that has turned against Lear nor the persistence of moral commitment in a world that does not reward virtue. The Fool embraces this new and bitter knowledge with what appears to be a stoic acceptance of what one can neither foresee nor control and now offers wisdom of a darker timbre:

He that has and a little tiny wit,
With hey, ho, the wind and the rain.
Must make content with his fortunes fit,
Though the rain it raineth every day. (III. ii. 74–77)

With the Fool thus stymied, his rationality overwhelmed by the facts of experience, it is up to Edgar as Poor Tom to probe the deeps of the situation, to reveal that Lear is crushed by evil, by the perverse will of others, rather than by simply folly.

The different worlds that Tom and the Fool inhabit are immediately evident when they first meet: the Fool's first reaction to Poor Tom is to recoil from him in horror: "Come not in here, Nuncle, here's a spirit. Help me, help me" (III. iv. 39–40). The Fool, who had stoically accepted the desperate conditions of his life with Lear, encounters a realm of experience that he cannot cope with. Like the Fool, Tom speaks of evil in the world, but in very different accents: evil for him is not simply folly, but an irruption of the supernatural into the world of man. It is the consequence of sin committed in concert with the Foul Fiend:

Take heed o' the foul fiend. Obey thy parents, keep thy word justly, swear not, commit not with man's sworn spouse, set not thy heart on proud array. (III. iv. 78–80)

The gulf between their responses to experience gapes wide when, hearing Tom's outcry, "The foul fiend bites my back," the Fool can offer only his timid response: "He's mad that trusts in the tameness of a wolf, a horse's health, a boy's love, or a whore's oath" (III. vi. 18–19). The Fool's response relates to nothing—it is essentially a non-sequitur, as the Fool is still resorting to the prudential language of the proverbs, now discredited by the grim facts of the play. What is needed is the semantic of diabolism introduced by Tom.

The time at which the Fool actually disappears is, I think, highly suggestive: he disappears without notice shortly after Lear, struggling to understand his situation, poses the desperate question:

> Then let them anatomize Regan; see what breeds about her heart. Is there any cause in nature that breeds these hard hearts? (III. vi. 75–76)

It is a question for which the Fool has no answer, and he has, for all intents and purposes, outlived his usefulness. The question, in fact, calls for a careful anatomy of the "hard hearts" of the play, an anatomy that uncovers significant differences in the manifestations of evil in the play. It is Tom's task to lead the way as the play goes on to perform the anatomy requested by Lear, the inquiry into the source of the evil that festers in the play's heart of darkness. Edgar, in short, is required to enter the concepts of sin and diabolical energy into the calculus of the play.

The primary subjects of the anatomy, of course, are Goneril and Regan, but the play performs its anatomy of evil on Edmund as well. What should be noted is that the anatomy of Edmund yields results that are significantly different from those offered by the anatomy performed on Goneril and Regan—the difference lying in what might be called his pragmatic sense of evil. From his opening soliloquy, when Edmund forthrightly tells all to the audience, he is a known quantity. He lives unabashedly by the law of the jungle and will go to any length to serve his own interests. His animal ethic, hypostatized by the Nature that is his goddess, allows him to do whatever he must do to secure his own advancement:

> Well, my legitimate, if this letter speed,
> And my invention thrive, Edmund the base

> Shall top th' legitimate. I grow, I prosper,
> Now, gods, stand up for bastards. (I. ii. 19–22)

He is ready to betray his father to Cornwall, though he knows full well the dire consequences of that betrayal, and he is ready, in Act Five, to have Cordelia and the King killed. But, significantly, he takes no special joy in his villainy—being in this respect significantly unlike Iago, who schemes for both "sport and profit." His reaction to the amorous advances of the sisters is characteristic: he is intrigued, even amused perhaps, by his quandary as he mulls over his decision: "Which of them shall I take? / Both? One? Or neither?" (V. i. 57–58).

But it is important to note that he is not up to murdering Albany with his own hands: "Let her who would be rid of him devise / His speedy taking-off' (V. i. 64–65). Conscience, to be sure, will not make a coward of Edmund, and yet, in the betrayal of his father, there is something like a twinge of guilt, or at least a recognition of the abominable character of the act:

> If I find [my father] comforting the King, it will stuff his [Cornwall's] suspicion more fully—I will persevere in my course of loyalty, though the conflict be sore between that and my blood. (III. v. 19–22)

It is, thus, not entirely surprising to learn—in Act Five—that Edmund in his dying moments is not unrelievedly evil, being stirred to recall the writ placed on Lear and Cordelia:

> I pant for life. Some good I mean to do
> Despite of mine own nature. (V. iii. 242–43)

The play's anatomy of the "hard hearts" of Goneril and Regan occurs not in the "trial scene," where Lear intended it to take place, but in the blinding of Gloucester. The difference between Edmund's villainy and that of the sisters is almost palpable. The anatomy requested by Lear, we should note, does take place, and in the very next scene after Lear has uttered his command, "Then let them anatomize Regan." The anatomy takes place in the blinding, where we are exposed to what must be seen as remorseless malice as the daughters of Lear, like harpies, swoop over the helpless Gloucester:

> *Reg.* Hang him instantly!
> *Gon.* Pluck out his eyes. (III. vii. 4–5)

And, as Cornwall gouges out one eye of Gloucester, Regan calls for yet more satisfaction: "One eye will mock another; th' other too" (III. vii. 69) The daughters are, we know, outraged that Gloucester has given support to Lear in a situation that threatens them, but their malice is so excessive to the situation that it can almost be labeled as a motiveless malignity, an indulgence in cruelty for its own sake.

It is a cruelty compounded by one fact that is largely lost on a modern audience: that Gloucester's captors are violating (as Macbeth so notoriously does) the primal law of civilization: the bond of sacred trust between host and guest that is a necessary condition for social intercourse. It is this fundamental ethical intuition that Homer incorporates in *The Odyssey*, where the measure of one's civility is the way one treats the *xenos*, the stranger received as "guest-friend." Nausicaa, for example, invokes this principle when, finding the stranded Odysseus, she instructs her attendants:

> ...this man, a wretched wanderer has come here,
> Whom we must look after, for all strangers and beggars
> Are in the care of Zeus, and a gift, even small, is friendly.
> Come, maidens, give food and drink to the stranger. (VI. 206–09)

Conversely, the guest-house relationship imposes solemn obligations upon guests, who are, as Telemachus reminds the boorish suitors of Penelope, to respect the person and property of the host:

> ...if your own spirit can feel the resentment,
> Get out of the halls, partake of other dinners,
> Eating your own goods, visiting each others' homes.

But if this seems better and preferable to you,
To use up one man's livelihood scot-free,
Waste on. But I shall call on the eternal gods for help.
So that Zeus may grant there to be acts of retribution.... (II. 138–144)

Thus, as Gloucester's captors prepare to inflict their unspeakable revenge on him, we are reminded of the circumstances that make the act especially atrocious, the fact that it is "friends," to whom he has extended hospitality, who are torturing him:

Good, my friends,
You are my guests. Do me no foul play, friends. (III. vii. 30–31)

Moreover, the notorious blinding scene, perhaps for viewers the most visceral and psychologically searing of all episodes in Shakespeare (beyond even the death of Cordelia) compels the audience to "see feelingly" the unnatural malice of the act: Shakespeare's version of the theater of cruelty. If we have not to this point seen that the evil in the hearts of the daughters is of a different kind and more horrid than that of Edmund, the play, in this unsparing representation of torture, compels us to look upon reality without blinders. There is more to Lear's predicament than the wages of folly, and Edgar's intuitions of diabolical energies are ever more convincing.

It is Albany who finally rivets Edgar's intimations of the diabolical to the acts of the daughters. Appalled by their treatment of Lear and Gloucester, he initially denounces their acts as bestial:

What have you done?
Tigers, not daughters, what have you perform'd?
A father, and a gracious aged man,
Whose reverence even the head-lugg'd bear would lick,
Most barbarous, most degenerate, have you madded. (IV. ii. 40–43)

But Albany's invective does not yet take the measure of the abominations committed by Goneril and Regan, and Albany goes on to denounce Goneril in the idiom earlier introduced by Edgar:

> See thyself, devil!
> Proper deformity shows not in the fiend
> So horrid as in woman. (IV. ii. 59–61)

> Howe'er thou art a fiend,
> A woman's shape doth shield thee! (IV. ii. 66–67)

The progress toward this kind of knowledge is Lear's destiny as well: when Lear is asked by Goneril "a little to disquantity your train" (I. iv. 249), Lear sputters, "Darkness and devils! ... yet have I left a daughter," little realizing that the devils and darkness have yet to emerge in force. Lear, feeling increasingly the stings of what he perceives as injustice, rails against a world in which the rich and politically well-placed abuse their power with impunity: "Robes and furr'd gowns hide all. Plate sin with gold/ And the strong lance breaks" (IV. vi. 163–64) But equally prominent is his obsession with sexuality, and the "luxury" of which all are guilty and which establishes the bond between the worlds of man and of the beasts:

> Die for adultery? No,
> The wren goes to't, and the small gilded fly
> Does lecher in my sight. Let copulation thrive. (IV. vi. 111–13)

In a purely natural world, where the pretense of virtue is nonexistent, sexuality is guiltless. Lear has, for the moment, accepted Edmund's reading of the world. It is hypocrisy to assume that humanity, so akin to animality, is capable of chastity, just as the beadle who lashes a whore "hotly lusts to use her in that kind/ For which he [whips her]" (IV. vi. 160–61). But, like Albany, Lear ultimately finds the imagery of bestiality wanting and his idiom veers from the bestial to the diabolical:

> Down from the waist they are centaurs,
> Though women all above;
> But to the girdle do the gods inherit,
> Beneath is all the fiend's; there's hell, there's darkness,
> There is the sulphurous pit, burning, scalding,
> Stench, consumption. Fie, fie, fie, pah, pah! (IV. vi. 123–28)

The daughters justify Lear's hard judgment, as their common lust for Edmund draws them into a bitter rivalry; the lust that impels them will not stop at the murder of husband or sister, and Sin has decisively replaced Folly as the cause of human disorder.

Edgar is now ready to act, to precipitate the downfall of the three involved in the coils of lust. The manner in which he restores justice is especially significant, for Edgar sets aright the subverted, "upside-down" world of Lear by elaborating a series of meticulously appropriate paradoxes: brought down initially by the forged letter of Edmund, Edgar uses the letter intercepted from Goneril to incriminate the conspirators and thus allow Albany to assert himself against Goneril:

> Shut your mouth Dame,
> Or with this paper shall I stople it. Hold, Sir,
> Thou worse than any name, read thine own evil. (V. iii. 153–55)

In the same spirit of paradox, Edgar is translated by Shakespeare in a reckless anachronism from pre-Christian Britain to the High Middle Ages—to face Edmund in a trial by combat. The irony is patent: Edmund, who in his opening soliloquy rejects all customs and conventions, as meretricious, the mere "curiosity of nations," now appeals to the unwritten code of knighthood of the Middle Ages, this most hierarchical of all times to establish his position: he need not accept a challenge from one of unknown rank:

> What safe and nicely I might well delay
> By rule of knighthood, I disdain and spurn. (V. iii. 143–44)

The relentless paradox of the episode culminates in the victory of the meek Edgar over the strong and wily Edmund—by using precisely the means most familiar to Edmund: cunning. It is, as the exasperated Goneril points out, a classic case of "the cozener cozened."

> This is practice, Gloucester.
> By th' law of war, thou wast not bound to answer
> An unknown opponent. *Thou are not vanquish'd,*
> *But cozened and beguiled.* (V. iii. 150–53; emphasis mine)

The paradoxes surrounding the mortal wounding of Edmund effectively restore order to the world—in what appears to be manifestation of poetic justice. This return of order is formally signaled when Edgar unmasks and proclaims his identity:

> Let's exchange charity.
> I am no less in blood than thou art, Edmund;
> If more, the more th' hast wrong'd me.
> My name is Edgar, and thy father's son.
> *The gods are just, and of our pleasant vices*
> *Make instruments to plague us:*
> *The dark and vicious place where thee he got*
> *Cost him his eyes.* (V. iii. 165–72; emphasis mine)

The location of the speech, at what appears to be the resolution of the play, grants it an impressive authority—seeming to offer the final word on the significance of what has transpired. And this impression is strengthened by Edmund's assent: "Th' hast spoken right, 'Tis true, / The wheel is come full circle. I am here" (V. iii. 172–73).

But we should not, I suggest, accept too complacently what Edgar proposes, for the play goes on to challenge Edgar's judgment. Indeed, the "just gods" who have visited upon Gloucester the same kind of darkness as that in which he had sinned seem far too stern and forbidding to yield solace to the attentive viewer. Gloucester, nothing more than *l'homme moyen sensuel*, seems to pay exorbitantly for a casual adultery. But what is even more evident is that Edgar, whose penetration into the mystery of evil represents an advance over the Fool's assumption that evil is the consequence of folly, has himself a too-naive view of the divine economy, for in seeing Gloucester's blinding as heaven-sent punishment for adultery, he is simply re-contextualizing the "common sense" of the Fool: his new calculus of evil includes the forces of supernatural evil, but it suggests that human suffering yet remains understandable—as the inexorable punishment for sin. Despite the machinations of the Foul Fiend, the world of Edgar is still, to this point, open to reason, still ordained by "the clearest gods."

Edgar is, in fact, repeating the mistake made earlier by King Lear, who, after his capture by Edmund and Albany, reacts to his imprisonment by assuring Cordelia that the two "will sing like birds i' th' cage and take upon us the mystery of things, as if we were God's spies" (V. iii. 9, 16–17). The play suggests otherwise: that neither Lear nor Edgar is qualified to be God's spy.

The death of Cordelia bares the shallowness of Edgar's optimism that he can penetrate the secrets of divine economy. If evil cannot be understood as the consequence of folly, neither can it be understood as necessarily the consequence of sin; though the wages of sin may be detected in the fates of Cornwall, Goneril, Regan, and Edmund, we can ascribe the death of Cordelia to neither folly nor sin. Her radiant innocence has offered no refuge from the harshness of the world.

This world, then, is not, as Proverbs would have it, one where "the curse of the Lord is on the house of the wicked, / But the dwelling of the just He blesses' (3:3). Though Edgar would cling tenaciously to that optimism, the darker Wisdom Books, Job and Ecclesiastes, are surer guides. Edgar, in presuming to know the mysteries of God's ways, has re-enacted the errors of Job's questioners, who are roundly chastised by the Lord for their arrogance. Edgar must, rather, follow Job in submitting to the mystery of God's dealings:

> I have dealt with things I do not understand;
> things too wonderful for me, which I cannot know.

The tone of the play is similarly captured in Ecclesiastes, which insists upon the inscrutability of God and the futility of all human aspirations and endeavors: "Vanity of vanities, saith the preacher, vanity of vanity. All things are vanity." In this reading of the world, God is in his Heaven, but not all is right with the world. All man can do is to observe the time, to enjoy the fleeting intervals of pleasures that life offers, and resign himself to misfortune when it comes—as it inevitably will at some time or other, regardless of one's moral worth:

> All this I have kept in mind and recognized; the just, the wise, and their deeds are in the hands of God. Love from hatred man cannot tell; both appear equally vain, in that there is the same lot for all, for the just and the wicked, for the good and the bad, for the clean and the unclean, for him who offers sacrifice and for him who does not. As it is for the good man, so is it for the sinner; as it is for him who swears rashly, so is it for him who fears an oath. *Among all things that happen under the sun, this is the worst, that things turn out the same for all. Hence the minds of men are filled with evil, and madness is in their hearts during life; and afterwards they go to the dead.* (Eccl. 9:1–3; emphasis mine)

In such a world one cannot hope to find causes for suffering, and Lear, like Edgar, has it wrong throughout. Lear's attitude is clear from the beginning; in his staging of the "love-contest" intended to establish the reasons for his generosity, he would reward each daughter in proportion to the love she manifested to him. But when Cordelia's silence denies him his "cause," he responds wrathfully, "Nothing will come of nothing," thus framing a central question of the play, the role of causality in human experience.

The formula "nothing will come of nothing" is a familiar one in the ancient world, expressing the belief that the universe is infinite (as opposed to the finite universe of Christianity, created *ex nihilo*). The logical implication is that the universe is material and governed by the laws of cause and effect. Thus Lear's outrage at Cordelia's rebuff—she, the favored one—had cause to love him—and his later outrage at her sisters, who likewise have, as he reminds Regan, cause to love him but are flouting the "dues of gratitude" (II. iv. 177).

> Thy half of the kingdom hast thou not forgot.
> Wherein I thee endowed. (II. iv. 178–79)

Regan's reply, "Good sir, to th' purpose," exposes her indifference to Lear's reasoning. Causality, it is clear, does not obtain in the moral order; gratitude cannot be created. It is a lesson, though, that Lear does not understand, as he seeks—in his agonizing disappointment—reasons for the malice of his daughters: "Is there any cause in nature that makes these hard hearts?" If evil exists, thinks Lear, there must be a cause. This same presumption dictates his reaction to Cordelia when they are re-united, for the child he has spurned has reason to hate him:

> I know that you do not love me, for your sisters
> Have, as I remember, done me wrong;
> You have some cause, they have not. (IV. vii. 73–75)

The secret that Lear cannot yet grasp is offered in Cordelia's "No cause, no cause": Love, she states, simply is, uncaused and unconditional, just as evil simply is, uncaused and beyond rational explanation. Cordelia's rejection of cause is at once her rebuttal of Lear's "Nothing will come of nothing" and of his desperate anatomy of evil, his probe into the "cause of these hard hearts."

The last, and hardest, lesson for both Lear and Edgar, both of whom have ceaselessly sought causes, is the causeless death of Cordelia. And even now Lear speaks in the language of causality demanding that the world make sense:

> Why should a dog, a horse, a rat, have life,
> And thou no breath at all? (V. iii. 305–06).

But no answer is forthcoming—only the astounding silence of Cordelia.

The truth that transfixes us is that God has not, and will not, indulge our causal speculation, for that would be to make Him less than He is. In the death of Cordelia, Shakespeare is embodying the hard-earned wisdom of Job, which is echoed in the language of a later thinker, Nicolai Berdyaev:

> It is absolutely wrong to apply the category of causality to God and the relation between God and the world. It is suitable only to relations which belong to the phenomenal world. God is not the cause of the world any more than he is master and king, any more than he is power and might. God determines nothing. *When people speak of God as the creator of the world, they are speaking of something immeasurably more mysterious than a causal relationship.* (Emphasis mine)

After Lear's death Edgar is left to countenance the appalling mystery of things as he sees the "nothing" that Cordelia now is, and is unable to believe that something can indeed come from nothing. It is a chastened Edgar who states, "The weight of this sad time we must obey, / Speak what we feel, not what we ought to say" (V. iii. 322–23), what we ought to say being, ostensibly, some pious formulation extolling the justice of the gods and outlining the reasons for what has transpired. Such a formulation would, in these harrowing circumstances, be gross impiety toward the gods, who themselves choose to remain silent.

Notes to *King Lear*: Tragedy and the Anatomy of Evil

1. All references are to *King Lear* in *The Arden Shakespeare*, ed. Kenneth Muir (London and New York: Methuen, 1987).
   Editors: The essay was left otherwise without citations and left unrevised at the time of Fortin's death.

HERMENEUTICAL CIRCULARITY AND CHRISTIAN INTERPRETATIONS OF *KING LEAR*

René Fortin

Attempts to redeem *King Lear* by appealing to intimations of Christian transcendence in the play have been summarily, if not vehemently, dismissed by secular critics. Christian critics, we are told by W. R. Elton and others, are simply wrong because they do not attend to the "facts" of the play; seeking to escape the dire significances of the tragic vision, they are in effect guilty of wishful thinking, of imposing their own a priori assumptions upon the play. "The record" of *Lear* interpretations, says Nicholas Brooke, "is of a long series of strenuous efforts to circumvent the pain; and it is accompanied by a will to release large and encouraging affirmations once the pain is evaded."[1] Brooke insists that the greatness of *King Lear* derives, rather, from the "perfect completion of its negation and in the superb energy with which it is enforced" (p. 77).

Recently, however, René Wellek has posed an intriguing question: whether it is possible to conclude that there is indeed a single correct interpretation of the tragedies.[2] Wellek's question is worthy of further consideration, for perhaps the root of the controversy between secular critics and "Christian" critics is the fact that our criticism lacks a solid hermeneutical base. It is quite evident that the typical interpretation of *King Lear* (and of the other tragedies as well) is offered as the "right" interpretation, setting forth the meaning of the tragedy all would derive if they would only see the play aright. But perhaps we are now ready to awaken from our dogmatic slumber and reexamine the implicitly Lockean assumptions which have governed our critical practice. For time after time in the past several decades we have been cautioned that perception and cognition are highly complex activities and that the perceiving eye and mind are actively engaged in constituting or shaping the truth they are naively supposed merely to register.[3] The conceptual model of a purely objective critical encounter, such as that called for by Morris Weitz (a model which would have the critic as spectator attempting to "see the object exactly as it is"), seems highly questionable at this time.[4] It is now almost *de rigueur* in critical essays to offer ritual obeisance to E. H. Gombrich and his demonstration that our vision is largely a matter of projection, of seeing only what we are prepared to see.[5] Specifically in literature the now familiar paradigm of the "included spectator" indicates an awakening to the creative participation of the viewer of a play,[6] while Norman Rabkin's view of the complementarity of Shakespearean meanings has made remarkable inroads; Shakespearean structure, Rabkin tells us, sets up "the opposed elements as equally valid, equally desirable, and equally destructive, so that the choice the play forces the reader to make becomes almost impossible."[7] Specifically about *King Lear*, Rabkin states, "We find ourselves able at almost any point in the play to read it as godless or divine; these are the terms implicit in the action of *King Lear* and explicit in its language."[8] E. D. Hirsch, who has been a stalwart defender of "objective interpretation," nonetheless concedes the shaping role of the interpreter:

> The object of interpretation is precisely that which cannot be defined by the ontological status of a text, since the distinguishing characteristic of a text is that from it not just one but many disparate complexes of meaning can be construed.... the object of interpretation is no automatic given, but a task that the interpreter sets himself. He decides what he wants to actualize and what purpose his actualization should achieve.[9]

In this context Marvin Rosenberg's condescending observation about the "redemptionist" readers of *King Lear* impresses me as especially provocative: "All this [devastation] cannot prevent those who will from seeing exaltation in Lear's final vision of Cordelia's death, or from believing that what Lear has learned was worth the suffering. *We perceive what we are prepared to, need to, perceive*" [italics mine].[10] Rosenberg goes on, of course, to dismiss such a response as tawdry sentimentality and to offer the real, objective truth about *King Lear*, that it is a play which ends in totally unrelieved "general woe" (p. 326).

Rosenberg's observation, however, raises the intriguing question whether it is only the "redemptionist" readers who are to be numbered among "those who will"; for it is difficult to determine precisely how the secular critics can lay claim to an epistemological transcendence denied other critics. Perhaps we have here, as Maynard Mack has suggested, merely a sentimentality of a different kind.[11] I do not propose, I hasten to add, that secular readings of *King Lear* are wrong; indeed they are often quite persuasive and should be heeded. I wish rather to suggest that to consider the secular reading as exclusively valid is as much an act of dogmatic assertion as is the comforting vision offered by the Christian interpreters, since the assertion in either case is based upon a selection of evidence as well as a selective interpretation of that evidence. It is difficult, when one considers the Joseph's coat of *Lear* interpretations, to dismiss the specter of the hermeneutical circle so prominent in Bultmann's exegetical theory:

> All understanding, like all interpretation, is...continually oriented by the manner of posing the question and by what it aims at.... Consequently, it is never without presuppositions; that is to say, it is always directed by a prior understanding about which it interrogates the text. It is only on the basis of that prior understanding that it can, in general, interrogate and interpret.[12]

One need not follow Bultmann's speculation into the intellectual swamp of relativism to appreciate the usefulness of the caveat; if critical objectivity is at all possible, as E. D. Hirsch insists it is, one does not easily attain it.[13] Interpretations of Shakespeare's plays are, and will continue to be, colored by personal predispositions since an active, personal response is inherent in the critical effort. But that this is the case is not to be regretted, for the great diversity of interpretations is our most eloquent witness to the wealth of Shakespeare's world as well as our best defense against critical dogmatism.

The final scene of *King Lear* provides the best opportunity to pursue these questions, for in the death of Cordelia lies the most formidable challenge to any affirmative, religious view of the tragic experience. The Christian critic's attempt to wrest comfort from the dire outcome of the play is decisively repudiated by the secular critic because the events of the play—its "facts"—supposedly contradict the central tenets of Christianity. But what specifically are these tenets? If we examine closely the secular arguments, we find (1) that nothing short of poetic justice would validate a religious argument; (2) that a truly Christian play would have to dramatize the miraculous intervention of the gods or otherwise catch them red-handed as they intrude into the affairs of men; and (3) that the universe in which the tragic ordeal takes place would have to be transparently meaningful. Nicholas Brooke, for example, states: "I have never been clear what constitutes a 'Christian play.' I should have supposed that label would involve some effort to justify God's ways to men, to make the mysterious less inscrutable" (p. 74). He later adds, "Poetical justice has been dealt out to Oswald, but embarrassingly, the gods didn't do it themselves," just as it is Edgar—and not God—who provides the "miracle" that saves Gloucester (pp. 80, 78). Elton likewise attaches great importance to miracles as signs of God's benevolent Providence: "In an unprovidential universe, it is suggested, miracles are absent and prayers are generally [?] ineffective. Such mention of miracles dramatically recalls to the spectator their absence—a sharply contrasting beam of tenuous light in a grimly dark and God-forsaken world."[14] Finally, Rosenberg joins this chorus with his utter certitude about the vacancy of Lear's final vision: "On this ultimate stage of fools, no one—except possibly Lear dying in illusion—is so foolish as to see any evidence of divinity at work.... Death everywhere, of the good as well as the 'bad'" (pp. 325–26).

Such responses cannot be peremptorily dismissed even by the Christian interpreter, for the question of poetic justice and of the benign concern of the gods for man is at the very heart of the play. From the outset of *King Lear* the characters express faith in the concern and loving-kindness of the gods: the gods, Lear feels, will at once take his part against his daughters; Cornwall's servants pray that the blinding of Gloucester be speedily avenged; Albany sees the killing of Cornwall as evidence that the "justicers" are above; and Edgar constantly assures his father that the gods are sensitive to human anguish:

> ...therefore, thou happy father,
> Think that the clearest gods, who make them honors
> Of men's impossibilities, have preserved thee. (IV. vi. 72–74)[15]

What we notice, however, is a far less hospitable universe. As many commentators have pointed out, a conspicuous feature of the structure of *King Lear* is its irony, the rhythm of expectation and frustration to which the characters are subjected.[16] It has been too infrequently noted, however, that the viewer is himself victimized by the same ironies. Our familiarity with the play—we all know how it ends—has largely blunted these ironies for us; like trained hounds we have been over the course before and are not likely to be led astray by false scents, as Lear, Albany, and Edgar are. But the "naive spectator," the first-time viewer of the play, who lacks our synchronic, spatial sense of the play's form, would hardly be so fortunate—especially if he is familiar with the earlier *Leir*. The naive spectator, rather, is constantly being assured that all will be well; he is comforted by the discreet loyalty of Kent, by the early and persistent rumors of civil wars that will bring down the house divided of Goneril and Regan, by the tender care of Edgar (as Poor Tom) for his father, and especially the perpetual promise of the return of Cordelia. What is especially noteworthy is how early the viewer is given these assurances: we hear of the "likely wars toward," for example, in the first lines of Act II, while Kent offers us the promise of the "almost miracle" of Cordelia's return in Act II, scene ii—significantly before Lear's ordeal begins in earnest. It is as if the play is taking great pains to buffer the viewer from anguish, assuring him that the darkness is only temporary.

The peculiar cruelty of *King Lear*, of course, is that this promise is violated, most glaringly in the manner in which Cordelia—"Great thing of us forgot" (V. iii. 238)—dies. Though we do see some measure of what could be taken for "rough justice" in the deaths of Cornwall, Oswald, Edmund, Goneril, and Regan, there is in the death of Cordelia no poetic justice, no "dark and vicious place" (V. iii. 174) to account for her murder, no discernible incense thrown upon her sacrifice. The viewer is tempted, after this unconscionable mischief of the wanton gods, to accept as his the "cheerless, dark and deadly" world described by Kent (V. iii. 292).

But does the play insist that we do so? Do the "facts" of the play, particularly its excruciating final scene, make *King Lear* absolutely incompatible with a Christian worldview? Any critic intending to offer an unequivocal reading of its ending should recall that he is witnessing a play that has throughout insisted upon the problematics of seeing and that this theme dominates the final lines of Lear:

> Do you see this? Look on her, Look, her lips.
> Look there, look there. (V. iii. 312–13)

Five times in his final fourteen words Lear refers to vision. As Rosenberg has aptly stated, *King Lear* dwells upon "the necessity and difficulty of seeing to know.... seeing and knowing are never certain in *Lear*, for the play's dialectic insists upon ambiguity" (p. 344). Thus Lear's final statement presents to the viewers the ultimate challenge to vision: everything depends upon what is actually seen—or not seen—in these final moments. But here is perhaps the most devastating irony of the play: we do not and cannot see what Lear sees. What we see is merely Lear seeing. Philip Hobsbaum is at least partially right in arguing that "we cannot, to put it crudely, know whether or not Lear dies smiling. At the end of the play we are in exactly the same position as the spectators on stage.... Most of the critics who have dealt with the play seem to me wrong in opting for one or the other of these possibilities [hope and despair]: the values are more complex than that."[17]

Hobsbaum's comment is particularly useful when we consider the scene in the light of Bertrand Evans' concept of discrepant awarenesses, for the concept may be especially relevant, though in a different way than most would imagine.[18] For where comedy typically offers to the viewer a cognitive perspective superior to that of the central figure (we know, for example, that Cesario is really Viola), it is possible that in *King Lear* it is the central figure who has the privileged vision, with the viewer able to see only from afar. Such a conclusion would be supported by the logic of the play, which postulates suffering as a precondition to accurate vision:

> Let the superfluous and lust-dieted man,
> That slaves your ordinance, that will not see
> Because he does not feel, feel your pow'r quickly.... (IV. i. 67–69)

Thus Lear, because he has suffered, may indeed see more than the survivors (Edgar, Kent, and Albany), who seem to see nothing more than "general woe" (V. iii. 321), and more than the spectators, whose suffering is at best vicarious. In short, if we accept what Rosenberg has said, that the play dwells upon "the necessity and difficulty of seeing to know," then we must be careful about arrogating to ourselves a clarity of vision superior to that of Lear, for what he sees, or cannot see, must remain for us only a matter of inference.

In order to be convincing, a Christian reading of *King Lear* must bravely push on beyond the "redemption" scenes of Act IV and take in fully the devastatingly ironic death of Cordelia. It is true, as secular critics have argued, that the death of Cordelia suggests the failure of the gods to provide the "chance which does redeem all sorrows" (V. iii. 268), the saving miracle that would attest to their beneficence. Their failure to do so is particularly agonizing because it has occurred in a universe that seemed to support a faith in poetic justice but which instead decisively reasserts its opaqueness; we are left blindly staring at that which passeth all understanding.

But for the Christian critic the opaqueness of the *Lear* world is no insurmountable obstacle, for the very structural ironies which purportedly impeach the Christian worldview provide, when seen from a different perspective, a strong support for a Christian reading. To begin with, if the absence of visible supernatural intervention is to be the cudgel to beat down Christian interpretations—or Christian interpreters—one had better take a second look at the traditional beliefs of Christianity, for it is not at all presumed in the mainstream of Christian orthodoxy that God will intervene on call for his faithful; nowhere is a God of sweetness and light promised to man on this earth. Saint Paul, for example, preaches constantly that God is beyond human knowing: "How incomprehensible are his judgments and how unsearchable his wayes" (Rom. 11:33).[19] St. Augustine similarly speaks of God's "hidden equity that cannot be searched out by any human standard of measurement, though its effects are to be observed in human affairs and earthly arrangements."[20] Moreover, in Shakespeare's own time Reformation theology, under the twin influences of St. Paul and St. Augustine, forcefully elaborated the concept of a "hidden God" whose power and purposes are not to be fathomed.[21] In the words of Luther, God is "He for whose will no cause or ground may be laid down as its rule or standard.... God is wholly incomprehensible and inaccessible to man's understanding."[22] It is true that commentators, especially in the Catholic tradition, insisted upon the rationality of God, but even these writers were careful to respect the *mysterium tremendum*; Richard Hooker, for example, was strongly influenced by St. Thomas Aquinas and was therefore eager to defend the "light of reason" against the fideistic and voluntaristic emphases of the Reformers, but he nevertheless writes:

> The book of this law [the eternal law of God] we are not either able nor worthy to open and look into. That little thereof which we darkly apprehend we admire, the rest with religious ignorance we humbly and meekly adore.[23]

The ordeal of Lear and the death of Cordelia are, to be sure, hard to cope with, but they do not contradict the image of God held in either Catholic or Protestant Christianity. In fact, an ear attuned to scripture would discern in Lear's ordeal resonances of the Book of Revelation:

> I knowe thy workes, that thou art neither colde nor hote.
>
> I wolde thou werest colde or hote. Therefore, because thou art lukewarm, and nether colde nor hote, it will come to passe, that I shall spewe thee out of my mouth.
>
> For thou saist I am riche and increased with goods, and have neede of nothing, and knowest not how thou art wretched and miserable, and poore, and blinde, and naked. (Rev. 3:15–17)

I think it is evident that the verses point to central themes of the play and suggest much about its imagery. The lesson that Lear learns in his suffering is that he has been morally callous; it is a lesson that he learns by becoming himself poor, naked, and—symbolically through his madness—blind. The suffering of Lear, seen against this background is at once punitive and propaedeutic, a necessary condition to his redemption:

> I counsel thee to bie of me golde tryed by fire, that thou maist be made riche, and white raiment, that thou maiest be clothed and that thy filthie nakednes do not appeare: and anoint thine eyes with salve, that thou maist se.
>
> As manie as I love, I rebuke and chasten. (Rev. 3:18–19)

Lear's "wheel of fire," the garment in which he is clothed after his wanderings, and the regained sight which allows him to see the daughter he has rejected in his blindness assume a more specific significance in the light of this Scriptural passage. The suffering of Lear may be construed as the activity of a loving, albeit stern, God.

There still, of course, remains the death of Cordelia. It is true, as many critics have averred, that Christian interpretations generally ignore the final excruciating scene of the play: "This object poisons sight; / let it be hid" (*Oth.* V. ii. 363–64). It is, however, equally true that secular interpreters tend to view the death of Cordelia as an isolated episode, apart from the rich context that the previous four acts of the play have provided.

Because this context has been effectively explored elsewhere, I shall limit myself to brief remarks about how it may support a Christian reading. First, what is especially remarkable about the final scene is its recapitulatory nature, its gathering up of themes which developed earlier in the play. It should be noted, for example, that the Lear whom we view in the final scene has come full circle, being in much the same position as he was in Act I: calling upon his one true daughter to utter the words needed to sustain value in his life and once again receiving as answer the silence which is the alpha and omega of the play:

> What is't thou sayst? Her voice was ever soft,
> Gentle and low, an excellent thing in woman. (V. iii. 274–75)

But Cordelia's failure to speak now may be no more a denial of value than was her earlier silence, particularly when one construes that silence in the light of other themes and images. Above all, Lear's lament over the dead Cordelia, "And my poor fool is hanged" (V. iii. 307), recalls the motif of folly which has been so prominent earlier in the play. We have seen folly constantly associated with virtue: in the Fool's poignant commitment to Lear despite his own worldly wisdom which counsels a different course; in the supererogatory loyalty of Kent, who serves Lear despite his unjust banishment; and particularly in the superfluity of Cordelia's loving forgiveness. Virtue, for all its foolishness, yet survives in an otherwise bleak world. The Christian reader will have little difficulty seeing in such instances of unlikely goodness reminiscences of the Pauline theme of Christian folly in the First Epistle to the Corinthians.

> For brethren, you se your calling, how that not manie wise men after the flesh, not manie, not manie noble, are called.
>
> But God hathe chosen the foolish things of the worlde to confounde the wise, and God hathe chosen the weake things of the worlde, to confounde the mighty things. (1:26–27)[24]

It is part of the Pauline scheme of things that true virtue be seen as folly or otherwise unpublished; Cordelia directs us to this view when she calls upon "All blest secrets, / All you unpublished virtues of the earth" (IV. iv. 15–16) to remedy her father's distress.[25]

For a prominent feature of *King Lear* is that virtue, in a world overwhelmed by evil, chooses to or is compelled to conceal its presence, to operate covertly. The list of "unpublished virtues" in the play is impressive; it includes Kent and Edgar, who fulfill their obligations in disguise; Gloucester, who summons up unexpected moral strength to assist his king and to bear his own ordeal patiently; the servants of Cornwall, who unexpectedly lash out at the cruelty of their master; and finally, Cordelia, who can publish her love for her father neither at the beginning nor at the end of the play.

But does the list of unpublished virtues end there? No one, I think, will deny that the question Lear addresses to the dead Cordelia, "Why should a dog, a horse, a rat, have life, / And thou no breath at all?" (308–309), is really addressed to the gods who would allow such an abomination. The Christian interpreter, recognizing that Lear has been throughout his ordeal surrounded by goodness which he has had difficulty perceiving, may have warrant enough to see the dead Cordelia as but a further instance of a pattern which points beyond to the gods, the ultimate unpublished virtues of the world. The apparent absence of redeeming goodness has thus far proven to be no guarantee that it does not exist.

And thus a play which begins with a king announcing "darker purposes" which lead to the temporary loss of a daughter ends with a Higher Power (or powers) announcing infinitely darker purposes and apparently bringing the same victim to distress. The Christian viewer will accept the harsh fact that the world offers no cheap consolations but need not necessarily infer that God has forsaken that world.

Rather, the Christian reader who is responsive to the Biblical echoes of the play may view the play as an attempt to demythologize Christianity, to reassert the hiddenness of God against the presumptuous pieties and shallow rationalism of the Edgars and Albanys of the world. In the death of Cordelia the viewers are once more confronted with the Judaeo-Christian God who, from the Book of Job on, has chosen to remain hidden and refuses to render account of His "darker purposes" to man. As Ivor Morris has indicated, *King Lear* is preeminently a play of stripping—of clothing, of language, of social masks—in order to unveil what is most fundamentally real (p. 184); in Act V it is God himself who is stripped, divested of the conventional images man has created for him. The God who emerges in the final events of the play is not the majuscule God as prime mover and creator of all, nor God as supreme justicer, nor even the God of translucent love to whom Cordelia seems to point. He is rather an unaccommodated and unaccommodating God who refuses masks of any kind, who denies us either the explanations we seek or the miracles which would make such explanations unnecessary. He is the minuscule God of Pauline theology who denies both signs and wisdom:

> For seing the worlde by wisdome knewe not God in the wisdome of God,
> it pleased God by the foolishenes of preaching to save them that beleve:

> Seing also that the Jewes require a signe, and the Grecians seke after wisdome.
>
> But we preache Christ crucified: unto the Jewes a stumbling block, and unto the Grecians foolishness. (1 Cor. 1:21–23)

For the Christian interpreter the death of Cordelia need not, cannot, be explained away; as "stumbling block" it supports rather than contradicts Revelation, the true Biblical God, even and perhaps especially that of the New Testament, being a God of faith seen but through a glass darkly, whose promises are beheld from afar. The ending of *King Lear*, in short, presents a demythologized Christianity that offers mystery rather than justice and that is founded upon hope rather than fulfillment; once more the language of Paul offers the best commentary:

> For we are saved by hope: but hope that is sene, is not hope: for how can a man hope for that which he seeth?
>
> But if we hope for that we se not, we do with patience abide for it. (Rom. 8:24–25)

Such a Christian reading again, is not intended as *the* authoritative reading of *King Lear*; it is offered, rather, in an attempt to show that a Christian response to the play may be in conformity with both the "facts" of the play and with the doctrines of Christianity. Such a response, however, does not invalidate the secular reading, since even the most adamantly Christian of interpreters must feel the force of Edgar's admonition to "speak what we feel, not what we ought to say" (V. iii. 326). What *King Lear* strongly suggests is that the lion of tragedy need not be devoured by the lamb of theology, for, as Paul Ricoeur has suggested, tragedy survives the most ardent hermeneutical efforts of Christian thinkers:

> Killed twice, by the philosophical Logos and by the Judaeo-Christian Kerygma, [tragedy] survived its double death. The theme of the wrath of god, the ultimate motive of tragic consciousness, is invincible to the

> arguments of the philosopher as well as of the theologian.... As soon as meaninglessness appears to swoop down intentionally on man, the schema of the wrath of God looms up and tragic consciousness is restored. (p. 326)

To assert that *King Lear* admits both secular and religious interpretations is not, however, to argue for critical relativism, to consider the play as a *tabula rasa* awaiting any critical impression whatever. We must, as Murray Krieger has stated, "accept the hermeneutical gap that separates every critique from the work," but we must do so without denying the intersubjective nature of poetic communication; "at some level," says Krieger, "in spite of persuasive epistemological skepticism, all of us share Dr. Johnson's hard-headed, rock-kicking impatience with the unbridgeable private worlds of solipsism."[26] It is evident that the play, despite its apparent multivalence, creates its unique frame of discourse, channeling inquiry into specific areas of speculation and compelling attention to clearly-defined overwhelming questions. Thus a Christian interpreter can agree with much that Brooke, Elton, Rosenberg, and Stampfer have observed about the play: *King Lear* indeed dramatizes man's quest for justice; the folly, callousness, and brutality of which humanity is capable; the apparent injustice which man may suffer. It also dramatizes the unlikely perdurance of virtue under the most trying of conditions, as well as the moral awakening of several under the pressure of adversity. Calculations about what all of this adds up to may differ, and differ markedly, but it is most probably true that any interpretation of the play which denies that these are central concerns is simply wrong.

The open form of tragedy, its respect for the limits of human experience, allows readers to draw different conclusions: enough is given to allow interpreters to "see feelingly," to infer an interpretation based upon their own personal experience of the play; but enough is withheld to compel respect for the tragic mystery, to remind us that our conclusions are, after all, nothing but inference. If we learn anything from *King Lear*, it is that we all must see in our way, that a personal response is mandated by the tragic structure, but that our own vision is necessarily limited. Perhaps this humbling truth, hermeneutical as well as theological in its implications, is the play's most valuable revelation.

NOTES TO Hermeneutical Circularity and Christian Interpretations of *King Lear*

1. Nicholas Brooke, "The Ending of *King Lear*," in *Shakespeare 1564–1964*, ed. Edward A. Bloom (Providence, RI: Brown University Press, 1964), p. 77.
2. "A. C. Bradley, Shakespeare, and the Infinite," *Philological Quarterly*, 54 (1975), p. 98.
3. Perhaps the most useful survey of this problem is in E. D. Hirsch, Jr., *The Aims of Interpretation* (Chicago: University of Chicago Press, 1976).
4. Cf. M. H. Abrams, "What is the Use of Theorizing About the Arts?" *In Search of Literary Theory*, ed. Morton W. Bloomfield (Ithaca, NY: Cornell University Press, 1972), pp. 31–35.
5. E. H. Gombrich, *Art and Illusion* (New York: Pantheon, 1960); esp. ch. 9, "The Analysis of Vision in Art."
6. Robert Hapgood's "Shakespeare and the Included Spectator," *Reinterpretations of Elizabethan Drama*, ed. Norman Rabkin (New York: Columbia University Press, 1969), is, of course, the seminal article.
7. Norman Rabkin, *Shakespeare and the Common Understanding* (New York: The Free Press, 1967), p. 12.
8. Rabkin, pp. 10–11; for a similar view, see Helen Gardner, *Religion and Literature* (New York: Oxford Univ. Press, 1971), pp. 35–36, 86–87.
9. E. D. Hirsch, Jr., *Validity in Interpretation* (New Haven: Yale University Press, 1967), pp. 24–25.
10. Marvin Rosenberg, *The Masks of King Lear* (Berkeley: University of California Press, 1972), p. 326.
11. Maynard Mack, *King Lear in Our Time* (Berkeley: University of California Press, 1965), p. 115.
12. Cited in Paul Ricoeur, *The Symbolism of Evil* (New York: Harper, 1967), p. 351.
13. See especially Hirsch's "Appendix I. Objective Interpretation," in *Validity in Interpretation*, pp. 209–44; the essay first appeared in *PMLA*, 75 (1960).
14. W. R. Elton, *King Lear and the Gods* (San Marino: Huntington Library, 1966), p. 236.
15. All references to the plays are to *The Complete Signet Classic Shakespeare*, ed. Sylvan Barnet (New York: Harcourt, 1972).
16. See, e.g., Elton's "Irony as Structure," pp. 329–34.
17. Philip Hobsbaum, *Theory of Criticism* (Bloomington: Indiana University Press, 1970), p. 161.
18. See Bertrand Evans, *Shakespeare's Comedies* (London: Oxford University Press, 1960), esp. p. viii.
19. All Biblical references are to the Geneva Bible (1560), facsimile ed. (Madison: University of Wisconsin Press, 1969).
20. Cited in Morris, p. 147.
21. See Paul R. Sellin, "The Hidden God: Reformation Awe in Renaissance English Literature," in *The Darker Vision of the Renaissance*, ed. Robert Kinsman (Berkeley: University of California Press. 1974). p. 175.
22. Cited in Morris, p. 147.
23. *Laws of Ecclesiastical Polity* (New York: Everyman's Library, 1925), I, 153.
24. For a fuller treatment of the relevance of the Corinthian letters, see Roger Cox, *Between Heaven and Earth* (New York: Holt, 1969).

25. I have discussed the theme of "unpublished virtues" at greater length in "Shakespearean Tragedy and the Problem of Transcendence," *Shakespeare Studies*, 7 (1974), pp. 307–25.
26. Murray Krieger, "The Critic as Person and Persona," in *The Personality of the Critic*, ed. Joseph P. Strelka (University Park: Pennsylvania State University Press, 1973), pp. 87–88.

SHAKESPEAREAN TRAGEDY AND THE PROBLEM OF TRANSCENDENCE

René Fortin

I

The sessions of critical thought about Shakespeare's metaphysics are anything but sweet and silent. On the one side we hear the theologizers of Shakespeare argue their case, insisting that every rift in the plays is loaded with Christian ore, that indeed the tragedies should be recognized as quasi-allegorical adumbrations of the Christian mysteries. Thus, G. Wilson Knight's assertion that "each of Shakespeare's tragic heroes is a miniature Christ"[1] has been, for better or worse, extensively explored in subsequent criticism, while Roy Battenhouse, probably the most conspicuous and most influential of today's theologizers, has recently argued that "the ultimate archetype for the tragic hero [is] a figurative Adam," and that tragic heroism in Shakespeare is, in fact, a *parody* of the Christ story:

> Adam is related to Christ by analogy, in the way in which the Old Adam in every man is related to the potential new Adam in him: the first is but the mistaken shadow-version of the second. From this point of view, the agony and "sacrifice" we see in a typical hero is not at all identical with Christ's but rather its rival analogue.[2]

But the secularizers of Shakespeare resist this theological treatment of Shakespeare's work, countering that Shakespeare's tragedies, and indeed all tragedies, are pervasively secular, essentially Manichaean or agnostic.[3] Sylvan Barnet's defense of the secularist position is representative of this view:

> Shakespeare was a writer of, among other things, tragedies, and his tragedies show the material fall of heroes. In the great plays this fall is generally accomplished by an increased awareness of the nature of life, but such profit is gained at the expense of life. Shakespeare had an Anglican education, and the ethics in the plays partake of Christian ethics, but they are not based, as Christian ethics in fact are, upon the eschatology of the Christian system.[4]

Those critics who choose not to be perplexed in the extremes are left to choose the labyrinthine middle ground, where things are but are not, where the critic giveth and the critic taketh away. In this middle ground, the reader, after being assured that Shakespeare's plays have no religious or philosophical dimensions, is more than likely to be solemnly initiated to the *real* religious and metaphysical meaning of the plays. Bradley, for example, argues that Shakespeare "practically confined his view to the world of nontheological observation and thought" but then adds that the ultimate power in the tragic world is a cosmic moral order which shows itself akin to good and alien to evil."[5] And, despite his conviction that the tragedy question cannot be posed or answered in religious terms, Bradley comes embarrassingly close to describing *Hamlet* as a religious drama.[6]

Roland Frye is no surer guide. Though he is convinced that "the weight of evidence and of critical opinion is in favor of the secular analysis of Shakespeare," he nevertheless states that "a familiar understanding of Christian doctrine in historical perspective...contributes to a fuller understanding of Shakespeare's art...."[7] The convolutions of Frye's argument can best be appreciated by noting that the authorities he marshals to "furnish a theological validation of [Shakespeare's] primarily secular approach to literature" are, remarkably, Luther, Calvin, and Richard Hooker.[8]

This critical befuddlement provides ample testimony that the place of religion in Shakespeare cannot easily be determined. The historical test, which would bear witness to Shakespeare's tragic meaning by establishing the religious expectations of his audience, is called into question by nothing less than history itself. However much the historical critic would like to take refuge in the residual medieval pieties of the Renaissance world, he runs afoul, if he is at all thorough, of disconcerting counter-evidence—the growing anxiety about the "trepidation of the spheres" and about the New Philosophy which finds expression most prominently in the poetry of John Donne. The Shakespearean moment, we are told in *Hamlet*, is a "drossy age" in which man acts as if "the world were now but to begin, / Antiquity forgot, custom not known..." (V. ii. 181; IV. v. 103–104).[9] It is, most significantly, an age uncomfortable with myth and miracle:

> They say miracles are past, and we have our philosophical persons, to make modern and familiar, things supernatural and causeless. Hence is it that we make trifles of terrors, ensconcing ourselves into seeming knowledge when we should submit ourselves to an unknown fear. (*AWW*, II. iii. 1–6)

If the historical test is at best inconclusive, the contextual test is no more satisfactory. Certainly we can affirm by counting images that Shakespeare used a religious idiom familiar to himself and his viewers, and by tracing image patterns, we can even establish that these image patterns have dramatic substance, that is, that they are to be taken seriously. But we cannot assume that they necessarily point to a religious interpretation of the action. When Richard II describes himself as a Christ-figure, we must, for example, consider first, that he is a medieval king who would naturally resort in his ordeal to the semantic of Christianity, and secondly, that he is by personality prone to self-dramatization and self-exculpation. Thus his image of himself as a Christ-figure would be emotionally uplifting for him but would nevertheless invite the sceptical appraisal of the viewer. Richard's appeal to the mysteries of Christianity, one could argue, says nothing about the Christian mettle of the character or the play, much less of the playwright. And so with such other religious manifestations as the several "miniature Christs" who, in the words of Roland Frye, "appear in such weltering profusion as almost to crowd all other actors from the stage."[10]

On the other hand, it is equally hard to dissolve the imagery and language of the plays into some miraculous manna that satisfies everybody's craving for meaning without having a taste or character of its own. The religious imagery of many plays is far too insistent, precise, and coherent to be dismissed as mere dramatic artifice or as a *lingua franca* of the Shakespearean theater. The involved reader of *Hamlet* or *Othello* will inevitably feel that the religious questions dwelt upon in the plays are of some moment, that Hamlet's anxiety about resolving the religious ambiguities of his experience is somehow an integral part of the play's meaning, just as the dark vision of damnation imagined by Othello is more than a merely poetic consummation of the play's action. The intuition of a supernatural reality seems, in short, to be an indissoluble part of the tragic hero's—and, by extension, the audience's—experience.

How are we then to get beyond this perplexity? I would suggest as a first step that the controversy about religious meanings be recognized as the result of naive theologizing (engendering an equally naive anti-theologizing). The crux of the problem seems to be that the religious significance of the tragedies is often approached as "given," with the result that the critic establishes prematurely the ethical and metaphysical bases of judgment. Thus a religious symbol occurring in a key passage is seen as validating the Christian significance of a tragedy, allowing the critic then to read theological meanings back into any passage of the play. Conversely, the absence of overt Christian references (as in *King Lear*) is often seized upon as decisive evidence of the secularity of the plays. What seems needed, many readers will agree, is an approach that will do justice to the evidently valid perceptions of both the humanists and the theologizers.

Perhaps it would be profitable for critics to follow the lead of contemporary students of religion and to recognize the possibility of an *inductive* theology, such as that expounded in Peter Berger's recent *Rumor of Angels*.[11] This inductive theology could be described as a thoroughly unbiased anthropology ready to take into account all of the dimensions of human life and consciousness; it would begin with the facts of human experience and strive to discern "signals of transcendence within the empirically-given human situation."[12] Berger goes on to describe these signals of transcendence as "phenomena that are to be found within the domain of our natural reality but that appear to point beyond that reality."[13]

What is especially important from the critic's point of view is that this concept of inductive theology offers the possibility of acknowledging religious experience in the tragedies without compromising the integrity of secular experience. Accordingly, Shakespearean tragedy, while remaining "this-worldly" in its utter fidelity to perceptible human experience, may nonetheless uncover within the heights and depths of this experience signals of transcendence, phenomena which point to a religious dimension in human life. In this tragic world it is not the religious symbols that reveal the significance of the dramatic action, but the dramatic action that validates (or often invalidates!) the "revealed" symbol. Theological insight is earned rather than given, for the heroes of the tragedies as well as the critics. Moreover, because of the anthropological (that is, humanistic) basis of these tragedies, we are offered at best only intimations of a meta-empirical reality, the probability but not the certitude that a Something Other exists. We are offered not a theological confession of faith but a dramatic world which admits of, without compelling, belief.

Indeed, the prominence of two related patterns of thought in the great tragedies invites us to read Shakespeare's tragedies as a deliberate search for an inductive theology. The first of these patterns is a preoccupation with paganism in its various manifestations, particularly in its interaction with traditional Christianity. In *Hamlet* Shakespeare, by deliberately introducing Christian elements into the originally pagan narrative, creates a tension between a pagan Teutonic ethos and the Christian ethos. In *Othello*, Othello's conversion to Christianity must withstand the pressures put upon it by the paganism of his own background as well as the neo-paganism of Iago. In *King Lear* the originally Christian source is purged of all Christian references and transformed to an austere paganism, while in *Macbeth* the Christian world is invaded by the occult in the form of the demonic witches. The intention of this tragedy seems to be to explore the relationship between "natural man" and "religious man," to penetrate as deeply as possible into the concept of Natural Man in order to determine whether man is indeed sufficient unto himself, whether he is indeed the measure of all things.

The second major pattern I would describe as the progressive penetration of the tragedies into negative transcendence. From *Hamlet* on, what we observe is a penetration into the mystery of evil, with each tragedy bringing us progressively closer to the springs of evil. We are gradually encouraged to believe that the natural explanation of evil is inadequate, that some supernatural hypothesis must be resorted to in order to account for the iniquity of man. Paradoxically, it is the affirmation of the mystery of evil, expressed in the imagery of diabolism, that lends credibility to the companion mystery, the mystery of good. For the barriers of reason, once breached, cannot be reconstructed, and the unsentimental affirmation of negative transcendence, that is, of metaphysical evil, prepares one to believe in a positive transcendence. It is thus the uncanny evil of Iago that authenticates the virtue of Desdemona, as it is the perversity of Goneril and Regan that testifies to the transcendent goodness of Cordelia. In this intuition Shakespeare anticipates Wallace Stevens, who writes in his "Esthétique Du Mal":

> The death of Satan was a tragedy
> For the imagination. A capital
> Negation destroyed him in his tenement
> And, with him, many blue phenomena.

It is an intuition voiced also by Chesterton:

> The world can be made beautiful again by viewing it as a battlefield. When we have defined and isolated the evil thing, the colours come back into everything else. When evil things have become evil, good things, in a blazing apocalypse, become good. There are some men who are dreary because they do not believe in God; but there are many others who are dreary because they do not believe in the devil.[14]

II

Shakespeare begins the journey to the heart of darkness with *Hamlet*. A remarkable feature of *Hamlet* is Shakespeare's manipulation of his sources to introduce Christian elements into an erstwhile pagan setting. Belleforest, well aware that revenge was inconsistent with the "official" Christian ethos of the Renaissance, was careful to insist in his very first paragraph that the Hamlet narrative was based upon a pagan ethic:

> You must understand, that long time before the kingdome of Denmark received the faith of Jesus Christ, and imbraced the doctrine of the Christians, that the common people in those dayes were barbarous and uncivill, and their princes cruell, without faith or loyaltie, seeking nothing but murther, and deposing (or at least) offending each other, either in honours, goods, or lives.[15]

By this appeal Belleforest offers an easy way out of the ethical difficulties, allowing the Christian viewer to suspend moral judgment of Hamlet's revenge motive and lend his sympathy to the hero. But Shakespeare, while maintaining the pagan atmosphere of the revenge story, seems to go out of his way to introduce into this story a relatively developed Christian ethos. The *Hamlet* that emerges is not, to be sure, a Christian play, but it is certainly no longer a pagan play. Rather, it is a play in which two incompatible moral contexts are held in tension.

The Christian elements in the play have been so well elaborated elsewhere that I shall limit myself to a few observations. They include a ghost that is decidedly more Christian than Senecan—that indeed describes itself as a purgatorial spirit "confined to fast in fires" (I. v. 11)—and a multitude of references to Christian eschatology and Christian liturgy, ranging from the "angels and ministers of grace" (I. iv. 39) invoked by Hamlet to the "churlish priest" who is berated by Laertes for the maimed rites accorded to Ophelia:

> I tell thee, churlish priest,
> A ministering angel shall my sister be
> When thou liest howling. (V. i. 233–35)

They significantly include Hamlet's own Christian perceptions, particularly after his "change of heart" in Act IV, where he expresses belief in a "special providence," in a "divinity that shapes our ends, / Rough-hew them how we will" (V. ii. 208–10; ii. 10–11). *Hamlet* is unquestionably among the most Christian of the tragedies in language and imagery.

And yet it cannot be described as unequivocally Christian because each Christian element seems to be neutralized by a corresponding pagan element. The ghost, for all of its Christian credentials, imposes upon Hamlet a mission that is totally incompatible with the Christian moral system. And Hamlet, though he does entertain severe doubts about the nature of the ghost, wondering whether it is a "spirit of health or goblin damned" (I. iv. 40), never once explicitly questions the mission of revenge, though revenge is abhorrent to Christian thought. Any suggestion that he is repelled by the task on moral grounds can only be inferred from his several vague remarks about conscience and scruples as causes of his delay. Moreover, Hamlet, despite his association with Wittenberg (in Shakespeare's—though not in the original Hamlet's—time a citadel of Lutheran thought), is remarkably inconsistent in his eschatological views, to the extent that we cannot determine whether or not he believes in God and immortality. If in one instance he can refer to a God who has "fixed / His canon 'gainst self-slaughter" (I. ii. 131–32), he is equally capable in another instance of questioning the existence of an afterlife:

> To sleep—perchance to dream: ay, there's the rub,
> For in that sleep of death what dreams may come
> When we have shuffled off this mortal coil
> Must give us pause. (III. i. 65–68)

He elsewhere utters a statement that seems to be an explicit confession of unbelief:

> this most excellent canopy, the air, look you, this, brave o'erhanging firmament, this majestical roof fretted with golden fire—why, it appeareth nothing to me but a foul and pestilent congregation of vapours. (II. ii. 296–99)

Even the redeemed Hamlet who returns from his sea voyage to speak so confidently of a special providence, of a heaven ordinant in his good fortune, cannot be comfortably accepted by the audience. For it is possible to interpret his quietism as a submission to pagan fatalism rather than to the will of God. Bradley, for one, finds that Hamlet's statements at this point "seem to express that kind of religious resignation which, however beautiful in one aspect, really deserves the name of fatalism rather than that of faith in Providence...."[16] The strongest support for this view is Hamlet's mood in the graveyard scene, where we seem to have a concrete re-statement of Hamlet's view of man as a "quintessence of dust" (II. ii. 304); a spiritually renewed Hamlet would presumably view death in the light of his Christian faith, but Hamlet's macabre humor about the final absurdity of death reveals nothing whatever of a Christian hope in resurrection:

> ... Alexander died, Alexander was buried, Alexander returneth to dust; the dust is earth; of earth we make loam; and why of that loam whereto he was converted might they not stop a beer barrel? (V. i. 196–99)

Even more disconcerting is his rejoicing over the killing of Rosencrantz and Guildenstern, whom he has had executed "not shriving time allowed" (V. ii. 47) and therefore placed in jeopardy of eternal damnation. This action, made possible—according to Hamlet—by divine intervention, is inconceivable as the action of a morally sensitive person and severely undercuts Hamlet's pretensions of spiritual renewal.

The ambivalence which surrounds Hamlet is maintained to the very end. Whatever the arguments forwarded to find religious meaning in his "the rest is silence" (V. ii. 347), it is hard to dispel the sense of an awesome finality in the lines. Ironically, our chief source of consolation in the final scene is Horatio, who has hardly impressed the viewers as a religious person, in his "Good night, sweet prince, / And flights of angels sing thee to thy rest" (V. ii. 3 48–49). It is the sceptic in the play who most strongly endorses belief in Christian immortality.

The world of *Hamlet*, we must conclude, is in fact two worlds, a Christian world, and a pagan world that affords man little sign of a benevolent

Providence or hope of an afterlife, a world in which man is nothing but a quintessence of dust or a plaything of mysterious agencies. Hamlet's crucial question "What should such fellows as I do crawling between earth and heaven?" (III. i. 127–28) expresses the hopelessness of this pagan vision. But the play does suggest, however vaguely, that there is something more than natural in man's experience and even that the mystery of evil is somehow more present to man than the mystery of good. The question of transcendence, however negative, is posed most insistently by the irreducible ghost; but the ghost's precise meaning is engulfed in darkness, and we no more than Hamlet can come to a reliable conclusion about its significance. As Mack has stated, what the play finally dramatizes is

> man in his aspect of bafflement, moving in darkness on a rampart between two worlds, unable to reject, or quite accept, the one that, when he faces it, "to-shakes" his disposition with thoughts beyond the reaches of his soul—comforting himself with hints and guesses.[17]

In *Othello* the confrontation between the pagan world and the Christian world is embodied in the conflict between Othello, the baptized pagan, and the cynical Iago. Othello's tragedy stems from the fact that his love for Desdemona is undermined by Iago, who rejects the possibility of altruistic love, considering love "a sect or scion" (I. iii. 331) of lust, that is, a mere sublimation of biological urges. Othello, whose love for Desdemona is based upon an intuitive faith in her goodness, is finally persuaded to share Iago's cynicism.

Like *Hamlet*, *Othello* is conspicuously Christian in language and imagery, and Othello's loss of faith in Desdemona is equated with the loss of his Christian faith. After Iago's subversion has succeeded, Othello is ready, as Iago had predicted, "to renounce his baptism, / All seals and symbols of redeemed sin" (II. iii. 326–27); and when Othello discovers his tragic error, he naturally reverts to the semantic of Christianity, vividly picturing his own damnation for throwing away "a pearl... / Richer than all his tribe" (V. ii. 347–48). Moreover, he reads his fall as the result of a diabolical plot, portraying himself as an Everyman seduced by the Devil:

> Will you, I pray, demand that demi-devil
> Why he hath thus ensnared my soul and body? (V. ii. 300–301)

There is indeed warrant for believing in the diabolism of Iago, who is—despite his mask of secularly—surrounded throughout the play with images of the diabolical and is, in fact, quite fond himself of using such imagery; the following is but one of many examples:

> Divinity of Hell!
> When devils will the blackest sins put on,
> They do suggest at first with heavenly shows,
> As I do now. (II. iii. 333–36)

Moreover, his "motiveless malignity," the fact that none of the motives he offers for his malice toward Othello is convincing, is entirely consistent with his status as a quasi-allegorical figure of metaphysical evil. The implications of the kind of imagery used by Othello and Iago are, it seems to me, quite clear: on one level the action of *Othello* approximates that of the medieval morality play, with Desdemona, as Iago's mighty opposite, becoming a Merry-Good Angel figure vying for the soul of Othello-Everyman.

These are familiar arguments, and within certain limits, they are quite convincing. But again, as in *Hamlet*, the play offers another equally convincing possibility—that the tragedy of Othello is entirely immutable to natural causes. From this perspective Iago is a realistic character who, impelled by a spirit of cynicism, probes latent weaknesses in Othello to effect the destruction of his love. The love of Othello can be said to fail, not because of supernatural forces, but because of its own radical deficiencies. From the very beginning of the play Othello seems himself to be aware of these deficiencies—the differences of race, age, and class, as well as the military occupation which prompts Roderigo to describe him as "extravagant and wheeling stranger" (I. i. 135). It should be noted that Othello is curiously defensive from the very start; he stresses in his first major speech the services he has done for the state and points out his noble descent, "from men of royal siege" (I. ii. 22). Later, confronted by hostile senators, he insists that lust has nothing to do with his marriage, "the young affects / In me defunct" (I. iii. 263–64). And, as Iago's plot develops, Othello again broods about differences in social background, race, and age:

> Haply, for I am black
> And have not those soft parts of conversation
> That chamberers have, or for I am declined
> Into the vale of years... (III. iii. 263–66)

It is this exposed nerve that Iago attracks in his temptation scene, when he reminds Othello of the "country disposition" (III. iii. 201) of Venetian women and dwells upon the theme of "clime, complexion, and degree" (III. iii. 230).

Thus Othello's loss of faith in Desdemona seems prepared for; the tragedy of Othello is not, in this reading, that product of metaphysical forces represented by Iago—nor is it even caused by Iago. Rather Iago serves only to catalyze social pressures inherent in Othello's situation from the beginning. The romantic love simply cannot withstand the pressures placed upon it by reality.

What I have described, in fact, are the two extreme positions in the contemporary debate about *Othello*.[18] Briefly stated, the question is whether the natural forces ranged against Othello are necessary and sufficient causes for his fall, or whether it is necessary to postulate supernatural agencies. Is, in fact, the religious world view constantly referred to in the play, like love, merely a sublimation of grosser realities, a projection of purely human intuitions? Or is the symbolic aura surrounding both Iago and Desdemona an intimation that natural human experience in its most intense moments reaches out to supernatural dimensions? The answer in *Othello* is, I think, noncommittal; as in *Hamlet* we are given two worlds, discrete and self-sufficient, but we are denied any decisive judgment.

King Lear seems to be a further step in this direction. Inverting the procedure he followed in Hamlet, Shakespeare carefully excises every overt trace of Christianity from an originally Christian story.[19] His object seems to be to explore further the question raised in the earlier tragedies, whether it is possible or necessary to discover supernatural dimensions in human experience. More specifically, the basic question seems to be whether man's evil can be attributed to natural causes: it is Lear himself who, in the mock-trial of Goneril and Regan, most directly approaches the question:

> Then let them anatomize Regan. See what breeds about her heart. Is there any cause in nature that makes these hard hearts? (III. vi. 74–76)

The ordeal of King Lear impels him to re-examine the traditional conceptions of man. It is important to note that even in *Lear*, despite the pagan setting, the world view is initially religious. Lear, for example, swears by Apollo and by Jupiter (I. i. 160, 178), expresses confidence that the heavens will love old men (II. iv. 184–85), and refers to "high-judging Jove" (II. iv. 223). Similarly Kent, pitying Cordelia, prays, "The gods to their dear shelter take thee, maid" (I. i. 182), and even Edmund, despite his own unbelief, appeals to Gloucester's faith in a transcendent moral order:

> ... I told him the revenging gods
> 'Gainst parricides did all the thunder bend. (II. i. 45–46)

But we are, I think, to interpret these as facile appeals to transcendence and therefore doomed to be disappointed. As G. Wilson. Knight has said, "the 'gods' so often apostrophized are, however, slightly vitalized; one feels them to be figments of the human mind rather than omnipotent ruling powers—they are presented with no poetic conviction. And exactly this doubt, this questioning, as to the reality and nature of the directing powers, so evident in the god-references, is one of the primary motives through the play."[20] Thus a significant phase of Lear's ordeal is his crisis of confidence in his pagan gods, in the benevolent moral order that will vindicate him. Despite his prayers and curses, the rain and thunder torment, not Goneril and Regan, but Lear himself, and his easy reliance upon benign gods is frustrated:

> I tax not you, you elements, with unkindness.
> I never gave you kingdom, called you children;

> You owe me no subscription....
> But yet I call you servile ministers.... (III. ii. 16–18, 21)

From this awareness of an indifferent cosmos Lear moves to his next phase, an acceptance of a purely natural definition of man, a concept of man as no more than a clever animal with a capacity for sophistication or guile:

> Is man no more than this? Consider him well. Thou ow'st the worm no silk, the beast no hide, the sheep no wool, the cat no perfume. Ha! here's three on's are sophisticated. Thou art the thing itself; unaccommodated man is no more but such a poor, bare, forked animal as thou art. (III. iv. 97–102)

This is essentially an acceptance of Edmund's Nature, the "goddess" who is a hypostatization of a world whose fundamental law is the law of the jungle, self-interest; it is a world in which virtue and altruistic love are inconceivable. Lear's "unbutton here," his stripping of his clothing, formalizes his intuition that there is no discontinuity between man and animals.

But this is an intermediate stage quickly bypassed as the action progresses, for we notice the gradual emergence of two kinds of villainy: the "natural" villainy of Edmund, motivated by resentment of his state and ambition for self-advancement, and the almost gratuitous villainy of Goneril and Regan. Where Edmund is amoral, almost cavalier in his villainy, Goneril and Regan practice an aggressive immorality, disclosing a viciousness that surpasses normal selfishness. Despite G. Wilson Knight's judgment that "the good and bad elements [in Lear] are...natural, not, as in *Macbeth,* supernatural,"[21] what we are finally compelled to acknowledge is precisely that the cruelty of Goneril and Regan is inconceivable in animals, that the human capacity for evil surpasses even the bitter logic of the jungle. This progression of understanding can be located specifically in the reactions of Albany to the deeds of Goneril and Regan:

> Tigers, not daughters, what have you performed?
> A father, and a gracious aged man,

> Whose reverence even the head-lugged bear would lick,
> Most barbarous, most degenerate, have you madded. (IV. ii. 40–43)

> See thyself, devil:
> Proper deformity seems not in the fiend
> So horrid as in woman (IV. ii. 59–61)

> Howe'er thou art a fiend,
> A woman's shape doth shield thee. (IV. ii. 66–67)

It is not enough for Albany to consider the daughters as predators; the intensity of their cruelty begs for a more metaphysical explanation.

Albany has at this point accepted the intuition of evil first offered by Edgar as Tom o' Bedlam, whose insane ramblings dwell obsessively upon the presence of diabolical powers. Despite some critical scepticism regarding the significance of Tom's semantic of hell,[22] it seems probable to me that the imagery of diabolical possession that pervades his speeches, from his initial "Away! the foul fiend follows me" (III. iv. 45), overtly states what seems to be a central intuition of the play—that rational and natural explanations of evil are inadequate. Edgar, like Albany, prepares us to accept the metaphysical depths of the deeds of Goneril and Regan. Thus if Lear's early religiosity is shattered by his experience, his suspicions of negative transcendence—of "darkness and devils" (I. iv. 243)—are confirmed.

But we are not left with this counsel of despair, for if the insistent evil in the play has broken down the pales and forts of reason, it has thereby provided access to good. It is not necessary to see Cordelia as a "Christ-figure" (though there seems warrant enough for granting her some such anagogical significance) to recognize that her love has in it something more than natural, that, indeed, all love and altruistic behavior is incomprehensible unless the mystery of the human condition is acknowledged. As West has suggested,

> Does Cordelia, as an exception to natural evil, draw Lear's understanding of nature somehow beyond nature? Lear's understanding rises—as

> it touches Cordelia, anyway—toward a conscious remission of self-interest, a conscious community with the beloved, that in natural creation only man seems persistently capable of. This feeling concern for another, this surpassing love, is a kind of doubling on nature's tracks, is a transformation of nature's law of self, a departure from the predation so constant in unalloyed nature and a rising superior to it. Through love we can put up with one another's natural faults and filths better than an impartial observer might expect. Is this a kind of supernature, of spirituality, in us and from beyond us? Several higher religions have said something of this sort.[23]

But Cordelia is only the highest and clearest manifestation of what the perceptive viewer has detected throughout the play, the perdurance of simple human goodness in a world apparently overwhelmed by evil. Fully as important as the monstrosity of the sisters is the theme of "unpublished virtues" (IV. iv. 16), given dramatic substance by the loyalty of Kent and the Fool, the humane reactions of Cornwall's servants to the blinding of Gloucester, and the moral regeneration of Albany and Gloucester. It is true that these virtues are inconspicuous—Edgar and Kent, significantly, are in disguise, while Cordelia's presence is for a time kept secret—but we are nonetheless given favorable indications, even before evil has achieved full dominance, that virtue is only temporarily eclipsed. The "unpublished virtues," rising beyond self-interest and even reaching at times the splendid absurdity of sacrifice, point to a dimension of grace in human behavior, to some kind of discontinuity between man and nature—a motiveless benignity as incomprehensible as the motiveless malignity of the villains.

If Lear is at all redeemed, it is in these terms: that his penetration of the evil of Goneril and Regan makes it possible for him to come to terms with the inexplicable love of Cordelia; and growing from this perception, Lear is willing again to take upon himself the mystery of things. G. Wilson Knight describes Lear's regeneration in these terms:

> Slowly, painfully, emergent from the Lear Naturalism we see a religion born of disillusionment, suffering, and sympathy: a purely spontaneous,

natural growth of the human spirit, developing from nature magic to "God."[24]

However, *King Lear* cannot be said to affirm unequivocally the traditional Christian world view. Despite the anagogical intimations of Cordelia and the other unpublished virtues and despite the fact that the evil forces have been defeated with the deaths of Goneril, Regan, and Edmund, "the bounty and the benison of heaven" (IV. vi. 221) is called into question by the gratuitous death of Cordelia. Is Lear's final "Look there, look there—" (V. iii. 312) then to be read as an intuition of human immortality which would redeem all human suffering, or should we construe it as a final desperate lament? No decisive answer to the questions posed by the tragedy is given; instead, as Stampfer has pointed out,

> Certainly almost every possible point of view on the gods and cosmic justice is expressed, from a malevolent, wanton polytheism...to an astrological determinism...from an amoral, personified Nature-goddess...to "high-judging Jove." But the very multitude, concern, and contradictory' character of these references do not cancel each other out, but rather show how precarious is the concept of cosmic justice... Despite the pagan setting, the problem of theodicy, the justification of God's way with men, is invoked by so many characters, and with such concern, that it emerges as a key issue in the play.[25]

What the play has suggested more strongly than ever is that the religious hypothesis is at least as convincing as the natural hypothesis, which seems incapable of accounting for the mystery of human vice and virtue.

In *Macbeth*, the last phase of his penetration into evil, Shakespeare is finally able to posit the existence of supernatural agencies. Though it would have been possible to present Macbeth's tragedy as a fully secular fall, as the tragedy of a great man undone by his ambition, Shakespeare introduces into the plot the demonic witches whose presence unequivocally establishes the metaphysical dimensions of evil.

The witches have long been an acute source of embarrassment to many of Shakespeare's critics; Johnson, for one, was appalled by their crudity:

> A poet who should now make the whole action of his tragedy depend upon enchantment, and produce the chief events by the assistance of supernatural agents, would be censured as transgressing the bounds of probability, be banished from the theater to the nursery, and condemned to write fairy tales instead of tragedies....[26]

But however embarrassing this residual Gothicism may be to enlightened critics, the witches resist being exorcised; other manifestations of the "supernatural" in *Macbeth*, such as the dagger or the apparition of Banquo's ghost (which are seen by Macbeth alone), may be explained as mere projections, as images of guilt welling up from Macbeth's fevered imagination, but the witches, especially since they were also seen by Banquo, must be accepted as embodiments of supernatural evil somehow distinct from the inner evil of Macbeth. Their indissoluble reality, whatever their precise identity, confirms beyond any reasonable doubt the several intuitions of diabolism voiced in, for example, Macbeth's reference to "night's black agents" (III. ii. 53), in Lady Macbeth's reference to "murd'ring ministers" (I. v. 46), and in the porter's description of himself as "porter of hell gate" (II. iii. 1).

Shakespeare is careful, however, to protect the human dimensions of Macbeth's crime; the witches' powers are so circumscribed that they cannot compel Macbeth to perform his deed, nor, it seems clear, have they even inspired it. The witches, despite Macbeth's reference to their "supernatural soliciting" (I. iii. 130), seem more to "wait upon nature's mischief" (I. v. 48) than to take the initiative. Bradley's assessment of their role is still most convincing:

> while the influence of the Witches' prophecies on Macbeth is very great, it is quite clearly shown to be an influence and nothing more. There is no sign whatever in the play that Shakespeare meant the actions of Macbeth to be forced on him by an external power, whether that of the Witches, or of their "masters," or of Hecate. It is needless therefore to

> insist that such a conception would be in contradiction to his whole tragic practice. The prophecies of the watches are presented simply as dangerous circumstances with which Macbeth has to deal....[27]

And yet, though the witches do not *cause* the actions of Macbeth, they are more intimately related to these actions than Bradley suggests. They seem, indeed, to body forth what the ambiguous ghost in *Hamlet*, the inscrutable enigma of Iago, and the moral horror of Goneril and Regan have adumbrated in the earlier plays—that the intensity of evil requires a metaphysical hypothesis. Macbeth's sins, in this dramatic embodiment of the mystery of evil, are at once his own and the product of diabolical forces, the inner and outer evil existing in some mysterious relationship incomprehensible to man. With more assurance than ever before, the tragic world of Shakespeare is able to reassert the traditional conception of evil as simultaneously the evil within and the evil without.

Again, in *Macbeth*, the defeat of his conspiracy of evil is inexplicable. Perhaps no one understood better than Shakespeare that virtue is intrinsically undramatic and unconvincing, for once more in this play the "unpublished virtues"—the seemingly bland and impotent good people such as Malcolm and Macduff—are the implausible agents of the defeat of Macbeth's titanic evil. Despite the imagery of holiness that surrounds their cause (for example, the saintly aura of King Edward), we are prepared to believe in the transcendence of goodness, in the "grace of Grace" (V. viii. 72) only because we have believed in the deep damnation of Macbeth.

An important feature of the tragic pattern I have tried to describe is that it is comprehensive enough to include both secular and theological approaches to Shakespeare. To speak of Shakespeare's tragedies as theological in their ultimate reaches requires, however, an understanding of theology as something more than a deductive system of truths pertaining to supernatural dimensions of human experience. Roland Frye, who has, in my opinion, presented the most formidable challenge to the theologizers of Shakespeare, implicitly defines theological drama as drama in which supernatural religious concerns are directly and overtly given dramatic form. The following questions which he poses are indicative of this concept:

> Does a play's inception, its development through crucial or pivotal incidents, and its ending accord in some meaningful way with the structures of theological doctrine? Are the conflict and "competition" of the play related to the divine order with sufficient consistency and force to make the divine references a major influence, or are such references more accurately described as theoretical and supportive? Is the divine presence in rejection and acceptance, judgment and mercy sufficiently strong in the play to shape or even to affect the major actions of the plot and of the characters? Are the internal struggles of the characters directly and meaningfully related to God? Is guilt directly and primarily associated with a character's relations to God through his relations with others, or is that guilt primarily concerned with his relations to society and to himself? Is conscience kept within a framework which is primarily social and personal, or is that primary framework meaningfully and consistently embraced in the larger order of divine will?[28]

On the basis of these questions we may accept Frye's verdict that Shakespeare's plays are not—in his sense of the word—theological. But the concept of an inductive theology allows us to see more clearly the implications of Shakespeare's tragedies. In such an approach, the theological structure is neither given or assumed; if it is initially present, it is placed in tension with the plot—as a hypothesis to be tested rather than an a priori solution to the problem of existence. The theological thrust of Shakespeare's tragedies is inquisitive rather than affirmative and apodictic; briefly stated, the recurrent questions in the tragedies are whether or not the religious hypothesis is valid or necessary, whether or not the Christian faith in a benevolent Providence can be corroborated by the hard facts of life.

Shakespeare's relentless exploration of secular experience in his tragedies, along with his attention to signals of transcendence, to intimations of meta-empirical reality, suggests that his understanding of Christianity was profoundly humanistic; for the Christian experience revealed in the tragedies, though ultimately transcendent. is primarily, to use Frye's words, social and personal. Moreover, the remoteness of God in the tragedies, noticed by Frye and Clifford

Leech,[29] among others, seems rather the result of this humanistic conception of the Christian experience than of a secular purpose. If God is not for most Christians precisely Pascal's *Deus absconditus*, he is certainly less immediately present to them than Frye implies. As Schillebeeckx has stated:

> Even human history does not show us God. Precisely because he demonstrates his effective presence in this world in his own way, he seems to be absent.... Man can thus reach out to God only as to someone who is absent from the normal totality of created things.... Thus all appearances speak against the existence of God. Our human insight finds it impossible to justify his providence.[30]

Shakespeare's tragedies are secular because they faithfully depict a Christian experience that is itself tentative and secular; we are denied our theophanies, burning bushes, or pillars of fire, being given at best only the shadowy outlines of a pattern that vindicates human striving. Yet from this human striving, in its moments of peak intensity, issue signals of transcendence.

Notes to Shakespearean Tragedy and the Problem of Transcendence

1. G. Wilson Knight, *Principles of Shakespearian Production* (1936; rpt. Baltimore, 1949), p. 166
2. Roy W. Battenhouse, *Shakespearean Tragedy: Its Art and Its Christian Premises* (Bloomington, 1969), p. 91.
3. I. A. Richards. *Principles of Literary Criticism* (New York, 1928), p. 246; Clifford Leech, *Shakespeare's Tragedies and Other Studies in Seventeenth Century Drama* (London, 1950), p. 18.
4. Sylvan Barnet, "Some Limitations of a Christian Approach to Shakespeare," in *Approaches to Shakespeare*, ed. Norman Rabkin (New York, 1964), p. 22—the article was first published in *ELH*, 22 (1955).
5. A.C. Bradley, *Shakespearean Tragedy* (1904; Greenwich, CT, 1965), pp. 30, 37. See also Battenhouse, pp. 68–69, for a commentary on Bradley's inconsistencies regarding the metaphysical or religious implications of Shakespeare's tragedies.
6. Bradley, p. 147.
7. Roland Mushat Frye, *Shakespeare and Christian Doctrine* (Princeton, 1963), pp. 60, 51.
8. Frye, p. 60.

9. All references to the plays are to *The Complete Pelican Shakespeare*, ed. Alfred C. Harbage (Baltimore, 1969).
10. Frye, p. 34.
11. Peter Berger, *A Rumor of Angels* (Garden City, NY, 1969).
12. Berger, p. 65.
13. Berger, pp. 65–66. In order to support his claim for the validity of religious experience, Berger attempts to "relativize the relativizers," that is, to neutralize the sceptical Feuerbachian argument that all religious experience is merely a projection of man's own "better nature"—see esp. pp. 57–59.
14. G. K. Chesterton, *Charles Dickens: The Last of the Great Men* (New York, 1942), p. 204.
15. "The Hystorie of Hamblet," in Sir Israel Gollancz, *The Sources of Hamlet* (1926; rpt. New York, 1967), p. 179.
16. Bradley, pp. 122, 123; see also Battenhouse, pp. 157, 158; Battenhouse, far less ambivalent than Bradley, states that "Hamlet has become resigned to a fatalism. He would view his own human condition as that of a person not responsible for his madness, although we have heard him praise rashness only a moment before. Hamlet's reasoning harbors contradictions which he is too confused to fathom."
17. Maynard Mack, "The World of Hamlet," in *Shakespeare: Modern Essays in Criticism*, ed. Leonard F. Dean (New York, 1961), p. 241.
18. For representative arguments for either position, see M.R. Ridley, *New Arden Othello* (Cambridge, Mass., 1962), p. lx; and Leah Scragg, "Iago—Vice or Devil," *Shakespeare Studies*, 21 (1968), pp. 61–62.
19. See William R. Elton, *King Lear and the Gods* (San Marino, CA, 1966), pp. 63–67.
20. G. Wilson Knight, *The Wheel of Fire* (1930; New York, 1957), p. 187.
21. Knight, *Wheel of Fire*, p. 187.
22. Knight, *Wheel of Fire*, p. 188; see also Elton, pp. 92–93.
23. Robert H. West, *Shakespeare and the Outer Mystery* (Lexington, Kentucky, 1968), pp. 158–59.
24. *Wheel of Fire*, p. 191.
25. Judah Stampfer, "The Catharsis of King Lear," in *Shakespeare's Tragedies: An Anthology of Modern Criticism*, Laurence Lerner, ed. (Baltimore, 1963), p. 153. Stampfer, however, finds that the issue is flatly resolved by the denouement of the play, which "destroys any basis for providential justice" (p. 155). The essay first appeared in *Shakespeare Survey*, 13 (1960).
26. *Samuel Johnson on Shakespeare*, ed. W. K. Wimsatt, Jr. (New York, 1960), p. 99.
27. Bradley, p. 285.
28. Roland M. Frye, "Theological and Non-Theological Structures in Tragedy," *ShakS*, 4 (1968), pp. 146–47.
29. Frye, "Structures," pp. 136–38; Leech, p. 11.
30. E. Schillebeeckx, O.P., *God and Man* (New York, 1969), p. 22.

POETIC JUSTICE IN SHAKESPEAREAN TRAGEDY: "THE JUSTICE OF IT PLEASES"

René Fortin

I

Among one's first lessons in literary scholarship is that the concept of poetic justice is wholly foreign to Shakespearean—or, for that matter, any—tragedy. It is a concept commonly associated with the righteous fulminations of Thomas Rhymer, who valued edification before truth:

> Rather may we ask here what unnatural crime Desdemona, or her Parents had committed to bring this Judgement down upon her; to wed a Blackamoor, and innocent to be thus cruelly murder'd by him. What instruction can we make of this Catastrophe?[1]

The most glaring instance of Shakespeare's violation of poetic justice, of course, is the arbitrary death of Cordelia, and accordingly it is here, in *King Lear*, that we find the most desperate contrivance to salvage the ideal, in Nahum Tate's "improved" version, where Lear and Cordelia happily survive. One measure of the popularity of this improvement in the 18th century is Dr. Johnson's ardent defense of it:

> Shakespeare has suffered the virtue of Cordelia to perish in a just cause, contrary to the natural ideas of justice, to the hope of the reader, and, what is yet more strange, to the faith of chronicles...a play may doubtless be good, because it is a just representation of the common events of human life, but since all reasonable beings love justice, I cannot easily be persuaded, that the observation of justice makes a play worse; or that,

> if other excellencies are equal, the audience will not always rise better pleased from the final triumph of persecuted virtue. In the present case the publick has decided. Cordelia, from the time of Tate, has always retired with victory and felicity.[2]

The romantic critics, it is clear, were more able to countenance Shakespeare's irregularities; and poetic justice, at least from Lamb's scornful attack on Tate, was virtually banished from the stage: "A happy ending! As if the living martyrdom that Lear had gone through—the flayings of his feelings alive—did not make fair dismissal from the stage of life the only decorous thing for him."[3]

And so the matter stands to this day. Charney, for example, finds "a certain glibness...in formulations which insist that there is a system of rewards and punishments in Shakespeare that has ceased to function in ordinary experience."[4] We have evidently learned our lesson well, and we recognize that, after peering into the abyss, there is scant consolation in conventional pieties: the lesson of tragedy is that we are to "speak what we feel, not what we ought to say" (*Lear,* V. iii. 325).[5]

But is poetic justice so alien to the spirit of tragedy as the past two centuries have assumed? Is it in fact possible, as Brooks and Wimsatt have argued, that the concept of poetic justice "is not adequately treated by a summary dismissal"?[6] A. C. Bradley, for one, while confessing to turning "with disgust from Tate's sentimental alterations," nonetheless wonders, "Are we so sure that we are right when we unreservedly condemn the feeling which beyond question comes naturally to many readers of *King Lear* who would like Tate as little as we?"[7]

Poetic justice, I suggest, has been a major consideration in tragedy from the beginning. It is the ideal, though at best only dimly realized, often yearned for by the choruses of Greek tragedy—especially, as we would expect, in the tragedies of Aeschylus. In *Agamemnon*, for example, the Chorus expressly rejects the traditional view that misfortune, in an inexorable law of compensation, necessarily follows upon "high good fortune," and preaches instead the new gospel that the virtues are duly rewarded and the evil punished:

> Far from others I hold my own mind;
> only the act of evil
> breeds others to follow,
> young sins in its own likeness.
> Houses clear in their right are given
> children in all loveliness?[8]

The spirit of tragedy survives, of course, because such pious hopes are seldom gratified, and, if they are gratified, one is impressed above all by what the victory has cost. Accordingly, Aristotle rules out poetic justice as unworthy of tragedy, arguing that it does not effectively provide the catharsis of pity and fear that is the end of tragedy:

> There are three forms of plot to be avoided (1) a good man must not be seen passing from happiness to misery, or (2) a bad man from misery to happiness. The first situation is not fear-inspiring or piteous, but simply odious to us. The second is the most untragic that can be; it has not one of the requisites of tragedy; it does not appeal to the human feeling in us, or to our pity, or to our fears. Nor, on the other hand, should (3) *an extremely bad man be seen falling from happiness into misery. Such a story may arouse the human feeling in us, but it will not move us to either pity or fear*; pity is occasioned by undeserved misfortune, and fear by that of one like ourselves; so that there will be nothing either piteous or fear-inspiriting in the situation.[9] (emphasis mine)

What should be noted is that the underlying norm in Aristotle's description of the tragic hero is the extent to which his fortune or misfortune fulfills the demands of justice. The third pattern, the "extremely bad man [who falls] from happiness into "misery," clearly excludes poetic justice from the precincts of tragedy because the evil-doer's misfortune is most patently deserved; since pity is aroused by undeserved misfortune, the audience would then heartily applaud the misfortune of the protagonist and thus remain insulated from tragic tensions: tragedy, the formula implies, cannot survive a too-evident working out of justice.

But the first two situations cited by Aristotle suggest the opposite as well: that tragedy cannot survive if what is represented is flagrantly unjust. Both instances are disallowed because, in allowing virtue to suffer misfortune and vice to be rewarded, they deliver unequivocal indictments of the moral order, outraging the "human feeling" that demands a just moral universe.

In this context we can understand the basis of Aristotle's call for a tragic protagonist who is "the intermediate kind of personage, a man not pre-eminently virtuous and just, whose misfortune, however, is brought upon him not by vice or depravity but by some error of judgment...." (145a). The key to Aristotle's formula for the tragic hero is the enigma surrounding *hamartia*, the flaw—be it an act of ignorance or of temporarily perverse will—that brings about the hero's downfall.[10] The very ambiguity of the hero and his motivation as he commits his great error enshrouds him in mystery and allows for the full play of the tragic tensions. The justice of his fate we can neither deny nor assert, and we are left in a world where poetic justice is an ideal that is perhaps adumbrated but not clearly attained.

Interestingly, though, Aristotle does not altogether ban poetic justice from the precincts of tragedy. In discussing the effectiveness of "matters of chance," Aristotle concedes that chance may operate in a tragic plot as long as there is at least the appearance of design, going on to provide an example that, in effect, reinstates poetic justice as a serviceable—and even, in fact, powerful—element of tragic form:

> ...as for instance when the statue of Mitys at Argos killed the author of Mitys' death by falling down on him when a looker-on at a public spectacle; for incidents like that we think not to be without a meaning. (1452a)

The incident described by Aristotle, from his perspective as a disbeliever in a personal God, is a matter of pure chance, but would likely be interpreted by believers as divine retribution, (as indeed it was by Plutarch in his *De sera numinis vindicta*), as the purest kind of poetic justice, and therefore, says Aristotle, as an incident capable of arousing tragic emotions.[11]

The example is instructive, for the implication is that poetic justice is more than simply the proportional distribution of rewards and punishments: beyond the "even-handedness" (*Macbeth* I. vii. 10) of justice lies an aesthetic dimension, a particular fittingness in the kind of reward and (especially) punishment administered that testifies publicly to divine intervention. In the purest form of poetic justice, "the justice of its pleases" (*Othello* IV. 1. 209)—as well as satisfies—the moral sense of the community. This kind of poetic justice, while not specifically Christian, is nonetheless highly congenial to the Christian mind, which is disposed to see "figures in all things" (*Henry V* IV. vii. 33), for it is, in the exactness, the precision, and even the wit of the justice that is administered, God's way of proclaiming his abiding interest in His creation. In its most familiar manifestation it shines forth in the *contrapasso* of Dante, the divine irony that so delights the readers of *The Inferno*: sowers of discord, who split apart human communities, are themselves torn apart; the uncommitted in life spend an eternity as non-persons, rejected by Heaven and even by Hell itself; flatterers are bogged down—as they so patently deserve to be—in a swamp of excrement; soothsayers who unlawfully scanned the future are condemned to look backward through eternity.[12]

Poetic justice is a concept of major importance in Shakespearean tragedy, where it is revealed as bristling with ambiguities. Shakespeare is not, of course, trying to justify the ways of God to men or, like the comforters of Job, trying to discern the rationale behind human suffering. Poetic justice, rather, is at the very center of Shakespearean tragedy because it reflects the way in which humanity tries to cope with adversity. It is an expression of confidence, in the face of radical insecurity, that the world has not turned against us and that we have it within us to control our destiny.

The desire for poetic justice obsesses tragic heroes and their audience as well. For we as viewers yearn for the quick and easy re-assurance that evil cannot, will not, effectively infest our world. What the tragedies proclaim, though, is that poetic justice cannot be legitimately hoped for, for the concept of poetic justice is consistent with neither the facts of human experience nor the traditional beliefs of Christianity.

In fact, the desire for poetic justice, wherever it is manifested, is shown to be an aberration, an impious assertion of the self over God. In the case of Hamlet and Othello, poetic justice takes the form of the hero's arrogation of divine prerogatives, of assuming the authority to pass judgment upon and cleanse the world. In *King Lear* poetic justice inheres in the plot as a temptation to presume upon the concern of God, upon God's eagerness to intervene in human affairs in order to thwart evil.

Shakespeare's final word on poetic justice is uttered in *Macbeth*, where the idea of poetic justice is in fact affirmed: despite the opaqueness of the moral order, there is, the play asserts, a moral intelligence that limits the encroachments of evil in the world of man. But, and the point is crucial, it does so in its own good time.

The world does not conform to man's rage for order in the way man would wish, and the plays of Shakespeare suggest that a quite different response is needed: the virtue of patience, which, in recognition of human limits, calls for reverent submission to the mystery of existence.

II

The seductive appeal of poetic justice is what entangles us in the world of Hamlet. Poetic justice taps the primal human impulse to retaliate, swiftly and decisively, against personal injury.[13] Thus viewers, seeing Hamlet as the victim of Claudius, demand prompt, energetic action by Hamlet, but they instead are taunted by a plot in which the hero does not, or cannot, take action, in which "enterprises of great pitch and moment...lose the name of action" (III. i. 85–87). Goldman has aptly described the peculiar dramaturgy of *Hamlet*:

> The "problems" of the play point, finally, to the subtle means it employs for manipulating one of our most fundamental theatrical appetites: the desire for action that makes sense, especially for action that seems complete and resolved.[14]

Thus what the audience observes is a hero who, having promised instant action—"Thy commandment all alone shall live in the book and volume of my brain" (I. v. 102–103), offers a spectacle of inactivity (or pointless activity), to the extent that as late as Act IV, he is heard lamenting, "I do not know / Why yet I live to say 'this thing's to do'" (IV. iv. 43–44). The viewer's experience is one of intense frustration or perplexity, "the pattern of interrupted action and blocked significance" thwarting the "fundamental theatrical appetite" for action—in this case, the enactment of poetic justice—that the plot has promised to satisfy.[15]

What should be noticed about *Hamlet*, though, is the viewer's uneasy suspension between aesthetic and ethical considerations. As the implications of Hamlet's acts become evident, poetic justice is likely to emerge for the viewer as a question to be scanned rather than a solution to be hoped for—whether or not Hamlet himself admits misgivings about what he has dedicated himself to. The very heroism that is so aesthetically satisfying is, from an ethical perspective, recognized as a passion for bloody revenge, as when Hamlet boasts,

> Now could I drink hot blood,
> And do such bitter business as the day
> Would quake to look on. (III. ii. 390–92)

The Ghost's account of his death, it should be noted, lays upon Hamlet the burden of seeking revenge, but without specifying its nature. Hamlet, however, infers from what he hears that he is to seek a particular kind of revenge:

> Thus was I, sleeping, by a brother's hand
> Of life, of crown, of queen, at once dispatched,
> Cut off even in the blossom of my sin,
> Unhousel'd, disappointed, unanel'd,
> No reck'ning made, but sent to my account
> With all my imperfections on my head. (I. v. 74–79)

The very precise reference to the sacrament in the Ghost's account underscores the special horror of the murder: in being "unhousel'd, disappointed, unanel'd," Hamlet the Elder was deprived of the saving graces of the Holy Eucharist, Penance, and Extreme Unction—and thus in jeopardy of eternal damnation. Hamlet's legendary delay, initially at least a consequence of his distrust of the Ghost, tends to obscure the fact that he will seek, not only to kill Claudius, but to kill him in exactly the same circumstances as his father was killed: in a state of deadly sin and without the saving graces of the sacraments. The notorious Prayer Scene dramatizes the moment when Hamlet fully realizes that nothing less than poetic justice will serve the purpose, for to kill a praying Claudius would reward him with heaven:

> A villain kills my father, and for that
> I, his sole son, do this same villain send to heaven.
> Why, this is hire and salary, not revenge. (III. iii. 74–76)

To this point the majority of the viewers have freely gone along with Hamlet; they have yearned for the decisive strike that will redeem the time and they have bristled with impatience at whatever served to delay that stroke. But the implications of Hamlet's utterance, if it is to be taken at face value, are profoundly disturbing. Dr. Johnson says it, I believe, for most of us: "This speech, in which Hamlet, represented as a virtuous character, is not content with taking blood for blood but contrives damnation for the man he would punish, is too horrible to be read or uttered."[16] The effect of Hamlet's utterance is curiously dual: viewers totally caught up in the tensions of the plot, here at their highest point, are likely to feel once more cheated out of the resolving act they have so eagerly awaited; the more reflective viewers, on the other hand, are likely to feel disappointment, not with Hamlet's inaction, but in the reasons he offers for his inaction. For here, at last, Hamlet's quest for poetic justice emerges as an unmasked passion for total revenge, and sensitive viewers are likely to balk: revenge, despite Laertes' later assertion, should indeed "have bounds" (IV. vii. 128).

Yet, in the complex dynamics of the play, the viewers' consternation is only temporary. Though Hamlet's desire to kill Claudius in a state of sin is no momentary aberration—Hamlet clearly dedicates himself to poetic justice for the remainder of the play—even the most sceptical of the viewers are likely to find themselves succumbing once more the "momentum of good will" that the play generates for Hamlet and to applaud his deeds and accept the justifications for his actions.[17] Thus we not only endorse Hamlet's killing of Polonius—"Take thy fortune; / Thou find'st to be too busy is some danger" (III. iv. 32–33)—but also even find cause for laughter in his dispatching of "this foolish prating knave" who is now "most secret and most grave" (III. iv. 214–15). And similarly we applaud Hamlet's wit in his counterplot against Rosencrantz and Guildenstern: "For 'tis the sport to have the enginer / Hoist with his own petard" (III. iv. 206–207). It is a deadly sport that we, and Hamlet, savor: intercepting Claudius' "exact command" that he be beheaded "no leisure bated, / No, not to stay the grinding of the axe," Hamlet re-writes the commission to read that Rosencrantz and Guildenstern are to be "put to sudden death, / Not shriving time allow'd" (V. ii. 19; 24–25; 45–46). Turnabout is fair play, we are invited to conclude, even though Hamlet once more contemplates the eternal damnation of his enemies. Horatio's (typically) subdued reproach, "Why, so Guildenstern and Rosencrantz go to't" (V. ii. 56) makes little impression upon us and we are, for the moment at least, assuaged by Hamlet's apology: "Why, man, they did make love to this employment" (57).[18]

The motif of poetic justice is especially prominent in the final scene of the play, the major business of which, in fact, may be described as the wholesale dispensing of poetic justice. A dying Laertes confesses: "As a woodcock to mine owne springe, Osric. / I am justly kill'd with mine owne treachery" (V. ii. 306–307). And Hamlet, seeing his mother poisoned by Claudius, forces the King's own poison upon him with the bitter taunt, "Drink off this potion! Is thy union here? / Follow my mother" (326–27), receiving as he does so the approbation of Laertes: "He is justly serv'd. / It is a poison temper'd by himself' (327–28).

The scene is so constructed as to nudge the viewers into a reassessment of the poetic justice they had so ardently sought throughout the play. Horatio, in case the viewers have missed the point and remain mired in moral complacency, concludes his grim rehearsal of the plot by calling attention to the pattern of poetic justice in the "deaths put on by cunning" and the "purposes mistook / Fall'n on th' inventors' heads" (83–85).

It is above all the prominence of the "baser natures" (V. ii. 60), Rosencrantz and Guildenstern, in this most gripping of dramatic resolutions, that is troubling: long since forgotten by the audience, they nonetheless preoccupy the dying Hamlet, who rues that he "cannot live to hear the news from England" (354) and dies before the returning ambassadors can "tell him his commandment is fulfill'd / ... Rosencrantz and Guildenstern are dead" (370–71). Why, in so flagrant a violation of dramatic economy, are we reminded of the fates of such inconsequential creatures—by a playwright, moreover, who did not hesitate to consign to limbo the Fool in *King Lear* after his dramatic function was exhausted? The answer, evidently, is that their deaths "not shriving time allow'd" highlight the enormity and persistence of Hamlet's passion for poetic justice.[19] The "sport" that delighted Hamlet—and his viewers—in his pursuit of Claudius ("O, 'tis most sweet / When in one line two crafts directly meet" (III. iv. 209–10) and in his witty dispatching of Rosencrantz and Guildenstern stands now in high relief as the *bella vendetta* of the Italianate revenger who is satisfied with nothing less than the eternal damnation of his enemies.[20] The very fact of seeking revenge, according to Sandys, is "to usurp Christ's office [to judge the living and the dead] to act as if God had resigned his own right into one's hands."[21] How much more arrogant it is to predetermine God's judgments upon immortal souls by killing them deliberately in the "blossom" of their sins. Part of the involved viewers' complex response to Hamlet's final moments is a desire to dissociate themselves from what appears to be unbridled and even gleeful violence.[22]

The audience's final estimate of Hamlet, however, is not one of horror or revulsion, for in the final moment of the play the viewers are, remarkably, able to have it both ways. In the death of Claudius they receive the consummation they have so devoutly wished, the release of energy that the drama has promised, as well as the satisfaction that the villain receives what he so patently deserves. And yet they are spared alienation from Hamlet by the circumstances of his death. The killing of Claudius is invested with an almost religious awe because it is not perceived as contrived by Hamlet. The killing is put on by "forced cause" rather than cunning, and Hamlet, apparently responding by reflex to the treachery of Claudius, seems less an agent than an instrument—as if a Higher Power, impatient with human bungling, finally asserts itself to set the time aright. However tarnished the image of Hamlet may have been for some viewers, the play leaves us with an impression, at least equally strong, of a "Sweet prince" who, "had he been put on, / [Would] have prov'd most royal" (V. ii. 397–98).

III

In *Othello* Shakespeare once more dramatizes the seductive appeal of poetic justice. Like Hamlet, Othello seizes upon poetic justice as the necessary response to the wrongs he has suffered—as the heroic way to restore integrity to his world and maintain his personal dignity. But there is a crucial difference in the dynamics of the play: here, because of the unimpeachable innocence of Desdemona, the viewers resist the purposes of the hero and instead witness from the outset the pathology of the hero's craving for poetic justice. *Othello*, unlike *Hamlet*, is a play in which the viewers dread the predictable unfolding of the plot that will constitute the dramatic experience.

The concept of poetic justice plays an important role in *Othello*, for it is only by disguising his wrath as poetic justice that Othello is able to countenance the horror of his design. Having seen in Bianca's hand the handkerchief with "magic in the web" that decisively incriminates Desdemona in his eyes, Othello, after some vacillation, is consumed by fury: "I will chop her into messes. Cuckold me!" (IV. i. 200), and then asks Iago for poison. But Iago provides Othello with the inspiration that he needs:

> *Iago.* Do it not with poison; strangle her in her bed,
> Even the very bed she has contaminated.
> *Oth.* Good, good; the justice of it pleases. (207–209)

Fury is to wear the guise of justice in this fiction of righteousness,[23] a fiction in which Othello casts himself for several roles. He casts himself as a judge, urging Desdemona, "If you bethink yourself of any crime / Unreconcil'd as yet to heaven and grace, / Solicit for it straight" (V. ii. 26–28); as a priest-sacrificer, offering up a bloodless victim: "Yet I'll not shed her blood" (V. ii. 3); as a priest-confessor: "Therefore confess thee freely of thy sin" (53). What is evident is that he has enormous difficulty in maintaining his several fictions: his kiss of

Desdemona melts his icy resolve as judge ("O balmy breath, that doth almost persuade / Justice to break her sword" (16–17), just as her denial that she has been false threatens his role as sacrificer and "makest me call what I intend to do / A murder, which I thought a sacrifice" (64–65).

But it is as a priest-confessor that Othello is most glaringly inadequate. After urging Desdemona to pray for forgiveness and assuring her that "I would not kill thy unprepared spirit" (31), Othello totally loses control when Desdemona expresses regret over the death of Cassio, moving Othello to deny her the time for reconciliation with Heaven:

Des. But half an hour!
Oth. Being done there is no pause.
Des. But while I say one prayer!
Oth. It is too late! (82–83)

The innocence with which the audience is ready to credit Desdemona should not be allowed to palliate the horror of Othello's act: once more in the name of poetic justice a victim is to be killed "not shriving time allow'd." The implications of Othello's poetic justice, that he is usurping God-like prerogatives, are exposed in Othello's implicit association of himself with God: "This sorrow's heavenly; It strikes where it doth love" (21–22), an allusion to Hebrews (12:6, "For whom the Lord loveth, he chasteneth."

Othello's pretense that his killing of Desdemona was an act of poetic justice momentarily crumbles when Emilia informs him that Cassio is not killed, evoking Othello's response: "Then murder's out of tune / And sweet revenge grows harsh" (115–16). But the lapse is of short duration: Othello manages to re-create his fiction, insisting to Emilia that he "did proceed upon just grounds / To this extremity" (138–39), and even after he is convinced that his wife was chaste, asking that he be viewed as "an honorable murderer, if you will, / For naught I did in hate, but all in honor" (294–95).

Othello's last act as hero is, befittingly, an act of poetic justice, his killing of himself: the hero of Venice kills the enemy of Venice, doing the state one last service in killing an enemy alien. But it is, like his earlier enactment of poetic justice, a flawed act, possibly entailing his eternal damnation and failing to redeem him in the eyes of the beholders. Gratiano's terse comment, "All that is spoke is marr'd" (357), suggests the scepticism with which this last stroke of poetic justice is greeted, while Lodovico's "This object poisons sight, / Let it be hid" (364–65) underscores the extent of Othello's fall from grace.[24]

In both *Hamlet* and *Othello* the passion for poetic justice leads the hero into a presumptuous reliance upon human initiative; it is the great temptation of the hero to exceed limits. In a sense, the hero's failure is that he lacks patience, a concept with theological as well as psychological meaning: in the face of adversity the hero must resign himself to his ordeal and wait upon the will of God; he must resist the all-too-human impulse to lash out against what he perceives as evil until he is sure that he can act in perfect conscience. Paradoxically, the better part for the hero may be not to act, to allow himself to lose the name of action and instead adopt the alternative to heroic self-assertion that is suggested in Ophelia's mad ramblings, "I hope all will be well. We must be patient" (IV. v. 68).[25] It is a suggestion that Hamlet, after his eagerness for revenge, appears disposed to adopt in the Fifth Act: "The readiness is all. Since no man, of aught he leaves, knows what is't to leave betimes, let be" (V. ii. 218–20).

The crowning paradox of *Hamlet* is that the very delay that earlier discomfited the audience urgently awaiting the release of the dammed-up dramatic energies now emerges as the main source of his attractiveness. It is Hamlet's resistance to the instant gratification of the easy way, however obscure his motives, that defines his unique brand of heroism.

Othello's pursuit of poetic justice is likewise a failure of patience, based on a need for immediate clarification of his ambiguous relationship with Desdemona: "No! to be once in doubt / Is once to be resolv'd" (III. iii. 179–80). Patience, which could have averted the disaster, is only once, and only briefly, considered by Othello as a possible response—and just as quickly rejected:

> Had it pleas'd heaven
> To try me with affliction, had he rain'd
> All kinds of sores and shames on my bare head,
> Steep'd me in poverty to the very lips,

Given to captivity me and my utmost hopes,
I should have found in some place of my soul
A drop of patience; but, alas, to make me
The fixed figure for the time of scorn
To point his slow unmoving finger at!
... Turn thy complexion there,
Patience, thou young and rosy-lipp'd chérubin—
Ay, there look grim as hell! (IV. ii. 47–55; 62–64)

Thus Othello follows his "compulsive course" (III. iii. 454), lacking even the patience to allow Desdemona her final prayers; "'Tis too late" (V. ii. 84). The seductiveness of poetic justice, so easily confused with righteous action and heroic self-assertion, is here exposed in all its horror—as an act of ruthless revenge.

IV

Of all the plays, it is *King Lear* that addresses most explicitly the problem of divine justice. From the very core of the action arises the question whether belief in a benign moral order, given the facts of human experience, is at all warranted—and the play offers no easy answers.[26] The setting of the play is austerely pagan; Shakespeare has eradicated all elements of Christianity and revealed religion from his proximate sources. And yet what characterizes many of the characters is a confidence that there are supernatural powers who will answer the prayers of humans in distress. Thus we witness Lear, rebuffed by his daughters, appealing to divinity for retribution:

All the stor'd vengeances of heaven fall
On her ingrateful top! (II. iv. 161–62)

Let the great gods,
That keep this dreadful pudder o'er our heads,
Find out their enemies now. (III. ii. 49–51)

O, heavens!
If you do love old men, if your sweet sway
Allow obedience, if you yourselves are old,
Make it your cause; send down, and take my part. (II. iv. 189–92)

The gods, of course, do not take Lear's part when he is plunged deeper and deeper into misery, as they emphatically do not avenge Gloucester's blinding, the act which most unsparingly—until the final scene—confronts the question of divine justice. It is an act that prompts the servant's assertion, "I'll never care what wickedness I do, / If this man come to good" (III. vii. 99–100). Still, the characters, notably Albany, cling to the hope that all will be well, as when Albany, appalled by the abuse of Lear by Goneril, states:

If that the heavens do not their visible spirits
Send quickly down to tame these vilde offenses,
It will come,
Humanity must perforce prey upon itself,
Like monsters of the deep. (IV ii. 46–50)

Here is a piety that is able to find comfort even in the blinding of Gloucester since, at least, the blinding has exacted the price of Cornwall's life: "This shows you are above, / You justicers, that these our nether crimes / So speedily can venge!" (IV. ii. 78–80).

What should be noted, parenthetically for the moment, about the poetic justice implicitly described by Albany are, first, its superficiality, in that Albany is able to draw comfort in Cornwall's death while the misery of the blinded Gloucester trails limply as an after-thought, and secondly, the conditions stipulated by Albany: the gods must work visibly, and they must work quickly if they are to retain his confidence. These are conditions that the play will hardly satisfy. But Albany's optimism, at this point, is not discredited and serves an important function in the play's strategy: that of guiding the audience into expecting a happy outcome.

The strategy of *King Lear* is to toy with the audience's expectations of poetic justice, a strategy that can be fully appreciated only if we can assume the perspective of a first-time viewer: such a viewer, probably familiar with the story of Lear from its most likely source, the earlier *True Chronicle History of King Leir* or from Holinshed's *Chronicles*, would be unaware of the re-working of the conclusion and would respond unsuspectingly to the false signals given by Shakespeare's play. And he would be all the more taken aback because the designation of *King Lear* as a "True Chronicle Historie" would appear to inhibit any major innovations in the plot.[27] And so the viewer is enticed by what might be called the plays "buffering" technique, which largely insulates the audience from the anguish of the tragedy and, at key junctures of the play, leads the viewers, like the characters themselves, to hope for and to expect the fulfillment of the hopes.[28] From the outset of Lear's ordeal the viewers are assured that the king's situation is not as desperate as it would appear. Lear, for example, is unlike the other tragic heroes in that he is not left to suffer in isolation; in his distress he is surrounded, at various times, by the Fool, the disguised Kent, Gloucester, and Edgar—figures who can, admittedly, provide meager comfort for Lear but who nonetheless assure the audience that Lear is not totally forsaken. The audience is moreover informed early on of "likely wars toward, 'twixt the Dukes of Cornwall and Albany" (II. i. 10–11) and is thus encouraged to expect the vulnerable "house divided" of Lear's enemies. Shortly after, Kent offers news that is more overtly comforting:

> Nothing almost sees miracles
> But misery. I know [this letter] 'tis from Cordelia,
> Who hath most fortunately been inform'd
> Of my obscur'd course; [reads]—"and shall find time
> From this enormous state—seeking to give
> Losses their remedies." (II. ii. 165–70)

And even as Lear gropes his way in darkness toward the heath, Kent reminds the viewers once more, not only that the quarrels between Albany and Cornwall have intensified, but, more importantly, that Cordelia's forces have secretly landed and "are / At point to show their open banner" (III. i. 33–34).

The viewers, in short, are inclined to share Gloucester's conviction that "these injuries the King now bears will be reveng'd home" (III. iii. 11–12).

Beyond this there develops a redemptive pattern that injects meaning into the sufferings of Lear and Gloucester. The once-haughty Lear finds in his humiliation a compassion for others, for the "poor naked wretches" whom he had ignored throughout his life:

> O, I have ta'en
> Too little care of this! Take physic, pomp,
> Expose thyself to feel what wretches feel,
> That thou may'st shake the superflux to them,
> And show the heavens more just. (III. iv. 32–36)

Gloucester likewise profits spiritually from his ordeal. Even before his blinding, Gloucester is moved by the distress of Lear to the extent that he will risk his life for him: "If I die for't (as no less is threaten'd me), the King my old master must be reliev'd" (III. iii. 17–19). After his blinding, Gloucester enlarges his circle of compassion, finding in his misery a God-sent opportunity to minister to the needs of others:

> Heavens, deal so still!
> Let the superfluous and lust-dieted man,
> That slaves your ordinance, that will not see
> Because he does not feel, feel your power quickly;
> So distribution should undo excess,
> And each man have enough. (IV. i. 66–71)

Edified by the cleansing effects of the suffering, the viewer is swept along to Dover, where Lear will be reconciled with Cordelia and where Edgar will reveal himself to Gloucester as the dutiful son he has always been. Moreover, further assurance is given by the letter intercepted by Kent that will expose the duplicity of Goneril. Time will, the viewer is assured, unfold what plighted cunning has hid, and the stage is set for the play's big moment:

Lear. Do not laugh at me,
For (as I am a man) I think this lady
To be my child Cordelia.
Cor. And so I am; I am. (IV. vii. 67–70)

All losses are restored and sorrows end; there remain only the technicalities of winning the battle and, in the ideal scheme of things, of Edgar and Cordelia recognizing what the viewers—and Nahum Tate—have suspected all along—that they are the meek who will inherit the kingdom. What else could one expect in a play that has run its over-three-hour course than a graceful consummation?

But such is not to be the case. In a battle that occurs almost parenthetically off-stage and occupies all of eleven lines of verse, the forces of Cordelia are defeated and Lear and Cordelia are captives of Edmund and Albany! The viewer, undoubtedly startled, is however, not yet dismayed, for once more calamity promises to be averted as Albany assumes control, exposing Goneril and Regan and declaring his protection of Lear and Cordelia, who are to be used "as we shall find their merits and our safety / May equally determine" (V. iii. 44–45). Furthermore, the excruciatingly patient force of poetic justice begins at last to assert itself, as Regan dies of a poison administered by Goneril, who, then out-manned by Albany, commits suicide. In a final stroke of poetic justice, the nameless Edgar bests Edmund in combat, in a manner befitting Edmund's history—the cozener is cozened, as Goneril points out:

This is practise, Gloucester.
By th' law of war thou wast not bound to answer
An unknown opposite. Thou art not vanquish'd.
But cozen'd and beguil'd. (V. iii. 152–55)

The play, from every indication, has reached its "promised end." But in its perverse strategy, it refuses to grind to a halt. In what might appear to be an uncharacteristic scrupulosity about loose ends on the part of Shakespeare, the audience is detained by Edgar's laborious dilation of his pilgrimage with Gloucester, followed by his prolonged account of his meeting with Kent, then the announcements of the deaths of Goneril and Regan, and finally by the appearance of Kent to greet his master: "I am come / To bid my king and master aye good night. / Is he not here?" (235–37)

The devastating response of Albany, "Great thing of us forgot! / Speak, Edmund, where's the King? And where's Cordelia?" (237–39), jolts us with the realization that the major figures of the play have been forgotten by both play and viewers for over two hundred lines. And there is yet more perversity. Despite a momentary flurry of concern, the bodies of Goneril and Regan offer yet more distraction, with Edmund taking the time to speculate about his relationship with them:

> Yet Edmund was belov'd!
> The one the other poison'd for my sake,
> And after slew herself. (240–42)

Finally we hear Edmund's declaration: "Some good I mean to do...for my writ is upon the life of Lear and Cordelia," and Edgar, after yet more fumbling, rushes at long last to the rescue. But Lear enters with the dead Cordelia and we know it is too late: Albany's pious prayer, "The gods defend her!" (257) is obviously not heeded.

Cordelia's death is an outrageous blunder taking place as the play leisurely goes about the business of tying up loose ends. It is doubly outrageous because it emerges as a violation of an implicit contract between the play and audience lulled into a false sense of security by misleading signals.[29] The "clearest gods" appealed to by Edgar (IV. v. 73) have not abandoned their mysterious ways; they have not come down, as he and Albany desired, visibly and quickly, to set things aright. The death of Cordelia starkly exposes these hopes as misplaced, and the world is shown as offering no guarantee to the virtuous. Neither the play nor nature can provide an answer to Lear's heart-rending question: "Why should a dog, a horse, a rat, have life / And thou no life at all?" (V. iii. 307–308)

The design of *King Lear* seems clearly to confront the issue of poetic justice and to call into question any hope of attaining it. What should be noted is that, despite the pagan setting of the play, the question is posed in specifically

Christian terms: the emblematic aura surrounding Cordelia, the rich allusiveness to Scripture, the redemptive patterns that recall the morality tradition, all invite a re-assessment of the Christian theology in the light of the dire outcome of the play.[30] Is there, in such a world, any basis for belief in Divine Providence? Is the world as God-forsaken as it appears to be? The side-piercing sight of the dead Cordelia appears to deny the viewer any comfort.

But the attentive viewer will recall that there is more to the play than the dead Cordelia. There is, after all, the suggestion of a moral order manifested in the "redemptions" of Lear and Gloucester—however one may define these—-as well as in the purging of evil in the deaths of Goneril, Regan, Cornwall, and Edmund. Evil, for all its apparent supremacy, is finally and improbably vanquished.

Even more likely to be overlooked are the quiet "miracles" of goodness, acts of quiet heroism performed by the meek and lowly in the play, like the servant who kills Cornwall and the servants who, at their own risk, tend to the unfortunate:

> *3 Serv.* I'll fetch some flax and whites of eggs
> To apply to his bleeding face. Now heaven help him! (III. vii. 106–07)

> *Old Man.* I'll bring him [Edgar] the best 'parel that I have,
> Come on't what will. (IV. i. 49–50)

The selfless acts of these "unpublished virtues" do not, to be sure, efface the horrors of the world of *Lear*, but they do point to a companion mystery to the mystery of evil: the mystery of good embodied in the irrational perdurance of human virtue in a world that does not consistently reward it. In the light of Christian theology, it is through such acts of gratuitous selflessness that God manifests Himself to man: the order of nature is irradiated by the order of grace through such human mediations:

> But God hathe chosen the foolish things of the worlde to confound the wise, and God hathe chosen the weake things of the worlde to confound the mighty things. (1 Cor. 1:27)[31]

Even the death of Cordelia is utterly consistent with Christian theology. The fact that the gods do not visibly intervene on her behalf discredits, not a providential interpretation of events, but a popular, debased version of Christian theology that in fact sentimentalizes the mystery of Divine Providence. The visibility of God has never been a cornerstone of Christian Faith and Hope; indeed, as St. Paul asserts, the invisibility of God is a condition of Hope.

> For we are saved by hope: but hope that is sene, is not hope: for how can man hope for that which he seeth? But if we hope for that we se not, we do with patience abide for it. (Rom. 8:24–25)

Once again in the tragedies patience is counterpoised with poetic justice. In *King Lear* Shakespeare has exploited the pious hopes of both characters and viewers that Providence will act as they presume it will—visibly and quickly—and then exposed these hopes as ill-founded. The gods cannot be presumed upon to act as servile ministers for human concerns; they owe man no subscription. Shallow pieties cannot survive the brute realities of the Lear world; rather, what is needed in such a world is the kind of patience for which Lear strove throughout the play: "You heavens, give me that patience, patience I need!" (II. iv. 271).[32]

V

Macbeth, I suggest, may be seen as a reprise of *King Lear*, as if Shakespeare, fearing that he had overstated his case in *King Lear*, reconsiders the problem of poetic justice and returns to a more affirmative verdict. The core of the action in *Macbeth* is the precise working-out of poetic justice against Macbeth, the glaring exception to Aristotle's doctrine that the tragic hero must suffer *undeserved* misfortune. The most conspicuous feature of the play is that he gets precisely what he deserves, and in so precise a way as to argue for a supernatural ordination of events.

Macbeth, it should be noted, is the only truly clear-sighted tragic hero in the canon: Unlike Brutus, Hamlet, Othello, or Lear, Macbeth knows exactly what he is doing and what consequences he will face, acknowledging that he has "mine eternal jewel / Given to the common enemy of man" (III. i. 67–68). A large part of the viewer's fascination with Macbeth resides in the fullness of his commitment to what he realizes will entail his damnation: the murder of a king, also a kinsman, and also a guest—this last involving a violation of the most sacrosanct of primal pieties, the duty of hospitality to guests.[33]

In the soliloquy in which he braces himself for the murder of Duncan, Macbeth carefully anatomizes the situation he will thrust himself into:

> If it were done, when 'tis done, then 'twere well
> It were done quickly. If th'assassination
> Could trammel up the consequence, and catch
> With his surcease, success, that but this blow
> Might be the be-all and end-all—here,
> But here, upon this bank and shoal of time,
> We'ld jump the life to come. (I. vii. 1–7)

It is important to note the implications of this act: Macbeth is describing a timeless act, an act that, like the *fiat lux* of God, would be perfect in itself and unattended by consequences beyond its own absolute completion. He is, in defiance of human limits, "o'er-leaping the banks and shoals of time" in an attempt to transcend all limits. Thus, in response to the taunt of Lady Macbeth, "Not time, nor place / Did then adhere, and yet you would make both," Macbeth resolves to dare do more than "may become a man" (I vii. 51–52; 46), and declaring himself "master of his time" (III. i. 40), kills Duncan.[34]

What is crucial is that Macbeth, even in contemplating the act, recognizes that he will call poetic justice upon himself: the act of violence will "teach / Bloody instructions, which, being taught [will] return/To plague th'inventor" (I. vii. 8–10), and "even-handed justice," in an image that has strikingly migrated from *Hamlet*, will "commend th'ingredience of our poison'd chalice / To our own lips" (10–12).

The retribution that he anticipates is swift and unmistakable. Having murdered sleep, Macbeth and his wife are afflicted by "these terrible dreams / That shake us nightly" (III. ii. 18–19). Having killed Duncan in the name of perfect freedom, Macbeth finds himself imprisoned:

> I had else been perfect,
> Whole as the marble, founded as the rock,
> But now I am cabin'd, cribb'd, confin'd, bound in
> By saucy doubts and fears. (III. iv. 19–20; 22–23)

And daring in his killing of Banquo to "Cancel and tear to pieces that great bond / Which makes me pale" (III. ii. 49–50), Macbeth finds himself utterly without bonds of love or loyalty:

> My way of life
> Is fall'n into the sere, the yellow leaf,
> And that which should accompany old age,
> As honor, love, obedience, troops of friends,
> I must not look to have. (V. iii. 22–25)

Time is above all Macbeth's nemesis. The hero who would o'erleap "the banks and shoals of time" and have his future in an instant is often depicted as trying to master time, to outrun events. He is literally, for Duncan, a swift horseman who "rides well and [whose] great love, sharp as his spur, hath holp him / To his home before us" (I. vi. 22–24), while his desire for the crown is figuratively a horse spurred on by ambition (I. vii. 25–26). He is able temporarily to "beguile the time" (I. v. 63) and hopes to find security in acting swiftly, as when his mistrust of Macduff prompts him to act:

> Strange things I have in head, that will to hand
> Which must be acted ere they be scann'd. (III. iv. 138–39)

But the first unequivocal signal that Macbeth is not the master of his time is Macduff's escape to England. For once Macbeth finds himself lagging behind events and, with a desperate resolve, he vows to re-assert his mastery of time:

> Time, thou anticipat'st my dread exploits:
> The flighty purpose is ne'er o'ertook
> Unless the deed go with it. From this moment
> The very firstlings of my heart shall be
> The firstlings of my hand. And even now,
> To crown my thoughts with acts, be it thought and done. (IV. i. 144–49)

Once again we note Macbeth's wish for the coalescence of thought and act, the divine prerogative, in the phrase "be it thought and done."

Macbeth's great soliloquy, not surprisingly, begins as a meditation upon time and its ravages. Macbeth, having mocked the time, now finds himself trapped by plodding time in a world without meaning:

> She should have died hereafter;
> There would have been a time for such a word.
> Tomorrow, and tomorrow, and tomorrow,
> Creeps in this petty pace from day to day
> To the last syllable of recorded time. (V. v. 17–21)

His conclusion, that life is absurd, "a tale told by an idiot, full of sound and fury / Signifying nothing," ignores the excruciating appropriateness of his situation: he is living in a world of his own making, its irrationality the consequence of his irrational killing of Duncan. What he suffers, moreover, is a precisely ironic fulfillment of his dissembling utterance at the death of Duncan:

> Had I but died an hour before this chance,
> I had lived a blessed time; for from this instant
> There's nothing serious in mortality;
> All is but toys: renown and grace is dead,
> The wine of life is drawn, and the mere lees
> Is left this vault to brag of. (II. iii. 91–96)

At the conclusion of the play Macbeth continues to suffer by the book, as Macbeth's irrational violations of time and place dictate the manner of his undoing. Having violated place in the murder of his guest, he now looks upon the woods moving toward Dunsinane; the final stroke of poetic justice is the mockery he suffers at the hands of time, when he encounters Macduff, "From his mother's womb / Untimely ripp'd" (V. viii. 15–16) and realizes that his dream of god-like freedom ends in the nightmare of his being chained like a wild animal: "They have tied me to a stake; I cannot fly / But bear-like I must fight the course" (V. vii. 1–2). With the defeat of Macbeth reason and order are once more within reach, as Macduff proclaims "the time is free" and Malcolm vows to "perform in measure, time, and place" the healing acts of a virtuous king (V. ix. 21; 39).

Macbeth would appear to be a special case in Shakespearean tragedy in its unequivocal affirmation of poetic justice. Unlike Hamlet, Othello, or Lear, Macbeth unquestionably gets what he deserves and his downfall is so rational, so precise and appropriate, that it argues for some ordering intelligence. And yet the difference is but one of degree: far from rejecting poetic justice as utterly alien to the spirit of tragedy, each tragedy gives, in the downfall of the wicked, evidence of a moral design in the universe. Laertes' condemnation of Claudius serves as a typical reminder that retribution finally overtakes evil-doers: "He is justly serv'd. / It is a poison temper'd by himself" (V. ii. 327–28).

Tragedy nonetheless loses none of its sting, for the great moral design includes that dread interim when evil is rampant and the good are overwhelmed by it. God's time is not man's time, and the only recourse while waiting the "judgment of the heavens" (*Lear* V. iii. 231) is to strive, like Lear, to be the "pattern of all patience" (III. ii. 37). And even this reverent submission, Lear learns, cannot fend off disaster. The grip of evil upon the world, though short-lived, exacts its awesome cost. Even in *Macbeth*, despite its insistence on poetic justice, viewers are compelled to hear of the slaughter of the innocent (IV. iii. 2–9) and to witness the horrid murder of Lady Macduff and her children. Her comment is an agonizing reminder of the devastating economy of Providence, which performs its wonders not in "measure, time, and place"—as we would have it, but when and where it will:

I have done no harm. But I remember now
I am in this earthly world—where to do harm
Is often laudable, to do good sometime
Accounted dangerous folly. (IV. ii. 73–77)

The concept of poetic justice embodies the ambiguity surrounding the Christian belief in Divine Providence. The God of the tragedies may be a Hidden God, but He is not an absent one, and therein lies the problem faced by the inhabitants of the tragic worlds: the problem of human limits. What the mystery of human existence calls for is a delicate poise between over-reliance upon divine intervention on the one hand and, on the other, a precipitous recourse to human initiative. The heroes find in the urgency of their tragic ordeals that they must choose when to act or not to act, when to retaliate, and when to "let be." In these tragic worlds one could do worse than to be guided by the sober wisdom of Ecclesiastes:

> And moreover I have sene under the sunne the place of judgment, where was wikednes, and the place of justice where was iniquitie. I thoght in mine heart, God will judge the just and the wicked: for time is there for everie purpose and for everie worke. (Eccl. 3:16–17)

Notes to Poetic Justice in Shakespearean Tragedy: "The Justice of It Pleases"

1. Thomas Rhymer, "A Short View of Tragedy," in *The Critical Rhymer*, ed. Curt A. Zimansky (New Haven: Yale University Press, 1956), p. 161.
2. Samuel Johnson, "Notes on the Plays" (1765), *Johnson on Shakespeare*, ed. Walter Raleigh (London: Oxford University Press, 1952), p. 160.
3. Charles Lamb, "On Shakespeare's Tragedies" [1808], in *The King Lear Perplex*, ed. Helmut Bonheim (San Francisco: Wadsworth, 1960), p. 115.
4. Maurice Charney, *How to Read Shakespeare* (New York: McGraw-Hill, 1971), p. 115
5. All citations from the plays are from *The Riverside Shakespeare*, gen. ed. G. B. Evans (Boston: Houghton-Mifflin, 1974).
6. W. K. Wimsatt and Cleanth Brooks, *Literary Criticism: A Short History* (New York: Knopf, 1964), p. 206.

7. *Shakespearean Tragedy* (New York: Fawcett, 1965), p. 207.
8. *The Agamemnon*, trans. Richmond Lattimore (Chicago: University of Chicago Press, 1959).
9. *The Poetics*, trans. Ingram Bywater, in *Aristotle's Rhetoric and Poetics* (New York: Random House, 1954), p. 238.
10. For discussions of the problematic *harmartia*, see Gerald Else, *Aristotle's Poetics: The Argument* (Cambridge: Harvard University Press), pp. 378–85; Wimsatt and Brooks, pp. 39–44.
11. See Else, p. 334: "The nub of the matter is this: Aristotle did not believe in any god or other supernatural agent who could or would push a statue over upon a murderer."
12. Dante specifically refers to the *contrapasso* in Canto 28, vs. 130ff.; the sowers of discord are found in Canto 28, the uncommitted in Canto 3, the flatterers in Canto 18, the soothsayers in Canto 20.
13. For the appeal of revenge as poetic justice, see the fine articles by Michael Cameron Andrews, "Revenge and the Critical Mirror," *English Literary Renaissance*, 8 (Winter 1978), esp. pp. 14–16, and Richard T. Bruecher, "Fantasies of Violence: *Hamlet* and *The Revenger's Tragedy*," *SEL* (Spring 1981), pp. 269–70.
14. Michael Goldman, *Shakespeare and the Energies of the Drama* (Princeton: Princeton University Press, 1972), p. 76.
15. Goldman, p. 87.
16. In *The New Hamlet Variorum*, ed. H. H. Furness (Philadelphia and New York: J. B. Lippincott, 1918) I, p. 283. See also Robert G. Hunter for a typical contemporary response: "To stab a kneeling, defenseless man while he is trying to purge his soul of sin is as damnable an action as it is possible to devise...[and] the motives that prevent Hamlet's committing a damnable act are themselves damnable"—in *The Mystery of God's Judgments*, (Athens: University of Georgia Press, 1976), p. 113.
17. E. A. J. Honigman, *Shakespeare: Seven Tragedies* (London: Macmillan, 1976), p. 55.
18. R. G. Hunter, pp. 121–22, concedes the ruthlessness of Hamlet toward Rosencrantz and Guildenstern but argues that it appears not intended to repel us when we experience the play in the theater. Eleanor Prosser, *Hamlet and Revenge* (Stanford: Stanford University Press, 1971), is also troubled but disposed to let Hamlet off, conjecturing rather timidly that this survival of the vindictive Hamlet is one of the play's "loose ends" (pp. 227–29).
19. Howard Felperin comments, "This self-styled Virtue [Hamlet's] is indictable by the end of the play for a series of offenses ranging from breach of promise through involuntary slaughter to premeditated murder." Hamlet, says Felperin, claims "the metaphoric license to kill of the old figure of *Vindicta Dei*..."—in *Shakespearean Representation: Mimesis and Modernity in Elizabethan Tragedy* (Princeton: Princeton University Press, 1976), p. 63.
20. See Harold Skulsky, *Spirits Finely Touched* (Athens: University of Georgia Press, 1976), pp. 71–86. Skulsky finds in Hamlet's treatment of Rosencrantz and Guildenstern decisive proof that *Hamlet* is "a tragedy of spiritual decline arrested only, if at all, by the brief madness of the Prince's last anger" (p. 82). For the "Italianate revenger," see Prosser, pp. 190–92; 265ff.
21. The quotation is from Edwin Sandys, *The Sermons* (1585), cited in Prosser, p. 7. See also Felperin, p. 167: "Hamlet...had been given to shaping plots in imitation of divine justice...."
22. See Prosser for an interesting instance of ambivalence: after seeing "the tragic cycle in its full horror," Prosser is disposed to accept Horatio's canonization of Hamlet: "His word is to be heeded. And in Horatio's eyes, Hamlet has somehow been granted salvation—but in spite of, not because of, his revenge" (pp. 239–40).

23. This point has often been made; see Derek Traversi, *An Approach to Shakespeare* (Garden City: Doubleday, 1956), p. 134.
24. The Eliot-Leavis school, which finds Othello unredeemed, has gradually lost its influence; see D. J. Palmer, "The Self-awareness of the Tragic Hero," *Stratford-upon-Studies*, 20 (1984), for a balanced verdict that acknowledges both the ironic and heroic possibilities of the end: "Othello's suicide does not vindicate him or reinstate a glory gone forever, but it does authenticate the man that Cassio is left to describe as 'great of heart.' In that sense it is adequate to the occasion" (p. 149)
25. I explore the concept more fully in "Desolation and the Better Life: the Two Voices of Shakespearean Tragedy," *Shakespearean Quarterly*, 32 (Spring 1981), pp. 80–94.
26. The diversity of response to *King Lear* is remarkable, ranging from the darkest pessimism—in critics who find the play's meaning residing in the death of Cordelia—to a sober exultation, in critics who stress the regeneration of Lear. W. R. Elton's influential study, *King Lear and the Gods* (San Marino: The Huntington Library, 1966), takes to task critics who find comfort in religious beliefs: see esp. pp. 3–8.
27. According to Joseph Wittreich, Shakespeare's transformation of his sources is an attempt to secularize the Christian myth of Apocalypse: *"Image of That Horror": History, Prophecy, and Apocalypse in King Lear* (San Marino: The Huntington Library, 1984), p. 127.
28. Stephen Booth provides a detailed and perceptive analysis of the false signals conveyed to the audience in *King Lear, Macbeth, Indefinition, and Tragedy* (New Haven: Yale University Press, 1983), pp. 6–17.
29. Booth, p. 11: "Shakespeare presents the culminating events of his story after the play is over." See also pp. 7–17 for a provocative discussion of the audience's uneasiness in the final scene.
30. For Christian patterns in *King Lear*, see Oscar James Campbell, "The Salvation of King Lear," *ELH*, 15 (1948), pp. 93–109; Roy Battenhouse, *Shakespearean Tragedy: Its Art and Christian Premises* (Bloomington and London: Indiana University Press, 1969), and Paul N. Siegel, *Shakespearean Tragedy and the Elizabethan Compromise* (New York: N.Y.U. Press, 1957), esp. pp. 185–87). Many (most?) critics, while acknowledging the intimations of Christian elements in the play, deny that the meaning is finally Christian; see, e.g., Felperin, pp. 94–96; 102–103.
31. Scriptural quotations are from the Geneva Bible. Two critics who explore the relationship between grace and nature in the tragedies are Virgil Whitaker, *The Mirror up to Nature* (San Marino: The Huntington Library, 1965), pp. 210–11; and Wilbur Sanders, *The Dramatist and the Received Idea* (Cambridge: Cambridge University Press, 1968), p. 265.
32. Whitaker, pp. 47ff., reaches a similar conclusion about the importance of patience in the tragedies.
33. The fascination, of course, does not account for the play's grip upon an audience. According to Booth, viewers in some deep way identify with Macbeth: "For the length of *Macbeth* we are like supernatural beings, creatures capable of being mentally comfortable with infinite possibility" (p. 115). Ironically, in this play (if Booth is accurate) we are in the position of resenting poetic justice—in the one play when it would be the appropriate moral response to hope for it.
34. The phrase "master of the time," of course, is used in another context—when Macbeth releases his guest to fill the time till the banquet. But it is nonetheless telling about Macbeth's own aim to master the time, an ambition that is beyond his powers to achieve. So says Sanders: "Macbeth runs, time runs; and time is continually gaining on him, anticipating him" (p. 270).

DESOLATION AND THE BETTER LIFE: THE TWO VOICES OF SHAKESPEAREAN TRAGEDY

René Fortin

Jacobean tragedy, according to Maynard Mack, is characterized by the interplay of antiphonal voices, each positing a possible response to the tragic conflict. The first and dominant voice is the heroic: a resonant, hyperbolic idiom that proclaims the greatness of the hero as he vies with the malignant forces ranged against him. The second voice is the subtler, muted voice of the anti-heroic, "expressive of a suppler outlook than the hero's and of other and less upsetting ways of encountering experience than the hero's hyperbolic, not to say intransigent, rigorism."[1] The aptness of this observation is easily verified. One may detect the voices in close proximity, for example, in the Ghost scene in *Hamlet*, where Horatio's anti-heroic counsel of prudence—"What if it tempt you toward the flood, my lord, / Or to the dreadful summit of the cliff?"—is met by the authentic heroic idiom of Hamlet:

> My fate cries out,
> And makes each petty artere in this body
> As hardy as the Nemean lion's nerve.
> Still am I call'd. Unhand me, gentlemen.
> By heaven, I'll make a ghost of him that lets me! (I. iv. 69–79; 81–85)[2]

But the ear that is attuned to the varied music of the tragedies will, I suggest, discern in the tragedies a further elaboration of the pattern: the interplay of the antiphonal voices *within* the tragic hero himself. From within the tragic hero occasionally sounds an antiheroic voice which hints at the futility of heroic striving and counsels rather the way of prudence, moderation, and patience.

These antiphonal voices give expression to the hero's dilemma, his urgent need to choose between the heroic and anti-heroic in a world wherein neither response seems wholly adequate.[3]

I

The heroic voice, embodying the humanistic ideal, sings of arms and the man, calling for the protagonist to face his predicament with fortitude and valor. It is the voice of manly and often violent action, of self-assertion in word and deed, and that one hears most resoundingly in *Othello*:

> Let him do his spite;
> My services which I have done the signiory
> Shall out-tongue his complaints. (I. ii. 17–19)

> Keep up your bright swords, for the
> dew will rust them. (I. ii. 59)

> He that stirs next to carve for his own rage
> Holds his soul light; he dies upon his motion. (II. iii. 173–74)

This superb self-assurance, the ringing confidence of a man in full control of his world, is what we value most about the hero. As "one of us," though drawn in larger scale, he represents the best that we as mankind have to offer against the forces that would diminish us. But the fact, also, is that he is in important respects not *quite* "one of us," for his very greatness, his heroic stature, tends to set him off from our own world of quotidian concerns. He is an individual who is proud of his uniqueness and who intends his deeds as a monument to the "I" that, alone and against great odds, has performed them. Thus his ultimate concern is his glory, which will be memorialized in the tale that will be told about him.[4]

This aspiration to be the epitome of mankind exposes for Shakespeare the darker, demonic side of the heroic will, for in his intransigent drive to make "ambition virtue" (*Othello*, III. iii. 350), the hero imperils himself and the society he inhabits. Such an extreme is presented in caricature in the person of Fortinbras, who "for a fantasy and trick of fame" (*Hamlet*, IV. iv. 61) would lead twenty thousand men to their deaths. But bravado is a temptation to which all heroes are subject. Macbeth speaks for them when he says, "I dare do all that may become a man; / Who dares do more is none" (I. vii. 46–47). To dare do more is precisely the temptation of the hero. In the exercise of the public manly virtues—aggressive action, physical valor, masculine fortitude, and self-reliance—the hero threatens to quench his true humanity, to "cancel and tear to pieces the great bond" of mankind (*Macbeth*, III. ii. 49). In his furthest reaches, the hero is tempted to view himself as godlike, to arrogate to himself divine prerogatives. He shares the danger of Coriolanus, whose proud insistence upon playing "the man [that] I am" (III. ii. 16) swells into the hubristic self-assertion that is noticed by others throughout the play:

> You speak a' th' people
> As if you were a god, to punish; not
> A man of their infirmity. (III. i. 80–82)

> What he bids be done is finish'd with his bidding. He wants nothing of a god but eternity and a heaven to throne in. (V. iv. 22–24)

Inevitably, the tragic pattern leads to moments of desolation in which the hero, faced with the challenge of killing a king, of surviving the infidelity of a wife, or of commanding the respect due to a king and father, recognizes the limits of his heroic posture. He acknowledges that he is not a god but merely a man, sharing in the "naked frailties" (*Macbeth*, II. iii. 126) of the race.[5] One recalls Lear's declaration that "aye" and "no" was "no good divinity" (IV. vi. 99–100), or Coriolanus' lament, "I melt, and am not / Of stronger earth than others" (V. iii. 28–29). The images that cluster around these moments of desolation are familiar enough: images of nakedness, melting, shrinking, bondage, beggary, and folly or madness. All are avatars of the anti-heroic way.[6]

II

The moments of desolation which all heroes confront are not, however, merely a retreat from heroic extremity. They represent, rather, the crucial phase of a propaedeutic process that summons the hero to values of a totally different order. The pattern is dimly figured in Cleopatra's utterance, "My desolation does begin to make / A better life" (V. ii. 1–2). From the desolation brought upon the hero by the failure of the masculine code of honor comes the vision of the "better life"—of gentleness, compassion, acceptance—that gleams most splendidly in Lear's struggle for patience:

> Come let's away to prison:
> We two alone will sing like birds i' th' cage:
> When thou dost ask me blessing, I'll kneel down
> And ask of thee forgiveness. So we'll live,
> And pray, and sing. (V. iii. 8–12)

This antiphonal voice, low-keyed and characteristically monosyllabic, articulates that within the hero which is hypostatized in Cordelia, Desdemona, and (less transparently) in Ophelia: the "feminine" response to experience that is the way of selfless acceptance.[7] Each hero, that is, feels within himself (though in various ways and with varying intensity) the call of the higher ideal voiced by Cordelia:

> We are not the first
> Who with best meaning have incurr'd the worst.
> For thee, oppressed king, I am cast down,
> Myself could else out-frown false Fortune's frown. (V. ii. 3–6)

The anti-heroic way culminates in a perception of human reality that seems at heart to be religious and that would, for an Elizabethan audience, have a specifically Christian ring. The thwarted hero—symbolically naked, shrunken in stature and dignity, and reduced to beggary or bondage—would have been seen as undergoing a purgative suffering, such as that described in Revelation 3 of the Geneva Bible:

> For thou saist, I am riche & increased with goods, & haue nede of nothing, and knowest not how thou art wretched & miserable, and poore, and blinde, and naked.
>
> I counsel thee to bie of me golde tryed by the fyre, that thou maiest be made riche, & white raiment, that thou maiest be clothed and that thy filthie nakednes do not appeare: and anoint thine eyes with eye salue, that thou maist se.
>
> As manie as I loue, I rebuke and chasten. (verses 17–19)

In its assertion of the value of emptiness (the paradoxical "something" which comes from "nothing"), the anti-heroic paradigm adumbrates a further ideal. For the anti-heroic way finally points to the way of kenosis, emulative of the "emptying" of Christ, as described in the Pauline hymn:

> Let the same minde be in you that was euen in Christ Jesus, Who being in the forme of God, thought it no robbery to be equal with God: But he made him self of no reputation, and toke on him the forme of a seruant, and was made like vnto men, and was founde in shape as a man. He humbled him self, and became obedient vnto the death, euen the death of the crosse. (Philippians 2:5–8)

In its fullest development, the anti-heroic voice decries the way of heroic self-assertion and sings rather of the way of selflessness and patience.[8] The pattern of the anti-hero way is given, not by Hercules, Alexander, or Caesar, but by Christ, who enacted the paradox that one gains all by losing all, that the way to true fulfillment is the way of emptiness.

The conformity of the Shakespearean pattern to the Christian mysteries does not, it should be noted, constrain the plays within a rigid dogmatic mold. Reduced to human scale after their god-like striving, the Shakespearean heroes all enact in their way the primordial pattern which underlies all tragedy: the death of a god. While it may be construed in specifically Christian terms, then, the kenotic pattern links Shakespeare to Athenian tragedy and, ultimately, to the most primitive rituals of man. The *gnothi seauton* of tragedy, which wars against the *hubris* of the hero, is finally ecumenical in the deepest sense.[9]

But the kenotic voice does not replace the heroic voice. The dominant voice of tragic heroes is still the heroic, and it is decidedly as heroes rather than as saints, martyrs, or Christ-figures that we think of Hamlet, Othello, and Lear. The kenotic ideal, moreover, is only dimly perceived by many of Shakespeare's heroes and is finally found to be unattainable; what characterizes all of them is their resistance, in varying degrees, to the kenotic ideal.[10] The anti-heroic or kenotic is a dissenting voice, then, but one which refuses to be stilled and which asserts its claims throughout the plays. In his interior antiphony the hero reveals his struggle to cope with the ambiguities of tragic heroism; at the same time, he reveals to us Shakespeare's own profound distrust, despite its splendor, of the heroic impulse. The conflict of the two ideals, the secular heroic and the religious kenotic, is expressive finally of the ambiguity of the human condition itself.[11] The woe or wonder of Shakespearean tragedy is most penetrating when we hear the kenotic voice as counterpoint to the dominant heroic music.

The importance of the kenotic voice may best be observed, perhaps, in *Hamlet*, *Othello*, and *King Lear*. One finds that Shakespeare's distrust of heroic ideals becomes more and more pronounced as one moves through the tragedies. The tragedies may be seen, indeed, as an attempt to answer the central question posed by Hamlet: "Whether 'tis nobler in the mind to suffer..." or "to take arms against a sea of troubles" (III. i. 56, 58).

III

In *Hamlet* the question is not easily answered. From the very first soliloquy, in which Hamlet rues his "too too sullied flesh" (I. ii. 129), he oscillates between the heroic way and the anti-heroic or kenotic way of patience. The heroic timbre of Hamlet's voice is easily recognized throughout the play: it is sounded early and clearly in the Hamlet whose "fate cries out" to him (I. iv. 8), and in the hero who is eager to engage in "enterprises of great pitch and moment" (III. i. 85) in an effort to set the time aright. His credentials as hero are impeccable: he is Prince of Denmark, "the glass of fashion and the mould of form" (III. i.

153–54), and the ways of the hero, particularly the hero's concern for glory and honor, are attractive to him, as he reveals when he contemplates the career of Fortinbras:

> Rightly to be great
> Is not to stir without great argument.
> But greatly to find quarrel in a straw
> When honor's at the stake. (IV. iv. 53–56)

But the anti-heroic side of Hamlet is also prominent, in the Hamlet who considers the world an "unweeded garden" (I. ii. 135), a "sterile promontory" (II. ii. 299), or a prison (II. ii. 245ff.), the Hamlet who considers all men to be either "arrant knaves" (III. i. 128) or "the quintessence of dust" (II. ii. 308). However one may interpret it, there surfaces early in Hamlet a skepticism which undermines his heroic resolve and which raises the question whether *any* man can be a hero: "Use every man after his desert, and who shall 'scape whipping?" (II. ii. 528–29).

The dramatic tension of the first three acts of the play stems from the struggle of the hero in Hamlet to be delivered. As the Prince comes closer and closer to executing his revenge, his heroic voice assumes an increasingly shrill tone: "O, from this time forth, / My thoughts be bloody or be nothing worth" (IV. iv. 65–66). It is a disturbingly vehement hero who, in order to attain an absolute revenge, refuses to kill Claudius while he is praying: "Why, this is hire and salary, not revenge / ... Up sword, and know thou a more horrid hent" (III. iii. 79, 88). Acting at this point as if "revenge should have no bounds" (V. i. 128), Hamlet has assumed the extreme stance of the hero, abandoning all moderation and even claiming for himself the divine prerogative of adjudicating the fate of a soul. This is heroic frenzy at its highest pitch, all-too-reminiscent of the "hellish Pyrrhus...roasted in wrath and fire" (II. ii. 463, 461). But the pitch is not maintained. After his "casual" killing of Polonius, Hamlet is dispatched to England, whence he will return apparently transformed.

The interim is Ophelia's. Deepened by her tragedy, she speaks the idiom of the kenotic way—now in explicitly Christian language—which will later be re-echoed in Hamlet's appearance. It is the kenotic voice that is heard in Ophelia's distribution of the flowers, particularly in the rue which "we may call herb of grace a' Sundays" (IV. v. 182–83), and in her prayer for the community of sinners: "God a' mercy on his soul! / And of all Christians' souls, I pray God. God buy you" (IV. v. 199–200). There is just enough coherence in the "unshaped" utterance of Ophelia to disclose a call for hope and patience—"I hope all will be well. We must be patient" (IV. v. 68)—and a summons to resign oneself to the will of God: "Lord, we know what we are, but know not what we may be" (IV. v. 43–44).

Ophelia, in short, prepares the stage for Hamlet's return. In this, the first of the great tragedies, she incarnates in her prophet-like insights the higher ideals of the kenotic way—ideals which will later, and more incandescently, be manifested in Desdemona and Cordelia.[12]

When Hamlet returns from his sea-voyage, we are ready for the sparer orchestration of his language. In the ostensibly regenerated Hamlet "set naked on your kingdom" (IV. vii. 43–44), we sense a new humility before the "divinity that shapes our ends." We hear a new religious tonality in his references to the "special providence" that overwatches him and that is "ordinant" in his schemes (VI. ii. 10, 48, 219, 220).[13] The kenotic voice thenceforth rings clearly, particularly in the graveyard scene, where Hamlet proclaims the grim democracy of death: "Alexander died, Alexander was buried, Alexander returneth to dust; the dust is earth..." (V. i. 208–10). Hero and rogue, sage and fool, king and beggar, tyrant and slave—all are, like Ophelia, creatures "native and indued" to the element of clay. "Alas, poor Yorick," and "Alas, poor Alexander" (V. i. 184).

But the heroic instinct is nothing if not tenacious. Even the "regenerated" Hamlet who has felt the chill of the grave still feels the stirring of the heroic pulse, and we are not entirely surprised to hear the heroic accent in his easy dismissal of the "baser natures" who intruded between the two "mighty opposites" (V. ii. 60–62), or in his challenge to the furious Laertes: "Yet have I in me something dangerous, / Which let thy wisdom fear" (V. i. 262–63). The heroic impulse clings to the very end, asserting itself in Hamlet's final moments, when he expresses concern about his "wounded name" and commissions Horatio to tell his tale (VI. ii. 344).[14] Glory and honor, "the last infirmity of noble minds," still have their appeal for Hamlet—as well as for the viewers who "pale and tremble."

The final moments of the play are especially rich in interplay between the two voices. Hamlet's death draws from Horatio the poignant invocation of "flights of angels" to sing the Prince to his rest. From Fortinbras, it draws the heroic note: Hamlet's death is the death of a hero, and the proper tribute will be the "soldiers' music, and the rite of war" which will speak loudly for him (V. ii. 360, 399). Even in Hamlet's death the voices cannot harmonize: Horatio and Fortinbras split between themselves the kenotic and heroic voices of Hamlet. Indeed, the voices in this final scene follow so closely upon each other that antiphony almost yields to polyphony. Perhaps a truer reflection of our experience than either the angelic choirs or the martial music is the "silence" of Hamlet's parting utterance, a silence which best communicates the burden of the mystery.[15]

One reason why the resolution of *Hamlet* is so immensely satisfying is that at the end each paradigm is present. There survives in Hamlet the appeal of the hero to which we, as "wonder-wounded hearers" (V. i. 258), spontaneously respond: we feel a sense of release in Hamlet's long-delayed and hard-won break-through to decisive action. But the reverence we feel for Hamlet as a prince "out of our star" stems equally, I suggest, from his resistance to heroic action; we sense that, in his notorious penchant for delay, he is groping for a finer way than that of heroic action and that he may be groping for something like the patience of the kenotic ideal. Hamlet's death is, to be sure, the death of a hero, but there is in it a suggestion of mystery. We may be sensitive to the ironies of the final scene and to a clinging to self in Hamlet, and yet still respond to the overtones of his death. And, like Maud Bodkin, we may see the hero as finally a sacrificial victim or martyr:

> ... Our exultation in the death of Hamlet is related in direct line of descent to the religious exultation felt by die primitive group that made sacrifice of the divine king or sacred animal, the representative of the tribal life, and, by the communion of its shed blood, felt that life strengthened and renewed.[16]

IV

The situation of the hero in *Othello* is less ambiguous. The question posed by the play at the end—whether the "immediate jewel" (III. iii. 156) of a good name is worth the "pearl / Richer than all his tribe" (V. ii. 347–48)—is more easily answered. It is the giving and forgiving voice of Desdemona that should have prevailed, although Othello seems not to have heard it, or at least not until it was too late. The famous Othello music is the really the heroic voice, and it resounds through much of the play—even after Iago's filching of Othello's good name, a theft that threatens to disable the noble Moor as a hero.

A soldier without honor is no hero, of course, and Othello, thinking himself stained by Desdemona's infidelity, bids farewell to his occupation, "the pride, pomp, and circumstance of glorious war" (III. iii. 354). But he does so in a remarkably heroic idiom:

> Farewell the plumed troops, and the big wars
> That makes ambition virtue! O, farewell!
> Farewell the neighing steed and the shrill trump,
> The spirit-stirring drum, th' ear-piercing fife.... (III. iii. 349–52)

One would expect Othello, at this point of desolation, to begin to glimpse, if from afar, the kenotic way; but what we find rather is a reaffirmation of the heroic way, though in a different modality.[17] Othello adopts the new heroic posture of the revenger, resolving to take decisive action in the face of dishonor:

> If there be cords, or knives,
> Poison or fire, or suffocating streams,
> I'll not endure it. (III. iii. 85–87)

Decision, not patience, is the way of the hero.

> I'll see before I doubt; when I doubt, prove;
> And on the proof, there is no more but this—
> Away at once with love or jealousy! (III. iii. 190–92)

It is thus in the posture of a hero that Othello dedicates himself to revenge, for his will be a public act, executed in the interests of honor and justice: "Yet she must die, else she'll betray more men" (V. ii. 6); "O, balmy breath, that doth almost persuade / Justice to break her sword" (V. ii. 16–17). The accent of heroic hyperbole is clearly audible in the language of Othello as he attempts to sublimate his wrath:

> Like to the Pontic Sea,
> Whose icy current and compulsive course
> Nev'r feels retiring ebb, but keeps due on
> To the Propontic and the Hellespont,
> Even so my bloody thoughts, with violent pace,
> Shall nev'r look back, nev'r ebb to humble love,
> Till that a capable and wide revenge
> Swallow them up. (III. iii. 453–60)

The proud and unswerving will of the warrior is asserted in Othello's "compulsive course" and in his rejection of the "humble love" which is the true alternative to the heroic way. And his vengeful will carries him, as it did Hamlet, into the excess of assuming divine prerogatives. We receive early intimations of this titanic pride in Othello's reference to the "mortal engines whose rude throats / Th' immortal Jove's dread clamors counterfeit" (III. iii. 355–56). The metaphor implies that to be a war-hero is to be godlike in power. And it is a similar God-like stance that Othello takes in his judgment and punishment of Desdemona. An Elizabethan audience would have been alert to the blasphemy in Othello's statement as he prepares to kill Desdemona: "This sorrow's heavenly; / It strikes where it doth love" (V. ii. 21–22), an echo of the familiar Biblical verse, "As manie as I love, I rebuke and chasten" (Revelation 3).[18]

In the meantime the kenotic voice that would call Othello to patience is not entirely unheard in the play. There are a few instances when Othello's "compulsive course" is slowed and he is drawn to the gentler way of "humble love":

> O, the world hath not a sweeter creature! She might lie by an emperor's side and command him tasks. (IV. i. 184–85)

> Hang her, I do but say what she is. So delicate with her needle! An admirable musician! O, she will sing the savageness out of a bear. (IV. i. 187–89)

> Had it pleas'd heaven
> To try me with affliction, had they rain'd
> All kinds of sores and shames on my bare head,
> Steep'd me in poverty to the very lips,
> Given to captivity me and my utmost hopes,
> I should have found in some place of my soul
> A drop of patience. (IV. ii. 47–53)

In this last instance the kenotic voice is heard most clearly, but it is no sooner heard than rejected:

> Turn thy complexion there,
> Patience, thou young and rose-lipp'd chérubin—
> Ay, here look grim as hell. (IV. ii. 62–64)

The ideal of patience which Othello resists throughout the play is embodied in Desdemona, who, after momentarily harboring resentment against Othello, chides herself for being an "unhandsome warrior" (III. iv. 151) and professes a love that can transcend the harshness of Othello's behavior toward her:

> My love doth so approve him,
> That even his stubbornness, his checks, his frowns—
> Prithee unpin me—have grace and favor in them. (IV. iii. 19–21)

The simple homely detail of "Prithee unpin me" reminds us that Desdemona is no Cordelia. Her plight is made even more pathetic by her almost preternatural innocence (some would call it ingenuousness) and by her almost total mystification about Othello's behavior. Her quiet strength is thus even more remarkable when she accepts her situation in a spirit reminiscent of Hamlet's "readiness is all":

> All's one. Good Father, how foolish are our minds! (IV. ii. 23)[19]

> Good night, good night. God me such uses send
> Not to pick bad from bad but by bad mend. (IV. iii. 104–105)

Her final speech, with the noble lie exculpating Othello—"Nobody; I myself. Farewell!"—concludes with her astonishing request: "Commend me to my kind lord" (V. ii. 124–25). Though one may argue that Desdemona's final actions are not explicitly redemptive—as was the death of Christ—one can hardly deny that she here embodies the humble love and self-renunciation that constitute the kenotic way.[20] In rejecting the "unhandsome warrior" that resides in all human breasts, she stands in starkest contrast to Othello, now literally the "unhandsome warrior" engaged in his last grim campaign.

Except for the few moment of self-doubt mentioned above, the kenotic voice within Othello himself is virtually stilled until the final moments of the play. But in the "insupportable...heavy hour" (V. ii. 98) when Othello must face the loss of his wife, his honor, and his occupation, as well as endure the searing shame of having been duped by Iago, the voice emerges. It is heard clearly in his meek acknowledgement of the loss of his identity—"That's he that was Othello; here I am" (V. ii. 284)—and in his self-flagellation as a "fool, fool, fool" (V. ii. 323). The new Othello who struggles to be born is especially audible in his plea to Cassio for forgiveness: "I do believe it, and I ask your pardon" (V. ii. 301).

Despite these kenotic impulses, however, the heroic temper resists softening. Nothing is more revealing of Othello's stubborn resistance to humility than the fact that he cannot be finally disarmed, stripped of the weapon that is emblematic of his heroism. He is first disarmed by Montano, evoking Othello's response, "I am not valiant either, / But every puny whipster gets my sword"

(V. ii. 243–44). Symbolically "naked" (i.e., unarmed as well as stripped of all he values), he verges upon a liberating self-recognition: "But why should honor outlive honesty? / Let it go all" (II. 245–56). He cannot "let it go all," however; his inability to accept the spiritual nakedness which is the precondition of his regeneration is signaled by his reappearance with another weapon, "a sword of Spain, the ice-brook's temper" (I. 253), which was concealed in his chamber. Sword in hand, he is once more the hero:

> Behold, I have a weapon;
> A better never did itself sustain
> Upon a soldier's thigh. I have seen the day
> That with this little arm and this good sword
> I have made my way through more impediments
> Than twenty times your stop. (V. ii. 259–64)

But even this titanic effort to reconstitute his heroic image cannot prevail over the reality of his situation, and the heroic ardor at once dwindles: Do you go back dismay'd? 'Tis a lost fear; /Man but a rush against Othello's breast / And he retires. (II. 269–71) After his ineffectual thrust against Iago, Othello is once more disarmed, and left only with his lame justification for the killing as an "honorable murder" (V. ii. 294).

This swing between self-assertion and self-renunciation continues into the final moments of the play. Othello's great final speech is a remarkable interweaving of the kenotic and heroic voices. Despite the hints of self-exculpation, there surfaces a new humility in the Othello who prays others to "speak of me as I am, nothing extenuate" (V. ii. 342) and who describes himself as a "base Indian [who] threw a pearl away / richer than all his tribe" (V. ii. 347–48). The new self which Othello seems to be struggling to free is above all manifested in the unheroic and "womanly" tears which flow from his "subdued" eyes (V. ii. 348).

But the heroic clinging to self is equally in evidence. The soldier whose first major utterance in the play referred to the services he had performed for the state reminds the audience once more of his heroic role. And his concern for the tale that will be told about him bears vestiges of the hero's pride:

Set you down this;
And say besides, that in Aleppo once,
Where a malignant and a turban'd Turk
Beat a Venetian and traduc'd the state,
I took by th' throat the circumcised dog
And smote him—thus.(V. ii. 351–57)

The heroic temper surfaces for the last time, in other words, in Othello's "bloody period." Visibly a hero, he ends his life performing a last service to the state, that of killing a criminal.

The ambiguity of the final moments is maintained when Othello falls upon the body of Desdemona: "I kiss'd thee ere I kill'd thee. No way but this, / Killing myself, to die upon a kiss" (V. ii. 358–59). The vast gulf between the kenotic and the heroic is paradoxically crystallized in the almost homophonous verbs "kiss" and "kill." Othello was indeed, as Cassio says, "great of heart" (V. ii 361), but this fate poses more insistently than Hamlet's the question of whether heroism is worth the price.[21]

V

Ironically, Shakespeare's closest approach to the kenotic way takes place in *King Lear*, the most pervasively "pagan" of the plays. The Lear experience may be seen as a passage from the exalted status of hero-king through the various avatars of the anti-heroic—babe, fool, madman, beggar, prisoner—to a final realization of the kenotic ideal and its awesome cost. The godlike Lear, the imperious arch-hero of his world, must be emptied of self and engulfed in the "nothing" that is so prominent a leitmotif in the play. He becomes a babe to his daughters, a fool to his fool, a naked beggar among naked beggars, an outcast among outcasts, and a madman striving to "outscorn the to-and-fro conflicting winds and rain" in a world gone mad (III. i. 11).

The kenotic voice is heard in Lear's struggle for patience and forbearance. Even early in Act II, when Lear finds Kent in the stocks, he very untypically tries to quell his rising anger: "I'll forbear, / And am fallen out with my more headier will..." (II. iv. 109–10). And shortly after, still before his ordeal begins in earnest, he responds to Goneril's rejection of him by striving for patience: "I can be patient, I can stay with Regan" (II. iv. 230). Henceforth Lear's education is a progression to "nothingness"; humbled, he learns to "see feelingly" and to acknowledge his kinship with the "poor, naked wretches" who must, like himself, "bide the pelting of this pitiless storm" (III. iv. 28–29). It is a new humility before both the gods and man that Lear dredges from his distress, and the imperious voice of the king is eventually replaced by the intensely spare, monosyllabic speech of the anti-hero:

> Here stand I your slave,
> A poor, infirm, weak, and despis'd old man. (III. ii. 19–20)

> I am a very foolish, fond old man
> Fourscore and upward, not an hour more or less;
> And to deal plainly,
> I fear I am not in my perfect mind. (IV. vii. 59–62)

> You must bear with me.
> Pray you now forget, and forgive; I am old and foolish. (IV. vii. 83–84)

But Lear's passage to the kenotic way is a fitful one, for in each instance when he strives for patience, his "headier will" prevails and the heroic temper continues to lash out. Often, in fact, the kenotic and the heroic meet within the very same speech:

> You heavens, give me that patience, patience I need!
> You see me here, you gods, a poor old man,
> As full of grief as age, wretched in both. (II. iv. 271–73)

Here as elsewhere, the prayer for patience is followed by a resurgence of the heroic will:

> If it be you that stirs these daughters' hearts
> Against their father, fool me not so much
> To bear it tamely; touch me with noble anger,
> And let not women's weapons, water drops,
> Stain my man's cheeks! (II. iv. 274–78)

The "women's weapons" which Lear now despises will later come to have value for him, for they are associated through the play with Cordelia. Upon her return to Britain, she is moved by the ordeal of her father, but, as the Gentleman inform us,

> Not to a rage; patience and sorrow strove
> Who should express her goodliest. You have seen
> Sunshine and rain at once; her smiles and tears
> Were like a better way. (IV. ii. 16–19)

> There she shook
> The holy water from her heavenly eyes
> And, clamor-moistened, then away she started
> To deal with grief alone. (IV. iii. 29–31)

The imagery which surrounds her here and elsewhere in the play makes of Cordelia a sublimated version—with intimations of transcendence—of the "pattern of all patience" (III. ii. 37) seen in less luminous form in Ophelia and Desdemona. In them the pattern is dimmed by the madness of Ophelia and the naïveté of Desdemona. Cordelia, in a sense, is the hypostasis of the kenotic way. Her "No cause, no cause" (IV. vii. 74)—one may detect an echo of Othello's "It is the cause, it is the cause"—is the quintessential expression of the way of self-abnegation, and one expects nothing less from her than her calm and serene acceptance of her capture: "We are not the first / Who with best meaning have incurr'd the worst" (V. iii. 3–4).

In Shakespeare the boisterous heroic way mysteriously meets its match in the muted and even silent responses of the women. And it should be noted that the common fate of the women offers no promise that the kenotic way is a refuge from tragedy. Ophelia, Desdemona, and Cordelia are all victims of malignant forces and suffer far beyond their deserving. Their fates may serve to deepen the mystery of evil, but their submission to their fates suggests a way of meeting adversity beyond the heroic.

Of all the heroes, it is Lear who, in his reconciliation with Cordelia, comes closest to accepting the kenotic mystery. Even facing the prospect of captivity with his daughter, Lear is able to renounce the world. In his aria-like "Come let's away to prison" speech he sings of the values of love and forgiveness, apparently in possession of a peace that passeth understanding.

But even now the heroic voice is ready to ring out. Lear vows that no earthly power will ever separate him from Cordelia:

> He that parts us shall bring a brand from heaven,
> And fire us like foxes. Wipe thine eyes;
> The good years shall devour them, flesh and fell,
> Ere they shall make us weep! We'll see 'em starved first. (V. iii. 22–25)

And after the death of Cordelia, it is the hero in Lear who takes pride in killing "the slave that was a-hanging thee" (V. iii. 275), who boasts of the "good biting falchion" that he wielded in his heartier days (V. iii. 277). But the voice of the hero quickly fades into that of the tired old man: "I am old now, / And these same crosses spoil me" (V. iii. 278–79). The heroic way is out of reach now, and the imperative mood which one associates with the early Lear fades into the interrogative: "Why should a dog, a horse, a rat have life, / And thou no breath at all?" (V. iii. 306–308). Equally out of reach is the kenotic way of unquestioning acceptance: Lear's intonation of "never, never, never..." (V. iii. 309) is neither defiantly heroic nor beatifically accepting. This is not the voice of saint, of hero, or (as some would have it) of howling animal: it is the elemental voice of man "perlex'd in th'extreme" before the mystery of evil. As in *Hamlet*, it is silence, the "word unheard" of Cordelia, that best sums up the mystery of the play.[22]

VI

The anatomy of heroism does not end here. In Macbeth, Antony, and Coriolanus, the limitations of human self-assertion are more surely depicted. Despite their resistance of the kenotic way, all end up as shrunken, shriveled versions of themselves. Antony is defeated by a "boy" and mastered by Cleopatra. Coriolanus at last discovers that he has always been his mother's son and dies with the taunt "Boy of tears" ringing in his ears. While Macbeth, reduced to the "dwarfish thief" who is denied even the tale that would make something of his life of sound and fury, is succeeded by the "boy" Malcolm.[23]

The problem of the subsequent plays, in Robert Frost's words, is "what to make of a diminished thing." Two developments are particularly worth noting: the pastoral setting (or its equivalent) of the last plays and the dominance of the women. The escape into the pasture, the antithesis of the heroic world, represents a renunciation of the heroic posture. And the cumulative weight of the long pastoral tradition accounts in part for the diminished, docile, and fallible heroes of these last plays. One can hardly, for example, conceive of Coriolanus meekly consenting to carry logs to win the hand of Virgilia. Heroism, it would seem, is now possible only for those who, like Guiderius and Arviragus in *Cymbeline*, have learned the humility of the pastoral way, or who, like Posthumus, have suffered the purgative ordeal of bondage: "Most welcome, bondage! for thou art a way, / I think, to liberty" (V. iv. 3, 4).

The corollary development is the emergence of the Imogens, Hermiones, and Marinas, who confirm what the tragedies have already intimated, that the way of true fulfillment is the kenotic way. It has been Shakespeare's women, though we have not sufficiently noticed it, who have all along been the "strong, silent types." Though the heroes despise, like Lear, the tears which are "women's weapons" (II. iv. 277), such tears are proven to be better weapons than manly swords. In desolation and repentance lies the better life.

Shakespeare's last hero is Prospero, and it is in keeping with the new humility that, having done his work, he discards the cloak and book which are the source of his "rough magic." The proud posture of the self-sufficient hero is abandoned as Prospero affirms that "the rarer action is / In virtue than in vengeance" (V. i. 27–28). Our last view of Prospero, and of the Shakespearean hero, is as a "naked" supplicant beseeching viewers to grant him his release from the bondage which, the play implies, we all share: "As you from crimes would pardoned be, / Let your indulgence set me free" (Epilogue, 19–20). The final voice of the canon is the kenotic voice which has struggled to be heard from the beginning of the tragic phase and which, as the voice of "nobler reason" (*Tempest*, V. i. 26), has at last stilled all fury.

Notes to Desolation and the Better Life: The Two Voices of Shakespearean Tragedy

1. Maynard Mack, "The Jacobean Shakespeare: Some Observations on the Construction of the Tragedies," in *Essays in Shakespearean Criticism*, ed. James L. Calderwood and Harold E. Tolliver (Englewood Cliffs: Prentice-Hall, 1970), p. 26. The essay first appeared in *Stratford-upon-Avon Studies*, 1, ed. John Russell Brown and Bernard Harris, in 1960.
2. All references to the plays will be to *The Riverside Shakespeare*, gen. ed. G. Blakemore Evans (Boston: Houghton-Mifflin, 1974).
3. Mack, p. 32, holds a similar view.
4. For an enlightening approach to the psychology of the hero see Matthew N. Proser, *The Heroic Image in Five Shakespearean Tragedies* (Princeton: Princeton Univ. Press, 1965).
5. See G. K. Hunter, "The Last Tragic Heroes," *Stratford-upon-Avon Studies*, 8 (New York: St. Martin's Press, 1967), pp. 20–21. Hunter finds in the last tragedies "the moral ambiguity of heroes who are both godlike and *inhuman*" (italics his). My point is that the moral ambiguity is present throughout the canon; even before the tragic phase one may detect skepticism about the hero, e.g., in the *Henriad*.
6. According to Mack, the hero passes into his antithesis, then reaches a third phase which "represents a recovery of sorts—in some cases, perhaps, even a species of synthesis" (p. 43).
7. I am uncomfortable with the masculine-feminine dichotomy, but the paradigm seems implicit in Shakespeare. Of course, the paradigm is often distorted or inverted: in *King* Lear Albany is certainly "feminine" while Goneril is decidedly "masculine," and the roles are flagrantly reversed for a time in *Macbeth*. The paradigm has less to do with biological sex than with moral disposition, though Shakespeare's Cordelias and Imogens may suggest that the "feminine" response to experience is natural for women.
8. I have found valuable support for my approach in Roy W. Battenhouse, *Shakespearean Tragedy: Its Art and Its Christian Premises* (Bloomington and London: Indiana University Press, 1969); Ivor Morris, *Shakespeare's God* (London: George Allen and Unwin Ltd., 1971); and Reuben Brower, *Hero and Saint* (New York: Oxford University Press, 1971), esp. pp. 416–20. John M. Steadman, in "The Arming of an Archetype," *Concepts of the Hero in the Middle Ages and the Renaissance*, eds. Norman T. Burns and Christopher Regan (Albany: State University of New York Press, 1975), finds the kenosis of Christ to be a dominant pattern in Milton's

poetry. Much of what Steadman says is equally applicable to Shakespeare's work, though, of course, Shakespeare's use of the kenotic paradigm is much more oblique than Milton's.

9. See Northrop Frye, *Anatomy of Criticism* (Princeton: Princeton University Press, 1957), p. 217. Frye notes that in many tragedies the hero "begins as a semi-divine figure, at least in his own eyes, and then an inexorable dialectic sets in to work which separates the divine pretense from the human actuality." E. J. Tinsley, *Christian Theology and the Frontiers of Tragedy* (Leeds: Leeds University Press, 1963), pp. 11–13, argues that Christ acted "in a way which is the reverse of the tragic hero's manner." This comment, while perceptive, highlights the danger inherent in the kenotic paradigm: of transforming the hero into an anti-Christ or into a grotesque parody of Christ. It is imperative that the moral ambiguity of tragedy be maintained and that the heroic paradigm, with its immense appeal *to all* viewers, be given its just due.
10. See Steadman, p. 180: in the best of cases, the paradigm of the kenotic hero is impossible to realize fully. It is largely because of the ambiguity of the hero's response to the kenotic ideal that the paradigm of the *felix culpa*, though initially attractive, does not provide an adequate basis for tragedy. What makes tragedy tragic is that one cannot finally establish whether or how the fall of the hero is indeed fortunate.
11. Brower, p. 419.
12. Cf. Battenhouse, pp. 240–41, 292.
13. The qualification "*ostensibly* regenerated" is important. Though I am convinced that we are invited to find a new disposition in Hamlet, I am not convinced that the transformation is as complete or as unequivocal as most would have it.
14. Brower, p. 311, comments on Hamlet's concern about his name.
15. On the death of Hamlet and its implications, there is a remarkable range of response. Brower, pp. 311–12, perhaps best captures the dialectic. See also Morris, p. 417, Battenhouse, p. 263, Patrick Crutwell, "The Morality of Hamlet—'Sweet Prince' or 'Arrant Knave'?" *Stratford-upon-Avon Studies*, 5 (London: Edward Arnold Ltd., 1963), p. 128; Harold Skulsky, *Spirits Finely Touched* (Athens: University of Georgia Press, 1976), p. 82. The varied responses attest to the play's openendedness.
16. Maud Bodkin, *Archetypal Patterns in Poetry* (1934; rpt. London: Oxford University Press, 1968), p. 21.
17. Proser, p. 130.
18. Skulsky, p. 237, makes a similar point.
19. I use the F1 "Father," which seems to me more appropriate than "faith," which G. B. Evans adopts from Q1.
20. Battenhouse, p. 97, finds that "at the core of the play's meaning is a Christlike martyrdom, fumbling though it be."
21. The death of Othello evokes a range of responses, but not to the extent that Hamlet's does; for representative responses, see Robert G. Hunter, *Shakespeare and the Mystery of God's Judgments* (Athens: University of Georgia Press, 1976), p. 156; Proser, p. 110; Brower, pp. 27–28; Skulsky, p. 244.
22. The traditional controversy still rages, with Morris, p. 237, and Battenhouse, pp. 292–93, insisting with Bradley upon the play's affirmations, and Hunter reaffirming the Elton position and stressing the "sense of cosmic emptiness" (p. 194).
23. See G. K. Hunter, "The Last Tragic Heroes" (n. 5 above) for a fuller treatment; I am also indebted to Dwight Cathcart, "The Conscience of Posthumus," a paper submitted to the 1976 ISA Congress.

THE CRUCIFIX AND THE POST: A NOTE ON THE CHRISTIAN THEME IN *GULLIVER'S TRAVELS*

Brian Barbour

I

When, in his survey of "Swift and Religion" in the *Cambridge Companion*, Marcus Walsh remarks that unlike Swift's earlier work, *Gulliver's Travels* was "not...obviously Christian" he is speaking for the Common Reader as well as for the high critical tradition.[1] But obviously much depends on that *obviously*. A couple of critical generations earlier and probably with Kathleen Williams in mind,[2] R.S. Crane had taken a no-nonsense secular line and attempted to close any fissures in that *obviously* by declaring that *GT* needed to be read in "a broadly human and non-sectarian sense." And he tightened his stricture by insisting that had Swift "meant his story to be a contribution to Christian apologetics" then (*obviously*?) he would have done so by either "attacking current doctrines incompatible with the dogma of original sin" or by "insisting on the reality of divine grace and the scheme of redemption," the only conceivable ways, apparently, that a literary work could enact a Christian point or theme or grow out of a Christian worldview.[3] But a work need not engage in apologetics to be Christian and Walsh's *obviously* still leaves us with an opening, however small. Consider, for example, Howard Erskine-Hill, no particular partisan of the secular. In his useful handbook on *GT* he has to allow that "the *Travels* is...remarkably silent about the Christian faith," adding that "Christianity itself has no explicit role in the *Travels*."[4] *Obviously* here morphs into *explicit* but we sense that unlike Crane, but like Walsh, Erskine-Hill is not quite willing to issue a straightforward denial. Although Christianity is "not explicit," he says, "it should not be forgotten."[5] Both Walsh and Erskine Hill are hedging their bets. Neither wants to definitively rule out the presence of a Christian something-or-other in *GT*, yet each acknowledges that Christianity's felt presence is implicit only and, for many readers, perhaps most, frankly invisible.[6] And thinking about other priest-authors—Donne, Herbert, Hopkins—one may be drawn to agree.

And yet what is not obvious or explicit may well be implicit and vital; and it is perhaps possible to re-examine the text, especially certain key passages, some well-known, some routinely ignored, ask some relevant questions, and thereby re-open and possibly expand the fissure Crane tried to seal. It is the purpose of this paper to do just that, to show how Swift quietly instantiated a major Christian theme in the book and to argue that a proper recognition of this theme opens a wider appreciation of the total meaning of both the Fourth Voyage and of *GT* as a whole, its radical criticism of the basic intellectual assumption of its secularizing age. For the fact is Swift has written a deeply Christian book about apostasy and the coming surge in rationalistic agnosticism. *Qui habet aures audiendi, audiat*. It is a consummate Swiftian irony: if we miss his point we thereby prove it.

II

It could be said that from the time of the Philippian jailer onwards,[7] coming to a clearer sense of the Christian presence depends on asking the right question or questions. If, for example, we come to *GT* expecting that an Anglican priest must—to write a Christian book—engage in "Christian apologetics," we are not going to get anywhere. Swift was not that kind of priest nor was he that kind of writer. It seems to me that the overwhelming question one has to ask is, *Why does Gulliver lose his Anglican faith*? That is the key, the *quaestio quaestionum*, and with it are associated the secondary questions, *When and How does this occur*? These are matters that can be profitably discussed in the text, and if they are matters Swift does not dwell on, that lack of insistence is a part of his overall literary strategy. Erskine-Hill put his finger on an important point when he remarked that the typical "eighteenth-century reader would...have seen Gulliver as a man without religion."[8] Just so. For the Gulliver of the Fourth Voyage is in fact a man without religion. But Erskine-Hill did not appreciate or follow out his own valuable insight. Gulliver was not always so bereft.

For lose his faith Gulliver most certainly does. We can see the result of this loss in the well-known passage in Part IV, Chapter V where he is explaining European wars to the master Houyhnhnm:

> Difference in Opinions hath cost many Millions of Lives: For Instance, whether *Flesh* be *Bread*, or *Bread* be *Flesh*: Whether the Juice of a certain *Berry* be *Blood* or *Wine*: Whether *Whistling* be a Vice or a Virtue: Whether it be better to kiss a *Post*, or throw it into the Fire: What is the best Colour for a *Coat*, whether *Black*, *White*, *Red*, or *Grey*; and whether it should be *long* or *short*, *narrow* or *wide*, *dirty* or *clean*, with many more. Neither are any Wars so furious and bloody, or of so long Continuance, as those occasioned by Difference in Opinion, especially if it be in things indifferent.[9]

This specious synopsis which glides over Reformation issues[10] in the anxiously belittling voice of the newly converted would win many a *philosophe's* smiling approval. The governing terms "opinions" and "indifferent" deftly frame serious but hidden theological quarrels over the Eucharist and transubstantiation, the liturgy, sacred music, sacramentals and sacred statuary, vestments, and ecclesiology—all rendered trivial here in a *reductio ad absurdum*. And the final distancing sneer—"in things indifferent"—is a smooth technique for undercutting Christianity without appearing to mention it at all; in fact it is a prescient anticipation of Voltaire's strategy: *écrasez l'infâme*. But the passage goes beyond witty Deism or salon posturing towards outright atheism. We ourselves might pass it by as no more than conventional Enlightenment propaganda, but in the movement from rationalism to Deism to assumptive atheism Swift was recording an advancing historical development.

Still, if this passage shows the loss, where is the faith Gulliver has apostasized? It is certainly nowhere evident in Book IV; the submerged imagery, however, tells a larger story. For what in the passage Gulliver dismisses as a *post* he had earlier (in Part III) venerated as a *crucifix*. And that shift from *crucifix* to *post* marks both the change in Gulliver himself and also Swift's sense of the menacing secular "progress" happening all around him, the larger theme of the *Travels*.

It is useful at this point to recall that Part III of the *Travels* was written *after* Part IV, so we can legitimately infer that the purpose of Part III lies in large part in preparing and comically clarifying and sharpening Swift's darker philosophical and religious critiques in Part IV, making them less easy to avoid. On the philosophical side Part III more openly mocks the premise of Cartesian rationalism that "reason alone is sufficient." But on the religious side it establishes Gulliver as a fairly devout believing Anglican, and this gives us the right perspective for seeing his apostasy in the Fourth Voyage.

How does it do this? It will be recalled that in Chapter I of the Third Voyage the pirate crew which seizes Gulliver's ship includes a Dutchman of some authority who becomes inflamed with rage when Gulliver appeals for his aid as "a Brother Christian." In his wrath the Dutchman tries to have Gulliver thrown overboard, and when that fails he succeeds in having him set adrift on the ocean, alone, "in a small Canoe" (130–31). Alberto Rivero rightly notes that Swift despised the Dutch both politically and religiously; here as later the stress falls on the religious distinction between "Dutch" and "Christian."[11] By the Seventeenth Century, with Calvin dead, with the Synod of Dort, TULIP and the suppression of Arminianism, with the "flowering of the Calvinist republic,"[12] Holland had come to replace Geneva as the *de facto* center of European Calvinism—and in Holland even displaying a crucifix was generally forbidden. "Dutch" therefore had become, as here, a surrogate term for "Calvinist" and thus a focus for that Presbyterian Dissent Swift so thoroughly despised.[13]

Bearing the Dutch / Christian distinction in mind, we come to "the Business of the Crucifix." In Chapter XI Gulliver has left Luggnagg and has reached Japan from where he hopes to return to Europe by means of the Dutch shipping that is trading with the empire. It is a requirement for any European leaving Japan that he trample on a crucifix as a sign of disrespect, something that the Dutchmen as Calvinist iconoclasts have no hesitation doing. But Gulliver, though he is claiming to be Dutch to make his escape, finds the demand repugnant and wants nothing to do with the ceremony. He may be forced to temporize in order to secure his escape, but he is unwilling to dishonor the central symbol of his faith. Trapped by precedent and expectation, he appeals directly to the Emperor. "[I asked] his Majesty...to excuse my performing the

Ceremony imposed upon my Countrymen [i.e., the Dutch] of *trampling upon the Crucifix*" (183). The Emperor, startled by so unprecedented a request, notes that Gulliver is "the first of [his] Countrymen who ever made any Scruple on this Point," and therefore "he began to doubt whether I were a real Hollander or no; but rather suspected I must be a CHRISTIAN" (183). This is a tense moment and Gulliver's escape hangs in the air. But because Gulliver is travelling under the protection of the King of Luggnagg and chiefly to gratify that King by this "uncommon...favour" (183) the Emperor disregards his suspicion and grants Gulliver's request, freeing him from the requirement. At the same time he warns Gulliver that the affair must still be managed "with dexterity" (183) because the Dutch—whom the Emperor distinguishes from Christians—are even more fanatical about the ceremony than are the pagan Japanese. "For he assured me, that if the secret should be discovered by my Countrymen, the *Dutch*, they would cut my Throat in the Voyage" (183–84). So the Emperor arranges for Gulliver to slip out quietly and he gives "the Commanding Officer...Orders to convey me safe thither, with particular Instructions about the Business of the Crucifix" (184).

Gulliver might now seem safe but Swift continues to drive the point home. Before they leave port some of the Dutch crew grow suspicious and begin to press Gulliver about whether or not he has performed the required ceremony, while one "malicious Rogue" goes to an officer and reports that Gulliver "had not yet *trampled on the Crucifix*." Happily, the officer, having been instructed to leave the matter alone, rebukes the informer, and Christian Gulliver escapes doing what "the real Hollanders" had no compunction doing.

What are we to make of this passage, especially given its salient position, its insistence, and its difference in tone from the reason-gone-silly hijinks of the earlier part of the Third Voyage? Two things stand out. First, Swift is drawing a general distinction between Dutch Calvinism, unmoored from sacramentals and by implication easily secularized, and Gulliver's presumptive and more Incarnational Anglicanism that takes honoring the crucifix very seriously. In Swift's mind it is the difference between a Christianity almost wholly subjective and one grounded in authority and tradition. Second, as to Gulliver himself we see that his Anglican Christianity is serious enough that he would run the risk of jeopardizing his escape from Japan. Though he is hardly faced with martyrdom, he is dead set on refusing to dishonor the crucifix. It is this seriousness of commitment that Swift predicates as basic to Gulliver's character when he departs just four months later on the Fourth Voyage. Gulliver's Christianity appears as a theme in the text now because it is needed now, to frame by contrast the apostasy of Part IV that characterizes the "Differences of Opinion" passage, where that once-revered crucifix is now casually dismissed as a "post." How and why does this change occur and Gulliver lose his faith?

III

Clearly Gulliver has no secular Road-to-Damascus or Aldersgate experience, but just as clearly he does experience an inverted or parodic conversion: from Christianity to atheism. Swift emphasizes the importance of the change by placing it right at the structural center of the Fourth Voyage, the opening paragraph of Chapter VII. And he uses the language of religious conversion to invoke the paradigm and thus underline its parodic nature. After less than a year among the Houyhnhnms, Gulliver tells us, he had experienced a profound, if gradual, inner change:

> But I must freely confess, that the many Virtues of those excellent *Quadrupeds* placed in opposite view to human Corruptions, had so far opened mine Eyes, and enlarged my Understanding, that I began to view the Actions and Passions of man in a very different Light; and to think the Honour of my own Kind not worth managing. (217–18)

The eye imagery with its latent Pauline suggestions is all-important. For perspective, consider Jonathan Edwards' contemporary account (1742) of his conversion experience, also a slowly developing inner change: "My sense of divine things gradually increased, and became more and more lively, and had more of that inward sweetness. The appearance of everything was altered."[14] *Opened mine Eyes and enlarged my Understanding / The appearance of everything was altered*—The substance of the two accounts is reversed but the epistemological form is substantially the same. In less than a year Gulliver moves from solid Anglican Christianity to assumptive atheism. Why and how does this happen?

We can best address these questions by recalling that although Gulliver had been a faithful if somewhat colorless reporter through the first three voyages, in the Fourth Voyage he finally lives up to his name and becomes an unreliable narrator. As the example of, say, Poe reminds us there are many different ways for a narrator to be unreliable. In Gulliver's case his unreliability is found not in misrepresenting facts or in psychological estrangement but in *gullibility*, his inability to properly sort out, understand, and judge the things he sees and reports. In brief, under the influence of and seeking the approval of the Houyhnhnms[15] Gulliver comes to accept two falsehoods, two examples of "the thing that is not," falsehoods that are connected, that have an inherent order, that reinforce one another, and that together mark his loss of Christian faith. The first and most decisive is the Cartesian motto that serves as the grand maxim of the Enlightenment: "*Reason* alone is sufficient to govern a *Rational* Creature," a phrase expressed in indirect discourse by the Houyhnhnm Master in this fullest form (219) immediately after the conversion passage but which is present in various cognate wordings another half dozen times. As the master expresses it, this is the absolute premise of the Houyhnhnms. And it indicates just what the Conversion is to. For Swift the heresy—and we should call it that—lies not in "reason" but in "reason *alone*" and its "sufficiency."[16] In this way *sola ratio* takes its place alongside the Reformation maxims Swift so distrusted, *sola scriptura, sola fide, sola gratia*, each of which with its stress on *sola* opened the hermeneutical door to subjectivity, autonomy and human pride. [17] For Swift, Christianity was not a matter of *sola* anything but was solidly grounded on the objective bases of authority and tradition, not the inner experience of the self no matter how profoundly felt. He wanted nothing to do with what his age called Enthusiasm.

The second falsehood is opened by the first: under peer pressure Gulliver accepts the premise that human beings are Yahoos, and thus, in self-hatred, so is he. If Part III is Swift's commentary on the sufficiency of reason *alone*, the second half of Part IV dramatizes the clouding of Gulliver's judgment and his increasing unreliability as a narrator.[18] What Swift does with his Houyhnhnms and Yahoos is breathtakingly simple and crushingly effective. He separates the two defining human qualities of Reason and Passion and then re-assigns them to creatures that in appearance have traditionally stood for their opposites. So, for example, in Plato's *Phaedrus* (or, for Swift, more laterally, Racine's *Phèdre*) horses are used to symbolize the powerful, unruly, hard-to-govern passions; and humanity, of course, is defined by reason, the index of which is language, though not by reason alone.[19] In *GT* neither species is properly human since the defining qualities exist only in separate creatures. That the Yahoos seem human to the Houyhnhnms, and then to Gulliver himself, is only a matter of their confusing surface appearance with reality. In Gulliver's first sight of the Yahoos he correctly identifies them as "Animals" (189), seeing them naked, without language, and walking mostly on all-fours. It is the master Houyhnhnm who first pushes the Gulliver–Yahoo connection and then later insists on it, and eventually Gulliver's resistance to it collapses. The entire issue demonstrates Gulliver's unreliability and is a tacit comment on the Houyhnhnms' Cartesian rationalism which cannot grasp essences or natures and thus is stuck at the surface of things. After the libidinous attack of the female Yahoo Gulliver will insist that he could "no longer deny that I was a real *Yahoo* in every Limb and Feature" (225)—drawing on this reverse bestiality to predicate an unreal "real."

The Yahoos are by no means human and Gulliver's insistence should not mis-lead any careful reader.[20] But Gulliver's strained identification of human = Yahoo is finally less important than its reflex, his foolish idealization of the Houyhnhnms and his blank insensibility in the face of their loveless dystopia, both predicated on the "sufficiency" of "reason *alone*." There is no need here for a line-by-line analysis of these falsehoods, especially since it would only add details to Samuel Holt Monk's justly famous study of Swift's use of the theme of Pride to define Gulliver's moral confusion.[21] That confusion can be caught in a single sentence, the one that opens Chapter VIII: "As I ought to have understood human Nature much better than I supposed it possible for my Master to do, so it was easy to apply the Character he gave of the *Yahoos* to myself and my Countrymen" (223) where the imperative *ought* compromises its integrity, logic collapses, and the alluring *easy* governs the acceptance that follows. Or consider Gulliver's praise of what he calls the Houyhnhnms' two "principal Virtues," *Friendship* and *Benevolence*, social virtues much touted by, for example, *les philosophes*. Even though the Conversion Passage touts these "reasonable" virtues, one is hard-pressed to find evidence of either virtue in the text. Gulliver provides no example of real friendship and no relationship among the Houyhnhnms goes beyond casual acquaintanceship or the purely functional.[22] Gulliver does allow that their friendships were marked by Decency and Civility, but that mincing praise is not exactly a vision out of Book VIII of the *Nichomachean Ethics*. Swift's own friendships–Pope, Arbuthnot, Gay—certainly had a depth and joy that the Houyhnhnms do not know.

Benevolence is even more of a bluff but of a different kind. Benevolence, after all, is only good will. It is directed outwards but it consists essentially of a feeling, and it always runs the danger of self-congratulation for that feeling, especially in an environment of unfeeling Philistines. But as a feeling it really demands little of the self and should not be confused with the Christian's virtue of charity, not a feeling but an act, especially since in the same Part IV we have such a dramatic contrastive example of Christian charity in Captain Pedro de Mendez. It is historically unfortunate that only eleven of Swift's sermons have come down to us, but Walsh stresses how strongly and consistently Swift in the pulpit emphasized charity to his congregation as the cardinal element in Christian living, and he also reminds us of the place of that virtue in Swift's own life, his generosity towards the poor, including his testamentary provision for the poor children of St. Patrick's.[23] Benevolence carries no cost and fits smoothly into the general emollient Houyhnhnm environment. Benevolence is only charity's lean shadow and Gulliver the erstwhile Christian who would not tread upon the crucifix would have recognized this. In any event, as we reflect on the society of the Houyhnhnms, civil or otherwise, it is neither Friendship nor Benevolence that sticks in the mind, but that fatal phrase debated by the General Assembly, "Whether the *Yahoos* should be exterminated from the Face of the Earth," (228) so violently opposite to the imputed Benevolence but so consistent with Gulliver's newfound willingness to use Yahoo skins and Yahoo "Tallow" for his own practical needs.[24] What would have been once unthinkable is now simply assumed, an intellectual pattern not without its parallels.

"Exterminated" is one of the two most seriously charged words in the entire four parts of the *Travels*. "Copulation" is the other. In the land of the

Houyhnhnms Swift has shown us a flattened loveless dystopia, a world of reason alone, lacking not just passion, *eros*, but love in all the varieties of C.S. Lewis' fourfold taxonomy, and he shows how Gulliver embraces and praises it. Thus he is blankly stupid in the face of Pedro de Mendez's kindness and charity—reason alone can neither identify nor respond to it. But there is worse and Swift focusses that worse in a single powerful word. In Chapter XI Gulliver at last reaches home and the joyous embrace of his family. But the joy is all on their side not his. The whole point of the Fourth Voyage and the Christian theme is brought before us:

> For, although since my unfortunate Exile from the *Houyhnhnm* Country, I had compelled myself to tolerate the Sight of *Yahoos*, and to converse with Don *Pedro de Mendez*; yet my Memory and Imaginations were perpetually filled with the Virtues and Ideas of those exalted *Houyhnhnms*. And when I began to consider, that by copulating with one of the *Yahoo*-Species I had become a Parent of more; it struck me with the utmost Shame, Confusion, and Horror. (244)

The irony of the entire passage is consummate, but it is "copulating" that most sticks in the mind, with its degradation of human intimacy and familial nurture, embraced by the man who has abandoned his Christianity, sacrificing it to the Enlightenment idols of Benevolence and the "Sufficiency" of Reason Alone. It is not Friendship and Benevolence that define the Houyhnhnms but *exterminated* and *copulating*.

To sum up: by collating the Apostasy passage, the Crucifix passage, and the Mock-Conversion passage we can trace Gulliver's decline following after Swift's insistence on his Christianity in Book III. Accepting the falsehood that "Reason alone is sufficient" destroys both Gulliver's Christian faith and his sense of what it means to be human. Swift allows this theme to emerge late in the *Travels* so it can subtly direct both the Fourth Voyage and underline the total meaning of the entire work. Gulliver's loss of faith is meant to be seen as paradigmatic. Swift knows that the winds of doctrine are blowing with increasing force and steadiness from secular quarters, and what he feared for his countrymen was a moral and spiritual disorientation, an intellectual confusion leading to a moral inversion where true virtue is no longer recognized and vice—Pride, especially—is hailed in its place. Thus *GT* can be read as an essay in the history of ideas, a logical unfolding when Reason *alone*—Rationalism—is deemed sufficient, cut off from the nurture and protection of tradition and authority; and the Crucifix, stripped of its sacred dimension, is reduced by naturalism to nothing more than a piece of wood, a Post. Swift makes no effort to explore Gulliver's spiritual life, but he shows that his Christian faith, while more firmly grounded than Dutch Calvinism, is not necessarily proof against the allure of the autonomy of reason. Gulliver the erstwhile Christian embraces the great falsehood and we mark what discord follows: apostasy, moral confusion, instability of judgment, loss of love. Swift the churchman informs Swift the writer and the result is a prescient warning, a canny understanding of just how the logic of that ideal will play out historically in intellectual and moral blindness. And to drive the point home he went on to write *A Modest Proposal*. If we miss Swift's point here, we are proving it.

F. R. Leavis was wrong in his famous judgment.[25] Thinking of the Blake who presided over the proto-Hegelian Marriage of Heaven and Hell, we can find Swift remarkable for intelligence indeed.[26]

Notes to The Crucifix and the Post: A Note on the Christian Theme in *Gulliver's Travels*

1. Walsh, p. 161.
2. "Swift's characteristic ways of thinking and of writing are intimately related to the conditions of his time. His ideas are, for the most part, those of his classical Christian heritage..." Williams, 1958, Preface. Monk's essay may also have played a part in Crane's insistence.
3. Crane, pp. 148, 149.
4. Erskine-Hill, pp. 82, 77.
5. Erskine-Hill, p. 77.
6. Victoria Glendinning voices the conventional view: "*Gulliver* is about morality, but it is not about Christianity." Glendinning, p. 187. But from focusing on parodies of Eucharistic imagery John Cunningham argues that "primitive Christianity runs more deeply in *Gulliver's*

Travels than has perhaps been recognized" (p. 346). Since Landa discussions of Swift's own Christianity usually tilt towards churchmanship rather than belief, and when belief more likely concerned with *A Tale of the Tub*. But see Hammond.

7. Acts 16
8. Erskine-Hill, p. 2.
9. *Gulliver's Travels*, p. 207. This is the Norton Critical Edition edited by Alberto J. Rivero (2002), based on the 1726 edition of Benjamin Motte, as emended. It reproduces Swift's typography and orthography and it also gathers much useful recent criticism. All subsequent references will be incorporated into my text.
10. Though it should be noted that apart from the Eucharist this is largely a Dissenter's pasquinade concerned not with central theological questions but with secondary religious issues more easily mocked.
11. "Although at the time of Gulliver's voyage England and Holland had joined forces in the Grand Alliance against France, the two sea powers continued to vie for commercial supremacy. As several passages in the *Travels* attest, Swift despised the Dutch for their religious tolerance, which he equated with atheism, and for their political duplicity against which he warned in *The Conduct of the Allies* (1711)" (p. 130, n. 9). There is a fine overview in Downie of the related question of Swift's *domestic* politics and the topical political satire, if any, of *GT*.
12. "The seventeenth century saw the flowering of the Calvinist republic," McNeill, p. 267.
13. Ehrenpreis is one of the few to comment on this passage, but omitting the historical dimension he draws a bland inference: "The implications are clear enough. We are being asked to regard the tolerant Dutch as not truly Christian." p. 460.
14. Edwards, p. 285.
15. Denis Donoghue says that Gulliver is "brainwashed." Donoghue, p. 93.
16. And we should bear in mind that the greatest of all Swift's satirical attacks on the "sufficiency of reason alone," *A Modest Proposal*, is a product of this same period.
17. Cf. Gregory, 113. "The credo of modern philosophy, the various expressions of the Enlightenment, and nineteenth-century notions of progress would be that *sola ratio* would achieve what *sola scriptura* manifestly could not." This outlook is precisely what Swift feared and hated.
18. My use of *unreliable* should be understood as innocent of Theory, more Booth than Barthes. For a robustly contemporary discussion of unreliability as a quality of the text see Janine Barchas in Rivero.
19. And in any case Reason in the tradition is a more robust power than the brittle and reductive rationalism displayed by the Houyhnhnms.—"He [i.e., the master Houyhnhnm] knew it was impossible that there could be a Country beyond the Sea or that a Parcel of Brutes could move a wooden Vessel whither they pleased upon Water" (p. 199; and cf. 225–26). *Vide* Burtt and MacIntyre.
20. Those critics who insist that the Fourth Voyage is about the Yahoos and Gulliver's and/or Swift's identification of them with human beings are working with very thin textual evidence. Of the sixty-five or so pages in Book IV only about three actually bring the Yahoos on stage and into the action. Another three or four pages (in Chapter VII, the Conversion chapter, of all places) go to characterize them, and of course they are mentioned throughout. But clearly the center of Book IV is the Houyhnhnms, their doctrine of the sufficiency of reason alone, and its effect on Gulliver, not on the Yahoos and Swift's alleged misanthropy.

21. Monk, p. 128. "Deluded by his worship of pure reason, he commits the error of the Houyhnhnms in equating human beings with Yahoos."
22. The apparent affection of the Sorrel Nag for the departing Gulliver (he "always loved me," p. 238) is of course to be read as comic-sentimental.
23. Walsh, p. 164.
24. See Rawson for a thorough airing of this issue.
25. Leavis, p. 87: "We shall not find Swift remarkable for intelligence if we think of Blake." His opening judgment in that essay, equally famous, is a happier one: "Swift is a great English writer," p. 73.
26. *In memoriam beatam Mabel Wallace Barbour, auia mea, quae mihi dedit primum librum de* Gulliver's Travels.

Works Cited

Barchas, Janine. "Prefiguring Genre: Frontispiece Portraits from *Gulliver's Travels* to *Millenium Hall*." *Studies in the Novel*, 30 (1998), pp. 260–86. Excerpted in Rivero, *infra*, pp. 467–480.

Burtt, E. A. *The Metaphysical Foundations of Modern Science*. Atlantic Highlands, NJ: Humanities Press, 1952.

Crane, R. S. "The Rationale of the Fourth Voyage." *Gulliver's Travels: A Casebook*. Richard Gravil, ed. London: Macmillan, 1974, pp. 148–56.

Cunningham, John. "Perversions of the Eucharist in *Gulliver's Travels*." *Christianity and Literature*, 40 (1991), pp. 345–64.

Donoghue, Denis. "Swift and the Association of Ideas," *England Their England: Commentaries on English Language and Literature*. New York: Knopf, 1998.

Downie, J. A. "The Political Significance of *Gulliver's Travels*," in *Swift and His Contexts*. John Irwin Fischer, et al., eds. New York: AMS Press, 1989, pp. 1–19. Reprinted in Rivero, *infra*, pp. 334–52.

Edwards, Jonathan. "Personal Narrative." *A Jonathan Edwards Reader*. John Smith, et al., eds. New Haven and London: Yale University Press, 1995, pp. 281–96.

Ehrenpreis, Irvin. *Swift, The Man, His Works, and the Age*, 3 vols. Cambridge: Harvard University Press, 1962–1983. Volume 3: *Dean Swift*.

Erskine-Hill, Howard. *Jonathan Swift: Gulliver's Travels*. Cambridge: Cambridge University Press, 1993.

Glendinning, Victoria. *Jonathan Swift*. London: Pimlico, 1999.

Gregory, Brad. *The Unintended Reformation: How a Religious Revolution Secularized Society*. Cambridge: The Belknap Press, 2012.

Hammond, Brean S. *Jonathan Swift*. Dublin: Irish Academic Press, 2010.

Higgins, Ian. *Swift's Politics: A Study in Disaffection*. Cambridge: Cambridge University Press, 1994.

Landa, Louis. *Swift and the Church of Ireland*. Oxford: Clarendon Press, 1954.

Leavis, F. R. "The Irony of Swift." Leavis, *The Common Pursuit*. London: Chatto and Windus: 1952, pp. 73–87.

Lewis, C. S. *The Four Loves*. New York: Harcourt, Brace Jovanovich, 1960.

MacIntyre, Alasdair. "Why the Enlightenment Project of Justifying Morality Had to Fail," in *After Virtue*, pp. 49–59. Notre Dame: University of Notre Dame Press, 1979.

McNeill, John T. *The History and Character of Calvinism*. New York: Oxford: Galaxy Books, 1967.

Monk, Samuel Holt. "The Pride of Lemuel Gulliver." *Sewanee Review*, 63 (Winter 1955), p. 48–71.

Rawson, Claude J. *God, Gulliver, and Genocide*. New York: Oxford University Press, 2001.

Rivero, Albert J., ed. Jonathan Swift. *Gulliver's Travels*: Based on the 1726 Text. New York: W.W. Norton: 2002.

Walsh, Marcus. "Swift and Religion." *The Cambridge Companion to Jonathan Swift*. Christopher Fox, ed. Cambridge: Cambridge University Press, 2003, pp. 161–176.

Williams, Kathleen. "Gulliver's Voyage to the Houyhnhnms," *ELH*, 18 (1951), pp. 275–86.

_____. *Jonathan Swift and the Age of Compromise*. Lawrence: University of Kansas Press, 1958.

HUME, AUSTEN, AND FIRST IMPRESSIONS

Rodney Delasanta

"Saint David," his friends in Scotland and England called David Hume. And in France, where he spent some years as secretary in the British Embassy during the reign of Louis XV, he was called "le bon David." It is easy to understand why. When Jean Jacques Rousseau alienated friends and critics alike with bizarre behavior that today would probably be diagnosed as paranoia, Hume invited Rousseau to come live with him in England. It took almost a year before Rousseau became unbearable even to Saint David, and thus the attempt to provide his colleague sanctuary from bitterly failed friendships in Paris and Geneva—such as those with Diderot and the Baron von Grimm—came to naught. But the invitation and hospitality were magnanimous and earned Hume considerable repute among the philosophers.

"Tender-hearted" is the phrase from William James that comes to mind in describing Hume's benevolence. Yet when we move from his practical ethics to his radical empiricism, "tender-hearted" must give way to its Jamesian contrary: "tough-minded." For it is hardly an overstatement to claim that philosophy has never recovered from Hume's tough-minded uprooting of metaphysics from its preeminent place in the traditional philosophical landscape. Indeed, *après moi le déluge* could have been as aptly applied to him as it was to Louis XV, his almost exact contemporary. Recall the devastating last paragraph from his *Enquiry Concerning Human Understanding.* "If we take in our hand any volume of divinity or school metaphysics...let us ask, *Does it contain any abstract reasoning concerning quantity or number?* No. *Does it contain any experimental reasoning concerning matter of fact and existence?* No. Commit it then to the flames: for it can contain nothing but sophistry and illusion." Kant, who credited Hume with awakening him from his dogmatic slumber, tried to snatch any future metaphysics from the bonfire that Hume ignited, though with only limited success; and Hegel, contra Kant, rammed through a metaphysics that eventually collapsed under the weight of its own Prussian improbabilities.

But when the smoke finally cleared, Hume emerged the Pyrrhic victor, for it is his heirs who have called most of the shots in what is left of philosophy in our time. To metaphysical questions like "Does God exist?" or "Is the will free?" or "Is the soul immortal?" many of the greatest modern philosophers have answered with Wittgensteinian improvisations on Hume: "We cannot think what we cannot think; so what we cannot think we cannot say either." Or, more mysteriously, "What we cannot speak about we must pass over in silence." An honest appraisal, some would say, of the limitations of human reason, but hardly a celebration of philosophical achievement. Oddly enough, while many analytical philosophers in our day hesitate, in homage to Hume, to construct even the simplest proposition for fear of falling into self-inflicted traps of metaphysical "nonsense," their physicist colleagues, less fussy about the theoretical limits of human knowledge, peer through their Hubble telescope at infinity.

At the risk of reducing the complexity and humanity of Hume's thought, especially his later essays and his six-volume *History of England*, to what a maverick such as Mortimer Adler called a "philosophical mistake," I intend, first, to revisit what seems to be the problematic first principle upon which Hume's radical empiricism depends, and then to enlist among the animadverters that most unlikely of respondents, Jane Austen.

Early in the *Enquiry*, Hume makes the startling epistemological claim, over and over, that "the most lively thought is still inferior to the dullest sensation" because "all our ideas or more feeble perceptions are copies of our impressions or more lively ones." And again: "All ideas, especially abstract ones, are naturally faint and obscure," whereas "all impressions, that is, all sensations, either outward or inward, are strong and vivid." To test the validity of an idea, therefore, "we need but enquire *from what impression is that supposed idea derived*" (emphasis added). This Humean elevation of impression, or sensation, to primacy of epistemological place—and his correlative humbling of idea to "feeble" impression—undercuts the classical Aristotelian and Scholastic commonplace that what distinguishes human from animal knowledge is its power to universalize ideas from their source in sense impressions. True, Aristotle and Aquinas would have agreed with Hume that there is nothing in the intellect that is not first in the senses (there are no innate ideas in their epistemological quivers either), but they would have taken ardent issue with his notion that in transforming impression into idea the epistemological enterprise was becoming "enfeebled." On the contrary, the primacy of idea over sense impression, central also to Platonic thought, though not arrived at transempirically, is what had made possible any kind of truth claim about the human capacity to know itself, to know the world, or to know that which transcends the self and the world.

Moreover, if the qualitative distinction between idea and impression is reversed, no truth-claim—not even the self-evident one about cause and effect—remains tenable. The consequence is a debilitating nominalism which subverts the ancient maxim that the proper object of the intellect is the idea, the universal, freed from its unknowability in the senses, and then proceeds to credit that very unknowability as the criterion, or the boundary (to use Locke's term), of knowledge itself.

The major victim of Hume's radical empiricism, as historians of philosophy never tire of telling us, is the very knowability of the connection between cause and effect. Sense knowledge can tell us only that effect *follows* upon cause, because the mind, bounded by the senses, cannot legitimately infer any idea of causality from impressions of mere contiguity. Sequence, yes; causality no. As Hume writes,

> Suppose a person, though endowed with the strongest faculties of reason and recollection, to be brought on a sudden into this world; he would, indeed, immediately observe a continual succession of objects, and one event following another; but he would not be able to discover any thing farther. He would not, at first, by any reasoning, be able to reach the idea of cause and effect, since the particular powers, by which all natural operations are performed, never appear to the senses; nor is it reasonable to conclude, merely because an event, in one instance,

> precedes another, that therefore the one is the cause, the other the effect. Their conjunction may be arbitrary and casual.

Recall the implications of this interdiction of cause and effect on the enterprise of philosophy itself. Before Hume, most philosophers would have agreed that "to know" meant the same as "to know the causes of things." (Scientists to our own day naively continue to operate under this misconception.) Aristotle's metaphysical doctrine of the four causes—material, formal, efficient, and final—ranged from physical knowledge of phenomena to the Unmoved Mover itself. Aquinas extrapolated from causality to Uncaused Cause and even enlisted this profound metaphysical idea as a preamble to Revelation: from *ratio* to *fides*, as it were. After Hume's demolition of the idea of knowable causality, however, such Thomist preambles came to be considered quaint. Metaphysics had not only been severed from theology—the *ancilla* no longer in the queen's employ—but even from quotidian thought.

It is quotidian thought, however, sustained by what some have called metaphysical realism, that has a way of circling back through the pantry window even when it has been denied epistemological entry through the front door. According to Emile Myerson, "man practices metaphysics just as he breathes, without thinking about it." Gabriel Marcel agrees: "By the mere fact of our existing we are already up to our eyes in metaphysics." John Searle has said it better: "Metaphysical realism is not a thesis or a theory; it is rather the condition of having theses or theories or even of denying theses or theories. This is not an epistemic point about how we come to know truth as opposed to falsehood; rather it is a point about the conditions of the possibility of communicating intelligibly. Falsehood stands as much in need of the real world as does truth." To paraphrase Dostoevsky, without metaphysical realism, anything is permissible—even the trumping of ideas by sense impressions.

I have long thought that the best curative to Humean radical skepticism is the experiential witness of writers who often "know" better than professional philosophers themselves. (Paradoxically, even Hume seemed to "know" better when he was not writing epistemology and savaging metaphysics. As we can see from his later, more literary work, he did not let his empiricism blind him to human realities.) Jane Austen is such a writer who "knows" better, whose novels are admirable examples of metaphysical realism writ small—and exquisite. Like other writers disconcerted by reigning philosophical doctrines (Voltaire by Liebniz's, Blake by Newton's, Emerson by Locke's, Melville by Emerson's), Austen stands as a splendid corrective to the assumptions of radical empiricism. Whether she intended to or not, for example, the famous opening sentence of *Pride and Prejudice* controverts Hume's proposition that what little we know of truth is entirely indentured to sense impressions and that, beyond those sense impressions, no acknowledgment of universal truth is warranted. By simply writing her novels and expecting them to be read and understood, Austen seems to be saying that, although truth has its *ressourcement* in sense impressions, its accessibility and transmissibility are made possible by a process of intellection that concedes the legitimacy' of universal propositions.

I am not the first to propose that Austen might well be enlisting Hume in the argument of her novel. A premier critic of Jane Austen, Tony Tanner, has opined that an intelligent woman like her, well read in the fiction of her time, could not but have read the reigning philosophers too, even though his own reading of *Pride and Prejudice* unaccountably enlists Hume as an epistemological ally of Austen rather than as a target. In any event, it seems that Hume's nimbus was present in Austen's choice of title before she settled on *Pride and Prejudice*. Tellingly, she originally called it *First Impressions*. What the novel teaches us is that impressions, however "strong and vivid," are hardly superior to ideas, however "faint and obscure." Strong and vivid—and immediate—are Elizabeth Bennet's disdainful impressions of Darcy's pride; equally so are Darcy's of Elizabeth's prejudice. But by the end of the novel they both sort out and think through those strong and vivid impressions, gradually discern their fallibility, fall deeply in love, and marry. In fact, despite Austen's characterization of Elizabeth as the most intellectually alert and morally sympathetic person in the novel, she is betrayed by other first impressions as well. Not only is she wrong about Darcy, she is also wrong about Wickham, whose attention she initially welcomed. But before long, Wickham is revealed to be the would-be seducer of Georgiana, Darcy's young sister, and the actual seducer of Lydia, Elizabeth's feather-brained sibling, whereas Darcy turns out to be the champion who quietly rescues the Bennet family from the disgrace of Lydia's mindless elopement. Darcy, of course, has his own fallible first impressions beyond his misapprehension of Elizabeth: he also errs in convincing his friend Bingley to break off relations with the splendid Jane, Elizabeth's sister, because of his first impressions of the Bennet family.

If Austen's original tide of the lost first version of *Pride and Prejudice* can be read as a teasing animadversion against radical skepticism, its famous opening line—"It is a truth universally acknowledged that a single man in possession of a good fortune must be in want of a wife"—ironically recapitulates and subverts the formulaic phraseology of Hume's *Enquiry* itself. In Section V, for example, where he argues that rational indubitability is really the product of custom or habit, rather than of any justifiable inference of universals from particulars, Hume writes: "We only point out a principle of human nature, *which is universally acknowledged* and which is well known by its effects" (emphasis added). In Section VIII, "Of Liberty and Necessity," while questioning the traditional claims of free will, he writes, "*It is universally acknowledged* that there is a great uniformity among the actions of men...that human nature remains the same." And again, a few paragraphs later: "...readily and *universally do we acknowledge* a uniformity in human motives and actions as well as in the operations of body." Still later, when Hume argues that the simple conjunction of events should not be misinterpreted to constitute cause and effect, he writes "that this regular conjunction *has been universally acknowledged* among mankind" as causality. I count four more instances in the *Enquiry* of similar phraseology. Of course, Hume is *denying* that universal acknowledgment constitutes any admission of universal truth (because universal truths are patently unknowable), whereas Austen has taken the universal idea to be a metaphysical given and has proceeded to write fiction that dramatizes its knowability.

If the errancy of first impressions is the theme of *Pride and Prejudice,* it is the very leitmotif of Austen's later novel, *Emma*, judged by many to be her best. When a heroine of common sense like Elizabeth Bennet, *simpatica* both to her creator and to the audience for whom she was created, can for a time be victimized by first impressions, it is little wonder that Jane Austen would allow, nay encourage, some of her other heroines to follow suit. Wealthy, willful, and indulged by a doting and witless father, Emma's seemingly harmless vocation is matchmaking, at which she can boast an early success by having arranged the marriage of her governess to a widower neighbor. However, her attempt to couple her attractive but impoverished protégée, Harriet Smith, with the eligible village rector, Mr. Elton, turns out to be a comic mismatch that dominates a good deal of the plot. Harriet has already revealed an interest in Robert Martin, a responsible local farmer, but his low-born state immediately disqualifies him in Emma's eyes as a suitable partner for Harriet. In what turns out to be the first in a series of spectacularly errant first impressions, Emma totally misreads Martin's character: "He is very plain, undoubtedly...but that is nothing compared with his entire want of gentility. I had no right to expect much, and I did not expect much; but I had no idea that he could be so very clownish, so totally without air. I had imagined him, I confess, a degree or two nearer gentility."

Whereas in Austen's earlier novel it took two characters, Elizabeth and Darcy, to dramatize the follies of pride and prejudice, in *Emma* they are fused into a single character. Because she is proud of her wealth and social station, Emma benignly intends to extend its privileges, as much as society will allow, to her friend—for whom marriage to a mere farmer is unthinkable. Hence her prejudice against Martin, who for her is worthy of no more serious consideration than mindless first impressions. Of course, Harriet is mortified by Emma's hasty demolition of her intended, but she backs off and allows her affections to be redirected toward the unsuspecting Mr. Elton. Strangely, not only is Emma unaware of Elton's indifference to Harriet, but she is also oblivious to the court that Elton is paying to herself. That Austen is indicting the perils of first impressions is evident in her description of Emma's plan to scuttle Martin's bid for Harriet's hand in order to free her for Elton. Fearing that competing busybodies may already have considered the suitability of a match between Harriet and Elton, Emma comforts herself by thinking that no one else could have preceded her "in the date of the plan, as it had entered her brain during the very first evening of Harriet's coming to Hatfield." A rush to judgment, Emma's sagacious neighbor, Mr. Knightley, calls it, as he scolds her for "abusing the reason you have.... Better be without sense, than misapply it as you do," adding that Emma is speaking "nonsense, errant nonsense, as ever was talked!" Knightley will become Emma's husband by the end of the novel, of course, so this criticism of the woman he loves is reluctant and self-lacerating.

The Harriet/Elton imbroglio is not the only one in the novel. Emma is wrong in thinking that Frank Churchill is romantically interested in her, wrong in thinking that Knightley is romantically interested in Jane Fairfax, wrong in surmising the identity of the gift giver in the case of Jane's pianoforte, wrong finally in thinking that Knightley is romantically interested in Harriet when in fact he is only interested in Emma herself. No other Austen heroine is so thoroughly victimized by her first impressions and the consequences thereof. The novel is a veritable comedy of errors but especially a comedy of failed first impressions, "strong and vivid" though they may be, that are contravened by Jane Austen's metaphysical realism, "faint and obscure" as it allegedly is.

One can surmise why David Hume would have thought it necessary to mount such a devastating campaign against metaphysics (while elsewhere feeling quite comfortable making all kinds of phenomenological generalizations about a range of human experiences, events, thoughts, and feelings) or why Jane Austen, if I am reading her right, would have taken cryptic novelistic issue with his brand of radical empiricism. It was a de rigueur stance for the philosophes of the day, of course, beholden as they were to the empirical method of science, to vilify metaphysics and metaphysicians. Voltaire's witty derision is typical: "Metaphysicians are like curious travelers who having entered the antechamber of the harem of the Grand Turk and having observed from a distance the comings and goings of a eunuch, would venture to guess how many times His Highness had caressed his odalisque that night." Perhaps the rationalists from Descartes to Malebranche and Leibniz had so overstated their metaphysical claims that Voltairean sallies and Humean enquiries were inevitable. When Pangloss comes, can Martin the Manichee be far behind?

But these putative epistemological correctives, it seems to me, mask a not-so-hidden agenda among the radical empiricists. Peter Gay has described the character of the Enlightenment as neo-pagan, less in the sense of moral dereliction than in its fulminations against Christianity. "Thou hast conquered, O pale Galilean," Swinburne could still lament a century later in the spirit of the Enlightenment, "the world has grown gray from thy breath." Most

Enlightenment intellectuals would have agreed that one solution to the ills of mankind was to *écrasez l'infâme*, Voltaire's injunction to crush the "infamous thing"—that is, Christianity. (They must have rejoiced to see half their wish granted when the Jesuits were suppressed in 1773.)

As for Hume's motives, one suspects that his agnosticism was less the consequence of his radical empiricism than his radical empiricism was the consequence of his agnosticism. The latter seems more likely, especially as the targeted *infâme* was Catholicism, which Hume held in contempt. In the *Enquiry* he called Catholics "devotees of superstition" and Catholic liturgy "mummeries." Moreover, because Catholicism had for centuries based its apologetics on a synthesis of faith and reason, one manner of contributing to the Enlightenment's crushing of the *infâme* was to demolish its metaphysical supports. If God's existence was putatively demonstrable by arguments from causality, then severing the epistemological connection between cause and effect would, higher up the great chain of being, unlink the idea of First Cause from the idea of God and do collateral violence to any attendant metaphysical speculation. Hence Hume writes: "We can never be allowed to mount up from the universe, the effect, to Jupiter, the cause; and then descend downwards, to infer any new effect from that cause." But then, as if to distance himself from the implications of this dislocation, he implores philosophers to leave religion to the fideists: "Our most holy religion is founded on *Faith*, not on reason; and it is a sure method of exposing it to put it to such a trial as it is, by no means, fitted to endure."

It is a familiar argument with respect to religion: fides, si; ratio, no. Descartes used something like it in his *Discourse on Method*, but one senses that there was actually some faith left in Descartes' fideism. A century later, however, despite Hume's honorific description of Christianity as "our most holy religion," the remnant of his faith was clearly gone; he spends the rest of the passage cryptically mocking Christianity's most sacred beliefs, not only the miracles from the Old Testament but also the chief miracle from the New, the Resurrection itself.

Jane Austen, like Samuel Johnson before her, belonged to a different Enlightenment, one that did not seek to enlighten by extinguishing the Light. The daughter of an Anglican clergyman, she was well aware of the failures of Christianity and even took some delight in satirizing its less than holy ministers, like the Rev. Collins and Mr. Elton. But in any final analysis she was a believer whose faith, though not shouted from the housetops, nevertheless remained firm. The editors of the 1998 Norton critical edition of *Mansfield Park* saw fit, for example, to reprint one of her three prayers that have survived, probably via her sister, Cassandra. In it, she does not compromise those Christian doctrines embarrassing to so many Enlightenment intellectuals, as they were to Thomas Jefferson when he produced his miracle-free Bible, but confesses her faith openly and unambiguously: "...we implore Thee to quicken our sense of Thy mercy in the redemption of the world, of the value of that holy religion in which we have been brought up, that we may not, by our own neglect, throw away the salvation Thou hast given us, nor be Christians only in name." In a letter to her niece worried about the evangelical tendencies of a suitor, she writes unfideistically: "And as to there being any objection from his Goodness, from the danger of his becoming even Evangelical, I cannot admit that. I am by no means convinced that we ought not all to be Evangelicals and am at least persuaded that they who are so *from Reason and Feeling*, must be happiest and safest.... Don't be frightened by the idea of his acting more strictly up to the precepts of the New Testament than others" (emphasis added).

The most visible defense of the Christian way of life in her novels is the long exchange in *Mansfield Park* between Edmund Bertrand and Mary Crawford, his intended, in which Miss Crawford expresses dismay that a man like Edmund could possibly consider taking holy orders. We recall that the estimable Edward Ferrars also took Anglican orders in *Sense and Sensibility*, but with the exception of his foppish brother, Robert, there was no character in that novel to belittle his intention to do so—and thus force a Christian riposte. Mary Crawford's harsh judgments, by contrast, have the ring of the freethinker's salon about them, like Voltaire's Society of the Temple, or Franklin's Junto, or Hume's French coterie, and thus provoke an apologetic response from both hero and heroine of the novel.

A minister of the church, Mary Crawford complains to Edmund, prefers "an income ready made to the trouble of working for one, and [has] the best intentions of doing nothing all the rest of his days but eat, drink, and grow fat.... A clergyman has nothing to do but to be slovenly and selfish—read the newspaper, watch the weather, and quarrel with his wife. His curate does all the work, and the business of his own life is to dine." And then, training her guns on Dr. Grant, her brother-in-law clergyman who is at that very moment affording her his hospitality, she complains that he is "an indolent selfish bon vivant, who must have his palate consulted in every thing, who will not stir a finger for the convenience of any one, and who, moreover, if the cook makes a blunder, is out of humor with his excellent wife." Although this distemper is not equal to the sting of Voltaire's *écrasez*, it is clerical ridicule worthy of Diderot and his *Encylopédie*. But the theme of *Mansfield Park*, as Jane Austen herself identified it, is "ordination"—and Edmund's defense of his taking holy orders is not adventitious to the plot.

Indeed, it is Mary Crawford's unremitting anticlericalism that finally wears down Edmund's infatuation with her and convinces him that such a person could never become his wife. Her withering denunciation of Anglican orders—"At this rate, you will soon reform every body at Mansfield...and when I hear of you next, it may be as a celebrated preacher in some great society of Methodists, or as a missionary into foreign parts"—is the final indignity. Edmund pulls back from the expected marriage proposal—and from his first impression infatuation with Mary Crawford—and after a time recognizes that his wife must be one who, like Fanny Price (and her creator as well), can respect and admire his own sacerdotal commitment.

Thus does Jane Austen seem to controvert, at least in generic terms, the premier British representative of the Enlightenment both with respect to metaphysics and to religion itself. Unwilling to obey the Humean imperative that would commit volumes of divinity or metaphysics to the flames, she is closer to the Christian humanism of her older contemporary, Samuel Johnson, who when asked by James Boswell what he thought of the radical empiricists, answered with less than his characteristic charity: "Hume and other skeptical innovators are vain men and will gratify themselves at any expense. Truth will not afford sufficient food to their vanity, so they have betaken themselves to error: Truth, Sir, is a cow which will yield such people no more milk, and so they are gone to milk the bull." Austen's response is less Johnsonian but no less artful.

"BETWEEN TWO WORLDS": THE STRUCTURE OF THE ARGUMENT IN "TINTERN ABBEY"

Brian Barbour

For both were faiths, and both are gone.
(MATTHEW ARNOLD,
"Stanzas from the Grande Chartreuse")

I

There is a point to the political readings of "Tintern Abbey" that have proliferated in recent years, but the point is an ironical one.[1] I am not thinking of the obvious irony whereby a generation of commentators has become absorbed in what the poem does *not* say, for in contemporary intellectual life elegant elaborations of the impossible often vie for honors with humorless denials of the obvious. The deeper irony is that commentators have, against themselves (and Theory!) returned to Wordsworth's *intention*, though they have metamorphosed it to bring it into line with modern interests. For Wordsworth's intention in his great poem is certainly religious, however generically we might define that. And politics, surely, is the realm of the sacred for modern intellectuals; or, if "sacred" seems invidious, at least the area of ultimate concern. So scholars, on principle, have denied intention only to find that they have returned to it by another route; ignoring the experience *and* missing the meaning.

A secondary irony is that the political readings have proven to be deeply traditional in one sense. Scholarship has always treated "Tintern Abbey" piecemeal, raiding it for selected lines or passages to illustrate Wordsworth's ideas or some feature of his belief—usually associationist psychology or pantheism. Sometimes lines and passages have been set off against each other to demonstrate the poet's "incoherence" (or the critic's subtlety), but it is a rare critic who has seen the poem steadily and whole, recognizing in it the unfolding of a coherent intellectual drama. In general critics have looked upon the poem much as a great Elizabethan magnate saw a dissolved monastery: as an attractive ruin whose beautifully dressed stones could be carried off and put to better purposes. This piecemeal approach has proven so coercive that Hoxie Neale Fairchild, the foremost student of Wordsworth's religious views, declared that "the thought of this beautiful but hastily written poem has not been clearly defined."[2]

Literary criticism strives to achieve a continuing refinement of perception and statement, but its record with "Tintern Abbey" is not impressive, and the trend to political readings has not improved things. The situation is very odd. The New Criticism, we are told, saw poems only as self-contained, organic wholes divorced from any historical context. Yet the tradition of piecemeal readings of "Tintern Abbey" ignored such a basic "organic" question as how the five verse paragraphs of the poem relate to one another (despite Wordsworth's hinging them together while proceeding by contrasts), saw little internal development within the poem, and tended to regard the fifth verse paragraph as an extraneous afterthought because written slightly later. The political readings have sought to restore the historical context (a proper emphasis in my judgment), but by the familiar sleight-of-the-New-Historical-hand they have substituted contemporary politics for history and delivered a poem that is unrecognizable—a mutant poem of their own creation. In the present controversy we have commentators who are talking past one another and past the poem, barren assertion not deepening perception. For example, consider the recent work of M. H. Abrams. Abrams has indefatigably and wittily defended the poem against political encroachments and distortions, arguing that the plain sense of the text cannot be set aside for virtuous misreading. But in defending the poem he has raised its argument to such a high level of abstraction as to leave it virtually denatured:

> Put briefly, hence reductively: the poem that Wordsworth composed is a sustained lyric meditation, in a natural setting, about what it is to be

> mortally human, to grow older, and to grow up, through vicissitudes and disappointments, into the broader, sadder knowledge of maturity; about what in tins temporal process is inevitably lost, but also what may be gained, and for another person as well as the lyric speaker himself. (p. 379)

Surely many readers besides myself feel that this view leaves out something vital to their experience of the poem. And that such a generous and perceptive reader as Abrams would offer such a summary is testimony both to the barrenness of the current controversy and the relative failure of the older tradition.

Nevertheless, I believe there is fruitful middle ground for criticism and that a richer enjoyment of Wordsworth's great poem is possible. We are, after all, speaking of perhaps the most influential poem in English between *The Dunciad* and *The Waste Land*. In this paper I want to set aside other possible readings and focus on the central religious drama of the poem.[3] If we do that, I think that we can recognize a distinctive poetic intention operating through a carefully articulated structure, and that we can properly appreciate the spiritual problem the poet was attempting to solve. It is my purpose to show that "Tintern Abbey" presents the unfolding of a coherent intellectual drama—fundamentally religious, all parts of which are organically related—and to argue that the terms of the drama can only be appreciated when we set the poem in its proper intellectual-historical context.

II

First the context: "Tintern Abbey" is a poem that went far toward establishing a new intellectual outlook (Romanticism) and this success leads us to forget that it was written against the prevailing climate of opinion (the Enlightenment). Like Matthew Arnold, Wordsworth found himself between two worlds; but while his Victorian disciple "wandered" in unending bafflement, Wordsworth deliberately positioned himself there in an effort to define a new outlook, to think out a new approach to man's moral and spiritual life. The young poet who stood above the Wye that July day knew nothing of what we are pleased to call

Romanticism. But he felt with calm intensity within himself the century-and-a-half struggle between Christianity and the Enlightenment,

> one dead,
> The other powerless to be born,[4]

a struggle that he had somehow to resolve both as man and as man speaking to men—as poet. Christianity ("dead") was perhaps easily gotten rid of. Wordsworth had no profound grasp of it either as doctrine or experience and probably could not have distinguished it from Deism.[5] But there were numinous, religious qualities that had to be preserved—his experience of Nature had taught him that. The real problem, the real enemy, was the Enlightenment. The Protestant Christianity that Wordsworth had known was deliquescing, but what was psychologically profitable in it had to be preserved against the encroachments of a worldview ("powerless to be born") that would leave Nature lifeless and mechanized and the poet's own mind merely the passive receiver of stimuli. A world (like Godwin's, for example, from which he had recently escaped) that was defined by materialism, rationalism, and necessitarianism was no world for a poet. There had to be a third way.

That new worldview would be Romanticism. Like Blake and Coleridge, Wordsworth was concerned to work out a viewpoint that was directed against the Enlightenment and that would preserve the (generically) religious. Like them, he would often confuse this with Christianity. But in 1798 the issue seemed clearer. What appeared psychologically valuable in Christianity, cut off from any historical and doctrinal roots, could be regenerated by the creative genius of the poet, and the whole basis of man's spiritual and moral life could be re-established. The issue was (or seemed to be) humanity's moral freedom and our life in a world that *means something*, where we are not just the atoms of Democritus or Newton's particles of light but are vitally connected to a larger whole.

It is within this intellectual-historical context of declining Christianity and ascendant Enlightenment that Wordsworth wrote his great poem, a poem that enacts the intellectual drama he confronted. Both his instincts and his experience were against the Enlightenment, and though he had little interest in historical Christianity or its rejuvenation, those same instincts were ineluctably religious. And so, perhaps nagged at by the ambiguity of the river's name, Wordsworth stood in meditation above the ruins of the old abbey. The location was portentous, for it was at the site of the old religion, with its faith in the supernatural and its life of prayer, that he chose to celebrate the new religion, with its faith in Man and its Nature mysticism. This new religion, freed of the supernatural, however, would retain both priestly and prophetic elements and a clear moral focus. Yet no sooner was the new evangelium announced in the great "burthen of the mystery" passage of the second verse paragraph than the troubling question of the status of this *fides novus* arose. Was it, too, vulnerable, as Christianity had been, to the attacks and sneers of the philosophes? The climate of opinion was purely naturalist. Wordsworth's outlook was not metaphysical, partook of nothing supernatural. So what was its authority? Was it merely a fantasy or a private solace? Or more than that? Based as it was on the poet's own experience, could it be communicated to others? Such questions could be neither burked nor evaded. It was Wordsworth's genius to make them the very subject of the poem, and the facing of them the unfolding of a coherent intellectual drama. "Tintern Abbey" is irrefragably a religious poem in which Wordsworth sought to define and defend a realm of the autonomously spiritual—autonomous *contra* Christianity,[6] spiritual *contra* the Enlightenment. This double purpose is what provides the structure of the poet's argument, and to an examination of that structure we must now turn.

III

Abrams's summary simply ignores the third verse paragraph. But this is the very section that controls the poetic argument and is crucial to understanding the poem's unified structure. Conceptually and structurally it is at the heart of the poem. Let us take a bird's-eye view of the poem as a whole. Verse paragraphs one and two are each independent, yet they play off one another as statement and response. Paragraph one presents the world of nature, though Wordsworth is not a "Nature Poet" in the sense that Thomson, for example, was. The full Wordsworthian formula is *not* "Nature supplies"—the Enlightenment error—but "Nature plus thought leads to purified feeling." The difference in the two verse paragraphs is in the verbs: paragraph one presents the poet "beholding" nature; paragraph two shows him "[seeing] *into* the life of things" (emphasis added), an intellectual advance from surface to essence. The second verse paragraph climaxes on this moment of exultation, of nature mysticism. But then there arises the troubling question that actually holds the poem together, "If this / Be but a vain belief." What is the basis, the authority, for such putative "religious" moments in a world no longer willing to credit either metaphysics or revelation? And if the numinous is not "real," and the priestly cultus cannot be validated, then what guarantees the prophetic claims that such mystical moments nourish the poet's moral life? This implicit challenge lies at the very heart of the poem. The first two verse paragraphs have defined a belief; but the poet lives in a world where all such beliefs are subject to attack or ridicule. Is his belief also vulnerable? Is it true? What is his authority? The main task of the fourth verse paragraph will be to defend what has been defined and challenged, and paragraph five will proclaim that there is a social dimension to all he has presented.

With this overview in mind, let us look more carefully at the pivotal paragraph three, for it arises out of what has gone before and governs the defense that will follow:

> If this
> Be but a vain belief, yet, oh! how oft—
> In darkness and amid the many shapes
> Of joyless daylight; when the fretful stir
> Unprofitable, and the fever of the world,
> Have hung upon the beatings of my heart —
> How oft, in spirit, have I turned to thee,
> O sylvan Wye! thou wanderer thro' the woods,
> How often has my spirit turned to thee! (ll. 49b–57)[7]

We will examine what is meant by "this" (l. 49) in a moment, but for now the key phrase here is "vain belief."[8] What is the status of such experiences, the poet asks; are they like everything else under the sun? Wordsworth's basic strategy is to appeal to the spiritual while remaining entirely within the natural order. His answer, therefore, appeals not to Truth but to efficacy.[9] The repeated "spirit" suggests the poet's insistence that he is no materialist, and while he cannot determine the (so to say) ontological status of such moments, he knows what their effect is: they relieve his spirit when it is weighed down, depressed by the unhealthy and inhumane conditions of the urban world that Enlightenment thought is fashioning. "Fretful stir / Unprofitable, and the fever of the world" leads out to such characteristically Wordsworthian utterance as "The World is Too Much With Us," the sonnet to Milton, and the argument about culture ("For a multitude of causes, unknown to former times, are now acting with a combined force to blunt the discriminating powers of the mind, and, unfitting it for all voluntary exertion, to reduce it to a state of almost savage torpor") at the heart of the famous "Preface."[10] What Arnold was to recognize in its full form, Wordsworth intuited in its incipient phase: the human mind was building a world in which the human spirit could not live. The wonderful phrase "joyless daylight" vividly contrasts the "deep power of joy" that climaxes verse paragraph two, and captures the gist of the poet's case against the philosophes. The "daylight" of Enlightenment rationalism has no power for life; it brings no joy. Still, Wordsworth has no direct answer to the central issue of the status of such moments. His evocation of a form of life—"joy" nourishing the spirit, spontaneously and reflexively ("How oft")—must be seen, therefore, as an inward turning that roughly parallels Kant's "Copernican" shift from ontology to epistemology (the known to the knower) and Schleiermacher's translation of theology into psychology. In all three cases the movement is from the objective to the subjective. Wordsworth is saying in effect, "I cannot establish such moments as public and measurable facts, but I know from the depths of my being what their positive effect is on my life." With this inward turn the poet temporarily finesses potential objections. The third verse paragraph, then, sits at the heart of the poem and controls its structure. It is Janus-faced, looking back to the definition of paragraphs one and two and forward to the defense and proclamation of paragraphs four and five. Paragraph four will remake the argument while providing it with a firmer basis, lending historical weight to the joy/joyless contrast. And it will prepare the reader for paragraph five, which is both very different from the first four paragraphs and yet an organic development from them. The later sections are a defense of what the earlier sections have defined, an attempt to place Wordsworth's religious experience on a basis that will satisfy the troubling question of verse paragraph three: What is the status of stich belief? If we recognize that this is how the argument is organized, then we can see the whole poem unfold as a coherent intellectual drama that posits an autonomous spirituality against the reigning climate of opinion.

IV

The first and second verse paragraphs of "Tintern Abbey" initiate the developing drama. These two sections function together, with the second playing off the first. Together they effectively define Wordsworth's religious outlook, his autonomous spirituality. We need to examine them in some detail to appreciate how the poet is moving away from the Enlightenment but *not* back to Christianity. Something different is evolving through an argument that is cautious, indirect, and subtle. The first verse paragraph presents a view of nature that appears congruent with the Enlightenment. But this appearance, even while given, is subtly undercut: vision gives way to mind. And in the second paragraph we see the poet carry out a transformation of nature, and viewing nature, that in effect invents Romanticism. Paragraph one is grounded in nature; paragraph two responds with active mind. Seldom in the history of ideas has an example crystallized with such clarity. Even so, one distinction is necessary here. In the second and fourth verse paragraphs the poet presents climactic experiences of pantheism, moments of "numinous cosmic unity and interfusion" (Fairchild, III, 171). But this must not mislead us. It is the Enlightenment, not Romanticism, that puts its faith in nature; the Romantic faith is in man—an irreducibly spiritual being. Wordsworth is keen to celebrate nature but only as it is quickened and transformed by the human imagination.[11] With these prolegomena in mind, let us see how the drama unfolds.

The opening verse paragraph ought to satisfy any philosophe. Feeling is unmentioned. It is "Nature poetry"—written inside the tradition of eighteenth-century landscape verse with its meditative tone, generalized diction, and emphasis on the picturesque. And if that tradition was played out by the time it reached Wordsworth,[12] that only made it more subtly effective for his purposes: he could use it as both source and foil. What is the value of external Nature even if lifelessness and mechanism are not conceded? The answer, of course, is that it is radically incomplete without an answering human spirit. Paragraph one, then, operates on two levels, corresponding, roughly, to vision and mind. First, it is manifestly about external Nature as it impresses itself upon the poet's vision:

> Five years have past; five summers, with the length
> Of five long winters! and again I hear
> These waters, rolling from their mountain-springs
> With a soft inland murmur.—Once again
> Do I behold these steep and lofty cliffs,
> That on a wild secluded scene impress
> Thoughts of more deep seclusion; and connect
> The landscape with the quiet of the sky. (ll. 1–8)

The verbs are not particularly active—"behold," "view," "see"—but even here they bring the poet's mind to the central intellectual act of *connection*. There is a pleasant harmony of man and nature, past and present, earth and sky—but little more. "The quiet of the sky" may refer only to the absence of wind and cloud, but it is hard not to read it as implying a sky not just quiet but empty—a philosophe's sky and forerunner to all those portentously empty skies in Wallace Stevens.

But the phenomenal is not all; there are already subtle noumenal suggestions and a second level. We notice, for example, that the poet's mind is almost immediately led beyond the visible to invisible sources—"These waters, rolling from their mountain-springs"—with just a hint here of that *causality* so vilified by Hume and others. And notice how the paragraph develops: though the etymology is not completely certain, *religio* (respect for what is sacred) probably stems from *religo* (to tie together or be connected with). By odd, but apt, coincidence, the opening lines are clearly a version of *religo*, and the paragraph closes with a fine example of *religio*, or Wordsworthian natural piety:

> Once again I see
> … … … these pastoral farms,
> Green to the very door; and wreaths of smoke
> Sent up, in silence, from among the trees!
> With some uncertain notice, as might seem
> Of vagrant dwellers in the houseless woods,
> Or of some Hermit's cave, where by his fire
> The Hermit sits alone. (ll. 14b, 16–22a)

Geoffrey Durrant's comment on these lines is particularly helpful: "The sense of a life that can gratefully be lived in half-natural paradise is furthered not only by the word 'pastoral' but also by the description of the 'wreaths of smoke Sent up, in silence, from among the trees.' These words, to any reader of Homer and Virgil, must recall the wreaths of sacrificial smoke ascending from the groves in gratitude to the heavens. Overtones of the twenty-third Psalm, and of the poetry of the classical world, combine here to create a strong sense of a life protected by the gods."[13] So while the opening verse paragraph is "about nature," the lines are vibrant with other suggestions because the poet's mind is already moving in a religious direction.

"I thought that nature was enough," Emily Dickinson wrote in an epitome of the Romantic argument, "Till Human nature came."[14] The Enlightenment faith in nature, Wordsworth thought, was radically defective, partly because of its view of nature, but mostly because it had no real place for the answering human spirit. In the second verse paragraph human nature—activity of mind—strongly asserts itself. Wordsworth ceases to be "a lazy Looker-on on an external World"; he achieves, in Coleridge's well-known words, "that deep Thinking... attainable only by a man of deep Feeling."[15] Nature, mind, the feelings, spirit—the key elements of Wordsworthian religion are all here gathered. But note the wariness. He begins obliquely, under cover of an argument that is initially cultural:

> These beauteous forms,
> Through a long absence, have not been to me
> As is a landscape to a blind man's eye:
> But oft, in lonely rooms, and 'mid the din
> Of towns and cities, I have owed to them,
> In hours of weariness, sensations sweet,
> Felt in the blood and felt along the heart;
> And passing even into my purer mind,
> With tranquil restoration. (ll. 22b–30)

The governing contrast is Horation (country/city) but with a special urgency in Wordsworth's thought, for the city is no longer just the locus of moral corruption among wastrels: the industrial city—product of the Enlightenment and its view of nature—destroys the spirit of man. And if the poet's life in nature is marked by "repose" (l. 9), then what he knows in cities is "weariness" of spirit. And if the putative Hermit can sit "alone," the poet in the city experiences something dramatically different: not solitude but loneliness. This triple contrast—country, repose, solitude vs. city, weariness, loneliness—defines the cultural situation. Its fundamental character is implied by the aggressive simplicity of the simile ("As is a landscape to a blind man's eye").

But the poet has not just looked *at* nature; he has taken mental possession *of* it. Mental initiative, the mind active and constituent—Coleridge's "grow-ledge"—is the road to spirit.[16] "Forms" is philosophically precise (and anti-Humean), the universal abstracted from the particular, nature seized and transformed into concept and held vivid in memory. And it is through this intellectual doorway that landscape verse and the picturesque are left behind and Nature poetry is forever altered. For the poet maintains that these forms are the source of feelings and that the feelings, in their turn, renew him physically ("Felt in the blood and felt along the heart") and restore him on a higher plane ("my purer mind"). Here there is a blurring, probably deliberate, between the psychological and the spiritual that is necessary to the poetic argument. But the poem has only begun its great ascension: in the rest of paragraph two Wordsworth will set forth the religious argument he has carefully prepared for.

We can break it down like this: nature is the source of restorative feelings; those feelings, in turn, are the source of the poet's moral life; but the forms themselves on occasion, entering directly into and modified by the poet's spirit, induce his moments of mystical exaltation.[17] Nature provides the moments when the poet transcends nature; or as an older vocabulary would have it, *natura naturata* leads to *natura naturans.* The moral and the mystical become mutually validating, though the moral argument—the one allowed by the philosophes—is ultimate:

> feelings too
> Of unremembered pleasure: such, perhaps,
> As have no slight or trivial influence
> On that best portion of a good man's life,
> His little, nameless, unremembered, acts
> Of kindness and of love. (ll. 30b–35)

Love of nature, in the famous formula, leads to love of man.

The great mystical passage of the second verse paragraph is well understood and probably too familiar to need comment. We should note that its structure suggests a rising order of reality—physical, moral, mystical—and we should remember that this is entirely within the natural order. In this passage the supple movement of the verse beautifully enacts the poetic idea of physical suspension—in preparation for mystical fruition. Wordsworth identifies the entire experience as "gift," as something that comes *to* him, and the climax emphasizes both "harmony" and "joy," qualities that were only implicit in paragraph one, where everything stays on or close to the physical level:

> While with an eye made quiet by the power
> Of harmony, and the deep power of joy,
> We see into the life of things. (ll. 47–49)

The argument has transcended landscape verse. Wordsworth has taken the poem from a fairly simple and straightforward celebration of *natura naturata* to extraordinary and unlooked-for "religious" claims about nature mysticism and the moral life, from Nature to Man. His main vehicle has been the philosophical term "forms" colored by the quasi-religious "gift," but the contrast itself has been the main point. The argument is directed against the Enlightenment faith in a lifeless and mechanical nature, and it posits an autonomous spirituality—what Abrams calls a natural supernaturalism. Yet once the argument is made, the objections assert themselves, as we have seen. Is this only a vain belief? What validates it? There is, to hand, the pragmatic argument "But it works," conveyed by the joy/joyless contrast and the iterated "oft" and "spirit." But the poet is aware that something more is needed. The objections of verse paragraph three have to be met and the basis of the natural religion has to be elaborated. That basis can be neither a revelation nor a metaphysics, for the Enlightenment will not permit either. But they are not needed. The poet is no supernaturalist: he is content to operate within a natural order so long as the human spirit is acknowledged. The basis of his religion is ultimately in himself. The shift from faith to personal experience is momentous.

V

Wordsworth has defined his religious outlook, a realm of the autonomously spiritual, and has shown anxious awareness of the Enlightenment challenge to belief. Christianity is a faith in a revelation, a Person, and a metaphysical order of reality. Wordsworth is a naturalist; he can place his faith in none of these. The situation is later made more explicit by Arnold:

> For rigorous teachers seized my youth,
> And purged its faith, and trimm'd its fire,
> Show'd me the high, white star of Truth,
> There bade me gaze, and there aspire. ("Grande Chartreuse," ll. 67–70)

Wordsworth's purging was less formal and scholastic, but it was no less real. His religious outlook had to be proof against all naturalist objections. The shift, then, was from faith (i.e., in a transcendent order) to experience, for only that could be the rock on which the new religion could be built. The Romantic faith in man is located in the inner recesses of the spirit. In the structure of "Tintern Abbey" the fourth verse paragraph is a *defensus fidei*, an effort to show that the "this" of paragraph two is not "a vain belief." His autonomous spirituality will be presented as internal, subjective, naturalist, and unassailable.

Paragraph four meets the question of paragraph three and validates the claims of paragraph two by recounting the poet's inner history, the story of the growth of his spiritual life, a life nourished by nature. The argument is as supple as the verse, but we should note that it falls into two phases. First, as everyone knows, Wordsworth moves backward from *now* to *then* and takes us through three stages of his life in nature. This is basically an amplification of the second verse paragraph, but it is now given a historical ordering that amounts to a proof through the testing of time. Second, whereas the earlier presentation advanced along the trajectory physical, moral, mystical, paragraph four moves from the physical to the mystical and climaxes with the moral. This arrangement, and the actual moral argument, insure that his outlook will be safe from philosophes, evil tongues, and the sneers of selfish men.

If paragraph one looked backward in its evocation of physical nature, paragraph four is situated "now" and is characterized by "hope," a hope rooted in the recognition

> That in this moment there is life and food
> For future years, (ll. 64–65)

which seems, in part at least, sacramental. In the earliest stages of his experience the boy (like a philosophe?) had submitted himself entirely to nature:

> what I was when first
> I came among these hills; when like a roe
> I bounded o'er the mountains, by the sides
> Of the deep rivers, and the lonely streams,
> Wherever nature led. (ll. 66—70)

Outgrowing this passivity of mind, he reached a Thomsonian second stage in which nature was such a delight that it needed nothing more:

> For nature then
> (The coarser pleasures of my boyish days,
> And their glad animal movements all gone by)
> To me was all in all. (ll. 72–75)

This was the stage of 1793, evoked so effectively in the landscape verse of paragraph one. But what was missing, as the poet now knows, was mind and the autonomous human spirit. He had, unwittingly, foregone the hierarchy of faculties and lived by appetite, not by reason:

> Their colours and their forms, were then to me
> An appetite; a feeling and a love
> That had no need for a remoter charm,
> By thought supplied, nor any interest
> Unborrowed from the eye. (ll. 79–83)

This is exactly the situation transcended in paragraph two. And so the poet's personal history is an epitome of eighteenth-century attitudes toward nature, arranged in a clear hierarchy, pointing beyond the physical to the mystical and moral.

The third stage, post-1793: a redaction of the experience presented in paragraph two? It might seem so. But here the poet makes a subtle move that indicates once more how strongly the whole argument is moving under the presence of the objections of paragraph three. While the earlier trajectory followed more or less that of Christian tradition—physical, moral, mystical—Wordsworth's pantheism is more vulnerable than his morality to the charge of being "a vain belief." The Enlightenment, after all, had put "God in the dock" (in C. S. Lewis's famous phrase), had tried Him by the canons of its own Benevolence and found Him wanting. So mysticism cannot justify morality. But if Wordsworth can show a secure morality, then his full religious outlook, with its mysticism, will be proof against the philosophes. For that reason the famous lines of "cosmic unity and interfusion" are both *preceded and followed* by passages that emphasize the *moral* life.[18]

Wordsworth's autonomous spirituality takes its stand on mind, not eye or appetite, and on the simultaneous awareness of man's social being, the life of mutual obligation:

> For I have learned
> To look on nature, not as in the hour
> Of thoughtless youth; but hearing oftentimes
> The still, sad music of humanity,
> Nor harsh nor grating, though of ample power
> To chasten and subdue. (ll. 88–93)

"Learned" takes us away from the Enlightenment model of a passive mind and turns the moral argument around: it is the philosophes who are threatened with a "thoughtless" life no higher than the appetite. In this wonderfully phrased and cadenced and deeply moving passage, "The still, sad music of humanity" is Wordsworth's version of Virgil's *lacrimae rerum*, his awareness of the tears, the deep sadness, at the heart of all human endeavor which the "daylight" of the philosophes is powerless to affect. And this grave awareness, so compelling in itself, quietly secures him against any reproach that the religious mysticism to follow is merely private or fantastic.

The passage on pantheism needs little comment, as our concern is with the structure of the argument and the coherency of the intellectual drama.[19] But we should remind ourselves that it *is* pantheistic, that the "presence" that is invoked is immanent and impersonal, a "something" found in nature and in mind; it is *not* supernatural. The passage is followed by the moral climax; and note how "Therefore" indicates that these lines are intended as the formal conclusion to an argument:

> Therefore am I still
> A lover of the meadows and the woods.

> And mountains; and of all that we behold
> From this green earth; of all the mighty world
> Of eye, and ear,—both what they half create,
> And what perceive; well pleased to recognise
> In nature and the language of the sense
> The anchor of my purest thoughts, the nurse,
> The guide, the guardian of my heart, and soul
> Of all my moral being. (ll. 102–111a)

Criticism has paid generous attention to the "half create, / And what perceive" idea, so central to the Romantic concept of imagination. We should note its firm repudiation of' Lockean passivity, but our focus must be on the conclusion of the argument. It runs thus: nature anchors, nurses, guides, guards, and is the soul of the poet's moral life. Here is the ultimate validation of the poet's religious experience against the Enlightenment objection that "this" is no more than "a vain belief." But notice the character of the claim, for we are witnessing a subtle and important shift in intellectual history, one of the doors, in fact, that opens on modernity. Among the most controverted points in Christian history, at the very center of the Reformation split between Catholics and Protestants—a split used by the Enlightenment in its campaign to discredit Christianity, is the issue of the relation of nature and grace.[20] Does grace "perfect" nature, or overwhelm it? From that issue flows fundamentally diverse understandings of the Incarnation, Justification, and the Sacraments. What Wordsworth has done, with audacious wit, is to make nature replace grace: nature, not grace, is the source (and so on) of the moral life.[21] Nature perfects (human) nature and the order of grace is redundant. The poet has identified the main lines of development for that characteristic nineteenth-century project, the search for a purely naturalist, yet nonteleological, ethics. Wordsworthian morality, like Wordsworthian religion, has no need of the supernatural.

With this claim the drama of ideas is nearly done. The poet has defined and defended his autonomous spirituality in the face of anticipated Enlightenment objections. He has proven his mysticism by his morality, with its unimpeachable proof from benevolence. And he has established by experience that his spirituality "works" without need for metaphysics or the supernatural. There is but one further dimension to the religious question, one that extends both the definition and the defense. For verse paragraph five is far from extrinsic to the argument; it is, in fact, the evangelical section of the poem. Wordsworth's experience is not just private, a special accommodation for himself; it is social, communicable, available to others.

In paragraph five, with the argument basically secure, the religious matrix of the diction becomes pronounced. A concordance alone would convey the dominant interest: "prayer," "joy," "faith," "blessings," "holier," and, of course, the give-away phrase so regretted by the poet in his later years, "a worshipper of Nature." The entire paragraph, admittedly the slackest, is addressed to Dorothy, his "dearest friend," and is basically an evangelium. The Good News is, What I *have* already experienced you *will* experience; what nature[22] has ministered to me, she will, in future, minister to you. The same moral benevolence will be formed in you, and when it does we two will be a sort of "church":

> for [Nature] can so inform
> The mind that is within us, so impress
> With quietness and beauty, and so feed
> With lofty thoughts, that neither evil tongues,
> Rash judgments, nor the sneers of selfish men.
> Nor greetings where no kindness is, nor all
> The dreary intercourse of daily life,
> Shall e'er prevail against us, or disturb
> Our cheerful faith, that all which we behold
> Is full of blessings. (ll. 125–34)

The key phrase, "Shall e'er prevail against us," deliberately echoes St. Matthew 16:18: "And I say also unto thee, That thou art Peter, and upon this rock I will build my church; and the gates of' hell shall not prevail against it."[23] This much-discussed text about the foundation, authority, and indefectibility of the Church is interpreted by Catholics to substantiate the doctrine of papal primacy, an interpretation necessarily controverted by Protestants. As with his quiet undermining of grace, Wordsworth's implicit logic is that his autonomous spirituality transcends the barren, scandalous controversies of Christian tradition. Religious faith, of a new sort, has been reestablished and rendered secure on the rock of moral benevolence and mystical intuition. The challenge of the philosophes has been met.

VI

"Tintern Abbey" is a poem that can be variously read. As a spiritual drama it is carefully positioned. Wordsworth has gone to the unmentioned ruins of the old faith and has celebrated the new, effecting a momentous shift from the supernatural to the natural, from faith to experience, from communal prayer to private exaltation. And this new faith is carefully placed between the competing worldviews of the Enlightenment and Christianity, acknowledging both, partaking of both, yet invincibly itself. The poem defines and defends an autonomous spirituality, and this action is an unfolding intellectual drama—a drama of the poet's deepest self. The priestly element—the poem as ritual reenactment of the poet's discovery of the basis of his own spiritual life—releases the prophetic with its double aspect of the mystical and moral. Theology is transformed into psychology and the poet articulates a new answer to the old conundrum of nature and grace, a new vision of the moral life based on the purified feelings.

The poem does recover and secure something spiritual over and against the materialism of the Enlightenment. But the gains were temporary and the cost was high. Truth had to be tacitly abandoned; the poet had to turn from the objective order and abandon the tradition of moral reasoning; he had to relinquish revelation and metaphysics, the transcendent and supernatural. All this he was willing to do on the supposition that here in nature was the only world:

> ... the very world which is the world
> Of all of us, the place in which, in the end,
> We find our happiness, or not at all.[24]

But the "Immortality Ode" reminds us how precarious and short-lived Wordsworth's early happiness was. Energy is not eternal delight and neither is activity of mind. Autonomous spirituality eventually collapses under the strain of its own impossibility. "The mind can only repose," Johnson warns us, "on the stability of truth." In later life, still hoping to satisfy his spirit, Wordsworth moved between two worlds, melding his Romanticism with Christianity, thereby helping to foster the confusion that their natures are reconcilable, which is a dire part of the nineteenth century's legacy to our world.

Notes to "Between Two Worlds": The Structure of the Argument in "Tintern Abbey"

1. Political readings, here, means those readings and types of readings that M. H. Abrams has objected to (see Abrams, "On Political Readings *of Lyrical Ballads*," in his *Doing Things with Texts: Essays in Criticism and Critical Theory* [New York: Norton, 1989], pp. 364–91).
2. *Religious Trends in English Poetry*, 6 vols. (New York: Columbia University Press, 1949), III, 169.
3. For references to the political readings, see Abrams, pp. 415–19; among recent commentators Alan Bewell finds that "'Tintern Abbey' is first and foremost an anthropological history," while Keith G. Thomas argues that "continuity [of nature, experience, self] becomes the central issue" in the poem (see Bewell, *Wordsworth and the Enlightenment: Nature, Sian, and Society in the Experimental Poetry* [New Haven: Yale University Press, 1989), p. 35; and Thomas, *Wordsworth and Philosophy: Empiricism and Transcendentalism in the Poetry* [Ann Arbor: UMI Research Press, 1987), p. 65).
4. Arnold, "Stanzas from the Grande Chartreuse," in *The Poetical Works of Matthew Arnold*, ed. C. B. Tinker and H. F. Lowry (London: Oxford University Press, 1950), p. 301, ll. 85–86.
5. This is the gist of Fairchild's argument. According to him, "Wordsworth's religion...between 1797 and 1800...is not avowedly anti-Christian" (III, 170). But he argues that by "Christianity" Wordsworth generally understood a gentle mixture of Deism and sentimentalism. Wordsworth's "Romanticism" is anti-Christian but that is, so to say, *per accidens*. It is the Enlightenment that is his conscious adversary.
6. "Wordsworth ignores the Christian scheme of redemption so pointedly that one may as well say that he denies it.... There is no room for the Cross" (Fairchild, III, 170).
7. "Lines Composed a Few Miles above Tintern Abbey," in *The Poetical Works of William Wordsworth*, ed. E. de Selincourt, 2nd ed., 5 vols. (Oxford: Clarendon Press, 1952), II, 259–53. All further references are to this text.
8. And we should note here and throughout the poem the religious matrix of Wordsworth's diction.

9. One line of development from here will run through Emerson to William James. The ties between "Tintern Abbey" and Emerson's *Nature* are particularly close.
10. "Preface to...'Lyrical Ballads,'" in *Poetical Works*, II, 389.
11. The Enlightenment outlook Wordsworth is rejecting proposed lifeless nature and passive mind. Romantic doctrines of the Imagination are a version of philosophical Rationalism (the mind as start-point). Nature is transformed by active mind, and this complexus modifies the feelings. The feelings, in their turn, are the real source of both the moral and mystical modes of experience.
12. "'It is very true,' said Marianne, 'that admiration of landscape scenery is become a mere jargon. Every body pretends to feel and tries to describe with the taste and elegance of him who first defined what picturesque beauty was. I detest jargon of every kind, and sometimes I have kept my feelings to myself, because I could find no language to describe them in but what was worn and hackneyed out of all sense and meaning'" (Jane Austen, *Sense and Sensibility*, ed. Claire Lamont [Oxford: Oxford University Press, 1970], p. 84). If Marianne Dashwood has noticed this, we can be fairly confident Wordsworth would have as well!
13. Durrant, *William Wordsworth* (Cambridge: Cambridge University Press, 1969), p. 36.
14. Poem 1286, in *The Poems of Emily Dickinson*, ed. Thomas H. Johnson, 3 vols. (Cambridge, MA: Belknap Press of Harvard University Press, 1955), III, 893.
15. Letter 388, to Thomas Poole, 23 March 1801, in *Collected Letters of Samuel Taylor Coleridge*, ed. Earl Leslie Griggs, 5 vols. (Oxford: Clarendon Press, 1956), II, 709.
16. For a particularly useful discussion of this in Coleridge, which applies *mutatis mutandis* to Wordsworth, see Basil Willey, *Samuel Taylor Coleridge* (London: Chatto and Windus, 1972), esp. pp. 86–96, 120–41.
17. Peter Malekin has noticed a resemblance between Wordsworth's description of physiological changes here and similar passages in St. Teresa (see "Wordsworth and the Mind of Man," in *An Infinite Complexity: Essays in Romanticism*, ed. J. R. Watson [Edinburgh: Edinburgh University Press, 1983], pp. 1–25; esp. pp. 6–9).
18. In paragraph two "the feelings" are what nourish "that best portion of a good man's life"; in paragraph four the way into the mystical experience of pantheistic fusion is phrased, "I have felt / A presence that disturbs me with the joy / Of elevated thoughts." This double use of the feelings is, in part, another indication of how the poet is writing to forestall Enlightenment objections. Once the moral is conceded, the mystical can follow.
19. For a discussion of the substance of Wordsworth's religious views and of the Romantic religion in general from a thoroughgoing supernaturalist viewpoint, Fairchild's work has never been superseded. But for a naturalist viewpoint, and therefore one more sympathetic to Wordsworth, see Abrams, *Natural Supematuralism: Tradition and Revolution in Romantic Literature* (New York: Norton, 1971), esp. pp. 17–141. For a more recent view, linking Wordsworth to Plato and Whitehead, see Daniel Dombrowski, "Wordsworth's Panentheism," *The Wordsworth Circle*, 16 (1985), pp. 136–42.
20. "It is against a background of discussions about the nature of divine grace and its operation that the whole history of western Europe proceeds for the next hundred years [i.e., from 1517]" (Philip Hughes, *The Reformation in England*, rev. ed., 3 vols. in one [New York: Macmillan, 1963], I, 122).
21. The fullest treatment of this topic is still Elizabeth Geen, "The Concept of Grace in Wordsworth's Poetry," *PMLA*, 58 (1943), pp. 689–715; but she does not mention "Tintern Abbey." Wordsworth was not the only one offering a new formula for the old conundrum. A

generation earlier in America that philosophe of philosophes, Benjamin Franklin, had substituted Method for Grace as the source of moral perfection (see *The Autobiography of Benjamin Franklin*, ed. Leonard W. Labaree, et al. [New Haven: Yale University Press, 1964], p. 148).

22. The success of the poetic argument justifies this shorthand.
23. Jeffrey Baker notices this, and in the "neither...nor" construction he hears echoes of Romans 8:38–39 as well (see Baker, *Time and Mind in Wordsworth's Poetry* [Detroit: Wayne State University Press, 1980], p. 57).
24. *The Prelude* (1805), ed. Ernest de Selincourt, rev. Helen Darbishire (Oxford: Clarendon Press, 1959), Book X, ll. 726–28.

POE AND TRADITION

Brian Barbour

I

Poe has proven the most difficult American writer to put in proper perspective. There has been, for example, a historical reluctance to define the nature and location of his achievement; instead, it has been somewhat mystically distributed over four categories—poetry, criticism, journalism, fiction—and he has emerged as that figment so beloved of dead scholarship, an "influence." Even so lively and sensible a critic as F. O. Matthiessen succumbed to the tendency, and in his judicious essay in the *LHUS* he reached the conclusion that Poe was " an original creative *force*," implying that his ultimate value resided somewhere else than in producible texts.[1] In this view, which T. S. Eliot fostered, Poe is a figure in international Romanticism, a mediator of ideas and attitudes to authors more valuable than himself, chiefly Baudelaire. Eliot in fact, playing Atticus, went so far as to hint that had Baudelaire, Mallarme, and Valery been more competent in English they would have lost interest in Poe, but handicapped as they were they found him stimulating.[2] Separated like this from the words on the page, criticism might just as well serve up the figure of the daguerreotypes or The Legend for all that it advances real understanding.

Interlocked with this failure to define is the puzzling question of Poe's Americanness. As a hovering international influence he seems to lack native identity and much of a concern with his native land. Eliot asked rhetorically, "What is identifiably local about Poe?" and Matthiessen admitted that one consequence of the position he took was that Poe seems "remote from the main currents of American thought."[3] In his widely praised *Poe: A Critical Study*, Edward Davidson says, "My approach to Poe's mind and writing has been primarily through the critical and metaphysical theories of Coleridge," and he adds that as a result, "I may have increased the distance between Poe and his age or between Poe and the American experience."[4] This instinctive tendency, like so much in Poe studies, goes back to Baudelaire, who could not believe that the *poete maudit* of his construction could have anything to do with the land of Franklin except to shake its dust from his artistic feet: "From the midst of a greedy world, hungry for material things, Poe took flight in dreams. Stifled as he was by the American atmosphere, etc."[5] Killis Campbell is sometimes supposed to have disproved this, but the contrary tendency has never really sunk roots wide or deep. It is noticeable, for example, that the two most ambitious recent books on Poe, David Halliburton's *Edgar Allan Poe: A Phenomenological Study* (Princeton, NJ: Princeton University Press, 1973) and G. R. Thompson's *Poe's Fiction: Romantic Irony in the Gothic Tales* (Madison: University of Wisconsin Press, 1973) both analyze his work with tools cast in the die shop of Continental philosophy.

Killis Campbell stoutly denied all this. He heroically collected all the references to things American throughout the canon that he could find, showing for example that twelve of the seventy tales are set in America and that they refer to such New World phenomena as watermelons, Bowie knives, and Lewis Gaylord Clark.[6] He suggested that Poe's "tales not only reveal a genuine interest in the political and economic life of his day, but they also reveal a genuine concern about the social life of his time."[7] However, he does not actually *show* this or allow it to control his argument, for his topographical method of cataloguing references does not permit it, and after saying that "several early reviews touch on slavery" (the verb is significant) he proceeds to considerations of a different type.[8] The result for the critical heritage, I have said, is puzzling and the puzzle is exemplified, I think, in the work of the late Henry Bamford Parkes. Parkes was one of the most penetrating and intelligent students of American culture, a historian unusually sensitive to literature and capable or making first-hand literary-critical judgments. But in two books he published in the 1950s there is a tension amounting almost to contradiction in his remarks on Poe. In *The American Experience* (1959) he argued thus: "While Emerson, Thoreau, and Whitman were concerned with what America ought to be, Poe, Hawthorne, and Melville indicated what America actually was."[9] But in his textbook, written in 1953 and then later issued in new editions, he took the more conventional line: "His environment affected him only as he reacted against it and tried to escape into a dream world of his own creation."[10] Is Poe a writer wrestling with what America actually was or a Romantic anchorite withdrawn in the face of the harsh quotidian? Parkes was well situated to feel the force of Eliot's term for Poe: "an enigma"![11]

The provisional answer is, Both. And what the question thus dramatizes is that Poe's Americanness cannot finally be discussed apart from an effort to define his achievement. One can answer "both" because in his verse Poe is the Romantic anchorite indulging a grievance against an ugly world, but in his greatest tales—"Ligeia," "The Fall of the House of Usher," "William Wilson," "The Pit and the Pendulum," "The Tell-Tale Heart," "The Black Cat," "The Purloined Letter," "The Cask of Amontillado," "The Imp of the Perverse," perhaps one or two more—he grapples with the inner meaning of the American experience and provides a permanently valuable critique of our tradition. It is the purpose of this paper to show that Poe's tales matter in a way the poetry can not, and to show further that their artistic strength is inseparable from the insight they show into the American experience, the effort to become truly human in America.

II

When Poe began as a creative artist in the late 1820s, there was no living American literary tradition for him to inherit. This is why scholars as diverse as Campbell and Davidson, seeking to reverse Baudelaire's ahistorical impetus, turned inevitably to Coleridge in an effort to link Poe to the ideas of his time. There is nothing factitious about this as there was, perhaps, about Marshall McLuhan's effort thirty years ago to relate Poe to a Ciceronian ideal in the South[12]: Coleridge had the most seminal mind of his century and Poe, particularly (but not exclusively) in his criticism, consciously adapted himself to the greater figure. But writers inherit more than just other writers, and Malraux's dictum that it is the beautiful painting not the beautiful smile that inspires the artist is no more than a half-truth, good for the beginner without question but inapposite to the mature artist whose work grows out of, even as it seeks to correct, the life around him. L. C. Knights put it this way: "Now the possibilities of living at any moment are not merely an individual matter; they depend on physical circumstances and (what is less of a commonplace) on current habits of thought and feeling, on all that is implied by 'tradition'—or the lack of it."[13] As applied to Poe, this sense of tradition—current habits of thought and feeling and their related values and ideals—is both wider and more exclusive than the conventional sense: wider because literature is only part of social experience, more exclusive because its focus will be primarily American.

Poe's creative years coincided with the Age of Jackson, and it was within and against that tradition that his own sensibility developed. As a gifted artist he was alive to its weaknesses and limitations and saw more clearly than most where it fostered and where it thwarted human possibility, including normal sympathetic existence, friendship. Values and ideals lie at the center of tradition. "The central value of American culture in the early nineteenth century," John William Ward has argued, was "the assertion of the worth of the totally liberated, atomistic, autonomous individual."[14] The strongest tradition shaping society, in other words, denied both the efficacy of tradition and the reality of society. If this was sometimes a paradox, the times had given it proof. The resulting tendency was to locate the experience of being in the exercise of the will; making straight the way was a certain utilitarian sense of mind, a kind of didactic rationalism that emphasized the immediate solving of practical problems and derided speculation. The drive was towards domination by the self rather than towards integration with other selves and the consequent modifications of ego-assertion. Means usurped ends and rather easily, for the moral consequences of the will-to-dominate of the autonomous self were kept conveniently obscure by the utilitarian theory of mind. It is against these features of the prevailing tradition that Poe needs to be seen.

His most valuable stories use unreliable narrators to *embody* a critique of this tradition. "The Purloined Letter," as we shall see, has a dialectical structure in which an outlook is criticized by means of a positive value actually present, but this is not Poe's customary method. His task was to show his society that its central values were not humanly adequate (or, at least, that they contained unsuspected dangerous consequences) and that its ordinary way of thinking kept this out of view. The consensus ran all the other way. In the practical and material realm what Ward calls the central value was well established, having received its classic expression in Franklin's *Autobiography*. Now in the spiritual and intellectual realm Emerson was striving to redefine the *opportunity* offered by the American experience, yet with the same emphasis on the atomistic, autonomous self. As Professor Ward has noted, "No less than Jackson... Emerson held a vision of the good society which had at its center the atomic individual, moving freely and without constraint through space and society, dependent upon nothing beyond his own personality and unaided self."[15] The strongest moral voice within the culture was divided in its effect. Emerson was attacking American materialism, but he possessed no coherent social theory; by exalting atomism and individual will he unwittingly strengthened the development of society along lines in which materialism and will-to-dominate were increasingly normative and morally reputable. There was, in short, no effectively established critical position even identifying the fundamental problems. None, that is, outside the great fiction of the period, for the creators of Hurry Harry, Chillingworth, Ahab, and Montresor were not deceived about the nature of the self-willing, means-obsessed, atomistic individual.

The fundamental cultural dialectic of the period concerned the deepest meaning of the American democratic opportunity, something unparalleled in human history, the *novus ordo saeculorum*. And the two most authoritative voices insisted that it lay in autonomous individualism as *the* defining American characteristic. But the fiction writers offered a third way. It has gone strangely unnoticed or unremarked that all four writers—Poe, Cooper, Hawthorne, Melville—were—unlike Franklin and Emerson—Christians, however quirky in belief and practice, and that as Christians they saw a deeper meaning in the American democratic opportunity than just operating space for the dominating individual. They developed a powerful and sophisticated criticism of American individualism, showing that the American democratic opportunity really lay in *relationships*: in Friendship (Poe), Responsibility (Hawthorne), and Bi-Racial Brotherhood (Cooper and Melville).

But what habits of thought and feeling would the emerging dominant tradition engender? What were its consequences, beyond the immediate, for human life? Poe's basic technique arose as a way of exploring this tradition without having a recognized counter-tradition to invoke. It has to be said that the strangeness of his tales often mitigated their intended moral effect, although this was intended to provide a certain stark clarity. His most characteristic tales embody the central value of the self-willing, atomistic, autonomous individual, but they wrench us out of the lenitive atmosphere of American optimism to focus our attention on narrators whose willfulness expresses deep disorder within. We are obliged to see the moral consequences, the dark, hidden possibilities in what we naively believe. The stories force us to live through a world empty of nourishing relationships where characters exist in an atomistic void, condemned to the resources of their autonomous selves, a loveless world in which no one is recognized as a person. Two steady, interdependent criticisms are brought to bear: the tradition frustrates the person's growth to wholeness, even leaving, in the emphasis on domination as opposed to integration, a basic and dangerous confusion over what it means to be human; and the utilitarian habits of mind keep this growth obscured, unfelt, and unprepared for.

III

The poetry provides a clarifying contrast. Killis Campbell had to admit that he was "unable to find any specific reference to contemporary movements or to contemporary conditions"[16] in Poe's poetry, and this is a key to understanding why it is a lesser achievement than the tales. Much of it was early—more than a decade before his greatest fiction—and in it Poe deliberately sets his face against that close engagement with the American tradition that will mark his maturity. The chief characteristic of the verse is its incredible music: that is why we never quite forget the command it gains over our imaginations in adolescence, but this canorous power generally obliterates sense. In his poetry Poe is content merely to escape the quotidian world, to repudiate Enlightenment rationalism and the bourgeois values somewhat superficially conceived. He deliberately makes no effort to understand these things; instead, he stresses a counter-world of dreams, fairyland, and romance. "Remember, that *time* is money," Franklin enjoined the Young Tradesman, and this conveys more than just one of Poor Richard's maxims: it expresses a whole attitude towards experience, the straitened sensibility of restless America. In a relatively late (1844) poem Poe voiced his alternative[17]:

> By a route obscure and lonely,
> Haunted by ill angels only,
> Where an Eidolon, named Night,
> On a black throne reigns upright,
> I have reached these lands but newly
> From an ultimate dim Thule—
> From a wild weird clime that lieth, sublime,
> Out of Space—out of Time. ("Dream-Land")

The differences in values could scarcely be greater. Even when the subject does not proclaim this extreme insistence on dream-work, the rhythms and language work to the same end. The Beauty that Poe wants to evoke is deliberately set against a harsh, mundane reality. The whole effort of the verse is to repudiate the waking world and find compensation in an esoteric vision.

> Here once, through an alley Titanic,
> Of cypress, I roamed with my soul—
> Of cypress, with Psyche, my Soul.
> These were days when my heart was volcanic
> As the scoriac rivers that roll—
> As the lavas that restlessly roll
> Their sulphurous currents down Yaanek
> In the ultimate climes of the Pole—
> That groan as they roll down Mount Yaanek,
> In the realms of the Boreal Pole. ("Ulalume," VII, 102)

This effectively stresses the incantatory and hypnotic, so much so that we scarcely pay attention or believe in what he is saying. The effects are all worked up from the outside, not shaped by the crystallizing pressure of what he has to say[18]; and what is aimed at is a state analogous to intoxication.

In repudiating the actual world, Poe was forfeiting any possibility he might explore the themes of the atomistic society and the will-to-dominate that most deeply engaged him. With the bugbear of scientific rationalism it was the same:

> Science! true daughter of Old Time thou art!
> Who alterest all things with thy peering eyes.
> Why preyest thou thus upon the poet's heart,
> Vulture, whose wings are dull realities?
> How should he love thee? or how deem thee wise,
> Who wouldst not leave him in his wandering
> To seek for treasure in the jewelled skies,
> Albeit he soared with an undaunted wing?
> Hast thou not dragged Diana from her car?
> And driven the Hamadryad from the wood
> To seek a shelter in some happier star?
> Hast thou not torn the Naiad from her flood,
> The Elfin from the green grass, and from me
> The summer dream beneath the tamarind tree?
> ("Sonnet-To Science," VII, 22)

Like all Poe's verse this shows a rhetorical brilliance, but the poem is empty of critical intelligence. He doesn't know anything about the science he is protesting—it seems a mark of honor not to know. Instead, he is enjoying his pang and finding solace in the romantic poetico-mythological traffic. The "poetry" that he would contrast to "science" means the careful cultivating of specialized emotions separate from ordinary living. The point is explicit: even were there no science, poetry would seek to avoid contact with the actual: "To seek for treasure in the jewelled skies." The bent is all for withdrawal, for what Baudelaire first called "flight"; little by way of insight could emerge.

The tales offer an entirely different psychological orientation; they stand at a different angle to their creator. The Romantic lyric is usually uttered *in propria persona*, and for Poe that was always a dangerous temptation. The narrative mask of the tales, however, enabled him to get out from under the burden of self-consciousness that the poems carry: by the device of first-person narrators he was able to depersonalize his deepest concerns—a necessary preliminary to making them available—and yet in the expression give them great immediacy. The effect of the poetry is to proclaim, "I am Edgar Poe, a poet, and I scorn your values," while the tales simply say, "Here is the hidden reality of what you believe in; if you have ears, you will hear."

IV

We face an embarrassment of riches. To fully analyze Poe's finest stories along the lines I have been indicating would extend this paper to unconscionable lengths. For convenience, therefore, I would like to concentrate on four representative tales, examining them in some detail; two—"The Purloined Letter" and "The Fall of the House of Usher"—convey Poe's analysis of the American mind, and two—"The Cask of Amontillado" and "Ligeia"—display his insight into the will-to-dominate of the autonomous individual and its destructive consequences. Before proceeding, however, a word about the narrators. "The Purloined Letter" is unusual not only for its dialectic but also because the narrator is not the real subject. The most liberating moment in the history of Poe studies came when James Gargano demonstrated conclusively that Poe "often so designs his tales so as to show his narrators' limited comprehension of their own problems and states of mind; the structure of many of Poe's stories clearly reveals an ironical and comprehensive intelligence critically and artistically ordering events so as to establish a vision of life and character which the narrator's very inadequacies help to 'prove.'"[19] The popular view of Poe as the exotic creator of *frisson* identified him *with* his narrators, but in fact the tales are, so to speak, told *against* them. In a word, they are all *unreliable*. This accounts for the wide diversity of styles, for Poe invented ways to convincingly communicate the feel of a variety of psychic disorders.[20] And the function of the ironic structure is to open a moral perspective upon the experience.

"The Purloined Letter" is the last of those three tales—"The Murders in the Rue Morgue" and "The Mystery of Marie Roget" are the others—in which Poe is commonly recognized to have invented detective fiction. Holmes liked to point it out to Dr. Watson as a salutary lesson, and the argument that they two descend from Dupin and Poe's narrator—that the basic elements and configuration of the genre sprang Minerva-like from his head—is a familiar one. These tales are ordinarily called "ratiocinative," but the term is misleading inasmuch as it suggests that what is of greatest importance is a method of Holmes-like deduction whereby Dupin outwits the Minister D—. That piece of detection largely serves as a framework within which Poe can explore the question, What constitutes real intelligence?

Like many of the Romantics, Poe brought into literature a new interest in the workings of the human mind. So strong was this that it made him proof against one of the weaker Romantic tendencies, that towards Primitivism. "The theorizers on Government," he said, with the Contractarian philosophers apparently in view, "who pretend always to 'begin with the beginning,' commence with Man in what they call his *natural* state—the savage. What right have they to suppose this his natural state? Man's chief idiosyncrasy being reason, it follows that his savage condition—his condition of action *without* reason—is his unnatural state" (XVI, 6–7). Like Blake, Poe assimilated Rousseau to Locke as retrograde powers. Locke of course was "America's philosopher" and his view of the mind, filtered through Reid, Stewart, and the Scottish Common Sense school, was dominant in Poe's day. Though Locke is, properly speaking, an empiricist,

> his immensely influential theory of knowledge...had become increasingly identified during the course of the eighteenth century with purely natural and rationalistic ways of thinking. Locke conceived of the mind as a blank page on which ideas of the external world were inscribed through the senses, or as a kind of mechanical organizer of sensations which were fed to it by "experience." *This view appeared very well suited to explain the processes of scientific classification* and experiment or the formation of common-sense judgments on practical matters, *but it tended to create the*

> *assumptions that only the physical, the tangible, the measurable were real,* and that consciousness was a prisoner of the senses.[21] (my emphasis)

To anyone concerned with introspection and the primacy of the mind's own powers, Locke was the enemy.

In America, this diagnosis and consequent revolt are identified with the Transcendentalists. Using James Marsh's edition (1829) of Coleridge's *Aids to Reflection*, the American Transcendentalists took over the distinction between Reason and Understanding, but they gave it a quite un-Coleridgean emphasis, an emphasis which "The Purloined Letter" shows Poe rejected. For Coleridge, with his lifelong search for unity, Reason and Understanding were complementary powers of the mind, each valuable in its own sphere which corresponded roughly to the moral and the practical. Pure Reason, for example, had no place in politics where it could only result in Jacobinism. But the moral life depended on the promptings of an intuition lying deeper than the Understanding. With the American Transcendentalists this distinction tended to harden into a frozen posture. Reason became an honorific power whose twofold purpose was to communicate with the Over-Soul and to dishonor the "sensual" Understanding. Coleridge valued the Understanding on its own terms. He rejected Godwin because he saw that "philanthropy" can't be achieved if the "homeborn" elements that insure life's continuity and allow virtue to develop—the family, for instance—are done away with.[22] The Transcendentalists, however, were not looking for a means to *explore* reality in its various dimensions; they wanted a means to *discredit* the "sensual" Understanding. As an independent realm, to be valued for what it was, they had no interest in it. Intelligence here comes dangerously close to being freed (ambiguous word) from common experience.

In "Sonnet—To Science" we see the young Poe similarly solve the problem of the prevailing rationalistic outlook by simply rejecting it. In "The Purloined Letter," however, he tries to discern the limits of this outlook and show why it is inadequate as an account of intelligence. The interplay between the mind, the body, and experience suggests a viewpoint similar to Coleridge's and implicitly criticizes Transcendentalism.[23] It will be recalled that the story falls into three parts. In the first G—comes to Dupin's rooms, relates the problem, and details the steps he has already taken. Dupin listens and gives his ironic advice: "Make a thorough re-search of the premises" (VI, 37). The story turns on the different ways *thorough* is understood and which *premises* are being referred to. The second is quite short. A month has passed when G—returns still baffled. He says he is willing to pay a reward of fifty thousand francs for the letter, whereupon Dupin produces the letter and tells him to draw up his cheque. G—leaves and Dupin enters into a somewhat long-winded "explanation," most of which is concerned with G—'s failure as a "reasoner"; only the last couple of paragraphs treat the action by which Dupin foils D—and recovers the letter. The interest centers in the explanation.

Why does G—fail as a reasoner? Calling him "a functionary," Dupin says, "the remote source of his defeat lies in the supposition that the Minister is a fool, because he has acquired renown as a poet" (VI, 43). And speaking of D—, he adds, "As poet *and* mathematician, he would reason well; as mere mathematician he could not have reasoned at all" (VI, 43).

Clearly, the prevailing rationalistic outlook dominant in America is being criticized. Poe uses narration and dialogue to point up the restless energy of the superficial "functionary," and he contrasts this busyness with the calmer, more attractive rhythm of the reflective Dupin. Out of this comes their contrasting attitudes towards poetry. Dupin has been "guilty of certain doggerel" himself, while for G—anyone whose interests lie that way is a "fool" (VI, 34). Poetry, as the story reveals, though not to G—, is a form of knowledge, the necessary complement, intuitive and tending to the concrete, to mathematics, rational and tending to the abstract. As Dupin argues, both are necessary in a mutually fertilizing relationship before there is full intelligence. The rational principle cannot be divorced from intuitive perception without running the risk of reducing itself to mere cleverness. Or, we might say, a people that has no way of valuing poetry is committed to very limited ways of knowing.

G—is committed to his "microscope"; and with this goes a certain hubris: "'The thing is *so* plain. There is a certain amount of bulk—a space—to be accounted for in every cabinet. Then we have accurate rules. The fiftieth part of a line could not escape us'" (VI, 34). But somehow the letter does, ironically defining the limits of this way of thinking about the world. "'Then we examined the house itself. We divided the entire surface into compartments, which we numbered, so that none might be missed; then we scrutinized each individual square inch throughout the premises, including the two houses immediately adjoining, with the microscope, as before'" (VI, 36). That "two adjoining houses" is a nice comic touch, redoubled energy serving for the lack of insight. "'But,'" asks Dupin later, with delighted scorn, "'what is all this boring, and probing, and sounding, and scrutinizing with the microscope, and dividing the surface of the building into registered square inches?'" (VI, 42). Our question might well be, Why does Poe call it a microscope? He doesn't mean the familiar compound microscope, he means a magnifying glass; the thing was known and the term was present in the language for him to use (the *O.E.D.* gives 1665 for its first citation). Dupin points out that all G—can do in an unprecedented situation is extrapolate his method, which brings more and more of the tangible (like the two adjoining houses) under review. Poe calls the glass a microscope because he wants, through this linguistic extension, to identify G—'s method with that of scientific rationalism. This outlook, as Hochfield says, "tended to create the assumptions that only the physical, the tangible, the measurable were real." The story undermines these assumptions. The immaterial or spiritual, it argues, is not only real but primary.

Dupin is a poet and the story contrasts his mode of intelligence, the imagination, with G—'s.[24] The use of the "microscope" entails a loss of perspective, a loss, that is, of wholeness of vision. G—is committed to a reality that is measurable only, the surface of things. The tale's central irony is that even there he cannot locate the letter, for *seeing* in this sense depends on a prior act of mind. He is cut off, in Coleridge's well-known words, from "that deep Thinking... attainable only by a man of deep Feeling" and locked into a Newtonian system where mind "is always passive—a lazy Looker-on on an external world."[25] Poetry or the imagination is contrasted with the microscope; the latter divides while the former unifies. And the corresponding unity of the self in the act of knowing is its strength (just as its absence is Dupin's warrant for calling G—"a functionary"). Poe points out the limits of the dominant American mode of thought, but he also criticizes the orthodox alternative. For Dupin is no Transcendentalist, using Reason to discredit the "sensual" Understanding, finding satisfaction in inverting the dominant view. Intelligence, properly understood, is not detached intellect; it is rooted in the life of the body and is a function of the whole person. When the tale opens Dupin and the narrator are sitting in the darkness "enjoying the twofold luxury of meditation and a meerschaum" (VI, 28), and it is through this perspective that everything subsequent is to be seen and judged. "The high perception," as Melville was afterwards to put it, is here wedded to "the low enjoying power." Thought (or meditation: the stress falls on that ingathering that must precede activity) is from the outset of this exploration into the makeup of real intelligence intimately linked with feeling (evoked by the meerschaum), and where there is this co-presence even the darkness is not prohibitive.

Poe's criticism of the impoverished sense of mind dominant in utilitarian America is not merely negative; it proceeds from a human center. American thought has customarily oscillated between unleavened materialism and unrooted idealism; but Poe's groundwork is the wholeness of the person operating through the unifying activity of the imagination. It will be useful to keep this in mind when we come to stories more wholly negative in their critique.

Poe feels disdain for the aggressive didactic rationalism of G—but reaches a different evaluation of the narrator of "The Fall of the House of Usher" who also embodies an essential American attitude towards the mind. The distinction is a moral one, and it reminds us that Poe's social thought, *as realized in his fiction*, is more *ondoyant et divers* than the aristocratic haughtiness and contempt for the mob usually ascribed to him. Within the American tradition, from the White House down, there was widespread belief in the sufficiency of the common-sense of the common man.[26] Professor Ward has noted this paradox: "the rejection of training and experience...was an important aspect of nineteenth century American thought."[27] The age was convinced that mental discipline was otiose, that real intelligence didn't need formal training, that the mind's inherent powers were adequate to any situation. Underlying this was the assumption, given spurious legitimacy by the Declaration of Independence, that the most important truths were self-evident; and the phrase "common-sense" had received a sort of sanctity from its Revolutionary association. This outlook was of course necessary for belief in the autonomous self. What Poe saw were its limitations, that in most important matters there are qualifications that can only be gained by discipline and experience, developing natural aptitude. What Lionel Trilling once called "the general import" of "The Rime of the Ancient Mariner" applies *mutatis mutandis* to "Usher": "The world is a complex and unexpected and terrible place which is not always to be understood by the mind as we use it in our everyday tasks."[28]

"What ails Roderick Usher?" Roy Male has asked. "That is the central question of the story."[29] And Darrel Abel in his well-known essay adheres to this emphasis: "Five persons figure in the tale, but the interest centers exclusively in one—Roderick Usher. The narrator is uncharacterized, undescribed, even unnamed."[30] But as usual in Poe the interest actually lies with the narrator. In this case he embodies the American belief in common-sense, but he is taken out of the plain and simple world where this view holds easy sway and he is tested by more severe events. To focus on Roderick, fascinating as he is, is to finesse Poe's intention and meaning. And Professor Abel seems misleading when he says the narrator is uncharacterized. The opposite is true, and this characterization is a basic element in the tale.

Poe uses tone and statement to establish the narrator as the ordinary man of common-sense. He is not unattractive. We see evidence of charity in his response to Usher's letter, and he has none of the hubris of Poe's swollen rationalists. But he accepts as axiomatic the adequacy of the untutored intelligence. The tale presents us with a mind incapable of the development necessary even for its own preservation. Consider the opening paragraph from the point where he first sees "the melancholy House of Usher":

> I know not how it was—but, with the first glimpse of the building, a sense of insufferable gloom pervaded my spirit. I say insufferable; for the feeling was unrelieved by any of that half-pleasurable, because poetic, sentiment with which the mind usually receives even the sternest natural images of the desolate or terrible. I looked upon the scene before me—upon the mere house, and the simple landscape features of the domain—upon the bleak walls—upon the vacant eye-like windows—upon a few rank sedges—and upon a few white trunks of decayed

> trees—with an utter depression of soul which I can compare to no earthy sensation more properly than to the after-dream of the reveller upon opium—the bitter lapse into every-day life—the hideous dropping off of the veil. There was an iciness, a sinking, a sickening of the heart—an unredeemed dreariness of thought which no goading of the imagination could torture into aught of the sublime. (III, 273)

Roderick is not around—he doesn't enter until the eighth paragraph—so this is usually allowed to provide atmosphere. But that account is exiguous, for Poe's theme, method, and the basic configuration of the tale are all outlined here. The theme emerges from the dialectical interplay between his untutored common-sense and the instreaming impressions which evade it. The method emphasizes his sturdy refusal to be affected by, or quite admit the reality of, phenomena that seem to lie outside the Newtonian framework until, at the end, he directly experiences what no common-sense can ever explain, no science account for.

"I know not how it was," he begins and sets out to undo that initial bafflement. The third sentence ("I looked upon the scene before me....") renders the movement of his mind and conveys the reasonable tone. His eye slowly scans the scene and particular images register one-by-one on his consciousness. The adjectives provide an interesting mix of the objective—mere, simple, few, white, decayed—and the subjective—bleak, vacant eyelike, rank—and this indicates the dialectical interplay. The sentence movement is extraordinarily slow and clogged; words are used in combinations the tongue and lips find awkward to make in passing over from one word to the next, giving the effect of great intellectual effort, of a mind puzzled by what lies before it and pondering each successive image in hopes of making a breakthrough. This sense of a search for order (the probable sense of *poetic*) is enriched by the anaphora, which in another context might have seemed frenetic. And this is furthered by the succeeding sentence with its series of false starts ("There was an iciness, a sinking, a sickening..."), implying the mind's reaching for and discarding in turn analogies which might generate understanding.

The effort fails. But he is not particularly disturbed, and the paragraph pivots, so to speak: "What was it—I paused to think—what was it that so unnerved me in the contemplation of the House of Usher?" (III, 273–74). *Think* here means something like "set up a chain of reasoning"—since the preceding perceptions have not arranged themselves into any sort of order—and it is in tension with *unnerved*, which the voice naturally stresses. "It was a mystery all insoluble; nor could I grapple with the shadowy fancies that crowded upon me as I pondered" (III, 274). The flat monotone smothers any concitation; whatever he might say, it is clear that he does not feel the experience as a mystery. And how much of the story is focused by that playing off of *grapple* (with its physical associations) and *fancies* (the word itself slightly dismissive)! Poe shows how the mind further smothers those "crowding fancies" by means of language which is highly abstract and undefining: "I was forced to fall back upon the unsatisfactory conclusion, that while, beyond doubt, there are combinations of very simple natural objects which have the power of thus affecting us, still the analysis of this power lies among considerations beyond our depth" (III, 274). How easily that is said! The undisturbed tone, his chief characteristic, continues to the end of the paragraph. But as the proleptic *mere* gives way to the experienced *shudder* after he looks into the tarn, we have the basic configuration outlined (and the ending adumbrated):

> It was possible, I reflected, that a mere different arrangement of the particulars of the scene, of the details of the picture, would be sufficient to modify, or perhaps to annihilate its capacity for sorrowful impressions; and, acting upon this idea, I reined my horse to the precipitous brink of a black and lurid tarn that lay in unruffled lustre by the dwelling, and gazed down—but with a shudder even more thrilling than before—upon the remodeled and inverted images of the gray sedge, and the ghastly tree-stems, and the vacant and eye-like windows. (III, 274)

The next paragraph begins with a casually thrown off "Nevertheless." Nothing is going to ruffle him, but it is clear that his apparent calm is not the expression of a firm inner poise. The rest of the tale develops this theme. The narrator's tone never changes no matter how hard he has to strain to account for phenomena, and this is the key to the tale as a whole. It indicates the strength of his need to domesticate the experience and keep up the illusion that everything is explicable within the general Newtonian framework. His untutored common-sense, lacking internal discipline, is unable to develop with the developing experience, and he has no other defense.

As the tale progresses, the narrator crosses the causeway, enters the house, goes deep within it to Usher's chamber, and finally—in the widely recognized analogy between House and head or brain—finds himself drawn into the recesses of Usher's mind: "It was no wonder that his condition terrified—that it infected me. I felt creeping upon me, by slow yet certain degrees, the wild influence of his own fantastic yet impressive superstitions" (III, 289–90). The *O.E.D.* gives "doorkeeper" for its first definition of *usher*, and Poe calls attention to the word in this sense: "The valet now threw open a door and ushered me into the presence of his master" (III, 277). This is a threshold world: having crossed the causeway the narrator leaves behind him the straight-forward world of common-sense; Usher opens the door on things undreamt of in the philosophies of, say, Benjamin Franklin and Ralph Waldo Emerson. The narrator's way of handling this unlooked for experience varies no more than his tone; the tone in fact is a function of a broader technique. From first to last he steadies himself by disclaimers, rational "explanations" of discordant phenomena, the cumulative effect of which is simply to undermine common-sense and authenticate the experienced actuality of the final, inexplicable event. They cluster around three moments: the opening when he is trying to stave off his uneasiness, the middle when Usher recites "The Haunted Palace," and the end when he desperately casts about for ways to deny that what is happening can be. It would not be convenient to quote them all and in full context, but perhaps a sampling from the first cluster will suggest their quality. Tone as always is important; sometimes it's only a matter of a strategic "but":

> There can be no doubt that the consciousness of the rapid increase of my superstition—for why should I not so term it? (III, 276)

> And it might have been for this reason only.... (III, 276)

> There grew in my mind a strange fancy—a fancy so ridiculous, indeed, that I but mention it to show the vivid force of sensations that oppressed me.... (III, 276)

> Shaking off from my spirit what *must* have been a dream. (III, 276)

And so on, right down to his assigning "the work of the rushing gust" (III, 296) for the final opening of the door by Madeline before she crosses the ultimate threshold. We notice, however, a progressive straining in these disclaimers, seen in the emphasis given to that last *must*, with its perceptible opening of doubt.

The tension he is under is nicely realized in the long paragraph that follows Usher's recitation of his poem:

> I well remember that suggestions arising from this ballad led us into a train of thought wherein there became manifest an opinion of Usher's *which I mention not so much on account of its novelty* (for other men have thought thus), *as an account of the pertinacity with which he maintained it*. This opinion, in its general form, was that of the sentience of all vegetable things. But in his disordered fancy, the idea had assumed a more daring character, and trespassed, under certain conditions, upon the kingdom of inorganization. I lack words to express the full extent, or the earnest abandon of his persuasion. The belief, however, was connected (as I have previously hinted) with the gray stones of the home of his forefathers. The conditions of the sentience had been here, he imagined, fulfilled, in the method of collocation of these stones—in the order of their arrangement, as well as in the many fungi which overspread them, and of the decayed trees which stood around—above all, in the long undisturbed endurance of this arrangement, and in its reduplication in the still waters of the tarn. Its evidence—the evidence of the sentience—was to be seen, he said (and here I started as he spoke), in the gradual yet certain condensation of an atmosphere of their own about the waters and the walls. The result was discoverable, he added, in that silent yet importunate and terrible influence which for centuries had moulded

> the destinies of his family, and which made him what I now saw him—what he was. *Such opinions need no comment, and I will make none.* (III, 286–87; my emphasis)

Within the paragraph a marked shift occurs. The first disclaimer is routinely made. By the end he has reached, for the only time in the tale, scorn. Why? Notice the way the third sentence from the end begins: "Its evidence—the evidence of the sentience—was to be seen, he said (and here I started as he spoke)…." The key here is the phrase inside the dashes, for it gives the effect of a mind suddenly growing alert to itself and realizing what is implied by that pronoun, the intimacy with Usher's beliefs that it insinuates. The effect is a delicate one, but it seems to indicate a sudden anxious rejection of a half-acceptance of what has been said in the previous sentence. The mind, braced now and solicitous to vindicate itself, impels him to "start" as Usher continues. The closing scorn is the self-conscious expression of the alerted and braced mind. But in the whole movement across the paragraph we have an indication of the strain under which he is operating. What we are seeing, in other words, is a variety of forms of resistance, but no growth.

As the story continues his grasp weakens. He loses any precise sense of calendar time and his disclaimers grow increasingly forced. Finally the last door is opened and common-sense is utterly routed. Madeline stands "without the door" (III, 296); when she crosses the threshold it is to bring death. Two possibilities lie open, death or flight, and, by instinct deeper than common-sense, he flies. Life is not defeated, but a certain way of regarding it most certainly is.[31]

Poe presents two aspects of the view of mind dominant in the American tradition, neither of them adequate. Real intelligence, we see, is a matter of sensibility and it has to be able to develop from within the new and unprecedented, not restrict itself to the already known and charted. The moral dimension of Poe's art is not always recognized, but it is there. He holds no animus against the common man clinging to his common-sense; he feels a certain sympathy for one whose tradition is so limited and, in the end, dangerous. But he does hold an animus against the theoretician of didactic rationalism whose arguments have determined what the common man has available to him, and who has wrongfully denied life in its depths. This moves in another direction, for such denial has important moral consequences. The American experience had given unprecedented scope to individual will: this could become unrestricted will-to-dominate when it disregarded life's moral complexity and was not controlled from below by a reverence for the mystery of the person.

V

The American tradition forced on Poe (as on Hawthorne and Melville) his great theme, the will-to-dominate, which is to say the will without any control operating from below and the ideal of the atomistic society forbidding rigorous control from outside. In Buber's familiar terms, the world of *It* displaced the world of *Thou*, manipulation prevailing over meeting and relationship. Poe emphasizes the cost. Other persons become looked upon not as beings to whom we are spiritually bound, but as mere objects in the external world, in short, as part of nature. The centrifugal impulse of society helped keep this obscure, but Poe seized on the hidden implications of this outlook and revealed them with prophetic insight. The will-to-dominate is, for Poe, always pathological and destructive no matter in what temperament it is expressed, and he is as quick to explore the consequences of Romantic will as of the rational didactic. The ironic structure and moral focus are turned on the narrators, romantic or rationalist, and the destructive possibilities of ideals too easily believed in are revealed.

"The Cask of Amontillado" presents a rationalist. It is a late work (1846), but it is for its clarity of development that one is tempted to call it the tale towards which all the others tended. Every word goes to characterize the narrator and at the same time to place him by moral standards of which he is insensible. The shaping irony lies in the fact that his rationalistic outlook is turned on events of a religious, indeed eschatological, nature. The time scheme and setting quietly enforce this. The affair with Fortunato lies fifty years in the past. Montresor was then on the bitter side of some disappointment, so he must be well into his eighties and near death as he relates his story to his Confessor ("You who so well know the nature of my soul," VI, 167). Against this situation

Poe rubs both Montresor's story and the attitude he takes in telling it. Like the Biblical fool, in his heart he does not fear God.

He is a man obsessed with his own cleverness. In his narrative he takes particular delight in this cleverness, but, unawares, reveals its terrifying human emptiness. The carnival "madness," for example, and Fortunato tricked out in motley initially emphasize, by contrast, his cool reason. And from the first we see him plume himself on his discipline. He is a connoisseur, and his study is himself: "It must be understood, that neither by word nor deed had I given Fortunato cause to doubt my good-will. I continued, as was my wont, to smile in his face, and he did not perceive that my smile *now* was at the thought of his immolation" (VI, 167). The narrator's view of human nature is of that type of reductive cynicism that usually goes by the name realist: "There were no attendants at home; they had absconded to make merry in honor of the time. I had told them that I should not return until the morning, and had given them explicit orders not to stir from the house. These orders were sufficient, I well knew, to insure their immediate disappearance, one and all, as soon as my back was turned" (VI, 167). He finds something exquisite in permitting Fortunato to insist that they go on to the vaults: "Putting on a mask of black silk, and drawing a *roquelaire* closely about me, I suffered him to hurry me to my palazzo" (VI, 169). He takes vulpine pleasure in his knowledge of what lies in wait:

> "Enough, he said, "the cough is a mere nothing; it will not kill me. I shall not die of a cough."
>
> "True-true," I replied. (VI, 170)

And his wit enables him to triumph even over the unexpected as when Fortunato gives him a sign from freemasonry and he pulls a trowel out from within his cloak. This sense of self is obdurate and proof against *any* appeal:

> "*For the love of God, Montresor!*"
>
> "Yes," I said, "for the love of God!" (VI, 175)

Against this, however, are two moments of inciting or prompting, their strength suggested by their being involuntary and physiological, life from out the depths protesting what the conscious mind is leading on to. These must be quelled and explained away, the grip of the rational mind reinstated. The first comes after the laying of the seventh tier. A period of silence has gone by and Montresor is curious about Fortunato's condition. He holds the torch above the opening and tries to see in: "A succession of loud and shrill screams, bursting suddenly from the throat of the chained form, seemed to thrust me violently back" (VI, 174). Though he has consciously desired this, something in him profoundly recoils: "For a brief moment I hesitated—I trembled. Unsheathing my rapier, I began to grope with it about the recess." This, I think, is a fine psychological detail. He is using the rapier to probe the dark, fearful interior; "grope" conveys just the right sense of loss of control: "but the thought of an instant reassured me. I placed my hand upon the solid fabric of the catacombs, and felt satisfied" (VI, 174). Here is the essence of his case. There is only the material world, the solid fabric, after all, safely there to the touch. He is restored.

The second comes in the final paragraph. No sound has succeeded his blasphemy about the love of God. Again he tries to get the torch to where he can still see in; he drops it through the tiny remaining hole and it hits the ground: "There came forth in return only a jingling of the bells" (VI, 175). A human being has been reduced beyond language to the uncoordinated twitchings of a nervous system: "My heart grew sick—." The inciting is clear, direct—and explained away: "on account of the dampness of the catacombs" (VI, 175). There is only the material world. Nothing else is real.

Montresor is characterized by his rationalistic outlook and haughty pride in himself. "Insult," we learn in the opening paragraph, he is far less able to bear than "injury." And it is a further point of this sense of honor that "the avenger" should "make himself felt as such to him who has done the wrong" (VI, 167). What he wants is a certain type of feeling, a feeling of domination. This is conveyed in the paragraph that precedes the fearful moment when he is forced to draw his rapier. Soon after beginning the wall he senses, with pleasure, that Fortunato's intoxication—a barrier keeping back full recognition of his plight—has worn off: "The earliest indication I had of this was a low moaning cry from the depth of the recess. It was *not* the cry of a drunken man. There was then a long and obstinate silence. I laid the second tier, and the third, and the fourth; and then I heard the furious vibrations of the chain. The noise lasted for several minutes, during which, that I might harken to it with more satisfaction, I ceased my labors and sat down upon the bones" (VI, 174). *Obstinate* is the key word. It indicates how badly Montresor wants to directly experience Fortunato's despair and take from that his *satisfaction*.

He is telling this is a last confession, and the irony is generated by the contrast between his rationalism pridefully centered on himself and the eschatological threshold he stands on. He does not feel contrition (without which there is no remission of sin) nor grasp the moral dimension of his story. For him its meaning is clear: he has had his vengeance, wreaked his will upon his enemy. The final sentence evokes his pride in his wit: "*In pace requiescat!*" (VI, 175). "May he rest in peace!" The phrase inverts an ancient liturgical formula (just as the opening sentence inverts a proverb); in doing so it completes Poe's meaning. The Latin Mass said in Poe's time ordinarily ended with the priest turning to the congregation and giving it his parting blessing, followed by the words, "*Ite missa est*"—"Go, the mass is ended." The only exception was the Mass for the Dead. In this there was no blessing; the priest simply turned and expressed the hope of the faithful: "*Requiescat in pace.*" Montresor's words are reflexive in their meaning, a point Poe underscores by inverting them. The ending co-operates in the placing of his moral obtuseness; it is he who has been dead in his humanity these fifty years.

Though there are still those who cherish the belief that "Ligeia" is about a woman who comes back from the dead through the agency of her will and another woman's body, the interpretation first developed by Roy P. Basler makes a response relevant to what Poe is offering. "Ligeia" shows "the power of frustrate love to create an erotic symbolism and mythology in compensation for sensual disappointment."[32] There is of course no Ligeia; she is wholly the creation of the narrator's fantasy, the product of an erotomania rooted, I would guess, in a habit of masturbation.[33] The account given by Joel Porte is more or less accurate, but his judgment—"The vitality of the world of dreams is the true underlying theme"—is quite wrong, if only by one word.[34] It is the power, not the vitality, of the world of dreams that is demonstrated, for the theme has to do with the way a diseased fantasy is the enemy of life. Like Montresor, the narrator here works his will upon another human being without any feeling for what he is doing; he is incapable of any living response to the individual and unique.

W. H. Auden has said somewhere that the tendency of the Romantic hero was to want to be God, and this story provides a case where the generalization applies. The story is quite simple and has a simple structure; there is a Ligeia-half and a Rowena-half. The first part is a fantasy; in the second part fantasy impinges on the real world with terrifying results. Poe uses the dark-heroine / light-heroine contrast and a marked shift in style to help establish the differences. The narrator, through Ligeia, experiences himself as worshipped ("idolatry" is a conspicuous word whenever his attention is directed towards her) in and through sexual passion. His response, in his throes, is to believe himself coming close to some ultimate knowledge, only to lose it. This knowledge is occasioned by Ligeia's eyes in moments of intense passion (Poe's pun could hardly be more pointed), and it is called a "sentiment" which he "feels." The key to the tale is the quote from Glanvill used as its epigraph. This is introduced by the narrator, not Ligeia, and he avers that it "never failed to inspire me with the sentiment": "'And the will therein lieth, which dieth not. Who knoweth the mysteries of the will with its vigor? For God is but a great will pervading all things by nature of its intentness. Man doth not yield himself to the angels, nor unto death utterly, save only through the weakness of his feeble will'" (II, 253). The will which operates is his, though he wants us to believe it is hers. If Ligeia, being all that she is, worships him, what must he be? And she will come back from the dead to go on worshipping him!

In the second half the narrator marries the real person, Lady Rowena Trevanion of Tremaine, probably thinking his sexual fantasies can be realized in the world of actual experience. The marriage chamber, at any rate, is arranged to that end:

> But in the draping of the apartment lay, alas! the chief phantasy of all.... The material was the richest cloth of gold. It was spotted all over, at irregular intervals, with arabesque figures, about a foot in diameter,

> and wrought upon the cloth in patterns of the most jetty black. But these figures partook of the true character of the arabesque only when regarded from a single point of view. By a contrivance now common, and indeed traceable to a very remote period of antiquity, they were made changeable in aspect. To one entering the room, they bore the appearance of simple monstrosities; but upon a farther advance, this appearance gradually departed; and step by step, as the visitor moved his station in the chamber, he saw himself surrounded by an endless succession of the ghastly forms which belong to the superstition of the Norman, or arise in the guilty slumbers of the monk. The phantasmagoric effect was vastly heightened by the artificial introduction of a strong continual current of wind behind the draperies—giving a hideous and uneasy animation to the whole. (II, 260–61)

What this seems to mean is that the draperies were decorated with figures that were lewd and which, by the air-current device, could be animated so as to become pornographic. Rowena recoils from her fate, but he finds a temporary pleasure in sexual cruelty: "That my wife dreaded the fierce moodiness of my temper—that she shunned me and loved me but little—I could not help perceiving; but it gave me rather pleasure than otherwise. I loathed her with a hatred belonging more to demon than to man" (II, 261). She experiences deep psychological anguish, while he finds himself reverting more and more to the fantast's world where the will meets no resistance. After a period she begins to decline physically—everything in this world is destructive of vitality—and he poisons her to hasten her along. His desire is to experience the climactic triumph of his fantasy. And so in the famous final paragraph he believes Ligeia is coming back through Rowena's corpse to continue her idolatry to him.

Poe's theme is a moral one: the triumph of fantasy is destructive of actual living with its demands. Rowena is not met with in the world of relationship; she is used by the narrator for his enjoyment in the world of *It*. Like Montresor, he is an imperious, autonomous self for whom others are atomistic objects to be manipulated. For them the will is neither disciplined by a sense of complexity nor controlled from below by a feeling for the mystery of the person. In each case this has consequences for the body. Speaking of "the Romantic retreat from the physical," John Fraser has noted that "the body has been suspect much of the time in American literature, perhaps because it is the body that most ineluctably sets limits to individual human ambitions."[35] These narrators, caught in the grip of a will-to-dominate, recognize no such limits while yet insisting on their own virtue. That situation mirrors in its way what has sometimes been called the irony of American history.

VI

Poe is a great writer and his tales richly repay a careful attention to their artistic detail and a careful consideration of his ideas and outlook. That outlook, governing his criticism of the autonomous individual, is rooted in his underlying Christianity and derives its form and energy from that tradition of thought. *Brotherhood—caritas*—peeks out in "Amontillado" but the whole subject is too large and weighty to be opened here. Any decent consideration of its several dimensions would have to bring in "The Black Cat" and "The Imp of the Perverse," at least, together with Poe's understanding and use of the Natural Law. Regardless, Poe's tales explore, as fiction can, the moral consequences of those ideals and values and consequent habits of thought and feeling that were regnant in the emerging American tradition. His achievement was to reveal, however obliquely, the human consequences of those habits and their assumptions, to cut through the fogbank of rationalized optimism and insist on their dark potential, to celebrate Friendship, Responsibility, and Brotherhood by showing their opposites. Unlike Cooper, Hawthorne, and Melville, he was not disposed to celebrate directly much in the American experience, and his work is almost wholly negative in expression and impact. Nevertheless, he was the great inaugurator. The thematic veins Poe's fiction opened were to yield the richest ore: *The Deerslayer; The Scarlet Letter; Moby-Dick, Bartleby; Huckleberry Finn; The Red Badge of Courage; The Great Gatsby; As I Lay Dying; Catch-22*—that is the great central tradition of American fiction. There is a sense in which American society defeated Poe. But not before he had taken its measure.

Notes to Poe and Tradition

1. "Edgar Allan Poe," *Literary History of the United States: History*, eds. Robert E. Spiller et al., 3rd ed. (New York: Macmillan, 1963), p. 342.
2. T. S. Eliot, "From Poe to Valery," *To Criticize the Critic and Other Writings* (New York: Farrar, Straus, 1965), pp. 35–36.
3. Eliot, p. 54. Cf.: "There can be few authors of such eminence who have drawn so little from their own roots, who have been so isolated from any surroundings," p. 29; Matthiessen, p. 341.
4. Edward Davidson, *Poe: A Critical Study* (Cambridge: Harvard University Press: The Belknap Press, 1966), p. vi.
5. "New Notes on Edgar Poe," *Baudelaire on Poe*, trans. Lois and Francis E. Hyslop, Jr. (State College, PA: Bald Eagle Press, 1952), p. 123.
6. Killis Campbell, *The Mind of Poe and Other Studies* (Cambridge: Harvard University Press, 1933), pp. 22, 119, 118.
7. Campbell, p. 25.
8. Campbell, p. 25.
9. Henry Bamford Parkes, *The American Experience* (New York: Vintage Books, 1959), p. 204.
10. *The United States of America: A History*, 3rd ed. (New York: Knopf, 1968), p. 287. The second edition was 1959.
11. Eliot, *To Criticize the Critic*, p. 55. More fecund than Campbell's was the work of Perry Miller. In *The Raven and the Whale: The War of Words and Wits in the Era of Poe and Melville* (New York: Harcourt, Brace, 1956) Miller showed how thoroughly Poe was immersed in the journalistic sub-culture of his day and that this helped to define his achievement. After Miller came a line of works including books by Edd Winfield Parks and Stanley P. Moss and culminating in the work of Robert D. Jacobs, all focusing on what Poe actually accomplished in his journalism and criticism. If it is true that this work concentrates on Poe's minor side, it has by virtue of that enabled us to see that this *is* the minor side, and it has cleared the ground for discussion of the tales and verse. Parks, *Edgar Allan Poe as Literary Critic* (Athens: University of Georgia Press, 1964); Moss, *Poe's Literary Battles: The Critic in the Context of His Literary Milieu* (Durham, NC: Duke University Press, 1963); Jacobs, *Poe: Journalist and Critic* (Baton Rouge: Louisiana State University Press, 1970).
12. Herbert Marshall McLuhan, "Edgar Poe's Tradition," *Sewanee Review*, 52 (1944), pp. 24–33.
13. L. C. Knights, *Drama and Society in the Age of Jonson* (London: Chatto and Windus, 1937), p. 177.
14. John William Ward, "Individualism: Ideology or Utopia?" *Hastings Center Studies*, 2 (September 1974), p. 13.
15. Ward, "Individualism," p. 12. I have transposed the names for emphasis.
16. Campbell, *The Mind of Poe*, p. 101.
17. Edgar Allan Poe, *The Complete Works of Edgar Allan Poe*, ed. James A. Harrison, 17 vols. (New York, 1902; rpt. New York: AMS Press, 1965), VII, 87. All quotations from Poe will be taken from this edition and will be incorporated into the text. The texts of the poetry cited agree with T. O. Mabbott's edition: *Collected Works of Edgar Allan Poe*, I (Cambridge: Harvard University Press, The Belknap Press, 1969).

18. "Its rhythm never lives for a moment, never once moves with an emotional life." William Butler Yeats, "Letter to W. T. Horton," *The Recognition of Edgar Allan Poe*, ed. Eric W. Carlson (Ann Arbor: University of Michigan Press, 1966), p. 43.
19. James Gargano, "The Question of Poe's Narrators," *College English*, 25 (December 1963), p. 178.
20. See Donald Barlow Stauffer, "Style and Meaning in 'Ligeia' and 'William Wilson,'" *Studies in Short Fiction*, 2 (1965), pp. 316–30.
21. George Hochfield, "An Introduction to Transcendentalism," *American Transcendentalism: An Anthology of Criticism*, ed. Brian M. Barbour (Notre Dame: University of Notre Dame Press, 1973), pp. 37–38.
22. Basil Willey, *Samuel Taylor Coleridge* (New York: Norton, 1973), p. 50.
23. During the explanation Dupin says, "What is true of *relation*—of form and quantity—is often grossly false in regard to morals, for example. In this latter science it is very usually *untrue* that the aggregated parts are equal to the whole." Poe is pointedly rejecting basic Transcendental doctrine. In *Nature* Emerson had averred, "The laws of moral nature answer to those of matter as face to face in a glass.... The axioms of physics translate the laws of ethics. Thus, 'the whole is greater than its part.'"
24. Thus in one paragraph Dupin uses these verbs: considered, reflected, regarded, felt, reflected, saw.
25. Earl Leslie Griggs, ed., *Collected Letters of Samuel Taylor Coleridge* (Oxford: The Clarendon Press, 1956), II, p. 709.
26. In his famous message establishing the spoils system, President Jackson declared that, "The duties of all public offices are, or at least admit of being made, so plain and simple that men of intelligence may readily qualify themselves for their performance." Quoted in Richard Hofstadter *Anti-Intellectualism in American Life* (New York: Knopf, 1963), p. 170. By intelligence Jackson meant a natural quality of the many as opposed to the training of the few.
27. John William Ward, *Andrew Jackson: Symbol for an Age* (New York: Oxford University Press, 1955), p. 48.
28. Lionel Trilling, *The Liberal Imagination* (New York: Anchor Books, 1953), p. xii.
29. In Charles R. Anderson et al., *American Literary Masters*, 2 vols. (New York: Holt, Rinehart, 1965), I, p. 17.
30. Darrell Abel, "A Key to the House of Usher," *University of Toronto Quarterly*, 18 (January 1949), p. 177.
31. The inevitable question, Is Madeline there or not? doesn't really matter. She is there for him. What does matter is that untutored common-sense has proven inadequate to what experience held in store.
32. Roy P. Basler, "The Interpretation of 'Ligeia,'" *Poe: A Collection of Critical Essays*, ed. Robert Regan (Englewood Cliffs, NJ: Prentice-Hall, 1967), p. 51.
33. See D. H. Lawrence, "Pornography and Obscenity," *Phoenix* (London, 1936; rpt. New York: Viking, 1972), pp. 170–87; esp. pp. 179–80.
34. Joel Porte, *The Romance in America* (Middletown, CT: Wesleyan University Press, 1969), p. 69.
35. John Fraser, *Violence in the Arts* (Cambridge, England: Cambridge University Press, 1974), pp. 68–69.

FLAUBERT AND THE SIN AGAINST THE HOLY GHOST

Rodney Delasanta

Hope is the thing with feathers, Emily Dickinson wrote. Had she composed a longer poem or lived a longer life, would she have come to agree with Gerard Manley Hopkins, in "God's Grandeur," that "the Holy Ghost over the bent / World broods with warm breast and with ah! bright wings"? Or would she have concurred with Flaubert, in *Un Coeur Simple*, that the Holy Ghost is really a stuffed parrot to whom simpletons, like his mockingly named heroine, Félicité, pray in their lunacy? From a poet who could lament in her last years that God's right hand "is amputated now / And God cannot be found," one cannot dismiss the latter likelihood.

Despair we have always had with us. Jesus warned against it in Luke's mysterious passage: "And whosoever shall speak a word against the Son of Man, it shall be forgiven him, but unto him that blasphemeth against the Holy Ghost it shall not be forgiven" (12:10). St. Benedict sought to deflect it from the prayer life of his monks by enjoining them, in the seventy-second (and final) precept of his *Rule*, "never to despair of the mercy of God." And when St. Thomas Aquinas distinguished between presumption (the sin against hope by excess) and despair (the sin against hope by defect), he tagged only the latter as unforgivable.

Rarely in the history of Western literature—until the mid-nineteenth century, that is—has the virtue of hope been sinned against in any final and irretrievable way. This or that devastated character falling into despair, yes, like Lear on the heath, railing at the storm when turned out of doors by his daughters, or Gulliver preferring to sleep with his horses when returned to his Yahoo family; but in each case the despairer is an aberrant measured against exemplars of hope: Cordelia and Kent in the former, and Captain Pedro de Mendez, the spurned Good Samaritan of Gulliver's fourth voyage, in the latter. Even Ishmael, in Melville's darkest novel, is saved from the vortex of the doomed *Pequod* by Queequeg's coffin and by the whaler *Rachel* in "search after her missing children." How distressing to realize, then, that a deliberate and irrevocable violation of hope should have constituted the clear intention of the premier practitioner of the realistic novel, Gustave Flaubert (1821–1880).

By Flaubert's time, of course, hope, coming after faith and before charity in the lineup of the three theological virtues, had undergone serious secular transformation. Certainly the Enlightenment had severed it from all eschatological promise; the provenance of hope to a Deist like Benjamin Franklin extended largely to the *civitas terrenis,* his kite and key the heavenly host, his street-swept Philadelphia the New Jerusalem. Later, the Romantics had tried to find hope in the countryside, but they presumed in the beneficence of Nature and in the innocence of the self. *Pace* Wordsworth, could any impulse from a vernal wood *really* teach "more of man, / Of moral evil and of good" than all the sages? And could anyone have been vain enough to obey the Emersonian injunction to "obey thyself," expecting thereby to touch the hem of the Transcendent? Flaubert thought not and said so with withering satire in *Madame Bovary,* his masterpiece.

For those who suspect that the catastrophes emanating from the Enlightenment have, over the slow pace of history, outdistanced its achievements, Flaubert's censure of the movement, via his mashing of the pharmacist Homais, seems just. Appropriately named, Homais is *man*—man alone—supremely confident in his own accomplishments and scornful of those superstitions, like primal falls and redemptions, that would compromise his newfound stature. Pompously self-reliant, he would cure the ills of the world by empirical fiat. It is from his apothecary's shop that the miracles of science issue and from his Comtean sagacity that uninvited dollops of the new morality are apportioned. His letters to the editor in the *Fanal de Rouen* dogmatize upon every conceivable subject: "There was no longer a dog run over, a barn burnt down, a woman beaten in the parish, of which he did not immediately inform the public, guided always by the love of progress and the hate of priests." He has named his sons Franklin and Napoleon. His poison helps to undo Emma Bovary long before she literally partakes of it from his laboratory, mockingly called Cafarnaum. He will outlast three doctors after Charles Bovary, "so effectively did he hasten to eradicate them." And for all this he will earn, as reward for his appalling career, the cross of the Legion of Honor. Hatred was the great spur to Flaubert's genius, and it is for the "enlightened" Homais that Flaubert reserves his singular contempt. Abandon all hope, ye who have presumptuously entered there.

Abandon all hope, also, ye who have succumbed to the siren call of Romanticism. By his own admission, Flaubert was in his youth addicted to the "disease" of Romanticism, and he wrote *Madame Bovary* as an act of self-exorcism. (He was supposed to have said, "Madame Bovary, c'est moi.") In the 1840s he wrote in a letter to his mistress, Louise Colet: "I am bored with great passions, exalted feelings, wild love affairs.... I prize common sense above everything else, perhaps because I so lack it." In another letter in which he complained about the sentimentality of Romanticism, he wrote: "I refuse to consider Art a drain pipe for passion.... No, no! Genuine poetry is not the scum of the heart," a metaphor that seems to mock Wordsworth's famous definition of poetry as "the spontaneous overflow of powerful feelings." In its place, Flaubert sought, in his own words, "to render ignoble reality artistically." The "ignoble reality" he tried to render was the hollow and sordid society of his time, half of which he thought was sick with romantic self-indulgence (the inanity of the French nation returning another Napoleon to a recreated emperor's throne in 1852 is a case in point) and the other half with bourgeois acquisitiveness. Emma Bovary is the most pitiful victim of the illusions of Romanticism, and of acquisitiveness (although Frederic Moreau of *A Sentimental Education* would come in a close second), and the tragedy that issues from those illusions—perhaps pathos would be a better word—is the subject of Flaubert's great novel.

First among the Romantic "Virtues" that Flaubert dissolves with his acidic realism, is *feeling*, Romanticism's vaunted mode of penetrating into the heart of reality: "I felt before I thought" was Rousseau's anti-Cartesian manifesto from his *Confessions*, just as in "Tintern Abbey" Wordsworth exalted the role of feeling into mystical intuition. In Emma Bovary, Flaubert diagnoses feeling not as the salubrious power that Rousseau and Wordsworth extolled, but as a neurosis. Later in the novel, Emma's feeling degenerates into psychosis and arsenic-induced suicide.

Nature too was high on the list of Romantic ideals. Wordsworth might claim her as "the anchor of [his] purest thoughts, the nurse, / The guide, the guardian of [his] heart, and soul / Of all [his] moral being"; but Flaubert, writing his novel shortly after Wordsworth's death, could see in the landscape of his native Normandy only "a mongrel land...without accent or character." Sainte-Beuve, the great critic of French literature, said that Flaubert saw in the rural countryside only "pettiness, poverty, conceit, stupidity, routine, monotony, and boredom," a far cry from the quasi-pantheistic celebration of nature in "Tintern Abbey" or in Thoreau's *Walden*.

Sincerity was another Romantic "good," much praised by its greatest writers. But Flaubert in *Madame Bovary* is utterly scornful of its vaunted efficacy. He memorably belittles the sincerity of romantic love in the description of the agricultural fair when Rodolphe's protestations of love to Emma intermingle with the announcements of prizes for the best manure and the best hogs. No less contemptuous of Romantic sincerity is Flaubert's rendering of the scene, in the last moments of their affair, in which a love-weary Rodolphe squirts a few drops of water on his goodbye letter to Emma in order to simulate tears. Like the Romantics who died young with decidedly *outré* ideas about sex—Byron and Shelley in particular come to mind—Flaubert in his youth could lyricize about "the most beautiful of human words—adultery, [which is] vaguely enveloped with an exquisite sweetness." But by the time he wrote his masterpiece that "exquisite sweetness" had soured into disgust. Emma's tawdry adultery in the bumpy back seat of a hackney cab, with curtains drawn, making the rounds of Rouen in the middle of the day, was not what the Romantics had in mind.

If Flaubert could so vivisect Enlightenment and Romantic hope, he was even more pitiless in anatomizing the species of hope traditional to Christianity. Admittedly, he seemed to prefer the peasant virtues of the abbé Bournisien, who is not above laboring in the fields with his parishioners, to the intellectual posturing of Homais. However, when it comes time for the priest to offer the balm of Christian hope to a frantic Emma, totally disillusioned with her marriage to Charles, he too fails. Stirred to momentary piety by the Angelus, Emma seeks out consolation from Bournisien, who is about to teach the catechism to a group of recalcitrant boys. To Emma's complaint that "she is suffering," the priest can only respond with a tired formula from St. Paul which says that we are all born to suffer. Incapable of imagining any suffering in Emma beyond the gynecological, he wonders why her doctor husband hasn't prescribed an appropriate medicine.

Meanwhile, the unruly boys wailing for the lessons to begin get more of the priest's attention, and he deflects Emma's signals of despair: "I've known housewives who didn't even have bread to eat," he says. To Emma's rejoinder that "there are women who have bread but no...," Bournisien interrupts by obtusely finishing her sentence with "fire in the winter." Further spiritual sparring yields no relief; the scene ends with the priest excusing himself in order to return to the catechism and Emma departing with the voices of Bournisien and his charges fruitlessly, mockingly, echoing in her ears: "Are you a Christian?" "Yes, I am a Christian." "What is a Christian?" "Me who, being baptized...baptized...baptized...." From such a ham-fisted sower of Christian seed, even the good ground would have sprouted thorns. What eventually follows is Emma's first adultery with Rodolphe.

Later in the novel, the assignation that Emma arranges with Léon in the Rouen Cathedral presents Flaubert with still another opportunity to disenfranchise Christian hope. For Léon, the cathedral's six centuries of architectural and iconic witness to the glories of Christianity serve only to frame Emma in a "a huge boudoir, the arches bending down to shelter in their darkness the avowal of her love." The intrusion of the verger, who stupidly assumes that the couple are tourists ripe for his packaged kerygma, briefly frustrates Léon's amorous strategies and briefly compromises Emma's initial resolve not to yield to them. The lovers' escape from his pedantic badgering is not made, however, without the verger's ludicrous, but ominous, insistence that on their way out they at least notice the sculptures of the Resurrection, the Last Judgment, Paradise, King David, and the damned consigned to the flames. For an aroused Léon and Emma, this is hardly the moment to dread the loss of heaven and the pains of hell; the couple flee Notre Dame de Rouen—the church of the Virgin, with its futile panoply of holy goads to virtue—and hail a hackney cab that will presently serve as their mobile cloister.

If Flaubert had ever read Alexander Pope's line that "hope springs eternal in the human breast," he summoned up all his narrative genius—in his description of Emma's death, wake, and funeral—to excise any remnant of it from *Madame Bovary*. The manner of her death is well known. In despair over her lovers' abandonment and hopelessly in debt, she commits suicide by devouring arsenic filched from Homais' Cafarnaum. At the vigil of her funeral, three characters, who represent the competing *weltanschauung* in Flaubert's day (as the Karamazov brothers do in Dostoevsky's), engage in competition for the last word. Chief among them is Emma herself, around whom, even in death, the Romantic aura lingers. Despite early signs of putrefaction, the grief-stricken Charles can still gaze at her veiled form on the deathbed and romantically venerate "the watered satin of her gown shimmering white as moonlight.... It seemed to him that, spreading beyond her own self, she blended confusedly with everything around her—the silence, the night, the passing wind, the damp odors rising from the ground."

But when, desperate to blend once more with her himself, Charles performs the ultimate romantic act of lifting her veil, "He uttered a cry of horror that awoke the other two." The other two are Homais and Bournisien, who have spent most of the vigil in fruitless polemic. Voltaire, d'Holbach, the *Encyclopédie*, priestly celibacy; confession, the Jesuits—all become topics of wrangling between them. Yet the most telling moment comes wordlessly when, after "time and again falling asleep—something of which they accused each other whenever they awoke—Monsieur Bournisien sprinkled the room with holy water and Homais threw a little chlorine on the floor." Here, dark realism surrenders to even darker symbolism, for Flaubert renders the hopelessness of the human condition by an opaque epiphany: against the irrevocability of death neither Romantic dreams nor the pitiful talismans of religion and science can hold sway.

This may well be narrative art at its dazzling best, but the discomfited reader hesitates all the same to concede Flaubert his carrion-comfort despair. Some critics have read *Madame Bovary* as a moral, even didactic, novel because it demolishes the sordidness of a corrupt civilization. Yet because Flaubert's brilliant diagnosis of his sick society is unaccompanied by even the most modest prognosis for amelioration ("Ah, love, let us be true to one another," Matthew

Arnold could plead in *his* moment of contemporary despair), it has also been read as an artful exercise in nihilism. For Flaubert closes his great opus, in the words of one critic, with neither a bang nor a whimper, but with a snarl. What he tells us is not only that the vicious prosper while the innocent suffer—no surprise there—but also that this Manichean rule brooks no exceptions. The meek clearly do not inherit Flaubert's scorched earth.

We know, of course, that Flaubert defended his art by appealing to its strict objectivity: "Nowhere in my book," he wrote, "must the author express his emotions or his opinions." Rather, he must remain detached and utterly impersonal, telling things as they really are and not as tender feelings would prefer them to be. But do his fictional chronicles of Toste and Yonville and Rouen in the 1840s tell things the way they *really* were? Flaubert's brilliant but self-serving line, now become a cliché, was that at this very hour his poor Bovary was suffering and weeping in twenty villages across France—to which the rejoinder might well be: Why does misery alone enjoy this privilege of universality? Should not its antinomies ask for equal time? Another village or two, somewhere, with a faithful Emma, a clever Charles, and an understanding curé? When reading Flaubert, should we not remind ourselves that at the other end of France, a year after the publication of *Madame Bovary,* Marie Bernarde Soubirous saw her astonishing visions at Lourdes? Did Flaubert, notwithstanding his genius, deliberately withhold some truths about the human condition?

Indeed, at those rare moments in the novel when Flaubert seems to relent and to crack open, ever so slightly, a Dutch door to hope, he quickly closes it again. Justin, Homais' adolescent helper who loves Emma from afar and whom she tricks into gaining access to the arsenic, is usually adduced as the best example of Flaubert's compassion. Yet his narrative carefully restricts Justin's love from connecting to anyone; it remains encaged, like the fenced unicorn. Only once is it noticed and even then it is cynically misunderstood: the grave digger Lestibudois, who secretly plants potatoes among his burial plots, spots Justin scaling the cemetery wall the night after Emma's funeral and decides that he has found the thief who has been stealing from his crop. Flaubert's mashing of the greedy grave digger in this scene trumps his compassion for the boy, whose love is sacrificed to the more compelling cause of high dudgeon.

One is moved to wonder: could not the author have sheathed his ironies this once and allowed Lestibudois to peek at Justin weeping over Emma's grave an instant *before* he scaled the wall? Similarly, after Charles dies and the remnant of his property is sold, was it not overkill to set the escrow at twelve francs, seventy-five centimes so as to guarantee that the impoverished orphaned daughter, Berthe, would be sent to work in a cotton mill? And how deeply would Flaubert's ironies have been compromised had he found a less wounding name than *Hippolyte* for the limping innocent who, through others' ambitions, suffered the amputation even of his clubfoot? Was it not gratuitously cruel to attach the name *Félicité* to the unhappy maid both of this novel and of *Un Coeur Simple*? Did narrative compulsion require that Charles' first wife, the widow Dubuc, "ugly, as dry as a bone, her face with as many pimples as the spring has buds," be named *Heloise*?

In an early short story, *Pigeon Feathers*, John Updike describes the adolescent fears of an innocent named David, who is precociously troubled by the inevitability and finality of death. At Lutheran catechism class, which he had valued as a Christian buffer to his dark thoughts, David is upset by his teacher, a young liberal pastor, who finesses the meaning of the Resurrection so as to deny its literal reality. He is further upset by his mother, who after admitting that she, too, in so many circumspect words, denied the Resurrection, casually asks him to take his new .22 rifle and rid the barn of pigeons that have rooked there. David reluctantly obeys his mother and shoots six pigeons, only dimly aware that by this act he too is somehow complicit in that killing of hope, the thing with feathers. It is a Flaubertian moment.

The story could have ended with this objective correlative unamended, and it would have if Flaubert had written it, but Updike—inspired perhaps by more orthodox Lutheran catechetics—recovers from this blasphemy against the Holy Ghost by allowing David the epiphany of examining one of the fallen birds before burying it: "He had never seen a bird this close before. The feathers were more wonderful than dog's hair, for each filament was shaped within the shape of the feather, and the feathers in turn were trimmed to fit a pattern that flowed without error across the bird's body.... And across the surface of the infinitely adjusted yet somehow effortless mechanics of the feathers played idle designs of color, no two alike—designs executed, it seemed, in a controlled rapture, with a joy that hung level in the air above and behind him."

Flaubert was incapable of such recovery. Four years before his death, and twenty after writing *Madame Bovary,* in ill health and beset by financial problems, he wrote *Un Coeur Simple*, a story in which he retrieved the name *Félicité* from his earlier novel and permitted himself a second chance to display his scorn. The story is a masterpiece, unquestionably, but Flaubert's scorched-earth strategies continue unabated. A simple-minded maid to Mme. Aubain, Félicité suffers a string of crushing losses throughout her life: an unfaithful lover, the death of her beloved sailor nephew, the death of her beloved young charge, Virginie, the onset of total deafness, the death of her beloved mistress, and—grotesquely climactic—the death of her beloved parrot. To cling to any vestige of hope, she has the bird stuffed and installs it on her shelf: "She enveloped him with a look of anguish when she was imploring the Holy Ghost and formed the idolatrous habit of kneeling in front of the parrot to say her prayers. Sometimes the sun shone in at the attic window and caught his glass eye, and a great luminous ray shot out of it and put her in an ecstasy."

Cruelty triumphs over compassion in this rendering of St. Teresa *manquée*. The story could only have been conceived and executed by a man who could write about himself thus: "I lead a bitter life, devoid of all external joy and in which I have nothing to keep me going but a sort of permanent rage, which weeps at times from impotence, but which is constant." The only relief Flaubert testified to was his art, his personal stay against confusion, but because he required it to bear the burden of his permanent rage it is variously antipathetic, unforgiving, vindictive, even vengeful against those who, like Félicité, would presume to hope. No less a critic than Jean-Paul Sartre called Flaubert's realism *spiteful*, and I am inclined to agree with an author who knew enough of spite—and of hopelessness. Sartre would never have phrased it thus, of course, but his is another way of saying that, materially if not formally, Flaubert sinned against the Holy Ghost.

In the last moments of *Un Coeur Simple*, that blasphemy crests. Félicité lies near death in the room above the courtyard where the Corpus Christi festival is being celebrated. The priest places the gold monstrance, containing the consecrated host, on the altar while the censers are "gliding to and fro on the full swing of their chains."

> An azure vapor rose up into Félicité's room. Her nostrils met it; she inhaled it sensuously, mystically, and then closed her eyes. Her lips smiled. The beats of her heart lessened one by one, vaguer each time and softer, as a fountain sinks, an echo disappears; and when she sighed her last breath she thought she saw an opening in the heavens, and a gigantic parrot hovering above her head.

One does not often encounter so exquisite an expression of unpitying contempt.

RESPONSIVE FORM: DOSTOYEVSKY'S NOTES FROM UNDERGROUND AND THE CONFESSIONAL TRADITION

René Fortin

Virtually no one would question the fact that Dostoyevsky in his *Notes from Underground* fulfilled his overt intention: to excoriate a Russian society whoring after the strange gods of modernity. Many critics have served us well in identifying for the uninitiated reader the various targets of Dostoyevsky's thrusts: Buckle, Bentham, Mill, Chernyshevsky, Dobrolyubov, Schiller, and others.[1] But exposing this rich historical context, while contributing to one's understanding of the work, does not account for the singular power and complexity of the novel. For this one must look to the confessional tradition, which we associate primarily with St. Augustine and Jean-Jacques Rousseau. The confession assumes in Augustine's hands a form that is responsive to his own myth of selfhood; form and substance are closely articulated. But when the Augustinian confession is used as a vehicle for Rousseau's confessions, it undergoes, in response to Rousseau's different myth of selfhood, a radical transformation; beginning with utterly different premises about the nature of man and of his relationship with God, Rousseau overturns many of the conventions of the genre, creating in fact what is virtually a new form within the same generic tradition.

Dostoyevsky's work, then, can be described as a synthesis of two antithetical literary forms within the same generic tradition; by harnessing the dialectical energies of these two mighty opposites Dostoyevsky creates a hybrid form of immense power and manages incidentally to create the prototype of an important modern genre, the confessional novel.[2]

With this confessional genre as context, it is possible to identify more precisely the narrator of the *Notes from Underground:* he is a composite of

Rousseau and Augustine, a Rousseauvian narrator struggling mightily to escape from the trap of Rousseauvian form—with its implicit values—and to gain the high ground of the Augustinian confession that would make him whole.

I

The Confessions of St. Augustine is, like *The Iliad*, so great a work that it at once creates and culminates a genre; it is the work by which all subsequent confessions are to be measured. Much of its greatness, to be sure, derives from the quality of the mind of the author and from the singular strength of his personality. But *The Confessions* is also a great work because it definitively stipulates the form of a confessional work. The confession which emerges from Augustine embodies formal elements which will henceforth characterize the genre: first, the problematic nature of the narratorial "I," who is present in the work as at once exploring subject and explored object, at once literary creator and literary creation; secondly, the narrator's intricate relationship with his audience, the readers whom he needs to fulfill the design of the confession.[3] Thus, beyond the obvious and inescapable question of what is being confessed, this most rhetorical of all genres requires us to consider carefully *how* the confession is offered, *why* it is offered, and *to whom* it is offered.

The matter of Augustine's confession is familiar indeed; one sees everywhere in *The Confessions* the soul of a man convinced of his sinfulness, of his utter unworthiness before God. We hear of the episode of the stolen fruit—perhaps the most widely misunderstood of Augustine's confidences—of his bondage to lust, of his engrossment in the pleasures of the secular theater, and, even, after his conversion, his shame over his intemperate grief at the death of his mother. Augustine conceals neither his sinfulness nor the pain that the act of confession is causing him: "Who can untie this most twisted and intricate mass of knots? It is a filthy thing! I do not wish to think about it; I do not wish to look upon it" (75).[4]

The Confessions, however, is more than a recital of failings, for Augustine finds in retrospect the guiding hand of God directing him at every turn through sin and blindness to his ultimate conversion, the moment of illumination in the garden where he receives the mysterious injunction to "Take up and read" the Bible. After reading a passage from St. Paul, Augustine is renewed: "Instantly, in truth, at the end of this sentence, as if before a peaceful light streaming into my heart, all the dark shadows of doubt fled away" (202). *The Confessions*, then, depicts moments of glory as well as moments of shame; the work is perhaps best described, as John K. Ryan has suggested, as a three-fold confession: "a confession of sins, a confession of faith, and a confession of praise."[5]

The complex nature of the confession mandates a multiple audience, which is itself three-fold. The rhetorical form of the work is that of a monologue addressed to God as interlocutor, at once the primary hearer of the confession, and, it should be noted, a partner in the creative act. In a curious circularity God is the hearer of a confession of which he is the ultimate source; it is Augustine who searches for self, but God who "finds": "That...which I know about myself I know because you enlighten me" (233). This first audience is crucial, but Augustine is also mindful of two other audiences, for it is clear that the confession is intended to be heard by both the writer himself, and the eventual reader of the work. Augustine's awareness that he is addressing several audiences is evident in the following passage: "To whom do I tell these things? Not to you, my God, but before you I tell them to my own kind, to mankind, and to whatever small part of it may come upon these books of mine. Why do I tell these things? It is that I myself and whoever else reads them may realize from what great depths we must cry unto you. And what is closer to your ears than a contrite heart and a life of faith?" (67).

Augustine, with his keen sense of paradox, recognizes the incongruity of revealing himself to an omniscient Being who, after all, knows Augustine better that he himself does. Clearly, Augustine's intent with regard to his first reader is not revelation. Rather, the confession issuing from the "contrite heart" is a plea for forgiveness, a song in celebration of the saving graces of God, and a stimulus to deepen his own love for God. Augustine reminds us elsewhere of these motives: "Let my soul praise you, so that it may love you, and let it confess your mercies before you, so that it may praise you" (113). "I confess to you, O Lord of heaven and earth, and I utter praise to you for my first being and infancy, which I do not remember" (48).

As the previous citations indicate, Augustine's second audience, in terms of importance, is himself. In this inclusion of himself as hearer of his own confession, Augustine highlights a crucial feature of the confessional genre, the bifurcation of the narrator's consciousness: the narrator, the "I" of the present, who is at once both speaker and hearer of the confession, is necessarily distanced from the "I" of the past, the character he is depicting. He views this character as an object, an "other" who must be objectively observed and dispassionately judged.[6] The narrator measures the benighted wanderer from the privileged position of one who is now enlightened, the "new man" Augustine has become through his conversion experience sitting in judgment upon the "old man" still in the bondage of sin.

Augustine's purpose, however, is not only to deplore his past sins and exult in his redemption; his painstaking re-creation of his former self is an attempt to gain self-knowledge, to come to grips with the mystery of evil and with the mystery that man is to himself: "Who am I, and what am I? Is there any evil that is not found in my acts, or if not in my acts, in my words, or if not in my words, in my will?" (205). "But do you, O Lord my God, graciously hear me, and turn your gaze upon me, and see me, and have mercy upon me, and heal me. For in your sight I have become a riddle to myself, and that is my infirmity" (262).

It is of major significance that Augustine continues to voice his anxieties about lacking self-knowledge even after his conversion, for Augustine, while he is aware that he has been to some extent enlightened by God, is equally aware of his perduring ignorance: "As to that which I am ignorant of concerning myself, I remain ignorant of it until 'my darkness shall be made as the noonday in your sight'" (233). The distance between the "I" as subject and the "I" as object is never fully closed in *The Confessions,* for the true confession will end only when the two "I's" will converge in an act of perfect self-knowledge—and this, Augustine knows, is beyond man's capability in this life.[7] In a sense the dynamic nature of the self compels man, having once begun to confess, to continue confessing until his death.

Augustine's third audience, his reader, is the least conspicuous of the three; in fact, Augustine addresses this audience only obliquely, as if they are eavesdroppers upon his colloquy with God. At times, however, Augustine addresses his audience more directly, even while maintaining the rhetorical form of a monologue with God. For example, after confessing the theft of the fruit, he cautions his readers against self-righteousness: "Let him not laugh to scorn a sick man who has been healed by that same physician who gave him such aid that he did not fall ill, or rather that he had only a lesser ill" (74). Why, Augustine wonders at one point, should a human audience be party to his confession: "What have I to do with men, that they should hear my confessions, as if they were to heal all my diseases?' ... Do you, my inmost physician, make clear to me with what profit I do these things" (230). Augustine does not need the absolution of the reader, for only his "inmost physician" is capable of that healing. But he does see his human audience as necessary in order that they might hear his proclamation of God's glory and, if they are unbelievers, perhaps be brought to the faith: "I will attempt to persuade them [doubters] so that they may become quiet and leave a way into themselves for your Word" (317).[8] For his fellow-Christians *The Confessions* are intended, in their revelation of the manifold mercies of God, as a reinforcement of their faith and, in their disclosure of the narrator's continuing weaknesses, as an appeal for prayer: "I beseech you, my God, show me to myself, so that to my brothers, who will pray for me, I may confess what wounds I find in me" (270). "But with what benefit do they wish to hear me? Do they wish to share my thanksgiving, when they hear how close it is by your gift that I approach to you, and to pray for me, when they hear how I am held back by my own weight? To such men I will reveal myself' (231).

Before this third audience Augustine assumes a dual role: in his torment over his continuing concupiscence Augustine confronts his readers as a penitent, submissively exposing his unworthiness and entreating his readers to pray for him. By virtue of his enlightenment, on the other hand, he is a teacher who has witnessed the goodness of God and who deems it his mission to proclaim that goodness to others. The confession, finally, is equally vital to both the narrator and the hearers of his confession; before the *mysterium tremendum* all men are diminished.[9]

In his *Confessions* St. Augustine has provided the paradigm for all future ventures in the genre. He has dictated its substance; the confession, quasi-sacramental in nature, will henceforth include: (1) an examination of self in a search for self-knowledge; (2) the narrator's remorse over his sinfulness; (3) a "conversion experience" which at once illuminates and renews the narrator; (4) a firm resolution to reform; (5) an attempt to reconcile himself with his readers; and (6) a sense of obligation to reveal his experiences to others for their welfare. In his formal contributions to the genre, Augustine, in seeing the need for psychic distance between the narrator and his created self, unveils the ironic potential of the genre. The narrator sees his character as self and non-self, example and exemplar, literary creator and literary creation, penitent and teacher, memory and mirror. The various roles designed for the multiple audience further highlight the intensely rhetorical nature of the genre, for the readers—or hearers—of his confession are, among other things, expected to absolve the narrator of his guilt, participate in his search for self-knowledge, rejoice in his reconciliation, pray for his perseverance, recognize their own guilt, and heed the narrator's pleas for moral reform. Finally, it should be noted that the readers are intended to begin their own confessions! The confession is, of all genres, that which most insists upon the active collaboration of the readers, the hearers of the confession without whom the confession would be meaningless.

II

Jean-Jacques Rousseau, for all of his professions of absolute sincerity, leaves implicit the major irony of his *Confessions*—the fact that they constitute his answer to St. Augustine. Although Rousseau does not once mention Augustine and his prototypical work, the very choice of his title—from a writer with a Calvinistic background and therefore steeped in Augustinian thought—impresses one as a tacit invitation to compare his *Confessions* with those of his predecessor. His ironic intent seems equally clear: to offer to the world a new version of the interior man, as he now appears in the Enlightenment.

Rousseau's work is, among other things, a direct frontal assault upon the Christian morality which informs the work of Augustine. It is a proud declaration of independence from the Christian conscience which, Rousseau would agree with Hamlet, makes cowards of us all, and a celebration of the natural man whose shining innocence dispels the dark shadows of sin, shame, and guilt. The crucial difference between Rousseau and Augustine, of course, one which determines the shapes of their lives as well as their works, lies in their conception of evil. Augustine's celebrated theft of the pears constitutes for him a symbolic re-enactment of the Fall; the pointless malice of an otherwise trivial act unveils the mystery of iniquity, the irrational eruption of evil from the depths of a soul blighted by Original Sin.[10] The analogous moment in Rousseau occurs when he is unjustly blamed for breaking a comb, the first violation of his innocence by society. He does not commit evil, it should be noted, he suffers it as an affliction from without. As a result of this radical difference, his *Confessions* will dramatically invert, in both form and substance, the Augustinian paradigm.[11] Where Augustine writes of an intrinsically sinful nature saved from error by grace, Rousseau writes of an innately good nature led astray by society; where Augustine rues his past self and seeks to distance himself from it, Rousseau cherishes this past self and seeks to recover it; where Augustine seeks an intimate bond with his audience, Rousseau recoils from an audience that he considers at least in part hostile and alienated.

Thus Rousseau asks us to admire "a just and good man, without bitterness, hatred, or jealousy, ready to acknowledge my errors, and still more prompt to forget the injuries I received from others" (1007).[12] He does, of course, divulge some of the more shameful episodes of his life: the thievery of the ribbon for which he allowed the innocent Marion to receive the blame, his various sexual embarrassments, his callous yearning for his friend's coat shortly after his death, and, above all, his desertion of his children. Rousseau indeed convicts himself of error but, it should be noted, not of sin. After revealing his life-long remorse about the ribbon episode, for example, Rousseau feels it necessary "to excuse myself as far as is conformable with truth," and he states that "never was wickedness further from my thoughts than in that cruel moment" (126). He reminds his reader that he was a youth at the time, and then even goes on to suggest that others were more to blame than he was:

> Had I been left to myself, I should infallibly have declared the truth. Or if M. de la Roque had taken me aside, and said: "Do not injure this poor girl; if you are guilty, own it," I am convinced that I should instantly have

> thrown myself at his feet; but they intimidated...instead of encouraging me. (127)

Yet again, while discussing the abandonment of his children, Rousseau states: "J'ai promis ma confession, non ma justification" but then he appeals to the innocence of his intentions:

> ... without exculpating myself from the blame I deserve, I prefer it to that resulting from their [his detractors'] malignity. My fault is great, but it was an error. I have neglected my duty, but the desire of doing an injury never entered my heart; and the feelings of a father were never more eloquent in favor of children whom he never saw. (553)

Like Augustine, Rousseau senses the distance between the narrator and the created self within the work, and, again like Augustine, he is writing primarily for himself, but he is far less interested in self-exploration and self-judgment than in finding consolation. What Rousseau seeks in reviewing his life is to recover what Wordsworth would later call "spots of time," moments enshrined in memory which, recalled in the present, yield once more their original delight:

> The remembrance of the finest portion of my years, passed with so much tranquility and innocence, has left in my heart a thousand charming impressions which I love to call to my recollection. (417–18)

> Precious and ever-regretted moments! Ah! recommence your delightful course; pass more slowly through my memory, if possible, than you actually did in your fugitive succession. How shall I prolong, according to my inclination, this recital at once so pleasing and so simple? (341)

The past as reverie: the distance between Rousseau as narrator and Rousseau as character is in constant jeopardy of breaking down as the narrator seeks to regain a lost innocence, to return to an earlier stage of his life. Moreover, what is especially striking about the Rousseau of the *Confessions* is how little troubled he is —unlike the author of the later *Dialogues* and *Rêveries*—by the mystery of self.[13] He is firm possession of his identity from the start, having acquired, at the age of five or six, "an uninterrupted knowledge of myself." (p. 8) Thus he declares later, "The real object of my confessions is to communicate an exact knowledge of what I interiorly am and have been in every situation of my life" (418).

Rousseau's transformation of the confessional tradition continues in his narration of his "conversion experiences." Rousseau, conforming to the requirements of the confessional genre, isolates within his history those decisive moments which shaped his life, but even these are deeply paradoxical. One such moment, his reading of the invitation to offer his celebrated "First Discourse," evokes the following response: "The moment I had read this, I seemed to behold another world, and became a different man" (540). The signals are familiar to readers of the confessional genre, but Rousseau then goes on to suggest that his memory of this climactic moment is somewhat vague, that he can remember only being urged by Diderot to write: "*I did so, and from that moment I was ruined. All the rest of my misfortunes during my life were the inevitable effect of this moment of error*" (541, italics mine).[14] What is depicted, it must be noted, is not the saving moment of illumination, but an error which blights the rest of his life. The moment is climactic, to be sure, and it does indeed bring about a transformation of self, but the conversion, if one can call it that, is a curse rather than a blessing.

A second such moment occurs when, after a sabbatical from society, Rousseau is persuaded to re-enter the intellectual circle of Diderot, Condillac, and Grimm. "Until then," writes Rousseau, "I had been good; from that moment I became virtuous, or at least infatuated with virtue.... I affected nothing; I became what I appeared to be.... *I was really transformed,* my friends and acquaintances scarcely knew me" (649–50, italics mine). Once more the idiom of conversion rings clear; but the careful reader who notes the antithetical relationship between virtue and goodness will recognize that Rousseau is once more sending false signals. Rousseau proceeds to disclose that, after six years of this new self, he returned to the countryside and became, to his great satisfaction, "the same Jean-Jacques I before had been" (651).

In thus transforming putative conversion experiences into what are essentially anti-conversions, Rousseau is interested in more than literary originality; he is, rather, giving expression to his deepest conviction, that the self is *given*, possessed at birth of all "those propensities nature had planted un my heart" (p. 18). It is this original self that is the true Rousseau, and any conversion is but a distortion of that original self, a betrayal of nature.

And yet despite his sense of his own worth and his proud refusal to be other than what he is intended to be by nature, Rousseau perceives in his last years the hollowness of his life; he feels abandoned in "the abyss of evil into which I am plunged" (927):

> How was it possible that, with a mind naturally expansive, I, with whom to live was to love, should not hitherto have found a friend entirely devoted to me, a real friend.... To what end was I born with such exquisite faculties? To suffer them to remain unemployed? The sentiment of conscious merit, which made me consider myself as suffering injustice, was some kind of reparation, and caused me to shed tears which with pleasure I suffered to flow. (665–66)

Rousseau's relationship with his all-important confessional audience, given his conception of his conscious merit and of his rebuffs by society, will inevitably be a complex one. Although he follows Augustine in initially addressing his confession to God, Rousseau is mainly concerned with his reading public.[15] But here Rousseau encounters an almost insurmountable obstacle to communication and confession, his conviction that this audience has already been poisoned by the conspirators against him: "They could never forgive my setting them, by my conduct, an example which, in their eyes, seemed to reflect upon themselves" (560), and he therefore, it should be noted, offers his confession primarily to a future generation of readers, as "a testimony in my favor, which, sooner or later, will triumph over the calumnies of mankind" (892). But the chilling audience of hostile contemporaries remains, and Rousseau is obliged to fend them off by rhetorical strategy. It is remarkable how seldom, in so intimate a confession, the reader's presence is explicitly acknowledged—even the obliquely addressed human reader of Augustine is more palpably embodied in the confession. But Rousseau, distrustful of his readers, carefully denies them through his rhetoric any genuine presence. As Vance has observed, the "I-Thou" relationship of genuine discourse, of *communication* in its etymological sense, is replaced here by an impersonal pronominal rhetoric: the readers, when they are not addressed in the third person as "le lecteur" or "mes lecteurs," are posited as "on," a tellingly impersonal third-person pronoun, or as an equally impersonal "vous"[16]:

> ... car je n'ai pas peur que le lecteur oublie jamais que je fais mes confessions pour croire que je fais mon apologie; mais il ne doit pas s'attendre non plus que je taise la vérité lorsqu'elle parle en ma faveur.... Qu'on juge si c'est là de quoi faire des tableaux agréables et leur donner un coloris bien attrayant. J'averti donc ceux qui voudront commencer cette lecture, que rien, en la poursuivant, ne peut les garrantir de l'ennui, si ce n'est le désir d'achever de connaître un homme, et l'amour sincère de la justice et de la vérité. (II, 21–22)
> [... for I am not under the least apprehension lest the reader should forget I make my confession, and be induced to believe I make my apology; but he cannot expect I shall conceal the truth when it testifies in my favor.... The reader will judge whether or not such a situation furnished the means of agreeable descriptions, or of giving them a seductive coloring! I therefore inform such as may undertake to read this work that nothing can secure them from weariness in the prosecution of their task, unless it be the desire of becoming more fully acquainted with a man whom they already know, and a sincere love of justice and truth.] (419–421)

"Let anyone judge..."—this characteristic relegation of Rousseau's reader to the third person betrays the tightly circumscribed role of the audience: to concur with judgments already made by the narrator. While seeking the approbation of his audience, Rousseau, it is clear, does not seek its absolution; his ideal reader is there to bear witness that there did once exist a just and sincere man.

In thus adapting the Augustinian genre to serve as a vehicle for his own values, Rousseau has in fact transformed confession to apologia. In his intense subjectivity, he has virtually closed the distance between the narrator and the created character that was so decisive in shaping the Augustinian confession, while simultaneously dissolving the intricate relationship with the audience, now remote and passive auditors of his words. For this, we have no better testimony than Rousseau's account of his private reading to a circle of "intimate friends":

> Thus I concluded, and every person was silent; Madame d'Egmont was the only person who seemed affected: she visibly trembled, but soon recovered herself, and was silent like the rest of the company. Such were the fruits of my reading and declaration. (1034)

The lasting popularity of *The Confessions* rewards Rousseau's confidence in his audience of future readers, but his disappointment in his immediate audience is almost palpable; he has failed to secure their partnership in his confession, and their brooding silence offers him only a judgment that he cannot accept.[17] He remains at the end of the work his only effective audience, awaiting the future readers who will read him with sympathy and admiration.

III

It is this mutated form of the confession that Dostoyevsky inherits and re-shapes for his own distinct purposes, creating a work that may be seen as part parody and part imitation of the Rousseauvian confession. The fact that Dostoyevsky originally contemplated publishing his *Notes from Underground* under the title *A Confession*, as well as his frequent allusions to Rousseau, clearly signals his intent: to invite comparison with his famous predecessor in the genre.[18] We learn from the tone of the allusions, however, that the narrator is anything but an unquestioning admirer of Rousseau; rather the narrator clearly shares Dostoyevsky's scepticism about Rousseau's *l'homme de la nature et de la vérité* and about the values that are implicit in *The Confessions*. Rousseau was, for Dostoyevsky, *l'enfant terrible* of the Enlightenment, the breeding-ground of the ideologies which Dostoyevsky thought were smothering the spirit of nineteenth-century Russia. What lends particular force to the narrator's confession, however, is his sense of complicity, for he has himself been caught up in Rousseauvian ideology and is thus struggling to expel demons within as well as demons without. In this he is reminiscent of Dostoyevsky, who had his own flirtations with secular humanism; as Mochulsky has observed, "Before penal servitude, Dostoyevsky was an idealist, a utopian, a socialist, a humanist. All these 'isms' were descended from Rousseau's axiom: 'man is by nature good.' After penal servitude, belief in 'natural goodness' was lost."[19]

The *Notes*, then, may be seen as Dostoyevsky's answer to Rousseau. Rejecting the values of Rousseau—in particular, the pelagianism that underlies his concept of the natural man—the narrator frantically struggles to discover the form of confession that would be truest to man's situation in the nineteenth century. But since the narrator cannot exorcise his personal demons, his confession falls short, and he must grudgingly admit his kinship with Rousseau. "The *Notes*," Matlaw has observed, "may even be considered as a parody of confession which, in religious terms, is ostensibly preceded by contrition, but here is replaced by proud (though ambivalent) self-defense. The confession is not Augustinian but Rousseauistic...."[20]

The Rousseauvian elements in the *Notes* are unmistakable. Part of the narrator's burden of guilt consists of his Rousseauvian past, his intoxication with the heady wine of romanticism. He confesses to having been a romantic dreamer in his youth, assured of his pre-eminent virtue and enraptured by sublime visions of the "good and the beautiful" (72):

> There were moments of such positive intoxication, of such happiness, that there was not the faintest trace of irony in me, on my honour. I had faith, hope, love. I believed blindly at such times that by some miracle, by some external circumstance, all this would suddenly open out, expand.... And what loving-kindness, Oh Lord, what loving-kindness I felt at times in those dreams of mine! in those "flights into the good and the beautiful": though it was fantastic love, though it was never applied

> to anything human in reality, yet there was so much of this love that one did not feel afterwards even the impulse to apply it in reality; that would have been superfluous. (72–73)[21]

These sentiments, except for the cutting irony of the love that was never applied to "anything human" would not be out of place in the pages of Rousseau. Even the narrator's repeated disclosures of his idleness—"The long and the short of it is, gentlemen, that it is better to do nothing! Better conscious inertia!" (56)—seem to suggest his kinship with Rousseau, who constantly sang the praises of "delicious indolence" (1025). The Underground Man's yearning for idleness has, like Rousseau's, an aesthetic basis; it would allow him to indulge his exquisite sensibility:

> Then...I should have been a sluggard and a glutton, not a simple one, but, for instance, one with sympathies for everything good and beautiful.... I should have found for myself a form of activity in keeping with it, to be precise, drinking to the health of everything "good and beautiful." I should have snatched at every opportunity to drop a tear into my glass and then to drain it to all that is "good and beautiful." (40)

But romantic idealism is the privilege of the young. The forty-year-old narrator of the *Notes* conveys to us by his tone what has happened to his dreams of the "good and the beautiful" and to his visions of emulating *l'homme de la nature et de la vérité*. His visionary gleam has fled, leaving him a solitary soul stranded in a world which he inhabits but does not really live in. His anguish in walking the streets of St. Petersburg (itself for Dostoyevsky a reminder of the ideological violence inflicted upon Russia by the Enlightenment) recalls Rousseau's bitter promenades "in the midst of the hootings of the dregs of the people, and sometimes through a shower of stones" (989). The Underground Man, however, encounters, not the hostility of the passers-by, but their total indifference:

> [Walking the streets] was a regular martyrdom, a continual, intolerable, humiliation at the thought, which passed into an incessant and direct

> sensation, that I was a mere fly in the eyes of all this world, a nasty, a disgusting fly—more intelligent, more highly developed, more refined in feeling than any of them, of course, but a fly that was continually making way for everyone, insulted and injured by everyone. (68)

All that remains of the narrator's earlier romanticism is his fierce ego, his determination to preserve "what is most precious and most important—that is, our personality, our individuality" (48). It is an egotism that takes the form of the *amour propre* of a sick and spiteful man sticking his tongue out at a world that despises him. Describing himself as a mouse, the narrator lays claim to being even more spiteful than his mentor: "There may even be a greater accumulation of spite in it (the mouse) than in *l'homme de la nature et de la vérité*. The base and nasty desire to vent that spite on its assailants rankles even more nastily in it than in *l'homme de la nature et de la vérité*" (32). The key to the *Notes* is the prominence of the confessional impulse, which contributes to the work both its form and its substance. It is important to note that the narrator's account of his life, once we have penetrated the ironies which he has erected around himself, is, in fact, a confession *about* a confession; what is being recounted are the narrator's attempts to wring from himself the confession that would liberate him: the confession (to the reader) of the failure of an earlier confession (to Liza) which emerges as the crucial episode in his life.

This episode begins when the Underground Man, crushed by the indignities heaped upon him by his former schoolmates, visits the prostitute Liza. After his night of sexual pleasure, the narrator, for reasons he cannot entirely fathom, begins to preach to Liza about the "holy mystery of love" (109) and succeeds in converting her. The conversion of Liza is genuine, but the narrator wonders about his own motives; he concedes that "it was the exercise of my skill that carried me away, yet it was not merely sport" (116). He is indeed himself caught up in Liza's emotions—"I began to have a lump in my throat myself" (115)—and once his objective has been reached, the narrator confesses to his great perplexity about what has transpired: "I was exhausted, shattered, in bewilderment. But behind the bewilderment the truth was already gleaming. The loathsome truth" (118).

We see for ourselves what this "loathsome truth" is when a grateful Liza returns his visit. The visit dismays the narrator because Liza sees him in his tattered dressing-gown, the hateful symbol of his poverty, and provokes him into what begins as a spiteful repudiation of his part in the conversion but soon changes into a confession: "Power, power was what I wanted then, sport was what I wanted.... I am a blackguard, a scoundrel, an egoist, a sluggard" (133). When Liza approaches him with compassion, he is at first genuinely moved, sobbing "They won't let me...I can't be good" (134), and then he weeps for several minutes in genuine misery. But he then perceives the incongruity of his situation and becomes ashamed of his hysteria: "The thought, too, came into my overwrought brain that our parts now were completely changed, that she was now the heroine, while I was just such a crushed and humiliated creature as she had been before me that night" (135). His feelings become ambivalent, the narrator at once being drawn to her and hating her; he is ashamed and yet experiences "a feeling of mastery and passion" which leads to his great betrayal, his seduction of his convert.

On the very brink of conversion, the narrator recoils from the forgiveness that is extended to him and aborts the confessional act. The impulse to confess persists, however, for after the betrayed Liza has left him, the narrator contemplates running after her: "To fall down before her, to sob with remorse, to kiss her feet, to entreat her forgiveness! I longed for that, my whole breast was being rent to pieces, and never, never, shall I recall that minute with indifference" (138). Once more repressing the impulse, however, he remains a moral cripple for the rest of his life. He reveals to us the "loathsome truth" that he is made to confront: "I was incapable of love...for, I repeat, with me loving meant tyrannizing and showing my moral superiority" (136). The *Notes*, then, reveal that the narrator, while approaching the fullness of the penitential act, rejects the conversion experience that would heal his soul and reconcile him to the human community. Seen from this perspective, the work does appear to be, as Matlaw has proposed, a parody of confession. The narrator's inability to transcend his self-consciousness, his egotism, leaves him—unrepentant, unforgiven, unconverted, unreconciled—trapped in what appears to be a parody of the Augustinian confession.

But the *ambivalence* of the confession, parenthetically adverted to by Matlaw, yet remains to be explored, for it is this very ambivalence that makes the work more than a simple parody. The confessions of the narrator—both to Liza and to the readers—are, it is true, failures, but the narrator's awareness and avowal of his failures prompt us to look beyond Rousseau to the paradigm which he has transformed. If the Underground Man is so mired in his contrariness that he cannot attain the liberation promised by the confessional act, it must be noted that he at least achieves some kind of illumination and is therefore capable of witnessing to values that he himself cannot attain. We can, I think, agree with Mochulsky in viewing the confession, however incomplete, as a religious one:

> In opposition to the innocent *homme de la nature* of humanism there stands the sinful man from underground; there is revealed the terrible spectacle of evil in the soul of man. By means of "negative argumentation," so characteristic of the writer, the fundamental lie of humanism is refuted: that it is possible to reeducate man through reason and advantage. Dostoyevsky objects, "No, evil is not overcome by education, but by a miracle. What is impossible to man, is possible to God. Not re-education, but *resurrection*."[22]

The Underground Man, having failed the test of Liza's love, recognized his guilt, his unworthiness, and his need for moral reform: "All salvation from any sort of ruin, and all moral renewal—is included in love and can only show itself in that form" (136). He recognizes, as the obverse side of his "loathsome truth," that his salvation would lie in the great mystery of love which he had appealed to so cavalierly in his conversion of Liza. Though he is, without "faith and Christ,"[23] incapable of the selflessness required by that love, his perception of its worth and of his failure to achieve it places him, despite his desperate evasions of the painful truth, as close to Augustine as he is to Rousseau.

Viewed from a formal perspective, the failure of the Underground Man is a failure to articulate the proper narratorial "I"; in tension between the self-sufficiency of his Rousseauvian self and the self-castigation of his Augustinian self;

the narrator can only sporadically maintain the proper dialectic between himself and the character he is depicting. Hence the ironies which impede his confession: at times the narrator so cherishes (however perversely) his past self that he totally closes the distance between the ironies directed against his readers. At other times, the psychic distance between the two selves is so magnified by the narrator's self-contempt that he is capable only of self-destructive ironies. In either case the proper confessional posture is beyond the narrator's reach.

The clashing selves of the narrator are manifested in the profusion of motives he offers for his confession: he is, we are told, writing because he wants to justify himself; because he seeks revenge; because he takes masochistic pleasure in humiliating himself; because he wants to test his ability to tell all about himself without, like Rousseau, lying "out of vanity"; because he would like to improve his style; and even because there is nothing better for him to do.[24] The Underground Man is so protean a character that we cannot totally discredit any of these motives. But among his motives for confessing, the narrator offers two crucial ones, motives that place him within the mainstream of the confessional genre: (1) a search for self-knowledge and (2) a search for forgiveness.

In his search for self-knowledge the narrator becomes the primary reader of his own work, which is, in fact, intended for no other readers: "I write only for myself, and I wish to declare once and for all that I write as though I were addressing readers, that is simply because it is easier for me to write in that form" (58). His confessions, as surely as they were for St. Augustine, are an attempt by the narrator to unveil the truth about himself. In his obsessive rationality, he finds his true self masked by the many ironic postures he has assumed. He has become, like St. Augustine, a riddle unto himself:

> Ech, I have talked a lot of nonsense, but what have I explained? How is enjoyment in this to be explained? But I will explain it, I will get to the bottom of it! that is why I have taken up my pen.... (30)

> Why, how am I, for example, to set my mind at rest? Where are the primary causes on which I am to build? Where are my foundations? Where am I to get these from? (38)

In the Liza episode lies the answer to his most insistent questions. The narrator admits that he is still, sixteen years after the event, tormented by his memory of Liza and that this torment is above all the reason why he decides to write his confession:

> Today, for instance, I am particularly oppressed by one memory of a distant past. It came back vividly to my mind a few days ago, and has remained haunting me like an annoying tune that one cannot get rid of. And yet I must get rid of it somehow. I have hundreds of such reminiscences; but at times one stands out from the hundred and oppresses me. For some reason I believe that if I write it down I should get rid of it. Why not try? (58)

The narrator cannot yet, even in retrospect, fully accept his guilt; he is still wedded to his initial reaction after the betrayal: that his rejection of Liza was for her own good, that "the feeling of insult will elevate and purify her...by hatred... h'm!, perhaps too, by forgiveness" (139). His rhetorical evasion of responsibility—though an apt turn of phrase—has the effect of translating his moral defeat into an aesthetic triumph of sorts: "I will add, too, that I remained for a long time afterwards pleased with the phrase about the benefit from resentment and hatred, in spite of the fact that I almost fell ill from misery" (139).

The narrator continues to cling to his saving fiction: he asks his readers: "...which is better—cheap happiness or exalted suffering? Well, which is better?" (139). But still there remains the misery, the admission that "all this is somehow a very evil memory" (139), to testify to the radical sincerity of the Underground Man. It should be noted that even in speaking of his failure to achieve the full form of confession, he has not entirely lost hope that Liza will extend—or has extended—to him the forgiveness he could not bring himself to ask for. It is equally significant that in his concluding paragraphs the narrator reveals in himself something of the true penitent in his admission that "I have felt ashamed all the time I've been writing this story; so it's hardly literature so much as corrective punishment" (139).[25]

The confession of the Underground Man is not, then, a parody of the true confessional form; it is rather a confession aborted by the divided soul of the narrator—much like those confessions addressed to his father in his youth:

> I was genuinely touched and penitent, I used to shed tears and, of course, deceived myself, though I was not acting in the least and there was a sick feeling in my heart at the time...it was all a lie, an affected lie, that is, all this penitence, this emotion, these vows of reform. (37)

If the confessional genre in its simplest manifestations dictates a complex relationship between narrator and reader, it is obvious that a narrator of so many-sided a personality as the Underground Man will have unusually complex relationships with his readers.[26] Just as, in his professed motives for confessing, the narrator is uneasily poised between the Augustinian and the Rousseauvian confession, so in his appeals to his readers will he follow both mentors.

The most flagrant wrenching of the confessional pattern is the narrator's reminder on several occasions that he is writing a confession that need be heard by no one but himself: "Why do I call you 'gentlemen,' why do I address you as though you really were my readers? Such confessions as I intend to make are never printed nor given to other people to read" (57). But the very fact that he has to resort to the fiction of a "non-reader" betrays his dependence, despite his almost total isolation from others, upon his readers; no confession, however perverse, can dispense with the hearer of the confession.[27] Thus the narrator reluctantly admits the readers into his confidence, even while insisting upon his total indifference to them: "Now, are you not fancying, gentlemen, that I am expressing remorse for something now, that I am asking your forgiveness for something? I am sure that you are fancying that.... However, I assure you that I do not care if you are..." (27).

As in the fantasies which the narrator confesses to having had in his earlier days, the reader is needed to hear a Rousseauvian self-glorification and to bear witness to the virtues of the Underground Man:

> I, for instance, was triumphant over everyone; everyone, of course, was in dust and ashes, and was forced spontaneously to recognize my superiority, and I forgave them all.... I confessed before all the people my shameful deeds, which, of course, were not merely shameful, but had in them much that was "good and beautiful." (74)

He has, however, no confidence that his fantasy will be gratified; rather he expects the condemnation of the audience. What is especially significant is his reaction to his presumably unsympathetic audience: he expresses an intense resentment against his readers precisely because they are his readers. This bitterness, we learn, is partly derived from shame, much the same reaction the narrator suffered when Liza's visit took place and which stifled the original confession of the narrator:

> Surely by now you must realize that I shall never forgive you for having found me in this wretched dressing-gown.... And I shall never forgive you for the tears I could not help shedding before you just now, like some silly woman put to shame! And for what I am confessing to you just now, I shall never forgive *you* either. (133)

The final italicized *you* is a reminder to the Underground Man's interlocutors within the story, and to the general reader, that all are caught up in the emotional dynamics of confession. We, as readers, have in fact seen much more than Liza has; we have seen the tattered robes of the narrator's soul and, because we have witnessed his spiritual poverty, we have called upon ourselves an even more intense resentment.

This barely masked resentment seethes over into positive aggression on several occasions; the narrator, for example, maliciously points out that there is something of the *voyeur* in the hearer of a confession, a morbid curiosity or even a prurient fascination that he is delighted to frustrate: "But enough...not another word on that subject of such interest to you" (34). He admits taking a voluptuous pleasure in his confession, like a man who moans incessantly over a toothache, while knowing "better than anyone that he is only lacerating himself and others for nothing" (36). The concept of "lacerating" (from Dostoyevsky's "nadryhvayet is razdrazhayet"—*tears* (verb) and *irritates*), a prominent word in the novelist's lexicon, reveals precisely what the narrator is up to: he is using his readers as he has used people all of his life—as partners in an essentially sado-masochistic relationship. His confessions are a form of sadistic revenge against his audience, a flaring out of the spite that consumes him: "It is nasty for you to hear my despicable moans; well, let it be nasty; here, I will let you have a nastier flourish in a minute" (36). After rejoicing in the nastiness he has inflicted upon his readers, he then taunts them by divulging the pleasure he finds "in the very feeling of his own degradation" (37), thus in effect transforming the reader who witnesses his self-degradation into an accomplice in an act of psychological perversion.

"*Hypocrite lecteur, mon semblable, mon frère*": Baudelaire's famous apostrophe to his readers captures something of the tortuous relationship between the narrator and his readers, the unwelcome but necessary adjuncts of his confessional act. The Underground Man views his audience as partners in his guilt; always, in confessing his own degradation, the Underground Man is careful to remind his readers that they share in his baseness—or even exceed it: "Observe yourselves more carefully, gentlemen, then you will understand that it is so" (37). The communal guilt he perceives is the focus of the work's conclusion; having terminated his own confession, the narrator includes the readers in his circle of guilt: "for we are all divorced from life, we are all cripples, every one of us, more or less" (139).

The narrator, finally, addresses the readers, before whom he had shamefully cringed, as people who are morally inferior to him, for his life, at least, is an examined life. His confession has stripped him of the fictions which sustain moral indifference: "I have only in my own life carried to an extreme what you have not dared to follow halfway, and what's more, you have taken your cowardice for good sense, you have found courage in deceiving yourselves. So that perhaps, after all, there is more life in me than in you" (140).

The confession has turned against the readers, who are now in no position to judge—or to forgive—the Underground Man. The injunction "Look into it more carefully!" (140) is a call from one who at least perceives his baseness for the readers to conduct their own self-examinations and to initiate, if they can, their own confessions. Despite his own failure to confess fully, and despite his resentment of his audience, the confessional narrator of the *Notes* emerges as a teacher and a moral guide.

The Underground Man's communication with the reader ends abruptly at this point: "But enough, I don't want to write more from 'Underground'" (140). But his confession has not ended. We have seen in Augustine that a perfect, and hence completed, confession is impossible; Dostoyevsky is likewise aware that a confession in its true sense is never really terminated, and thus the "spectral" author informs the readers: "(*The notes of this paradoxalist do not end here, however. He could not refrain from going on with them, but it seems to us that we may stop here*)."[28] The human self is never fully defined, and the narrator will go on searching for himself.

The Augustinian elements in *Notes from Underground* are, despite the ironic qualifications, quite unmistakable: the narrator offers his confession out of remorse and describes it as "corrective punishment." Though he failed to obtain absolution from Liza or from the readers, he maintains the tenuous hope that somehow his confession will purge him of his "evil memories." He does undergo an Augustinian conversion experience, a privileged moment which could have changed the course of his life, and though he cannot accept it, he gains from the experience a degree of enlightenment, a perception of his moral situation. This insight is made possible by the narrator's ability to view himself, on occasion, as "other," thus creating the dialectic between self and non-self that is needed for the confessional narrator. Finally, he is able, after great reluctance, to include his audience in the confessional act—first, as the potential absolvers of his sins, and secondly, as the erring brothers who must be called to a new life.

The celebrated ironies of the *Notes*, of course, do violence to this Augustinian pattern; at any moment remorse is likely to revert to resentment, confession to self-congratulation, humble submission to defiant assertion of self. But these remaining vestiges of the Rousseauvian natural man are not enough to cancel out the Augustinian man who is struggling to be delivered, laboring to return the confession to the Augustinian form.

Dostoyevsky, by re-opening the distance between narrator and character which Rousseau had closed, regains for the confession the enormous potential for irony which is inherent in the genre. In so doing, he restores to the genre its "intrinsicate knot," the intricate and almost symbiotic relationship between the narrator and created self, narrator and audience, that characterizes the genre. Once more the confession becomes a two-way transaction. Moreover, by adding a fictive narrator, himself subject to objective scrutiny as well as sympathy, Dostoyevsky introduces a further dialectic, that between author and narrator. The hybrid form he develops from materials passed on to him by Augustine and Rousseau paves the way for the modern confessional novel, which has so often reflected the ambivalences of modern man.

Notes to Responsive Form: Dostoyevsky's Notes from Underground and the Confessional Tradition

1. A useful sampling of critical backgrounds may be found in *Notes from Underground*, trans. Serge Shishkoff, ed. Robert G. Durgy (New York: Thomas Crowell Co., 1969). See especially Joseph Frank, "Nihilism and *Notes from Underground*," pp. 149–203 for the historico-political context.
2. Peter M. Axthelm, in *The Modern Confessional Novel* (New Haven and London: Yale University Press, 1967), finds in the *Notes* "a prescription for the genre of the modern confessional novel" (p. 13).
3. See James Olney, *Metaphors of Self: The Meaning of Autobiography* (Princeton: Princeton University Press, 1972) for a valuable description of the genre: Olney states that Augustine's is a "double autobiography," for "instead of describing the events of a philosopher's life as they happened in the past, he portrays himself acting out the life of a psychologist and a philosopher as that life comes into being and is now" (p. 45).
4. All references to Augustine are to *The Confessions of St. Augustine,* trans. and ed. by John K. Ryan (Garden City, NY: Doubleday, 1960).
5. Ryan, p. 29.
6. Eugene Vance, "Augustine's *Confessions*: A Grammar of Selfhood," *Genre* (March 1973), pp. 4, 5.
7. Vance, p. 9.
8. Robert E. Sayre, *Examined Self* (Princeton: Princeton University Press, 1974), pp. 10–11, stresses the didactic urgency of Augustine's confession.
9. See Thomas O'Donnell, "T. E. Lawrence and the Confessional Tradition: Either Angel or Beast," *Genre* (Summer 1976). O'Donnell highlights the tension between the confessional narrator's sense of uniqueness and his representative nature (p. 140).

10. See Christie Vance, "Rousseau's Autobiographical Venture: A Process of Negation," *Genre* (March 1973), pp. 100–101.
11. C. Vance, pp. 100–101.
12. References to Rousseau will be drawn from *The Confessions of Jean-Jacques Rousseau*, trans. W. Conyngham Mallory (New York: Tudor, 1928). Occasional references in French will be to *Les confessions*, ed. Michel Launay (Paris: Garnier, 1968), 2 vols.
13. I hope it will be understood that I am discussing the author of *The Confessions* and not the whole man. As Christie Vance has pointed out, *The Confessions* is but the first installment of an autobiographical venture which includes *The Dialogues* and *The Reveries*; in these later works, Rousseau gives evidence of a more self-critical attitude and is more willing to acknowledge the ambiguities which bedevil him.
14. Vance takes note of this reversal, pp. 100–101.
15. Vance, p. 102.
16. Vance, p. 102.
17. Vance, p. 103: "The attempts to incorporate the enemy reader into the text itself...testifies to the failure of this text to produce the other." Sayre, p. 6, cites as a prominent feature of the work its "exclusion of everything but ego."
18. M. M. Bakhtin refers to this proposed title in "Monologue Speech of the Hero, and Narrative Discourse in the Stories of Dostoyevsky—*Notes from Underground*," in *Notes*, ed. Durgy, p. 203. Ralph Matlaw sees Rousseau as the "propounder" of the recurrent phrase, *l'homme de la nature et de la vérité*, in "Structure and Integration in *Notes from Underground*," Durgy, p. 184.
19. Konstantin Mochulsky, *Dostoyevsky: His Life and Work*, trans. Michael A. Miniham (Princeton: Princeton: Princeton University Press, 1967), p. 210).
20. Matlaw, p. 184.
21. Citations to the text of *Notes from Underground* will be from *Three Short Novels of Dostoyevsky* (New York: Dell, 1960), translated by Constance Garnett.
22. Mochulsky, p. 257.
23. The phrase is from the famous passage excised by the censor: "...where from all this I deduced the need for faith and Christ—that is suppressed" (Mochulsky, p. 256). See also Axthelm, p. 26: "The world view at the end of *Notes from Underground* recalls Augustine's cry that 'every man is a liar,' with its implication that truth must be sought in theological terms."
24. Most of these motives are stated or are at least implicit in Book XI of Part One, pp. 56–59.
25. Matlaw, because of the failure of the confession, denies that it is genuinely intended as a corrective punishment.
26. See Bakhtin, esp. pp. 204–206, for a sensitive description of this complex relationship.
27. See Mochulsky, pp. 132, 133.
28. Bakhtin, in a somewhat different framework, has much to say about the dialogue which cannot end—pp. 207, 213, 214. I refer to the author as "spectral" because he enters the work only in an introductory footnote and in a concluding parenthesis. Nevertheless, he introduces into the work a further dimension of irony, erecting yet a further barrier between the reader and the truth he is challenged to perceive.

DOSTOEVSKY ALSO NODS

Rodney Delasanta

Those of us who thought we were well informed about 1054 and all that were stung by the viscerally hostile reaction of many Orthodox Christians to John Paul II's recent Pauline pilgrimage to Greece, Syria, and Malta. Whereas ecumenism in the West seems to have succeeded in muting anti-papal rhetoric among most Protestants, the East is still quite capable of hurling public insults at the Bishop of Rome and the Catholic Church itself.

It would be folly to understate the abounding historical reasons for this disdain and presumption to think that any brief chronicle is explanation enough. From the *filioque* controversy in the Nicene Creed to Eastern perceptions of papal overreach; from the Latin Crusaders' incomprehensible sack of Constantinople in 1204 to Western impotence against the Ottoman capture of that "Second Rome" in 1453—there are numerous sources of suspicion and animosity. Nor have Catholic incursions into Russian Orthodox provenance in more recent times endeared Rome to the East. Father Willard Francis Jabusch was right in reminding us in *Commonweal* of Alexander Nevsky's mythic heroism in saving Russia for Orthodoxy against the invading Teutonic Knights in the thirteenth century and, in the seventeenth, the Polish massacre of monks, women, and children at the Russian monastery of Optina Pustin. Recent overzealous proselytizing, especially in Ukraine, has also left the Orthodox wary of Catholic intentions.

Notwithstanding these and countless other reasons for friction, there are no two forms of Christianity that are at their base more theologically compatible than Catholicism and Orthodoxy because—need it be said?—the doctrines they share were already in place long before the schism in 1054. To name only a few: God as a Trinity of Persons (despite the *filioque* flap); Christ the Redeemer as the Incarnate Son of God (no mere ethicist he); the centrality of the sacraments to divine worship, especially the Eucharist; the claim of ecclesial authority through apostolic succession (despite Orthodox refusals to accept Petrine authority); and the veneration of the Virgin Mary as the Mother of God. Also instructive is Catholicism's own perception of its separation from Orthodoxy on the one hand and Protestantism on the other. Catholic catechetics before Vatican II, for example, would routinely distinguish between Orthodox and Protestant Christianity by declaring the former to be only in schism from Rome while describing the latter as heretically separated.

It is thus probably right to say that, despite the official state of schism and mutual excommunication (the latter not lifted until 1967 by Pope Paul VI and the Patriarch Athanegoras), Catholics still thought of Orthodox believers as spiritual kin with whom they had considerably more in common than with Protestants. And they also assumed, gratuitously as it now seems, a semi-benign reciprocity of Orthodox feelings towards them. After all, if France and Germany could forgive each other for two world wars in the twentieth century (with a carnage much bloodier than Constantinople in 1204), couldn't Orthodox and Catholic Christianity, whose raison d'être is forgiveness itself, do the same? How surprising and disappointing, then, to hear the Pope slandered as "the two-horned grotesque monster of Rome" when he landed in Athens. I was living in Switzerland in 1969 when Paul VI made a first-ever papal visit to Geneva, and I can attest to the fact that he was received more hospitably in that gray *civitas dei* of John Calvin than John Paul was in Orthodox Athens.

On second thought, though, my disappointment at anti-Catholic Orthodox ire is not entirely surprising, for I have routinely been forced to abide it while reading my favorite nineteenth-century novelist, Fyodor Dostoevsky. Now, obviously, Dostoevsky was Russian Orthodox, not Greek, but the depth of his hostility to Rome belongs to a species that might be called pan-Orthodox. Perhaps if we can begin to understand the depth of Dostoevsky's disdain we can extrapolate from it to understand how, over a century after his death, much of Eastern Christianity is still not on speaking terms with its Western cousins.

Even the cursory reader of Dostoevsky must know that he was on the side of the angels in the great Christian/Secularist *psychomachia* that has been waged since the Enlightenment. Having taught some of his novels in my Western Civilization classes, I can say that he has touched my students and me in a manner that no other Christian apologist (Pascal, say, or Kierkegaard, or his contemporary John Henry Newman) has quite succeeded in doing. As the most prophetic writer of the nineteenth century, Dostoevsky saw the coming triumph of secularism with an extraordinary clarity: whether by way of the dyspeptic narrator of *Notes from Underground* railing against the invasive "anthill" culture of the secularized West; or the impoverished student Raskolnikov in *Crime and Punishment* experimenting with utilitarian ethics in order to rationalize his murder of the money lender; or the roster of abusive characters in *The Idiot* deprecating the holiness of Prince Myshkin; or the demonic Stavrogin and Peter Stepanovich in *The Devils*, with their pitiful cell of Russian Nihilists, plotting to overthrow all that is holy to Christian Russia; or Ivan in *The Brothers Karamazov*, so converted to Western atheism that he could easily overwhelm his saintly brother, Alyosha, in dialectic. Against what he acknowledged to be compelling arguments for the culture of disbelief, Dostoevsky did not offer philosophical counterarguments but instead, in the spirit of the Gospels, Christian parables: the Magdalene-like redemptive love of fallen women—Liza, Sonia, Nastasya, and Grushenka—who illuminate his major novels; the kenotic love of the "holy fool," Prince Myshkin, the greatest Christ figure in literature since *Don Quixote*; the lover of children, Alyosha Karamazov, who transforms the pathos of the illness and death of the consumptive youngster Ilyusha into an occasion for belief in the Resurrection.

Dostoevsky's was an authentic Christian voice that said "no!" to the new secular world order that sought to uproot Christianity, both Western and Eastern, from what was left of Christendom in his time. Its shibboleth had been voiced by Voltaire: *écrasez l'infame!* The rational eighteenth-century Enlightenment assumed that a benevolent deism would supplant its superstitious predecessor and usher in a *novus ordo saeculorum* free of all traces of supernaturalism and superstition—something like El Dorado in *Candide* or Monticello at Charlottesville. Dostoevsky knew better and saw that what deism had become in the nineteenth century was a halfway house, as Jonathan Swift had predicted, to atheism.

Thus do I gratefully admire Dostoevsky's profound insights into the mysteries of the Christian faith, while at the same time admitting bewilderment that these epiphanies should be accompanied by a crude anti-Catholicism that seems wholly unworthy of a giant of world literature. If I as a Catholic reader can revere him so, I mutter to myself, especially in consequence of his Russian Orthodox spirituality, should he not have tolerated my Catholicism, or at least muted his disrespect for it? East is East and West is West, but to my unsophisticated American eye the spiritual respect of the West for the East has gone cruelly unrequited.

The most obvious example of this in Dostoevsky's fiction, as we all know, is the "Grand Inquisitor" chapter of the greatest Christian novel ever written, *The Brothers Karamazov*. Even when I am reminded that the narrator of that episode is Ivan, the brother tormented into atheism by post-Enlightenment Western ideologies, Dostoevsky nevertheless seems to have gone out of his way to describe Catholic Christianity as not only having abandoned Christ, but literally sent him packing. In the grim person of the aged and bloodless Spanish cardinal Inquisitor, Dostoevsky has reduced the Catholic Church to a Christless institution that delivers bread to its faithful only in exchange for a surrender of their freedom. I confess to moments, in exegetical desperation, when I have tried to mitigate Dostoevsky's Catholic-baiting by suggesting to my students that perhaps what he was really doing with the Grand Inquisitor was typologically describing, by way of a sixteenth-century antetype, nineteenth-century liberalism captivated by atheistic socialism or communism. In short, maybe he was literally describing Spanish Catholicism, but with the proleptic intention of warning against some rough beast, its hour come round at last, slouching towards Moscow to be born.

But I have come to the conclusion that such apologetics are more than a little naive. Of course, in Dostoevsky's mature novels, we must take care in determining which character might speak for Dostoevsky himself. Certainly, there are some parallels with Fr. Zosima in *The Brothers Karamazov* just as there are with his disciple, Alyosha Karamazov. But above all others is the voice of the one character whom Dostoevsky deliberately created as a Christ figure, Prince Myshkin in *The Idiot*. To read anti-Catholic fulmination coming from him (as opposed to, say, Ivan Karamazov) is to hear the anti-Catholicism of Dostoevsky himself.

Consider this rather long passage from Chapter 7 of Part 4, near the end of the novel, which describes the Epanchins' engagement party at which Myshkin's admiration of his beloved Aglaya is interrupted by news that a certain Pavlishchev has been converted to Catholicism.

> "Pavlishchev was a clear-headed man and a Christian, a true Christian," the prince declared suddenly. "How could he submit to a faith—that is unchristian? Catholicism...is no more than an unchristian faith...even worse than atheism.... Atheism only preaches nullity, but Catholicism goes further; it preaches a distorted Christ, a Christ it has calumnied and defamed, the opposite of Christ! It preaches the Antichrist.... Roman Catholicism believes the Church cannot remain on earth without universal temporal power.... [It] is not even a religion but very definitely the continuation of the Holy Roman Empire, and everything in it is subservient to that idea, beginning with faith. The Pope usurped the earth, an earthly throne, and took up the sword, and since then everything has been going on that way, except that to the sword they have added craft, deceit, fanaticism, superstition, villainy.... They have bartered everything, everything for money, for base earthly power. And isn't that the teaching of Antichrist? How could they fail to create atheism? Atheism has come from them, directly from Roman Catholicism! ... Among us only exceptional classes of people don't believe, those... who have lost their roots. But there, in Europe, awesome masses of the people themselves are beginning to lose their faith—first from darkness and lies, and now from fanaticism, from hatred of the Church and Christianity....
>
> "For socialism too is an offspring of Catholicism and the essential Catholic ideal. It, too, like its brother atheism, springs from despair in opposition to Catholicism as a moral presence, to replace the lost moral

> power of religion, to quench the spiritual thirst of parched humanity, and to save it not through Christ but also through violence! ... Our Christ, whom we have preserved and they have not even known, must shine forth in opposition to the West! Not by falling like slaves into Jesuit traps but by carrying our Russian civilization to them; we must now stand before them."

Prince Myshkin's harangue is the most withering attack on Catholicism in the entire Dostoevsky canon. What makes the timing of it especially odd is that it was written in 1867–1868 while Dostoevsky and his wife were residing for short periods in Dresden, Geneva, Vevey, Milan, and Florence. They must have been aware of the progress of Italian unification, which by the time Dostoevsky was writing *The Idiot had* stripped the papacy of everything in the Papal States, except a tenuous control of Rome itself, and which, three years later, would make a de-papalized Rome the capital of a united Italy. The Pope would retire to the papal precincts, refuse Italian indemnification, and eventually declare himself a prisoner in the Vatican. It seems a strange time for Dostoevsky to have raised such a polemic over the pitiful remains of papal temporal power, which had not presumed to inject itself seriously into European politics since the Thirty Years War, some two and a half centuries earlier. To see Catholicism in 1867 as "the continuation of the Holy Roman Empire," or the Pope as "a usurper of the earth," would, in the words of Dostoevsky biographer Joseph Frank, "be looked on by the majority of his compatriots with the same rather frightened and pitying incredulity as that displayed by the Epanchins' guests" in the novel.

One might even entertain the thought, though it may seem bizarre at first, that there was as much for Dostoevsky to approve of as to condemn in Pope Pius IX. True, Ultramontanism was cresting and by 1870 would culminate in Vatican I and the definition of papal infallibility (at the very time that the Pope was politically deposed by Victor Emmanuel). But Pius' whole career since the revolutions of 1848 had been directed against the same dominations and powers at which Dostoevsky, too, took aim. Shortly before the publication of *The Idiot*, the Pope had issued the encyclical *Quanta Cura*, to which was attached the Syllabus of Errors. Eamon Duffy has described it as a "now familiar Vatican

Jeremiad" against the notion that "the Roman Pontiff can and should reconcile himself with progress, liberalism, and recent civilizations."

Many of the syllabus' eighty condemnations—in Duffy's words, of "Indifferentism, Freemasonry, Socialism, Gallicanism, Rationalism"—concerned developments that equally disturbed Dostoevsky. Doesn't his condemnation of the "nihilist" characters in *The Devils*—Stavrogin, Peter Stepanovich, et al.—constitute his own syllabus of errors? Are any of Pius' diatribes more withering than Dostoevsky's denunciation of these figures, whom he compares to the legion of devils (from Luke 8:32–35) cast out of the possessed man and permitted to enter a herd of swine that plunge into the sea? Considering the furor caused by the Syllabus of Errors throughout liberal Europe, it is hard to believe that Dostoevsky, who read French fluently and devoured daily newspapers both at home and abroad, would not have known of its existence and would not have been grudgingly forced to admit, if only to himself, that he and the Pope were facing the same implacable enemy. Is not the enemy of my enemy my friend?

Not, apparently, with Orthodox true believers, then and now. Yet in our own time should one not expect more of the Patriarch of All Russia, Alexei II, when considering the prospect of a papal visit to Moscow? Of course, as Fr. Jabusch has made clear, Alexei has his own reasons for foot dragging. All politics, even Russian Orthodox politics, is local. Still, should he not acknowledge that this is a pope whom many have credited as having contributed enormously to the fall of atheistic communism—and in his own country? Pope Leo, who faced down Attila the Hun at the gates of Rome fifteen centuries earlier, confronted a less dangerous foe. But now, thanks in part to the efforts of the Pope and Polish Solidarity, the Soviet Union is no more; the Russian Orthodox Church has been restored; persecutions of Eastern Christians have ceased; individual churches and seminaries have been reopened; ex-Communists may be seen ceremoniously crossing themselves—and the Pope has apologized to the Orthodox for the sins of Catholics in the past.

For those of us with long enough memories, all this seems miraculous, the kind of miracle prayed for at every pre-Vatican II Latin Mass which ended with the so-called Last Gospel. How many remember that the reading of the opening verses of John's Gospel was directed at "the conversion of Russia"? How many have noticed that something resembling that conversion has actually happened and that it would not have been done without the ministrations of a Polish pope? Under the circumstances why should we not expect Alexei to welcome his brother Patriarch, and brother Slav, to Moscow to sing a Slavonic Te Deum in thanksgiving?

The old reason—fear of Roman Catholic domination—can explain only some of the hostility. Maybe examining Dostoevsky's phobias can help, one of which was, in fact, Poland. When reading Dostoevsky, one cannot help but notice that the Polish character is always in the wrong, especially when he is identified as a Catholic. Grushenka's former lover in *The Brothers Karamazov*, for example, who comes back to her only when he learns that she has acquired a small fortune, is a Pole caught by Dimitri cheating at cards. In *The Idiot*, the faithless Aglaya's beloved, whom she marries instead of Prince Myshkin, is a Polish émigré count (a fake one, as it turns out), who succeeds in luring Aglaya into the confessional "of a certain celebrated Catholic priest" and thus "gaining complete ascendancy over her mind." With minor, unnamed Polish characters, Dostoevsky's favorite epithet is "obsequious." The disdain is also present in his correspondence: in a letter from Geneva to his friend Maikov in St. Petersburg, Dostoevsky defends himself against bureaucratic questioning of his loyalty to the Czar by "ask[ing] him to free me of the suspicion of betraying the Fatherland and in having relation with the Polacks.... I hate the Polacks and love my Fatherland." Finally, in what must be the most petulant example of ethnic pique on record, Joseph Frank tells us that Dostoevsky loved classical music, especially Mozart and Beethoven, but not Chopin, because he was a Pole.

Maybe Dostoevsky's habitual dismissal of all things Polish is a consequence of the seventeenth-century horrors at Optina Pustin, or the more recent Polish rebellion of 1863, which he deplored. Still, with all deference to Fr. Jabusch's reading of Polish culpabilities, it may be argued that Russia was more sinning than sinned against in its relations with its Slavic cousin to the west. A century after Optina Pustin, Russia cynically colluded in a series of three partitions, with Austria and Prussia, that resulted in the complete disappearance of Poland from the map of Europe. Chopin did not compose his Polonaises in Paris of the 1830s and 1840s merely as romantic folk celebrations but in commemoration of the failed rebellion of 1830 which provoked a stream of Polish refugees to Paris fleeing Russian oppression in their homeland. Indeed, Chopin's last concert before his premature death was a benefit for these refugees, who at his funeral in Paris in 1849 sprinkled Polish earth over his grave. When we add to these political causes of strife the un-Orthodox phenomenon of Poland's historic Catholic loyalties, we can better understand Dostoevsky's Polish phobia, and perhaps the phobias of the current Orthodox churchmen. Ironically, Dostoevsky may have explained some of this in a memorable line from *The Brothers Karamazov*: "I did him dirt and forever after did I hate him."

I have not meant, of course, to disparage Dostoevsky's greatness or Orthodox holiness. As a great writer and a good man, he understood Christianity *de profundis* and was able to transmit that understanding with an unmatched power. He has warned us, with a prescience that would have terrified even him had he seen it played out in history, especially on his native soil, that "without God all is permitted." Malcolm Muggeridge once said that Stalin's great mistake was denying his people access to the Gospels while permitting them to read their Dostoevsky—and Tolstoy. Dostoevsky's literary presence in our time has kept the votive candle to Christian faith lighted. His fiction, I make bold to say, can be, and has been, a channel of grace. Some of my students have confided to me that *The Brothers Karamazov* actually converted them away from the *novus ordo saeculorum*—insidiously present in every corner of their lives, even on their dollar bills—to a renewed belief in Christ.

Nevertheless, Dostoevsky, like Homer, also nods—and in that nodding reveals some disturbing reasons for the continued enmity between Eastern and Western Christianity. Certainly, his notion that the future of Christianity would be exclusively connected to the Christ of Russian Orthodoxy—him "whom we have preserved and *they have not even known*" (to quote Prince Myshkin)—was exploded in October 1917. And Dostoevsky's fantasy that this Russian Christ "must shine forth in opposition to the West"—that the East must not "fall like slaves into Jesuit traps but carry our Russian civilization to them"—seems to have gotten it backwards. Were he alive today, would he have recognized the great irony that, had it not been for the providential nexus of two scorned adversaries, Catholicism and Poles, Ivan Karamazov might have had the last word?

THE GREAT GATSBY AND THE AMERICAN PAST

Brian Barbour

"If he'd of lived, he'd of been a great man. A man like James J. Hill. He'd of helped build up the country."
(Mr. Gatz to Nick Carraway)

I

The Great Gatsby is a brilliant but sometimes brittle book. The social observation and notation are exact, yet the novel lacks the density of the accomplished novel of manners. Its method is that of poetic suggestion rather than detailed accumulation. A careful symbolism is used to suggest a depth that sometimes isn't there. It is admired as a critique of the American Dream, yet the way its admirers see it making that critique seems to me to be wrong. To set Gatsby off against the Buchanans threatens to seriously imbalance the novel's meaning because the Buchanans can't hold down their side of the scale. Fitzgerald hated the Buchanans and what he saw them as standing for, but there are moments when one might wonder if the hatred was sufficiently controlled by understanding:

> Slenderly, languidly, their hands set lightly on their hips, the two young women preceded us out onto a rosy-colored porch, open toward the sunset, where four candles flickered on the table in the diminished wind.
>
> "Why *candles*!" objected Daisy, frowning. She snapped them out with her fingers. "In two weeks it'll be the longest day in the year." She looked at us all radiantly. "Do you always watch for the longest day of

> the year and then miss it? I always watch for the longest day in the year and then miss it."
>
> "We ought to plan something," yawned Miss Baker, sitting down at the table as if she were getting into bed.
>
> "All right," said Daisy. "What'll we plan?" She turned to me helplessly: "What do people plan?"
>
> Before I could answer her eyes fastened with an awed expression on her little finger.
>
> "Look!" she complained; "I hurt it."
>
> We all looked—the knuckle was black and blue.
>
> "You did it, Tom," she said accusingly. "I know you didn't mean to, but you *did* do it. That's what I get for marrying a brute of a man, a great, big, hulking physical specimen of a—"
>
> "I hate that word hulking," objected Tom crossly, "even in kidding."
>
> "Hulking," insisted Daisy.[1]

He has captured here with impressive exactness the feeling of the Buchanan life in all its sterility, emptiness, and confusion. The egotism behind the thought and feelings is clear. But the tone is too simplistic, too filled with spite. The only possible response—and it is too easily arrived at—is scorn.

Fitzgerald knew the danger here and his method of attacking it is significant. That method is to force our attention not on the scene itself but on the moral consequences of the debased feelings that sustain the dialogue. Thus:

> "You make me feel uncivilized, Daisy," I confessed on my second glass of corky but rather impressive claret. "Can't you talk about crops or something?"
>
> I meant nothing in particular by this remark, but it was taken up in an unexpected way.
>
> "Civilization's going to pieces," broke out Tom violently. "I've gotten to be a terrible pessimist about things. Have you read 'The Rise of the Colored Empires' by this man Goddard?"
>
> "Why, no," I answered, rather surprised by his tone.

> "Well, it's a fine book, and everybody ought to read it. The idea is if we don't look out the white race will be—will be utterly submerged. It's all scientific stuff; it's been proved."
>
> "Tom's getting very profound," said Daisy, with an expression of unthoughtful sadness. "He reads deep books with long words in them. What was that word we—"
>
> "Well, these books are all scientific," insisted Tom glancing at her impatiently. "This fellow has worked out the whole thing. It's up to us, who are the dominant race, to watch out or these other races will have control of things." (p. 13)

The tone here is more ironic, but the significance of the passage lies in its moral reordering of what has preceded it. Tom's confused racism throws the whole long dinner scene into a new and darker perspective and we are forced to reevaluate the simple scorn of our response. The Buchanans may be despicable, but they are also dangerous. The racism dialogue acts as a kind of frame for the scene, the upshot of which is that our attention turns from what the Buchanans *are* to what they *represent*.

Fitzgerald repeats this technique in Chapter II. The long party scene in Tom's and Myrtle Wilson's hideaway hardly rises above the level of bathos until the end:

> Some time toward midnight Tom Buchanan and Mrs. Wilson stood face to face, discussing in impassioned voices whether Mrs. Wilson had any right to mention Daisy's name.
>
> "Daisy! Daisy! Daisy!" shouted Mrs. Wilson. "I'll say it whenever I want to! Daisy! Dai—"
>
> Making a short deft movement, Tom Buchanan broke her nose with his open hand. (p. 37)

The method and significance are here the same as they were before. The moral consequences of the bathos, not the bathos itself, are what is being insisted on. He uses the frame technique for a third time in Chapter III, though this time with reverse effect. After the bathos of the drunks and the wrecked car has been established, the frame technique throws the scene into perspective, but by dissociating Gatsby from the life he watches over.

It may seem that I am laboring over the obvious or even perversely refuting my own earlier remarks, but what I am trying to establish is the kind of representative quality the Buchanans have. For they are not meant to be taken as adequate representatives of the American leisure class ("the rich"); rather they represent a deep and permanent tendency in American life, one that surfaces most spectacularly in the leisure class but which is by no means confined to it. The quality they represent, the tendency they embody, is a moral complacency that finds material wealth both self-validating and its own end. The truth about the Buchanans is that they are blind to any values or standards beyond the ones they enact. It is not that they repudiate any deeper wisdom about life and its ends; it is that they are unaware of any such wisdom. "The curse of ignorance," according to Socrates in the *Symposium*, "is that a man without being good or wise is nevertheless satisfied with himself: he has no desire for that of which he feels no want." It is this curse of ignorance that they embody and moral complacency is the quality they represent. Their debased feelings—their infantilism—have the most serious consequences for human life; but the material wealth which validates the moral complacency also makes thinking about ends and consequences unnecessary. The novel lacks the necessary density and roundedness for the Buchanans to be accepted as anything like adequate representatives of the American leisure class. Read like that the novel is not just brittle but absurd. But they represent a quality, a permanent tendency that runs all through American life and which finds its source in Benjamin Franklin.

II

The Great Gatsby is about the American dream—so the truism goes. But the truism in this case is too clumsy, for there are actually two American dreams and *The Great Gatsby* is about them both and the way they interact. It is convenient to employ metonymy and identify these two dreams with the two figures who first articulated them and thereby brought them to consciousness: Franklin and Ralph Waldo Emerson.

Franklin's dream is the dream of *freedom-from* that D. H. Lawrence complained about so bitterly in *Studies in Classic American Literature. The Autobiography* is a book shaped by fear, the fear of arbitrary power—tyranny—that prevents a man from becoming himself. The form this fear takes is economic. What does Franklin teach us? That a man has to acquire a certain amount of necessary wealth so that his destiny will be in his own hands and not those of his creditors. Without wealth no man is free—that is the book's secret motto. It is no use being superior about this motto. Franklin was articulating something deep in human consciousness and something given power by the intellectual and political currents of the time. America can be the land of the free because in America every man can acquire the minimum wealth necessary to be his own man. It's a dream not far different from Jefferson's, and it was certainly never intended to license the Robber Barons. But what we must pay attention to is its focus and direction. It is a view that looks exclusively to the past and defines itself in relation to that past. In a way it is transfixed by that past to the extent that it never turns its face forward and asks itself where it is going and what its consequences are. It is so exclusively concerned with *getting free* that it has no energy left for exploring the meaning of its freedom. The wealth that bestows freedom validates itself. Vulgarized, what this means is that wealth is not just means but end; because it means freedom it need not be questioned by any standard beyond itself. (That the emergence of this idea happened to coincide with the vulgarization of certain aspects of Calvinist theology—the Puritan Ethic argument—was doubly unfortunate, for not only was a possible higher standard for judgment lost, but the new tendency received a firm moral—sometimes religious—endorsement.) Having become free, Franklinian man is spared the necessity of having to ask himself, What for? What is my freedom for?

Franklin himself did not entirely escape this vulgarization. It is present in *The Autobiography* in two distinct ways. The first and most famous of these is the schedule of virtues that is attached to the plan for moral perfection. All that needs to be said about them was said long ago by Lawrence. They are hopelessly trivial and the sense of life they betray is likewise trivial. The second is to be found in the basic structure of the book itself. The principle of organization is the anecdotal moral lesson. He retails little events from his past and then points out the lesson to be learned. Franklin was a skilled comic writer and his life gave him a fund of rich material, but because there is no deeper sense of life working through and organizing the material it becomes hopelessly repetitious and finally just boring. One reads up to the famous plan and perhaps a little beyond, but the book is unreadable straight through and no one is likely to mind that it went unfinished.

The Autobiography, nevertheless, is the most influential book ever written by an American. It organized, expressed, and made eminently respectable a concept of human life that is seriously deficient but which does not know itself to be so. The view it expresses is the bourgeois outlook of Main Street, and its American dream has been casually and complacently erected into the implicit goal of American life. What makes it pernicious is that the value-words on which it depends, especially freedom, are invoked but not defined. In the nature of the case they cannot easily be, but there is present no reason for feeling that they *should* be. The Franklinian dream, then, is one of self-validating materialism that is ignorant about the inner, positive meaning of the freedom it posits as its end, and is in fact complacently blind with respect to any positive moral values or genuinely spiritual sense of human life. The Buchanans embody it in its least attractive form.

Emerson's role as an antipode to Franklin has never been adequately stressed, yet it is possible to say that his whole career was a quarrel with the Franklinian spirit and the Franklinian dream. "Quarrel" is perhaps inadequate to suggest that in every line he indited Emerson was warring against the Franklinian outlook. The main thrust of his career was an attempt to take the American dream away from the Franklinians ("the Party of Memory," he called them) and to redefine it in moral and spiritual terms. For Emerson, too, the meaning of America was associated with freedom, but he set out to explore the nature and consequence of that freedom and to determine its effect on human life. He too articulated an American dream, but one moral and spiritual and always in the state of becoming. It is not a little significant that when—as in *The American Scholar* and *Self-Reliance*—Emerson goes on the attack he writes against an attitude that he posits in unmistakable Franklinian imagery: the "iron lids" of the "sluggard intellect" that never rises above "mechanical skill" and so results in a spirit that is "timid, imitative, tame"; or "the reliance on Property" no matter if it comes through "gift, inheritance, or crime" that marks "the want of self-reliance."

Self-reliance is the foremost Franklinian virtue; it is also the title of Emerson's most powerful essay, and the fundamental differences between the two American dreams can be seen by comparing the inner meanings the concept had for the two men. For Franklin it is a reliance on one's self as an accumulator of wealth; that is, it is a means for becoming free from the power of another. It is indivisible from the credit-enhancing self-discipline which is the highest mark of character. Because this self-reliance *works*—i.e., because it does lead to wealth—the inevitable tendency is to over-value this self of the marketplace, to feel secure in its power and certain of its capacity. And this in turn leads to the moral complacency that abandons any rigorous scrutiny of means and ends and which does not feel itself to be called on to answer any of the deeper questions about life. Its self is a satisfied self. This is most easily seen in the pitch-note of optimism (or, at its most vulgar, backslapping, flank-rubbing geniality) which has always keyed the Franklinian dream and which is not an optimism that has taken the measure of things, but is only a lack of contact with or concern for any adequate concept of Evil or with the tragic sense. Franklin rose above this through his ideal of public service. But often no such ideal exists, and after the status of leisure has been attained, there is no sense of what to do with it. Life flattens out into a string of "Tomorrow and tomorrow and tomorrow...." "'What'll we do with ourselves this afternoon?' cried Daisy, 'and the day after that, and the next thirty years?'" (p. 118).

For Emerson self-reliance was based on trust, but it was decidedly not a trust in the ordinary self of the marketplace. That self had to be redeemed. Self-reliance begins with a reliance on God, or at least the Oversoul, and it moves through a purgation of the ordinary self. That movement is from the ordinary self existing at the level of Franklinian materialism to the new self that has left materialism behind in order to live in the spirit. "The one thing in the world, of value, is the active soul." The whole of Emerson's thought is contained in that one sentence with its startling reassessment of the concept of *value*. Where Franklin is concerned with being and having, Emerson is concerned with being and becoming. Where Franklin is concerned with accumulating energy, Emerson is concerned with releasing it. Where Franklin looks to the past to secure his definition and meaning, Emerson looks to the future. Freedom is the condition for man's exploration of the new, higher self. "This one fact the world hates: that the soul *becomes*; for that forever degrades the past, turns all riches to poverty, all respect to shame."

It is difficult to translate the Emersonian vision, with its strong overlaying of mysticism, into the language of ordinary discourse. At his greatest moments Emerson was operating at the frontiers of language, and he knew what obstacles that raised to communication. But it is enough to note the positive, idealist structure of the Emersonian dream, and to note too the stern standard of *character* which Emerson assumed. He had nothing to offer triflers. The real secret of the Emersonian self is that, in contradistinction to the Franklinian self based on wealth, it depends on the moral ground of its own bedrock puritanism. Much of its power lies in its promise to free the ordinary self from the materialism, stagnancy, and moral complacency of the enacted Franklinian dream. Its promise is in the future; it lies in becoming and poses the deepest of moral challenges. In attempting to articulate it, Emerson threw Franklin's dream into a new perspective. Once both are brought to consciousness, the moral deficiency and adolescent cast of Franklin's become glaring. One has to leave it behind and pursue the higher truth. Emerson was a true moral teacher: he called on men to change their lives. His vision involved nothing less than a fundamental revaluation of the meaning of the American experience. The new self is to be a moral self whose duty is to be always becoming, always extending and newly articulating the possibilities of life. "The truth was that Jay Gatsby...sprang from his Platonic conception of himself. He was a son of God..." (p. 99).

III

Information about Gatsby is scattered piecemeal throughout the novel and accumulates slowly for the very good reason that Nick Carraway has to realize the significance of Gatsby's career and this realization does not come easily. The last piece of the puzzle is provided by the novel's oddest character, Gatsby's father, who does not enter until the last chapter. What he provides pushes the novel to the full limits of its depth and significance. He takes from his pocket a tattered copy of *Hopalong Cassidy* and shows Carraway Gatsby's boyhood schedule scribbled inside the back cover. This schedule associates quite explicitly Gatsby's youthful dreams with the Franklinian version of the American Dream. But Gatsby is not associated with that dream; his is of a different order altogether.

When Gatsby dismisses his servants at the start of Chapter VII he is registering his attitude toward wealth. He cares nothing for it in itself; its only value is as a means to something beyond itself, some fuller, more graceful sense of life of which Daisy is the symbol. Gatsby's is a version of the Emersonian dream: in a great imaginative act he has created himself and set out to explore the possibilities of life. The Franklinian dream was the dream of his youth, but he repudiated that youth and the dream associated with it. Part of his "greatness" lies in his having transcended the limits of the Franklinian world, but it is his fate that this Emersonian greatness will go largely unwarranted in a world whose fundamental postulates are Franklinian, postulates he cannot entirely escape. But Gatsby's dream matured, while America's did not. It is again Mr. Gatz who drives this point home. Throughout the novel Gatsby is consistently misunderstood by those who speculate about him, but none hits wider of the mark than his own father:

> "He had a big future before him, you know. He was only a young man, but he had a lot of brain power here."
>
> He touched his head impressively, and I nodded.
>
> "If he'd of lived, he'd of been a great man. A man like James J. Hill. He'd of helped build up the country." (p. 169)

The concept of greatness is perfectly representative, the representation underlined by the standard invoked. Greatness for Mr. Gatz lies within the Franklinian vision of America. His desire for his son is that he become another Tom Buchanan. The real nature of Gatsby's greatness takes shape against this concept.

The Franklinian dream leads only to the dead end of money, and the characteristic animus held against the leisure class throughout the novel is associated with their lack of any enlarging vision. The Buchanans possess wealth and its concomitant freedom but they have no idea of living. They just drift "here and there unrestfully wherever people played polo and were rich together" (p. 6). Their concept of life never extends beyond a game. What the novel dramatizes, then, is the conflict between the two American dreams, one whose idea is material wealth and leisure (a restless leisure), the other whose ideal is less restricted and finally spiritual. But the novel argues its point even more closely. The Emersonian dream of the self depends to a certain extent on wealth also, although on wealth as means not as end. The freedom this wealth produces is *freedom-to*, a positive value, one that looks forward to becoming. One way of seeing the conflict is to say that there has been a fundamental confusion of material and spiritual values and that the novel dramatizes this confusion which is deep in American life. The confusion can account for Gatsby's failure—i.e., his unwise location of the meaning of his dream in Daisy.

But Carraway offers another choice. In his final meditation he notes that Gatsby's dream of the future really lies in the past, "somewhere back in that vast obscurity beyond the city, where the dark fields of the republic [roll] on under the night" (p. 182). The transcendental vision collapsed under the weight of the Civil War: that is a primary datum of American intellectual history. Another is that in the vast accumulation of wealth that followed, few noticed that it was gone. Where it endured (John Jay Chapman) or resurges (Martin Luther King) it is a quirk: the American dream is a Franklinian dream. The Emersonian dream is in the possession of the scholars. The older vision was temporarily challenged by Emerson but his dream, which in part was not of this world, ended and the older vision reemerged and changed with the new conditions. It was Horatio Alger, not Emerson, who articulated the sense of the postwar world.

Gatsby's failure is an index of the inability of the Emersonian dream to be focused adequately in this world, which is another way of saying that he fails because he is too innocent. It is a very telling fact that Emerson did not like, and could see no reason to read, fiction. He had no sense that works of art act their moral judgments. His mind, which had a curious eighteenth-century cast to it, wanted just the moral values, stated pure and simple. He truly was once-born. But we must draw back here from the gates of allegory and focus on Gatsby. Gatsby embodies the Emersonian dream, perhaps the most attractive quality in American life, and its weakness is his failure. His dream is so beautiful that he assumes that whatever triggers it must also have its haloed quality. The dazzle of the dream leaves his eyes too weak to gaze on ordinary life. Daisy's value for him is purely symbolic; like his shirts or his servants she means something beyond herself. His vision implicitly evaluates American civilization even as it gives dignity and purpose to his life. But while the Franklinian dream is complacently ignorant about the ends of life, the Emersonian dream runs the danger that the dreamer may be transfixed by his end. He may lose his contact with ordinary living.

IV

The Great Gatsby dramatizes the conflict between the two American dreams. It does this because its characters represent fundamental tendencies in American life, and the novel acts its meaning on this representative level. It reveals a profound insight into the American past and the meaning of that past in the present. Fitzgerald dramatizes with a sure touch the moral consequences of the conflict and the moral differences between the two dreams. Moreover, he lays his finger on what is tragically missing in American life: an articulated awareness of moral evil. Both the Franklinian and Emersonian dreams lean too heavily on the thin reed of optimism. What is wanted is the oaken staff of Jonathan Edwards or the tragic sensibility of Abraham Lincoln. The novel, on the literal level, like Gatsby's clothes, always just misses being absurd. But on a different level it reveals, on the part of its author, a rare inwardness with something that one can only call the meaning of American history.

Notes to The Great Gatsby and the American Past

1. F. Scott Fitzgerald, *The Great Gatsby* (New York, n.d.), p. 12. This and all subsequent page numbers refer to the Scribner Library Edition.

HOST-ESS AND PRIESTESS: SACRAMENTAL IMAGERY IN *MRS. DALLOWAY*

René Fortin

The real question confronting the literary critic, despite Edward Albee, is not who is afraid of Virginia Woolf, but who understands Virginia Woolf. There is general agreement about her formal contributions to the modern novel, but the ultimate significance of her art is a matter of dispute. Walter Allen, for example, in *The Modern Novel* (New York, 1964), finds her ultimate significance quite limited; granting her some moments of revelation and illumination, he warns, however, that these "sometimes don't amount to much more than a series of short, sharp, feminine gasps of ecstasy." Other critics are more generous, conceding that some substance is to be found in her novels, though they cannot quite agree as to precisely where this substance lies: the novels, accordingly, have been read in the light of Bergson, Freud, Plato, British empiricism, and even Chinese quietism.

Mrs. Woolf has, in addition, been castigated by Erich Auerbach in *Mimesis* (Garden City, NY, 1957) for her nihilistic philosophy, her "turning away from the practical will to live and producing, in *To the Lighthouse*, a book filled with good and genuine love but also in its feminine way, with irony, amorphous sadness, and doubt." R. W. B. Lewis' *The Picaresque Saint* (Philadelphia, 1959) pushes the point further, taking exception to her "fading fragilities, the sigh that extends into a delicate death rattle...." He argues that she, along with the other death-obsessed writers of her literary generation, moved "away from actual life as fatally infected by death and toward an imaginative life made whole and luminous by art...art was the answer given back by the first generation to the universal pressure of death." This diversity of critical opinion is little less than startling; one might well agree with Shakespeare's Cicero that

> Indeed, it is a strange-disposed time:
> But men may construe things after their fashion,
> Clean from the purpose of the things themselves.

I am convinced that *Mrs. Dalloway* is very much at the center of the Woolf problem and that grasping the meaning of this novel would contribute greatly to a clearer assessment of Virginia Woolf's thought. I am convinced, moreover, that this novel can be made accessible to the reader, not by imposing a philosophical system upon it, but by carefully examining the traditional religious symbols and values which the novel explores. The fundamental problem of *Mrs. Dalloway* is the fragmentation of the modern world, the loss of unity within society and within the individual himself. And though the novel implies that Christianity has been a monumental failure in its attempt to safeguard the unity of man, it nevertheless engages in a careful re-assessment of traditional Christian values. The imagery of this novel, in fact, suggests that the central action of the heroine is to find an adequate substitute for Christianity and, specifically, for the sacramental sense of reality which it fostered. Only by a restoration of this sacramental sense of reality, Virginia Woolf argues, can man regain his integrity, his wholeness.

The precision with which the problem is stated is remarkable, for the spiritual vacuum of modern society is initially dramatized by an extremely suggestive parody of sacramental imagery. From Mrs. Dalloway's encounter with a government vehicle in the early part of the novel emerges one of the central metaphors. The vehicle is described with religious imagery: "But now mystery had touched them with her ring; they had heard the voice of authority: the spirit of religion was abroad with her eyes bandaged tight and her lips gaping wide." After the car is stopped by a policeman and then allowed to proceed when identification is shown, the religious imagery becomes even more specific:

> Clarissa guessed; Clarissa knew of course; she had seen something white, magical, circular, in the footman's hand, a disc inscribed with a name—the Queen's, the Prince of Wales's, the Prime Minister's?—which, by force of its own luster, burnt its way through...to blaze among

> candelabras, glittering stars, breasts stiff with oak leaves, Hugh Whitbread and all his colleagues...

The white, magical, circular disc possessed of religious significance hardly needs the additional notion of "Whitbread" to be identified with the Host of the Eucharist, or at least the ironic modern equivalent of it. The function of Christianity in this secular age, the passage hints, has been assumed by the government; it is the government which is invested with authority and mystery, which provides a sense of community to the populace. The ironic tone leaves no doubt that the government is considered unworthy to take on the functions abdicated by Christianity.

Immediately after the car vanishes, an airplane appears, writing an indecipherable message across the sky, "as if destined to cross from West to East on a mission of the greatest importance which would never be revealed..." The airplane (which, in its West to East flight, significantly reverses the historic course of Christianity) is interpreted as a religious phenomenon by various people. To Septimus Smith, the airplane heralds the "birth of a new religion," inspiring in him an ecstatic perception of the unity of being:

> ...leaves were alive; trees were alive. And the leaves being connected by millions of fibres with his own body, there on the seat, fanned it up and down; when the branch stretched he, too, made that statement. The sparrows, fluttering, rising, and falling in jagged fountains were part of the pattern...

To another observer, the airplane was a "symbol...of man's soul; of his determination to get outside his body, beyond his house, by means of thought, Einstein, speculation, mathematics, the Mendelian theory...." (p. 41). And to yet another observer, the airplane is related to that symbol which it supersedes, the cathedral with its altar and cross "the symbol of something which has soared beyond seeking and questioning and knocking of words together and has become all spirit, disembodied, ghostly...."

But the new religion symbolized by the airplane is also fraudulent: its "marvelous revelation" is first mysterious, then insignificant when it is finally decipherable. The message which the airplane is communicating is the word "toffee"; the airplane, identified with the strange gods of science and technology, with the kind of speculation that has replaced traditional thought, offers no solace to man: its "mission of the greatest importance" is to serve commerce. Other and more obvious perversions of the religious instinct are the cults of the Goddess Proportion and the Goddess Conversion. The Goddess Proportion, around which has grown the cult of respectability, conformity, and efficiency, has as her high-priest Sir William Bradshaw, the psychiatrist, who "not only prospered himself, but made England prosper, secluded her lunatics, forbade childbirth, penalized despair, made it impossible for the unfit to propagate their views until they too shared his sense of proportion." Sir William, in his complacency and shallowness, feels that there is nothing wrong with the modern psyche that common sense cannot overcome.

But the Goddess Conversion, a sister Goddess of whom he is also a dedicated worshipper, is more insidious, for she "feasts on the wills of the weakly, loving to impress, to impose, adoring her own features stamped on the face of the populace." This goddess, that is, represents the will for power, the tyranny of a strong personality over a weaker one. Miss Kilman, the zealous Christian who would bludgeon others into her convictions, is another devotee of the Goddess Conversion, whose tyranny extends into all human relationships, even that of love: "love and religion [muses Mrs. Dalloway] would destroy the privacy of the soul."

Much of the religious imagery, therefore, is charged with a powerful irony extended to expose the fraudulence and oppressiveness of the modern versions of religion. Mrs. Dalloway, in fact, twice professes herself to be an atheist (pp. 43, 118, Harbrace Modern Classics Edition), and she is even bitter in her denunciation of religion:

> Love and religion! How detestable they are! ... The crudest things in the world, she thought, seeing them clumsy, hot, domineering, hypocritical, eavesdropping, jealous, infinitely cruel and scrupulous, dressed in a mackintosh coat, on the landing; love and religion.

But the religious imagery is much more subtle than it would seem to be, for despite the bitter antagonism against religion expressed through Mrs. Dalloway, the novel moves through its religious imagery into an admittedly tentative and partial but nonetheless significant affirmation. The complexity of meaning inherent in the religious imagery emerges above all in the characterization of Septimus Smith, who lurks enigmatically on the periphery of Clarissa Dalloway's life. Septimus Smith is initially perplexing: what are we to make of a Christ figure in an atheistic, anti-religious novel? The insanity of Septimus, suggesting a continuation of the ironic view of religion, is certainly to be taken into account. But the unmistakable sympathy with which he is treated by the author as well as the eventual identification of Septimus and Mrs. Dalloway compel us to find at least some residual significance in the Christ analogue. Septimus and the traditional Christian values which cling to him cannot be entirely dissolved by irony.

In my opinion, he can best be understood as a device of intensification (reminiscent of the Gloucester sub-plot in *King Lear*). His function is apparently to provide a heightened version of Mrs. Dalloway, with whom his spiritual kinship is later asserted. Where Clarissa is hedged in by her domestic environment, Septimus, his perceptions intensified by his insanity, penetrates the boredom of life to reveal at once its horror and its glory. He is ecstatic in his visions of beauty: "The trees waved, brandished. We welcome, the world seemed to say; we accept; we create. Beauty, the world seemed to say...all of this, calm and reasonable as it was, made out of ordinary things as it was, was the truth now: beauty, that was the truth now. Beauty was everywhere."

But he is flagellated as well by the sordidness of existence:

> This was now revealed to Septimus; the message hidden in the beauty of words. The secret signal which one generation passes, under disguise, to the next is loathing, hatred, despair. For the truth is...that human beings have neither kindness, nor faith, nor charity beyond what serves to increase the pleasure of the moment.

The agony of Septimus is precisely that of Mrs. Dalloway, but raised to a higher power; isolated like her, he yearns for the unity and integrity of existence which would give significance to his life. What is at stake in this novel is the very worth of life itself, and the struggle is waged especially in the tortured mind of Septimus, "the Lord who had come to renew society...the scapegoat, the eternal sufferer...." Whether or not Septimus consummates his symbolic redemptive role is kept in suspense throughout; even at the very moment before his suicide, Septimus is ambivalent about life: "But he would wait [to commit suicide] till the very last moment. He did not want to die. Life was good. The sun hot. Only human beings—what did *they* want?"

The suicide of Septimus is crucial to the meaning of the novel; but significantly, its implications are cloaked in ambiguity. For Mrs. Dalloway, who is expectedly very much moved by his death, is nonetheless inconsistent in her appraisal, viewing it alternately as a triumph and a disaster. Her first reaction borders on jubilation:

> Death was defiance. Death was an attempt to communicate; people feeling the impossibility of reaching the centre which, mystically, evaded them; closeness drew apart; rapture faded, one was alone. There was an embrace in death.

But she then re-assesses the situation:

> Somehow it was her disaster—her disgrace. It was her punishment to see sink and disappear here a man, there a woman, in this profound darkness, and she forced to stand here in her evening dress.

Neither is this, however, the final statement of her altitude. After a further consideration of the death, she concludes that "she felt somehow very like him—the young man who had killed himself. She felt glad that he had done it; thrown it away.... He made her feel the beauty; made her feel the fun." Her final estimate is vaguely affirmative, and the precise meaning of Septimus' death remains a matter of conjecture. Despite this ambiguity, however, Septimus Smith has fulfilled his strategic function: to focus our attention upon the religious dimensions of the novel.

It is against this background of religious imagery, transvaluated or often ironic in effect, that Mrs. Dalloway's actions take on a precise meaning. This precise meaning begins to unfold when she is described as a nun: "...she felt like a nun who has left the world and feels fold around her the familiar veils and the response to old devotions.... It was her life, and, bending her head over the hall table, she bowed beneath the influence, felt blessed and purified...." The image of the nun is appropriate in many ways; above all, it immediately points to the isolation of Mrs. Dalloway, who even in her marriage cannot effectively communicate with another person. She has renounced conjugal life, unable "to dispel a virginity preserved through childbirth which clung to her like a sheet."

But the nun image expands in significance as the novel develops; in this early description of Mrs. Dalloway there is already implicit the sacredness with which Mrs. Dalloway feels life is—or should be—permeated. She seeks to penetrate through the veil of ordinary human experience to the mystical center. These moments of illumination (attained, according to her testimony, only in encounters with other women) bridge the gap between persons to provide moments of communion: "Only for a moment, but it was enough. It was a sudden revelation.... Then, for that moment, she had seen an illumination, a match burning in a crocus; an inner meaning almost expressed. But the close withdrew; the hard softened."

The great affirmation of which she is capable is that the human personality is sacred; she looks upon the mystery of the human soul with reverence and almost religious awe. It is important, therefore, to detect the tension in her yearning for unity, for communion. Human beings, she feels, must attain unity, but they must attain it without losing individual integrity; a soul must make contact with, but must neither dominate nor submit to another. This is for Mrs. Dalloway the "supreme mystery," the delicate balance between isolation and involvement: "Here was one room; there another. Did religion solve that, or love?" She continues elsewhere:

> And there is a dignity in people; a solitude; even between husband and wife a gulf; and that one must respect, thought Clarissa, watching him open the door; for one would not part with it oneself, or take it against his will, from one's husband, without losing one's independence, one's self-respect—something, after all, priceless.

To establish the kind of communication which would not violate the mystery of the soul is the self-appointed mission of Clarissa Dalloway. And her parties, for which she is the object of polite scorn or, at best, condescension, are her means of establishing this delicate relationship. She is the "perfect hostess" (p. 9) whose special gift is to unite, to be "composed so for the world only into one centre, one diamond, one woman who sat in her drawing-room and made a meeting-point, a radiancy no doubt in some dull lives, a refuge for the lonely to come to, perhaps."

But the parties are more than social gatherings; it is crucial to note that they are described quite precisely as "offerings":

> But suppose Peter says to her, "yes, yes, but your parties—what's the sense of your parties?" all she could say was (and nobody could be expected to understand): They're an offering; which sounded horribly vague...she felt if only they could be brought together; so she did it. And it was an offering; to combine, to create; but to whom? An offering for the sake of offering, perhaps. Anyhow, it was her gift.

The precise sense in which her parties are offerings is revealed by her relationship with Septimus: just as Septimus, if he were to consummate his archetypal redemptive mission, would offer himself to save mankind, so does Mrs. Dalloway, through her parties, offer herself as sacrifice; she is "the woman who was that very night to give a party; of Clarissa Dalloway; of herself."

Furthermore, the virtual identification of Septimus and Mrs. Dalloway reveals the extent of her offering: the death of Septimus in the course of her party is, symbolically, the death of Clarissa herself. It was, in fact, Virginia Woolf's original intention to climax the party with the death of the heroine;

the "Introduction" to the Modern Library edition (New York, 1928) quotes her, "...in the first version, Septimus, who later is intended to be her double, had no existence. Mrs. Dalloway was originally to kill herself, or perhaps merely to die at the end of the party." We may see traces of this original intention in her husband's warning that Mrs. Dalloway's parties are "bad for her heart" (p. 183) and in the prefigurative vision of Peter Walsh: "...and the sudden loudness of the final stroke tolled for death that surprised in the midst of life, Clarissa falling where she stood, in her drawing room" (p. 75).

The conclusion is, I think, inescapable: a party which involves an offering, a sacrifice in the form of a symbolic death, and a sense of communion in the participants obviously invites identification with the Mass. Mrs. Dalloway, in her parodic Mass, is indeed the "perfect hostess," offering herself, like Christ, as priest and victim to restore the integrity of man.

It would certainly seem, therefore, that the inseparable Christian mysteries of the Holy Eucharist and the Mystical Body are directly and profoundly involved in the meaning of *Mrs. Dalloway*. Virginia Woolf sees disunity everywhere in human experience: man is isolated from man, lacking the "something central" around which a corporate society could form. He is, moreover, split in his own experience, tortured above all by irreconcilability of matter and spirit. Mrs. Dalloway's genuine love for her husband, as we have seen, cannot express itself physically, while Septimus is himself disgusted by "the getting of children, the sordidity of mouth and belly!" (p. 134). It is significantly these Christian mysteries of the Eucharist and the Mystical Body which fit the Christian to his world and his world to him; through them the integrity of human experience is restored. In the words of the theologian Matthias J. Scheeben:

> ...the significance of the Eucharist comes to this, that the real union of the Son of God with all men is ratified, completed, and sealed in it, and that men are perfectly incorporated in Him in the most intimate, real, and substantial manner, so that, as they are His members, they may also partake of His life. The concept of our real and substantial incorporation in Christ [the Mystical Body] is the fundamental idea of the mystery of the Eucharist.

The implications of this incorporation in Christ, it should be noted, are not exclusively spiritual; mankind does not become a society of angelic beings tolerating the temporary embarrassment of corporeality. The effect of man's incorporation in Christ through the Eucharist extends to man's material life; as another scholar has expressed it:

> ...the Eucharist does not melt matter into pure spirit or make angels out of men in history. The sacramental strategy is to respect, while it reinforces, the created handiwork of God. The Word is made Flesh. The sacrament of the altar is fleshly. And from it, like ever-widening circles from the rock dropped at the center of the dark pool, flows the sacramental principle, reclaiming place and time, but destroying nothing. Nature is consecrated and renovated by the sacramental action.

The parody of the Eucharist at the beginning of the novel—the white, magical, circular disc—has, in effect, revealed the central action of the novel: a search for a renewed sacramental sense of reality which would re-establish the integrity and significance of human experience. In a very precise sense, Mrs. Dalloway does not *find* this sacramental sense, she *becomes* herself the sacrament which will make man whole.

To point out Mrs. Woolf's careful parody of the Christian mysteries and her indebtedness to Christian sacramental doctrine serves to define the issues which the novel probes. But we must remember, in pursuing her meaning, that the symbols are transvaluated, that, in other words, their dogmatic content is radically altered. The author evidently had little sympathy for Christianity, and she is most decidedly not urging a wholesale return to the Christian communion. Her exact meaning, in fact, is blurred by a gentle and all-pervasive irony from which even Septimus and Mrs. Dalloway cannot entirely escape. However, we may conjecture with some certitude that the novel is a statement of secular humanism: the vague hope that man will find a renewed harmony in his life lies in the possibility of self-redemption. Mrs. Dalloway's appraisal of her action reveals the central tragedy of her life, that there is no God to whom (and in the more accurate Christian sense, with whom) the Sacrifice can be offered.

"...it was an offering; to combine, to create; but to whom? An offering for the sake of offering, perhaps. Anyhow, it was her gift" (p. 185). In the absence of anything else, man must become his own sacrament.

This much is, I think, quite clear. But a radical uncertainty lingers in other areas. Throughout the novel, horror of the flesh has been symptomatic of psychic maladjustment (in a much more than merely Freudian sense—though I am not discounting Freudian interpretations, I feel that Mrs. Dalloway's psychological problem is symptom rather than cause for her anguish, the issues in the novel far transcending psychology). The tone of the novel conveys what clearly seems to be a criticism of the angelism of Mrs. Dalloway, Septimus, and Miss Kilman. The virginity which Mrs. Dalloway has been unable to dispel in her marriage is but another example of the time that is out of joint; in symbolic terms, the bells of Big Ben—symbolizing the masculine and physical nature of love—continue to ring two minutes before the bells of St. Margaret's, symbolizing the feminine and spiritual nature of love (cf. pp. 72–75, 193). This inability to reconcile sex and soul, the novel implies, is the peculiar spiritual sickness of modern man. And yet, the "sacrifice" of Mrs. Dalloway apparently does nothing to reconcile sex and soul. Despite the relative success of the party, there is no indication that the transformed and almost transfigured Mrs. Dalloway has come to terms with her fleshliness. Her affirmation of life in this novel is at best tentative, since the "sacrament" of Mrs. Dalloway has brought about a limited communion between people but has apparently not redeemed the world of matter.

POETIC FORM IN "JOURNEY OF THE MAGI"

Brian Barbour

We had the experience but missed the meaning.
(T. S. ELIOT, *The Dry Salvages*)

It is odd that T. S. Eliot's most accessible poem, "Journey of the Magi," has been routinely approached as a biographical signpost rather than as "excellent words in excellent arrangement and excellent metre" (Eliot, *Sacred Wood*, ix). Eliot, after all, is the one who early on made the eloquent plea from which so much that is valuable in modern criticism derives, a plea for an approach to poetry that respects its *integrity*: "when we are considering poetry we must consider it primarily as poetry and not another thing" (*Sacred Wood*, viii). Yet it is the poem's apparent status as an expression of Eliot's spiritual journey and formal conversion that seems to arrest most attention—another oddity considering Eliot's negative views on regarding poetry as the direct transcription of the poet's inner state. And it is odder still that so little thinking has been directed to the poem's form when we consider that it is not only accessible but quite popular. Recall for a moment the Eliot section in a typical anthology—the *Norton*, say; "Prufrock" and "The Waste Land" are there, of course, as are "Tradition and the Individual Talent" and "The Metaphysical Poets"; *Four Quartets* is represented by "Little Gidding." And all of this is as it should be, for each of these works is of major intrinsic and historical importance. But "Journey of the Magi" is included too, despite its lesser status, and the reason, of course, is that students, who find the other poems, and even the prose, daunting, find this work accessible. So it is a poem that is much read and much discussed, at least in the classroom. And yet some elementary formal points have never been addressed.

This is not because the poem has lacked commentators. It is granted its routine page in the standard books. It has been cranked through the Derridean contraption and had its integrity severed into four synchronic "texts" (see Harris). And it has received its share of consideration in critical journals, where one expects the focus to be tightly drawn and the explication to be vigorous. Yet it would not be misleading to say that criticism of the poem keeps reverting to the same four points: (1) The first lines were lifted from Lancelot Andrewes's Nativity Sermon of 1622, and modified. (2) The rich imagery of the second part is proleptic, its Christian, symbolic import not yet established in history. (3) The psychological portrait of the magus in part three shows a man puzzled and in anguish. (4) The poem as a whole, and taken with "Song of Simeon," marks a stage in Eliot's own conversion, an event of the same year. But the first of these is misleading; the third has to be recognized as rooted in the second; and the conversion theme needs to be studied as it emerges dramatically in the verse, not glanced at as a function of the poet's biography. Criticism, therefore, needs to examine the neglected question of the poem's form, if only to push past these four points and open up further lines of discussion.

Almost everyone recognizes that the poem is a dramatic monologue. And there is a general consensus that as with Eliot's other works of this type—"Prufrock," "Portrait of a Lady," "Gerontion"—we are on safe ground only when we discuss the speaker, that both audience and occasion are indeterminate in keeping with Eliot's modernist taking of the form inward, that what we have here is something like what Hugh Kenner first called "Prufrock," a "zone of consciousness" (*The Invisible Poet*, 40). But the implicit analogy is simply misleading. "Journey of the Magi" is really quite traditional in its use of the poetic form and is filled with suggestions which, if not solidly Browningesque, nevertheless point in a single discernible direction. From these suggestions both audience and occasion can be inferred, and once these details are understood the poem's irony of situation comes into focus and the theme becomes clear. Any reading that neglects these formal features of the work can never really penetrate to its thematic and experiential center.

I suggest that the *audience* in the poem (the "you" of line 31) is St. Matthew; that the *occasion* is the Evangelist's searching out of the magus to gather information about those events of "a long time ago" (l. 32); that the dramatic monologue is precipitated by the magus's reading of (or, more likely, listening to) a different account of the journey (the first five lines), which St. Matthew has gotten earlier from a second magus and probably polished; that the poem develops as the magus responds to this earlier version; and that the *theme* of conversion emerges because the Evangelist's presence generates a profound irony of situation. And when we read the poem in this way we can see that the old magus's real journey has not ended, that his ultimate destination was not the manger but the cross.

What details support this suggestion? There are at least five. First, there is the matter of the time scheme, the poem's historicity. Line 32 tells us that the journey took place "a long time ago," an indefinite reference but one that allows my suggestion. St. Matthew was Christ's contemporary; he would have been gathering material for his gospel as early as the late 40s or early 50s. As an arbitrary convenience we might date the drama as occurring in the year 50, but what is really important, central in fact, is that the Crucifixion and Resurrection have occurred without the magus's knowing about them. The gospel cannot have spread very far. The year 50 gives the magus great but not impossible age, and the poem everywhere sounds like the voice of an old man. A second detail is the parenthetical "you may say" of line 31. This imputes the audience and seems to authorize the listener to repeat, interpret, or in some way use the magus's recollections. Third, and closely linked, there is the peculiarly forceful urgency of lines 33–35:

> but set down
> This set down
> This.

This detail clearly indicates that the auditor is taking down, and being invited to interpret, the old man's memories. There is one point that he wants transcribed exactly; one feature of the story that mustn't be overlooked. These three details together clearly point to a scribe, but it might be objected that they could point to any scribe, perhaps a servant of the magus, and while suggestive are not entirely conclusive.

Let us turn, then, to the last two. They are the matter of the single quotation marks around the first five lines and the marked poetic shift that occurs at line 6.

It is generally known that Eliot lifted the first five lines from Andrewes's 1622 sermon and modified them for his own purposes. Scholarship, since F. O. Matthiessen first identified the source in 1947, has established this beyond question; but what scholarship establishes is sometimes misleading for criticism. Clearly the lines have to have a poetic function within Eliot's text. Consider how unlikely it is that even the most devout and learned Anglican—and the poem was published in a large edition for the Christmas trade—upon reading those lines would register them as Andrewes's. Eliot happened to be himself steeped in Andrewes at the time (see *For Lancelot Andrewes*, 22–23), but basically he used them because he needed a second voice to precipitate the poetic drama. They must be understood as being read by, or to, the magus and thereby occasioning his own flow of memory. Those inverted commas are peculiar. It is notorious that throughout his work Eliot lifted words, phrases, and lines from other sources and melded them into his own verse. But generally he did not signal this by use of quotation marks, preferring to reserve them for dialogue or, in at least one instance ("Sweeney Agonistes"), to indicate a reading out. And that is how they function here, as a second voice, not as some kind of anachronistic prologue from the great Caroline divine. Either the listener speaks them or the magus reads them (probably the former; recall how "Gerontion" begins: "Here I am, an old man in a dry month, / Being read to..."), but they are a different voice and provocative.

This is corroborated by the fifth and last of the poetic details that establish audience and occasion. It is surely every reader's experience that as he passes from the first five lines to the sixth he notices a marked shift in tone, rhythm, diction, and feeling. Eliot changed Andrewes slightly, but *not* to meld him into his poem; he wants us to register the difference. The voice becomes more intimate and conversational, less formal. The language becomes more particular, while the rhythms tighten and become more nervous and springy. The feeling grows more intense. Whereas the first five lines are somewhat general, loose, and distant ("A cold coming we had of it"), line 6 is vivid, forceful and immediate:

> And the camels galled, sore-footed, refractory.

From line 6 through line 20 of the first section the abstractions of the opening give way to concrete, highly specific details of this sort. Notice how the large looseness of phrasing that marks the opening contrasts with the anaphora and intensity of lines 12–15:

> And running away, and wanting their liquor and women.
> And the night-fires going out, and the lack of shelters.
> And the cities hostile and the towns unfriendly
> And the villages dirty and charging high prices.

The entire first section is built on just such basic poetic contrasts, all moving in the direction of a greater intimacy and realism. When we reach line 16, "A hard time we had of it," with its deliberate echo of the opening, both "hard" and "time" have been charged with a forceful poetic meaning. I suggest that this is because with line 6 we begin to get the voice of the magus proper, responding personally to the somewhat detached, almost mandarin, summary that he has been reading (or listening to). Though the opening is a modified version of Andrewes. it functions in the poem as a second magus's voice, another account of the journey. And as the magus responds, the drama ensues. The poem moves from an impersonal description to a deeply personal re-enactment of a life's intensely pondered, central experience.

The evidence is circumstantial; the Evangelist is not present by name. But taken together these five details point to an audience of someone who, having presented the magus with an earlier account of the journey, now is taking down the old man's memories. The person who best fits this role is St. Matthew, gathering material to write his gospel. (It is suggestive, to say the least, that the work of Dibelius (1919) and Bultmann (1921) which established *formgeschichte* had just appeared, stimulating a new interest in what lies behind scripture.) As with traditional dramatic monologues, "Journey of the Magi" has a discernible speaker, audience, and occasion. In the rest of this paper, I want to follow out the ways these formal features establish the basic irony of situation and show how St. Matthew's presence deepens and enriches the poetic thought.

The poem presents two journeys, related through paradox: it narrates the arduous physical journey and then dramatizes the even more difficult and incomplete spiritual one. The first, the actual historical journey made by the magi from the East, is recounted in vivid detail. It has the necessary *from-to* structure and culminates in the rich, Empsonian ambiguity of "satisfactory" in line 31. It is a journey from uncertainty,

> With the voices singing in our ears, saying
> That this was all folly,

to certainty, from a star in the East to a birth, from the heavens to the earth, from the darkness of the first section "At the end we preferred to travel all night" to the light of the second "Then at dawn we came down to a temperate valley." In summarizing this journey, the magus employs an almost Cartesian vocabulary which the poem then undermines:

> There was a Birth, *certainly*.
> We had *evidence* and no *doubt*. (emphasis added)

And yet this philosophical, evidential certainty is not satisfactory. The more the journey continues on to the end the more perplexing it becomes.

The second journey, then, is the spiritual journey, which nearly reverses the physical. Hugh Kenner first pointed out that the rich imagery of the second section is strangely uncharged for the magus (*Invisible Poet*, 248), and the reason is the peculiar historicity of the drama. Having been present at the Nativity, the magus yet knows nothing of those events—the Passion and Resurrection—that, for us, inform the imagery with its significance. The spiritual journey leads to the deepest perplexity and. indeed, alienation. This is partly indicated by one fine detail in part two, where Eliot presents the magi as arriving "at evening" (l. 30), which deftly mixes the dark/light imagery of the journey itself and prepares us for the spiritual twilight of part three. In fact, the uncharged imagery of part two—concentrated on the day of their arrival, presumedly the January 6th of tradition—serves as an objective correlative of the magus's inner state in part three, where we see him haunted by the question. What did it all *mean*? The physical imagery embodies his spiritual condition: it is there, but its significance is hidden from him.

Consider, then, this recounting of the journey's end in light of St. Matthew's presence in the drama. Notice, for example, what happens to that peculiar word "information" in line 29—"But there was no information, and so we continued"—a line that is virtually a synecdoche of the old man's spiritual experience. (Cf. "Where is the knowledge we have lost in information," *Choruses from 'The Rock'*) Note the rich complexity. St. Matthew has come to the magus to obtain privileged information about a more or less private experience. The magus gives it and in doing so reveals that he is in anguish for want of knowing (a) what his information *means*, and (b) the necessary complementary information of the kerygma. The Evangelist, on the other hand, (a) knows what the magus's information means, and (b) possesses the complementary "information" which is of far greater intrinsic worth than anything the magus knows. St. Matthew's presence, then, gives the poem a doubleness of theological focus which enables the imagery of part two to have its dual status: anterior to the Redemption and therefore empty for the magus: posterior and charged for the audience and us. This doubleness draws to its full significance in the oft-noticed (see Franklin and Brown) concluding word of the second section: "it was (you may say) satisfactory." The parenthetical remark/gesture dramatizes a certain drawing back at the end into something between understatement and velleity. The key word is the ambiguous "satisfactory," emphasized by rhythm and position, which for us, though not the magus, evokes the Thirty-Nine Articles, expiation, and the Atonement: a satisfaction begun with the Nativity but only completed in the Passion and Resurrection ("*vine*-leaves" and "*wine*-skins"). The dramatic irony generated by the Evangelist's presence makes the theological dimension of the word present to us even as it is hidden from the speaker.

With part three the difficult physical journey has ended, but the old magus's perplexity and spiritual anguish remain. It is not a question of regret, for he says "I would do it again," but of deep bafflement. The most important experience of his life is still vividly present to him, but its meaning is utterly elusive; it has left his spirit wounded, his life incomplete. The poetry forcefully evokes the bafflement:

> All this was a long time ago, I remember,
> And I would do it again, but set down
> This set down
> This: were we led all that way for
> Birth or Death? There was a Birth, certainly,
> We had evidence and no doubt. I had seen birth and death,
> But had thought they were different; this Birth was
> Hard and bitter agony for us, like Death, our death.
> We returned to our places, these Kingdoms,
> But no longer at ease here, in the old dispensation,
> With an alien people clutching their gods.
> I should be glad of another death.

These lines convey an intensity that surpasses anything earlier in the poem. The philosophical language and certainty of the senses serve largely to contrast the deeper uncertainty of spirit. For the magus is unable to say if it was birth he observed or death. He knows that the event was not happenstance, for they "were...led." But why? Wherefore? Polarities collapse, certainties dissolve, as a new order of reality emerges. The inner drama revolves slowly around the unfathomable paradox: "this Birth was / Hard and bitter agony for us, like Death, our death." Eliot has taken his poem on a long journey from the numbing banalities of Christmas cards.

Baffled by the meaning—by the apparent absence of meaning, the epiphany that revealed so little—the old man turns to the result, alienation from everything "in the old dispensation." The Birth he saw began the death of his old world, old life, but did not, with the same certainty, give him anything new. The certainty of the senses and individual experience has been undermined without the compensating certainty of faith—"the substance of things hoped for, the evidence of things not seen" (Hebrews 11:1). Like many of Eliot's characters, the magus is fixed in a painful middle slate, between birth and death, between Death and Birth. Yet without knowing it, because of something, someone, who has come to him freely, graciously, from outside himself, he is moving to the still point, the center of the Christian mystery, where death (to self) is the way to birth (in Christ). It is appropriate that his language—agony, death—unwittingly evoke the Crucifixion—"three trees on the low sky" and "dicing for pieces of silver."

From a Christian perspective alienation may be ultimately a good thing, a preparation for conversion. For conversion always hinges on the awareness of its need. Some fifty years of the magus's life have passed in a hard catechumenate. But conversion also hinges on someone proclaiming the gospel, voicing the kerygma. "How then shall they call on him in whom they have not believed? And how shall they believe in him of whom they have not heard? And how shall they hear without a preacher?" (Romans 10:14). It is here at the moment of maximum anguish that the reader can most keenly feel the force of the Evangelist's presence in the drama. As Eliot conducts his poem forward to its wonderful concluding line, he has brought together the seed and soil for the life of faith: "I should be glad of another death." The double focus gives the line an unconscious proleptic meaning, somewhat parallel to that given "satisfactory" at the end of section two. We read it two ways. In his psychological discouragement, the magus yearns for release and the freedom of death. But at the theological level, and obscurely, the death he would be glad for is the unknown Redemptive Death. According to St. Paul, "The whole of creation has been groaning in travail until now" (Romans 8:22), and the magus typifies this condition. But, like the poem itself, he has reached a verge. With this double focus the drama ends, but it has opened an awareness and sounded a resonance which imply that for the magus there is going to be a second epiphany. A third voice is about to enter and the different drama of conversion is about to begin. He has had the experience; now he is to learn its meaning.

In "Journey of the Magi" the dramatic details and the dramatic logic together point to the presence of St. Matthew. He is the audience that gives the poem its greatest richness and deepest meaning. His search for background information about Jesus is the poem's occasion, and speaker, audience, and occasion all co-operate to define the full poetic significance. And the conversion theme subtly emerges from the interplay of poetic detail just as surely as, say, the marriage negotiations in "My Last Duchess." Meaning is inextricable from form, and by considering the poem "primarily as poetry and not another thing" we can see how it can reach out into "the spiritual and social life of its time and of other times" (*Sacred Wood*, viii). For the magus also, Eliot shows, "the end is where we start from" ("Little Gidding," l. 216).

WORKS CITED IN Poetic Form in "Journey of the Magi"

Brown, R. D. "Revelation in T. S. Eliot's 'Journey of the Magi.'" *Renascence* 24: 136–49.

Eliot, T. S. *For Lancelot Andrewes: Essays on Style and Order.* London: Faber, 1928.

_____. *The Sacred Wood: Essays on Poetry and Criticism.* London: Methuen, 1950.

Franklin, Rosemary. "The Satisfactory Journey of Eliot's Magus." *English Studies* 49 (1968): pp. 559–61.

Harris, Daniel A. "Language, History and Text in Eliot's 'Journey of the Magi.'" *PMLA*, 95 (1980): pp. 838–56.

Kenner, Hugh. *The Invisible Poet.* New York: Harcourt, 1959.

Matthiessen, F. O. *The Achievement of T. S. Eliot: An Essay on the Nature of Poetry*, 3rd ed. New York: Oxford University Press, 1958.

MARITAIN'S *ART AND SCHOLASTICISM*

Brian Barbour

"WOE TO ME IF I DO NOT THOMISTICIZE."

Jacques Maritain (1882–1973) was perhaps the greatest Catholic philosopher of the twentieth century—a seminal thinker in several areas of philosophy, the embodiment of a living Thomism, a key influence on the U.N. Declaration on Universal Human Rights and on the Second Vatican Council, the major inspiration of the several Christian Democratic political parties of Europe and Latin America—but his background was very different.[1] He was born into a family superficially Liberal Protestant and closely connected on his mother's side with the fiercely secular and anti-clerical Third Republic and its ambiguous, comforting ideals of humanity and progress. As a youth Maritain reacted against the bourgeois element in this heritage and looked to an equally vague and comforting socialism as the road to this progress. While a student at the Sorbonne (1900) he met Raïssa Oumansoff, a refugee from Russia's pogroms, and they formed an immediate personal attachment enlarged by shared cultural ideals and a certain intellectual and spiritual sympathy. But their delight in high culture was undercut by the otherwise frustrating shallowness of their environment and the absence of any nourishing intellectual and spiritual wisdom. The result was a sort of suicide pact.[2] For a year, they would search for some reason to live and, if they found none, well, the conclusion seemed inevitable. This inverted youthful idealism was to be forestalled, however, and their lives changed forever, by three providential encounters.

First, the poet and man of letters Charles Péguy introduced them to the philosophy lectures of Henri Bergson at the Sorbonne, lectures that they had somehow missed. Bergson was to prove decisive for Maritain's intellectual life because he opened for him the reality of metaphysics, which the regnant materialism, skepticism, and positivism had closed off, thereby freeing Maritain's intelligence to follow its natural bent. Second, after their marriage the Maritains met up with the strange, fascinating, prophetic figure of Léon Bloy (*The Pilgrim of the Absolute*, Raïssa would entitle her collection of his writings), a writer whose radical commitment to sharing the sufferings of Christ was lived out among the Parisian poor. In the depths of Bloy's love for Christ, the Maritains saw their own spiritual quest fulfilled and within a year (1906) they were baptized and received into the Church, Bloy acting as their godfather. Third, not long after their conversions, Raïssa, lying ill, was advised by her spiritual director Humbert Clerissac, a Dominican priest, to read St. Thomas Aquinas, a finding she quickly shared with Jacques. In that third encounter the two lines of Maritain's intellectual and spiritual quest drew together and were complete. "*Vae mihi, si non thomistizavero*," he would say, going forward, obliquely echoing St. Paul (1 Cor. 9:16)—"Woe to me if I do not Thomisticize." Maritain would write some sixty books in a long lifetime though only one, a short one, on Aquinas himself. Nevertheless, Aquinas' thought informs and vitalizes everything else he wrote.

There is no space here to trace the long, rich arc of Maritain's career, but we should note the extraordinary range of his philosophical interests: metaphysics, aesthetics, epistemology, anthropology, ethics, social and political philosophy, the philosophy of history—and various sub-fields within most of these. He lectured at universities in France, England, Canada, and the United States, where he taught at Notre Dame and Princeton, retiring from the latter in 1952. After World War II, he was the French Ambassador to the Vatican and he became a close friend and advisor to Giovanni Battista Montini, later Pope Paul VI, who singled him out for praise at the conclusion of Vatican II. For half a century Maritain was a major intellectual figure who in all his work showed that the thought of Thomas Aquinas was not a reliquary, nor was it something to be learned and repeated by rote, nor worshipped as the only and eternal philosophical standard, but it was to be assimilated, reflected on, understood until its living force could quicken the modern thinker as he faced the decidedly different exigencies of the modern world. Raïssa Maritain, never robust, died in

1960. After that, Maritain associated himself with The Little Brothers of Jesus, and lived in their religious house near Toulouse in the south of France, and it was there that he died in 1973. He and Raïssa are buried in the Alsatian village of Kolbsheim, about fifteen miles from Strasburg.

"ART IS A VIRTUE OF THE PRACTICAL INTELLECT."

Art and Scholasticism (1920)[3] is a book that draws on the work of Scholastic philosophy, chiefly that of Thomas Aquinas. Since none of the Scholastics wrote a formal treatise on either art or the artist, Maritain constructed his essay from their writings on metaphysics and ethics by reading between the lines and dwelling on the asides, the subordinate clauses, so to say, wherever the two topics happen to come into play. *Art and Scholasticism* is a work grounded in the Scholastic love of distinctions and built through inference, contemplation, synthesis, and extension. As such it models Maritain's whole approach to Aquinas and Thomism.

What does Maritain have to say about Art? The key phrase comes early on: "*Art is a virtue of the practical intellect.*" This is the theme of the opening chapters and the governing idea of the entire book. What does it mean? Maritain begins in high Scholastic fashion with a number of distinctions about the intellect that allow him to focus his subject and reach his key idea: Speculative / Practical; Doing / Making; Prudence / Art. Art belongs to the Intellect (not, mark, the feelings), the *Practical* Intellect, and it is a matter of Making (not, mark, "creating"). His sense of art here is quite broad, broader than our usual idiom: rather than just the Fine Arts (music, sculpture, painting, literature), he means all products of artisans, however grand or humble, Leonardo's drawings or the village tinsmith's candle-holder. Under Practical Intellect the distinction between Making and Doing leads to the distinction between Prudence (Doing), which has reference to the actor, and Art (Making), which has reference to the thing made. The good of Prudence is in the person; *the good of Art is in the object itself, not in the Maker*. Art, therefore, is not a matter of the artist's feelings nor does its value come from its origin in the artisan's inner life. Its good ("virtue") lies in itself, quite apart from the artisan, in how well it is made.

Made, crafted, not "created." In short, Maritain is developing an idiom and a view of art that runs counter to the presuppositions of Romanticism, which are the presuppositions of our own time.

This objective view of Art as craft is intertwined with what Maritain says about the Artist (Chapter IV) especially the maker of the Fine Arts (Chapter VI), and these chapters, together with Chapter V on Beauty, are the heart of the book. (Artist, Artisan, and Maker are all correlative terms for Maritain.) For perspective on the Artist, recall T. S. Eliot's dedication of *The Waste Land*, "For Ezra Pound / *il miglior fabbro*"—the better maker, the better craftsman. In his use of Dante, Eliot is doing more than just thanking Pound for his editorial work. He is implying a view of art and the artist that parallels Maritain's. For both of them the artist is a maker, a craftsman whose attention is not on himself but on working out the good of, the perfection of, the work of art. And he is able to do this not because he is a higher type of person ("genius") with a uniquely interesting inner life, but because he has worked to perfect the *habitus* of art. Now recall what the very Romantic Walt Whitman says at the start of *Song of Myself*: "I celebrate myself, and sing myself." The song of the self is decidedly *the* Romantic subject and in this expressive theory the poet's feelings and experience are enlisted to validate the poetry: "I am the man, I suffered, I was there." Again, contrast Eliot: "[The] more perfect the artist, the more completely separate in him will be the man who suffers and the mind which creates.... It is not in his personal emotions that the poet is in any way remarkable or interesting.... The business of the poet is to express feelings which are not in actual emotions at all.... Poetry is not the expression of personality, but an escape from personality."[4] Maritain would—certainly did—agree.

For both Eliot and Maritain, the emphasis falls on the objective nature of art, not on the subjective life of the artist. Drawing on Aquinas, Maritain pushes this further and introduces that odd word and valuable notion, *Habitus*: "Art is a *habitus* of the practical intellect." Without this *habitus* the would-be artist is essentially a *poseur*, playing at being an artist, one of that unhappy contingent that identifies artistry with talking about the art they are going to create but have not, or with living an artistic "lifestyle," or with striking approved "artistic" attitudes. Maritain's view is practical: "Art confers only the power of making well.... It operates for the good of the work done.... Art in no wise tends to make the artist good in his specifically human conduct" (unlike prudence). The artist's focus has to be entirely on the work and on solving the artistic problems that the work sets. Once the artist turns his attention to himself, the art goes wrong.

Habitus comes from the common verb *habeo*, to have, but it is more or less untranslatable. The temptation is to just go with "habit," but Maritain explicitly rejects that move, calling habit "mere mechanical bent and routine," something that "resides in the nerve centers," something like an athlete's muscle memory, perhaps, or the painter's drawing skill. *Habitus* is of the spirit, a virtue, a quality. Perhaps to see just what Maritain is getting at, we can blend several notions, including natural aptitude or capacity; spiritual insight; disinterested commitment; disciplined development; connaturality; an attitude that is un-self-regarding but is *riveted* on the perfection of the work as the proper artistic end. Flannery O'Connor, who called *Art and Scholasticism* "the book I cut my aesthetic teeth on," can help us here. Thinking of the Romantic exaltation of the artist (so easily superior to the bourgeois Philistine), she says, "I even dislike the concept *artist* when it sets you above, all it is is working in a certain kind of medium to make something right.... The idea of making it right is what should be applied to all making. St Thomas said the artist is concerned with the good of that which is made, that art is a good-in-itself."[5] Notice her focus and emphasis: *making it right*; *a good-in-itself*.

The Romantic view of the artist as isolated genius creating out of his own originality was conveniently summarized long ago by Logan Pearsall Smith: It is "the notion that the artist, and above all the poet, has the power of creating a new heaven and a new earth, a world more real perhaps than the actual one, a universe of the mind, concrete, autonomous, independent...out of the depths of the poet's own mind."[6] In the allusion to Revelation 21 ("new heaven and new earth"), we remember W. H. Auden's observation that at his extreme the Romantic wants to be god-like, limitless, without restraint on his capacity to experience. On the other hand, for Maritain, Eliot, and O'Connor, the artistic energy of the practical intellect, *habitus*, is directed to working out the artistic logic, the technical and more-than-technical problems, the perfecting of the work. "The artistic *habitus* is concerned only with the work to be done." The knowledge involved is often—generally?—tacit and connatural, and instead of appearing as a genius, the true artist may seem tongue-tied, unable to give an explicit, rational "reason" for his or her work. After the initial stirring, or what Hopkins calls "the fine delight that fathers thought," the problems of art are problems of execution, practical ones within the maker's *habitus*, guided only by the relentless imperative to get the thing *right*. As O'Connor said, "When I write I am a maker. I think about what I am making. St Thomas called art reason in making. When I write I feel I am engaged in the reasonable use of the unreasonable. In art the reason goes where the imagination goes."[7] Hence the familiar, somewhat puzzling, and, to the lazy-minded, apparently mannered, answer that the artist may give to the question, "What does it mean?" *The work itself is what it means.* Which is to say, "meaning" is the entire coordinated ensemble of the elements of the work acting symphonically. So against the eyes-a-sparkle isolated genius of Romanticism, spinning out his new world from within, Maritain presents a view of the artist humbly acquiring his or her *habitus* through discipline and within a tradition, a handing-on: first as an apprentice, then as a journeyman, watching, listening, pondering. And within that structure of life interior capacity is stirred, connaturality is quickened, and youthful energy feels its way forward, riveted, he says, on the object to be made.

"TO WHAT SERVES MORTAL BEAUTY?"

Habitus follows what Maritain calls "The Rules of Art," and no phrase is more likely to rankle our Romantic certainties. But by Rules here Maritain means something *intrinsic* to the work, not extrinsic, and most certainly not a *method*. Nor does it have anything to do with *Les Regles* of the Classical Period, so lovingly charted by Boileau and so thoroughly demolished by Dr. Johnson.[8] To repeat, "the artistic *habitus* is concerned only with the work to be done." The Rules are what *habitus* follows in working out the logic or necessity of the formal cause of the specific work, solving the technical problems inevitably thrown up by the medium and by the exploratory nature of the artist's thought and which must be solved if the artist's focus is on the work's perfection. Again the emphasis falls on connaturality: there is no predetermined set of Rules written down somewhere, and the Rules are likely to be different for every achieved work. Nor could the artist in every instance necessarily explain, beyond a general statement of intention, just what he is doing or where the work is going, though he would know when he got there. As Maritain puts it, "With the *habitus* or virtue of art exalting his mind from within, the artist is a *master making use of* rules to serve his ends.... [H]e holds—through them—matter and reality." And as a coda, he reminds us, "there is always an infinity of ways in which it can be *beautiful*." The artist knows when the work is "right," but he may not necessarily know how he knows.

The discussion of Beauty is Maritain's transition from Art in general to the Fine Arts. Art in the generic sense has for its end a practical purpose—health for the physician, a ship for the shipbuilder—and that end is understood beforehand. But the end of the fine arts is Beauty and that is a different matter, not known beforehand in anything like the same way. "The sole end of art," he argues, "is the work itself and its beauty." Beauty is one of the transcendental properties of being and as such is one of the proper objects of the intellect. *Id quod visum placet*, Aquinas says: "that which, being seen, pleases." Maritain is inclined to say that the beautiful artistic object[9] delights, and that that delight comes in and through the artist's discovery of, realization of, a something in the secret depths of being.[10] Steeped in tradition and discipline, the artist is also an explorer, and his or her discoveries lead the mind on—his or her own mind as well as the mind of the viewer, let us say—towards the transcendental where, in wonder, it can repose. Beauty delights the intellect through the senses, and the intellect participates in the artistic object and receives it rather than (as in the sciences) abstracting from it.[11] Because the Beautiful is connatural to man *qua* man, it is something the artist—and the qualified receiver—discovers in each of its various and unexpected occurrences.[12] It has such power that it can draw us beyond the beautiful object itself to dim awareness of, contemplation of, not the artist but the Creator. This is the logic behind that saying of Dostoevsky's in *The Idiot*, which Solzhenitsyn reminded us of and made his own in his Nobel Prize Address: "Beauty will save the world," a world, presumably, that has abandoned the True and can no longer recognize the Good.

Beauty is directed to contemplation, Maritain says, and the realm of the spirit. "The work which involves the labor of the Fine Arts is ordered to beauty: insofar as it is beautiful it is an end, an absolute, self-sufficient; and if, as work to be done, it is material and enclosed in a kind, as beautiful it belongs to the realm of the spirit and dives deep into the transcendence and the infinity of being." But the very self-sufficiency of Beauty carries with it its own danger, one the Romantic sensibility is particularly vulnerable to, that the reader or observer will rest content with the beautiful object *qua* object, making of it an idol, and be uninterested in its call from the realm of the spirit, impervious to its glimpse of transcendence. And yet even at this level, Beauty, "mortal beauty," is efficacious to the spirit, and serves a greater purpose. Few human beings have ever responded to being and Being with a deeper sense of delight in beauty than Gerard Manley Hopkins, a particular favorite of Maritain's, and Hopkins was keenly aware of the danger we are noticing, asking (in the poem of that name), "To what serves mortal beauty?" and answering simply, "Dangerous." The danger lies in satisfaction ("does set dancing blood") with the *mortal* object and stopping there. Hopkins captures the dangerous satisfaction of that dancing blood in the responder's cry, "O-seal-that-so" where "seal" suggests encasing and closing the object, a "Stop right there, that's enough, that's enough for me," with no thought of anything beyond the merely mortal.

> To what serves mortal beauty—dangerous; does set danc-
> ing blood—the O-seal-that-so feature, flung prouder form
> Than Purcell tune lets tread to?

But *Enough!* need not be the only response, and Hopkins thinks the danger worth running, because quite another "service" of "mortal beauty" is possible.

> See: it does this: keeps warm
> Men's wits to the things that are; what good means—

—so that both Truth and the Good are served. Hopkins, Maritain, and Dostoevsky are at one in this regard. Beauty, an end in itself, nevertheless provides us with a glimpse of being, awakens us to its call, stirs our dull roots, warms our wits to the things that are. Poetry, like philosophy, begins in wonder.

"HUMAN REASON LOST ITS GRASP OF BEING."

Art and Scholasticism is both a positive doctrine and a closely related critique. Why did Maritain write it, and why did he write it when he did? It was his second book. His first, six years earlier (The Great War intervening), was on Bergson, and it was both an appreciation and a critique from the perspective of Thomism. Since Bergson's work had played such a vital role in Maritain's life and intellectual development, truth demanded that he carefully identify and criticize what he now saw as the deficiencies and errors in that philosophy. Having done so, he was ready to unfold his own thought and his choice of philosophical area was undoubtedly prompted by the fact that Raïssa was a poet and that they were both highly cultivated in the fine arts. Moreover, just as Maritain had had to bid farewell to Bergson's work, so too he needed to work through and criticize the enthrallment to Baudelaire's Romanticism that had marked his adolescence. *Art and Scholasticism* appeared in 1920, at exactly the same time as Eliot's *The Sacred Wood* and his famous essay on "The Metaphysical Poets" (1921) and, together with Dostoevsky's fiction, Maritain's book and Eliot's essays constitute a major critique of Romanticism.[13]

The "–ism" is important and we should think about why. As a concept, Romanticism is notoriously difficult—some would say impossible—to define, but it is rooted in common practice and perfectly useful in specific literary contexts. As Dr. Johnson said of light, we may not be able to define it but we know it perfectly well, regardless. Romanticism, as it is commonly used in literary criticism (romantic versus classic as alternating stylistic tendencies is another matter) refers to one of three things: (1) The Romantic Period (the years for which vary in different countries: in England from the 1790s to the 1830s; in America from 1836 to 1860; Germany in the 1770s is the usual start-point), which is something long past and done with; (2) an entirely new way of understanding and valuing literature, different from that operating in all previous literary eras[14]; (3) a worldview.[15] The second and third meanings begin to operate fully in the Romantic Period, and they continue to thrive and reinforce one another today. The Romantic Period is gone but Romantic*ism* continues as a major factor in our culture, helping shape our world. For Maritain, this matters beyond Raïssa's poetry and his own Baudelairean past, for the root issue is metaphysical, and he saw in Romantic*ism* both the product of, and an energizing force of, modern intellectual and spiritual confusion.

Romantic*ism* is so dominant and pervasive in our culture that it is nearly invisible unless searched out; otherwise, it is taken for granted as the natural, ordinary, inevitable way of thinking about art and about valuing human experience. *Art and Scholasticism* was part of Maritain's searching out. His next important book, *Three Reformers* (1925),[16] traced the development of modern subjectivity, the enabling principle of Romanticism, from the sixteenth to the eighteenth centuries through the careers of Luther, Descartes, and Rousseau. There is a deep thematic unity in these three books, for Maritain wanted to understand and place Romantic*ism* within a larger intellectual context. The metaphysical pivot of modern culture came, of course, with Descartes, and it is a considerable oddity in the history of ideas that the father of modern rationalism should be present in the tentacular roots of Romanticism, itself a reaction against rationalism and so much concerned with the primacy of feeling. But if we want to get at the start of what C. S. Lewis called "The Poison of Subjectivism," we had best begin there.[17]

At the heart of Maritain's thought is what we might call the anti-*Cogito*: *Being is*. It would seem that there is no escape from this truth and this start-point for the intellect, but for all kinds of reasons modern thought wants no part of it. For Maritain, this turning away from being, from its necessity for the intellect, is part of the "historical misfortune" of modern civilization. For with the Cartesian *Cogito*, "Human Reason lost its grasp of Being," and with that it also lost its hold on Truth, Goodness, and Beauty.[18] In his post-*Art and Scholasticism* writings, Maritain was concerned to work out the metaphysical, epistemological, and social and political implications of this loss. Romantic*ism* is largely a reflex of this loss and we should place his thinking about it in this context.

In his great essay, "Christian Humanism," Maritain traces these implications in broad historical terms through the arts, technology, and social and political philosophy.[19] But for a focus specifically on the results for Romanti*cism*, we can perhaps employ a proxy, someone whose philosophical positions are generally different from Maritain's but whose deep agreement with him on this issue is all the more confirmatory. Isaiah Berlin begins by sketching our common intellectual patrimony:

> Since the Greeks, and perhaps long before them, men had believed that to the central questions about the nature and purpose of their lives and of the world in which they lived, true, objective, universal, and eternal answers could be found.... It was assumed that all the truly central problems were soluble in principle even if not in practice.... [This] proposition underlies most classical and Christian thought. What was common to all these views was the assumption that there existed a reality, a structure of things, a *rerum natura*, which the qualified inquirer could see, study, and, in principle, get right.... This was the great foundation of belief which Romanticism attacked and weakened.[20]

Like Maritain, Berlin sees the great metaphysical shift operating behind the new principles of art. From Homer to Jane Austen there had been a consistent metaphysics underlying all literature, however different the works themselves, but that viewpoint was to be now disregarded and a new one installed.

> The common assumption of the Romantics that runs counter to the *philosophia perennis* is that the answers to the great questions are not to be discovered so much as to be invented. They are not something found, they are something literally made, something that man creates, as he creates works of art; not by imitating but by an act of creation.

From metaphysics to epistemology, to ethics, to art, and from art to this new and inflated conception of the artist, Berlin spells it out:

> Hence the new emphasis on the subjective and ideal rather than on the objective and the real, on the process of creation rather than on its effects,

> on motives rather than consequences, on the quality of the vision, on sincerity of purpose rather than getting the answer right, on activity, movement, on the flow that cannot be arrested.... Hence, too, the celebration of all forms of defiance against the "given." Hence the worship of the artist, whether in sound, word, or color, as the highest manifestation of the ever-active spirit, and the popular image of the artist in his garret, wild-eyed, wild-haired, poor, solitary, mocked-at; but independent, free, spiritually superior to his Philistine tormentors.

It was the Romantics, we recall, who thought the road of excess led to the palace of wisdom, who revered Prometheus, who thought that poetry would replace religion,[21] and who thought that the hero of *Paradise Lost* was Satan.[22]

This brief excursus into the "–ism" is meant to show how Maritain's metaphysical concerns lie beneath his aesthetic argument and to illustrate the place of that argument in literary history.[23] *Art and Scholasticism* gives us the anti-Romantic view of art and the artist, and their relation through Beauty to being; and it connects these themes with other unfolding aspects of Maritain's philosophical thought. At all times he was concerned with being, with the objectivity of truth, and he saw the shift from Being to Thought that underlies Romantic*ism* as the major source of modern intellectual confusion and spiritual evil. Maritain's was an especially fertile mind, rich in contemplation, not given to treating a subject and then restlessly abandoning it. His love of art and the artist was an abiding one. Besides a small book on his friend, the painter Georges Roualt, he would turn to the fine arts a second time in a late major work, *Creative Intuition in Art and Poetry* (1953), in which he works out a non-Romantic epistemology of the artist, showing in great detail that poetic knowledge is a real, though non-discursive, knowledge that nourishes the spirit, and once again showing his delight in beauty, his respect for the maker, and his sense of the sheer pluriform superabundance of meaning and significance in the greatest works of art.

NOTES TO Maritain's *Art and Scholasticism*

1. "Perhaps" is hedging, of course, to allow mention of Maritain's contemporary and friend, Étienne Gilson (1884–1978), and the great proponent of virtue ethics, Alasdair MacIntyre (1929–), like Maritain a convert. Incidentally, both Maritain and Gilson disliked the designation *Neo-Thomist*. Each considered himself a Thomist, pure and simple.
2. Raïssa describes the resolve they reached one day after a long conversation in the Jardin des Plantes: "Before leaving the Jardin des Plantes we reached a solemn decision which brought us some peace: to look sternly in the face, even to the ultimate consequence—insofar as it would be in our power—the facts of that unhappy and cruel universe, wherein the sole light was the philosophy of skepticism and relativism.... But if the experiment should not be successful, the solution would be suicide; suicide before the years had accumulated their dust, before our youthful strength was spent. We wanted to die by a free act if it were impossible to live according to the truth." *The Memoirs of Raïssa Maritain: We Have Been Friends Together* and *Adventures in Grace* (Garden City: Image Books, 1961), pp. 67–68. *Friends*, from which the quote comes, first appeared in 1942; *Adventures* in 1945.
3. *Art et Scolastique* (Paris: Libraire de l'Art Catholique). There was a second French edition in 1927, which included "Frontières de la Poésie" and a third and final edition in 1935. The first English translation of 1930, by J. F. Scanlan, the edition in hand, was based on the second French edition, and the second English edition, of 1962, translated by Joseph W. Evans, was based on the French third. "The Frontiers of Poetry" and "An Essay on Art" were added to the later editions where they provide somewhat simpler versions of the same basic argument.
4. Whitman, *Song of Myself*, Sections 1, 33; Eliot, *The Sacred Wood*, 2nd ed. (London: Methuen, 1928), pp. 54–58. The first edition—like *Art et Scolastique*—was 1920. The quotes are from "Tradition and the Individual Talent."
5. *The Habit of Being: The Letters of Flannery O'Connor*, ed. Sally Fitzgerald (New York: Farrar, Straus, and Giroux, 1979), pp. 216, 214. I have left O'Connor's punctuation unaltered.
6. *Words and Idioms: Studies in the English Language* (Houghton Mifflin: Boston and New York, 1926), pp. 128–29. The section, a classic, is entitled "Four Romantic Words."
7. *Conversations with Flannery O'Connor*, ed. Rosemary M. Magee (Jackson and London: University Press of Mississippi, 1987), p. 39. O'Connor's advice to the neophyte writer was to learn to stare.
8. Boileau, *Art Poétique* (1674); Johnson, *Preface to Shakespeare* (1765).
9. "Object" here is to be understood to include musical and literary works as well as sculpture and painting.
10. Hence *Imitation* (Chapter VII) is of that original delight in being; it is not external copying. Literalists—and they are many—generally misunderstand this point.
11. According to C. S. Lewis this participation / reception results (or can) in an enlargement of our being, the proper good of all the fine arts. Lewis, *An Experiment in Criticism* (Cambridge: Cambridge University Press, 1962), p. 137 and *passim*.
12. It will be noticed that much that Maritain says about the artist's *habitus* and the work's Formal Cause has (*mutatis mutandus*) great correlative importance for the viewer, or, let us say, (with literature in mind) the literary critic. There is a necessary *habitus* for the literary critic and without it he or she is likely to be indifferent to the Formal Cause in the work under discus-

sion. It is disastrously easier to *use* a work of art than to *receive* it. This is a large, independent topic that can be no more than noted here, while remembering Eliot's sadly ignored words about "the integrity of poetry," that "when we are considering poetry we must consider it primarily as poetry and not another thing." *The Sacred Wood*, Preface to the 1928 Edition, p. viii.

13. We ought also to remember the now largely forgotten figure of T. E. Hulme (1883–1917), whose posthumous book *Speculations*, ed. Herbert Read (London, 1924) was an energizing attack on the "–ism." It contained the famous *aperçu*, "Romanticism is spilt religion." It was Hulme who introduced Bergson to the English-speaking world with his translation of *Introduction to Metaphysics* (1913) and with some vigorous lectures in London that same year. He was killed fighting in France in September 1917.
14. For example, the Lamp replaces the Mirror as the operating metaphor for literary method, originality replaces truth as the goal aimed at, and "Poetry is the spontaneous overflow of powerful feelings."
15. For example, self-realization not self-knowledge is the chief aspiration; ethical decisions are grounded in feelings; and "the road of excess leads to the palace of wisdom."
16. *Trois Réformateurs: Luther, Descartes, Rousseau* (Paris: Librairie Plon, 1925); Englished as *Three Reformers: Luther, Descartes, Rousseau* (London: Sheed and Ward, 1929).
17. C. S. Lewis, "The Poison of Subjectivism," in *Christian Reflections*, ed. Walter Hooper (Grand Rapids: Eerdmans, 1967), pp. 72–81; see also Lewis, *The Abolition of Man* (New York: Macmillan, 1947), especially Chapter Two, "The Way."
18. "What [Descartes] saw in man's thought was *Independence of Things*." *Three Reformers*, p. 55 (Maritain's emphasis).
19. 1942. See *The Range of Reason* (New York: Scribner's, 1953), pp. 185–99. The essay is the best introduction to, and overview of, Maritain's thought; it is largely a précis of what is probably Maritain's greatest book, *Humanisme Intégral: Problèmes Temporels et Spirituels D'Une Nouvelle Chrétienté* (1936); translated into English by Margot Adamson as *True Humanism* (London: G. Bles, 1938); and later by Joseph W. Evans as *Integral Humanism* (New York: Scribner's, 1968; South Bend: Notre Dame, 1973).
20. Berlin, Preface to H. G. Schenk, *The Mind of the European Romantics: An Essay in Cultural History* (Garden City: Anchor Books, 1969), pp. xiv–xv. The succeeding quotes are from pp. xvi–xvii. For ease of reading I have somewhat condensed Berlin's syntax. The voice is his but the viewpoint is congruent with Maritain's. For Berlin's own more developed and sympathetic views see Berlin, *The Roots of Romanticism*, ed. Henry Hardy (Princeton: Princeton University Press, 1999).
21. But to be fair to Matthew Arnold, in the notorious passage from "The Study of Poetry," he has ethics in mind, "poetry as a criticism of life."
22. The contemporary obsession that art be "transgressive" has behind it a deep grudge against being and any metaphysical order.
23. It is not meant to suggest that there are not great Romantic works, for there clearly are, nor to suggest that a certain Christian decorativeness or bourgeois morality or earnest piety will somehow make a mediocre work into a masterpiece. Maritain's final two chapters make that clear. To make Christian art, he says, be a Christian and have the *habitus* of art. Gilson was characteristically more blunt: "*Piety never dispenses with technique*." "The Intelligence in the Service of Christ the King," in *A Gilson Reader*, ed. Anton C. Pegis (Garden City: Doubleday, 1957), p. 40.

HOME AND THE USES OF CREATIVE NOSTALGIA IN *DOCTOR ZHIVAGO*

René Fortin

We need hardly be reminded of Pasternak's comment that "art is as realistic as activity and as symbolic as fact" to suspect the presence of symbolic patterns in *Doctor Zhivago*.[1] The novel, in its oscillation between the lyrical episodes tracing the troubled Zhivago-Lara love relationship and the historical episodes documenting the devastation caused by the Revolution, seems to invite the reader to detect the symbolic patterns and to penetrate to "the hidden, secret part of content" that, Zhivago tells us, constitutes the form of art.[2] A recent study of the novel which has based its exploration of the symbolic patterns on the statement that "all great, genuine art resembles and continues the Revelation of St. John" (p. 90) has, in my opinion, contributed much to our understanding of the novel.[3] But I would like to propose another complementary approach that seems to me equally fruitful. The reader is guided in this approach by the meditations of Zhivago while returning to Moscow from Meliuzeievo:

> The first real event since the long interruption was this trip in the fast-moving train, the fact that he was approaching his home, which was intact, which still existed, and in which every stone was dear to him. This was real life, meaningful experience, the actual goal of all quests, this was what art aimed at—homecoming, return to one's family, to oneself, to true existence. (p. 164)

What is especially evident in this passage is the prominence of home imagery: it is intimated that Zhivago's return to his home is a symbolic as well as a literal act and that homecoming is one of the ultimate ideals of human life. Indeed, an examination of this central homecoming symbol uncovers historical, religious, and aesthetic dimensions, with the novel itself being an embodiment of the initially mystifying statement that all art aims at homecoming.

As one would expect in a novel about the Bolshevik Revolution, the home theme has significant historical implications: the primary effect of the War and the Revolution for Zhivago is to destroy his home in Russia, to reduce Russia itself to "homelessness and savagery" (p. 160). He is personally separated from Tonia, "their home, and their former, settled life where everything, down to the smallest detail, had an aura of poetry and was permeated with affection and warmth" (p. 160). After returning from the War to Moscow and a reunion with Tonia, Zhivago is again driven from home by intense poverty and takes refuge in Varykino, where he rediscovers the primal joy of establishing a home:

> What happiness, to work from dawn to dusk for your family and for yourself, to build a roof over their heads, to till the soil to feed them, to create your own world, like Robinson Crusoe, in imitation of the Creator of the universe, and, as your own mother did, to give birth to yourself, time and again. (p. 277)

But the new home at Varykino is again destroyed when Zhivago is captured by the partisan forces of Liberius, with whom he serves until his escape three years later. Zhivago's flight takes him to Yuriatin, where he meets Lara again. Shortly after he returns to Varykino, this time with Lara, and the home theme again becomes very prominent; it is especially high-lighted when Lara, seeing her daughter constructing a doll house amid the disorder at Varykino, states: "Look at that instinct for domesticity. It just shows, nothing can destroy the longing for home and order" (p. 433). It is during this episode at Varykino that we are offered Lara's fullest analysis of the direction of Russian history:

> All customs and traditions, all our way of life, everything to do with home and order, has crumbled into dust in the general upheaval and reorganization of society. The whole human way of life has been

> destroyed and ruined.... You and I are like Adam and Eve, the first two people on earth who at the beginning of the world had nothing to cover themselves with—and now at the end of it we are just as naked and homeless. (pp. 402–403)

On this most obvious level, therefore, the home theme is an expression of Zhivago's resentment of the Bolshevik Revolution, precisely because it jeopardizes the very values associated with home, the reverence for hallowed traditions that constitute "the whole human way of life." The Revolution, we are told, is a violation of the nature of history itself, which for Zhivago is like the forest, "eternally growing, ceaselessly changing...the life of society moving invisibly in its incessant transformations" (p. 453). History, in short, is evolutionary, a process which maintains continuity with the past—with man's "home," in its gradual transformations of human life.

It is important to note this acceptance of transformation and renewal in Zhivago's view of history in order to recognize that his distaste for the Revolution as it developed is based not on a mindless conservatism or a sterile nostalgia for a bygone era, but on a sophisticated organic view of history that stresses continuity amidst change. The view of history held by Zhivago conforms with that implicit in Pasternak's assessment, in *Safe Conduct*, of the Marburg school of philosophy, which Pasternak praises for its "originality, i.e., the vital place it occupies in a tradition vital to one section of contemporary knowledge."[4] What Zhivago—and Pasternak—value in history is originality, but an originality that is a fresh development of a tradition rather than a patricidal repudiation of it.

Thus Zhivago reveals that he was initially enchanted by the ideals of the Revolution, but suffers disenchantment when he discovers that the Revolution violates the organic rhythms of history in its obsession for radical, instantaneous change, in its contempt for the past and its vital traditions.[5] The Bolshevik Revolution, says Zhivago, is the product of "fanatical men of action with one-track minds...who overturn the old order in a few hours or days" (p. 454).

Whereas home symbolizes serenity and order for Zhivago, the central metaphor for the Revolution is that of motion. "Mother Russia," says Zhivago, "is on the move, she can't stand still, she's restless and she can't find rest..." (p. 146).

Motion as the anti-home metaphor is articulated in the opening chapter, which is entitled "Five O'Clock Express" and describes, among other things, the suicidal leap of Zhivago the father from a speeding train, and reaches its culmination when Zhivago himself suffers a fatal heart attack in a moving trolley, with meditations on speed as virtually his dying thoughts (p. 490). In between these episodes, Zhivago is constantly kept in motion by social upheavals, being driven from Moscow to the front, then to Meliuzeievo, returning to Tonia in Moscow and shortly thereafter retreating to Varykino. He is then abducted by the forces of Liberius, but escapes eventually to Yuriatin where he again meets Lara. Because of the threat of political persecution, he again takes flight to Varykino with Lara, and it is there that he is finally separated from her. In the last stage of his life Zhivago returns to a Moscow that can no longer provide a home for him. That the pattern of Zhivago's life—and the structure of the novel—is one of enforced motion is hardly accidental: we are to recognize that Zhivago is caught up in the forces of contemporary history. The stability and order represented by the home symbol cannot survive the violent motions of history, and Zhivago's attempts to create a home with Tonia, with Lara, and finally with Marina in Moscow inevitably fail.[6] Shortly before his death, in fact, Zhivago recognizes that frantic motion is the essential characteristic of modem life and that he must reject, to conform to the pressures of the time, the language of pastoral simplicity; he decides to develop a new language of urbanism which will capture the spirit of the city "incessantly moving and roaring outside our doors and windows" (p. 489). One measure of Zhivago's defeat is that the imagery of the bustling city and of the roaring locomotive replaces the pastoral landscape which has given him, at Varykino, his moments of joy and serenity.[7]

The home symbol reaches beyond its topical context to embody finally the deepest religious insights in the novel; "home" is offered by Pasternak as the primary symbol of man's nature and of his destiny. The very identity of man, Zhivago asserts, is sustained by his ability to create a home; we recall his ecstasy in Varykino over his ability to "create your own world, like Robinson Crusoe, in imitation of the Creator of the universe, and, as your own mother did, to give birth to yourself, time and again" (p. 277). We learn further from the philosophy of Zhivago's Uncle Nikolai, which Zhivago implicitly accepts, that man, in a larger sense, is characterized by his ability to create a home in history; history for Nikolai is "another universe, made by man with the help of time and memory in answer to the challenge of death" (p. 66). It is a view of man-in-history, Nikolai tells us, that is based on a "new" interpretation of Christianity; given hope and dignity by Christ's redeeming presence in time, "man does not die in a ditch like a dog—but at home in history, while the work toward the conquest of death is in full swing; he dies sharing in this work" (p. 10). This new interpretation of Christianity, to be more specific, is based upon the freedom and individuality given man by Christ; invested in this dignity, man becomes an integral part of the historical process overseen by God, and even a god-like partner in the process of shaping the world. As Sima, a follower of Uncle Nikolai, asserts with Zhivago's tacit approval, "Individual human life became the life story of God, and its contents filled the vast expanses of the universe... Adam tried to be like God and failed, but now God was made man so that Adam should be made God" (p. 413).[8]

The most mystifying of Zhivago's religious speculations are those which attempt to encompass the problems of death and immortality; and here again the home symbol seems to provide a key. It should be noted, first of all, that the novel's Christian view of man-in-history is significantly heterodox in its version of the conquest of death. For Zhivago and Lara there is apparently no personal immortality in the ordinarily accepted sense of the word; man conquers death by accepting it as part of a total design, living on only in his work and in the memory of others.[9] Any hope for the survival of the soul seems grounded in a vaguely pantheistic rather than traditionally Christian faith, consisting in a belief in man's oneness with the universe and his consequent participation in the cosmic processes of death and rebirth. The doctrine is most fully stated by Lara: "The vegetable kingdom can easily be thought of as the nearest neighbor of the kingdom of death. Perhaps the mysteries of evolution and the riddles of life that so puzzle us are contained in the green of the earth, among the trees and the flowers of graveyards" (p. 493). Elsewhere, in trying to find consolation for the death of Zhivago, she is consoled by the memory of having shared with him "a sublime joy in the total design of the universe, a feeling that they themselves were a part of that whole, an element in the beauty of the cosmos"

(p. 501). The imponderable mystery of death is therefore implicitly assimilated in the imagery of home: man is at home in the universe in death as in life, death being a return to the All—the final homecoming.

The symbol of homecoming which dominates much of the thought of *Doctor Zhivago* underlies as well the conception of art that is developed in the novel. In order to understand Zhivago—and Pasternak—as artists of homecoming, we must first appreciate the significance of Lara, who is at once the inspiration and primary subject of Zhivago's poetry. Zhivago's description of her is crucial:

> Ever since his childhood Yuri Andreievich had been fond of woods seen at evening against the setting sun. At such moments he felt as if he too were being pierced by shafts of light. It was as though the gift of the living spirit were streaming into his breast, piercing his being and coming out at his shoulders like a pair of wings. The archetype that is formed in every child for life and seems for ever after to be his inward face, his personality, awoke in him in its full primordial strength, and compelled nature, the forest, the afterglow, and everything else visible to be transfigured into a similarly primordial and all-embracing likeness of a girl. Closing his eyes, "Lara," he whispered and thought, addressing the whole of his life, all God's earth, all the sunlit space spread out before him. (p. 343)

It seems immediately evident that in this passage Lara is elevated to the status of symbol, but the rich significance of this symbol is not fully appreciated until the reader detects that this passage is linked with an earlier episode in the novel. The forest imagery, above all, invites us to recall the Dantesque vision suffered by Zhivago as a child shortly after the death of his mother; he dreams of being stranded alone in a dark forest, which he identifies with the whole world, but this dream is relieved by a vision of incandescent order:

> This inaccessibly high sky once came all the way down to his nursery, as far as his nurse's skirt when she was talking to him about God.... There the heavenly stars became the lights before the icons, and the Lord God

> was a kindly Father, and everything more or less fell into its right place.... At that time, with the whole of his half-animal faith, Yuri believed in God, who was the keeper of that forest. (p. 87)

"The archetype that is formed in every child for life" is thus more sharply defined: Lara is an incarnation of this earlier vision which transformed the menacing dark forest of reality into a place of serenity and splendor. She is associated with, among other things, the dead mother of Zhivago (and, by extension, with Mother Russia), with a world that is home because as Zhivago's childhood vision revealed, it is benevolently ruled by God.[10] In this sense art is a homecoming in that it involves a return to the intuitions of childhood. It is a return to the primal archetype that is the source of inspiration, a return to one's original intimations of the sacred which touches upon human existence.

The means by which this return to the primordial archetype is effected is the poetic power of naming; Zhivago, in a further meditation on Lara which centers on his first encounter with her, states:

> Often since then I have tried to define and give a name to the enchantment that you communicated to me that night, that faint glow, that distant echo, which later permeated my whole being and gave me a key to the understanding of everything in the world. (p. 427)

Art for Zhivago is then the struggle to capture in language the living essence of the intuition graven in his memory and incarnated by Lara; the poet strives to "give a name" to the ineffable. The theory of poetry which underlies this statement reveals, in its insistence upon the power of naming, the primal impulse of Pasternak's art: we are reminded specifically of Adam who created his "home" by language, by naming the beasts of the field. The aesthetic of naming proposed by Zhivago is essentially that which Pasternak expounded in *Safe Conduct*.

> We cease to recognize reality. It appears in some new form. This form appears to be a quality inherent in it, and not in us. Apart from this

> quality everything in the world has its name. It alone is new and without name. We try to give it a name. The result is art.[11]

There is a second sense in which art is identified with homecoming. Poetry, we have seen, creates a home for the poet by naming—and therefore renewing his contact with—the archetypes of childhood; but poetry creates a home for the archetype as well. To name, suggests Zhivago, is to give a home to that which is named, for language is "the home and receptacle of beauty and meaning" (p. 437), and the archetype that is hypostatized in art by being given shape, aesthetic form, thereby renews its residence among men.

The theory of poetry as homecoming is not so idiosyncratic or arcane as it would initially seem; it is, I think, instructive to compare Pasternak's view of poetry as homecoming with the aesthetic theory that Heidegger developed in his essays on Hölderlin, "Remembrance of the Poet" and "Hölderlin and the Essence of Poetry."[12] In these essays Heidegger asserts that it is the poet, not the philosopher or theologian, who brings man into contact with Being. The essential poetic role is that of mediator, by means of language, between the gods and the people. What is especially significant about Heidegger's theory is that in his "Remembrance of the Poet," an essay based on Hölderlin's "Homecoming," he places strong emphasis on the central poetic acts of naming and returning to the source. For the reader of Pasternak the following statements from that essay will have the ring of familiarity:

> to name poetically means: to cause the High One himself to appear in words, not merely to tell of his dwelling-place, the Serene, the holy, not merely to name him with reference to his dwelling-place.[13]
>
> The writing of poetry is not primarily a cause of joy to the poet: rather the writing of poetry *is* joy, is serenification, because it is in writing that the principal return home consists.[14]

The nature of Pasternak's art becomes more understandable when it is seen in the light of Heidegger's aesthetic of homecoming. The nostalgia that is so prominent in *Doctor Zhivago* emerges as much more than Pasternak's longing for lost innocence; it is the vital essence of his art, the homecoming that Heidegger refers to as the primal act of the poet. Zhivago's immersion in the past, in the visions of his childhood, and in his memories of Old Russia is an act of re-creative memory, a return to the source of creativity, true originality, true existence. *Doctor Zhivago* is on one level a parable lamenting a lost Russia, a lost home. But it is, beyond that, a witness to Pasternak's faith in the ability of art to reconstitute the primordial archetypes that symbolize man's unity, his at-homeness, with the universe. Thus the novel is itself an achievement of homecoming.

Notes to Home and the Uses of Creative Nostalgia in *Doctor Zhivago*

1. *Safe Conduct: An Autobiography and Other Writings* (New York: New American Library, 1958), p. 59. *Safe Conduct* was originally published in 1931.
2. Boris Pasternak, *Doctor Zhivago*, trans. Max Hayward and Manya Harari (New York: Pantheon Books, 1958), p. 281. All subsequent references to *Doctor Zhivago* will be to this edition.
3. Mary F. Rowland and Paul Rowland, *Pasternak's Doctor Zhivago* (Carbondale and Edwardsville: Southern Illinois University Press, 1967); see esp. p. 16.
4. On p. 38. Pasternak studied philosophy at Marburg before World War I.
5. See, for example, p. 160: "In the same group were his loyalty to the revolution and his admiration for it. This was the revolution in the sense in which it was accepted by the middle classes and in which it had been understood by the students, followers of Blok, in 1905." Much later in his life Zhivago is described as mourning "that distant summer in Meliuzeievo when the revolution had been a god come down to earth from heaven..." (p. 454).
6. It is suggested by Mary and Paul Rowland, p. 45, that the three women in the life of Zhivago symbolize "distinct classes of Russian society."
7. In a sense, of course, Zhivago is not defeated; he has succeeded in creating his art and his spirit permeates the final chapter of the novel, where a cautious optimism prevails. For the symbolic use of the locomotive and streetcar, see Rowland, pp. 89–91, 190.
8. Rowland, pp. 25–27, provides an excellent summary of this religious view of history and its opposition to Marxist-Leninst thought.
9. A manifestation of this kind of survival is the book of Zhivago's writings, which, in the final sentence of the novel, is "communicating" with Dudorov and Gordon: "And the book they held seemed to confirm and encourage their feeling" (p. 519). The novel's fullest exposition of the concept of immortality such as it is apparently understood by Pasternak himself is offered by Zhivago shortly before Anna Ivanovna's death, pp. 67–68: "However far back you

go in your memory, it is always in some external, active manifestation of yourself that you come across your identity—in the work of your hands, in your family, in other people.... You in others—this is your soul."

10. See also Rowland, esp. p. 44.
11. *Safe Conduct*, p. 57.
12. Martin Heidegger, in *Existence and Being*, introd. by Wemer Brock (Chicago: Henry Regnery, 1949). The essays were first published in, respectively, 1944 and 1936. It is not my purpose in this essay to allege any direct influence, although this influence seems highly probable. The former student of philosophy at Marburg would almost certainly have known of the work of Heidegger, who himself taught at Marburg from 1923 to 1927. It is equally probable that the Heideggerian influence asserts itself by way of Rilke, whom Pasternak admired immensely. The art of Rilke, in a sense, is a poetic rendition of Heidegger's key concepts.
13. *Existence and Being*, p. 263.
14. *Existence and Being*, p. 260.

"HIS TREES STOOD RISING ABOVE HIM": PHILOSOPHICAL THOMISM IN FLANNERY O'CONNOR

Brian Barbour

What is first precipitated in the mind's conception is being. A thing is knowable because existence is pointed to. Therefore being is the proper object of mind.
(THOMAS AQUINAS, *ST* I, q. 5, a. 2)

Human Reason lost its grasp of Being.
(JACQUES MARITAIN on the Cartesian Revolution in Philosophy)

I feel I can personally guarantee that St. Thomas loved God because for the life of me I cannot help loving St. Thomas.
(FLANNERY O'CONNOR, in a letter to "A," August 9, 1955)

"He wanted it all in his head."
(Old Tarwater on Rayber, *The Violent Bear It Away*)

Despite its intrinsic importance, Flannery O'Connor's Thomism is not a topic that receives much attention.[1] Nor is its existence much taken for granted or subsumed in the many exegetical discussions of her fiction. On what would seem to be an important, indeed central, topic a remarkable silence obtains. There are at least four reasons why this should be so. First, literary studies and advanced literary training do not include Thomism in the curriculum. And while there is a sense in which literary *criticism* is of necessity implicitly Thomist (it begins with the senses, i.e., the text), literary *theory* is implicitly Cartesian (beginning not with the text but with ideas) and therefore not pre-disposed to cultivate so foreign, not to say retrograde, a field. Moreover, those whose training has been only in Theory are often handicapped by a tendentious and skewered view of the history of philosophy ("Plato, Descartes, Kant"). Second, O'Connor's Thomism is so pervasive, so deftly assimilated into the action and idiom of her work as to be nearly invisible to many of her readers. Third, and following from the first two, there thus seems little incentive to pursue her myriad references to, and habitual praise of, Aquinas. The stories seem complete, or complete enough, without them. And fourth, many of her readers simply identify and dismiss Thomism as Catholicism, a category mistake. *Ars longa, vita brevis*. And yet, she was insistent, and she was a person who knew her own mind.

If we did happen to be looking for the Thomism in O'Connor's work, what is it we would be seeing? Consider a passage like the following. It is tucked into Chapter IX of *The Violent Bear It Away* and it is what we could call an ordinary example of O'Connor Thomism:

> Once out of sight of the boy, he felt a pressure had been lifted from the atmosphere. He eliminated the oppressive presence from his thoughts and retained only those aspects of it that could be abstracted, clean, into the future person he envisioned. (*Collected Works* 441)

The *he* is Rayber, the *boy* is Tarwater, the time is five days after Tarwater's arrival at Rayber's door with the announcement that Old Tarwater, their relative, is dead, and that he, Tarwater, "had done the needful" and burnt the old man's house and body, defying the old man's charge to give him a Christian burial. Rayber's initial response had been something like elation. Here was a boy he could now raise "according to his own ideas," in contrast to his own son Bishop, who is mentally deficient and therefore "useless." But Tarwater has stubbornly refused Rayber's overtures, insisting that he will not become "a piece of information in [Rayber's] head." It is this refusal to be co-opted that is the source of the pressure. Notice how O'Connor gives it a certain tactile force in the awkward phrasing "oppressive presence," so manifestly in tension with "his thoughts," thoughts specified as "abstracted." Once he has reached that level of abstraction, freed from the weight of actuality, Rayber can see the future boy he envisions. Both the diction and the mental action indicate that these sentences stand as a critique, from a Thomist perspective, of Rayber's Cartesian epistemology. He subordinates being to thinking, metaphysics to epistemology, and what thinking then has in mind is only itself, not its putative, actual, object.[2] This is the way Rayber's mind works, and that working is the focus of O'Connor's Thomistic critique.

A one-off? A passage that just happens to lend itself to this sort of analysis? Then consider this from just a few pages further on. Rayber has driven aimlessly out into the countryside and finds himself at Powderhead, the old man's place that Tarwater burnt. Intrigued, he moves in for a closer look.

> Suddenly he realized that the place *was* his. In the stress of having the boy return to him, he had never considered the property. He stopped, astounded by the fact that he owned all of this. His trees stood rising above him, majestic and aloof, as if they belonged to an order that had never budged from its first allegiance in the days of creation. His heart began to beat frenetically. Quickly he reduced the whole wood in probable board feet into a college education for the boy. His spirits lifted. (*CW* 444–45)

Here is the same implicit conflict between Descartes and Thomism, but now the stress is on metaphysics rather than epistemology. It begins with pride in possession: "The place *was* his," "the property," "he owned all of this." But while Rayber is taking all this in (and notice that the nouns are all abstract), possession—"his trees"—begins to turn into something different. "His trees stood rising above him, majestic and aloof, as if they belonged to an order that had never budged from its first allegiance in the days of creation. His heart began to beat frenetically." What is happening here, below the level of Rayber's consciousness, as it were, is something that brings him to the verge of a metaphysical epiphany, an experience of the trees not as *his* trees but as *trees*, trees in all their tree-ness, trees *qua* trees in all their staggering *whatness* and mystery, trees *treeing*, trees as Adam might have seen them in their prelapsarian glory, majestic indeed. No wonder his heart begins to beat frenetically. But if he should accede to that intuition and give himself to that metaphysical recognition, he will effectively overturn his entire life, everything he has constructed for himself out of his own head. Thus the next sentence is a violent turn back to Cartesian comfort, made in two decisive steps, "quickly," lest he falter. The trees are first reduced to *lumber* (property), and then lumber is abstracted further into *a college education*. Once that abstraction is complete, "his spirits lifted," and they lift both for the comfort of the idealized vision and for the momentary resolution of the interior conflict, a conflict at the heart of the novel itself as well as of his character, and one best understood in its Thomistic terms.[3]

If this analysis is at all correct, then it follows that to read O'Connor well one has to be able to recognize—even in such small passages—the Thomism that characterizes her thought and pervades her writing, that enabled her to reveal the *claritas* of being in the humble particular of a mule's hind quarters. I want to argue that O'Connor's Thomist critique of Descartes—*Esse* vs. *Cogito*—is the meta-narrative of her fiction, at least from "Good Country People" (1955) to the end, the keystone in her arch. Aquinas was of course both theologian and philosopher, and the *theological* emphases in O'Connor's fiction are generally recognized, if somewhat erratically explored: the centrality of baptism as the decisive Christian act, the action of grace which always operates through secondary causality, the noticeable absence of Hollywood "miracles," the many allusions to Scripture, and so on. But the *philosophical* aspects—there are six—have gone neglected. It is the purpose of this paper to identify the six and to provide examples of how they are working in the fiction.

I

No one doubts O'Connor's admiration for Aquinas the philosopher. She herself spells it out as for example in letters to her old teacher Helen Greene: "My philosophical notions don't come from Kierkegard (I cant even spell it) but from St. Thomas Aquinas" (*CW* 897); to her close friend "A" (Betty Hester): "I couldn't make any judgment on the *Summa* except to say this: I read it for twenty minutes every night before I go to bed.... I feel I can personally guarantee that St. Thomas loved God because for the life of me I cannot help loving St. Thomas" (*CW* 945); and to her friend from Iowa days, the writer Robie Macauley (*CW* 934) with her wry designation of herself as a "hillbilly Thomist," a phrase she evidently used just the once, though it has for obvious reasons caught on—at least as a label. Moreover, references and allusions to Aquinas crop up regularly in her letters and abound in her non-fiction prose. It is clear that he was a living, pervasive presence in her thought, not some odd antiquarian interest but a nourishing and shaping power. Off her own witness, then, her Thomism has to be taken as a given, and it is distinctly *her* Thomism. In the non-fiction, for example, she rarely quotes Aquinas directly, preferring summary and paraphrase ("St. Thomas says..."), easing his technical Scholasticism into her own colloquial idiom;[4] while in the fiction she deftly absorbs the concepts into the structure and action. So our concern is pragmatic: the different ways her Thomism actually works in the stories. And while Thomism grounded her thought and nourished her sensibility, she was not a philosopher but an artist, and it is the drama and consequence of ideas, especially the central conflict between *Esse* and *Cogito,* that commanded her interest. This was probably the point she was making when she remarked to John Hawkes, "I am a Thomist three times removed and live amongst many distinctions. (A Thomist three times removed is one who doesn't read Latin or St. Thomas but gets it by osmosis)" (*CW* 1149).[5] So her direct interest in Aquinas was enriched by modern Thom*ism,* the living tradition of Aquinas' thought, as it was manifested in the great lay Thomists of the twentieth century on whom she also drew: Jacques Maritain, Etienne Gilson, A.C. Pegis, and Joseph Pieper. In their work, by careful study as well as by "osmosis," she found her own Thomism clarified and deepened.[6]

Thomism is found in O'Connor in six ways: (1) as a metaphysics of being; (2) as an epistemology of moderate realism; (3) as a historical narrative showing the consequences of the loss of the first two; (4) as a view of man as a *composite* of body and soul (not a ghost or an angel in a machine); (5) as a natural law morality; (6) as an objective aesthetics, the one feature commonly recognized. These six, which interpenetrate, ground her thought and give shape and themes to her stories, as she was always quick to acknowledge. For example, once we are aware of them we can hear all of them in just a scrap of conversation that she had with the interviewer Betsy Lockridge (*Conversations*, 38–39): "I can accept the universe as it is—I don't have to make up my own sense of value"—1, 2, and perhaps 6. "I can apply to a judgment higher than my own"—5. "I believe that a person is always valuable and responsible"—5 again. "When I write I am a maker"—6. "St. Thomas called art reason in making"—6. "We have reduced the uses of reason terribly"—2, 3, and probably 4. The point is that Thomism is pervasive in her thought, not some occasional option. She once warned Betty Hester that "if you live today you breathe in nihilism," but clearly Thomism was her filter.

But Thomism does more than shape O'Connor's narratives and provide her with themes. It grounds the very nature of her fiction, her basic outlook and the kind of art she made. O'Connor was a comic satirist—"Mine is a comic art, but that does not detract from its seriousness," she told Lockridge (*Conversations* 38), and she was broadly in the Jonsonian tradition of moral comedy. An obvious enough point but one that calls for some consideration, for satire is notoriously difficult to write under twentieth and twenty-first century conditions where the diminishment or disappearance of common moral and intellectual standards undercuts its effort at judgment. F. R. Leavis, for example, thought it all but impossible and considered Eliot's "Coriolan" poems as notable and rare exceptions. Yet O'Connor was able to write comic satire easily, almost naturally. How was this possible? Besides her native ironic wit, her satire had three distinct sources. First was her Thomist realism. She was endlessly amused by the folly of her Cartesian characters with their "clear and distinct ideas" frustrated by the protean unpredictabilities of quotidian life. Second was her South, a story-telling region (and therefore closer to the concrete and specific), with a common *mythos* available to every level of society ("Christ-haunted" and steeped in Scripture), and with a distinctive idiom that supported both.[7] And third was her Catholicism intertwined with her Thomism (they are not the same thing!). This gave her confidence in reason, in a transcendental order, and in objective truth, enabling her to hold her characters, for all their freakishness, to universal moral standards.[8] Her strategy was generally to assume the standards her vision gave her and to dramatize their violation. "What [the Catholic writer] sees at all times," she wrote, "is fallen man perverted by false philosophies," no weak or relativist position (*Mystery and Manners*, 177). It is time to examine the six elements of Thomism that figure in the fiction. We will take them up in reverse order.

II

"I have sent you *Art and Scholasticism*," O'Connor wrote to Betty Hester in April of 1957. "It's the book I cut my aesthetic teeth on.... He [Maritain] is a philosopher and not an artist but he does have great understanding of the nature of art, which he gets from St. Thomas" (*CW* 1030). The first two sentences, well known to O'Connor's admirers, generally mark the limit of interest in her as a Thomist, hillbilly or otherwise. What Maritain took from Aquinas and passed on to O'Connor was remarkably similar to what Eliot was saying at just the same time. Each presented an objective view of art and the artist that rejected Romantic subjectivity and proposed instead an older, impersonal approach, one that did not exalt the poet and his feelings but put the focus resolutely on the art object as something crafted, made, carrying within itself its own artistic purpose and logic.[9] And this is what O'Connor responded to.

Briefly then, Maritain's book is synthesized from various *apercus* found scattered across Aquinas' moral philosophy and theology. Art, broadly conceived, is an intellectual virtue of the practical order. As such it is close to Prudence but it differs in this way that while Prudence is concerned with doing and the person, Art is concerned with making and the object. Prudence's concern is with the means to our moral ends; Art is an end in itself. "Art operates for the good of the work done," Maritain says, adding that "art in no wise tends to make the artist good in his specifically human conduct" (15), addressing and directly undercutting the basic Romantic myth of the artist. By this approach, then, the work of art is impersonal and autonomous. O'Connor often echoed these views in her letters, conversations, and essays. And she also used them, *inter alia*, to stress that art could never be hijacked for pious purposes. As she told Fr. John McCown with her usual gimlet-eyed directness, "The novel is an art form and when you use it for anything other than art, you pervert it. I didn't make this up. I got it from St. Thomas (via Maritain) who allows that art is wholly concerned with the good of that which is made; it has no utilitarian end." And then veering away from any possibility of being understood in an "art for art's sake" sense, she added, "If you do manage to use it successfully for social, religious or other purposes, it is because you make it art first" (*The Habit of Being* 157).

O'Connor felt the need to push back against the Romanticism of the age. She could be deadly wry in remarking on the pretentiousness of the artist and his "vision," someone creating out of his own mind a new heaven and a new earth. Instead she saw her task as finding the meaning in the world God made, not expressing her own feelings or exalting her personal "vision".[10] She particularly disliked any extolling of the writer as a Shelleyean hierophant "with words expressing what the ordinary person understands not," or *vates* dwelling on himself and proposing himself as an unacknowledged legislator for the world. "I even dislike the concept *artist* when it sets you above," she wrote Hester. "All it is is working in a certain kind of medium to make something right. The material is no more exalted than any other kind of material and the idea of making it right is what should be applied to all making. St. Thomas said the artist is concerned with the good of that which is made, that art is a good-in-itself" (*CW* 1029). O'Connor could be pretty caustic about "Creative Writing" because she thought such programs overplayed the artist-as-special-person line and played down the hard truth that writing is hard work, disciplined hard work, needing what, following Maritain, she called the *Habitus* of art—a combination of natural talent, discipline, connaturality, disinterestedness, tacit appropriation of tradition, and a commitment to the good of the work itself, its formal cause; *dignum et justum est.*

While rejecting the artist as exalted figure, she always allowed that the artist's imagination and reason could be *prophetic*—even while insisting that this prophetic ability conferred no intrinsic superiority. It simply meant one was endowed with imagination, a gift. Her authority for this was once again St. Thomas via Maritain. "According to St. Thomas, prophetic vision is not a matter of seeing clearly but of seeing what is distant, hidden. The Church's vision is prophetic vision; it is always widening the view. The ordinary person does not have prophetic vision but he can accept it on faith. St. Thomas also says that prophetic vision is a quality of the imagination, that it does not have anything to do with the moral life of the prophet" (*CW* 1116). Her shorthand for this insight was that the writer-as-prophet was "a realist of distances" (*M&M* 179), someone who could approximate the remote and familiarize the wonderful, showing the reader the implications and consequences hidden in actions and ideas. Descartes, after all, thinking of the *Cogito* had no idea what was hidden in the *ergo sum*.

That being said (and in scandalously brief compass), how do these ideas about the autonomy of art and the disinterestedness of the artist play out in O'Connor's fiction? I want to suggest two different ways. First, as action within the story: in "The Enduring Chill" she directly satirizes the Romantic myth of the artist as it has been swallowed and digested by Asbury like so much unpasteurized milk. One of her favorite techniques is the expanding and re-working of stereotypes and clichés—the judge who gets the book thrown at her, the philosopher left without a leg to stand on, the old lady who lets the cat out of the bag, the woman being eaten out of house and home (by a bull!), the character who cannot see the forest for the trees—because so much of our lives is spent among unrecognized clichés frustrating thought and debasing feeling. In "The Enduring Chill" she pushes the Romantic stereotype of subjectivity pretty far. Poor Asbury! What a hilarious farrago of Romantic pretense he embraces: art is the path to salvation—if there is salvation, maybe it's Death that's the ideal; *epater le bourgeois!*; the Joycean artistic soul is bound in restraint by the very society he so eagerly denounces; Kafka's sufferings are a hagiographic ideal, together with the famous letter to his father outlining all the ways his father had failed him, cramped him, ruined him. O'Connor neatly varies this last point: the letter is not to the father but to the mother; Asbury eagerly quotes (but actually misquotes) Yeats (and the widening gyre of all metaphors!) to his "ignorant" mother, carefully explaining to her that it *is* Yeats; and it ends with the wonderful comic bathos of his final cry, "Woman, why did you pinion me?"—a line so uproariously funny that it would take an Oscar Wilde to do it justice. As the action unfolds it is this Romantic claptrap that leads Asbury to the unpasteurized milk escapade and his physical undoing. And with her swift change of tone and direction, she brings Asbury and his self-regarding pretentiousness into clear satiric critique with a single acerbic line from Father Finn ("from Purrgatory," of course)—"The Holy Ghost will not come until you see yourself as you are," a task not eagerly welcomed by this would-be Romantic artist.

The second way O'Connor's Thomistic aesthetics comes into play is with its emphasis on the autonomous and impersonal. Consider "Temple of the Holy Ghost" and "Good Country People." In each story the central character is a self-portrait of the artist, but their relation to O'Connor is more like that of "Dante" to Dante, "Chaucer" to Chaucer, or Prufrock to Eliot than Paul Morel to Lawrence or Eugene Gant to Thomas Wolfe. What is remarkable is her own self-knowledge in creating two very different characters who lack that very quality and who are filled instead with pride. Each is a projection of vices or dangerous possibilities O'Connor recognized in herself, and there is certainly no self-idealizing[11]. The little girl in "Temple" is a partial portrait of what O'Connor took herself to be at that age, manifesting characteristics that O'Connor saw as distinctive of Catholic smugness—"long on logic, definitions, abstractions."[12] Hulga, on the other hand, presents us with O'Connor as she thought she would have been without the Church, filled with pride and the gas of nihilism, "the stinkingest logical positivist you ever saw," as she said to Betty Hester (*CW* 948). So one in the Church, one out, both remarkably unidealized versions of O'Connor herself. O'Connor's ability to coolly and dispassionately observe negative features in herself and then dramatize them objectively, blending them into the narrative drama, testifies to her deep artistic integrity, her commitment to "getting it right" that she took from Aquinas via Maritain. A recent emphasis on "Good Country People" as a biographical transcript of a failed romance is enormously reductive and utterly misses this point.

III

Thomistic anthropology and natural law morality are fundamental to O'Connor's fiction, but they are nearly invisible and best seen through contrasts. The human person as a *composite* of body and soul, the soul as the form of the body, provide her with a perspective for satirical judgment of Cartesian dualism. Take, for example, "The Life You Save May Be Your Own," a straightforward enough story in all conscience, but one often oddly mischaracterized through a failure to grasp its tone. The title comes from a seemingly ubiquitous public service advertisement put out in the 1950s by the AAA motor club and directed at the appalling number of highway deaths in those pre-seatbelt days. Mr. Shiftlett—Tom T. Shiftlett—the shiftless, one-armed, unredeemable[13] con man is the focus of the satire. He certainly meets his match in Lucynell Crater, determined to unload her daughter, and the comic action turns on these two grifters trying to con one another over a deal in which Mr Shiftlett can have the unused automobile rusting near the barn but only if he will take the daughter with it. Early on Mr. Shiftlett, trying to impress, asks the question, "What is a man?" and he goes on to answer that he is one, that despite his loss of an arm he has—and the announcement is preceded portentously by a rapping on the floor, Mr. Shiftlett specializing in The Dramatic Pause,—"a moral intelligence." That *sounds* impressive but is only part of the huckster's spiel. And, O'Connor says, "the old woman was not impressed with the phrase." One con artist recognizes another. And of course the action belies it, as does a later admission that is quietly decisive, at the height of the negotiations when he almost overplays his hand, demanding some money for a honeymoon:

> "Listen here, Mr. Shiftlett," she said, sliding forward in her chair, "you'd be getting a permanent house and a deep well and the most innocent girl in the world. You don't need no money. Lemme tell you something: there ain't any place in the world for a poor disabled friendless drifting man."
>
> The ugly words settled in Mr. Shiftlett's head like a group of buzzards in the top of a tree. He didn't answer at once. He rolled himself a cigarette and lit it and then he said in an even voice, "Lady, a man is divided into two parts, body and spirit."
>
> The old woman clamped her gums together.
>
> "A body and a spirit," he repeated. "The body, lady, is like a house: it don't go anywhere; but the spirit, lady, is like an automobile: always on the move, always…" (*CW* 179)

The spirit / automobile connection is a wry comic variation on the Cartesian ghost in the machine and it helps to place and judge Mr. Shiftlett.

A second example of the body-spirit split can be seen in Hulga of "Good Country People." There is more to say about Hulga as the Cartesian Protagonist, but for the moment it is enough to consider the scene in the loft where lofty Hulga, dead certain of her mind's control of her body and of everything else, is first introduced to that fatal counter-argument to mind-body dualism, necking.

> The kiss, which had more pressure than feeling behind it, produced that extra surge of adrenalin in the girl that enables one to carry a packed trunk out of a burning house, but in her, the power went at once to the brain. Even before he released her, her mind, clear and detached and ironic anyway, was regarding him from a great distance, with amusement but with pity. She had never been kissed before and she was pleased to discover that it was an unexceptional experience and all a matter of the mind's control. (*CW* 278)

This misplaced confidence is her undoing as the necking intensifies and the scene reaches its climax in a moment of comic irony where she loses not her virginity but her wooden leg. The human person, O'Connor reminds us, is a unity, a composite.

Natural law morality is pervasive in O'Connor's work, but this is not to say very much because so too is it in most of the world's great literature. The idea that the human person is governed by practical reason and inclined to do the good and to avoid evil is, or was, our common human patrimony.[14] The Enlightenment denied it, of course, and O'Connor recognized the working out of that denial in the culture surrounding her. Modern culture, she saw, has lost its grasp on natural law morality and has become deeply subjectivist and relativistic. Her dealing with this theme can be seen in her use of the words "good" and "true," those transcendental properties of being that in her fiction are revealed to have lost their traditional force and to have become little more than empty counters in banal discourse. But to lose *good* is also to be unable to recognize *evil*, to move unwittingly into Nietzsche's territory. O'Connor's word for this was *nihilism.* She noticed this in an example from *The Waste Land.* Madame Sosotris, that "famous clairvoyante," may have "had a bad cold" but "nevertheless"

> Is known to be the wisest woman in Europe,
> With a wicked pack of cards.

What are we to make of *wicked* here? After all, we are dealing with the Black Arts even if in a stylized comic way. Clearly the word does not carry its traditional force. In fact Eliot has caught it hovering between the traditional and the modern, at the very moment it was transmogrifying into its exact opposite, the modern intensifier meaning something strongly positive.[15] And with that change we are *beyond* good and evil and are truly in the waste land.

In O'Connor's first collection, three of the ten stories have the word *Good* in the title, pointedly used in the empty sense, and that is not accidental. She wants to suggest that the good, like the true, has been emptied of its traditional moral force and reduced to vague cliché. Consider this bibliographical point. In February of 1955 when she had written "Good Country People" in just four days, O'Connor asked her editor, Robert Giroux if she could get the story into the manuscript for *A Good Man Is Hard to Find and Other Stories*, a manuscript set to go to the printers. Two stories could be cut, she said, "Afternoon in the Woods" and "A Stroke of Good Fortune." In the event only one had to go, there wasn't that much to choose between them, so the one she kept was the one with *Good* in the title. Both stories are apprentice work and neither amounts to much. But keeping the one with *Good*, helps to reinforce the overall emphasis and thereby lends a humble modicum of support to the two very great stories, "A Good Man Is Hard to Find" and "Good Country People."

Briefly then, in "Stroke" Madame Sosostris has morphed into Madam Zaleeda, a palm reader now, and she promises Ruby Hill that following an illness she will receive a stroke of good fortune—which Ruby eagerly interprets as a house "in a subdivision" and not, decidedly not, the pregnancy that it turns out to be. Ruby does not want children—the question asked by Lil's friend in *The Waste Land*, "What you get married for if you don't want children" more or less hangs in the air throughout—and she is unable to see anything *good* in the bearing of new life. The story is about being unable to judge what is truly good.

"A Good Man Is Hard to Find" is the name of a blues song from the Twenties recorded by Bessie Smith. It caught O'Connor's eye in a news story about a seven-year old child (!) who won an award for singing it. And then, just before she wrote, it was featured in the movie *Meet Danny Wilson* (1952) where it was sung first by Shelly Winters and then by Frank Sinatra! In other words, the title phrase is of a piece with the rest of the weightless world of pop culture emphasized in the first, or comic, half of the story. Its importance climaxes in the pivotal episode at Red Sammy's where the dialogue indicates that neither *good* nor *true* carries any real weight or force. The grandmother and Red Sammy are comically unable to rise above reinforcing one another's clichés.

> "You can't win," he said. "You can't win," and he wiped his sweating red face off with a grey handkerchief. "These days you don't know who to trust," he said. "Ain't that the truth?"
>
> "People are certainly not nice like they used to be," said the grandmother.
>
> "Two fellers came in here last week," Red Sammy said, "driving a Chrysler. It was a old beat-up car but it was a good one and these boys looked all right to me. Said they worked at the mill and you know I let them fellers charge the gas they bought? Now why did I do that?"
>
> "Because you're a good man!" the grandmother said at once.
>
> "Yes'm, I suppose so," Red Sam said as if he were struck with the answer.
>
> ..."A good man is hard to find," Red Sammy said. "Everything is getting terrible. I remember the day you could go off and leave your screen door unlatched. Not no more."
>
> He and the grandmother discussed better times. The old lady said that in her opinion Europe was entirely to blame for the way things were now. She said the way Europe acted you would think we were made of money and Red Sam said it was no use talking about it, she was exactly right. (*CW* 141–42)

With the Marshall Plan well-trashed and foreign policy nicely settled, and with the comforting satisfaction brought on by easy agreement over the hackneyed, the dialogue trails off, comic, but one might think, not greatly serious. Yet the careful reader notices what has been done to both *good* and *true*.

What is usually not noticed or understood is what O'Connor did next. In the original version of the story in *The Avon Book of Modern Writing* (1953), the transition from Red Sammy's to the darker second half is made with the words, "Outside of Toomsboro *the highway was being paved and they had to detour on a red dirt road*" (my emphasis).[16] The revised version, the one everyone reads, inserts here almost two pages of new material concerning the grandmother's story of the ante-bellum mansion, and this insertion changes things immensely. "'There was a secret panel in this house,' she said craftily, *not telling the truth* but wishing that she were" (my emphasis). In the original version the accident is caused by the bouncing of the car on the bad road, shaking the cat out of the bag. It is the Highway Department that puts them on that road. But in the more carefully developed final version, it is the grandmother's elaborate falsehood, her lie, that is the cause.

The grandmother has only a loose regard for truth. She lives pretty largely within the superficial world of popular culture set out in the story's first half, and her thinking and feeling are guided by that, as is her vocabulary.[17] She is not a "liar" in the usual sense; she is a casual manipulator who has no real sense that there should be in language an adequation of word to thing, to use a Thomist phrase. Unfortunately, in the story's second half she is no longer in that world. This is dramatized immediately after the accident in her initial dialogue with The Misfit, very different from her last conversation with Red Sammy.

> "Good afternoon," he said. "I see you all had you a little spill."
> "We turned over twice!" said the grandmother.
> "Oncet," he corrected. "We seen it happen." (*CW* 146)

That phrase "he corrected" is the essence of the story, the defining difference between casual exaggeration and real truth, grounded in the nature of things. We have just moved from the banality of popular culture into the stricter definitions of the natural law. That difference is extended from the true to the good as Bailey is hauled off into the woods:

> "Bailey Boy!" the grandmother called in a tragic voice but she found she was looking at The Misfit squatting on the ground in front of her. "I just know you're a good man," she said desperately. "You're not a bit common!"
>
> "Nome, I ain't a good man," The Misfit said after a second as if he had considered her statement carefully. (*CW* 148)

In the two scraps of dialogue the two words are cleansed of their banality and restored towards their true meaning, and they again carry their proper moral force. In The Misfit's world, truth is truth and good and evil are very different. The corrected grandmother will die redeemed, of course, and The Misfit's famous epitaph is a just one. "'She would of been a good woman, if it had been somebody there to shoot her every minute of her life.'" But its justice is earned only in the grandmother's final seconds of life when her head clears and she first sees the *Truth*, "'Why you're one of my babies! You're one of my own children'!"—and then does the *Good*: "She reached out and touched him on the shoulder" in a final gesture of love. Even the order has a Thomistic logic: first the intellect, then the will.

"Good Country People" uses the title phrase to effectively convey the triviality of the world Joy / Hulga has to endure each day and to make plausible her cynical response to it, her "ironic and detached" view of all that her mother's farm has to offer. It is used at least seven times to make this point, but the last use, at the climax, is by Hulga herself, shocked, outmaneuvered, and bewildered: "Her voice when she spoke had an almost pleading sound. 'Aren't you', she murmured, 'aren't you just good country people?'" The effect here is to cancel her prideful assumption of superiority and close the gap between the triviality of her mother's discourse and the misanthropic self-indulgence of her own. She is craving the solace of the cliché.

To summarize this discussion of O'Connor's use of natural law principles, then: the Good and the True are transcendental principles of being, and she uses them in such a way as to remind us of this, and at the same time to remind us of their debased and harmful current use, our casual emptying of their true significance, our heedless drifting into the banal, beyond good and evil. "We have reduced the uses of reason terribly," she remarked to Lockridge (*Conversations* 39), and her use of *Good* is meant to illustrate that fact.

IV

Although none of her characters attempted to extract sunbeams out of cucumbers or carve mutton into rhomboids, O'Connor may have been the most anti-Cartesian writer since Swift. The historical narrative she found in Maritain and Gilson criticized Descartes' shift from being to thought in metaphysics and from knowledge to thinking in epistemology. The ensuing subjectivism and dualism led eventually to a variety of false philosophies, and O'Connor was keenly aware of such arguments as Gilson's in *The Unity of Philosophical Experience* (which she greatly admired) and Maritain's in "Christian Humanism," (from *The Range of Reason* which she reviewed). As Maritain put the gist of it, with Descartes there occurred a "failure of philosophic Reason.... Human Reason lost its grasp of Being," and this led to a changed outlook and the new set of attitudes that underwrite "enlightened" modernity. In her copy of Aquinas O'Connor marked for special attention a passage in which A.C. Pegis noted the starkness of the difference, putting the metaphysical argument into historical terms:

> We are the heirs of generations of philosophical speculations according to which man is a *thinker* and a *mind*. Now it is a fact that the Thomistic man is a knower rather than a thinker, and he is a composite being rather than a mind. In fact, St. Thomas does not even have in his vocabulary a term corresponding to the term thinker: you cannot translate such a term into Thomistic Latin. If we are to judge matters as St. Thomas has done, we are bound to say that the European man became a thinker after he ruined himself as a knower; and we can even trace the steps of that ruination—from Augustinian Platonism to the nominalistic

> isolationism of Ockham to the despairing and desperate Methodism of Descartes. For what we call the decline of medieval philosophy was really a transition from man as a knower to man as a thinker—from man knowing the world of sensible things to man thinking abstract thoughts in separation from existence.[18]

"From man knowing the world of sensible things to man thinking abstract thoughts in separation from existence"—that defines pretty well a type of a figure that O'Connor was much concerned from with 1955 onwards, from the time, that is, when she crafted the archetype of the Cartesian Protagonist in the Joy / Hulga of "Good Country People." After Joy / Hulga there followed Mr Fortune ("A View of the Woods"), Asbury ("The Enduring Chill"), Rayber and Tarwater (*The Violent Bear It Away*), Julian ("Everything that Rises Must Converge"), Sheppard ("The Lame Shall Enter First"), and Ruby Turpin ("Revelation"), all variations on the Cartesian type—a type that Old Tarwater memorably sums up in a phrase about Rayber, "He wanted it all in his head. You can't change a baby's pants in your head" (*CW* 378). *Mystery and Manners* is replete (at least sixteen instances by my count) with O'Connor's Thomistic insistence that *knowledge begins with the senses*.[19] The Cartesian Protagonists all want it all in their heads.

Joy / Hulga is the archetype. Her identification with Descartes is through a pattern of allusions and is unmistakable (more than for any of the others), beginning with the simple fact that she is a philosopher, that she identifies with that consciousness she never lost when her leg was blasted off, that she is absolutely convinced that the mind is an independent force in control of the body's sensations ("Her mind, throughout this, never stopped or lost itself for a second to her feelings" is her conscious assessment of herself in the necking). The one philosopher she quotes is Malebranche, a follower of Descartes. And then there is the typographical peculiarity of her fierce challenge to her mother—"'If you want me here I am—LIKE I AM,'" where the typeface alludes to both *Cogito, ergo sum* but also, and blasphemously, to Exodus 3.14, the very passage that Gilson loved to cite as Revelation's warrant for thinking about God as pure act. She is also absent during the conversation her mother and Manley Pointer have about the *good* and about *truth*, a dialogue that partly mimics the one between the grandmother and Red Sammy, though here the terms are given a stronger positive sense. And then there is the Heidegger passage, the one that so unnerves her mother when she sees it marked in one of Hulga's books. In it Heidegger is scoring easy points against science because, unlike philosophy, it veers away from thinking about Nothing. And presumably Hulga is using this later on with Manley Pointer. But what is really important is what she *doesn't* mark, doesn't take in, is unconcerned for, namely Heidegger's great themes: *Dasein*, facticity, our loss of wonder, our surrender to technology, our bland and blind indifference to being. There is no underlining of his great provocative question, "Why is there not just nothing at all?" Hulga the Cartesian has no interest in such themes.[20] On the other hand, she has quite literally enacted the *Cogito*, remaking Joy as Hulga in a supreme act of her own thought ("She saw it as the name of her greatest creative act"). And all of this is mixed into the innocence / experience theme, and the bawdy story structure (The Travelling Salesman and the Farmer's Daughter) to show how unaware of *the real* she really is.

Two points are especially relevant. First, O'Connor is a fiction writer not a philosopher, and she is concerned to subject ideas to the pragmatic test, a realist of distances who wants to bring out the implications of things perhaps too easily held.[21] With Hulga and the other Cartesian Protagonists her concern is with the anterior attitudes hidden in the outlook, the peculiar vulnerability they generate, and the consequent capacity for deception and for self-deception. "'I don't have illusions,'" Hulga tells Manley Pointer, voicing her greatest one. "'I'm one of those people who see *through* to nothing.'" Second, Hulga's lofty attitude and supreme self-confidence in her ability to see *through* everything all the way to Nothing are captured in her tone, her habitual delivery that defines the gap between herself and the Hopewell farm. And yet the action is cross-grained and will reveal her innocence, indeed her naïveté. She may think she sees *through* things, but the action suggests she is unable to see even simple things as they are. And as for seeing through to Nothing, that is a judgment, and she is unable to judge people or things at their real worth. Moreover, she is unable to perceive the story, the bawdy comic story, she is caught up in, and of which she is the butt. Even the imagery works against her: are there two lakes there, or just one? How do the speckled wildflowers get moved from the pink hillside to the green lake or lakes? Why does she not notice that he has removed her glasses? The topography of the farm she lives on seems to have escaped her notice.

There is no need to trace this out in its artistically splendid detail, for the epistemological problem has been identified. But her vision is crystallized in a single paragraph:

> During the night she had imagined that she seduced him. She imagined that the two of them walked on the place until they came to the storage barn beyond the two back fields and here, she imagined, that things came to such a pass that she very easily seduced him and that then, of course, she had to reckon with his remorse. True genius can get an idea across even to an inferior mind. She imagined that she took his remorse in hand and changed it into a deeper understanding of life. She took all his shame away and turned it into something useful. (*CW* 186)

A few minutes of heavy necking undermines this fantasy, and she is exposed to the cold cruelty of Manley Pointer, her vulnerability heightened by the comic parody of the seduction scene and her painful, if non-sexual, ravishment. It is ironically apt that she should be left in the *loft*, unable to come down, churning with impotent rage for the full and final reversal of all that she has believed.

V

Metaphysics is the keystone in the arch of Thomism and it is inseparable from knowledge. It is a basic principle of Thomism that being is the condition of knowing and that "the idealist thinks whereas the realist knows."[22] In O'Connor this means that *ideas* and *thinking* are always suspect terms. Her characters are tempted to prefer *thinking*—i.e., his or her own ideas, own inner world where there is no let or hindrance—to *knowledge*—i.e., of things in the outer, shared, objective world in all its otherness: abstraction *from* rather than participation *in*. This is the struggle of the Cartesian Protagonist. In Hulga we see the results but not the form itself, something we glimpsed however with Rayber and the trees. In *The Violent Bear It Away*, O'Connor puts the matter in large-scale form and not once but twice,[23] once for Tarwater, once for Rayber. Each has a moment of intuition when the singular gives way and the character stands in the presence of being itself. The passages are closely parallel but they diverge in one crucial way, for while Tarwater's demands that he recognize being as *true*, Rayber's demands that he recognize it as *good*, something to be *loved*. To frame the issue, O'Connor first distinguishes her three characters in relevant Thomistic terms. First, Rayber, "who had no child of his own and wanted one of his dead sister's to raise *according to his own ideas*" (CW 331). Next, Tarwater, "...the boy, who had *ideas of his own*..." (CW 332). And finally, Old Tarwater's Thomistic admonition to the boy: "It's no part of your job *to think for the Lord*. Judgment may rack your bones" (CW 335; all emphases mine).

It is difficult to briefly situate Tarwater's moment because of the complexity of O'Connor's technique of story-within-story and memory-within memory, but it comes in Chapter I as he is digging Old Tarwater's grave. He is recalling the old man's teaching about *freedom* (which Tarwater habitually confuses with autonomy) and about the lordship of Jesus, "madness," he thinks, and as he does so resentment begins to color everything.

> He tried when possible to pass over these thoughts, to keep his vision located on an even keel, to see no more than what was in front of his face and to let his eyes stop at the surface of that. It was as if he were afraid that if he let his eye rest for an instant longer than was needed to place something—a spade, a hoe, the mule's hind quarters before his plow, the red furrow under him—that the thing would suddenly stand before him, strange and terrifying, demanding that he name it justly and be judged for the name he gave it. He did all he could to avoid this threatened intimacy of creation. (*CW* 343)

The demand for naming is a demand for truth, to speak the truth of things, which is to have knowledge of them and to grasp their nature, their essence, even things as humble as the mule's hind quarters, and that he adapt himself to that truth. This goes against his every desire for autonomy,[24] even against his grudging willingness to be a prophet. He will be a prophet so long as it is on his terms, terms drawn from the more colorful passages of Ezekiel and the drawings of William Blake.

> When the Lord's call came, he wished it to be a voice from out of a clear and empty sky, the trumpet of the Lord God Almighty, untouched by any fleshly hand or breath. He expected to see wheels of fire in the eyes of unearthly beasts. (*CW* 343)

Rather than name things justly, he wants them to conform to his ideas. O'Connor is using the metaphysics and epistemology of Thomism to criticize the emerging Cartesianism against which Tarwater must struggle.

The corresponding Rayber passage is somewhat longer and decidedly more chilling. For one thing it turns not on the mule's hind quarters but on Bishop, Rayber's "useless" son whom he once tried to drown, and towards whom he practices indifference. "That's only Bishop," he tells Tarwater when they first meet, and there is a good deal packed into that *only*. For Rayber Bishop is a *problem*, one he has not yet been able to solve.[25]

> His normal way of looking on Bishop was as an *x* signifying the general hideousness of fate. He did not believe that he himself was formed in the image and likeness of God but that Bishop was he had no doubt. The little boy was part of a simple equation that required no further solution, except at the moments when with little or no warning he would feel himself overwhelmed by the horrifying love. (*CW* 401)

The second sentence is simply blasphemous, an expression of Rayber's deep hatred of God. As the passage continues we recognize the parallel with Tarwater's:

> Anything he looked at too long could bring it on. Bishop did not have to be around. It could be a stick or a stone, the line of a shadow, the absurd

> old man's walk of a starling crossing the sidewalk. If without thinking, he lent himself to it, he would feel suddenly a morbid surge of the love that terrified him—powerful enough to throw him to the ground in an act of idiot praise.

We should note both *without thinking* and *lent himself to*; the first indicates the Cartesian, the second the pull towards participation in, not abstraction from. The demand in his case is to affirm the *goodness* of being, for the will should love that which is good. And this is precisely what he refuses. O'Connor then draws the line taut from the Cartesian to the utilitarian, that other fatal "false philosophy."[26]

> He was not afraid of love in general. He knew the value of it and how it could be used. He had seen it transform in cases where nothing else had worked, such as with his poor sister. None of this had the least bearing on his situation. The love that would overwhelm him was of a different order entirely. It was not the kind that could be used for the child's improvement or his own. It was love without reason, love for something futureless, love that appeared to exist only to be itself, imperious and all demanding, the kind that would cause him to make a fool of himself in an instant. It began with Bishop and then like an avalanche covered everything his reason hated. (*CW* 401)

There is no need for further comment. Love, here, is the properly ordered response to the transcendental goodness of being, a goodness that Rayber refuses to allow because it does not correspond to what is "in his head." It should be clear by this point how O'Connor's Thomism is what is at play throughout.

Her use of metaphysics defines her two characters and their differences. Each will resist the metaphysical intuition, but they will suffer different fates. Tarwater will come to accept the hard truth that his ideas have been wrong; Rayber will know the success of solving the problem of Bishop—and the shock of emptiness when he hears his son being drowned and he feels nothing.[27]

VI

This look into O'Connor's philosophical Thomism is not to be thought of as exhaustive of any of the six aspects nor even of the Thomism in any one story. Rather it is designed as a series of signposts to assist the interested reader. That said, I would like to end by noting two stories where Aquinas himself puts in an appearance, cameos as it were, where allusions to his legendarium are woven into the story—tacit tributes by O'Connor to The Philosopher.

"The Comforts of Home" is theological, not philosophical and so need not detain us. The protagonist's name is Thomas but this Thomas is more like an anti-Thomas, a modern materialist not a medieval thinker. In a letter to John Hawkes, O'Connor pointed out the theological issue: this Thomas is "face to face with his own evil—which is that of putting his own comfort before charity" (CW 1147). The element of serio-comic parody is developed through the name, the youthful Aquinas's experience with the prostitute his brothers sent to his room to deter him from the religious life, and from an allusion to the "Dumb Ox" story. This modern Thomas puts himself, not God, at the center and the apex, and is satisfied with material comforts like an electric blanket: an image of modern man who has lost his way.[28]

"A Temple of the Holy Ghost" is O'Connor's only "Catholic" story, that is to say one with a Catholic protagonist and perspective, Catholic ritual, and a Catholic understanding of the Eucharist and its sacramental action. As such it too is "theological" not "philosophical" and outside our purview, but there is an important point of epistemology that is both philosophical and theological. The child-protagonist, the O'Connor self-portrait, is smart and knows it and she is pridefully contemptuous of those who are not. But the action reveals the limits of both her knowledge and her mode of knowing, and does so in clear Thomistic terms. Briefly then, in the porch scene after Wendell has sung two Protestant hymns, the two convent girls requite him with the *Tantum Ergo*, and he, confused by the Latin, remarks, "That must be Jew singing."

> The girls giggled idiotically but the child stamped her foot on the barrel. "You big dumb ox! she shouted. "You big dumb Church of God ox!" she roared and fell off the barrel. (*CW* 202)

She evidently does not know that for his taciturnity "The Dumb Ox" was the sobriquet hung on the young Aquinas by his fellow students,[29] and that Aquinas is the author of *Tantum Ergo*,[30] familiar to Catholics from the devotion of Benediction, common in those days. The child knows the hymn but not its author. This gap, her childish concept of martyrdom, and her view of rabbit reproduction all indicate the limits of her knowledge (as distinct from her knowingness, her prideful attitude).[31]

This conceptual limitation bears on the child's spiritual growth. After hearing about the hermaphrodite at the fair, something she is unable to understand, she has a dream in which the figure is identified as a temple of the Holy Ghost. The hermaphrodite is in fact a serious parody, one that invokes the *paradigm* of Christ as one person with two natures. Both parody and paradigm are beyond the child's knowledge. But the next afternoon at Benediction, during the *Tantum Ergo*, her mind empties and "she began to realize that she was in the presence of God," and when the priest raises the monstrance she has an image of "the freak at the fair." Soon after, her face is mashed by the crucifix on the nun's rosary, an anticipation of the Christian life less dramatic than her Walter Mitty images of martyrdom. And at the end she sees the sun as "an elevated Host drenched in blood," and "the red *clay* road hanging over the trees" (my emphasis; the clay of common life). The images, the dream, are felt rather than understood; they are mysterious not discursive. And as such they represent a mode of knowledge Aquinas called *per modum inclinationis* as opposed to *per modum cognitionis*. Maritain comments on the difference this way: "A moral philosopher may not be a virtuous man and yet know everything about the virtues,"—*per modum cognitionis*. "A virtuous man may possibly be wholly ignorant in moral philosophy, and know as well—probably better—everything about virtues, through connaturality"—*per modum inclinationis*.[32] This important epistemological distinction is what O'Connor is using. The connatural mode is the one the girl is learning via the Eucharist, the better path for those of common clay on the spiritual life.[33] That is how O'Connor understands the sacraments to work. And the epistemological distinction shapes and informs the story. The child's growth is from one mode of knowing to the other, ending in calm of mind all glibness spent.

VII

Philosophical Thomism, then, is fundamental to O'Connor's thought and it animates and orders a large part of her fiction. In fact, much of that fiction has to be seen as a Thomistic critique of the central pathologies of modern (and post-modern!) life and thought. Her letters show that from 1955 onwards she was dogged by academic responses that she found ludicrous, reductive "interpretations" casually indifferent to her craftsmanship, grounded in bizarre misunderstandings of her *donées* or her intentions. That ludicrousness is now, unfortunately, well-established in all-too-much academic scholarship, seriously compromising appreciation of the nature and value of her work. To be sure, an understanding of O'Connor's *philosophical* Thomism is *not* The Key to All Mythologies. But without a lively awareness of how and why she was using it, how vital it was to her vision and her fiction, any response to her work is unnecessarily compromised, if not vitiated. All six aspects are important but the gravest is the historical narrative connecting metaphysics with epistemology for the Cartesian Protagonist. From Rayber, whose spirits lifted as he reduced his trees to his ideas, to the prideful child reduced to awed silence and "lost in thought," in an inexpressible connaturality, Thomism framed and informed the characters O'Connor created and the stories she had to tell. Not to see this is to miss a good deal of what that fiction has to offer.[34]

Notes to "His Trees Stood Rising Above Him": Philosophical Thomism in Flannery O'Connor

1. Four partial exceptions, all of which lean towards the theological side: Helen R. Andretta, "A Thomist's Letters to 'A'," *The Flannery O'Connor Bulletin*, Vols. 26–27 (1998–2000), pp. 52–72; Frederick Christian Bauerschmidt, "Shouting in the Land of the Hard of Hearing: On Being a Hillbilly Thomist," *Modern Theology*, 20 (January 2004), pp. 163–82; Jae-Nam Han, "O'Connor's Thomism and the 'Death of God' in *Wise Blood*," *Literature and Belief*, 17 (1997) pp. 115–127; Marion Montgomery, *Hillbilly Thomist: Flannery O'Connor, St. Thomas and the Limits of Art*, 2 vols. (Jefferson, NC: McFarland and Company, 2006). There are bits and bobs in some of the books, of course, especially the better ones, but nothing focused or developed and generally leaning to the theological side. See Frederick Asals,

Flannery O'Connor: The Imagination of Extremity (Athens: University of Georgia Press, 1982); Henry T. Edmondson III, *Return to Good and Evil: Flannery O'Connor's Response to Nihilism* (Lanham, MD: Lexington Books, 2005); Ralph C. Wood, *Flannery O'Connor and the Christ-Haunted South* (Grand Rapids, MI: Eerdmans), 2004. Christina Bieber Lake has some prescient remarks about O'Connor and Descartes, *The Incarnational Art of Flannery O'Connor.* (Macon, GA: Mercer University Press, 2005).

2. "What a deliverance it would be for us, if we could recognize the elementary truth that the object of epistemology is not *thought*, which is only the consciousness of an act of knowledge, but *knowledge* itself, which is the grasp of an object." Etienne Gilson, *Methodical Realism* (Fort Royal, VA: Christendom Press, 1990), p. 122. Cf. the moment when Tarwater tells Rayber he has "done the needful": "He gazed through the actual insignificant boy before him to an image of him that he held fully developed in his mind" (*CW* 388).
3. A thrifty O'Connor will make similar use of the same trope in "A View of the Woods," where for the life of him Mr. Fortune can't understand why a mere view of the landscape should be counted as of more worth than "progress," by which he means converting the landscape into money.
4. An indication of how deeply she meditated upon him.
5. In *Flannery O'Connor's Library: Resources of Being* (Athens: University of Georgia Press, 1983), Arthur Kinney lists these primary holdings in Aquinas: *Philosophical Texts*, ed. Thomas Gilby (New York: Oxford University Press, 1951; pb. 1960); *Introduction to St. Thomas Aquinas*, ed. with an introduction by A. C. Pegis (New York: Modern Library: 1948); *Truth (Quaestiones Disputatae: De Veritate)*, 3 vols. (Chicago: Regnery, 1952); *Treatise on Law, On Truth and Falsity, and on Human Knowledge* (Chicago: Regnery, 1949). The Pegis volume was her main text and *vade mecum* until she acquired her *De Veritate* in 1960. It should be noted that she also read and used non-Thomists like Gabriel Marcel, Romano Guardini, and Teilhard de Chardin.
6. The books of special importance and influence for her were Maritain, *Art and Scholasticism* (New York: Scribner, 1930); Maritain, *The Range of Reason* (New York: Scribner, 1952); Gilson, *The Unity of Philosophical Experience* (New York Scribner, 1952); Gilson, *Reason and Revelation in the Middle Ages* (New York: Scribner, 1938); Pieper, *Leisure: The Basis of Culture* (New York: Pantheon, 1954); and Pegis' Introduction to his edition of Aquinas (see note 4, *supra*). Maritain and Gilson also wrote books on literature and on painting and Pieper was deeply interested in literature. The newcomer to Aquinas and Thomism is usually directed to the final three chapters of G. K. Chesterton, *Saint Thomas Aquinas* (New York: Sheed and Ward, 1933), but for a firm grasp of the concepts, arguments, and consequences of Thomism as understood by O'Connor he or she could hardly do better than the chapter on Aquinas in Gilson, *History of Christian Philosophy in the Middle Ages* (New York: Random House, 1955), pp. 361–386. More latterly, there is Fergus Kerr, *Thomas Aquinas: A Very Short Introduction* (London: Oxford University Press, 2009).
7. Cf. "I have Boston cousins and when they come South they discuss problems, they don't tell stories. We tell stories" (*Conversations* 71).
8. "Whenever I'm asked why Southern writers particularly have a penchant for writing about freaks, I say it is because we are still able to recognize one. To be able to recognize a freak, you have to have some conception of the whole man, and in the South the general conception of

man is still, in the main, theological." "Some Aspects of the Grotesque in Southern Fiction," in *CW* 861.

9. For a fuller exposition on this point see my Introduction to Jacques Maritain, *Art and Scholasticism* (Providence, RI: Cluny, 2020), pp. i–xvii. Rowan Williams, *Grace and Necessity: Reflections on Art and Love* (Harrisburg, PA: Morehouse, 2005), gives a fine exposition of Maritain's thought as it leads on to *Creative Intuition in Art and Poetry* (1953). *Grace and Necessity* has a chapter on O'Connor with some outstanding theological reflections, but the literary exegesis is cramped by a certain stiffness in the face of O'Connor's ironic comedy and an unfortunate lapse into political correctness and the irrelevant Bakhtinian view of O'Connor's narrators.
10. As she wrote to Betty Hester, "the moral basis of poetry is the accurate naming of the things of God" (*CW* 980). And to Cecil Dawkins, "I admire a saying of Braque's that he made about painting—'I like the rule that corrects the emotion'" (*HB* 486).
11. And the same is true of Asbury, her third "portrait of the artist."
12. Cf. "Smugness is the Great Catholic Sin. I find it in myself and don't dislike it any less." To Betty Hester, *CW* 983. And, "We too much indulge ourselves in the logic that kills, in making categories smaller and smaller, in prescribing attitudes and proscribing subjects. For the Catholic, one result of the Counter-Reformation was a practical overemphasis on the legal and logical and a consequent neglect of the Church's broader tradition." "The Catholic Novelist in the Protestant South" (*M&M* 205). The text in *CW* is different but the same basic idea can be found there as well.
13. O'Connor to John Hawkes: "I can fancy a character like the Misfit as redeemable but a character like Mr. Shiftlett as being unredeemable" (*CW* 1108).
14. There is a classic Thomistic exposition of the natural law and its metaphysical premises, brilliantly distilled into just six and-a-half pages, in the final chapter of John Courtney Murray, S.J., *We Hold These Truths: Catholic Reflections on the American Proposition* (New York: Sheed and Ward, 1960); Image pb., pp. 310–317. O'Connor apparently did not own this book, at least it is not listed in Kinney, but she certainly was familiar with Murray and undoubtedly knew this argument, if only through "osmosis."
15. Ricks and McCue note that the OED's first citation for this change–as slang–is from Fitzgerald's *This Side of Paradise* (1920). See "Commentary" in *The Poems of T.S. Eliot*, Volume I, edited by Christopher Ricks and Jim McCue (Baltimore: Johns Hopkins Press, 2015), p. 611. Eliot's "wisest" parallels and strengthens the point.
16. *The Avon Book of Modern Writing*, eds. William Phillips and Philip Rahv (New York: Avon, 1953). "A Good Man Is Hard to Find" is found in pp. 186–99. The passage O'Connor altered is on p. 191. It is the only change she made, and it is of such great importance that its neglect is hard to understand. But then again most of the artistic elements in this, O'Connor's most famous story—structure, wordplay, rhythm, play of tone, handling of conventions–have been largely ignored.
17. In order of appearance: newspapers (the sports page), television ("rabbit ears"), radio ("queen for a day"), cartoons (patrolmen and billboards), comic books, movies and pop fiction ("Gone with the Wind," a favorite O'Connor target), and pop music ("Tennessee Waltz")—all rich sources of cliché. The entire first half is saturated, providing the appropriate context for her dialogue with Red Sammy; there are no such references in the second, or Misfit, half.

18. *Introduction to Saint Thomas Aquinas*, ed. Anton C. Pegis (New York: The Modern Library, 1948). See "Introduction," p. xxiv. This was the edition O'Connor habitually read.
19. This is O'Connor's paraphrase, not a direct quotation. She rarely quoted Aquinas directly, preferring to run his concepts through her own idiom. *Nihil in intellectu quod prius non fuerit in sensu* was a favorite Scholastic tag, often used against Platonists. It is not found in either of the *Summas* but O'Connor likely came upon it in *De Veritate*, q. 2, a. 3, arg. 19, where Aquinas is using it for heuristic purposes. Aquinas' epistemology can be found in *ST* I, qq. 78, 79, 80, 84.
20. O'Connor held Heidegger in high regard. "Heidegger writes a good deal about the poet's business being to name what is holy. His essays on Holderin are very rich." To Beverly Brunson, *CW* 925. Heidegger's relation, relations, or possible relation / relations to Thomism and Being is / are typically complex and obscure. But see William Barrett, *The Illusion of Technique* (New York: Anchor Books, 1979), pp. 121–248; and David Bentley Hart, "A Philosopher in the Twilight," Hart, *A Splendid Wickedness and Other Essays* (Grand Rapids, MI: Eerdmans: 2016), pp. 91–104.
21. "America is therefore one of the countries where the precepts of Descartes are least studied and are best applied." Marked by O'Connor in her edition of Tocqueville, *Democracy in America*, vol. 2 (New York, Vintage: 1945), p. 4.
22. Gilson, *Methodical Realism*, p. 128.
23. Once for the almost-blind and once for the hard of hearing?—in a much-overused line from her.
24. Almost his first thought after the old man dies comes as he looks out at the farm: "I'm going to move that fence" (*CW* 337). O'Connor here blends the autonomy theme with the desire to shape things according to his own ideas.
25. We should note here O'Connor's use of Gabriel Marcel's problem / mystery distinction to deepen her characterization of Rayber. When Rayber first sees Tarwater at the door he first sees "a fascinating problem." Marcel, *The Mystery of Being*, 2 vols. (Chicago, Regnery, n.d.) [O'Connor's are signed and dated 1953]. Marcel, of course, was no Thomist.
26. At the end of Chapter VI Rayber suddenly recalls "an old rage" at the physician who told him he should be grateful that Bishop's health was good, that he had "seen them born blind as well, some without arms and legs, and with a heart outside."

    "How can I be grateful," he had hissed, when one—just one—is born without a heart outside?"

    "You'd better try," the doctor had said. (*CW* 205–06)

    The submerged imagery of *hissed* is a quiet evaluation. It should be noticed that there are in Rayber traces of Ivan Karamazov.
27. "Rayber and Tarwater are really fighting the same current in themselves. Rayber wins out against it and Tarwater loses; Rayber achieves his own will and Tarwater submits to his vocation." To Alfred Corn (*CW* 1170).
28. The virtues of this lovely story were first made clear to me by my former students Ealish Cassidy and Laura Wells.
29. And Albert the Great is supposed to have rebuked his students by saying that one day the dumb ox would roar. It is a well-known story.
30. The two-stanzas of *Tantum Ergo* are the conclusion of Aquinas' great hymn to the Eucharist, *Pange Lingua Gloriosi*, still sung today in Corpus Christi processions.

31. It is noticeable that the child does not recognize the allusions to 1 Corinthians 3 and 6 that the girls giggle over and that give the story its title. Catholic ignorance of scripture was something O'Connor constantly deplored.
32. Maritain, *The Range of Reason*, (New York: Scribner, 1953), Chapter III, "On Knowledge through Connaturality," pp. 22–29. The quote is from p. 23.
33. Her virtue / knowledge is only incipient and the red clay road is a long one. On the ride home she is quick to observe "three folds of fat in the back of [Alonzo Myers'] neck and she noted that his ears were pointed almost like a pig's." Grace builds on nature—and nature can be fairly intractable.
34. In memory of Joseph W. Evans and Francis J. O'Malley, beloved teachers, and of Rene Fortin and Rodney Delasanta, beloved colleagues, beloved friends.

Works Cited

Andretta, Helen R. "A Thomist's Letters to 'A'," *The Flannery O'Connor Bulletin*, Vols. 26–27 (1998–2000): pp. 52–72.

Aquinas, St. Thomas. *Introduction to St. Thomas Aquinas*. Edited and with an Introduction by Anton C. Pegis. New York: Modern Library, 1948.

_____. *Philosophical Texts*, Selected and edited by Thomas Gilby. New York: Oxford University Press, 1951; pb,, 1960.

_____. *Treatise on Law, On Truth and Falsity, and on Human Knowledge*. Chicago: Regnery, 1949.

_____. *Truth (Quaestiones Disputatae: De Veritate)*, 3 vols. Chicago: Regnery: 1952.

Asals, Frederick. *Flannery O'Connor: The Imagination of Extremity*. Athens: University of Georgia Press, 1982.

The Avon Book of Modern Writing. Edited by Phillips, William and Philip Rahv. New York: Avon, 1953 (pb.).

Barrett, William. *The Illusion of Technique*. New York: Anchor Books, 1979.

Bauerschmidt, Frederick Christian. "Shouting in the Land of the Hard of Hearing: On Being a Hillbilly Thomist," *Modern Theology*, 20 (January 2004): pp. 163–82.

Chesterton, G. K. *Saint Thomas Aquinas*. New York: Sheed and Ward, 1933.

Edmondson, Henry T. III. *Return to Good and Evil: Flannery O'Connor's Response to Nihilism*. Lanham, MD: Lexington Books, 2005.

Eliot, T. S. *The Poems of T. S. Eliot*, Volume I. Edited by Christopher Ricks and Jim McCue. Baltimore: Johns. Hopkins Press, 2015.

Gilson, Etienne. *History of Christian Philosophy in the Middle Ages*. New York: Random House, 1955.

_____. *Methodical Realism*, Front Royal, VA: Christendom, 1990.

_____. *Reason and Revelation in the Middle Ages*. New York: Scribner, 1938.

_____. *he Unity of Philosophical Experience*, New York: Scribner, 1937.

Hart, David Bentley. *A Splendid Wickedness and Other Essays*. Grand Rapids, MI: Eerdmans: 2016.

Han, Jae Nam. "O'Connor's Thomism and the 'Death of God' in *Wise Blood*." *Literature and Belief*, 17 (1997): pp. 115–127.

Kinney, Arthur F. Comp. *Flannery O'Connor's Library: Resources of Being*, Athens: University of Georgia Press, 1985.

Lake, Christina Bieber. *The Incarnational Art of Flannery O'Connor.* Macon, GA: Mercer University Press, 2005.

Marcel, Gabriel. *The Mystery of Being*, 2 vols. Chicago: Regnery, n.d.

Maritain, Jacques. *Art and Scholasticism.* New York: Scribner, 1930; new edition with an Introduction by Brian Barbour. Providence, RI: Cluny, 2020.

_____. *The Range of Reason*, New York: Scribner, 1953.

Montgomery, Marion. *Hillbilly Thomist: Flannery O'Connor, St. Thomas and the Limits of Art*, 2 vols. Jefferson, NC: McFarland and Company, 2006.

Murray, John Courtney, S.J. *We Hold These Truths: Catholic Reflections on the American Proposition* (New York: Sheed and Ward, 1960.

O'Connor, Flannery. *Conversations with Flannery O'Connor.* Edited by Rosemary Magee. Jackson: University Press of Mississippi, 1987.

_____. *Collected Works*, New York: Library of America, 1988.

_____. *Mystery and Manners: Occasional Prose.* Edited by Robert Fitzgerald and Sally Fitzgerald. New York: Farrar, Straus, & Giroux, 1969.

_____. *The Habit of Being.* Edited by Sally Fitzgerald. New York: Farrar, Strauss, Giroux, 1979.

Pieper, Joseph. *Leisure: The Basis of Culture.* New York: Pantheon, 1954.

Williams, Rowan. *Grace and Necessity: Reflections on Art and Love.* Harrisburg, PA: Morehouse, 2005.

Wood, Ralph C. *Flannery O'Connor and the Christ-Haunted South.* Grand Rapids, MI: Eerdmans, 2004.

LEWIS AND CAMBRIDGE

Brian Barbour

"Say not the struggle nought availeth..."

Although he held the Chair of Medieval and Renaissance Literature at Cambridge for the last nine years of his life and published three books with Cambridge University Press, C. S. Lewis (1898–1963) is almost always identified in the popular mind with Oxford. There are good reasons for this. First, Lewis was Oxford bred. He came up to University College as an undergraduate in 1917 and, except for his war service, he was at Oxford continually until the end of 1954. During that time he was successively an undergraduate (with Firsts in Mods, Greats, and English), a freelance tutor in philosophy, a Fellow of Magdalen and tutor in English, and a university lecturer in the English Faculty. Second, it was at Oxford that Lewis wrote the books that first brought him fame—as a literary scholar (*The Allegory of Love* [1936]), as a Christian apologist (*The Screwtape Letters* [1942] and *Broadcast Talks* [1942][1]) and as a writer of children's stories (*The Chronicles of Narnia* [1950–1956]). Third, his autobiography, *Surprised by Joy* (1955), ends with him still in Oxford. Fourth, Lewis's circle, The Inklings, was exclusively an Oxford gathering. Finally and contrastively, the years Lewis spent at Cambridge were also the years of "Shadowlands"—his friendship with and marriage to Joy Davidman and his loss of her to cancer—and the intense, emotional nature of that experience has driven interest in Lewis's academic career into the background. The convergence of these lines can make his seem exclusively an Oxford story, and there are people conversant with several areas of Lewis's work who register surprise at learning that he was ever at Cambridge.

But Oxford, characteristically, was of two minds about Lewis—his popularity was a stumbling block, his Christianity a scandal—and never honored him. Cambridge—it is a great irony—did honor him. This is the story of Lewis and Cambridge.

LEWIS AND LITERARY STUDIES

It is ironic because first and last Lewis was hostile to "Cambridge English," a perspective that informs, shapes, and sometimes mars nearly all his literary scholarship. Late in his Cambridge period Lewis was talking shop with George Watson, a junior colleague who also had migrated from Oxford, and they were comparing the English Schools at the two universities. "We don't have a School of English," Lewis grumbled. "We have a school of Literary Criticism." This was Cambridge's boast: it was nothing if not critical. But in that boast Lewis heard folly.

It was the Oxford approach that he favored. Like J. R. R. Tolkien, Lewis began teaching for the Oxford English School in 1925, and by 1931 he and Tolkien had pushed through a reformed syllabus that exactly suited them. The emphasis fell on what Lewis would call "learning," not on criticism. Anglo-Saxon was required (read as literature, not as a sourcebook on language), literary history was emphasized, the Middle Ages were central, and the syllabus ended with the Romantics at 1830. Along the Cam things were organized very differently, particularly after the Tripos reform of 1928. Cambridge made Anglo-Saxon optional, stressed "practical criticism," paid little attention to literature before "the Shakespearean moment,"[2] and routinely lectured and examined on contemporary figures. The two approaches were different and distinct; as different as literary history and literary criticism; as distinct as, say, Oxford and Cambridge—or as C. S. Lewis and F. R. Leavis.

Lewis, always suspicious about teaching literary criticism, had no sympathy with Cantabrigian insistence. "The essential discipline of an English School is the literary-critical"—that dictum of Leavis's Lewis stood solidly against; while what Leavis derided—"there is no more futile study than that which ends with mere knowledge *about* literature"—was for Lewis an essential.[3] What, then, should an English School do? Lewis thought its basic concerns should be "background" and "intention"; criticism would emerge from these but should be kept at a distance. The Oxford syllabus dealt with what Lewis called "old books," and he recognized that it was all too easy to approach these as though they were current books and thus disastrously misread them.[4] By background Lewis meant the whole context of a work: the historical and intellectual framework of its time, the conventions of its genre, and the expectations of its audience. He also included the work's semantics, its hard words, especially ones that had changed their meanings over time. Lewis disliked intensely what he called "chronological snobbery"—"the uncritical acceptance of the intellectual climate common to our own age and the assumption that whatever has gone out of date is on that account discredited"—and he especially liked the sheer difference of the past.[5] Because he did not view poetry as a source of quasi-religious value in the present, he respected it on its own terms. Knowledge of background was the best means of insuring respect for intention, and such respect gave critical reading an ethical dimension. The duty of the English School was to impart such learning.

The emphasis on old books was combined with an older approach to poetry. Like his bête noire T. S. Eliot, Lewis held an impersonal theory of poetry: poetry was essentially "making" and not essentially "expressing." The poem was something shaped, *poiêma*, as well as something said, *logos*; it was not the outpouring of the poet's inner life. His sympathy lay with Alexander Pope's *Essay on Criticism*, not William Wordsworth's "Preface" to *Lyrical Ballads*, and the notion that either a poem's value or its meaning was a function of the poet's personality Lewis repudiated *simpliciter*. This impersonal, objective approach served him as a safeguard against reading old books as though they were new. While "practical criticism" also insisted on the reader's response to "the words on the page," Cambridge tended to read old books primarily for the light they threw on modern problems. This approach implicitly tips the balance toward *logos*, and in assigning value Cambridge tended toward the Romantic emphasis on the poet as superior personality. Lewis was unremittingly hostile to this interpretive approach and unsympathetic to evaluation as well. His idea of university English—background and intention—certainly implied a view of literary criticism, but he wanted it left implicit, not made the focus of attention—as Cambridge made it.

Both Leavis and Lewis had tripartite models of literary criticism, but the resemblance was only numerical.[6] Leavis saw the English School as "training" the student in literary criticism—a training that affected perception, analysis, and judgment. For Lewis, by contrast, literary criticism consisted in understanding intention, receiving the work, and experiencing an inner enlargement. The center was reception, and he dismissed the Cambridge center—analysis—as using a work rather than receiving it. Lewis wanted to keep literary criticism out of the foreground of literary study where he thought it too easily and too quickly became evaluative. Understanding was his goal. Two of his three Cambridge books were addressed to the problems of clarifying background and discerning intention; the third developed an approach to criticism that centered on reception and tried to exclude evaluation.

Lewis's antagonism to Cambridge English rested on issues far graver than ordinary Oxbridge rivalry. By the early 1930s Cambridge meant several related things for Lewis. One was the pedagogical and critical approach outlined above, deriving its general principles from I. A. Richards and its specific applications from Leavis and *Scrutiny*. For convenience's sake this program can be called "Leavis." Lewis was antagonistic to "Leavis," and to the man himself. But Lewis had a certain reluctance, not absolute, to attack Leavis; this is clearly discernible in his Cambridge period. One reason was Leavis's famous refusal to discuss criticism on theoretical grounds. It was a critic's job to evoke response and appeal to established standards, Leavis argued, not to engage in bad philosophical discussion; and Lewis respected this. Another reason was Leavis's combativeness, which often made him the object of unfair disparagement; Lewis, however strong his disagreements, maintained a sense of fair play. While he disliked Leavis and *Scrutiny*, they were not the *radix malorum*.

Regarding Richards, however, Lewis's antagonism was absolute and unremitting. *Scrutiny* had large cultural ambitions derived from "the function of criticism at the present time." Lewis knew that this Arnoldian tune was dangerously seductive, that it had seduced Matthew Arnold himself into believing poetry could replace religion. Richards, waving the baton of theory, had collected Arnold's ideas and formulated them within his own psychological and subjective theory of value, infusing them with new life in a contemporary "scientific" idiom.[7] Richards also had an Enlightenment belief in education as soteriology. Poetry, he argued, was our most certain source of value, and the successful reading of poetry was the best preparation for an ethical life. As he put it in *Science and Poetry*, "Poetry is failing us, or we it, if after our reading we do not find ourselves changed; not with temporary change...but with a permanent alteration of our possibilities as responsive individuals in good or bad adjustment to an all but overwhelming concourse of stimulations."[8]

Lewis saw this broad outlook—the critical approach and the claim of salvation through poetry—as intellectually and morally dangerous, potentially destructive. In a letter to a different adversary, Brother George Every, S.S.M., he made his objections clear: "I am sure you are right in tracing the *extreme* Richardian (and the Leavisian, so far as it derives from him) view to subjectivism. Since the real wholeness is not, for them, in the objective universe, it has to be located inside the poet's head. Hence the quite disproportionate emphasis laid by them, as by the Romantics before them, on the poet—to the exclusion of the object dealt with, the work of art as a *thing*, and the reader."[9] While literature was a useful tool for diagnosing the modern malaise, it did not necessarily follow that it provided the needed prescription or that it was that prescription. Richards and Leavis were Apostles of Culture who gave literature the wrong kind of seriousness.[10] Like T. S. Eliot, Lewis rejected the Romantic-Arnoldian argument. Literature was not ersatz religion.[11] But this coincidence of viewpoint entailed no larger harmony of outlook. For the third thing Cambridge meant was T. S. Eliot. And Lewis's antagonism to Eliot was personal and irrational.

LEWIS VS. CAMBRIDGE, 1934–1944

The story of Lewis and Cambridge, then, combines three tightly related themes—biographical, intellectual, institutional—and begins long before 1954. The first period runs from 1934 to 1944; in it Lewis taught twice at Cambridge while nevertheless presenting himself as its adversary. Then from 1944 to 1954 Lewis had almost nothing to do with Cambridge, in person or in print. The second period—his real Cambridge period—lasts from 1954 until Lewis's death in 1963.

T. S. Eliot, oddly enough, launches the story of Lewis and Cambridge. Although Eliot had been a research student at Oxford's Merton College shortly before Lewis himself went up, to Lewis he seemed to smack of Cambridge. Not only had Eliot delivered his Clark Lectures there in 1926, but Eliot's poetry first drew serious critical notice from Richards and then from Leavis. Much of the historical and critical core of Leavis's thought clearly derived from Eliot as well. The young Lewis had hoped to win recognition as a poet. Like many an Oxbridge undergraduate, he published a book of verse, and he then brought out another shortly after winning his fellowship at Magdalen.[12] But between 1919 and 1926 the shadow of Eliot and literary modernism had fallen across English poetry, forcing Lewis to recognize that there probably would never be any considerable public for his kind of verse. Perhaps this initiated the antagonism,[13] or perhaps Eliot was simply the particular focus of Lewis's general dislike of literary modernism. But the irrationality of Lewis's animus is unmistakable. For he must have seen that his views and Eliot's were largely congruent on a whole range of important issues. After their conversions they were the two most prominent Anglican laymen of their generation, and although they were differently situated within the church neither hesitated to brand as Modernism all efforts to make Christian teaching conform with passing fashion.[14] On the issue of general humane culture both lamented the rise of the machine and its effect on general civilized living—the writer of "De Descriptione Temporum" ought to have felt sympathy for the author of "Choruses" from *The Rock,* Their views on poetry were also similar, as we have seen. Lewis thought of poetry as *poiëma*, something made; Eliot dedicated "The Waste Land" to Pound as *il miglior fabbro*. Lewis objected fiercely to the Arnoldian idea of literature as religion; so too did Eliot. Lewis should also have liked Eliot's remark that "poetry is superior amusement," since this was a point he himself repeatedly made in his own fashion.[15] Above all, both held an impersonal theory of poetry; this affinity first brought them in contact and led to Lewis's involvement with Cambridge.[16]

Sometime late in 1929 the unknown young don sent Eliot at *The Criterion* a much worked-over manuscript outlining his views on impersonality in poetry.

Eliot was slow to respond, so in April 1930 Lewis wrote asking him for a decision on the manuscript, in which, he reminded Eliot, "I contended that poetry never was nor could be the 'expression of personality' save *per accidens*, and I advanced a formal proof of this position," adding, "I believed that you had some sympathy with this contention."[17] In the event, Eliot returned the manuscript and Lewis put it aside to continue his research into medieval love poetry. But when he came to rewrite it, he found fresh negative evidence for his ideas about impersonality in a recent book on John Milton by the Cambridge lecturer E. M. W. Tillyard.[18]

The revised version was published in *Essays and Studies*.[19] Lewis argued forcefully for his view that what mattered was not the poet but the poem: "We do not know whether the story of the sonnets was Shakespeare's own story or not; we do not know whether Milton really grieved for the death of Mr. King or not; and if we know that Shelley had really met Keats, we do not know it in and by appreciating *Adonais*." He found the opposite view articulated by Tillyard, who had claimed of *Paradise Lost* that "the poem is really about the true state of Milton's mind when he wrote it."[20] Lewis could see the hopeless muddle in the phrase "really about" and he had little difficulty in disposing of Tillyard's view. There the matter might have stood, but Tillyard wrote a reply, published in *Essays and Studies* the following year (1935). Tillyard claimed that he agreed with a great deal of what Mr. Lewis said, so Mr. Lewis must be partly right, but not with everything Mr. Lewis said, so Mr. Lewis must be partly wrong. In 1936 Lewis, with his Johnsonian relish for argument, replied in lofty kind ("Dear Dr. Tillyard...I am, my dear Sir, with the greatest respect, Your obedient servant..."). Thus the matter stood as a mannerly and somewhat mannered literary controversy between opponents who were in some sense representative figures of the differing outlooks of their two English Schools. But Tillyard had not yet had his full say, so when he wrote a second response it was decided to put this together with Lewis's rejoinder and a third response from Tillyard as a short book, *The Personal Heresy: A Controversy*.[21] The world could then judge between Oxford and Cambridge.

Besides his Johnsonian relish for argument, Lewis had a weakness for paper logic and a tendency to run with the bit between his teeth. These qualities are on display here and, while Lewis's is clearly the superior position, the argument proves longer on logic than on sensibility. As it continued the controversy became a matter of hairsplitting, growing increasingly abstract so that in the end few praised it and no one wished it longer. But two things are noteworthy. One is that Lewis—"professional controversialist and itinerant prizefighter," as he once waggishly put it[22]—had a deeply irenic spirit beneath a pugilistic exterior. His controversies were always impersonal and often ended with the participants finding a good deal of common ground, whereas Leavis's controversies (for example) tended to end in anathematizing and deeply personal wounding. From a certain perspective Lewis was really not all that good at polemics. The other noteworthy point is that Lewis was now publicly engaged, in the lists, contra Cambridge. Much would follow.

While Lewis was jousting with Tillyard, the Cambridge English School was undergoing a climacteric that would eventually involve him. By 1936 Mansfield Forbes, one of the School's founders and leaders, was dead, and I. A. Richards had begun his slow withdrawal toward China and Harvard.[23] In the same year, Leavis was given a university appointment and elected to a Fellowship at Downing. Thereafter until his retirement in 1962 he would do battle with "official Cambridge" from within the faculty and the faculty would be divided. All of this must have dismayed H. S. Bennett. And it is Bennett—not Richards, Tillyard, or Leavis—who becomes the key figure in the story of Lewis and Cambridge. As Cambridge English was undergoing its changes, he began to cultivate Lewis's acquaintance.

The relations between Bennett and *Leavis*, on which our story equally depends, are impossible to sort out completely. The facts are few and simple. Bennett and Leavis were close friends in the 1920s, working together at Emmanuel College; they both married students from Girton who became formidable critics in their own right, Joan Bennett and Q. D. Leavis; but by the middle thirties there was deep and lasting enmity between them. Bennett, a scholar with special interest in the Middle Ages (best known for *The Pastons and Their England*), also interested himself in administration and was almost always on the Faculty Board or the Appointments Committee of the English faculty. He probably became aware of Lewis through the latter's long-running debate with Tillyard, but this initial awareness was strengthened at a pivotal moment. For just as Cambridge was changing in ways Bennett found unhappy, in 1936 Lewis published his great work, *The Allegory of Love*, on Bennett's own scholarly period. Here was a potential ally.

Nineteen thirty-six was the crucial year. Bennett was a man of considerable academic influence, an influence extending well beyond Cambridge. Herbert Grierson, recently retired, turned seventy, and that spring a festschrift was planned with contributors lined up from all over Britain and the United States, including five each from Oxford and Cambridge. One of the Oxford contributors was Lewis. Bennett may have been involved in this solicitation, but even if he was not, he and his wife did invite Lewis to spend the New Year's holiday (1937) at their house in Cambridge, where they talked shop and faculty politics.[24] When Lewis left, he sent the Bennetts his contribution on John Donne written for the Grierson volume, for Joan Bennett had by that time made metaphysical poetry her specialty.[25] Lewis's essay was a fine critical and scholarly study, clearly rooted in the material of *The Allegory of Love*. And the "itinerant prizefighter" poked through.

The subject of Donne had provided Lewis an opportunity too good to miss. This relatively forgotten poet had, in effect, been discovered for the twentieth century by Eliot in his famous review of Grierson. In "The Metaphysical Poets" (1921), together with "Tradition and the Individual Talent" (1919) and his essay on Andrew Marvell (1921), Eliot had broached a whole critical view of the history and development of English poetry which Leavis had elaborated in his great book of 1936, *Revaluation: Tradition and Development in English Poetry*. Lewis, accordingly, found Eliot, Leavis, and Richards—"Cambridge"—all under his guns.

In both substance and form, Lewis's essay on Donne was a blast at Cambridge, though only Richards is mentioned directly and then only in a footnote.[26] The declared purpose was to describe the essential characteristics of the style and matter of Donne's love poetry and place it in a historical context. But beneath this surface Lewis's essay attacks Richards and the Richardian sense of poetic value and Eliot and Leavis and their view of the history of English poetry as elaborated by Leavis in *Revaluation*. The allusions are unmistakable. First, there is a parody of Richards: "Those who object to 'emotive terms' in criticism may prefer to read '...used by an accomplished poet to produce an attitude relevant not directly to outer experience but to the central nucleus of the total attitude-and belief-feeling system'" (*SLE*, p. 108). Second, there is a page on the need to understand metrics to understand Donne, alluding to the dismissal of metrics and scansion by both Richards and Leavis (pp. 113–14). Then there is a remark about "the present popularity of Donne [and] the growing unpopularity of Milton: (p. 106), implicating both Eliot and Leavis.[27] And there is a jab at Leavis alone in a remark about hearing in Donne "the living voice."[28]

Beyond these allusions, the substance of the paper calls into question Eliot's and Leavis's view of literary history in general and its expression in Leavis's chapter "The Line of Wit" in particular. There Leavis makes Donne a living (that is, contemporary) voice and places him with Ben Jonson as the two originators of the Line of Wit in which English poetry most vigorously develops before the consequences of Eliot's "dissociation of sensibility" take effect in the eighteenth century. Lewis turns this view on its head, placing Donne at the end of a medieval line as someone who kept poetry of Thomas Wyatt's type artificially alive a generation longer and arguing that very little could or did develop from this dying line. With his love of paradox, Lewis ends his paper by slyly admitting Donne's considerable influence on seventeenth-century poetry, specifically on the great devotional poetry of the period. This he calls "a commonplace of criticism"—so much for Eliot and Leavis! The essay is a tour de force.

Lewis was now in full stride. The Grierson festschrift came out in 1938; the following year saw the publication of both *The Personal Heresy* and a volume of Lewis's essays with the provocative title, *Rehabilitations*—a transparent allusion to Leavis's *Revaluation* and the whole series of "Revaluations" that had been going on in *Scrutiny*.[29] As Lewis makes clear, the title "Rehabilitations" refers to the design of the whole work:

> A man is seldom moved to praise what he loves until it has been attacked. The first six essays in this book, which give it its title, were all in various degrees provoked in this way. The first two defend great romantic poets against popular hatred or neglect of Romanticism. The third and

> fourth defend the present course of English studies at Oxford against certain criticisms.... The fifth is partly a defence of the many popular books which have, I believe, so greatly increased my power of enjoying more serious literature as well as "real life"; but it is much more a defence of disinterested literary enjoyment in general against certain dangerous tendencies in modern education.... The sixth...probably I should not have written...if I had not been stimulated by the contempt sometimes expressed for Anglo-Saxon poetry. (p. vii)

The book does not show Lewis at his best, but it does fairly characterize his view of Cambridge English and the Cambridge Three—Eliot, Richards, and Leavis. What he loves is under attack; let us observe his defense.

The first two essays, "Shelley, Dryden, and Mr. Eliot" and "William Morris," comprise Lewis's quirky defense of Romanticism.[30] The former stands Eliot on his head for praising John Dryden and dispraising Percy Bysshe Shelley. Lewis does the reverse and, with his fondness for paradox, claims to do so on the grounds that Shelley is the more *classical* poet (Lewis's word). "Shelley... is a poet who must rank higher than Dryden with any critic who claims to be classical; ... he is superior to Dryden by the greatness of his subjects and his moral elevation (which are merits by classical standards), and also by the unity of his actions, his architectonic power, and his general observance of *decorum* in the Renaissance sense of the word; that is, his disciplined production not just of poetry but of the poetry in each case proper to the theme and species of composition" (*SLE*, p. 194). Lewis argues generally against the dangers of evaluation, of establishing canons of preference for Dryden that denigrate Shelley, and proceeds by showing that Dryden falls short of classical norms which Shelley fulfills. This forced paradox somewhat obscures the deeper reaches of Lewis's thought, which is that good reading should include both Dryden and Shelley. But while he uses the devil's tools against the devil, the essay on Morris is a piece of special pleading that fails to persuade. Regardless, with transparent irony, Lewis adopts an epigraph from Richards's *Principles* to get launched, and invokes his essay for the Grierson volume to develop one of his key anti-Cantabrigian themes:

> As the lovers of Morris now are, the lovers of Donne once were, and not so very long ago. It is possible that a critical revolution may yet embarrass these scattered and inoffensive readers with the discovery that what they regard as a private, shamefaced, indulgence has all along been a gratifying proof of their penetration and "contemporaneity." The thing is feasible because even the sternest theories of literature cannot permanently suppress an author who is so obstinately pleasurable. It is certain that the common cries against Morris, where they are not mere ignorance, are based on *a priori* dogmatisms that will go down at a touch. (*SLE*, pp. 219–20)

For Lewis the one infallible critic is Time, and Enjoyment is the burden of the argument. Against these two, all theories are so much straw. Lewis adumbrates here the position that he will finally develop in *An Experiment in Criticism*.

In the third and fourth essays of *Rehabilitations* the "certain criticisms" of English Studies at Oxford are not specified, but they probably originated in undergraduate dissatisfaction with the design of the Oxford curriculum as opposed to Cambridge's more glamorous version in which Eliot, William Butler Yeats, James Joyce, and D. H. Lawrence were all being lectured on. "Our English Syllabus" is the stronger of the two essays. It was first read to Oxford undergraduates, so the "Our" is denotative and intramural, but its further implication is also clear: "Our" opposes "Their" and so does the argument, which distinguishes "learning" from "education" and "training" with their Richardian and Leavisian overtones. University English consists in learning, in finding out hard things that one does not know, like Anglo-Saxon, for example, or older, forgotten meanings of words, or the background and context of a poem. It is not a matter of reading what is current:

> We naturally wish to help the students in studying those parts of the subject where we have most help to give and they need help most. On recent and contemporary literature their need is least and our help least. They ought to understand it better than we, and if they do not then there is something radically wrong either with them or with the

> literature. But I need not labour the point. There is an intrinsic absurdity in making current literature a subject of academic study, and the student who wants a tutor's assistance in reading the works of his own contemporaries might as well ask for a nurse's assistance in blowing his own nose. (p. 91)

That last remark is Lewis being silly, but the difference from Cambridge is clearly emphasized.

The fifth essay, "Highbrows and Lowbrows," is specifically directed against Richards and the hygienic program in his work that was being carried out by Leavis and *Scrutiny*.[31] It is also an early run for ideas that will finally come to fruition in *An Experiment*, where Lewis will think hard about the modern form of differentiating between the Few and the Many. Here one notes the appeal to Enjoyment, the animus against evaluation, and the desire that reading be as inclusive as possible. One also notes how Lewis throws the Arnoldian term "disinterested" back against the Neo-Arnoldians, implying a misunderstanding and misappropriation.

In the sixth and final essay, "Christianity and Literature," Lewis brings together his two greatest interests. At first glance the essay seems very odd. He begins by dividing matter and form within Christian literature, sets matter aside, points out that form will be the same whatever the matter, and concludes: "Of Christian Literature, then, in the sense of 'work aiming at literary value and written by Christians for Christians,' you see that I have really nothing to say and believe that nothing can be said."[32] Since virtually all Western literature, from *Beowulf* to the early twentieth century, falls into this category either directly or by contrast, this seems a trifle exclusive. But Lewis wants to get to something else, and he will risk outrageous paradox to get there. His real concern is to point out the incompatibility between modern criticism and the basic outlook of the New Testament. "I think there is so great a difference of temper that a man whose mind was at one with the mind of the New Testament would not, and indeed could not, fall into the language which most critics now adopt." The idiom of modern criticism—of Cambridge criticism, though the point is left unspecified—is largely derived from the Romantic worldview. "What are the key-words of modern criticism? *Creative*, with its opposite *derivative*; *spontaneity*, with its opposite *convention*; *freedom*, contrasted with *rules*. Great authors are innovators, pioneers, explorers; bad authors bunch in schools and follow models." Lewis is again concerned with the Personal Heresy, now more effectively, and he proceeds to an essential point: the idiom of modern criticism reveals a habit of making literature into a substitute for religion, finding there the "values" needed for ordinary living. Modern man, fleeing the Philistine City of Man, has erected the City of Art and called it the City of God. Lewis's insight into this muddle—seeing it for what it is, recognizing its seductiveness, and making necessary distinctions—is one of the permanently valuable parts of his legacy. "The unbeliever is always apt to make a kind of religion of his aesthetic experiences.... Pater prepared for pleasure as if it were martyrdom."[33]

By 1939, then, despite certain private misgivings, Lewis stood doughtily engaged against Cambridge English. But Cambridge was evolving; H. S. Bennett watched with displeasure the rise of Leavis (whose students were winning a disproportionate share of Firsts). With Forbes dead, with the *fainéant* Sir Arthur Quiller-Couch occupying what was at the time Cambridge English's only professorship, and with Richards leaving, Bennett perhaps saw Lewis as someone with the force and ability to resist a Leavisian ascendancy. One of the oddest incidents in the story of Lewis and Cambridge was Bennett's arrangement that Lewis come to lecture for a full term for the Honours Degree in Cambridge English.[34] The Lecture List in the Cambridge University *Reporter* for October 7, 1938, announces "C. S. Lewis: Sixteenth Century Literature," for Lent term. By January 10, 1939, the *Reporter* specifies "C. S. Lewis: 'Prolegomena to Renaissance Literature,' Tu. 5.15." It is hard to imagine a worse time to lecture in Cambridge than 5:15, but Lewis enjoyed himself immensely. He was in the enemy camp, emphasizing the importance of background, and he gave full rein to his sense of paradox. "I go to Cambridge to lecture once a week this term," he wrote to A. K. Hamilton Jenkin. "Did I tell you I have discovered the Renaissance never occurred? That is what I'm lecturing on. Do you think it reasonable to call the lectures 'The Renaissance' under the circumstances?"[35] "The Renaissance never occurred" became one of Lewis's favorite phrases, indicating that his lectures were an early version of his Clark Lectures

(1944), themselves the germ of his Oxford History of English Literature volume. He also met Richards, probably for the first time, and the two adversaries were cordial enough; Richards sent Lewis a copy of *The Philosophy of Rhetoric* (1936).[36] But by this time the tramp of German boots could be heard in the Sudetenland, and all concerned would soon have other worries. Lewis's lectures were not repeated.

Lewis's energy and productivity during the war years are astounding. Besides four well-known works of apologetics—*The Problem of Pain* (1940), *The Screwtape Letters* (1942), the three parts of *Mere Christianity* (1952), and *Miracles* (1947)—he made his broadcast talks, lectured to large numbers of Royal Air Force groups, gave the British Academy Shakespeare Lecture ("Hamlet: The Prince or the Poem?"), lectured on education at Durham (*The Abolition of Man* [1943]), and delivered two sets of lectures on literature: the Ballard Lectures at Bangor (*A Preface to "Paradise Lost"* [1942]) and the Clark Lectures at Trinity College, Cambridge. But before all this, during 1939–1940, he once again took up the cudgels against "the whole school of critical thought which descends from Dr Richards" and a certain naive syncretism that he saw developing in the pages of *Theology*.

In the darkening years of the late 1930s Alec Vidler had become Editor of *Theology* and decided to promote discussion of general cultural issues from a Christian perspective. He invited a number of "literary collaborators" to participate, including Brother George Every, S.S.M., Michael Roberts, Charles Williams, J. Middleton Murry, Eliot, and Lewis—a very mixed theological bag. Lewis had his reservations from the start, and by March 1939 Every's review essay, "The Necessity of Scrutiny," confirmed them.[37] Reviewing *Scrutiny* (and seven related books—four by the Leavises, one by Eliot, two by D. H. Lawrence), Every quoted with approbation: "There is a necessary relationship between the quality of the individual's response to art and his general fitness for humane living" (p. 177). Lewis, privately furious, wrote to Vidler: "Each number makes it clear to me that my only use to you in literary matters can be that of permanent opposition, for I find myself in sharp disagreement with Mr. Roberts and Brother Every.... The hint in Brother Every's paper that good taste is essential to salvation seemed to me precisely one of our greatest enemies...

there is a danger of making Christianity itself appear as one more highbrow fad."[38] Vidler wrote back, thanking Lewis for the warning:

> So far, I confess, there seems a danger that *Theology* may be falling into the hands of a certain literary clique, but I am determined to avoid that, if possible. It so happens that George Every was one of the first to urge upon me the importance of giving attention in *Theology* to literary matters, and he made many suggestions. As this was a new development in *Theology*, it is natural that this fact should have coloured the first few numbers. While I wish Every and his friends to have an opportunity of saying what they want to say, I do not intend that *Theology* shall be an exclusive organ for their views, and I shall welcome any opportunity of making this clear.[39]

Lewis was, for the moment, mollified: "As long as I can occasionally contribute an article on the opposite side, I am content."[40] But his unhappiness over this latest indication of the influence of Cambridge English increased in July with the appearance of S. L. Bethell's "Poetry and Belief."[41] Bethell argued for a distinction between the official, declared beliefs of an age and its implicit, lived-out beliefs, concluding: "It is these implied beliefs which are most important for criticism, far more important than any creed to which a writer may consciously draw attention" (p. 25). On this basis he went on to argue in Cambridge fashion for the importance of evaluative criticism, and he cited Richards on "objectless beliefs." Bethell's piece was certainly more critical of Cambridge ideas than Every's had been, but its invocation of both Richards and Eliot prompted Lewis to respond.

I will not trace this debate in its every detail, but certain aspects bear directly on our story. Lewis, determined to isolate the Cambridge position, began with a flourish of overstatement that placed so absolute a division between Culture and the New Testament that Bethell was moved to say, "Mr Lewis's position logically implies an heretical theology, which I know he would formally repudiate—the Calvinistic doctrine of total depravity, according to which the values of the positive order are without positive relation to supernatural values, and natural good and evil come alike under God's arbitrary condemnation"—a charge Lewis hotly denied.[42] His real concern was the uncritical acceptance of Richards's ideas about poetry. Tracing their descent from Arnold, Lewis says, "This great atheist critic found in good poetical taste the means of attaining psychological adjustments which improved man's power of effective and satisfactory living all round, while bad taste resulted in a corresponding loss. Since this theory of value was a purely psychological one, this amounted to giving poetry a kind of soteriological function; it held the keys to the only heaven that Dr Richards believed in."[43]

The argument dragged on throughout 1940 until Lewis himself called a halt in December with his "Peace Proposals for Br Every and Mr Bethell." Summing up, he said, "My general case may be stated in Ricardian terms—that culture is a storehouse of the best (sub-Christian) values. These values are in themselves of the soul, not the spirit.... They will save no man.... The work of a charwoman and the work of a poet become spiritual in the same way and on the same condition." And he added, irenically, "My fear was lest excellence in reading and writing were being elevated into a spiritual value, into something meritorious *per* se."[44] In all this we recognize that it is Richards, not Leavis, whom Lewis finds most dangerous. And he refuses to blur the distinction or compromise the main point. Literature is a subordinate good; reading poetry is not morally efficacious; reading it well does not make one a morally superior person; the imagination can be a vehicle of grace but not its source. Lewis admits that Bethell has raised difficult and important questions about evaluation in criticism. But the thrust of Lewis's argument here and always is that literary study is cognitive whereas morality is a function of the will. To the response that evaluation is after all a matter of choice, Lewis counters: "No. That's still cognitive, and we should not be in the muddle of thinking that knowledge is the same as virtue." But, interestingly, he admits that the whole question is not one he can fully resolve: "My dilemma about literature is that I admit bad taste to be, in some sense, 'a bad thing,' but do not think it *per se* 'evil.'"[45] When we evaluate, on what basis do we judge? He would face this question but not resolve it in his next book.

A Preface to "Paradise Lost" (1942) sets out superbly the background and intention of Milton's poem. As usual, Lewis becomes involved with Eliot,

Richards, and Leavis, not always very wisely or cogently.[46] For example, his chapter on Eliot, "Is Criticism Possible?", is a serious flaw. This is not the place to rehearse "The Milton Controversy" or Eliot's famous change of mind about Milton, but Lewis's attack is gratuitous: it simply does not advance the argument. His remarks on Richards in "Defence of This Style" are more happily conceived. Lewis identifies real weaknesses in Richards's notion of Stock Responses, but he also loses himself in several pages of aimless hairsplitting that eventually drag in both Eliot and Lord Haw-Haw. Best of all is his page on Leavis and the famous chapter in *Revaluation*: "Dr. Leavis does not differ from me about the properties of Milton's verse. He describes them very accurately—and understands them better, in my opinion, than Mr. Pearsall Smith. It is not that he and I see different things when we look at *Paradise Lost*. He sees and hates the very same that I see and love."[47] But if this is so, where do the differences lie, and what do they tell us about literary criticism and the possibilities of justly evaluating? The differences must be both fundamental and anterior to the critical act. "Hence the disagreement between us tends to escape from the realm of literary criticism. We differ not about the nature of Milton's poetry, but about the nature of man" (p. 134). This insight governs something otherwise easy to misunderstand in Lewis, his repeated use of the Latin tag, *de gustibus non est disputandum*. This habit can look as though Lewis, the Christian apologist and defender of the Natural Law, is yielding to relativism. Actually, he is signaling that under contemporary circumstances some arguments may not be resolvable. There is not enough shared ground.[48]

In 1943 Lewis delivered the Riddell Lectures at Durham; later published as *The Abolition of Man,* they argue for the Tao (*lex aeterna*) and against naturalism and relativism. These lectures also engage him with Cambridge, for the subjectivity Lewis saw undermining modern education he traced, in part, to Richards's *Principles*. A second invitation to lecture at Cambridge came in 1944—this time not as the result of Bennett's maneuvering but at the behest of the Master and Fellows of Trinity College. Following Eliot's by eighteen years, Lewis's Clark Lectures elaborated those he had delivered at Cambridge in 1939 when he argued that "the Renaissance never occurred." These lectures became "New Learning and New Ignorance," the famous first chapter of Lewis's Oxford

History of English Literature volume, *English Literature in the Sixteenth Century, excluding Drama* (1954). That chapter is outside our purview, but consider the matter *in situ* just for a moment as Lewis developed his paradoxes. Remarkably, Lewis went to Cambridge under the aegis of Trinity, Macaulay's alma mater, with G. M. Trevelyan, the Master, in the Chair, there to demolish the Whig-history view of the Renaissance—the audacity was like preaching on the Real Presence before Calvin at Geneva: "Whatever else humanism is, it is emphatically not a movement towards freedom and expansion.... The war between the humanists and the schoolmen was not a war between ideas; it was, on the humanists' side, a war against ideas.... The great literature of the 1580s and 1590s was something which humanism...would have prevented if it could.... In the field of philosophy humanism must be regarded, quite frankly, as a Philistine movement: even an obscurantist movement. In that sense the New Learning created the New Ignorance."[49]

The Clark Lectures mark the end of Lewis's first Cambridge period. By 1944 he was the most prominent member of the Oxford English Faculty and, from within its strengths, a trenchant critic of Cambridge English. It is not, however, Leavis whom Lewis most strongly opposed but rather Richards (and, more broadly, Eliot). Lewis and Leavis had a shared concern: to make English Studies a real intellectual discipline, one worthy of university Honours study. But they interpreted their concern very differently. For Leavis, "the essential discipline" was "literary-critical" training in "perception, analysis, and judgement." Lewis ranked learning above criticism, placing the emphasis on the careful examination of background and identification of the author's intention. Those prerequisites were crucial for the full reception of the literary experience, and it was the learned man's duty to help clear the way for that. For more than ten years Lewis had been oddly involved with Cambridge, but his career as "professional controversialist and itinerant prizefighter" now seemed to be over, at least as far as Cambridge was concerned. Richards had left for America, the war was followed by domestic privation, and there were plenty of battles to fight in Oxford. During the whole ten-year period, 1944–1954, the only point of contact between Lewis and his old adversaries came in 1947 when he wrote to the *Times Literary Supplement* endorsing a letter by Leavis about Milton.[50]

But as all the world knows, Lewis's life look some odd turns in the 1950s, and in 1954 one of them led north from Liverpool Street Station. Stanley Bennett had decided to try again.

LEWIS AT CAMBRIDGE: THE CHAIR

On Monday, May 10, 1954, eight distinguished scholars gathered in the Old Schools at Cambridge to elect the first holder of the Chair of Medieval and Renaissance Literature, a chair virtually created for a man who had not bothered to apply for it when it was advertised, who was given to saying that "the Renaissance never occurred," and who when the chair was offered to him declined it—not once but twice. It cannot be said that Lewis was eager to go to Cambridge.

Bennett, the moving force in Lewis's translation, was approaching retirement. In the early 1950s Cambridge had the finest English faculty in the world, but it was not without its problems. For one thing it was bottom heavy. There were forty-two people teaching English in 1954, but a third of them had only college (as opposed to university) affiliation. Of the twenty-seven with university posts, only three were above the rank of Lecturer. There was one Professor (Basil Willey), two Readers (Bennett and F. L. Lucas), fourteen Lecturers, and ten part-time or affiliated members. There was no room for advancement for scholars like Joan Bennett, M. C. Bradbrook, David Daiches, John Holloway, Leavis, Theodore Redpath, and A. P. Rossiter. Moreover, the somewhat diffident Willey did not exercise forceful leadership, particularly when representing the interests of the English faculty within the university—hence the paucity of higher positions. Richards was long since gone and the faculty was, in a certain sense, dominated by the presence of Leavis, who was a source of ongoing tension—Leavis *contra mundum*, though of course he did have supporters. It was a faculty that, never particularly strong in the medieval period, seemed likely to grow weaker still with Bennett retiring. Bennett recognized the situation and set out to remedy it. If it is largely true that "the Chair was created for Lewis," it is equally true that Lewis and the Chair seemed to be a remedy for most of these problems: a second Chair, a forceful man, a medievalist, and a long-time adversary of Leavis. That it was "Leavis" Lewis opposed, the representative of Cambridge English rather than the man himself, was perhaps not clearly seen.

In its Statement of Needs, 1952–1957, the Faculty Board on which Bennett sat asked for a second Professor, one in Medieval and Renaissance, "since the King Edward VII holder [Willey] is mainly concerned with modern literature and thought." But England was still coming out of wartime austerity, Professorships were not to be had for the asking, and Bennett had to engage in some creative financing. On January 18, 1954, the *Reporter* announced that Bennett's Readership would be discontinued upon his retirement, and the English Faculty's Reserve Fund was to be transferred to the University's "Chest." That would provide a portion of the funds for a new Professorship, with the University making up the rest. On that basis, the Council of the Senate recommended that "there be established in the University on 1 October 1954 a Professorship of Medieval and Renaissance English, and that...the Professor of Medieval and Renaissance English treat the subject on literary and critical rather than on philological and linguistic lines." A scheme followed for the appointment of Electors and their terms. Applications for the Professorship were to be made "by 30 April 1954 to the Registrar at the Old Schools" with the election scheduled for May 10. The eight Electors could not have been friendlier to Lewis. Besides Bennett, they included Tillyard, his friendly adversary and fellow contributor to the Grierson volume, Willey (another Grierson contributor), F. P. Wilson (Lewis's old tutor), Peter Alexander, David Knowles (Regius Professor of Modern History), S. C. Roberts, and J. R. R. Tolkien—Lewis's closest academic friend. Wilson and Tolkien represented Oxford.

Yet Lewis did not apply. No one knows fully the reason why, though it seems that Lewis had encouraged someone else who was interested (G. V. Smithers, the philologist, then at Merton) and then felt obliged not to become a candidate himself.[51] And he was reluctant to leave Oxford, as he imagined would be required, since his brother, who had problems with alcohol, would be left alone. Nevertheless, the Chair should have been particularly attractive to Lewis in the spring of 1954, for although Lewis was not a man who brooded over insult, M. C. Bradbrook's words are largely true: "Oxford treated him shamefully" (private conversation). In 1947 Lewis had been passed over in favor of Wilson for the Merton Professorship of English Literature even though Lewis was clearly the most distinguished member of the faculty. In 1951 he had been defeated (by C. Day-Lewis) in an election for Professor of Poetry that was marked by a particularly bitter anti-Lewis campaign, another sign of Oxford's animosity.[52] In 1953 the Oxford English School had also gone through a bitter and divisive fight over reforming Lewis and Tolkien's 1931 curriculum by extending it from 1830 to 1914. Lewis found himself opposed by Lord David Cecil, an old Inkling, and he was chagrined to discover that Tolkien, although he voted with Lewis at the end, was now "soft" on the reforms. Lewis's side "won," but inconclusively. Meanwhile, the Inklings had dissolved so that by 1954 Lewis and Tolkien no longer enjoyed their earlier intimacy; a certain reserve had grown between them. Besides these negative considerations, there were positive ones as well. Cambridge is smaller than Oxford, and it was free of industrial suburbs for automobile manufacture; in 1954 it was still something of a country town with easy access to the countryside, a very important feature for a walker of Lewis's dedication.[53] The Chair at Cambridge would treble his salary.[54] There would be no more tutorials, no more of the daily grind of undergraduate teaching that he had been doing for thirty years. By statute a Cambridge Professor may not have pupils; his function is to offer lectures (and to supervise research, if he wishes). The combined considerations must have weighed heavily. But what happened after the election was comedy—and not wit but academic slapstick.[55]

When the Electors met on May 10, Lewis was chosen despite the absence of formal application. The following day the Vice Chancellor, H. U. Willink, wrote to offer Lewis the Chair: "I was asked by my colleagues [the Electors], who were unanimous with a warmth and sincerity which could not have been exceeded, to invite you to become the first holder of what we feel will be a Chair of great value to the University. Throughout the discussion stress was laid on the fact that we were electing to a first tenure, a moment of critical importance."[56] Lewis's response on May 12 was immediate. It must have surprised Willink and flabbergasted Bennett!

> I feel more pleased and honoured than I can express at your invitation; and the prospect (socially and academically considered) of migrating

> from Oxford to Cambridge would be more an incentive than a deterrent. The very regretful and very grateful refusal which I have to make is based on different grounds. Domestic necessities govern all our lives at present, and by moving I should lose an invaluable servant. I have, moreover, led another candidate to believe that I was not in the field. Thirdly, I come of a stock that grows early old and I already know myself to have lost a good deal of the energy and vigour which the first holder of this important chair most certainly ought to have. It is very difficult to say that the decision I have based on these reasons is now quite fixed without seeming to suppose, like a coxcomb, that you might press me. You will understand that my only motive is a wish to save you from any waste of time.[57]

Willink waited a day then wrote back, asking Lewis to reconsider and giving him a fortnight to think it over. Lewis again responded immediately and negatively, adding to his previous reasons:

> I am most moved by your extremely kind letter. But you offer persuasion to one who needs liberation. You knock at my door but I can't unlock it because I haven't the key. The more I look at it the less possible it seems to transport the peculiar domestic set-up of my brother, our man, and myself. There is a whole network of conveniences and life-lines already built up here (my brother, in your ear, is not always in perfect psychological health) which I really dare not abandon. I am assuming, of course, that your Chair involves residence at Cambridge, at any rate in term (as it certainly *ought* to).[58]

Was that last sentence a query? Or even a plea? Whatever, Willink by this time must have felt that he was being asked to play Mr. Collins to Lewis's Elizabeth Bennett. And so on May 16 he put an end to that: the offer of the Chair went out to Helen Gardner, the second choice; unlike Lewis, she considered the offer for some time.

Willink wrote to Gardner without formally consulting the Electors (though he talked to Willey). That same night Tolkien paid Lewis a visit. Their discussion resembles an earlier one in 1931 when Tolkien talked Lewis through a different set of objections. Then the issue had been Christianity; now it was going to Cambridge. By the time Tolkien left, Lewis had agreed to accept the offer. He mulled it over for three days, then wrote Willink—too late, of course. In the meantime, Tolkien wrote to Willink and Bennett on May 17 explaining that Lewis was now willing to accept. As he told Willink,

> Whatever may be strictly correct in an elector, it was clear to me that without some such talk the offer to Lewis would be a mere gesture. But in spite of the loss to Oxford I fell able to urge the case for Cambridge sincerely, since I do think that, besides being the precise man for the job, Lewis would probably be happy there, and actually be reinvigorated by a change of air. Oxford, has not, I think, treated him very well, and though he is incapable of "dudgeon," or of showing resentment, he has been a little dispirited.
>
> After our talk he said he would *accept*! It was as I thought: the chief obstacle is domestic. He has a house and some dependants [sic]—including his brother. He will not contemplate closing that establishment. But if he could be assured that Cambridge would provide him with the equivalent (more or less) of his rooms in Magdalen (which he will lose), in which to live during term and house a lot of his books—then I think you can have him. I suppose that depends on election to a fellowship, since "chairs" are not automatically attached to a college as here; but would there be much difficulty in that in this case?[59]

To Bennett, Tolkien added that he had to "overcome his scruples about G. V. S. I felt able to say in confidence that he would not be doing S. down." And he added that Warnie Lewis "backed me up."[60]

But Tolkien's visit had come too late. The game was now in Helen Gardner's hands. Lewis's party could only stand and wait.

During his correspondence with Willink, Lewis had been gradually changing his mind even as he acted precipitously, which left no room for proper consultation. Apparently Lewis had not looked into the matter carefully, but simply assumed that he would need to reside in Cambridge for the eight weeks of each Full Term and that he would be without a College. The first point was open to interpretation, however, and the second was not insurmountable—as Tolkien surmised. But was it too late? On May 19, somewhat shamefaced and of course knowing nothing of events in Cambridge, Lewis wrote to Willink accepting the Chair on the terms outlined by Tolkien:

> Since my last letter to you I have had a conversation with Tolkien which has considerably changed my view. He told me, first, that the electors would in no case elect a philologist. This is to me important, for it sets me free (in honour)—I had thought myself bound to refuse it by certain words I had already said to another candidate. If, as now appears, he is not effectively eligible, then I am not bound. He told me, in the second place, that full residence with an "establishment" in Cambridge was not thought necessary: that four days a week in term time (less or more—there wd. of course be periods of pressure when I might be there a fortnight or so) would fill the bill. Tolkien's lively mind sometimes leads him (with perfectly innocent intentions) to overstate things. Is his view correct? If so, it would remove my difficulty. As long as my normal housekeeping can be at Oxford, so that the life-lines I told you of are intact, and it is a question of rooms in Cambridge (could any College supply me with them?) I cd. manage well.... I have no right to assume these conditions—they seem too good to be true—but if they are real conditions I shd. like nothing better.[61]

Willink digested this news. Clearly nothing could be done until Gardner acted. In the meantime he thanked Tolkien and clarified the situation for him and Willey; then he sought advice about the question of residence under the relevant University statutes. On May 24, with the facts in hand, Willink finally replied to Lewis, telling him that the offer had gone out to "No. 2" but asking him to hold steady. The regulations about residence were not inflexible: "A Professor can be absent as much as he wishes outside Full Term provided that he is not *habitually* absent from a residence within 5 miles of Great St Mary's

Church (e.g., rooms in College) more than two nights in the week during Full Term." And Willink added a personal note, "Oh that my letter to Choice No. 2 had not gone on its way."[62] Ten days of waiting followed, and then on June 3 Willink received a letter from Gardner. She would not accept the Chair. She never divulged her reasons.

Willink now wrote to Lewis. "No. 2 has declined, and I am filled with hope that after all Cambridge will obtain the acceptance of No. 1." The question of residence had been clarified as to time, but Lewis still needed a place in Cambridge. As it happened, Willink was both Vice Chancellor and the Master of Magdalene, and as Vice Chancellor he advised Lewis to write the Master of Magdalene to inquire about the possibility of making his "Cambridge home within its walls." So on June 4 Lewis sent Willink two letters, one as the Vice Chancellor and one as the Master of Magdalene: "Dear Vice Chancellor, I feel much pleasure and gratitude in accepting the Chair of Medieval and Renaissance English," and "Dear Master, The Vice Chancellor...has suggested...that I should ask if there is any possibility of my making my Cambridge home in Magdalene."[63] Willink sent two replies, one in each role, and things were tidied up. A formula was reached—"Election from October 1st 1954 with dispensation until January 1st 1955"—that allowed Lewis time to settle his affairs in Oxford. Since he could not be formally elected a Fellow of Magdalene until January, Willink advised him how to reply to any other Colleges that might make him an offer. So at last it was done. C. S. Lewis was going, of all places, to Cambridge.

TEACHING CAMBRIDGE ENGLISH

In more than one sense he was in a new position. Lewis knew what Cambridge English was and knew he had no hope of changing it into anything resembling the Oxford syllabus he favored. Richards was gone these fifteen years, and Eliot was no longer a consideration. Cambridge now meant "Leavis"—training in practical criticism and emphasis on evaluation—and of course Leavis the man as well. Lewis would be a minority voice, a voice for "learning" as against "training." While he had no intention of coming to Cambridge as an itinerant prizefighter, he would not shirk from being a controversialist. As such it would take him a while to work out a modus vivendi. He was self-conscious and a bit unsure, especially at first.[64]

On Monday, November 29, at 5:00 p.m. Lewis gave his inaugural lecture, "De Descriptione Temporum," with Willink in the chair. The room in Mill Lane was so packed on this grand occasion that auditors were unable to take notes.[65] Lewis, who seemed to speak extempore, used the name of his Chair—Medieval *and* Renaissance—to develop one of his cardinal themes: the great break in Western culture did not occur at the Renaissance; that antithesis with the Middle Ages was Humanist propaganda. After canvassing other possible periodizations, Lewis proposed his own: "I have come to regard as the greatest of all divisions in the history of the West that which divides the present from, say, the age of Jane Austen and Scott." Everything before that really constitutes one period, Old Western Culture. After setting out his reasons for making the division decisive—politics, art, religion, and the rise of the machine—he concluded with a characteristic emphasis on background and intention: "It is my settled conviction that in order to read Old Western Literature aright you must suspend most of the responses and unlearn most of the habits you have acquired in reading modern literature."[66] This was what he had been telling Cambridge for twenty years.

One of Lewis's basic points was that the West was now post-Christian and that "post" was utterly different from "pre." But part of Cambridge, less pleased than Willink that Lewis had come, heard something very different: a call to arms for the restoration of Christendom. This fantasy aroused important opinion, and by February 1955 the "Humanists" were at the ramparts. An entire issue of *Twentieth Century* was devoted to alarming developments in Cambridge signaled by Professor Lewis's dreadful lecture. Twelve essays appraised the situation from a variety of disciplinary viewpoints. An "Editorial Note" took the high Voltairean line. "Most" of the contributors, it explained, were agreed "on the importance of free liberal, humane inquiry, which they conceive to be proper not only to a university community but to any group that claims to be civilized," leaving the reader to wonder which contributors did *not* accept these banalities. E. M. Forster set the tone. He had been worried, he said, over "certain tendencies in Cambridge." Nor were these worries recent. "Humanism" had been "threatened during the past ten years," and Religion was on the march.[67] Now religion can be a good thing, Forster allowed, so long as it was, well, Forsterean: "nothing could be more sensitive, cultivated, and understanding than Roman Catholicism in an English University" (p. 100). But the glad days were now past, and the great danger keeping Forster awake nights was Spiritual Authority. England could overnight turn into priest-ridden Ireland: "we might have authoritative fundamentalism over here too." As one looked out from King's upon the Backs and saw the Cam gently purling, the situation seemed especially grim: "the arbitrary theory of Original Sin" (p. 101) was cresting. And this fearful disaster stretched itself out before him because Humanism was being "elbowed out.... Its stronghold in history, the Renaissance, is alleged not to have existed" (p. 101). The crow was making wing to the rooky wood. Lewis had blown his trumpet. The walls of Humanism might fall.

What was going on here? Partly, it was a delayed reaction to that anti-Whiggish first chapter of *English Literature in the Sixteenth Century*, where Lewis reversed the conventional wisdom about the Humanists, assimilating them to the Puritans, and argued that they were retrograde in their outlook. More immediately, the issue was that both Professors of English (Lewis and Willey) and both Regius Professors of Modern History (Herbert Butterfield and Knowles) were well-known Christians and Cambridge tolerance had found its limits.[68] Lewis's lecture generated a small explosion of resentment, though one that rapidly disappeared. And he took it with detached good humor, as we see in a letter to Ruth Pitter: "I am having an 'impact,' whether 'joyous' or not. If you have seen the 'Cambridge Number' of *The XXth* Century [*sic*] you'll see that the Orthodox Atheists are v. alarmed at this influx of Christians (Butterfield, Knowles, and C.S.L.). They don't call themselves atheists, though, but 'Humanists,' tho' I doubt if they cd write very good Latin and I am sure that E. M. Forster (who is the silliest of the lot: disappointing, for I liked his novels) wd not really enjoy a meeting with Poggio or Scaliger."[69] In the April issue he wrote a response, widening the discussion while lowering its temperature. With dialectical skill he merely glanced at the religious issue while responding to the question of Culture raised by one of the two undergraduate contributors: "A 'faith in culture' is as bad as a faith in religion; both expressions imply a turning away from those very things which culture and religion are about." Building on this, "Lilies That Fester" repudiates the basic Richardian argument: "Those who read poetry to improve their minds will never improve their minds by reading poetry." Culture, if it comes, "must come as a by-product." Otherwise, Lewis warned, Culture could quickly become assimilated to utilitarianism, especially under current conditions where University class lists have great influence on future prospects. Under these conditions, "practical criticism"—the backbone of Cambridge English—becomes training "in the (not very difficult) art of simulating the orthodox responses." Enjoyment, the real end of reading literature, is frustrated. Atheists and Agnostics, Lewis said, should stand shoulder to shoulder with him against Culture in the defense of real culture.[70]

This was something of a sideshow, and not all of Lewis's life at Cambridge had such drama. By early 1955 he had found his footing and settled into a routine that lasted into the early 1960s. Though he had warned Willink that he had "lost a good deal of [his] energy and vigour," his output during this period did not noticeably slacken off, even given Mrs. Lewis's health problems, her death, and his own physical decline. From 1955 until his death Lewis published thirteen books, edited or introduced three more, and wrote forty-four articles, thirteen book reviews, seven poems, and four short stories. He also dealt personally with a huge volume of correspondence, a considerable portion of which was pastoral in nature and required careful and delicate consideration.

Lewis generally wrote in the evening during his Cambridge years. How were his days spent? By the Easter term 1956 he had settled into his Cambridge routine: in Michaelmas term his lectures were on what we know as *The Discarded Image* (1964); Lent term was relatively light, with Lewis providing two lectures in a "circus" (survey by several lecturers) on the medieval period; in Easter term he lectured on what became *Studies in Words* (1960); and for Long Vacs he gave as lectures a précis of *The Discarded Image*, "Imagination and Thought in the Middle Ages."[71] In his last years his attention turned to Edmund Spenser, on whom he was contemplating a book[72]; health problems—first Mrs. Lewis's, then his own—kept him out of Mill Lane in the spring of 1960 and most of 1961. Lewis also entered into the quotidian world of University English:

faculty boards and committee work, prize committees, supervising research, and, most onerous of all, examining. His Chair placed him permanently on both the Faculty Board and the Degree Committee for the English Faculty, and he served for six years (1956–1962) on the Appointments Committee as well. Lewis was generally bored by such work and, no doubt, did it somewhat perfunctorily. He was appointed by the General Board of the University, not the English Faculty, to a three-year term (1958–1961) on the Board of Research Studies, charged with general oversight of graduate research. In his letter of acceptance to Willink, Lewis had noted that "Tolkien also said all the Oxford members of the committee had warned you that I was not a great exponent of 'Research.'" Lewis himself had carried out a model of research in "English"—*The Allegory of Love*—but he was not enamored of the way universities were developing. Recall that he took nearly eleven years to write that book, a book he truly wanted to write. The increasing pressure on young scholars to "find a topic" and "do it up" in a hurry seemed to him trivial matter pursued for irrelevant ends.[73] Nevertheless, he took on six research students, three for the Ph.D., two for the M.Phil, and two for the M.Litt (one student worked with him for the M.Phil, and the Ph.D.). This effort crested in 1959–1960 when he was supervising five projects. But Mrs. Lewis died that year, which kept him away, and in 1960–1961 only one student, Francis Warner, was left.

Examining is the root canal of academic life: Lewis bowed to its necessity. In 1957 he was an Examiner for Part II of the Cambridge Tripos. But according to the *Reporter* (June 5, 1957) he was "unable to act"—that was the spring of Mrs. Lewis's first struggle with cancer and the bedside marriage—and had to be replaced by J. E. Stevens. In 1958 he examined for Part I, in 1960 and 1961 for Part II. The last time Lewis examined at Cambridge was in 1961, and it was on that occasion, during a break, that Lewis turned in conversation to his fellow examiner Leavis for support for his contention that in America there could be no universities in the true sense of the word. Leavis, who also had never been to America, solemnly agreed.[74] But we have delayed this meeting for too long.

LEWIS AND LEAVIS

Lewis and Leavis: everything leads to this, yet there is about the relationship something of the nature of Sherlock Holmes's "curious incident of the dog in the night-time": "'But the dog did nothing in the night-time.' 'That was the curious incident.'" Lewis came to Cambridge as the premier opponent of Cambridge English and of "Leavis." But it was "Leavis" whom Lewis opposed, not Leavis. Lewis was a controversialist of ideas. "Open lists and 'the rigours of the game' are what I want and offer," and it was never personal. In this he differed remarkably from Leavis, who personalized everything. Lewis took the measure of the situation and decided, immediately, that the day for papers such as "Shelley, Dryden, and Mr. Eliot" was in the past. Principled opposition could also be oblique.[75]

I do not want to deny the obvious. Lewis and Leavis never became friends. There were no afternoon teas with Lewis chatting up Leavis and his wife Queenie about Milton's dislodgement or Middle English metre, nor did Leavis drop by Lewis's rooms in Magdalene for the occasional sherry. But neither was there mortal conflict between them. Three aspects of the situation need stressing. First, both men refused to be drawn into any sort of confrontation. Whatever may have been in Bennett's mind at the founding of the Chair, there was never any public antagonism or personal hostility between Lewis and Leavis. One sign of Lewis's circumspection is expressed, I think, in the inscription on the manuscript of *An Experiment of Criticism* that he gave Bennett. It reads, "Dear Stanley—You confessed to a morbid passion for MSS. This is the only one I cd. lay my hands on. Yours [,] Clive."[76] What is intriguing here is that to the very end of his Cambridge career (*Experiment* came out in 1961) Lewis was deliberately "Clive," not "Jack," to Bennett, although they had known each other for thirty years, implying that he was keeping his distance from Cambridge's fratricidal conflicts. Second, there was an elaborately formal structure to their relationship that both Lewis and Leavis accepted. George Watson has recorded that "they were always courteous to each other, and in a manner so elaborate that when they sat on committees one was reminded of the formality of a tea party before the First World War. This was Edwardian decorum at its best."[77] John Holloway expressed it in a curiously similar metaphor. According to him their relations were as measured and formal as a minuet. Nor should it be thought that this external convention masked hidden rage. Watson has said that he "never heard Lewis speak ill of Leavis," while adding that "he plainly preferred not to speak about him at all" (p. 236). From the other side, J. M. Newton, certainly close to Leavis in those days, told me that in discussing Lewis, Leavis did not allow himself the same tone he habitually used for his colleagues; there was a noticeable difference. Whatever their intellectual differences, the two great antagonists respected one another.[78] And according to J. E. Stevens, in discussions within the English Faculty they often spoke on the same side of an issue.[79]

Third, there is a fact that one hesitates to press too hard, but during Lewis's tenure Leavis's position within the English Faculty improved noticeably. For example, when Lewis came in 1954–1955, Leavis had been a Lecturer since 1936 and had never served on either the Faculty Board or the Degree Committee (let alone the Appointments Board—Bennett was taking no chances). During Lewis's years he served every year on both. Moreover, in 1956 Lewis also recommended to Willey that Leavis be made Chairman of the Faculty Board in English: "My own thoughts hover between the (certainly safe) [Graham] Hough and the wild idea of Leavis. Is it just possible that if his nose were once rubbed in the actual working of the Faculty, if he were once the target of criticism instead of the critic, he might be cured? Of course we should suffer: but then we suffer already. I know it's risky: but malcontents have before now been tamed by office."[80] Nothing came of this particular "wild idea." Still, in 1959 Cambridge did for Leavis what Oxford never did for Lewis: it promoted him, in this case to Reader. And for several years a position was also found for Q. D. Leavis. The same issue of *The Times* (November 25, 1963) that reported Lewis's death also carried a story about a new ruckus in Cambridge. Leavis had not been reelected to the Faculty Board.

So on one level Lewis and Leavis is very largely the story of a dispute that didn't happen: "the dog did nothing in the night-time." Yet while the master did not bark, there was plenty of yelping by the pups. The Leavisites were chafing against the leash, and in 1960 they broke loose.

THE ATTACK OF THE LEAVISITES

In October 1953 *Scrutiny* ceased publication. Although the decision was his alone, Leavis never quite got over making it, for he felt that *Scrutiny* had been his life's work, and he was bitter about its "outlaw" status in Cambridge.[81] In that same month *Delta* began life as an undergraduate poetry magazine based at Queens' College. Random events, except that in the autumn of 1954 *Delta* moved to Downing, Leavis's College, and its new editor announced that in the future it would include criticism. From then on *Delta* tried to be *Scrutiny minor*, Leavisite in tone and outlook, and never more so than when denying it. (Leavis had little, probably nothing, to do with it, but that hardly mattered. It meant the pups would have to bark louder for his attention.) *Delta* continued to publish undergraduate verse, while complaining about its quality and dearth, but the center of gravity shifted toward essays and, especially, reviews (astringent). It seemed to occur to no one that poetry was unlikely to flourish in an atmosphere where every piece of writing was treated as a "case" to be "diagnosed," ransacked for signs of "immaturity," "superficiality," and "cleverness."[82] Regardless, *Delta* went its way, migrating to Corpus Christi and then Trinity, publishing reviews and articles that were nearly always negative—and generating normal undergraduate resentment. In the Summer 1955 issue (no. 6), for example, an editorial sniffed that "*Delta* has recently been attacked for its astringent reviews," and in November (no. 7) it proclaimed "the existence of two violently opposed camps in Cambridge criticism." And the division extended to student magazines as well. In early 1960 a skirmish broke out between undergraduates angry with each other and at the faculty. And Lewis, wandering into the middle of it, became a new target of Leavisite wrath.

It began in *Delta* in February 1960 with "The Approval Game," in which Simon Gray criticized severely a short story that had appeared in a previous number of *Granta* and had been praised warmly in both *Varsity* and *Broadsheet*.[83] Gray used this as an occasion "for tracing in some detail the structure of the Cambridge literary world," and he found it a very shaky structure indeed. A big problem was "the real nature" of the "interest in literature" in these other publications, a non-interest, of course, perfectly on display in some negative remarks published by *Broadsheet* the term before on—no surprise here—*Delta*.

Broadsheet then negatively reviewed *Delta* itself, cunningly exempting Gray from its stringencies, and Gray responded in a letter exempting no one.[84] An editorial response to Gray followed in *Broadsheet* on March 2. And then Lewis somehow got conscripted, for the following week there appeared in *Broadsheet* two paragraphs from him entitled "Undergraduate Criticism" which tersely reiterated some of his basic warnings about Cambridge English in general and "Leavis" in particular, sharpened by six years of experience with Cambridge undergraduates. How or why Lewis became involved in this parochial affair is probably no longer ascertainable. It is unlikely that he had any idea of the supercharged context:

> The faults I find in contemporary undergraduate criticism are these:
>
> (1) In adverse criticism their tone is that of personal resentment. They are more anxious to wound the author than inform the reader. Adverse criticism should diagnose and exhibit faults, not abuse them. (2) They are far too ready to advance or accept radical reinterpretations of works which have already been before the world for several generations. The *prima facie* improbability that these have never till now been understood is ignored. (3) Most European literature was composed for adult readers who knew the Bible and the Classics. It is not the modern student's fault that he lacks this background; but he is insufficiently aware of his lack and of the necessity for extreme caution which it imposes on him. He should think twice before discovering "irony" in passages which everyone has hitherto taken "straight." (4) He approaches literature with the wrong kind of seriousness. He uses as a substitute for religion or philosophy or psychotherapy works which were intended as *divertissements.* The nature of the comic is a subject for serious consideration; but one needs to have seen the joke and taken it as a joke first.
>
> Of course none of these critical vices are peculiar to undergraduates. They imitate that which, in their elders, has far less excuse.[85]

That was in March 1960, and there the matter might have stood. Lewis certainly had other things on his mind. The previous October Mrs. Lewis's cancer had become active again. In April Lewis and she took their trip to Greece, and on July 13 she died. Meanwhile the June number of *Delta* had come and gone with nothing said about Lewis's piece. The tempest was over, and the teacup could be washed up.

But by October *Delta* had new editors. Gray and Howard Burns had replaced Andrew Roberts, and Gray apparently had spent the Long Vac nursing a grievance,[86] for he weighed in with "Professor C. S. Lewis and the English Faculty," twelve rebarbative pages, abusive and patronizing, that were supercilious even by Cambridge standards. "The tone of Professor Lewis's small piece might well seem to many distasteful—distasteful in its arrogance, distasteful in its authoritarian self-righteousness, distasteful finally in the contempt for the undergraduate that it suggests" (no. 22, p. 9). The rhetoric and strategy were *faux*-Leavis, for Gray went on to link Lewis's sins with perceived failings in the Faculty as a whole and the Tripos Examination in particular. The piece was so derogatory that Donald Davie, *Delta*'s Senior Treasurer (faculty moderator), resigned immediately. *Varsity* (October 8, 1960) had the story on page 1: "Dr. Donald Davie, of Caius, has resigned from the senior trusteeship of Delta because he can no longer associate himself with what he describes as its 'whining and bullying tone.' This, he claims, is carried to an extreme in the latest issue, most of which is devoted to a critical examination of the English Faculty at Cambridge.... The main article attacks Professor C. S. Lewis' summary in Broadsheet, March 9th, of what he thinks is wrong with undergraduate criticism.... The issue also contains unfavourable reviews of four books by teachers of English at Cambridge.... Dr. F. R. Leavis, of Downing, said that he had been excessively busy and therefore unable to see the copy in question." Once again, there the matter might have stood. Gray was relatively insulated since *Delta* would not come out again until February, and when interviewed by *Varsity* Lewis indicated that he had never even heard of *Delta* and knew nothing of the article. But Davie's resignation was less easy to ignore, and on October 20 the matter gained national attention when *The Listener* published a leader, "English—Left and Right," commenting on *Delta*'s attack, predictably followed by letters from Burns, Gray, and then Leavis. The *Times Literary Supplement* of November 25 also commented on the attack in a leader, "Learning the Hard

Way." And in *The Spectator* Davie gave an account, "Literature into Life," which generated a gratuitously abusive letter from J. M. Newton, a reply by Davie, and further letters contra Davie by Gray and Burns.[87] By this time it was December 30, and Lewis had dropped from the combatants' sight amidst all their fury. He did send a letter to *Delta* (no. 23, February 1961) in which he set forth for the sciolists some home truths, and there the matter finally, mercifully, ended.

Leavis was not behind all this. Nor was it a case of his playing Henry II and asking, "Who will rid me of this foolish Professor?" It was largely a matter of Leavisites trying to win Leavis's attention by acting in ways they thought would please. We can see this in Gray's otherwise misleading and disingenuous memoir.[88] What of its effect on Lewis? In some ways it epitomized his Cambridge years. For example, there is this anecdote from *An Experiment in Criticism*.[89] "After a lecture of my own I have been accompanied from Mill Lane to Magdalene by a young man protesting with real anguish and horror against my wounding, my vulgar, my irreverent, suggestion that *The Miller's Tale* was written to make people laugh" (p. 12). For six years Lewis had kept his distance and his counsel. But the *Delta* controversy and incidents like this one led him to rethink his views on Cambridge English, evaluative criticism, and the injurious effect on the young of "Leavis."[90] That reconsideration is evident in the logic of his three books published shortly thereafter with Cambridge University Press. In them Lewis reasserts the importance of background and intention while also trying to undercut "Leavis"—especially evaluation in criticism. And the gap between "Leavis" and Leavis is not always clear.

THE LOGIC OF THE C.U.P. BOOKS

The Discarded Image (1964) sets out Lewis's concern for background. Lewis wrote four great books on literary history, *The Allegory of Love,* A *Preface to "Paradise Lost," English Literature in the Sixteenth Century*, during his Oxford years, and the last, *The Discarded Image*, at Cambridge. In the latter we can see fleshed out the argument of "De Descriptione Temporum," for the book demonstrates that the Medieval "Model" was also in essentials that of the

Renaissance and that large parts of it were still Johnson's. It was, however, decidedly not Blake's or Coleridge's: the decisive break, the most momentous in all literary history, fell there.[91] And Lewis's argument is that one cannot read intelligently earlier books without recognizing that their presuppositions are different from those that have governed literature since Romanticism. In other words, when reading earlier literature, Donne for example, we cannot "read on as we read the living." This is a familiar Lewisian argument, and it is untouched by the events we have been just discussing.

Studies in Words is another matter. Its concern is also background, with a focus on words rather than the larger Model, a "point of view" as he puts it, "merely lexical and historical" (p. vii). And its first eight pages provide a *locus classicus* for Lewis's argument about the hidden difficulties of approaching old books.

> If we read an old poem with insufficient regard for change in the overtones, and even the dictionary meanings, of words since its date—if, in fact, we are content with whatever effect the words accidentally produce in our modern minds—then of course we do not read the poem the old writer intended. What we get may still be, in our opinion, a poem; but it will be our poem, not his. If we call this *tout court* "reading" the old poet, we are deceiving ourselves. If we reject as "mere philology" every attempt to restore for us his real poem, we are safeguarding the deceit. Of course any man is entitled to say he prefers the poems he makes for himself out of his mistranslations to the poems the writers intended. I have no quarrel with him. He need have none with me. Each to his taste.[92]

But after the *Delta* controversy, Lewis wrote three additional chapters, "World," "Life," and "I Dare Say," that convey his reconsideration of the weaknesses and dangers of Cambridge English. They are anti-"Leavis" and also, now, anti-Leavis: obliquely ("I Dare Say," where the concern is background) and directly ("Life," where the concern is for a favorite Leavisism). And in his conclusion, "At the Fringe of Language," Lewis reviews the whole misguided emphasis of Cambridge English on evaluation from Richards on down.

"I Dare Say" is seven pages of oblique adversarial brilliance. In the "Introduction" Lewis had said of his own experience, "One saw increasingly that sixteenth- and even nineteenth-century texts needed such elucidation not very much more rarely, and in a more subtle way, than those of the eleventh or twelfth; for in the older books one knows what one does not understand but in the later one discovers, often after years of contented misreading, that one has been interpolating senses later than the author intended" (p. 1). Here he takes the throwaway phrase "I dare say," one we all use without ever thinking about it very carefully, and notices its various usages from Malory to the trial of *Lady Chatterley* before focusing in on the nineteenth-century novel. Taking Jane Austen as his example he says, "I find in her works many places where, I think, it cannot bear the modern sense; some where it may; and none where it must." In other words, "almost every instance of *I dare say* requires careful scrutiny" (p. 309). The larger point is deftly made after reviewing eight instances in her novels, and it has its Cambridge application: "Indeed, I am ashamed to remember for how many years, as a boy and a young man, I read nineteenth-century fiction without noticing how often its language differed from ours. I believe it was work on far earlier English that first opened my eyes: for there a man is not so easily deceived into thinking he understands when he does not" (pp. 311–12). An admonition to the author of *The Great Tradition*? *Qui habet aures, audiat.*

In "Life," Lewis's concern is with the word as a Lawrentian-Leavisian ejaculation of approval. After his usual historical survey and gathering of variations he reaches, inter alia, Lawrence, *Delta*, and Leavis.[93] Lewis amuses himself by assimilating Lawrence to W. E. Henley, or writing "Fr. [Martin] Jarrett-Kerr and Dr Leavis use *life* in the same sense, and I think their view is really the same as [G. K.] Chesterton's," knowing full well how that comparison would rankle! More seriously, Lewis shows that often Leavis uses "life" to mean "what I approve" (while admitting that he himself approves of many of the same things) and that this usage tends to degenerate into an empty intensifier. He then follows the word from Lawrence to Leavis and shows how in Lawrence it often is unfocused Romantic pantheism. Lewis shows how empty "life" often is in Leavis's rhetoric. But the case is not quite so simple as Lewis makes it, for if the word were only an empty counter Leavis could never have developed the important cultural criticism that he did, beginning with his attack on C. P. Snow and developing fully only after Lewis's death. "Life," with its Arnoldian antithesis "machinery," led Leavis to his valuable consideration of the "techno-logico-Benthamite" ascendancy in modern civilization.

"At the Fringe of Language" attacks evaluative criticism, a genre that almost always degenerates into adverse criticism. Lewis approaches the subject logically as a species, the genus of which is Richards's "conception of emotional language" (p. 314). After distinguishing language which expresses emotion from language which arouses it, he reaches abusive language. The odd thing, he says, is that "language meant solely to hurt hurts strangely little." The reason is not hard to find. "As words become exclusively emotional they cease to be words and therefore of course cease to perform any strictly linguistic function.... Hatred cuts its own throat" (p. 324). The language of literary criticism has to avoid this trap; it must be descriptive and objective. The evaluative critic, employing a term like "adolescent," writes "not to inform the reader but to annoy the writer." And after reviewing the inutility of such usage, he ends with an admonition that is also a plea directed to those whose training has been in "Leavis": "I would be glad if I could transfer to even one reader my conviction that *adverse* criticism, far from being the easiest, is one of the hardest things in the world to do well" (p. 328).

For this there are two reasons, one logical and one moral. Richards had raised the logical one: "Dr I. A. Richards first seriously raised the problem of badness in literature. And his singularly honest wrestling with it shows how dark a problem it is. For when we try to define the badness of a work, we usually end by calling it bad on the strength of characteristics which we can also find in good work. Dr Richards began by hoping he had found the secret of badness in an appeal to stock responses. But Gray's *Elegy* beat him. Here was a good poem which made that appeal throughout. Worst still, its particular goodness depended on doing so" (p. 328). But the other reason for avoiding evaluative criticism is moral: "The...difficulty lies within...what we think thoroughly bad, we hate.... Lower and still lower levels of hatred may open; we may dislike the author personally.... The book before us becomes a symbol of *l'infâme*" (p. 329). When this occurs literary criticism becomes "mere action—a blow delivered in a battle. But if it does, we are lost as critics." Here is precisely why Lewis did not want to teach evaluative criticism to undergraduates.

Studies in Words, then, has a double purpose: to reassert the importance of background and to undercut evaluation. The *Delta* controversy was a reminder of the danger of the critical *procédé* we have been calling "Leavis." Any experienced teacher knows that perception can be strengthened and analysis can certainly be taught. But judgment is a different kind of matter, for its roots lie in prudence, a part of the self anterior to the critical act.[94] Criticism requires humility—submitting one's imagination to the work, receiving it—while premature evaluation fosters pride. The young are only too glad to take an adversarial pose, for it plays to their normal rebelliousness and desire for recognition, and it enables them to hide their great weakness—inexperience—while using their perceptive and analytical strengths. Evaluative criticism too easily becomes a form of attitudinizing, a substitute for the hard task of receiving a literary work and carefully describing it. Lewis wanted to make evaluative criticism far harder.

We come now to Lewis's last and (excepting *Rehabilitations*) most deliberately anti-Cambridge book, but also the one in which he makes fully explicit his positive convictions. His four works of literary history set out Lewis's views about background and intention and their critical use; here he provides the complement, his presentation of a non-evaluative literary criticism. Lewis had always seemed to struggle with evaluation, and he had never defined reception. *An Experiment in Criticism* clarifies both and brings into focus something that had always been latent in his thought, the vulnerability of practical criticism to utilitarian distortion.[95]

"If we are to be critics," Lewis had said in *Studies in Words*, "we must condemn as well as praise" (p. 330). But what should we condemn? Authors? Readers? Or ways of reading? Cambridge English sought to distinguish good books from bad. But Lewis had shown the logical difficulty this entails, so he refocused the question. Good and bad, he says, can more profitably be predicated not of books but of ways of reading. We start with the distinction between the Few and the Many and then notice that the Many read in a way different from the Few—those for whom literature has a commanding presence in life.

The Many use books while the Few receive them. "A work of (whatever) art can be either 'received' or 'used.' When we 'receive' it we exert our senses and imagination and various other powers according to a pattern invented by the artist. When we 'use' it we treat it as assistance for our own activities.... 'Using' is inferior to 'reception' because art, if used rather than received, merely facilitates, brightens, relieves, or palliates our life, and does not add to it" (p. 88). Here is the essential distinction, and so far all is clear sailing, but Lewis heads for more troubled waters. For the Few—the literary—can also misread books, can use them. And this is just what the whole Cambridge project, in Lewis's view, had been doing: not developing real inwardness, "wise passiveness," but using literature for secondary, hygienic ends. Cambridge English largely rested on Richards's *Practical Criticism* (1929), one of the greatest of all pieces of literary research. And Lewis agreed with Richards in his negative findings: "For the fact is," he had admitted in *Rehabilitations*, "that those who have had no experience in the teaching of English are living in a fool's paradise as regards the ability of the average undergraduate to *construe* his mother tongue" (p. 61). But he disagreed with the positive program: however valuable it was in itself, literature was not a source of value, and reading it well was not the narrow gate leading to the good life. Instead of receiving literature, Cambridge, willy-nilly, was using it as a substitute for religion. In their misreading the Literary had assumed the view "that all good books are good primarily because they give us knowledge, teach us 'truths' about 'life.' Dramatists and novelists are praised as if they were doing, essentially, what used to be expected of theologians and philosophers, and the qualities which belong to their works as inventions and as designs are neglected. They are reverenced as teachers and insufficiently appreciated as artists" (p. 74).

Lewis is able to clarify a question that has haunted modern criticism ever since it was raised in the 1920s by Richards and Eliot, a question that Lewis himself struggled with earlier in his controversy with Every and Bethell and left open in his book on Milton: the relation of Literature and Belief. The distinction between using and receiving resolves the problem. Notice how the argument employs Richardian terms:

> In reading imaginative work, I suggest, we should be much less concerned with altering our own opinions—though this of course is sometimes their effect—than with entering fully into the opinions, and therefore also the attitudes, feelings, and total experience, of other men. Who in his ordinary senses would try to decide between the claims of materialism and theism by reading Lucretius and Dante? But who in his literary senses would not delightedly learn from them a great deal about what it is like to be a materialist or a theist?
>
> In good reading there ought to be no "problem of belief." I read Lucretius and Dante at a time when (by and large) I agreed with Lucretius. I have read them since I came (by and large) to agree with Dante. I cannot find that this has much altered my experience, or at all altered my evaluation, of either. A true lover of literature should be in one way like an honest examiner, who is prepared to give the highest marks to the telling, felicitous and well-documented exposition of views he dissents from or even abominates. (pp. 85–86)

In the end, Lewis acknowledges, to read well is to read critically. And to read critically is to employ permanent canons: "The accepted valuation of literary works varies with every change of fashion, but the distinction between attentive and inattentive, obedient and willful, disinterested and egoistic, modes of reading is permanent; if ever valid, valid everywhere and always" (p. 106). Good reading is, and always was and will be, attentive, obedient, disinterested. And it has its own proper order: "The effect must precede the judgment on the effect.... *We must receive it first and then evaluate it*" (p. 92; my emphasis). Having established his position, he then makes his final attack on evaluative criticism. This part of the book is mixed in its success. About evaluative criticism he is telling and witty. But he also overstates his case, generates an unfortunate confusion, and permits himself an unworthy jocular remark at Leavis's expense.

One of Lewis's best points about evaluative criticism is that "we invariably judge a critic by the extent to which he illuminates reading we have already done.... The truth is not that we need the critics in order to enjoy the authors, but that we need the authors in order to enjoy the critics. Criticism normally casts a retrospective light on what we have already read" (pp. 122–23). And Lewis is witty when he separates Arnold from Cambridge: "Criticism as Arnold conceived it I take to be a useful activity.... Evaluation plays a minor part" (pp. 119–20). But at that very moment he overstates his case: "Can I say with certainty that any evaluative criticism has ever actually helped me to understand and appreciate any great work of literature or any part of one?" And he goes further. "Can I, honestly and strictly speaking, say with any confidence that my appreciation of any scene, chapter, stanza or line has been improved by my reading of Aristotle, Dryden, Johnson, Lessing, Coleridge, Arnold...Pater, or Bradley?" Does Lewis really intend to answer his own rhetorical questions with a "No"? Well, from Aristotle to A. C. Bradley, excepting perhaps Samuel Johnson, evaluative critics were generally not practical critics. Practical criticism is a twentieth-century phenomenon. Using his rhetoric against the evaluative critics of the past, Lewis expects us to apply it to the practical critics of the present. But how many of us find every literary work equally transparent to our minds? And who among us has never had a scene, a chapter, a stanza, or a line illuminated for us—possibly by some son or daughter of Cambridge?

The glance at Leavis is not Lewis's best moment. After arguing that "one result of my system would be to silence the type of critic for whom all the great names in English literature—except for the half dozen protected by the momentary critical 'establishment'—are so many lamp-posts for a dog" (p. 112), he adds a denunciation of the "Vigilant School."[96] But after having got that off he finds his stride again, and he connects his argument with the pedagogical issues that he has been pondering for thirty years, issues that had flared up in the *Delta* controversy. Evaluative criticism kills receptivity. It ends in diminishing the enjoyment of literature itself while engendering a specious sense of superiority. "I remain...sceptical...about the necessity or utility of evaluative criticism.... Everyone who sees the work of Honours students in English at a university has noticed with distress their increasing tendency to see books wholly through the spectacles of other books. On every play, poem, or novel, they produce the view of some eminent critic. An amazing knowledge of Chaucerian or Shakespearian criticism sometimes co-exists with a very inadequate knowledge of Chaucer or Shakespeare. Less and less do we meet the individual response" (p. 129). Lewis knows that evaluation is the inevitable end of the critical act. But he wants to delay it, to permit it only at the end, when it wells up with its own inevitability and authority after the full reception and deep pondering of a whole range of comparative experiences. "Force till right is ready," Arnold said, "and till right is ready, force."

Experiment is too fine a book, and Lewis too good a writer, to end on this negative note. The Epilogue, which is justifiably well known, restates the central Lewisian case for reception of the full literary work, *logos* and *poiëma*, and it sets forth a renewed vision of what constitutes the specific good of literature, of "occupying our hearts with stories of what never happened and entering vicariously into feelings which we should try to avoid having in our own person" (p. 137). If using a work of literature "merely facilitates, brightens, relieves, or palliates" our lives, receiving it enlarges us from within. "The nearest I have yet got to an answer is that we seek an enlargement of our being" (p. 137). And is not his thought moving on more than one level as he evokes, in unforgettable terms, our desire for the specific good found in the *logos*?

> Good reading, therefore, though it is not essentially an affectional or moral or intellectual activity, has something in common with all three. In love we escape from our self into one other. In the moral sphere, every act of justice or charity involves putting ourselves in the other person's place and thus transcending our own competitive particularity. In coming to understand anything we are rejecting the facts as they are for us in favour of the facts as they are. The primary impulse of each of us is to maintain and aggrandise himself. The secondary impulse is to go out of the self, to correct its provincialism and heal its loneliness. In love, in virtue, in the pursuit of knowledge, and in the reception of the arts, we are doing this. (p. 138)

Here is the full reach of Lewis's case against Cambridge, the fulfillment of the logic of the C.U.P. books: learning as opposed to training, reception as opposed to evaluation, respect for the various parallel spheres of human activity, without confusion. It is a digest of thirty years of adversarial argument.

Notes to Lewis and Cambridge

Research for this paper was supported, in part, by a grant from the Committee to Aid Faculty Research, Providence College. For permission to study materials in their possession, thanks are due to the Librarians and Staff of the Bodleian Library, and especially the Keeper of Western Manuscripts; the staff of the Cambridge University Library; and the Master and Fellows of Magdalene College, Cambridge. I am grateful to the Master and Fellows of St. Edmund's College, Cambridge, for electing me a Visiting Fellow, thereby enabling me to carry out my research. Unpublished letters of J. R. R. Tolkien are used with the kind permission of the Tolkien Estate: © The J. R. R. Tolkien Copyright Trust, 1999. Extracts from unpublished letters by C. S. Lewis © 1999 C. S. Lewis Pte. Ltd.

1. Which together with *Christian Behaviour* (1943) and *Beyond Personality* (1944) is better known as *Mere Christianity.*
2. The opening sentence of Patrick Crutwell's very Cambridge book by that title was, "The 1590s are the crucial years" (London, 1954).
3. F. R. Leavis, *Education and the University: A Sketch for an "English School"* (London, 1943), pp. 34, 67–68. Leavis of course always regarded himself as an "outlaw" from official Cambridge, but for the purposes of this paper that is irrelevant. Lewis certainly regarded him as representative of Cambridge English.
4. "There are, I know, those who prefer not to go beyond the impression, however accidental, which an old work makes on a mind that brings to it a purely modern sensibility and modern conceptions." *The Discarded Image: An Introduction to Medieval and Renaissance Literature* (Cambridge, 1964), pp. vii-viii.
5. The term was flexible in Lewis's thought; the definition here is from *Surprised by Joy* (1955; reprint ed., Glasgow, 1977), p. 167.
6. As did I. A. Richards: "The qualifications of a good critic are three. He must be adept at experiencing, without eccentricities, the state of mind relevant to the work of art he is judging. Secondly, he must be able to distinguish experiences from one another as regards their less superficial features. Thirdly, he must be a sound judge of values" (*Principles of Literary Criticism* [New York, 1925], p. 114). Richards's first point bears some resemblance to what Lewis called "receiving." The third quarrels remarkably with Richards's own hygienic program.
7. From *The Abolition of Man* (London, 1947) one infers that Lewis saw Richards's schemata as destroying all objective value. He never uses this approach, however, to argue the consequent problematics of evaluation in criticism. Lewis was not against evaluation—that, after all, is what criticism is—but he thought it was best when it was a Johnsonian approbation of good readers over a long period of time.
8. I. A. Richards, *Sciences and Poetries: A Reissue of Science and Poetry (1926, 1935) with Commentary* (New York, 1970), p. 47.
9. February 4, 1941. C. S. Lewis Collection, Bodleian Library, MS Eng. lett. 220/2, leaf 137.
10. The context of the 1930s should not be forgotten, the pressures to acquiesce to Marxism were very strong, and Leavis and Richards stood up to them.
11. "When we are considering poetry we must consider it primarily as poetry and not another thing." T. S. Eliot, *The Sacred Wood: Essays on Poetry and Criticism* (London, 1920), preface to the 1928 ed., p. viii.

12. *Spirits in Bondage: A Cycle of Lyrics* (London, 1919) and *Dymer* (London, 1926). Lewis published both under the pseudonym "Clive Hamilton."
13. Tolkien, whose authority is great, did not think so (*The Letters of J. R. R. Tolkien*, ed. Humphrey Carpenter [Boston, 1981], p. 350).
14. Lewis disliked Eliot's High Anglicanism. In the notorious second chapter of *A Preface to "Paradise Lost,"* Lewis remarks about Eliot, "I agree with him about matters of such moment that all literary questions are, in comparison, trivial" (p. 9)—and then launches into a gratuitous attack that mars an otherwise superb book.
15. T. S. Eliot, *The Sacred Wood*, p. viii.
16. Humphrey Carpenter reports a foolish prank in the mid-1920s in which Lewis and several others put together a pastiche modernist poem and sent it to Eliot at *The Criterion*, hoping that its acceptance would expose modernism in verse as somehow bogus. It wasn't, and it didn't. Obviously, Lewis's view of Eliot was still evolving. See *The Inklings* (London, 1978), p. 21.
17. C. S. Lewis Collection. Bodleian Library, MS Eng. lett. 220/2: leaf 177. Eliot also rebuffed Leavis's one submission, "Mass Civilization and Minority Culture," something that later, in his more Lawrentian phase, helped push Leavis into "diagnosing" Eliot as a cultural "case."
18. E. M. W. Tillyard, *Milton* (London, 1930). For the rewrite Lewis also found an ambiguous statement by Eliot himself.
19. C. S. Lewis, "The Personal Heresy in Criticism," *Essays and Studies by Members of the English Association*, 19 (1934), pp. 7–28; reprinted in C. S. Lewis and E. M. W. Tillyard, *The Personal Heresy: A Controversy* (London, 1939), pp. 1–30. In the meantime, Lewis had begun to establish a name for himself with "What Chancer Really Did to *Il Filostrato*," *Essays and Studies*, 17 (1932), pp. 546–75.
20. Lewis and Tillyard, pp. 9, 2.
21. Brought out, incidentally, by Lewis's publisher, not Tillyard's, so Lewis got in the last word. The editor involved was Charles Williams.
22. *The Letters of C. S. Lewis*, ed. W. H. Lewis (New York, 1966), p. 159.
23. All memoirs and other accounts of the formation of Cambridge English emphasize that Forbes and Richards were the key figures (Forbes actually recruited Richards to lecture for the newly formed Tripos), together with H. M. Chadwick, the Anglo-Saxon specialist, who was decisive in cutting the English Tripos off from required Anglo-Saxon. Chadwick wanted students who were committed to the Anglo-Saxon world and the Heroic Age.
24. Lewis, *Letters*, pp. 157–58. Joan Bennett was also a contributor to the Grierson volume. Her essay was a "Reply" to Lewis.
25. She had published *Four Metaphysical Poets* (Cambridge, 1934). Because of the exigencies of hiring, she and Leavis were in effect rivals for a position in the late twenties and early thirties. And when Leavis left the Lecture List after 1931–1932 (not to return until the Michaelmas Term, 1937), she began lecturing on the seventeenth century, heretofore his area. In his several recountings of his conflicts with "official Cambridge" Leavis usually portrayed Tillyard as his arch enemy. M. C. Bradbrook told me that it was actually H. S. Bennett and not Tillyard. In any event, Bennett was the key figure in Lewis's going to Cambridge both in 1939 and in 1954 (Bradbrook, private communication; see also Bradbrook, "Nor Shall My Sword: The Leavises' Mythology," in *The Leavises*, ed. Denys Thompson [Cambridge, 1984], p. 32; Ian MacKillop, *F. R. Leavis: A Life in Criticism* [London, 1995], p. 128; and D. W. Harding, "No Compromise" in Thompson, p. 188).

26. The footnote refers to "the Richardian school (for whom all poetry equally is addressed to the nervous system)" (C. S. Lewis, "The Love Poetry of John Donne," in *Seventeenth Century Studies Presented to Sir Herbert Grierson* [Oxford, 1938], p. 76); the paper is reprinted in Lewis, *Selected Literary Essays*, ed. Walter Hooper [Cambridge, 1969], pp. 106–25). References will be to this volume, *SLE*, and will be given parenthetically in the text.
27. Leavis's notorious remark about Milton's "dislodgement" (*Revaluation* [London, 1936], p. 42) never quite got dislodged from Lewis's gorge. He was still alluding to it a quarter of a century later.
28. The allusion is to the first chapter of *Revaluation* ("The Line of Wit") where Leavis says (he is reviewing *The Oxford Book of Seventeenth Century Verse),* "After ninety pages of (with some minor representation) Fulk Greville, Chapman and Drayton, respectable figures who...serve at any rate to set up a critically useful background, we come to this"—"this" being the opening lines of "The Good-morrow"—and he comments, "At this we cease reading as students, or as connoisseurs of anthology-pieces, and read on as we read the living" (*Revaluation*, pp. 10–11).
29. C. S. Lewis, *Rehabilitations and Other Essays* (Oxford, 1939). The first of *Scrutiny's* revaluations was "John Webster," by W. A. Edwards (June 1933).
30. But see infra for a different emphasis. Lewis's views of Romantic*ism* ("the poison of subjectivism") will change considerably over the years, and they are unsettled even within this collection; what appealed to him in the Romantics was *Sehnsucht*, which he always associated with "Northernness."
31. It is not clear that Lewis knew that by this time Leavis had broken with Richards and his positivism in a brilliant review of the latter's *Coleridge on Imagination* (1934), "Dr. Richards, Bentham and Coleridge," *Scrutiny*, 3 (March 1935), pp. 382–402.
32. *Rehabilitations*, p. 185. The essay is more easily available in C. S. Lewis, *Christian Reflections*, ed. Walter Hooper (Grand Rapids, MI, 1971), and I quote from this text at p. 3.
33. *Christian Reflections*, pp. 6, 3, 10.
34. Bennett was on both the Faculty Board and the Appointments Committee in English in 1937–1938 and 1938–1939, the only person besides Quiller-Couch to serve on both boards both years. In 1938–1939 Bennett was also on the Appointments Committee in Music, Oriental Languages, and History, an indication of his influence. In 1946 it was he that announced Willey's appointment as Quiller-Couch's successor to the (surprised) Faculty Board of English (Willey, *Cambridge and Other Memories* [London, 1970], p. 117). And his *Chaucer and the Fifteenth Century* (1947) was the only Cambridge contribution to the Oxford History of English Literature.
35. January 22, 1939, C. S. Lewis Collection, Bodleian Library, MSS Eng. lett. copy 220/4, leaf 133.
36. The meeting was actually at Oxford. In the Richards Papers (Magdalene College Archives, Group F, Private Papers: I. A. Richards) there is a letter from Lewis dated March 11, 1939:

    Dear Richards,

    Thanks for the very delightful surprise packet—an unexpected present of a book is one of the things that still gives me the kind of pleasure that all presents gave me in childhood. I have nearly finished it, with more agreement than I anticipated and with absorbed interest whether I agreed or not.

    On p 126 I think we need a little more explanation about the Hopkins passage.

> I am afraid that many readers who don't know O. E. *Husl* and have forgotten *un-housel'd* in *Hamlet* will think that you think—or that you think Hopkins thought—that *housel is* a newly coined diminutive of *house*, whereas I suppose the most you claim is that he availed himself of the resemblance between the two words, helping it out with 'low-latched.' Yet I'm not sure what he means (in the dictionary sense) by 'latched.' Too much of this.
>
> We all enjoyed your visit very much. Thanks for the book and remember me to your wife.
>
> Yours
>
> C. S. Lewis

For a glimpse of Richards's unenthusiastic attitude to Lewis, expressed to Eliot, see *Selected Letters of I. A. Richards, CH*, ed. John Constable (Oxford, 1990), pp. 116, 164.

37. *Theology* 38:176–86.
38. March 11, 1939, C. S. Lewis Collection, Bodleian Library, MS Eng. lett. copy 220/4, leaf 156.
39. March 14, 1939, ibid., leaf 153.
40. March 16, 1939, ibid., leaf 154.
41. *Theology* 39:24–35.
42. Though in his response to Bethell he shifts to calling culture a subordinate good, tacitly accepting Bethell's rebuke. Lewis could be touchy about his Ulster background—but he also had a nose for Bulverism (substituting causes for reasons). The quotation is from *Theology* 40:357.
43. *Christian Reflections*, p. 12.
44. Ibid., pp. 23, 24, 28.
45. Ibid., p. 36.
46. Tillyard, despite several books on Milton, is unmentioned. For Lewis, Cambridge meant the other three. It is a noticeable curiosity that Lewis rarely mentions any Oxford colleagues, except for Tolkien. This concern for other critics is almost exclusively a concern contra Cambridge.
47. *A Preface*, p. 134. On January 20 of 1941, Lewis wrote to Brother Every, saying, "I've just written a review of Pearsall Smiths [sic] *Milton & His Modern Critics* for the Cambridge Review [sic]. What a perfectly ghastly book! I hope you understand that if I thought Smith's case for Milton the real and best one, I should join Leavis at once. Against all that bilge Leavis & Milion and I almost stand together: and Millon wd. resent *this* defence more than the attack" (C. S. Lewis Collection, Bodleian Library, MS Eng. leu. 220/2, leaf 137).
48. Lewis is anticipating Alasdair MacIntyre's point in *After Virtue* (Notre Dame, 1971).
49. C. S. Lewis, *English Literature in the Sixteenth Century, excluding Drama* (Oxford, 1954), pp. 23, 30, 31, 19.
50. "*The New Miltonians*—Sir, I would like to express my agreement, if not with the language which Dr F R. Leavis holds about your review (Nov. 1) of Mr Waldock's *Paradise Lost and Its Critics*, yet with his general contention that it deserves much more favorable treatment than your reviewer gave it. I agree with very little that Mr Waldock says, but I think he has given us a strong and clear presentation of a view that should be seriously considered. The tone and temper of his book deserve the praise which Dr Leavis gives them. C. S. Lewis" (*TLS* [November 29, 1947], p. 615). Considering the way Waldock treats Lewis, the disinterestedness

of this letter is remarkable. But as he once said to Vidler, "open lists and 'the rigours of the game' is what I want, and offer" (March 23, 1939, C. S. Lewis Collection, Bodleian Library, MS Eng. lett. copy 220/4, leaf 155).

51. Smithers, as a philologist, was ineligible under sec. II of the terms of the Chair ("That the Professor of Medieval and Renaissance English treat the subject on literary and critical rather than on philological and linguistic lines"). Tolkien, an elector, understood this, but Lewis, at first, did not.
52. Leavis would lose the election as well when he stood for it in 1961.
53. C. S. Lewis, "Interim Report," *Cambridge Review* (April 21, 1956), pp. 468–69.
54. From £600 per annum to £1950 (less £100 with a College appointment). In the 1950s Lewis's royalties were always more than twice his professorial salary. But Lewis of his charity quietly gave away a great deal of money.
55. Previous accounts of the election vary in accuracy. Green and Hooper give no details; Carpenter was unaware that Lewis turned the Chair down twice before Gardner became involved; Griffin tells of Tolkien using the threat of Gardner's nomination to persuade Lewis; Wilson gives a colorized version of Carpenter; Constable is detailed and accurate except for confusing Smithers with Fred Paxford, the Lewises' servant. See Roger Lancelyn Green and Walter Hooper, *C. S. Lewis: A Biography* (Glasgow, 1974); Carpenter, *The Inklings*, p. 231; William Griffin, *C. S. Lewis: The Authentic Voice* (Tring. Herts., 1988), p. 328; A. N. Wilson, *C. S. Lewis: A Biography* (New York, 1990), p. 245; John Constable, "C. S. Lewis: From Magdalen to Magdalene," *Magdalene College Magazine and Record*, 32 (1988), pp. 42–46.
56. May 11, 1954, Magdalene College Archives, Group F, Private Papers, F/CSL.
57. May 12, 1954, ibid.
58. May 15, 1954, ibid.
59. May 17, 1954, ibid.
60. Ibid. Someone other than Tolkien has annotated the "S." as "Smithers"—clearly the person referred to in Lewis's initial refusal to Willink.
61. May 19, 1954, ibid.
62. May 24, 1954, ibid. But as he said to Tolkien, "Lewis wrote too quickly and too definitely."
63. June 4, 1954, ibid.
64. For example, in Easter term 1955 he gave a series of lectures on Milton, knowing full well how different his views were from those prevailing in Cambridge. But after that, his challenge to Cambridge became oblique rather than direct.
65. Barbara Reynolds, "Memories of C. S. Lewis in Cambridge," *Chesterton Review*, 17 (1991), p. 379.
66. *SLE* (n. 26 above), pp. 7, 13.
67. *Twentieth Century*, 157 (February 1955), p. 99.
68. Might one add that the Associated Examining Board for the General Certificate of Examination—the "A Levels"—had just chosen *Screwtape* as a set text for the English syllabus? There had been a wartime and postwar religious revival in Cambridge, but by 1954 its strength had largely waned.
69. *The Letters of C. S. Lewis*, ed. Walter Hooper (San Diego, 1993), pp. 446–47.
70. C. S. Lewis, "Lilies That Fester," *Twentieth Century*, 158 (April 1955), pp. 332, 334, 338.
71. C. S. Lewis, *Studies in Medieval and Renaissance Literature*, ed. Walter Hooper (Cambridge, 1966), pp. 41–63.

72. Alistair Fowler wrestled these notes into a book: C. S. Lewis, *Spenser's Images of Life*, ed. Alistair Fowler (Cambridge, 1967).
73. "For Research as practised at this and other universities to-day I make no defence. I detest it" (C. S. Lewis, "Correspondence," *Delta: The Cambridge Literary Magazine*, 23 [1961], p. 7). Learning, however, was another matter. J. E. Stevens told me Lewis taught Anglo-Saxon privately in his rooms to all comers—faculty, graduate students, undergraduates.
74. Or perhaps it was the other way round. "In Cambridge I was party to a conversation between F. R. Leavis and C. S. Lewis, illustrious antagonists on many famous issues and occasions, who agreed however that there could not be in any serious sense universities on American soil because—and I don't remember which of the revered elders triumphantly produced this moth-eaten proposition—the United States was not a democracy but (wait for it!) a plutocracy. Sagely nodding and capping each other's observations, Lewis and Leavis would hear nothing of expostulations from me, or from another of the company lately returned from a year in the States" (Donald Davie, *These the Companions: Recollections* [Cambridge, 1982], p. 159).
75. Until the final chapter of *Studies in Words*, Lewis was content to provide an alternative to "Leavis"—practical criticism and evaluation—by his lectures. The single exception was a short essay in *Cambridge Review* in which he responded to some remarks of H. A. Mason's that disparaged literary history in favor of critical evaluation. Lewis argued for the autonomy of literary history—it "gratified a liberal curiosity"—and warned, as he had in "Lilies That Fester," that practical criticism runs the danger of being co-opted by utilitarianism ("Is History Bunk?" *Cambridge Review* [June 1, 1957], pp. 647–48).
76. C. S. Lewis Collection, Bodleian Library, MS Facs. c. 49. The Bodleian's is a photocopy. The original manuscript is in the Marion E. Wade Center, Wheaton College. The book's dedication is "To Stanley and Joan Bennett."
77. George Watson, "The Art of Disagreement: C. S. Lewis (1898–1963)," *Hudson Review*, 48 (Summer 1995), pp. 235–36.
78. "I asked him after he went to Cambridge how he got on with Dr. Leavis, a famous literary controversialist. He replied that...Leavis 'was all right,' he was 'saved.' He did not mean religiously, but that ultimately his values were the right ones" (Derek Brewer, "The Tutor: A Portrait," in *C. S. Lewis at the Breakfast Table and Other Reminiscences*, ed. James T. Como [New York, 1979], pp. 63–64). Lewis made basically the same remark to George Watson.
79. Holloway, Newton, Stevens, private communications.
80. October 26, 1956, C. S. Lewis Collection, Bodleian Library, MS Eng. lett. copy 220/4. Cited in Green and Hooper, *C. S. Lewis: A Biography* (n. 55 above), p. 289.
81. In 1963 Cambridge University Press reprinted the complete run: nineteen volumes plus an index (with a retrospect by Leavis). Bennett, a power at the Press, was out of the country when the decision was made.
82. To be fair, *Delta* did publish some estimable verse. Thom Gunn, Sylvia Plath, Ted Hughes, and D. J. Enright all appeared in its pages.
83. *Delta*, no. 20 (February 1960), pp. 20–27. The story was "The Fantasy Game," by Janet Burroway. *Granta*, *Varsity*, and *Broadsheet* were other Cambridge undergraduate magazines. This was a very parochial affair at first.
84. *Broadsheet*, vol. 8, no. 14 (February 17, 1960), and vol. 8, no. 15 (February 24, 1960).
85. *Broadsheet*, vol. 8, no. 16 (March 4, 1960).

86. Or nourishing a hope? Lewis's second paragraph traces the failings to their source. What better way to gain Leavis's attention and favor than to defend him?
87. *The Listener*, "English—Left and Right" (October 20, 1960), p. 668; *TLS*, "Learning the Hard Way" (November 25, 1960), pp. 749–50; Davie, "Literature into Life," *The Spectator* (December 9, 1960).
88. There were a couple of poetic aftershocks. In March 1961 Muriel [sic] Bradbrook published a poem in *Granta* (vol. 64), "On Reading Certain Items in *Delta* and the *Cambridge Review*," and one of Lewis's research students wrote a delightful broadside, "The Rape of the Muse," that remains, alas, unpublished.
89. Simon Gray, *An Unnatural Pursuit and Other Pieces* (London, 1985), pp. 211–28.
90. "Injurious" is not lightly chosen; see the "F. R. Leavis Special Issue" of *Cambridge Quarterly*, 25 (1996). Along with fine and admiring tributes to Leavis there are mixed in various memoirs, pained and painful, of those who tried to give literature the substitute-religious status that Leavis did. "I do not believe in 'literary values,'" he said, "and you won't find me talking about them; the judgments the literary critic is concerned with are judgments about life" (F. R. and Q. D. Leavis, *Lectures in America* [New York, 1969], p. 23). Here the balance between *poiëma* and *logos* is finally and completely destroyed. But to be wrong about literature in this way is also to be wrong about "life." See also R. L. Houghton, "What For—What Ultimately For?—the Leavises in the Sixties and Seventies," *Cambridge Quarterly*, 17 (1988), pp. 66–77.
91. Lewis, always protective of the Romantic poets, could be oblique. He speaks of "that great movement of internalisation, and that consequent aggrandisement of man and desiccation of the outer universe, in which the psychological history of the West has so largely consisted" (*The Discarded Image*, p. 42). Lewis, strangely, seems not to have known H. N. Fairchild's great work of literary history, *Religious Trends in English Poetry*, 6 vols. (New York, 1939–1968).
92. C. S. Lewis, *Studies in Words*, 2nd ed. (Cambridge, 1967), p. 3.
93. His comments on *Delta* provide an illuminating instance of Lewis's moral poise and intellectual disinterestedness. In a catalog of examples he quietly inserts this: "An undergraduate periodical praises an author's work because, 'like tragedy, it is ultimately for and not against life.'" And Lewis comments, "The undergraduate who values work because it is 'for and not against life' appears to me to mean by *life* exactly the Common Lot. The somewhat defiant reference to tragedy—which might be thought by some to be 'against life'—makes that clear. Apparently good literature must not suggest the Johnsonian, still less the Sophoclean, view of our destiny. *Life*, 'the sort of thing that happens,' must be in some sense or other commended. Whether because it is really commendable or because we had better dream it to be so, does not appear" (pp. 278, 281). The reference is to *Delta* (February 23, 1961), p. 28. From first to last Lewis disliked sentimental-religious appeals to The Tragic. The issue he cites is not the one that attacked him (and of course no names are given) but the one in which his letter appeared.
94. As Richards seems to have recognized. Recall his third qualification of the good critic: "He must be a sound judge of values." I take "be" to mean "prior to the hygienic program of reading poetry," which loosens the logic of the whole Richardian program. Early on, Leavis tried to finesse the difficulty by arguing that judgments should be comparative. But as we saw above (n. 90), he eventually abandoned this position.

95. Compare: "Readers, like artists and poets need the capacity for relaxed and attentive *listening.* Practical Criticism, explication, *can* become an externalizing routine, inhibiting that listening...[and] it can have the effect of unduly narrowing the range of reading which is an essential part of an education in English" (L. C. Knights, *Explorations 3* [London, 1976], p. 21). Here one of the greatest of all practical critics implicitly accepts Lewis's admonitions, although Knights goes on to argue that reception and practical criticism can be properly combined.
96. About the Vigilant School Lewis makes three points: (1) They make literature and life a seamless whole so that a fault in one is a fault in the other: "You can admire them as critics only if you also revere them as sages"; (2) they diminish the pleasure of literature: "The use of the guillotine becomes an addiction. Thus under Vigilant criticism a new head falls nearly every month. The list of approved authors grows absurdly small"; (3) they make reception of the literary work difficult to impossible: "Even if [the Vigilant philosophy of life] is right we may doubt whether such caution, so fully armed a determination not to be taken in. not to yield to any possibly meretricious appeal—such 'dragon watch with unenchanted eye'—is consistent with the surrender needed for the reception of good work."

APPENDIX: THE DIALECTIC

Brian Barbour and Rodney Delasanta

The combined craftsmanship of Brian Barbour and Rodney Delasanta, the Appendix—"The Dialectic"—supplied on the following pages serves as a strong illustration of the difference that Romanticism makes both in literature and in the broader worldview that signaled the Romantic change, the hidden assumptions that underlie modern literature. It is included in this volume as an aid to deeper, more fruitful readings of the essays of Fortin, Delasanta, and Barbour as well as the works and authors which they treat therein.

WORLDVIEWS

CHRISTIAN-CLASSICAL		ROMANTIC
Christian (God is both transcendent and immanent)	RELIGION	Pantheism (God is immanent but not transcendent) *May the Force be with you.*
Mind and matter	METAPHYSICS	Monism (mind *or* matter) generally, Idealism)
Reason (latterly Rationalism or Empiricism) The HEAD	EPISTEMOLOGY	Feeling and intuition; the HEART
Design (Aristotelian or Newtonian)	COSMOLOGY	Organic world
Hierarchical	SOCIETY	Atomistic
Subordinate within the hierarchy	INDIVIDUAL	Autonomous
Reason governs (*should* govern) the Passions	ANTHROPOLOGY	Feeling or Sensibility is superior to reason (i.e., to rationalism)
Objective	PSYCHOLOGY	Subjective
Moral order discerned by Right Reason. Natural Law	ETHICS	Anchored by Feeling (which is inspired by Nature). Relativistic
Wounded by sin but perfected by supernatural grace	HUMAN SITUATION	Man is without Original Sin; education cures evil
The Mean between the extremes of Excess or Defect	VIRTUE	*The road of excess leads to the palace of wisdom*
Pride	CAPITAL SIN	Conformity or Imitation
Historical; actual event	THE FALL	Psychological, reversible
Tradition and academic learning	EDUCATION	*The tigers of wrath are wiser than the horses of instruction*
Self-knowledge; judgment	IDEAL	Self-expansion, self-expression

We are perpetually moralists but we are geometricians only by chance. Socrates laboured to turn philosophy from the study of nature to speculations upon life; the innovators seem to think we are placed here to watch the growth of plants or the motions of the stars. Socrates was rather of opinion that what we had to learn was how to do good and avoid evil. (Samuel Johnson)

One impulse from a vernal wood
May teach you more of man,
Of moral evil and of good,
Than all the sages can.
(William Wordsworth)

LITERARY STYLES

NEO-CLASSICAL		ROMANTIC
Beauty is in order, balance, harmony	ESTHETICS	Beauty is in dynamic, organic unity
Mimesis ("imitation" of Nature)—The **Mirror**	METHOD	Self-expression—The **Lamp**
Truth ("The pleasures of sudden wonder are soon exhausted")	CHIEF CHARACTERISTIC	Originality
Instruction / Correction (Didactic)	INTENTION	Pleasure
Reason	CHIEF FACULTY	**Imagination**
"How rarely reason guides the stubborn choice"	THEME	Restless questing for the unattainable
The Universal (general truths)	FOCUS	The Particular (the image)
Craftsmanship. The "Rules"	TECHNIQUE	Self-expression / visionary
Uniformity / decorum	FORM	Variety
Elevated poetic diction	DICTION	Common speech ("A man speaking to men")
Aristocracy / Middle Class ("high mimetic")	SUBJECTS	Common people (low mimetic)
City ("He who tires of London has tired of life")	SETTING	Countryside: the individual alone with Nature
Socrates / Newton	HERO ADMIRED	Prometheus / Satan
Classical Greece, Rome	PERIOD ADMIRED	Medieval ("romances")
Epic / Tragedy / Comedy / Satire	CHIEF GENRE	Lyric (for personal expression) / ballad / ode
"The poet...holds up a faithful mirror of manners and of life"	THE POET	Genius / Visionary / Exalted, priestly figure
True wit is nature to advantage dress'd, What oft was thought, but ne'er so well expressed	DEFINITION OF POETRY	"Poetry is the spontaneous overflow of powerful feelings; it takes its origin from emotion recollected in tranquility"

ACKNOWLEDGMENTS & SOURCES

Grateful acknowledgment is made to the individuals and institutions which made the republication of these essays possible.

Rodney Delasanta and James Slevin, "*Beowulf* and the Hypostatic Union, " *Neophilologus*, 52 (1968), pp. 245–51.

Rodney Delasanta, "Nominalism and Typology in Chaucer, " *Typology and English Medieval Literature* (New York: AMS, 1992), pp. 121–139.

Rodney Delasanta, "Chaucer and the Problem of the Universal," *Medievalia*, 9 (1983), pp. 145–63.

Rodney Delasanta, "The Horsemen of the *Canterbury Tales*," *Chaucer Review*, 3 (1968), pp. 29–36.

Rodney Delasanta, "Alisoun and the Saved Harlots: A Cozening of Our Expectations," *Chaucer Review*, 12 (1978), pp. 218–35.

Rodney Delasanta, "*Quoniam* and the Wife of Bath," *Papers on Language and Literature*, 8 (1972), pp. 202–206.

Rodney Delasanta, "And of Great Reverence: Chaucer's Man of Law," *Chaucer Review*, 5 (1971), pp. 288–310.

Rodney Delasanta, "'Namoore of This': Chaucer's Priest and Monk," *Tennessee Studies in Literature*, 13 (1968), pp. 117–25.

Rodney Delasanta, "Sacrament and Sacrifice in the *Pardoner's Tale*," *Annuale Medievale*, 14 (1973), pp. 43–52.

Rodney Delasanta, "The Theme of Judgment in the *Canterbury Tales*," *Modern Language Quarterly*, 31 (1970), pp. 298–307.

Rodney Delasanta, "Penance and Poetry in the *Canterbury Tales*," *PMLA*, 93 (1978), pp. 240–47.

René Fortin, "Hope, Despair, and Faustus' 'Mangled Limbs,'" *Gaining Upon Certainty* (Providence: Providence College Press, 1994).

René Fortin, "Launcelot and the Uses of Allegory in *The Merchant of Venice*," *Studies in English Literature*, 14 (Spring 1974), pp. 259–70.

René Fortin, "*Julius Caesar*: An Experiment in Point of View," *Shakespeare Quarterly*, 19 (Autumn 1969), pp. 341–47.

Rodney Delasanta, "The Theme of Redemption in *I Henry IV*," *Cithara*, 12 (1973), pp. 58–73.

René Fortin, "*Hamlet* and the Mythic Hypothesis," *Tennessee Studies in Literature*, 18 (1973).

René Fortin, "*King Lear*: Tragedy and the Anatomy of Evil," *Gaining Upon Certainty* (Providence: Providence College Press, 1994).

René Fortin, "Hermeneutical Circularity and Christian Interpretations of *King Lear*," *Shakespeare Studies*, 7 (1974), pp. 113–25.

René Fortin, "Shakespearean Tragedy and the Problem of Transcendence," *Shakespeare Studies*, 12 (1979), pp. 307–25.

René Fortin, "Poetic Justice in Shakespearean Tragedy: 'The Justice of It Pleases,'" *Gaining Upon Certainty* (Providence: Providence College Press, 1994).

René Fortin, "Desolation and the Better Life: The Two Voices of Shakespearean Tragedy," *Shakespeare Quarterly*, 32 (1981), pp. 80–94.

Brian Barbour, "The Crucifix and the Post: The Christian Theme in *Gulliver's Travels*," *Renascence*, 74 (Summer 2021), pp. 145–56.

Rodney Delasanta, "Hume, Austen and First Impressions," *First Things*, 134 (June/July 2003), pp. 24–29.

Brian Barbour, "'Between Two Worlds': The Structure of the Argument in 'Tintern Abbey,'" *Nineteenth Century Literature*, 48 (September 1993), pp. 147–68.

Brian Barbour, "Poe and Tradition," *The Southern Literary Journal*, 10 (Spring 1978), 46–74.

Rodney Delasanta, "Flaubert and the Sin against the Holy Ghost," *First Things*, 121 (March 2002), pp. 33–37.

René Fortin, "Responsive Form: Dostoevsky's *Notes from Underground* and the Confessional Tradition," *Essays in Literature*, 7 (Fall 1980), pp. 225–45.

Rodney Delasanta, "Dostoevsky Also Nods," *First Things*, 119 (January 2002), pp. 35–39.

Brian Barbour, "*The Great Gatsby* and the American Past," *The Southern Review*, 9, N.S. (Spring 1973), pp. 288–99.

René Fortin, "Host-ess and Priestess: Sacramental Imagery in *Mrs. Dalloway*," *Renascence* 18 (Fall 1965), pp. 23–30.

Brian Barbour, "Poetic Form in 'Journey of the Magi,'" *Renascence*, 40 (Spring 1988), pp. 189–96.

Brian Barbour, "Maritain's *Art and Scholasticism*," Introduction to Jacques Maritain, *Art and Scholasticism* (Providence: Cluny, 2020), pp. i–xvii.

René Fortin, "Home and the Creative Uses of Nostalgia in *Dr. Zhivago*," *Modern Fiction Studies*, 20 (Summer 1974), pp. 203–210.

Brian Barbour, "'His Trees Stood Rising Above Him': Philosophical Thomism in Flannery O'Connor," *Renascence*, 70 (Fall 2018), pp. 245–71.

Brian Barbour, "Lewis and Cambridge" *Modern Philology*, 96 (May 1999), pp. 439–84.

CLUNY MEDIA

Designed by Fiona Cecile Clarke, the Cluny Media *logo depicts a monk at work in the scriptorium, with a cat sitting at his feet.*

The monk represents our mission to emulate the invaluable contributions of the monks of Cluny in preserving the libraries of the West, our strivings to know and love the truth.

The cat at the monk's feet is Pangur Bán, from the eponymous Irish poem of the 9th century. The anonymous poet compares his scholarly pursuit of truth with the cat's happy hunting of mice. The depiction of Pangur Bán is an homage to the work of the monks of Irish monasteries and a sign of the joy we at Cluny take in our trade.

"Messe ocus Pangur Bán,
cechtar nathar fria saindan:
bíth a menmasam fri seilgg,
mu memna céin im saincheirdd."

Made in United States
North Haven, CT
20 February 2025

66093406R00342